America's Changing Neighborhoods

America's Changing Neighborhoods

An Exploration of Diversity through Places

Volume 1: States and Neighborhoods: A–E

REED UEDA, EDITOR

GREENWOOD™

An Imprint of ABC-CLIO, LLC
Santa Barbara, California • Denver, Colorado

Library of Congress Cataloging-in-Publication Data

Names: Ueda, Reed, editor.
Title: America's changing neighborhoods : an exploration of diversity through places / Reed Ueda, editor.
Description: Santa Barbara, California : Greenwood, [2017] | Includes bibliographical references and index. | Description based on print version record and CIP data provided by publisher; resource not viewed.
Identifiers: LCCN 2017002036 (print) | LCCN 2017020316 (ebook) | ISBN 9781440828652 (ebook) | ISBN 9781440828645 (set : hbk : alk. paper) | ISBN 9781440846250 (vol. 1 : hbk : alk. paper) | ISBN 9781440846267 (vol. 2 : hbk : alk. paper) | ISBN 9781440846274 (vol. 3 : hbk : alk. paper)
Subjects: LCSH: United States—Population—Statistics. | Ethnic groups—United States. | Neighborhoods—United States. | Cities and towns—United States.
Classification: LCC HA214 (ebook) | LCC HA214 .A44 2017 (print) | DDC 973—dc23
LC record available at https://lccn.loc.gov/2017002036

ISBN: 978-1-4408-2864-5 (set)
  978-1-4408-4625-0 (vol. 1)
  978-1-4408-4626-7 (vol. 2)
  978-1-4408-4627-4 (vol. 3)
EISBN: 978-1-4408-2865-2

21 20 19 18 17 1 2 3 4 5

This book is also available as an eBook.

Greenwood
An Imprint of ABC-CLIO, LLC

ABC-CLIO, LLC
130 Cremona Drive, P.O. Box 1911
Santa Barbara, California 93116-1911
www.abc-clio.com

Contents

Preface

A major part of America's identity is the diversity of our people, who represent every race, ethnicity, and cultural background. The ethnic and immigrant neighborhoods that populate our country are unique microcosms, each with its own heritage and traditions. Exploring these groups of people, their origins and development, provides a better understanding of America's complex society.

Unlike other encyclopedias of American ethnic groups, *America's Changing Neighborhoods: An Exploration of Diversity through Places* presents groups in terms of the places where they have formed enclaves or communities. In other words, this work has a unique depth of treatment of American ethnic groups because it locates them in actual local places. It also has a scope of coverage that is based on geographic dimension. Ethnic populations are described in terms of their distribution and concentration across the United States and in specific regions and states.

Designed for student and non-specialist readers, this three-volume set comprises the following three parts:

1. **State Entries:** These 51 alphabetically arranged entries (including the District of Columbia) provide a summary of each state's racial and ethnic history, as well as its current ethnic and religious composition. Each entry includes a Historical Population table and a Population by Ethnic Group table. Cross-references are also provided to entries in the Neighborhoods section for neighborhoods and ethnic enclaves located within that state.
2. **Neighborhood Entries:** This section includes almost 180 alphabetically arranged entries providing description of important ethnic neighborhoods and enclaves throughout the United States. Each entry also includes cross-references to other enclaves in the same state and to neighborhoods and enclaves comprising the same ethnic or racial groups. Many entries also include sidebars offering brief information on interesting related topics. All entries in this section conclude with a bibliographic listing of relevant and current print and electronic information resources.
3. **Appendix of U.S. Enclaves with Highest Proportion of a Particular Ancestry:** This appendix includes brief summaries of the most important enclaves in the United States of almost 120 different ethnic and racial groups, for example, Australian enclaves, Belgian enclaves, Japanese enclaves, Palestinian enclaves, South African enclaves, and Venezuelan enclaves. Many of these summaries, which are arranged alphabetically, are accompanied by tables listing current population estimates for the group's major U.S. neighborhoods and enclaves.

America's Changing Neighborhoods also offers a lengthy introduction that contextualizes racial and ethnic enclaves and neighborhoods in the United States, as well as a useful bibliography of important general print and electronic information resources. The index provides further access to topics with all entries in all three sections.

Introduction: America's Diverse Places of Diversity

A Permanently Unfinished Country

At the turn of a new millennium, the American public wondered and worried about the impact of immigration on the environment, the economy, and the future of democracy. Experts vied with each other to describe how the globalization of immigration was giving birth to a "diversity" society, as rising immigration totals raised the prospect of a "minority majority," a white population outnumbered by "people of color," sometime in the 21st century. New questions brought attention to the possibility that The United States was being culturally recolonized, that long dominant European traditions were being supplanted by those of Latin America, Asia, and Africa.

We Are All Multiculturalists Now, a book published in 1997 by Nathan Glazer, an influential sociologist, illustrated the changes that had been transforming American national identity in the late 20th century. In the media, in politics, and even in academics, an irresistible tide of opinion portrayed multicultural diversity by emphasizing its novelty. All too often, the publicity and polemics heralding the age of multiculturalism made it hard to notice that the new diversity was a child of old historic patterns. The age was actually the latest stage in the creation of an immigrant nation, a process that stretched back to the first settlements in the region that became the United States.

From the Cold War to the first decades of the 21st century, the United States was transformed by a new cycle of immigration. A wave of newcomers arrived from Asian, Latin American, Caribbean, Middle Eastern, African, and Pacific Island countries. This mass movement was spurred by popular knowledge of opportunities in America, spread by the expansion of multinational corporations, electronic mass media, military installations, and international commerce.

The great migrations from Europe of the previous century could no longer be regarded as the culmination of nation building through immigration. Instead, they appeared in a new light, as a preliminary stage in a gigantic geographic realignment of world population that accelerated in the 20th century. John F. Kennedy recognized this open and unfinished process in his 1958 book, *A Nation of Immigrants*:

> The *continuous* immigration of the nineteenth and early twentieth centuries was thus central to the whole American faith. It gave every old American a standard by which to judge how far he had come and every new American a realization of how far he might go. It reminded every American, old and new, that change is the essence of life, and that American society is a process, not a conclusion. (Kennedy [1958] 1964, p. 68)

From its founding to the twentieth-first century, the United States diverged sharply in its development from the course taken by other nation-states. The successive waves of American immigrants established communities and enclaves that existed in a broad sphere of civil society. (Amy Harris/Dreamstime.com)

The communal, religious, informational, educational, and consumer needs of immigrants were provided by the familial and village networks transplanted to urban neighborhoods and farming outposts. Community life sprang from the self-initiated efforts of newcomers to organize themselves as American ethnic groups. Ethnic merchants and purveyors supplied commodities from the homeland. Priests, rabbis, and ministers shaped the transmission of religious and cultural traditions. The limited reach of American government allowed private initiative, entrepreneurialism, and mutual association to plan, finance, and deliver the services and goods needed by immigrants and their descendants, in contrast to advanced industrial nation-states that adopted centrally managed programs for accommodating immigrants.

The civic opportunities of liberal democracy provided areas for immigrants to build communal power. Democratic civic traditions protected the immigrant's right to express and preserve ethnic heritages. These traditions permitted political organization along ethnic lines to achieve economic and political interests. From there, such ethnically structured political organization controlled the election of city, state, and federal officials who represented their constituency. State officials did not sponsor or organize religious institutions, ethnic newspapers, ethnic language schools, or ethnic mutual aid societies. These were the responsibility of the immigrants themselves. Furthermore, the national culture and ethnic subcultures remained legally undefined in constitutional law, which made them open to new and changing influences.

As long as the newcomers in the era of globalization had opportunities to create a dynamic new life, they mixed across group boundaries at a pace that accelerated with each successive generation. This was, in fact, the course charted by the predecessors to the worldwide immigration in the late 20th century. Under conditions supportive of innovation and change in rebuilding lives, recent immigrants and their children gave new expression to the old tradition of integration and assimilation first established by immigrants of the age of industrialization in the 19th century.

The Continuing Role of Immigration

The waves of immigration in the early and late 20th century were the largest and most heterogeneous waves in history. As such, they aroused fears of social division and disorder. The new immigrants of the early 20th century, predominantly from Southern and Eastern Europe, as well as the global immigrants of the Cold War era, produced changes in poverty, occupational skill, cultural pluralism, linguistic diversity, fertility, and schooling. But their overall impact was far less drastic and their capacity for assimilation greater than described in the polemics of politics and journalistic editorials. Indeed, it is possible that the dynamic forces of the 20th-century American society quickened societal integration of newcomer groups to a pace that continued well into the 21st century. Although it is well known that New York City has a large Italian American population, most people did not realize how vast in extent it had grown by the start of the 21st century. While Manhattan had a famous Little Italy, there were actually 16 other Little Italies spread throughout the other boroughs of New York City by 2010. Chinatown was also well known as a large ethnic enclave in Manhattan, but there were 10 other Chinatowns located throughout the city. The life of ethnic populations can only be understood if they are seen within the total fabric of local neighborhoods that are constantly undergoing change and expansion.

By the Cold War era, the descendants of the new immigrants and the early Asian, Hispanic, and Caribbean immigrants achieved a significant level of inclusion and positive coexistence with surrounding groups. The Slavic, Jewish, and Mediterranean immigrants of the early 20th century assumed a central place in the regional culture of the industrial North, while the Mexicans in the Southwest, and the Chinese, Japanese, Koreans, and Filipinos of the Pacific Coast and Hawaii infused their cultural influences into these regions. As geographic and social mobility spread among the descendants of the early-20th-century immigrants, ethnicity became less significant in residential, occupational, and marriage choices by the late 20th century. The absorption of the enormous and various immigrant waves of the early 20th century made the national fabric more complex in its forms of cohesion and more dynamic in its inclusive processes. Because so many nativists doubted assimilation could be achieved, its success was vital for maintaining the idea that ethnic diversity was consistent with a democratic nationhood.

As a result, the nation was able to maintain a receptivity that would admit an even more diversified immigration in the second half of the 20th century. This wave, like its predecessor in the early 20th century, was noted for the variety of its national and racial groups. Like the early-20th-century immigration, this new wave of immigration probably contributed to a rise in social inequality because it included many poor laborers and refugees from Asia and Latin America. Furthermore, the post-1965 immigrants came from nations where cultural traditions were different from the popular culture brought by immigrants from Europe. The infusion of unprecedented and highly diverse new cultures intruded on the national process of cultural unification, even increasing cultural distances that had been shrinking as Southern and Eastern European ethnic groups incorporated themselves into American society. The global cultural migration increased non-European linguistic and cultural heritages. As a consequence, this wave of immigration generated pressure to enlarge the eclectic component of American national identity and the national culture to make them consistent with global heterogeneity.

American institutions promoted the integration of newcomers in the 1970s and 1980s, but experts and ordinary citizens wondered if American society's capacity for absorption was fast becoming overloaded. The negotiating and skirmishing that led up to the passage of the Immigration Reform and Control Act (IRCA) in 1986, which legalized undocumented immigrants, was probably a harbinger of a long-term struggle to redesign the whole system of American immigration.

Policies selecting for occupational skills and family reunification admitted newcomers who contributed to a modern, technological economy and who had the family investments to reside permanently and to acquire citizenship. The large contingent of blue-collar workers found among all groups, but particularly among immigrants from the West Indies, the Dominican Republic, and Latin America, contributed a vital input of low-wage labor for light manufacturing and service industries, which expanded in the postindustrial economy. The increasing globalization of communications had made these immigrants more familiar with American life, and even the English language, before their arrival than were many immigrants in the early 20th century, who hailed from the remote hinterlands of the Mediterranean and Eastern Europe.

Immigration in the 20th century promoted ethnic intermixing on a national scale, despite the initial cultural and social separateness of immigrants. Long-distance migration gradually spread out the regional cores of European, Hispanic, Asian, and West Indian immigrants who arrived in the early 20th century. By the 1980s, Asians and Mexicans, who were heavily concentrated in the far west before World War II, had become national minorities, settling on the East Coast, in the Midwest, and in the Southeast.

In an era of increasing globalization, immigrants continue to select the United States as the most attractive country of destination. An immigrant from El Salvador provided the following thoughts about his decision and the decision of others he knew to migrate to the United States:

A lot of people have asked me and asked a lot of other immigrants that come into this country, particularly during the past ten years, "Why did you come to the United States? Why didn't you go to Mexico? Why didn't you go to Panama or something like that?" The truth is that, particularly in the case of Latin America, there is only one country that is perceived by the majority of the population as a country not only that provides with safe haven but a country that can provide you also with opportunity of making a decent life, and that is this country. . . . That will explain why later, for example, my younger brother faced exactly the same risks as I did, and he actually had an even rougher experience, but eventually he left El Salvador and came into the States as well. Soon my father had also to leave, and then later my mother and my younger and older sisters also came to the States. (Namias [1978] 1992, p. 225)

Transitions in the Neighborhoods

With the decline of industrial employment and the intergenerational movement of early ethnic groups out of the central cities to the suburbs, immigrant enclaves began to lose their social foundations after World War II. But as the old immigrant America moved off the stage, a new influx recreated the civic and communal vitality that had ebbed as the European immigrant communities departed from their historic enclaves. A social transition was underway in which the cycle of ethnic succession replayed itself once more. Newcomers from India, Vietnam, Korea, China, Haiti, Jamaica, Colombia, the Dominican Republic, Iraq, Syria, Lebanon, Jordan, Egypt, and Turkey took over the neighborhoods that the Southern and Eastern European newcomers had once assumed from the departed Protestants and Anglo-Saxons. By the 1970s, the resuscitation of previously demoralized and declining transitional neighborhoods was taking root.

The process became visible in urban neighborhoods in cities across the nation. In the Elmhurst section of Queens and in Prospect Park and Sunset Park in Brooklyn, immigrants from Asia, the Caribbean, and Latin America rehabilitated residential and commercial establishments. In Los Angeles, Downtown, Westlake, the Wilshire district, Silver Lake, and North Hollywood became magnets for Asian and Latino newcomers who built homes and businesses. Hamtramck, a city near Detroit, once known as Little Warsaw for its predominantly Polish American population, became the unofficial capital of Arab and Muslim America. The Chicago neighborhood of Pilsen, the gathering place of Czech and other Slavic immigrants in the late 19th century, became Chicago's largest Latino neighborhood. By the 1980s, 95% of Pilsen's population claimed Mexican ancestry.

With the coming of immigrants from the Third World, the public life of the ethnic neighborhood was resurrected in new forms of entrepreneurship, consumerism, art, and entertainment, thereby creating a new worldwide communal culture. The web of consumerism and exchange created by immigrants was a manifestation of cultural globalization. It was visible in the Latino grocery that catered to Brazilian, Mexican, and Dominican shoppers or the Asian store that stocked Japanese, Chinese, Vietnamese, and Korean food products. Restaurants took shape along these plural lines: Kosher-Chinese, French-Cambodian, Cuban-Chinese, and Mexican-Japanese "fusion" restaurants caused surprise and novelty. (Indeed, emporia for virtually all ethnic culinary traditions had long followed the dictates of fusion, for they had constantly to adjust dishes to the tastes of American consumers.) By running food stands, restaurants, stores, markets, and newsstands, they created a new commerce that conveyed the cultural and lifestyle ingredients of Haitians, Jamaicans, Cubans, Indians, Koreans, Thais, Vietnamese, Brazilians, Colombians, Haitians, and Lebanese. As people purchased Latino music CDs, West Indian food, Indian videos, and Chinese magazines, they overlaid the surviving residue of previous Catholic and Jewish neighborhood culture with a new international culture.

The new international culture of commerce spilled out into the suburbs in the 1980s and 1990s. A 20-year resident of Somerville, Massachusetts, a "streetcar suburb" of European Catholic and Protestant multigenerational neighborhoods, chronicled the changing ethnic geography:

> Somerville is changing. . . . You see it in Union Square where there are Asian, South Asian, Caribbean, Portuguese and Latin American markets and Cambodian-French, Armenian-Lebanese, Portuguese, country Korean, Brazilian, Chinese, Indian, Greek and French bistro joints. . . . Haitians have started grocery stores, tailor shops, beauty parlors, clothing stores, restaurants and check-cashing places. . . . (Gross 1994)

The voluntary atmosphere of American social conditions supported the preservation of cultural heritages. American society permitted immigrants to separate into enclaves marked by geographic segregation. This situation fostered a semi-autonomous community life that supported maintenance of separate customs and institutions but still enabled members of the group to absorb and admit outside influences under self-regulated circumstances. Extrapolating from his study of the Italian and Jewish enclaves of Brooklyn, sociologist Jonathan Rieder stated, "Defying those theorists who direly predict the atomization of American life, countless Americans remain joined to one another by bracing ties of kinship, ethnicity, territory, religion, and status" (Rieder 1985, p. 31). This trend was not unique to the late-20th-century America. It has been noted that in the 19th century, especially in rural areas of the Midwest, "the foreign born gathered largely in settlements, some of them extending over several counties (Thomson 1920, p. 147).

The ethnic neighborhoods of American cities that disturbed so many acted as launch points to penetrate the borders of the host society. Immigrants used the neighborhood as a bridgehead from which to move into the mainstream. "For members of the immigrant generation," Alejandro Portes and Ruben Rumbaut pointed out, "spatial concentration has several positive consequences: preservation of a valued life-style, regulation of the pace of acculturation, greater social control over the young, and access to community networks for both moral and economic support" (Portes and Rumbaut 1990, pp. 53–58).

Journalists and scholars who observed the enclaves formed by recent immigrants found that a flourishing communal life enabled Asian, Hispanic, and Caribbean Americans to adapt positively and functionally. Enclaves provided an environmental support system for immigrant parents who wished to insulate their children from what they perceived as corrupting and demoralizing features of mass culture. The role of the immigrant enclave in filtering out disorganizing external influences was not new. Early in the 20th century, in Jewish, Greek, German, Armenian, and Italian communities in the industrial Northeast and Midwest and in Chinese, Japanese, and Korean communities in the far west, the cultural and social structures of the ethnic ghetto warded off extraneous disturbances and conserved the immigrant disciplines of industry, thrift, and mutual assistance.

Furthermore, because American communities existed in an expansive social and geographic ecology, a large number of groups could sort themselves out into niches, which did not bring them into constant collision and competition. The multiplying economic slots of industrial cities helped to lower intergroup competitive tensions. Immigrants from groups that were locked into conflictual relations with each other in the homeland—such as Germans and Russians, Jews and Poles, the Koreans and the Japanese, the English and the Irish—were able to coexist in mutual toleration. Social friction, conflict, and even sporadic violence occurred at points between members of these groups, but these newcomers could not mount collective persecutions of one another.

As among the immigrants who preceded them, the post-1965 worldwide immigrants invigorated the culture of neighborhood citizenship and democracy. They endeavored to become an active part of communal government and politics to increase their opportunities. Asians, Latinos, Caribbeans, Africans, Eastern Europeans, and Middle Eastern immigrants diligently prepared themselves for naturalization. They sought out contacts in the offices of municipal government to learn how they could apply for programs or services assisting them to rebuild their lives and obtain their rights as new citizens. They started neighborhood and civic organizations to lobby for vital services in their enclaves. Many foreign-born parents took unusual interest in improving the local schools where their children often became pacesetters in scholastic achievement. They learned how to lobby government officials so as to gain improvements in public facilities such as playgrounds, school buildings, and the thoroughfares where small-business commerce was transacted. The leaders for urban civic reform increasingly sprang from the ethnic associations and interest groups of the newest immigrant communities.

As one generation succeeded the next in the 20th century, the descendants of immigrants gravitated to wider connections defined by civic involvement, occupation, education, consumerism, and residency. The new communities of work, school, suburban lifestyle, and voluntarism diluted identification with an ancestral ethnicity by creating alternative identities and associations. As new cultural, social, and political ties directed to the outside world multiplied with each generation, the traditional bonds of inward solidarity could not contain members of the group who filtered into the mainstream.

Ethnic Enclaves and Pluralistic Cultures

Unlike the historic nation-states of the Old World, the United States developed a national self-image that emphasized heterogeneity, not homogeneity. The songs, sports, national dishes, slang, and dress of the Italians, Germans, Jews, and Irish transformed local neighborhood cultures during the immigration of the industrial revolution; in the postindustrial era, the cultural ingredients brought by Mexicans, Brazilians, Koreans, Filipinos, and Arab and Caribbean immigrants reshaped audience and consumer behavior.

In the pattern of American pluralism generated by immigrants, ethnic communities developed a capacity to adapt their heritage to a new surrounding culture with remarkable creativity and flexibility. The history of ethnic culinary styles expressed the capacity of the national culture to absorb new elements introduced by mass immigration. This process was illustrated vividly by the mainstreaming of German ethnic food, such as oatmeal, hot dogs, and hamburgers. According to the economist Thomas Sowell, the hot dog, like many ethnic foods, "was an improvisation in America (like chop suey and chow mein among the Chinese), rather than a direct import from the homeland. German street vendors selling cooked wieners in nineteenth-century Cincinnati produced the combination roll and frankfurter that became famous as the all-American hot dog" (Sowell 1981, p. 58). In the 1880s, the frankfurter was seen as an ethnic culinary novelty in areas with large German settlements. A century later, after the melting away of German ethnic communities, the hot dog was seen as the symbol of all-American food to be contrasted with "real" ethnic food. At a 1989 Fourth of July celebration in the multiracial suburb of Monterey Park, California, a Chinese girl hawked hot dogs, shouting, "Get your hot dogs here, they're so American," while a rival male vendor replied, "No, hot dogs are an American cliché. Expand your cultural experiences. Eat an egg roll." (Horton 1992, p. 238)

The popular creativity in blending elements of culture gained momentum from the quest for self-expression by the second generation, the children of immigrants. Their ethnic American identity was highly absorbent of different styles of art, music, dress, taste, amusement, recreation, and comportment in a milieu shaped by movies, radio, and mass spectatorship. In the tenements of the West End of Boston, the children of Jewish, Italian, and Irish immigrants blended their inherited lifestyles to create the ethnic American culture of the urban neighborhood. In the streets of Palama in Honolulu, the children of Japanese, Chinese, and Portuguese immigrants borrowed and shared to form a Hawaiian pan-ethnic "local" culture. While their parents had formed communities organized along regional antecedents, the children of immigrants created ethnic American communities, still set within enclaves, but built upon broader commonalities of "Americanized" lifestyle and popular behavior. Cultural accommodation produced enormous possibilities for the blending of particular elements into plural cultures.

Immigrants and their descendants charted a variety of ways to deal with the concurrent needs of joining the mainstream and of maintaining a different ethnic life. Parents who were born and raised in the home country negotiated a middle course as they raised their American-born children. As he became a parent, an immigrant scientific researcher from India, Dr. A. L. Sarkar, reflected on how his son will be growing up in the American mainstream, but still staying in touch with his heritage:

So, I don't think I would like to impose my decision on my child. At sixteen, having been brought up here, he's at the age where he thinks what he's doing, at least *he* thinks that. He becomes completely Americanized. . . . He still has some habits because we try to inject on him. We observe the festivals, we observe the values, we have fairly good, in fact very good, interaction with the community from back home. Being a large group here we get together almost every weekend or so. So he does get pretty good exposure to our culture, our values. (Namias [1978] 1992, p. 186)

Immigrants exhibited a dual capacity for recurrent reconnection with a unique heritage and creative self-transformation. Ethnic communities in the United States could be compared to a multiplicity of durable fragments repeatedly resetting themselves into new and unexpected patterns. The experiences of each immigrant group were expressions of the American pattern of ethnicity, endlessly renewing itself, endlessly reshaping a "permanently unfinished country" (Glazer 1985, p. 3).

American society permitted immigrants to separate into enclaves marked by geographic segregation. This situation fostered a semiautonomous community life that supported maintenance of separate customs and institutions but still enabled members of the group to absorb and admit outside influences under self-regulated circumstances. The voluntary conditions that attenuated particularistic ancestral identity also supported the preservation of cultural heritages.

Collective ethnic segregation was visible in the country as well as the city. The U.S. Bureau of Education found this clustering pattern among the rural ethnic communities in South Dakota in 1918:

Some counties—Hutchinson, for example—are largely peopled by German stock. In this county and in Hanson County the German-Russian Mennonites still live the quaint community life brought with them from Russia. German, not English, is the language of the villages, although in most of the schools English is the language of instruction. (Thomson 1920, p. 147)

Ethnic enclaves were cradles of a public culture that integrated village and kinship subgroups into American ethnic groups. By establishing and participating in parishes, mutual-benefit associations, and entertainment and recreational institutions, immigrants bridged the inherited differences of family and communal ties and discovered a broader identity defined as ethnic Americans. Community institutions such as schools, parks, and service agencies involved immigrants and their progeny in a shared culture of citizenship. In the ethnic enclaves, citizenship and ethnicity became defined in terms of residential and communal identity.

Immigrants and their descendants were absorbed in a democratic popular culture through participation in neighborhood institutions such as churches, schools, clubs, mutual benefit societies, union locals, and settlement houses. These agencies shaped a wider context for civic relations that came to define a Polish American, Italian American, or Japanese American collective identity that was more inclusive and synthetic than antecedent village identity. In this setting, immigrants and their children developed a public life that transcended the particularistic world of the neighborhood.

Historian Lizabeth Cohen described this pattern of outward growth in ethnic life in Chicago of the 1920s:

> In the course of adapting to change, ethnic institutions redirected people's sense of affiliation outward, beyond the narrow confines of the neighborhood. During the twenties, ethnic welfare agencies, mutual benefit societies, banking institutions, and church parishes all consolidated local and regional European loyalties into larger, national ethnic communities. What came to be defined as Jewish welfare agencies, Italian fraternal associations, Bohemian banks, and Polish parishes now serviced ethnic needs. Through some these new nationally defined institutions, such as fraternal orders, Chicagoans began to connect to a more national community within America. Ethnic organizations introduced workers to the world outside their neighborhoods while ensuring that it was still an ethnic one. As ethnic institutions competed more vigorously with mainstream counterparts, they grew to resemble them in crucial ways. (Cohen 1995, p. 95)

Moreover, immigrants played a direct role in creating the institutional building blocks for Americanization within a wider ethnic American collective life. Sociologist Nathan Glazer observed:

> If immigrants could not establish new polities, they could do just about anything else. . . . Immigrants could establish their own churches, and under the doctrine of state-church separation, these would neither be more favored nor less favored than the churches of the original settlers which had once been established churches. They could establish their own hospitals, cemeteries, social service agencies to their own taste. . . . The state, in effect, respected whatever any group more or less wanted to consider education, or health and welfare, or religion, or charity. (Glazer 1975, pp. 25–26)

Citizenship and communal ethnicity developed a reciprocally complementary relationship. Immigrants made local public institutions respond to a self-interest defined by ethnic ties and mobilized by group networks. In this fashion, the first and second generation participated in the disposition of public power and the shaping of the public interest. Subgroups divided by class, region, generation, traditionalism, and secularist ideology vied for control of mutual-aid and church organizations. Historian John Bodnar pointed out:

> Given the nature of this factionalism and innumerable divisions, such fragmentation left immigrant attitudes divided and insured immigrant communities would not last. The future path of the plain folk would be decided in institutions such as families, unions, businesses, or even political parties where a greater consensus was obtainable. (1985, pp. 150–65, 167–68)

The neighborhood institutions proved to be hospitable to dynamic and pluralistic forces. Through their operation as a gateway to involvement in broader political and cultural patterns of life, the self-identity of immigrants expanded beyond the sphere of family and regional origin.

Historian Oscar Handlin observed, "The man who joined a mutual aid association, who took a newspaper or went to the theater, was adjusting thereby to the environment of the United States. These were not vestiges of any European forms, but steps in his Americanization" (Handlin [1951] 1973, p. 165). Participation in urban public life and consumption of its services expressed and developed citizenship. As national ethnic associations were founded among Poles, Italians, Greeks, Mexicans, Jews, Japanese and virtually every sizable population formed through mass immigration, group leaders increasingly advocated an ethnic solidarity concurrent with Americanism. "National fraternals," Bodnar pointed out, "reached forward under the banner of Americanization and backward under the guise of ethnic identity in order to sustain the loyalty of large portions of immigrant communities" (Bodnar 1985, p. 125).

This was the historic process described by political scientist Lawrence H. Fuchs as "ethnic Americanization, in which ancestral loyalties (religious, linguistic, and cultural) are changed (and in some ways strengthened) to American circumstances even as immigrants and their children embrace American political ideals and participate in American political institutions." (Fuchs 1990, p. 20). Through civic activities in neighborhood communities, immigrants were self-initiated into democratic political traditions. Citizenship was a nexus that made possible political and civic alliances with elements of the native middle class and working class to achieve social reforms.

The new immigrants who were criticized as non-Nordic races merged into an official white community with respect to the rights of liberal citizenship that ensured equal access to the opportunities and resources afforded by urban, industrial communities. This community preferred shared participation in government. The state's avoidance of involvement in the maintenance of ethnic communities limited the tendency to turn government into a battleground for the promotion of group interests. The acquisition of citizenship allowed American national identity to compete with ethnic communalism.

For the new immigrants, individual private rights to opportunity were functional and effective in the major social and economic arenas. They concentrated on the full use of their individual rights to opportunity rather than on the pursuit of rights to equality of condition. Citizenship rights to equal opportunity organized ethnic relations into a fluid and shifting array of diverse groups structured by the individual exercise of civil and political rights. Widespread social mobility eroded social-class entrenchment of particular groups and produced a cumulative intergenerational rise in the social position of others. In the northern ethnic pattern, a ranked ethnic order moved closer to an unranked order.

A popular politics based on the territorial community mediated the politics of occupation and class. Popular exercise of the rights of citizenship threw a bridge across the divides of social class toward integration in the sphere of civic community and its institutions. The communities immigrants built served as the cradle for a new common culture of public life. They learned official American values and ideals in neighborhood institutions, which they turned into an ideology for democratic social inclusion. In union locals, they engineered a politics that blended class interests and ethnic interests to advocate the rights of immigrant workers and to define on their own terms their inclusion in American national identity.

Social mobility, acculturation, and citizenship prevented the isolation of groups and created possibilities for wider associations. There was an insistent and practical need to move outside the ethnic boundaries to survive and to make progress:

> The organization of American economic, political, and cultural life compelled individuals often to disregard ethnic lines. . . . The entrepreneur, aware of his own interests hired the most efficient hand, bought from the cheapest seller, sold to the highest bidder, or suffered in consequence. So, too, no group formed a majority secure enough to hold political power except on a very local level; those who sought office of advantages through politics were compelled to develop alliances that transcended ethnic division. (Handlin 1961, p. 130)

Between Different Ethnic Enclaves, Spaces for Mutual Interaction and Exchange

The immigrants who built America, in the phrase of German American historian Carl Wittke, arrived as outsiders to an official sphere of American culture. They were divided from each other in fragmented enclaves, organized according to particularistic homeland antecedents. But along the social margins between native and immigrant, and in the spaces between different ethnic colonies, an area for mutual interaction existed that accommodated cultural exchanges that created a variety of possibilities for intergroup contact. The public life of immediate neighborhood surroundings offered opportunities for novel forms of cultural exchange and combination. Historian Arthur Mann described how the cultural intermixing of New York City neighborhoods had been internalized in the personality and public persona of Fiorello LaGuardia, mayor of New York City, during the Great Depression:

> Tammany Hall may have been the first to exploit the vote-getting value of eating gefulte fish with Jews, goulash with Hungarians, sauerbraten with Germans, spaghetti with Italians, and so on indefinitely, but this unorthodox Republican not only dined every bit as shrewdly but also spoke, according to the occasion, in Yiddish, Hungarian, German, Italian, Serbian-Croatian, or plain New York English. Half Jewish and half Italian, born in Greenwich Village yet raised in Arizona, married first to a Catholic and then to a Lutheran but himself a Mason and an Episcopalian, Fiorello LaGuardia was a Mr. Brotherhood Week all by himself. (Mann 1959, p. 21)

In his study of the creation of Mexican American culture in early-20th-century Los Angeles, historian George J. Sanchez noted:

> In a consumer society, each Mexican immigrant alone, or in conjunction with family, embraced cultural change—consciously or unconsciously—through the purchase of material goods or by participation in certain functions. Neither the Mexican elite nor the Anglo American reformers intent on Americanization could completely determine the character of these private decisions. (1993, p. 186)

Political scientist Harold R. Isaacs incisively described the relationship between the individual and collective identity as follows:

> The problem is the striking of new balances between the "one" and the "many," between the individual as a single American citizen, and the individual as a member of some group, an identity he shares only with the other members of that group,

whether it be defined by racial, religious, or national origin. It remains the essence of the American theory and largely, indeed, of the American fact that one is "American" only as an individual. The American individual is free to associate with any kind of group to which he feels he belongs, and each such group is free to exist, to function, to live and grow according to its own genius and its own vitality. It does so, on its own, however, in the great private domain where every person retains his own individual freedom of choice. (Isaacs 1975, p. 213)

A journalist also noted, "Many things are possible in America, but the singleness of identity is not one of them," because the "dream of liberalism was not the multicultural society, it was the multicultural individual; and in America the dream came true" (Wieseltier 1994).

The cores of neighborhood subcultures were not only porous; they reached outward. Cultural horizons in ethnic neighborhoods widened as immigrant groups were reshuffled into communities defined increasingly by social class and generation. The new American ethnic communities of Polish Americans, Italian Americans, Jewish Americans, and Czech Americans emerged through the development of internal institutions that, in the process of competing with external and mainstream institutions for constituencies, came to internalize syncretic and transferred cultural elements. Immigrant parents took the first step toward launching their American-born children toward a new ethnic American identity. In the Japanese enclaves of the Hawaiian Islands, "the names of Yoshi, Yuki, and Haru become reincarnated into Elsie, Daisy, and Rose" (Smith 1937, pp. 247–48). Endowed with new American names, the children of immigrants, still inside their enclaves, engaged improvisationally and experimentally with the mainstream of "Americanized" lifestyle and public behavior through the consumption of popular culture.

According to historian Lewis A. Erenberg, a public sphere of assimilative and "cross-cultural" popular culture began to emerge from the end of the 19th century in urban enclaves as "new institutions of amusement and leisure were growing into general respectability, offering immigrant children and middle-class urbanities visions of a more luxurious and experiential life, one not bound by the old restrictive ways" (Erenberg 1981, p. 61). The old compartments of traditionalism, nativism, gender relations, and social class could not contain the fluid and expressive new forms of lifestyle that the children of immigrants created through consumerism. These became their vehicle for moving into a wider sphere of cultural identity.

A history of Coney Island (Kasson 1978) found that amusement parks and the emerging mass culture offered a particular opportunity for the foreign born and their children to participate in American life in a new way. Mass culture was inherently inclusive rather than exclusive; it encouraged access on many levels. In her study of Mexican American women in the cannery industry of the 20th century, historian Vicki L. Ruiz described the cultural creation of "cross-ethnic bridges" by focusing on the experiences in the 1940s of a worker named Maria Rodriguez:

"I had a Jewish friend. She was my work buddy," recalled Maria Rodriguez. "I never saw her outside the cannery but we were friends at work. Rodriguez and her buddy talked about issues of interest to adolescents. "We broke the ice by talking about Clark

> Gable. We were crazy about him." She continued, "Oh, I loved *True Story*, and she did, too. We'd discuss every little story. We even liked the ads." (Ruiz 1987, p. 34)

According to Ruiz, cultural boundary crossing produced a meeting of "parallel networks" so that "collective strategies, such as unionization, could be created and channeled across ethnic boundaries." "Second-generation Mexican and other ethnic women" shared "common aspirations and ideas" (Ruiz 1987, pp. 34–35). Young women in different ethnic neighborhoods followed the latest fads and shared Hollywood fantasies. Movie and romance magazines enabled these adolescents—and older women as well—to experience vicariously the middle-class and affluent lifestyles heralded in these publications. Gossiping about real celebrities or fictitious heroines entertained women as they performed rote assembly tasks and, in the process, nurtured important cross-cultural networks. As a result, Ruiz concluded, "Teenagers began to discuss with one another their problems and concerns, finding common ground not only in their status as cannery workers but as second-generation ethnic women coming of age during the depression" (Ruiz 1987, pp. 34–35).

Due to the creative efforts of immigrants and their children in their search for cultural self-expression, the United States experienced a recurrent process in which cultural hierarchies and partitions broke down. This process was fraught with resistance, friction, and conflict. But it eventually fostered and expanded communication among the many ethnic fragments and between the fragments and the national whole.

Oscar Handlin explained as follows:

> The will is not to change. But change comes. New words and ways insidiously filter in. Someone speaks and you can only look at him on the street there, miserable in your lack of English. Now phrases will be remembered, become familiar, enter into usage, be confounded with the old language. Someday the trolley signs will have a meaning and you will be interpreter for someone greener still. (Handlin [1951] 1973, p. 175)

Even under the controlling aegis of the Anglo-Saxon core culture, cultural accommodation produced enormous possibilities for the blending of particular elements into plural cultures. "Between assimilationism and radical multiculturalism," historian Sean Wilentz has pointed out, "there is a third conception of America as a miscegenated or Creole culture, born of oppression as well as opportunity—an America that is not something that must be assimilated to, but that is always (and often painfully) creating itself" (Wilentz 1994, p. 46). In this way, the immigrants who were culturally alien, poor, and powerless gradually but inexorably transformed the borders of American culture.

After two or three generations, localized subcultures grew intensely syncretic. Immigrant Americans did not submit passively to a uniform and unilateral core culture imposed upon them. Instead, they explored the creative possibilities for accomplishing assimilation as a give-and-take process. They defended their cultural heritages to force natives to adjust to them and propagated their particular traditions in the general culture. Immigrants and their descendants assimilated by creating a new pluralistic society into whose compartments, defined by different ethnic influences, they could be absorbed.

Each ethnic community created subcultures that assumed a place in—that became part of—the surrounding environment that affected all Americans. Over time, newer immigrants absorbed the residual cultural contributions of earlier immigrants. James Barrett, a historian who analyzed ethnic enclaves, found that acculturation and socialization were patterned by the historical ecology of ethnic subcultures, as much as by the forces of group cohesion or formal institutions like schools. "Late nineteenth-early twentieth century East European immigrants, for example, learned to deal with situations on a day-to-day, informal basis at the work place. It was often native-born and 'old' immigrant workers—primarily British, Germans and Irish—still steeped in their own ethnic cultures, who had the greatest influence on the new immigrants" (Barrett 1994, pp. 6–11). Natives too were compelled to adapt to the influence of new cultural worlds created by immigrants. Immigrants insisted on being accepted on terms of commonality and equality with natives. It was from this perspective that they were able to accommodate themselves to the demand from natives for Americanization. To immigrants and their descendants, Americanization represented the exchange of absorption in the core culture for democratic acceptance of their way of life. As historian James Barrett pointed out:

> "Americanism" is itself a contested term because it is not one, definable thing. Many people feel there is an important core: a society based on the Constitution, the Declaration of Independence and a political tradition. Beyond that, we are shaped fundamentally by a multi-ethnic, multi-racial population and everything that entails. (1994, pp. 6–11)

The "Bridging" Role of Immigrant Enclaves: A Template for All Communities

A historically constructed ecology of local subcultures mediated and bridged between immigrants and a wider American core culture. Gradually over the succession of generations, elements of local ethnic enclaves percolated into the mainstream core that had once dominated over them. The motion of this dialectical process was repetitive and cyclical, not linear. The ethnic parts, in time, constituted a new cultural whole that, in turn, had to absorb new and different ethnic parts carried into the arena of national history by successive waves of immigrants. In the evolution of mutual cultural exchange among different ethnic Americans and between ethnic Americans and native Anglo-Saxons, old universals were reformatted in new inclusive totalities that stood for wider patterns of cultural proprietorship. Sociologist Orlando Patterson attempted to describe the existence of this periodic pattern in concrete terms:

> Once an element of culture becomes generalized under the impact of a universal culture, it loses all specific symbolic value for the group which donated it. It is a foolish Anglo-Saxon who boasts about "his" language today. English is a child that no longer knows its mother, and cares even less to know her. It has been adapted in a thousand ways to meet the special feelings, moods and experiences of a thousand groups. . . .

What is true of language is also true of other areas of universal culture. . . . Jazz is now the music of the universal culture of America. . . . The universal culture's symbols and patterns . . . are shed of their ethnic specificities in the process of being universalized. They become the property of everyone. And, as such, they are enriched and developed by all. (Patterson 1977, pp. 149–50)

The history of ethnic culinary styles expressed the capacity of the national culture to absorb new elements introduced by mass immigration. The subtle reshaping of the national food culture by immigrants whose dishes had passed into wider circles beyond the ethnic enclave was a central pattern of American life. The process by which hot dogs, bagels, pizza, chop suey, ramen, and sushi became a standard part of a supermarket's items was actually a significant expression of the potency of the historic forces of assimilative pluralism in the United States.

In the pattern of American pluralism generated by immigrants, ethnic communities developed a capacity to adapt their heritage to a new surrounding culture with remarkable creativity and flexibility. This was a multiform and even refractory process, due to the procession of subgroups within individual nationalities that brought differing conceptions of religious and political identity from diverse localities and social strata in the homelands. At the center of their collective life lay experiments in modifying the variegated traditions of church, charitable and mutualist organizations, and schools. These adaptations accumulated into a pattern that would unify an ethnic American community and mold a new collective identity as Italian Americans, Japanese Americans, and Greek Americans, while providing the capacity for integration with the wider culture and its institutions. This was a group pattern of acculturation that required the capacity to accept cultural tension. In a study of the Jews of Boston, Ellen Smith noted the struggle to define a middle area between a Jew and a Bostonian, between being a member of a distinct community and a wider American community. It was an adaptive strategy that required the ability to live with degrees of contradiction and ambivalence. The leaders of Boston's Jewish community formed by immigrants from Central Europe played a key role in formulating this style of group adaptation and conveying its practical possibilities to later waves of Jewish immigrants from Eastern Europe. Smith described how Boston's Central European Jews "attempted to pass on . . . their model for living a consciously Jewish life in new ways, adapted to the advantages of Boston and America, and creative with the ambiguities that such a conjoined existence could bring" (Smith 1995, p. 65).

American immigrants were pioneers of a creative form of pluralism that can be described as consensual, voluntary, and inclusively democratic. They utilized the freedom afforded in the United States to merge with the wider community while maintaining connections with ethnic life. Their adaptive strategy was sufficiently flexible and fluid to accommodate successive and superimposed waves of newcomers from the changing home societies. New adjustments in the community's institutional life and outreach occurred as second and third generation descendants resettled in suburban enclaves, graduated from elite educational institutions, and intermarried.

The threads of the myriad histories of immigrant enclaves were imbedded within the weave of the wider society. The expansive economy, the process of urban growth, the fluid social structure, and the continuously expanding cultural pluralism produced by mass immigration provided a setting in which ethnic Americans could find niches for self-assertion and social accommodation. The building of relations between immigrants and the host society involved communicating and coexisting with a vast array of different neighbors.

Immigrants and their descendants experimented with a variety of ways to deal with the concurrent needs of entering the mainstream and of maintaining a different ethnic life. They exhibited a dual capacity for both cultural self-transformation and rededication to a unique heritage. Following the lead of cultural anthropologists, the historian Timothy L. Smith argued that a conception of immigrant culture as functionalist best captured its historical workings in the organization of group life and identity. The collective ethnic culture was not primordial and static, it was a living, changing resource that responded in sensitive ways to the pressures of survival and the attractions of social opportunity. Thus religion, according to Smith, was mobilized or activated by "the acts of uprooting, migration, resettlement and community-building." The old religion joined in new living ways with the adaptive social and psychic needs of present conditions. This active, functionalist relationship was innately dialectical and ambivalent.

> An intense interest in the religious meaning of their break with the past lay behind the preoccupation of both clergy and lay emigrants with religious organizations; and this interest stemmed from formidable psychic challenges. The individual's sense of responsibility for the decision to migrate was primary here. Loneliness, the romanticizing of memories, the guilt for imagined desertion of parents and other relatives, and the search for community and identity in a world of strangers all began the moment the nearest range of hills shut out the view of the emigrant's native valley. Longing for a past that could not be recovered intensified the emotional satisfaction of daring to hope for a better future. Separation from both personal and physical associations of one's childhood community drew emotional strings tight. Friendships, however, were often fleeting; and the lonely vigils—when sickness, unemployment, or personal rejection set individuals apart—produced deeper crises of the spirit. At such moments, the concrete symbols of order or hope that the village church and priest and the annual round of religious observances had once provided seemed far away; yet the mysteries of individual existence as well as the confusing agonies of anomie cried out for religious explanation. For this reason . . . migration was often a theologizing experience. . . . Preoccupation with the ethical dimension of faith was one outcome of such uprooting. (Smith 1978, pp. 1174–75)

This new preoccupation with religion did not produce replications or fossilizations of homeland religious styles. Instead, it produced future oriented and adaptive American-style Protestantism, Catholicism, and Judaism. Smith noted, "Once in America, immigrants uniformly felt that learning new patterns of correct behavior was crucial to their sense of well-being." Thus the development of immigrant religions reflected the need "to determine how to act in these new circumstances by reference not simply to a dominant 'host' culture, but to a dozen competing subcultures, all of which were in the process of adjustment to the materialism and the pragmatism that stemmed from the rush of both newcomers and old-timers to get

Pell Street in Chinatown in New York. It is the largest and oldest such enclave in the United States. (Sean Pavone/Dreamstime.com)

ahead." As Smith summarized, "This complex challenge to choose among competing patterns of behavior affected immigrants in all periods of American history; and they persisted in dealing with it on religious terms" (Smith 1978, pp. 1174–75).

Ethnic enclaves in the United States can be compared to a kaleidoscope of old fragments resetting themselves into new and unexpected patterns under changing surrounding pressures. The experiences of each immigrant group were expressions of the American pattern of ethnicity, endlessly renewing itself, endlessly reshaping national life. Most importantly, there existed a practical purposefulness and plan beneath these self-adaptations. According to historian Lawrence Fuchs, immigrants and their descendants endeavored to integrate "their ethnic identity, culture, and their stake among the American citizenry with some coherence." Fuchs also noted a study of the Chinese in Hawaii that demonstrated how among the second generation "the English language, Christian religion, and American business and political methods had been energetically adopted" (Fuchs 1961, p. 86).

As they became recognized in the sphere of public culture, the syncretic identities of ethnic Americans challenged cultural partitions and group stereotypes. The control of public images and ethnic identities depended on both external forces and agencies internal to ethnic communities. Native lawmakers, scholars, and journalists played a dominant role in this process. However, with the emergence from within the enclave of elites who could act as journalists, spokespeople, and politicians, immigrants gained a growing measure of influence in the field of public relations. They used the sphere of neighborhood and school for the strategic presentation of images and identities that legitimated the changing balance of assimilation and ethnic persistence in their lives. As such it provided immigrant ethnic minorities a chance to identify and clarify their position in American life, in their self-interest and on their own terms.

Just after the start of World War I, the Carnegie Corporation's authoritative 11-volume set of explorations in assimilation called the *Americanization Studies* series set forth a general model of intergroup cultural matching and overlapping called "Americanization." The series' volumes included a prefatory note announcing Americanization was a form of reciprocal assimilation, a harmonious and constructive process appreciative of the positive qualities in native and immigrant alike. It optimistically espoused Americanization as an ideal model for creating a new American community. The conception of Americanization was inherently inspirational and positive to counteract high intergroup tensions and mutual suspicion produced by the World War, labor conflict, and the acrimonious debate over immigration restriction. By announcing that "Americanization is the uniting of new with native-born Americans in fuller common understanding and appreciation to secure by means of individual and collective self-direction the highest welfare of all," by arguing that "Americanization should perpetuate . . . a growing and broadening national life, inclusive of the best wherever found," and by insisting the with "all our rich heritages, Americanism will develop best through a mutual giving and taking of contributions from both newer and older Americans in the interest of commonweal," the producers of the Carnegie Corporation Americanization Series described a democratic model of assimilation between native and immigrant that many priests and rabbis, as well as parents and their children, would have publicly endorsed as mirroring their own sense of how they were becoming American by contributing a part of their ethnic selves to the collective life of their native hosts (Thomson 1920). The German immigrant Carl Schurz, who was a liberal champion of the Revolution of 1848, articulated this view when he reminded other German Americans, "[W]e as Germans are not called upon here to form a separate nationality but rather to contribute to the American nationality the strongest there is in us" (Galicich 1989, p. 115).

Historians have studied public events in various immigrant communities that can be seen as epiphanies of the merger of ethnic heritages with national public life. In his analysis of a patriotic pageantry during World War I, historian John Bodnar observed:

> Immigrants characteristically expressed a mixture of ethnic and American interests. Thus, the Italian-American floats featured a caricature of the "queen of Italy" and groups of Italian-American school children carrying American flags. Slovenians numbering over 350 in the line of march, presented a truck carrying Slovene-American children and farmers pledging loyalty and a second truck filled with women in folk costumes. The group carried a banner that read, "Slovenians: We Are For America First, Last, and All the Time." Romanians created a float that depicted a man dressed as Uncle Sam "triumphing" over another figure that represented "autocracy." At the end of the parade each ethnic group carried its homeland flag to a stage dominated by a large American flag in the middle. (Bodnar 1992, p. 84)

In a study of the emergence of the Jewish community of Boston, historian William A. Braverman reported a signal event in 1915 that provided public recognition of the aspirations of American Jews as expressions of fundamental American ideals. Boston's reception of a weeklong conference of eight Zionist organizations reflected the acceptance of "the compatibility of Americanism, Zionism, and strong Jewish identity":

> Mayor James Michael Curley offered the Zionists the key to the city, and American and Zionist flags decked the streets. In the Public Garden, a large floral display featured a Star of David at its center. . . . The extent to which Zionism and American Judaism had lost their unpatriotic images was best expressed by the Boston Post when it editorialized at the end of the convention that "it was in a notable sense a popular gathering, representative not of class politics but essentially and collectively of American citizenship." (Braverman 1995, p. 88)

From the industrial revolution to the Great Society, ethnic leaders and those who represented the immigrant community to the wider society through journalism, politics, and other media defined assimilation as achieving the mutual overlap of American citizenship and collective legacies. In the public realm, they emphasized the inherent Americanism of their respective groups. The Irish Knights of Columbus, the Jewish Anti-Defamation League, the Mexican League of United Latin American Citizens, and the Japanese American Citizens League proclaimed that the values of their particular heritages corresponded to the official values of American life. Thus they argued that the love of democracy, or the work ethic, the family ethic, or the aesthetic sense were learned in their traditional subcultures so as to reinforce their American national identity, rather than to detract from it, as anxious nativists and Americanizers alleged.

One example of this matching principle was revealed in Milton Himmelfarb's description of how "Jews came to the United States" "already civic" because of "a Jewish tradition that affirmed the worth of government and out of their strong feeling for the social and communal" (Himmelfarb 1973, p. 242). The theme of the mutual relationship of citizenship and ethnicity was a way of defining assimilation as pluralistic assimilation rather than Anglo-conformity. This was the key to a democratic pluralism. In the more philosophical and articulate expressions of this ideal, it became a way of establishing the civic link between the universal and the particular. The legal scholar Milton Konvitz who described how the values of Judaism intertwined with those of the American founding in Judaism and the American Idea explained, "The ideas here presented have as their objective the softening of boundaries, the mitigation of differences, the removal of obstacles that stand in the way of those who know that common ideals do exist in this complex world in which we live and move and have our being" (Konvitz 1978, p. 9).

Achieving public acceptance through asserting the correspondence of ethnic traditions with American traditions while living in their enclaves occupied a central place in the adaptive strategies of immigrants. Immigrants and their descendants gained external respect and esteem by showing that their different and unique heritages contributed to American community. This strategy played into what historian Rivka Shpak Lissak described as "a more humanitarian method of assimilating new immigrants into American society" advocated by liberal progressives who "believed that cultural and social assimilation could be successful insofar as it created the least antagonism between immigrant traditions and ethnic identity and American ones" (Lissak 1989, p. 60). In this way, with the passage of generations, ethnic identity would merge into national identity.

Furthermore, finding the correspondences of the ethnic fragment to the national whole reaped subtle, psychic advantages. The inner conflict between the ethnic self and American identity and the alienation felt keenly by the immigrants and their children could be transmuted into a sense of belonging, participation, and, even, influence upon the surrounding culture. As they endeavored to shape positive public relations between themselves and the wider society by promoting the conflation of ethnicity and national identity, immigrants and their descendants gained an important degree of self-affirmation. Sociologist Andrew Greeley made reference to the constructiveness of this historical pattern when he hoped that in the future ethnic pride would be based on a sense of having something positive to contribute to society rather than on a sense of being different from the broader society. An educational policy centered on this principle served cultural exchanges that united ethnic groups with the nation and with each other.

Although nativists feared immigrant minorities as dangerous separate societies, in their neighborhoods, immigrants prompted and assisted each other to move into the wider world. The enclave allowed immigrants to regulate the pace of cultural and social change, preserve discipline, pool resources, and establish moral and economic support networks, all of which fortified the capacity for social mobility.

Journalist Joe Klein discovered in his investigations of New York City public schools that academic culture was being revitalized by the children of immigrants. Judith Khan, a teacher in Brooklyn, told him, "They have a drive in them we no longer seem to have. You see these kids, who aren't prepared academically and can barely speak the language, struggling so hard. They just sop it up. They're like little sponges" (Klein 1993, p. 26). Ms. Khan described a Haitian student who graduated and entered MIT in the same admiring tones that one of Mary Antin's teachers would have used to describe her, when as a child of poor Russian Jewish immigrant parents, she became a striving student-scholar in the Boston slums before World War I.

The enclave, with its social, cultural, and economic capital, also acted as a springboard for rising to a higher place on the social ladder. It was the launch point for the "tenement trail," the exodus of immigrants and their children to better neighborhoods, a geographic pathway toward upward social mobility. In Boston, they left the West End tenements of Boston for Allston and Brighton, and then the finer neighborhoods of Brookline and Newton. In Los Angeles, immigrants moved from Boyle Heights to Crenshaw Boulevard and Arlington Avenue, and then further to the Westside.

The continuous expansion of the American economy fortified the capacity of immigrants to capitalize fully on opportunity rights for self-initiated and self-guided progress. The growth of national economic power from the industrial revolution to the information revolution provided new fields in which immigrants exercised their rights for economic self-betterment. It thereby also sustained the social mobility that assured a fluid relation between immigrant communities and the class structure.

Immigrant ethnic enclaves never became isolated and national life depended on openness toward them. Even the Anglo-Saxon core became porous; the charter group could not preserve a totally separate sphere of existence. As a consequence of these transactional processes, immigrant communities evolved from an initial phase of differentiation to accommodation, integration, then consolidation in the patterns of national life. The United States stood apart from traditional plural societies such as India, Austria-Hungary, the Russian Empire, and the Ottoman Empire, due to the potency of the assimilative factor of its ethnic pluralism. Immigration was the principal shaping force of this absorptive factor. Immigration insured that the patterns of pluralism would not become preformed and predetermined. They would not turn into petrified cultural roots, but unfold progressively as living and creative forms capable of absorbing new traditions. Impinging recurrently on building a new society and its institutions, the periodic cycles of immigration composed a dynamic force that endowed the United States with an abiding capacity for social self-transformation. Because the ever-changing patterns of pluralism exercised an assimilative power, the United States, the immigration country par excellence, sustained itself as a unified democracy in the 20th century.

These open patterns of pluralism did not exist full-blown and continuously throughout the span of national history. They were historically "constructed," evolving gradually in a matrix of political and civic conditions that grew more racially inclusive over time. The involvement of immigrant groups in the patterns of assimilative pluralism followed a rough sequence corresponding to time of arrival. The group life of immigrants from Northern and Western Europe was incorporated within the dynamics of an assimilative pluralism in the earliest and most developed way. They were soon followed on that pathway by immigrants from Southern and Eastern Europe. Due to their unequal legal and social status, immigrants who were of non-European origin did not have the chance to participate centrally in the processes of acculturation and social mobility within the mainstream until after World War II. In the Cold War era, however, Asian, Hispanic, Caribbean, African, and Middle Eastern ethnic groups expanded through a new immigration, participated in from the creation of a new politics of equal opportunity, and moved into the heart of the matrix of assimilative pluralism. In the course of the 20th century, successive waves of immigrants broadened the social foundations of American communities toward the universal inclusion of ethnic groups. The participation of immigrant communities in inclusionary pluralism created a platform for an integrative pattern for all minorities. The movement of racial minorities—blacks, Latinos, and Asians—into this pattern had the potential to follow and grow toward a kind of pluralistic integration. The process that had first integrated European immigrants and other immigrants became part of an experiment to integrate the communities of racial minorities.

In the history of the United States, permeable boundaries between a multiplicity of immigrant communities came to define the character of ethnic relations. These boundary conditions and their outcomes depended on the existence of enclaves with bridges open and reaching out to other people and cultures. Because the public sphere allowed ample space for local expression and control, immigrants exercised extensive self-determination and self-maintenance in their cultural and social existence. Ethnic identity and American national identity coexisted in a kind of deregulated balance and transformed each other in the neighborhoods of the local community.

An Urban Framework for America's Enclaves

Across the North Atlantic world from the late 18th century to the early 19th century, mercantile enterprises and modern agricultural production began to support unprecedented levels of urban population growth. The surge of urbanization accelerated in the 19th century to the point that it began to seem cataclysmic rather than a smooth evolutionary change. From the start of the 19th century to the first decade of the 20th century, the percentage of Europeans who could be considered urban residents tripled and in the United States the proportion of urban dwellers multiplied sevenfold.

The United States began the 19th century far behind other countries in the level of urbanization, but began to catch up rapidly. In *The Age of Reform*, Richard Hofstadter, one of the 20th century's most perceptive historians, wrote that the United States was "born in the country and has moved to the city" (Hofstadter 1955, p. 23). The earliest surveys of the U.S. Census confirmed this statement. In 1790, only 1 of 20 Americans lived in urban areas (defined as population centers of 2,500 or more people). The urban population would climb upward so that by the Civil War 1 of 5 Americans lived in urban areas. In 1800, there were 33 cities in the United States, but by 1860, there were nearly 400 of them.

The emergence of giant cities signaled the arrival of the modern age of urban growth in the trans-Atlantic world. London and Paris, the twin colossi of Europe and, indeed, the world, housed well over two-and-a-half million and a million inhabitants, respectively, by the middle of the 19th century. New York City, the greatest metropolis of the Western Hemisphere with half a million inhabitants in 1850, lagged behind these two European giants in scale, but it occupied a not inconsiderable place in the next tier of the world's great cities of over half a million in population, along with Bombay, Calcutta, and Tokyo.

The largest cities in early-19th-century North America and Europe were primarily seats of government where administrative decisions were reached and warehousing and transshipment of commercial goods occurred. The rapid growth of great cities was associated with the intensification of these centralized functions. In the United States, before the Civil War, the cities of New York City, Philadelphia, Brooklyn, Baltimore, Boston, Cincinnati, St. Louis, and New Orleans expanded by performing these specialized roles.

The first factories in The United States sprang up in smaller cities located in the hinterlands of the Northeast to be near water power, charcoal supplies, and cheap rural labor. New England led the way in the establishment of small cities founded with the strategic purpose of housing manufacturing enterprises. Textile factory towns, such as Lowell, Lawrence, Waltham, Manchester, and Woonsocket, mush-roomed in the river valleys of Massachusetts, Rhode Island, New Hampshire, and Connecticut. Eventually, with the advent of steam powered machinery, manufac-turing enterprises shifted to the largest urban centers that had direct connections with railroads and ports and that were accumulating a large pool of low-cost labor through the arrival of migrants from the countryside and from foreign countries.

With the highest level of urbanization in the United States, the Northeast became the most culturally advanced part of the country. It became the foremost generator of human capital, the home of the most dynamic entrepreneurs, creative artists, inventors, intellectuals, and professional classes in the country. The most modern and extensive public school systems in the world were built in the Northeast. Cit-ies such as Boston, Philadelphia, and New York City developed into meccas of the nation's literary, publishing, and public cultural activities.

The rise of the modern city was not the result of a gradual evolution, a continu-ous and incremental development. Instead, it was convulsive, breaking sharply away from the structures of the past. The city in the age of industrialization emerged with new ways of thinking, feeling, working, and living that were introduced suddenly into the lives ordinary people. A new sense arose of time and environment as some-thing artificial, not as part of a natural order. The clock and the schedule replaced spontaneous activity. The built environment overshadowed pastoral fields and hills.

The sheer size of the 19th-century city, the magnitude and diversity of its popu-lation, constituted a radically different setting where the capacity for social regula-tion faced new challenges. Relationships between individuals were no longer governed by corporate and kinship groups, by the commune, the clan, or the guild that had once been accountable for the behavior of its members. The face-to-face interaction of rural village life could not be effectively transplanted in the new urban centers. Social relations on streets and sidewalks, on trains and in the marketplace had to be governed by impersonal standards. Public activities hinged on the employ-ment of standardized sets of knowledge, basic literacy, and numeracy. Behavior in public became increasingly regimented, especially in the factory, the market, and the common vehicles for transportation.

The 19th-century city produced a new style of social life. People more frequently encountered each other in purely instrumental and manipulative ways. The new industrial city encouraged human transiency and social mobility, which caused more superficiality in social contacts. It became harder there to know the whole person-ality or the background of others, especially the myriad newcomers who drifted in and out of the city. The city engendered a psychology of vulnerability to mono-lithic and overwhelming forces. Newcomers to cities were overcrowded in resi-dential and public areas and developed an unprecedented sense of living in anonymous mass units. The industrial economy of boom and bust produced sea-sonal unemployment that bred a haunting sense of insecurity. Routinized and degrading jobs ground down the worker's spirit.

Although the rural population of the United States continued to rise, from 36 million in 1880 to 50 million in 1910, the urban population jumped much more rapidly, from 14 to 42 million in the same period. About 10 million of the 28 million gained by the urban population, however, came from the American countryside. This vast rural to urban migration was vivid testimony to the unsettled economic and social conditions of the age.

The motives of millions who left the farms and small towns were represented in the character of Carrie Meeber, the protagonist of Theodore Dreiser's novel *Sister Carrie*, who found the city's excitement and magic to be irresistible. Carrie escaped to Chicago from a small Wisconsin town. Her story illustrated the plight of young people who were frustrated by the small cultural world of the rural and small-town America. Urban life was the new frontier—a place that promised a new job or a start in a new community—a "safety valve" for economic discontent, personal frustration, and social stagnation.

In the early 19th century, the largest American cities—Boston, New York City, and Philadelphia—had taken on a compact but amorphous shape. These cities resembled a crowded jumble of buildings and displayed hardly any systematic and efficient principles of land usage. Most people traversed the city on their daily business by foot or by common horse-drawn carriers that moved slowly and over short distances. Overcrowded apartment buildings housing the poor, industrial and construction laborers, and workers in harbor trades stood near their sites of work. Even the most fashionable residential and shopping districts, such as Boston's Beacon Hill, existed in the midst of the mix of subpopulations and enclaves. In the decades after the Civil War, the framework of American cities underwent a drastic change. Their physical form would emerge utterly transformed by the turn of the 20th century.

The first reaction of the newcomer to post–Civil War Boston, Philadelphia, New York City, or Chicago was frequently sheer amazement at its size. The application of technologies that used coal, gas, and electric power, as well as the availability of new construction materials (most importantly, iron and steel), resulted in the emergence of a new physical framework for the industrializing metropolis of the late 19th century. Civil engineers with the support of politicians and businessmen eager to promote development created a new spatial order and a new built environment for the changing urban population. Civil authorities successfully campaigned for urban renewal of neighborhoods blighted by narrow lanes, overcrowded tenements, and poor sanitation. Led by the example of Paris, large European and American cities installed new sewage and drainage systems. Optimism in the future of urban expansion was so great in Chicago that developers decided to lay sewer and plumbing lines beyond the radius of extant buildings in anticipation of the sprawling suburbs to come.

Urban planners redesigned streets to form more efficient spatial networks. They hired civil engineers to build bridges out of iron and steel and to dig tunnels that extended transportation into and out of the city. They also expanded city boundaries by increasing the distance of public streetcar routes, by extending railways and replacing horsepower by electricity. Streetcars ran with greater speed and covered more distance, thereby effectively connecting the burgeoning suburbs with the central city. The new science of bridge building and tunneling, on one hand, and the technology of motor power, on the other, were united first in the subways of London, Boston, and Manhattan (which were built with astonishing speed) and the elevated trains of Chicago and Brooklyn.

Cities increased their capacity to hold population in ever greater concentrations. New technologies afforded buildings of unprecedented height. The potential for steel and glass as construction materials had been demonstrated by the construction of London's famous Crystal Palace in 1851. Ever higher structures followed, and eventually the tallest built in Chicago and Manhattan in the last decade of the century earned the nickname of "skyscraper." New designs for densely packed apartment buildings (in Manhattan called the dumbbell tenement) enabled residential neighborhoods in the central city to house unprecedented numbers of people. As a result, the population densities of America's great cities rose to the highest levels found anywhere in the world. On Manhattan Island in New York City, the 10th Ward housed nearly 277,000 people per square mile in 1880, and, by 1890, it would hold a stupendous 334,000 people per square mile. This level of population density was achieved by packing people into overcrowded dwelling units. The largest American cities became leading centers of overcrowding. London was the most populous city in the world in 1881, but its rate of 7.9 persons per dwelling unit lagged behind Boston's rate of 8.3, Brooklyn's rate of 9.1, and New York City's rate of 16.4 in 1880.

The ingenuity of civil engineers enabled them to adapt different building projects to each other. The construction of the Manhattan subway system in the 1890s depended upon the application of earlier canal-building techniques to the task of digging tunnels for the subway lines. Engineers created novel solutions to the problem of train smoke that filled up railroad stations. New train stations such as Gare Saint Lazare in Paris and Manhattan's Penn Station and Grand Central Station solved the problem of locomotive smoke by being situated at the end of a long network of tunnels through which trains approached and expelled emissions before arriving in the station. Lessons learned in building the interior of train stations were later applied to solving the ventilation and lighting problems of larger steel structures, such as the skyscraper office building.

The cadre of creative geniuses who redesigned the city's built infrastructure were members of a trans-Atlantic fraternity of civil engineers. The leading engineers who designed the greatest bridges within urban centers included the German immigrant Johann Roebling; his American-born son, Washington Roebling; an Austrian immigrant, Gustav Lindenthal; and a Swiss immigrant, Othmar Ammann.

The application of new metal and power technology to the design of new systems of commuter transportation created the breakthroughs to a radically new urban landscape. The half-century of urbanization after the Civil War replaced the amorphous pedestrian city of the early 19th century with a metropolitan infrastructure of discrete districts that specialized in different functions, such as shopping, manufacturing, recreation, and residency, and which were integrated spatially through public transportation.

The Industrial City and the Problem of Order

The physical form of industrializing cities after Reconstruction had grown so large and complex as to become incomprehensible to the casual observer. It was difficult from any vantage point to perceive the city as a whole physical unit, as a single community. The overwhelming size and diversity of the city caused new problems in social communication—the circulation of information among social groups. Due to its size, internal diversity, and rapid changes, its inhabitants were less able to feel confident about their own understanding of their surroundings. Furthermore, the information they received from political leaders and newspapers was not free of deliberate distortion and misrepresentation of facts.

The drab routines of mass existence dulled sensibilities and had a perverse effect on social communication. William Wordsworth, the English poet, and P. T. Barnum, the American entertainment impresario, both realized that the urban grind caused people to crave sensational entertainment and vicarious experiences. The most popular newspapers and magazines competed to publicize the newest, but less verified news, and overlooked older but more accurate news. The print media aimed at stories with shocking or exotic content, supplying lurid details about atrocities, crimes, and disasters. Accurate information and valid knowledge about surrounding occurrences often did not filter through to the public.

The heterogeneity of the population made a precise shared vocabulary for communication difficult to establish. The various forms of popular communication involving printed texts and public speaking depended on invoking crude stereotypes and simplistic generalizations to get across only the most communicable concepts to an impersonal audience. The business of publishing presented information in a crude form to reach the widest possible audience, many of whom had only very limited ability to access printed text. Many immigrants were still struggling to learn English; even the native working class had only elementary literacy.

The industrial city appeared to many contemporaries as a relentless force for social fragmentation and the atomization of individuals. Small-town and rural critics of urban life feared that the forces of the city pulled people apart from their natural groups and left individuals exposed to victimizers and corrupting influences.

Middle-class people tended to obsess about these forms of disintegration in the life of the lower class. The urban lower class, they believed, led lives that were out of control, self-destructive, and downwardly mobile. They were lost in demoralizing and hostile surroundings, without familial, communal, or religious supervision.

The stresses of city life drove people to dull their pain by seeking outlets through excessive drink, drugs, and vice. Excessive escapist activity destroyed the capacity to act in a socially responsible fashion. Such escapism only reinforced dysfunctional and nonproductive behavior. Alcoholism, for example, could cause husbands to be idle, improvident, or to abuse or abandon their wives and children. The ultimate downward path was toward degeneration into the pauper or the degraded transient—the bum or tramp or prostitute without a family to offer care. Cautionary tales about personal self-destruction that led ultimately to pauperism, crime, and insanity captured the popular imagination of the urban public.

To sensitive contemporaries who witnessed the rise of industrial urban society, the new social atmosphere it created was a realm of bewilderment, of literally unnatural and disturbing experiences. It was an enormous pressure cooker, a centrifuge that tore away ruthlessly and relentlessly at inner will and rational control. The industrial urban environment caused an intensification of competitive stress, sensory stimulation, and displacement from orderly life patterns. The psychological result was a rise in nervous maladies sometimes called "neurosis" or "neurasthenia" and in more severe cases of a kind of self-destructive mania or insanity. The Reverend Josiah Strong inveighed against "nervousness" in his best-selling exposé, *Our Country: Its Possible Future and Its Present Crisis*, published first in 1885 and then in a second edition in 1891. By "bringing the country to the city, the inland cities to the sea-board, the seaports to each other," by "establishing industries on an immense scale," the "steam" revolution has "greatly complicated business; while severe and increasing competition demands closer study, a greater application of energy, a larger expenditure of mental power" (Strong [1885] 1891, p. 122). Strong prophesied that these developments, "this feverish activity of modern civilization" would have harmful moral consequences:

> Such excitements, such restless energy, such continued stress of the nerves, must, in course of a few generations, decidedly change the nervous organization of men. . . . We have seen that the progress of civilization brings men into more intimate relations, that closer contact quickens activity, that increased activity refines the nervous system, and that a highly nervous organization invites intemperance, and at the same time renders its destructive results swifter and more fatal. (Strong [1885] 1891, p. 130)

The rise of nervous disorders causing an epidemic of intemperance in the United States was only part of a trans-Atlantic pattern of moral and psychological pathology that bound together the vanguard societies of modern civilization. According to Strong, Great Britain, Belgium, Holland, and Germany, the European countries lying in the belt of nervous disorders, showed a marked increase in the use of alcohol during the last half century.

The occurrence of suicide began to attract worldwide attention as a peculiar problem of these urbanizing, industrializing, and commercializing societies. Scholars and social reformers in Europe and The United States found the phenomenon of suicide to be a key to the character of the new urban culture and probed for its causes. Some experts argued that biological traits could be related to suicide. For example, it was argued that the repressed personalities of Nordic Europeans predisposed more city dwellers of this ancestry to suicide than those with the sunnier dispositions of Mediterranean Europeans. Geography was invoked as a concurrent factor causing suicide. The colder, darker climate of the north caused depression and anxiety that had driven unstable persons to suicide. The sheer size of cities, however, did not seem sufficient to account for the phenomenon of suicide. London and New York City were the two largest cities in the Atlantic world, but they had the lowest per capita rate of suicide at the end of the 19th century.

The new science of sociology produced a new set of explanations for the mysterious causation of suicide that focused on the unique character of urban societies.

Sociologists believed that the stressful social conditions of urban life were the key. The city's social pace and dynamism outstripped the individual's adaptive ability, the industrial conditions of work were so dehumanizing and degrading as to create psychological depression, and the general competitive atmosphere of cities produced psychic stress and emotional exhaustion.

The eminent French sociologist, Emile Durkheim, tried to analyze all these causal factors in his famous treatise *Suicide* (1897). He inferred from a systematic ecological study that the cause of suicide was a socio-psychological state, particularly found among the professional and commercial classes of cities, called "anomie," a term he coined to signify social detachment or isolation. The atomization of individuals in the urban centrifuge created a lifestyle devoid of community, family, and meaningful intimate associations, a sociological emptiness that could lead all too often to despair and suicide.

The research on the pathologies of city life of European sociologists such as Durkheim, Georg Simmel, and Max Weber was studied in America. A stream of pessimistic social thought flowed between Europe and America, as the trans-Atlantic industrial revolution produced new and complex urban societies. Scholars and commentators created an international sociological discourse to explore common concerns about the capacity of new urban cultures to shape social existence. The negativism of their depiction of city life was partly due to the fact that personal deterioration and social disintegration were much more visible in the city than they had been in the country. Furthermore, they were gripped by an intellectual unease that came from an encounter with an unprecedented place, the great metropolis of industry, technology, and people in transit that had only existed for one or two generations. Many of the new urbanists took their critical perspective toward the city from the paradigm of rural society that still dominated European and American culture well into the 19th century.

The City as a Rough Frontier of Enclaves

Metropolitan police services that professionally protected public safety had only been in operation since the middle of the 19th century. In many urban centers, they found themselves overstrained with work. In Boston, the police barely kept up with rates of burglary, robbery, larceny, assault, and murder that reached a high point in the late 1870s. Organized thuggery confounded police departments everywhere. In New Orleans, street gangs such as the Spiders and the Yellow Harry Mob, overpowered available police forces. In Chicago, Regan's Colts—a huge youth gang—prowled the sidewalks around the turn of the century. These organized gangs and their counterparts in other cities were used as "muscle" by criminal syndicates and political rings.

The dark half-life, the underside of the urban social world, provided endless material for the publishers of police gazettes, dime novels, and a new genre of urban expose literature. In 1883, urban reformer Anthony Comstock published *Traps for the Young*, a shocking narrative of New York's gambling joints, bars, and theatrical shows. Comstock challenged the public: "Let the reader who has never visited this illuminated den go with me in imagination to see the wicked character of the place pictured as well as I am able to paint it."

Cheap pulp tabloids found an audience among the middle class reading public who, barricaded in suburban enclaves, thrilled vicariously at the vivid accounts of violent crime and lurid vice. These publications propagated the image of a nation that President Grover Cleveland's Attorney General Richard Olney thought bordered on anarchy. Frightening stories could prey on middle-class insularity and ignorance to produce an overpowering sense of degeneration at the center of industrial urban society where the rule of reason was being severely challenged, where the stabilizing culture of rational control forged by the middle class could not act effectively as an antidote to disorder.

That urban centers were turning into horrid slums was vividly evident to a congressional investigatory committee that held hearings on the conditions of New York City tenements. Edward Bellamy's *Looking Backward* (1888) also supplied a memorable and nightmarish description of a Boston slum that confirmed the worst fear of suburbanites in Dorchester, Roxbury, and Jamaica Plain:

> From the black doorways and windows of the rookeries on every side came gusts of fetid air. The streets and alleys reeked with the effluvia of a slave ship's between-decks. As I passed I had glimpses within of pale babies gasping out their lives amid sultry stenches, of hopeless-faced women deformed by hardship. . . . Like the starving band of mongrel curs that infest the streets of Moslem towns, swarms of half-clad brutalized children filled the air with shrieks and curses as they fought and tumbled among the garbage.

Urban expose journalism gained a new weapon in the 1880s when advances in flash photography made it possible to present degraded slum life with unprecedented, graphic clarity. The two most important uses of the new photographic technique occurred in Jacob Riis's *How the Other Half Lives* (1890), with its arresting pictures of poor immigrants, and Helen Campbell's *Darkness and Daylight; or, Lights and Shadows of New York Life* (1892). These two lengthy books described in melodramatic prose scenes wretched tenements, police stations, orphanages, gambling houses, opium dens, and all-night liquor dives, which produced the same effect on the Victorian public as oceanographer Robert Ballard's underwater videos of eerie wreckage and life forms on the ocean bottoms produced in our day. Pondering this new photographically enhanced urban journalism, the Reverend Walter Rauschenbusch wrote about men and women, who like African or polar explorers, plunged into the life of the lower classes and then wrote books about the experience as if describing an unknown race.

Popular writers described social disorganization in American cities that was part of a worldwide devolution into urban dystopia. Josiah Strong's *Our Country* lamented "our Cincinnatis have become Chicagos, our Chicagos New Yorks, and our New Yorks Londons," and warned that when the ignorant and vicious power" of urban America had "fully found itself, . . . the volcanic fires of deep discontent" would explode with terrible force (Strong [1885] 1891, p. 143). The fears articulated by

Strong were felt by enough people to inspire disaster novels that attained great popularity. Ignatius Donnelly's *Caesar's Column* (1891), an early example of science fiction, described a global social upheaval of the underclasses unleashed by a band of anarchists seeking to overthrow an international plutocracy. The uprising led by an Italian immigrant, a giant named Caesar Lomellini, first devastates New York City and then spreads across the globe to destroy civilization worldwide.

The explosive menace of urban life pictured in late-19th-century popular writings represented a change from the early-19th-century view of urban disorder. Ante-bellum critics had been concerned with the characterological effects of the city on the individual. They worried about immorality, the hardening of spirit, predatory coldness, sensualism, and the dissipated lifestyles that the city fostered. In the late-19th-century city, the fear of social disorder not only concerned these effects upon personality, but also fixated on an urban threat that could destroy American and world civilization. Barbarian hordes had taken over the city and they threatened soon to destroy the republic. In his fanciful novel, *The Iron Heel,* Jack London referred to the urban underclass as "the people of the abyss." The poor were no longer a pitiable group, but a depraved mob threatening at any moment to become a "resistless flood . . . sweeping all before it," as Jacob Riis had also worried. In his apocalyptic *Caesar's Column*, Donnelly portrayed them as a subhuman race, "the canaille."

To many contemporaries who lived in the industrial city, America's urban centers were nothing less than the battleground between the forces of civilization and progress, on one hand, and the forces of barbarism and degeneration, on the other. And, unhappily, it was not clear which side would emerge victorious from the Armageddon-like confrontation. Several real developments contributed to the popularization of a social-clash model of American society at the end of the 19th century.

An important process that stimulated the perception of inescapable social conflict was the shift in immigration from countries in Northern and Western Europe after 1890 to an immigration that flowed chiefly from Southern and Eastern Europe. The diversification of the immigrant population occurred in the largest cities. In the first decade of the 20th century, New York City, Chicago, and Boston were chiefly composed of immigrants and their children, most of whom were coming from Italy, Russia, Poland, Greece, and other countries of Southern and Eastern Europe. Anxious native-born Americans of British and Protestant origins interpreted this shift as introducing an inferior racial element that undermined society.

Another emerging social pattern that gave the impression of profound social cleavage was the increase in size of the industrial working class who owned no property and only possessed their labor power as their sole economic asset. By contrast, in the era before the industrial revolution, when farming dominated the economy, more people had had landed property or stood to inherit it.

Blue-collar work took place in settings that were physically dangerous and stressful. Work was tedious, regimented, and grinding. Under these conditions, blue-collar workers often lost their health and vigor rapidly. Twenty-years of working sixty or more house a week left many factory hands in their forties too debilitated to work a regular schedule.

In the industrial city's geography, working-class populations were starkly segregated from the middle class. The worker communities were in turn subdivided into enclaves by ethnicity. Commentators described the ethnic subdivisions in terms equivalent to what became understood as "balkanization."

Reformers such as Jacob Riis documented how working-class housing was poorly constructed and maintained, and degenerated easily into slums. Public sanitation services were not sufficient to keep sidewalks and streets from becoming filthy. In the 1880s, half the children born in Chicago did not live beyond early childhood due to epidemic disease and inadequate health care. General infant mortality was higher in urban centers than in rural communities. Those who dwelled in slum housing were actually the fortunate, because thousands of people in New York City, Chicago, Detroit, Pittsburgh, and Philadelphia were homeless in 1900.

The family life of the working class diverged profoundly from that of the middle class. Working-class families generally had several children, who entered the labor force well before adulthood, and were unshielded from street life. The household was subsistence oriented with wives often seeking employment; parents did not foresee the possibility for retirement in old age. In white-collar families, by contrast, parents usually had a small number of children, prolonged their schooling, insulated them from external influences, and planned for savings to support intergenerational social mobility and retirement.

The specter of "two Americas," a profoundly divided nation, was evoked by Jacob Riis's *How the Other Half Lives*. Its title implied how the two halves of American society were not only separate and discrete, but also how they were out of touch with each other. Riis wrote this book to bring about proper social communication between the two halves of society. He felt that his readers would learn how this social division had a powerful potential for destructive class hatred.

Building Social Capital in the Enclaves

In the last half of the 19th century, American cities did not fall apart, in spite of deepening social divisions and tensions. Instead, they began to create a public life that would bring together the urban multitudes. In new institutions and activities, city people built new types of social and civic relations that bridged groups with dissimilar origins. A new public culture had to counteract the atomization of individuals, social fragmentation, and the alienation caused by the divides of class, race, religion, and ethnicity.

City governments tried to invent new ways of building and managing an inclusive community. The city supplied the educational needs of children by reforming and expanding the system of public schools. The public school of the late 19th century adopted a reformed curriculum suited to the practical needs of citizenship and productive work in the changing urban world. The duties of city leaders also included providing places for religious worship, institutions for the care of dependent persons, recreational facilities, and public forums for cultural expression and civic celebrations. City leaders took very seriously the task of constructing public monuments and venerated spaces that stimulated civic patriotism.

The functional organization of urban activities stimulated new creative techniques to monitor public identities. Banks, businesses, schools, police forces, and government officials yearned for a kind of total index that would identify and locate every resident of a city so that each person could be made accountable for responsible activity in private and public life. In the 19th century, city directories, school enrollments, censuses, business directories, and police registers constituted together a rough total public index that treated everyone as an anonymous trackable unit, a "number." The growth of municipal agencies, requirements for official registration, and the responsibilities of public administration increased the number of sources that kept record files on the location and status of individuals.

Increasing state authority created a new establishment of coercive force, the professional police, which was formed in most large cities by the middle of the 19th century. Civil engineers introduced spatial rationalization into the city's geography to facilitate the rapid deployment of police or militias to quell crime outbreaks and violent upheavals.

The industrializing city afforded the freedom for new voluntary activities that expanded civil society. It allowed for the initiative of the civic minded to create new community ties and to foster the public interest. Individuals seeking a particularistic form of public community started mutual-benefit organizations. These voluntary associations multiplied rapidly throughout 19th-century cities and drew together the masses of newcomers to the city into organized memberships directed toward the collaborative pursuit of economic welfare, social activities, and cultural refinement. Many urban newcomers longed for the collective familiarity of village worlds they had left behind. Immigrants formed regional societies based on antecedents in particular villages in their homelands. Civic neighborhood clubs developed from the common public concerns of urban enclaves.

Philanthropic, religious, educational, recreational, and cultural organizations provided the institutional framework in which interpersonal bonds were formed, sociability stimulated, and public identity fostered. They formed the new public spaces where orderly building of support networks could aid individuals in gaining connections, status, and a voice that was heard in the community. In other words, these institutions were instruments for building intermediate levels of voluntary association—civil society—in the city. As such, they formed social capital, norms, and values that facilitated group collaboration.

The expansion of civil society fortified the bonds of community and cooperative potential in the volatile world of American industrial cities. The continuous flow of outsiders into the city pressured established organizations to redefine constantly their membership boundaries. They faced repeatedly the issues of whether to change or to loosen requirements for joining and how to reach out to new potential candidates for membership.

Legions of low-skilled workers who had little say or control over government institutions developed their own communal voluntary associations that they managed in their own interests and on their own terms. They formed ethnic lodges, mutual benefit societies, credit associations, recreational clubs, and churches that generated social capital.

The first collective acts of immigrant workers were to establish benevolent associations that operated on the principle of mutual social trust. From a club of countrymen, an immigrant obtained funds on loan that helped defray the cost of medical care, food, heating fuel, or a funeral service. For those living on the thinnest of wages and who had few allies and supporters outside the narrow circle of fellow immigrants, such benefits could provide the all-important margin of survival. Support for benevolent mutualist associations was widely spread and intensely popular, with local memberships of some clubs reaching over a hundred persons. In Pennsylvania factory towns, for example, a constellation of ethnic associations operated locally and were federated together nationally as the Polish National Alliance, the Greek Catholic Union, the First Catholic Slovak Union, and the National Croatian Society.

The scale of the industrial metropolis permitted other sources of communalism and social stability to form. The social structure and the geography of the city accommodated the establishment of myriad, self-sufficient residential enclaves defined by ethnicity and class. The enormous diversity of the economy of the industrial city permitted workers to form occupational segments within the labor force. Jews worked in the garment industry, the Irish in the building trades, and the Italians in construction. Geographic, social, and economic factors created an urban ecology that promoted segregation and self-segregation. The resulting compartmentalization of segments of the population reduced the areas for unregulated conflict between groups. It narrowed the horizon for insecurity and vulnerability to outsiders and intensified social supports within communities.

Segregation also cut in another direction. It could promote xenophobia, cultural insularity, and removal from wider channels of social and cultural contact. The intense communalism created by urban segregation drew energy from the continuous waves of immigrants who renewed the foreign culture and its particularistic power. Enclaves defined by ethnicity, race, and class often defended their sphere of existence against newcomers and outsiders rather than uniting with them.

The turn-of-the-century industrial city came to support many differentiated spheres of popular culture within its social boundaries. Each was equipped with its own expressive idioms and seldom overlapped with one another. Each sphere catered to different social subgroups. None was inclusive enough to incorporate the whole population. Cultural differentiation and segregation shaped theatrical entertainments that depended on paid spectatorship. The vaudeville theatre appealed to young middle-class people and was developed by a cadre of entrepreneurs like B.F. Keith who started to build his empire from his base in downtown Boston. The music hall was patronized by the working class. Some ethnic groups, such as Jews, Italians, and Chinese, operated their own theaters and staged their own performances.

By the turn of the century, new entertainment and educational forums centered in cities began to shape a more homogenized and inclusive style of mass culture. World's fairs held in Chicago, St. Louis, and San Francisco attracted immense and diverse crowds who mingled together and experienced a collective fascination with exhibits that displayed new technologies and the wonders of foreign lands. The rise

Every economic class found appeal in attractions like Coney Island, a place that offered afford-able entertainment, and it continues to be a major draw to this day. (Library of Congress)

of mass spectator sports also occurred in urban centers. Football and baseball teams first at the school and college level drew elite audiences, but as they were reorganized in regional professional leagues they began to attract a mass audience of paying spectators known as "fans." Boxing also expanded rapidly into one of the most popular spectator sports. Motion pictures, player pianos, and phonograph recordings multiplied in urban entertainment districts and were put on sale in a vast popular market for domestic consumption.

Entire districts in cities were transformed into preserves for cheap popular amusements and entertainments. In New York City, the Bowery, Coney Island, and the Tenderloin housed, according to one guidebook, "a class of resorts such as a respectable person would not like to be seen in." However, in these districts new institutions developed that broke down the cultural partitions separating elites, the middle class, and ethnic minorities. The cabaret and the nightclub drew members of respectable society who came to be entertained and to rub shoulders with a mixed crowd. These institutions for crossover intermingling thrived in areas like Manhattan's Broadway, which was transformed by outdoor electrical lighting into a gaudy and fantastic public playground of nightlife.

Population Growth and Social Structure

Native-born Americans of the mid-19th century, who were the great grandchildren of the generation that had founded the United States, were astonished by the rapid pace of change in their new republic. The United States began the 19th century as a nation with a miniature population in comparison to the countries of the Eastern Hemisphere. In 1800, the United States had only 5.3 million inhabitants, while France had 27.4 million, the German states had 23.0 million, and Britain had 20.8 million. The Asian countries of China, India, and the Ottoman Empire dwarfed the United States in population. Beginning the 19th century as a sparsely populated land, the United States started to expand at a growth rate surpassing those of European countries. From 1800 to 1850, the U.S. population quintupled to over 23 million inhabitants, while the populations of France and Germany grew by about a quarter.

Two forces propelled the unusually rapid rise of the U.S. population. The first had roots in the demographics of fertility. The United States achieved a high rate of fertility from 1800 that exceeded that of European countries. In 1800, an average of seven children were born to a woman by the end of her childbearing in the United States, compared to slightly over five in England, and slightly over four in France. Although the U.S. fertility rate gradually declined, it continued to lead over the fertility rates of France and England. The second factor that raised the pace of population growth in the United States was an accelerating rate of mass immigration. The number of foreign-born people annually entering the United States grew steadily from several thousand in the 1820s to over 300,000 in the 1850s. The vast majority of these newcomers came from Europe, producing a net loss for the population of European countries.

The number of Americans who lived in cities and towns grew faster from 1790 to 1860 than in any other time in American history. In 1790, 9 of 10 Americans derived their living from farming; in 1860, nearly half of all employed persons worked in nonagricultural occupations. The "face-to-face" society typical of village-size communities gave way to larger and denser settlements. These new centers attracted masses of people from a variety of distant places. The newcomers were increasingly anonymous to each other and struggled to build communal institutions. In the first quarter of the century, the master artisan's household of servants, journeymen, and apprentices lived and worked together to form an extended family. However, by the 1830s more and more workers toiled in factory-like shops where they were treated as "hands," and lived in poor and segregated neighborhoods without paternalistic care or supervision.

Working-class urban enclaves were fed by a swelling migration of poor, young laborers from the countryside, seeking jobs in the sprouting manufacturing shops. Increasingly, by the middle of the 19th century, immigrants from Canada, Ireland, Germany, Scandinavia, and other parts of Western Europe who sought urban employments settled into the worker enclaves.

Immigrants from Scandinavia and Germany also followed the flow of settlers to the territories around the Great Lakes, which were quickly being turned into new states. Norwegians and Swedes carved out farms in Wisconsin, Michigan, and Minnesota. They were joined by even more numerous German immigrants who fanned out widely to start farms in Ohio, Missouri, Iowa, Nebraska, and Texas.

From 1840 to 1860, the rapidly multiplying population of the United States was being reconfigured geographically as flows of migrants from the American countryside and from foreign lands steadily accumulated. The nation's population grew at the rate of doubling every 25 years. With a population of 31 million people in 1860, the United States was nearly as large as France, the most populous country in Europe. The United States was unlike any country in Europe, however, since it possessed a long, open borderland known as the western "frontier" that kept shifting further and further toward the Pacific Coast. The movement of people toward the frontier traced an ever-lengthening arc of settlement pointing to the west. As a result, the "geographic center of population," the point around which the national population was equally distributed in every direction, kept moving progressively westward. In 1790, it was located in Maryland; by 1860 it was in Ohio. As population surged to the west, the creation of new territories and then states followed regularly. A new state gained admission to the union on an average of every three years. The 16 states that composed the United States in 1800 multiplied to 33 states in 1860.

Industrial urban society developed into a stable and nationally dominant sector in the decades spanning the late 19th to the early 20th century. The rapid shift of resources and labor to urban centers caused by industrialization began to settle into a more regular and smooth pattern but retained continuing dynamism.

The growth of the city and the multiplication of urban centers meant an enlarged urban influence through production and distribution of goods, information, and values that reduced urban-rural differences. By 1920, the United States had 68 cities of at least 100,000 inhabitants, which was probably more cities of that size than existed in any other country in the world. The population of these 68 cities represented one-fourth of the total population of the United States.

American culture was being transformed through the urban control of industrial society. The demographic dominance of big cities had profound consequences for the socioeconomic order and for the mainstream culture of the country. In 1800, the United States was a country without a city of 100,000 people, whereas Europe had 21 cities of that size. By 1900, New York City was bigger than Berlin, Bombay, Calcutta, Edinburgh, and Tokyo, and was in size of population surpassed only by London.

Urban environments and urban forms of culture extended further and further from the central city, bringing their ethos of artificiality, heterogeneity, impersonality, competition, and transitory social relations to nearby regions. The suburbs succumbed to the congestion, overcrowding, moving masses, and dense arrangements of buildings of unprecedented height. As land became urbanized—rationally planned for functionalism and economic profit—it was formed into an exact grid of streets and blocks. Urban workplaces such as the office building and factory helped to spread the industrial discipline of employment. More and more Americans worked according to the clock and in large regimented units. Urban society crystallized into a new and permanent framework for shaping the collective behavior of the American nation.

Out from the big city came the urban styles, products, and consumer tastes that changed cultural horizons in small towns and rural communities. The national communication and transportation revolution centered in cities created wider markets for urban consumer trends and commodities. Ready-made clothing, appliances, household supplies, recreational equipment, and forms of mass entertainment radiated through all the areas of the country through the mail-order catalog and the circulation of magazines and newspapers.

This wide-ranging commercial process democratized consumer behavior and helped to raise the living standard of the ordinary American. The workday and the number of weekly workdays grew, but the workday also shortened gradually. Despite the low wages, wage rates rose continuously, while consumer products became increasingly affordable. Americans with more leisure and assets were being integrated into new communities of consumers that extended from the downtown to the suburbs.

The large cities of the country became centers for a new public school system that shaped upcoming generations to take their place in a complex modern society. Its classrooms included children of the new immigrants who came from Southern and Eastern Europe, the Caribbean, East Asia, and other distant parts of the world. The public school created a common peer group learning experience in which shared outlooks, civic understanding, and useful common knowledge were gained that in totality added up to a new sense of American national identity.

The coupled processes of industrialization and urbanization had created new separations among the American people but these processes also organized the population into new more inclusive communities. New communities developed out of innovative forms of functional collective activity: mass production, popular consumerism, entertainment and sports spectatorship, ethnic communalism, mutual-benefit fraternalism, and the public culture of cities. The industrializing city also created a new ecology of territorial communities: tenement districts, shopping districts, ethnic enclaves, and streetcar suburbs. The complex fabric of life in industrial cities acculturated Americans to democratic pluralism. A concept of group co-existence called the "melting pot" sprang out of the urban experience and came to symbolize a new America of dynamic changes, bewildering choices, and diversity.

Globalization and Immigrant America

Immigration to the United States occurred in a surrounding world of accelerating spatial movement and regional interconnectivity. From the onset of the Cold War, the global expansion of corporate businesses, mass media, military installations, and commercial exchanges created new networks of international contact that stimulated immigration to the United States. Informal support networks based on family or neighborhood connections helped immigrants to cross international frontiers of opportunity shaped by economic differentials between countries.

A Mexican immigrant, Graciela Mendoza Pena Valencia, recalled how her arrival in the United States was arranged by her uncle who had settled earlier in California. Graciela was 14 years old when her parents received a message: "My uncle wrote to my parents they have money for me to stay with them in Los Angeles. Is my mother's brother. That first day I come from Mexico, I come on the bus. . . . He take me to inspection" (Namias 1992, p. 177).

Worldwide immigration of the late 20th century increasingly became the byproduct of inter-state and intra-state activities: schemes for partition, repopulating new territories, civil war, ethnic cleansing, and the solution of domestic unemployment and economic underdevelopment. In the aftermath of World Wars I and II, "displaced persons" uprooted by armed conflict and governmental regime changes sought havens in foreign countries.

An important factor increasing immigration to the United States has been the expansion of forced migration. The global flow of refugees and IDPs (internally displaced people) swelled in the last decades of the 20th century with the expansion of intra-state conflict in the form of civil wars and ethnic cleansing programs. The United States became the leader in refugee resettlement and in granting asylum. In 2000, 72,500 refugees were resettled in the United States, while the next largest number of refugees resettled were 13,500 in Canada, 6,600 in Australia, and 1,500 in Sweden and Norway each. The refugees resettling in the United States reflected the leading sources of refugees, the countries of Central America, Eastern Europe, Asia, Africa, and the Middle East.

Forced migration assumed greater salience as postcolonial and emergent states grew more active in engineering population movements for the purposes of national and regional domination. The rise of intra-state conflict due to ethnic hostilities and violence between dominant and minority subgroups accelerated this trend. Regimes used military aggression to relocate or expel marginalized or excluded groups to consolidate control of their territory and nation. The militarization of ethnic conflict escalated into civil war or international war and thereby fed the growing streams of forced migrants. The world's refugee population grew to 30 million by 2000 as more people were put at risk of becoming forced migrants, due to war and attendant civil chaos.

The increasing integration of the international political order in the course of the 20th century linked U.S. immigration control policy in closer coordination with diplomatic relations. For example, the United States has vigorously utilized refugee admissions policies to further its alliances with foreign nations and to promote its interests against adversaries. This strategic use of refugee policies and programs became prominent during the Cold War. Thomas Blatt was able to gain admission as a refugee from Hungary in 1956 during this country's abortive revolution against Soviet communist domination. He recalled how suddenly and quickly his life changed after the unexpected events brought about political and military threats from the outside:

> I was twenty-three when I left; I had just finished college. I was reasonably adult so I remember everything in detail; in fact, the whole thing started at our university. . . . The university students . . . marched on October 23rd. . . . The uprising was a completely spontaneous matter. . . . Even the day it started there was no indication. . . . [The] tanks and everybody came in with two hundred thousand soldiers. It was just ridiculous at that point. On November 9th, we realized it's all over, and on

November 13th we left. I didn't want to get out of there, but it was hopeless. There was no serious possibility because the border was mined. Hungary was completely surrounded by Communist countries: Czechoslovakia in the north, Yugoslavia in the south, and of course Russia in the east and Romania in the southeast. (Namias 1992, pp. 146–54)

The wave of refugees who arrived from Cuba in the early 1960s illustrated the effects of Cold War policies that provided admission to those escaping from Communist regimes. Rodolfo de Leon came to Miami in 1962 as an 11-year-old boy with his mother and brother, followed soon after by his father, his maternal grandparents, two aunts, and an uncle. Long after his arrival, Rodolfo still looked at the world with the dual perspective of a refugee torn between two worlds. In the 1970s, he offered this reflection that probably represented the mental horizon of other Cuban Americans of his generation:

I would like to go back to my country. But I've been here such a long time! I'd like to be able to drive around the place where I was born, once in a blue moon, you know. And I like to be with my own people and say, that's where my father used to own his business, and that's where I lived, and this is where I played when I was a kid, and these are my people. . . . Do I think my parents are happy here? No. But they have to keep their myth up. They belong to another generation—old Cuba. (Namias [1978] 1992, p. 163)

The United States, like many countries in Europe, received a growing flow of undocumented aliens, whose numbers had mounted to several million illegal residents by 2000. The growth of an illegal alien population reflected the rise of state activism. Illegal immigration became severely problematic after the state installed more stringent admissions requirements that increased the numbers of excludable people who clamored for entry.

The need for controlling the labor market of the United States and Mexico led these two countries into agreements that coordinated binational economic relations with policies for interstate migration. During World War II, the United States and Mexico developed an international agreement in which "braceros," agricultural guest workers from Mexico, were allowed temporary employment in the United States. The bracer program lasted from 1943 to 1964. Under the leadership of President Bill Clinton, the United States and Mexico signed the North American Fair Trade Agreement (NAFTA) in 1995, aiming to strengthen the regional economy but also to contain the flow of migration, both legal and undocumented, to the United States by creating more employment in Mexico. NAFTA attempted to coordinate economic development in regions of Mexico that had high out-migration due to underemployment

As with the bracero program and NAFTA in the United States, the role of the state in creating and regulating flows of international migration has grown as interstate frameworks for cooperation have taken root. In the Middle East, in Europe, and in Asia, states sought to control and manage human resources through treaties to regulate international migration. The general trend toward political integration of the world affected global patterns of migration. The creation of the European

Union fostered migration between member states. The expansion of relationships between states that permitted immigrants to hold dual nationality also promoted immigration.

"Sun Belt" migration in the late 20th century to far western states made the United States bi-coastal. Waves of postwar migration flowed to the West Coast as descendants of European immigrants left the Midwest, South, and Northeast. New Asian and Hispanic migration transformed the Pacific Coast and spread eastward. New Asian immigrants arrived from China, Southeast Asia, the Philippines, and refugee communities of "boat people." To the U.S. mainland and Hawaii also came an unprecedented Pacific Islander mass migration from U.S. Samoa and former German Samoa, Tonga, Fiji, and French Polynesia.

Progressively widening patterns of intermarriage between people of European ancestry and people from countries in the Pacific region made Hawaii into the state with the highest proportion of "multiracial" Americans, according to the 2000 U.S. Census. The power and momentum of these processes appeared in the U.S. Census of 2000, which enumerated individuals by multiracial ancestry, and were reflected in the admissions control policies that have created an immigrant population of worldwide origins in New World receiver nations; in the role of the United States and other nations as countries of transit for temporary laborers; and in the unprecedented mass immigration of Africans and other newcomers from the developing world.

Journalists and scholars who observed the enclaves formed by recent immigrants found that a flourishing communal life enabled Asian, Hispanic, and Caribbean Americans to adapt positively and functionally. Enclaves provided an environmental support system for immigrant parents who wished to insulate their children from what they perceived as corrupting and demoralizing features of mass culture. The role of the immigrant enclave in filtering out disorganizing external influences was not new. Early in the 20th century, in Jewish, Greek, German, Armenian, and Italian communities in the industrial Northeast and Midwest and in Chinese, Japanese, and Korean communities in the far west, the cultural and social structures of the ethnic ghetto warded off extraneous disturbances and conserved the immigrant disciplines of industry, thrift, and mutual assistance.

As among the immigrants who preceded them, the post-1965 worldwide immigrants invigorated the culture of neighborhood citizenship and democracy. They endeavored to become an active part of communal government and politics to increase their opportunities. Asians, Latinos, Caribbeans, Africans, Eastern Europeans, and Middle Eastern immigrants diligently prepared themselves for naturalization. They did all the things earlier immigrants had done in terms of obtaining programs and services, education for their children, and engaging with local and civil governments.

Transnational Encounter, Shuttling between Worlds

Underlying what became popularly known as the "transnational" quality of the immigrants' experience was the rise of temporary and repeat migration as central patterns in the global movements of people. *New York Times* reporters examined these patterns by describing the dual dimensions of life facing Dominican immigrants in the United States as follows:

> Fernando Mateo has been shuttling between New York City and Santo Domingo since he was in utero. His pint-sized immigrant mother, belly swelling, flew back to her homeland so Mr. Mateo, now 40, could be born a Dominican. After that, his childhood was split between here and there, between a cramped Lower East Side Apartment and a pink house beneath a mahogany tree in the Dominican capital. As an adult, Mr. Mateo, a stocky man with a dimpled baby face, continues to lead a double life, with gusto. A dual citizen of the Dominican Republic and the United States, he wears a custom-made lapel pin that entwines the Dominican and American flags. He is fluent in Spanish and English, in the business handshake and the business hug, in yucca and plantains, bagels and lox. But there is nothing fractured about his existence. Every few weeks, Mr. Mateo, who owns a money transfer company, simply commutes between the Westchester County suburb of Irvington, where he lives, and Santo Domingo. Many a day, he and his wife, Stella, start out in blaring traffic on the Grand Central Parkway and end up on horseback in the verdant Dominican countryside, cantering down to a river to feast on rum and goat. "I believe people like us have the best of two worlds," Mr. Mateo said. "We have two countries, two homes. It doesn't make any sense for us to be either this or that. We're both. It's not a conflict. It's just a human fact." (Sontag and Dugger 1998, p. 1)

For modern immigrants like Mr. Mateo, the homeland is no longer something to be forsaken, released into a mist of memory or nostalgia. As the world has grown smaller, the immigrant experience has inevitably changed. Unlike the Europeans who fled persecution and war in the first half of this century, few modern immigrants abandon their motherlands forever, shutting one door, opening another and never looking back. Instead they straddle two worlds, in varying degrees, depending on where they came from and what they can afford. Some immerse themselves in two societies at once—economically, culturally, politically.

Immigration to the United States and departure from the old-country home, however, inevitably leads to subtle changes in life outlook even for newcomers who keep connected to both. After long years in a transnational mode of life, immigrants found that they neither fitted in smoothly with their roots in the United States or their roots in their homelands. An immigrant from Trinidad reflected thoughtfully about changes in herself and her perception of her roots:

> I think this is the struggle that you go through every day, havin' this yearnin' to go back since you came because, although you have lived here and you have accepted a lot of American customs, you still have ties with your *roots*. Take, for instance, me. I have been away since 1960; and I always think of Trinidad as when I left it. But then you go home periodically and you see that things have changed! It's not like what you left it as, but you still have that *yearnin'* to go back and try to fit in, although I know I can't fit in. When I go back home, I'm too accustomed to this life here in America: getting up in the morning, goin' to work, hustlin', hustlin', hustlin'. I think it's something that I trained myself into, and I wouldn't be able to go back home and be relaxed as I was when I was there as a kid. (Namias [1978] 1992, p. 189)

From the Cold War to the start of the 21st century, immigrants to the United States exhibited a new "double-ended connection" that held their lives in their

American host society together with their homeland places of origin. Transnational migration has intensified in the era of globalization, leading some to visualize the unfolding present and future in terms of the end of assimilationist patterns within the nation-state. Technology has reached unprecedented capacity for furthering communications and movement between home and host societies. Nevertheless, all is not unprecedented. Migrants who were not fully assimilated in one country or another existed in the past due to advances in international transportation and communication. Chinese immigrants in the 19th century; Italian and Slavic immigrants at the turn of the century; and West Indian immigrants, Mexican immigrants, and Puerto Rican migrants all developed features of transnational existence in their collective lives.

Flows of economic and social remittances created by immigrant communities have formed a vital conduit connecting the United States with homeland societies. Economic remittances sent by immigrants to relatives and organizations at home have helped boost economic activity in local communities. Social remittances—forms of social assistance provided to pay back received social favors or support—have furthered the workings of networks that facilitate chain migration. In the decades at the end of the 20th century, the provision of economic and social remittances through immigration has been facilitated by the rapid communication and cultural link-ups made possible by the global telecommunications revolution.

In the late 20th century, mass immigration returned to the United States on a scale comparable to the early 20th century. In the three decades after 1960, 15 million immigrants entered the country legally and probably 3–5 million entered illegally. The percentage of the foreign-born in the population rose to 11.5%, the highest level since 1910 when it reached 14.8%. In the last half of the 20th century, the United States had the greatest intake of immigrants of any country. In the size of its net international migrant stock in 2000, the United States towered above the rest of the world with an estimated 35 million. The next closest countries—the Russian Federation and Germany—lagged far behind at 13.3 and 7.3 million, respectively.

The global age of American immigration unfolding at the end of the 20th century, like the industrial era of immigration before it, was a time for re-evaluating the character of the nation and its destiny. New sources of immigration to the United States emerged on a global platform and the characteristics of newcomers became increasingly representative of worldwide cultures. By hosting the world's largest population of global migrants, the United States served as a key base of the human networks and intercultural linkages that forged the worldwide integration of societies and economies.

The Migrant Roots of National Diversity

The multicultural age of global American immigration unfolding at the end of the 20th century, like the industrial era of immigration before it, was a time for re-evaluating the character of the nation and its destiny. These were not unique developments on the compass of world history. In other lands and other eras, the arrival of new peoples through invasion, migration, or conquest challenged host societies to reappraise their institutions and identities. Confronting newcomers with alien habits and values, natives were compelled to take stock of their capacity for group coexistence.

In the final decades of the 20th century, experts vied with each other to describe how Americans were witnessing the birth of a diversity society. The publicists heralding the age of diversity made it hard to notice that the new diversity was a child of old historic patterns. The political and media culture hindered as much as helped citizens seeking to inform themselves in linking recent immigration to the human waves that preceded it, in seeing the multicultural present as part of a long and continuous succession of superimposed cultures, a historical palimpsest. All too often, the public saw the surface of diversity and concluded that it was wholly novel. Thus, some misjudged it as a new threat and others as a new utopia, when it was in reality a familiar outgrowth of roots deep in the national past.

By contrast, the middle decades of the 20th century, after restrictive legislation and the Great Depression staunched the great migrations of the industrializing era, were a time when scholars could take stock of immigration relatively free of the emotions and partisanship of immigration politics. At a Princeton American Studies symposium in 1942, the scholar David F. Bowers noted that the "origin and growth of the United States represented one chapter in the history of a great migration" that extended "over a period of four hundred years." "To find a movement comparable in magnitude, velocity, and social profundity," Bowers argued, "it is necessary to go back to the barbarian invasions of Rome, and beyond these to the wanderings of primitive tribes in prehistoric times." Looking backward after the industrial revolution, Bowers described three reasons why the United States among all countries "has probably been influenced most" by the impact of immigration (Bowers 1944, pp. 3–5):

> In the first place, it was among the earliest of the new nations to be colonized, and, therefore, one of those affected longest.
> In the second place, it has been the most important of the immigrant-receiving countries, admitting between 1820 and 1930 no less than 38 million immigrants, or about sixty per cent of the total number estimated for the period.
> And, in the third place, as a growing culture with few traditions of its own, it has always been alert to discover and to seize upon the arts and beliefs of other people. (Bowers 1944, pp. 3–5)

According to Bowers, the existence of these three historical conditions assured that "[f]oreign influences in America have poured in through many different channels, have affected in one way or another almost every phase of our national life, and have recreated continuously throughout our history" (Bowers 1944, pp. 3–5).

Indeed, the historical record that Bowers gazed upon showed that the immigration of the era of industrialization produced a social and cultural diversity rivaling and surpassing in certain respects the vaunted multiculturalism of the late 20th century. The fastest growth of immigration in American history occurred in the decades preceding the Civil War. The proportion of foreign-born in the American population reached its historic peak in the half-century after the Civil War. In this era, a majority of inhabitants in the nation's largest cities were immigrants or the children of immigrants. Asian immigrants composed a higher percentage of California's population in 1880 than in 1970. Before the turn of the century, the nation's metropolises included districts where non-English mother tongues, such as German, Polish, Italian, and Yiddish, were the chief medium of communication. Rural districts in the Midwest and Great Plains experienced just as much, if not greater, linguistic foreignization. In 1910, over fifty different languages were spoken by immigrants in the United States. The percentage of uneducated and unskilled immigrants in the population reached a historic benchmark in the decade after the turn of the century, when nearly one of four immigrants who entered the United States was illiterate and over 90% were blue-collar workers or farmers.

The United States was the first of the independent "immigration countries" that sought immigrants and in which immigration played a central historical role in the building of society and the state. Other such "new societies" emerged later under the aegis of a single state (Hartz 1964). Typical listings of these countries usually included Canada, Argentina, Brazil, Australia, and New Zealand. The major waves of immigration in these immigration countries emanated from European societies that constructed states based on a unified ethnic nationality, such as England, Denmark, Spain, France, Sweden, Portugal, the Netherlands, Italy, and Germany. These nation states served primarily as countries of emigration, within the matrix of international flows of migration in the industrializing era.

The United States was part of a world in motion. By examining currents of migration in their wider context, historians since World War II have created a complex picture of modern immigration history that is simultaneously particular and comparative, local and international, trans-continental and trans-oceanic. They have explored the possibilities of comparing different collective experiences to understand the significance of specific groups of migrants as well as the features of the total pattern of migration. The modern historical study of migratory experiences has revealed the importance of inter-regional and international connections shaping long-term social transitions to settled communities. The comparative vision of migration history is apposite to the spread of cultural globalization in the modern world.

The cumulative scholarship of immigration historians in the last fifty years has succeeded in overturning the simplistic characterization of societies as internally developed, pure and simple. They recast the notion of a country as a sealed "container" for the nation. Rather, England, Ireland, Scotland, Germany, Norway, Sweden, Denmark, the Netherlands, France, Poland, Italy, and the lands of the Austrian and Russian empires were, in a real sense, countries that transcended borders, because through in-migrations, out-migrations, and return migrations their social, cultural, and economic linkages extended into geographically distant places in other realms, in other states. Although certainly not an "immigration country" on the scale of the United States, Canada, Australia, or Brazil, these traditional Old World states appear through the lens of history as countries that have been significantly shaped and reshaped by long-distance currents of immigration and emigration.

The gradual expansion of immigration to a worldwide influx was the underlying factor that ensured the continuous restructuring of American communities in general stages. The history of the relation between immigration and American communities resembled a connected series of circles, a kind of spiral. The evolution of American society turned on cumulative stages of national creation and re-creation generated by three sequential cycles of immigration. They exerted a transformative effect on the structure of society, its cultural life, and its institutions of governance. From the beginning of the 18th century to the American Revolution, the first cycle of immigration brought non-English Protestant settlers, particularly from Northern Ireland, Scotland, France, and Germany. The presence of these immigrants shaped an eclecticism of national identity that informed the cosmopolitan ideal of citizenship adopted during the American Revolution. The second cycle began as the new republic received an immigration expanding from Catholic Ireland as well as Germany and Scandinavia in the middle decades of the 19th century. This wave formed the first great peak of the second cycle that was succeeded by a second and even larger peak of immigration originating chiefly from Southern and Eastern Europe, but also springing from East Asia, Mexico, and the Caribbean. The European newcomers of the second peak were labeled the "new immigrants" to contrast them with the "old immigrants" of the first peak. The second peak declined sharply in the late 1920s and the Depression era, marking the close of the second cycle. The second cycle of immigration emanated from the industrial and urban revolutions, supplying its mass human infrastructure, its new forms of communal collectivism, its media and consumer based culture, and its heightened ethnic pluralism. The third cycle of immigration began after the 1960s as the circuit of immigration touched every region of the world, making the United States history's first global immigration country. It was, however, an imbalanced immigration in which arrivals from Latin America and Asia, who were called "third-world immigrants," composed a large majority. The third great cycle of American immigration, referred to as the "worldwide system of immigration," galvanized the internationalization of the culture and the economy, expanded multiracialism, and facilitated the rise of political multiculturalism.

The cycles of American immigration were shaped by individual and collective calculations about the degree of opportunity afforded by structural conditions for migration to the United States. Immigrants by and large did not come from the most under-developed countries and they did not spring from the most deprived and stagnant orders of their homelands. They were rural and urban laborers who had already initiated adaptations to survive in the intersection of population pressure and limited resources. They were in the process of negotiating an unsettling transition and overcoming the insecure circumstances it produced. The experiences of this process made them "available" to the attractive forces of opportunities they perceived to lie outside their local worlds.

Nevertheless, because of a host of mediating sociological, subjective, institutional, and international factors, the existence of disparities between the United States and other societies was never sufficient to generate the characteristic patterns of American immigration. Scholars have gradually constructed a "systems" approach to immigration in which "micro-structures" of informal networks developed by immigrants interacted with "macro-structures" shaped by inter-state relations and world market relations to capture the actual complexities underlying the organization of the three great cycles of American immigration.

In the second half of the 20th century, spreading linkages with sending societies involving transnational businesses, mass media, military installations, and commercial exchanges stimulated immigration to the United States and configured its patterns and directions of flow. The mass migrations from Europe, once seen as definitive and conclusive of nation-building through immigration, appear to have been an early stage of a long-term global re-alignment of population that transformed the United States.

The diversity of the 1990s multicultural The United States was only the another impact of a historically continuous and widening spiral of international migration. It is true that peripheral communities on the geographic margins have long included a multiracial mix of ethnic groups. Chinese, Japanese, and Filipinos were historically numerous in Hawaii. These Asians along with Mexicans, Asian Indians, and blacks formed ethnic pockets in the Pacific Coast states and the Southwest. In the northern Midwest and Northeast and the South, a bipolar pattern of whites and blacks formed the racial dimensions of society. The globalization of post-1965 immigration bringing Hispanics, black Caribbeans, Asians, and Africans produced new mosaics in which minorities of color settled over the entire expanse of the nation. Multiracial patterns became characteristic of national society. A worldwide cultural pluralism began to find a reflection in American national identity and national culture.

Poor men and women from the countryside moving in search of better opportunities to nearby provinces, towns, cities, and neighboring countries became part of regional worlds in motion. These unrooted people frequently moved back and forth between distant workplaces and home. They formed a growing pool of migrant labor that spilled over into streams of immigrants travelling to the United States and other developing overseas areas. Many saw their move to the United States as an extension of the circular or transient currents of local migration and thus returned home after sojourns. Since World War II, the patterns of circular migration have particularly involved immigrants from Mexico who moved back and forth across the border, and Puerto Ricans and Caribbean immigrants who traveled by air between the home island and mainland destinations.

The decision to migrate turned always on their possession of two attitudes that set them apart from countrymen who stayed behind. These were an exceptional individual openness to risk-taking and the willingness to search for the widest fields of opportunity for their offspring—to invest in future generations. The conception of emigration to the United States as a "safety valve" providing a field to the opportunistic masses played upon the thoughts of influential European commentators and officials. In their view, emigration from their countries readjusted the balance between population and inherent economic resources. In Germany, the country that sent the greatest number of immigrants to the United States, a debate occurred throughout the 19th century, which focused on the possibilities of trans-Atlantic emigration as an overflow that relieved social pressure. The "Iron Chancellor" who unified Germany, Otto von Bismarck, claimed that the peopling of North America by Europeans was "the decisive fact in the modern world" (Bailyn 1986, p. 5).

Historian Klaus J. Bade suggested that for many emigrants their departure was "a manner of non-violent social protest against the living conditions in their homeland" and called for more research on this important topic. Bade argued,

> For many emigrants, departure was a gesture of nonviolent social protest against the living conditions in their homeland. Perhaps if millions of Germans had not had the opportunity to emigrate in the nineteenth century, and the majority of those who stayed had not had the chance to consider the dream of the New World as a real and viable alternative, the expectation of Karl Marx and Friedrich Engels, that the lost political revolution of 1848/49 would be followed by a successful social revolution, might not have turned out to be simply a false projection. (Bade 1997, p. 13)

The United States sprang from the seat of the world-historical process that elevated the role of migrations in the shaping of countries. At the very birth of national history, policymakers and opinion makers pointed to the exceptional and central role of immigrants in the United States. In *The One and the Many* (1979), University of Chicago historian Arthur Mann noted, "Next to Independence and the Constitution, that [policy] turned out to be the Revolutionary generation's most critical decision" (Mann 1979, p. 71). The founders made the United States the first country to decide to receive immigrants to fulfill its national destiny, to include them as participants in the project of nation-building. Defining the new republic as an immigration country sprang from a pragmatic commitment to an economic policy geared toward expansion and a population policy aimed at peopling the land. George Washington announced in 1783, "The bosom of America is open to receive not only the opulent and respectable stranger but the oppressed and persecuted of all nations and religions" (Commager 1951, p. 145). In the next two centuries, the nation's political leaders echoed Washington's theme that American nationhood stemmed from its role as an open country for the world's migrants, irrespective of their social origins. In 1852, the platform of the Democratic Party urged, "That emigrants and exiles from the Old World should find a cordial welcome to homes of comfort and fields of enterprise in the New; and every attempt to abridge their privilege of becoming citizens and owners of soil among us ought to be resisted with inflexible determination." In 1864, the Republican Party platform proposed, "That foreign immigration, which in the past has added so much to the wealth, development of resources, and increase of power to the nation—the asylum of the oppressed of all nations—should be fostered and encouraged by a liberal and just policy." Woodrow Wilson stated in 1915, that the role of immigration in American life was the result of "the traditional and long-established policy of this country, a policy in which our people have conceived the very character of their Government to be expressed, the very mission and spirit of the Nation" (Wilson 1917). Those who expounded on the character of America's nationhood asserted that the concept of immigrant nationhood—national development through mass immigration—was inseparable from the country's constitutional heritage. This relationship would be challenged periodically by restrictionists seeking to reduce immigration generally or to exclude particular groups. Those who argued for a restricted nationhood attempted to exclude the Chinese, Jews, Catholics, Italians, and Slavs. But their impact proved temporary. Over the long span of history, the idea of immigrant nationhood remained a pre-eminent factor of national identity.

By contrast with the United States, other countries resisted affording a prominent place to immigration and immigrants in the shaping of national identity. According to Dirk Hoerder, an expert in German migration history, "The German people experienced as much—or perhaps more—migration than most other people in the North Atlantic economies." Transfers of population from France, Austria, Bohemia, Poland, Denmark, and Poland occurred from the 17th century to the early 20th century; after World War II, Germany recruited laborers from Southern Europe and Turkey. However, the national experience of migration was never accepted by Germans "as a way of life" and "they rarely welcomed those who came to them" (Hoerder and Nagler 2002, p. 16). A German political leader remarked in 1991, "We [in Germany] are not an immigration country and we will not become one" (Kinzer 1991). Hoerder also pondered how "some nations accept ethnic pluralism and multiculturalism as part of their heritage, while other nations—with almost as many shifts in population and with histories of in- as well as out-migration—continue to resist the very idea" (Hoerder 2002, p. 16).

The openness to immigrants of the United States was a fundamental expression of its historic republican and democratic ethos. Political leaders recognized that newcomers possessed the ability to adopt a new identity and popular confidence in the capacity of natives to accept the foreign born. The nation's greatest statesmen recognized the connection between immigration and the egalitarian belief in the irrelevance of ancestral origin for becoming American and the decisive role of individual will in becoming American. Although respect for this ideal standard fluctuated in times of nativist activism, it had a primary place in democratic ideology. In a speech to the Knights of Columbus in New York City in 1915, Theodore Roosevelt avowed, "Our nation was founded to perpetuate democratic principles. Those principles are that each man is to be treated on his worth as a man without regard to the land from which his forefathers came and without regard to the creed which he professes. . . . Some of the very best Americans I have ever known were naturalized Americans, Americans born abroad. . . . Americanism is a matter of spirit and of the soul" (Roosevelt, T. 1920, pp. 48–49). Over a generation later, during World War II, his distant cousin Franklin D. Roosevelt echoed, "The principle on which this country was founded and by which it has always been governed is that Americanism is a matter of the mind and heart; Americanism is not, and never was, a matter of race and ancestry" (Roosevelt, F. D. 1994, p. 103). The pioneering historian of immigration, Oscar Handlin, pointed out in the first decade of the Cold War, "In our willingness to accept the persecuted and oppressed we also gave concrete evidence of our faith in the ability of all men to raise themselves to the same levels of freedom" (Handlin 1957, p. 173). When President Lyndon Johnson signed into law the Hart-Celler Act of 1965 ending nationality discrimination in immigrant admissions, he announced that the nation abolished a policy that was "a deep and painful flaw in the fabric of American justice" (Reimers 1985, p. 86).

The United States qualified as the greatest immigration country in world history not only in its national ideological commitment to serving as a haven of opportunity to the foreign born, but also in terms of the volume of immigration it received and the number of ethnic groups it accommodated. A comparative accounting of American immigration totals reveal America's historical role as a uniquely powerful magnet of international population movements. More immigrants went to the United States than to all other great immigration-receiving countries in the world combined. From 1820 to 1930, 38,000,000 people moved to the United States while 24,000,000 migrated to Canada, Argentina, Brazil, Australia, New Zealand, South Africa, and other areas. Canada received only 7,130,000, Argentine 6,200,000, Brazil 4,500,000, Australia 2,800,000, New Zealand 1,900,000, and South Africa 1,400,000. The United States attracted three-fifths of the population flocking to immigration countries. After a hiatus in arrivals from the Great Depression to World War II, the United States resumed its role as the world magnet of immigration. From 1945 to the early 1990s, 20 million newcomers flocked to the United States (Bernard 1950, pp. 201–04; U.S. Immigration and Naturalization Service 1991, p. 47).

American immigration reflected an unparalleled historic pattern of ethnic variation. From 1820 to 1945, Germany sent 16% of all American immigrants, Italy 12%, Ireland 12%, Austria-Hungary 11%, Russia 9%, Canada 8%, while England sent only 7%. Smaller fractions of the influx from 1820 to 1945 came from Asia, the Middle East, the Caribbean, and Latin America. By contrast, other English-speaking immigration countries drew their settlers almost wholly from other English-speaking nations. Eighty percent of immigrants to Australia came from Great Britain, while in Canada 37% arrived from Great Britain and another 37% from the United States. Immigration to Latin American societies also showed a narrow spectrum of national diversity limited chiefly to Iberian and Italian origins. In Argentina, 47% of the immigrants came from Italy and 32% from Spain; in Brazil, 34% came from Italy, 29% from Portugal, and 14% from Spain. Ethnic variety in American immigration increased in the late 20th century, especially with the rise of immigration from regions in Asia, the Caribbean, Latin America, the Middle East, and Africa from which few immigrants had come in the early 20th century. The Immigration and Naturalization Service reported admissions in 1990 from 30 Asian countries (including the Middle East), 17 Central and South American countries, 13 Caribbean countries, and 13 African countries.

In spite of the paramount role played by immigration and pro-immigration ideology, it would be a misjudgment to assume that throughout history, as a consequence, ethnicity had a constant and unambiguous presence, or that it was the preeminent force in shaping the social identity of inhabitants of the United States. In the history of American society, the majority of Americans did not think of themselves as immigrants, and more importantly, they probably did not think of themselves primarily as ethnics. Nor did they consistently assume that others had a clear ethnic identity springing from a line of descent or ancestry, or that this particularly mattered. Even in the era of ethnic revivalism since the 1960s, many

Americans displayed a marked lack of interest in centering their social identities on ethnicity. In 1972, a current population survey of the federal census bureau reported that 4 of every 10 white respondents declined to claim ethnic descent from any of the major ancestry groups. In 1973, sociologist Edward O. Laumann found that ethnic groups comprised chiefly of the third generation usually felt no deep ethnic identification (Laumann 1973, pp. 60–61). In the 1980 federal census, due to what two Harvard sociologists described as "the wide dispersion of ethnically mixed ancestry," 13.3 million respondents refused to identify with any ancestral nationality and wrote-in "American" or "United States" for their collective identity (Lieberson and Waters 1988, pp. 264–65).

The juxtaposition of the enormous pluralism of immigration and widespread ethnic assimilation came to define the social dynamics of the United States in a cardinal way. Social psychologist Thomas F. Pettigrew noted that in the United States "assimilation is not the opposite but a part of the same social processes as pluralism. The two conceptually separate phenomena are, in reality, inseparable parts of the same ball of wax, called *American society*" (Pettigrew 1988, p. 22). Under conditions without central state management, ethnic enclaves evolved on their own paths and the wider ethnic mosaic stood partly intact and partly dissolved in a melting pot. Because they were involved continuously and inescapably with centrifugal forces promoting external merger, immigrant communities formed a pluralism that integrated the total society. Sociologist William S. Bernard described this condition:

> The fact of the matter is that the United States has not assimilated the newcomer nor absorbed him. Our immigrant stock and our so-called "native" stock have each integrated with the other. That is to say that each element has been changed by association with the other, without complete loss of its own cultural identity, and with a change in the resultant cultural amalgam, or civilization if you will, that is vital, vigorous, and an advance beyond its previous level. Without becoming metaphysical let us say that the whole is greater than the sum of its parts, and the parts, while affected by interaction with each other, nevertheless remain complementary but individual. (Bernard 1964, p. 68)

An Ethnic Kaleidoscope of Diverse Communities

In the course of the Industrial Revolution and the westward movement, immigrants scattered across farming districts, small towns, and big cities, making it clear to Americans that the hallmark of their society was a diversity of communities. The image of the American people as ethnically eclectic became a popular and ubiquitous perception. Historian Frederick Jackson Turner described his memory of the social panorama passing into his hometown of Portage, Wisconsin, after the Civil War as a mixture of the following:

> Irishmen (in the bloody first ward), of Pomeranian Immigrants . . . in old country garbs, of Scotch with Caledonia nearby; of Welsh with Cambria adjacent; of Germans some of them university trained . . . of Yankees . . . of Southerners . . . a few Negroes; many Norwegians and Swiss, some Englishmen, one or two Italians, who all got on together in this forming society. (Saveth 1948, p. 123)

The United States provided a sharp historical contrast to the way postindustrial and postnationalist societies coped with immigration. In the United States, mass immigration that was central, not marginal, to the building of society preceded the founding of a national and industrial community. Immigration flowed from Great Britain, Ireland, Germany, and other parts of Western Europe in the form of colonization to a rural geographic periphery and brought the settlers who created the agricultural and mercantile economy in the 17th and 18th centuries. With the rise of a manufacturing, technological economy in the 19th century, the United States became a focal point for an internationalization of the labor market that created the human infrastructure for an industrial economy and urban expansion. In the late 20th century, economic globalization propelled new worldwide currents of migration that flowed into the United States.

The successive and continuous waves of immigrants established communities and enclaves that existed in a broad sphere of civil society and thus were left unmanaged in important ways by central government power. The communal, religious, informational, educational, and consumer needs of immigrants were provided by the familial and village networks transplanted to the urban neighborhoods and farming outposts. Collective life and identity sprang from the self-initiated efforts of newcomers. Ethnic merchants and purveyors supplied food and other commodities from the homeland; priests, rabbis, and ministers shaped the transmission of religious and cultural traditions. The limited reach of American federal, state, and municipal governments left a large public sphere in which private initiative, entrepreneurialism and mutual association planned, financed, and delivered the services and goods needed by immigrants and their descendants, in contrast to advanced industrial societies that adopted centrally managed programs for accommodating immigrants. Historian Oscar Handlin observed, "Social action in the United States . . . is presumed to come not within large unitary forms but within a mosaic of autonomous groupings, reflecting the underlying dissimilarities in the population" (Handlin 1961, p. 220).

Unlike the historic nation states of Europe and Japan, the United States developed an idea of nationhood that emphasized heterogeneity, not homogeneity. This self-concept was already developed in the early republic, but it had to compete with the view that the nation was constituted out of a dominant and homogeneous Anglo-Saxon core, an Anglo-American nation. In this vein, John Jay in Federalist No. 2 hailed the new republic as composed of "a people descended from the same ancestors . . . very similar in their manners and customs" (Jay 1961). The French visitor and philosopher Alexis de Tocqueville observed in *Democracy in America* that the United States consisted of "offsets of the same people," a single and culturally unified "Anglo-American" nation "connected with England by their origin, their religion, their language, and partially by their manners: they only differ in their social condition" (de Tocqueville 1956, p. 223).

The idea that American nationhood was attained through the accommodation of diversity, however, progressively eclipsed the self-image of national homogeneity. While the latter was invoked by elites, particularly by advocates of national causes as an inspirational collective self-image and philosophers seeking theoretical consistency, the former resonated with the migratory origins of a heterogeneous populace. A spreading and growing multiethnic population gave the latter the appearance of an increasingly abstract ideal and the former the life of a natural, palpable reality. The historian David Hackett Fischer has argued that even early Anglo-American society did not possess a single culture, but, instead, a quadruple set of complex regional cultures constituted of transplanted "immigrant" cultures from across Great Britain and Ireland (Fischer 1989, pp. 783–816). Moreover, other scholars have shown that the English were a demographic minority in all the colonies south of New England. A reanalysis of the first federal census of 1790 estimated that more than two of five whites in the United States were non-English in background (McDonald and McDonald 1980, pp. 179–99).

Historian Lawrence W. Levine commented on the multiple and composite character of ethnic communities as follows:

> Contemporary scholars have demonstrated again and again that, in penetrating the culture of a neglected group, historians often find more than they bargained for. What looked like a group becomes an amalgam of groups; what looked like a culture becomes a series of cultures. . . . The complexity I speak of is . . . the complexity of people and the cultures they create. (Levine 1989, p. 678)

The French immigrant Hector St. Jean de Crevecoeur described the provenance of pluralistic nationality in 1782 when he observed that the American was "neither an European nor the descendant of an European; hence that strange mixture of blood, which you will find in no other country. I could point to you a family whose grandfather was an Englishman, whose wife was Dutch, whose son married a French woman, and whose present four sons have now four wives of different nations" (St. Jean de Crevecoeur 1782). Oscar Handlin, pointed out that "on the eve of the Revolution, it was clear that a new nationality held together the people of the New World. . . . Heatedly Americans insisted that their English inheritance was only one, if the largest, of several" (Handlin 1963, p. 149). He and Lilian Handlin reminded their readers that Americans "turned the lack of common ancestry or unifying church into the dominant characteristic of their nationality. . . . Even before 1776 they were not simply transplanted Britons, but the offspring of all Europe, proud of their various antecedents" (Handlin and Handlin 1989, pp. 139–40).

The United States has historically been a country in which a democratic pluralism based on diverse communities formed the basis of society. While the history of European states centered on the construction of a homogeneous ethnic nation, the United States arose from an eclectic nationality shaped centrally by communal diversity. No single group could claim sole and uncontested possession of the communities in the country. All groups learned that minimally regulated communal coexistence with others was a fundamental social condition. The free interaction of cultural, economic and political forces emanating from diverse communities reinforced rather than detracted from national unity. As historian Hans Kohn observed, "[The] American idea of liberty—with its recognition of diversity in origins and religious background—has proved a stronger national cement and a more secure basis for ordered liberty and economic prosperity than bonds of common blood and religion or the uniformity of a closed society" (Kohn 1957, p. 149). The fluid contacts among a multiplicity of communities—ranging from those originating in colonial and industrial times to those built in the recent era of globalization—produced local social and cultural fabrics that changed recurrently into new unifying patterns of pluralism throughout the history of the United States.

Reed Ueda

Bibliography

Alba, Richard D. *Ethnic Identity: The Transformation of White America.* New Haven, CT: Yale University Press, 1990.

Archdeacon, Thomas. *Becoming American: An Ethnic History.* New York: The Free Press, 1983.

Bade, Klaus J. "From Emigration to Immigration: The German Experience in the 19th and 20th Centuries." In Klaus J. Bade and Myron Weiner, eds. *Migration Past, Migration Future.* Vol. 1. Oxford: Berghahn Books, 1997.

Bailyn, Bernard. *The Peopling of British North America.* New York: Alfred A. Knopf, 1986.

Barrett, James. "Americanization Then . . . and Now." *LAS Summer 1994 Newsletter.* Urbana: University of Illinois Alumni Relations Office, 1994.

Barton, Josef. *Peasants and Strangers: Italians, Rumanians, and Slovaks in an American City, 1890–1950.* Cambridge, MA: Harvard University Press, 1975.

Bernard, William S. ed. *American Immigration Policy.* New York: Harper and Brothers, 1950.

Bernard, William S. "The Integration of Immigrants in the United States," UNESCO, 1956. Quoted in Milton M. Gordon. *Assimilation in American Life: The Role of Race, Religion, and National Origins.* New York: Oxford University Press, 1964.

Bodnar, John. *Remaking America: Public Memory, Commemoration, and Patriotism in the Twentieth Century.* Princeton, NJ: Princeton University Press, 1992.

Bodnar, John. *The Transplanted: A History of Immigrants in Urban America.* Bloomington: Indiana University Press, 1985.

Bowers, David F. "The Problem of Social and Cultural Impact." In David F. Bowers, ed. *Foreign Influences in American Life; Essays and Critical Bibliographies.* Princeton, NJ: Princeton University Press, 1944.

Braverman, William. "The Emergence of a Unified Community, 1880–1917." In Jonathan Sarna and Ellen Smith, eds. *The Jews of Boston.* Boston: The Combined Jewish Philanthropies of Greater Boston, 1995.

Brown, Richard, and Herbert Bass. *One Flag, One Land.* Morristown, NJ: Silver Burdett, 1985.

Castles, Stephen, and Mark J. Miller. *The Age of Migration: International Population Movements in the Modern World.* New York: Guilford Press, 1993.

Center for Civic Education, National Standards for Civics and Government. Calabasas, CA: Center for Civic Education, 1994.

Chan, Sucheng. "European and Asian Immigration into the United States in Comparative Perspective, 1820s to 1920s." In Virginia Yans-McLaughlin, ed. *Immigration Reconsidered: History, Sociology, and Politics.* New York: Oxford University Press, 1990.

Cheng, Lucie, and Edna Bonacich, eds. *Labor Immigration under Capitalism: Asian Workers in the United States before World War II.* Berkeley: University of California Press, 1984.

Cohen, Lizabeth. *Making a New Deal: Industrial Workers in Chicago, 1919–1939.* New York: Cambridge University Press, 1990.

Commager, Henry Steele, ed. *Living Ideas in America.* New York: Harper, 1951.

Couvares, Francis. *The Remaking of Pittsburgh: Class and Culture in an Industrializing City, 1877–1919*. Albany: State University of New York Press, 1984.

Cullen, Kevin. Europe's "Unwelcome Mat: Immigrants Face a Bitter Backlash." *The Boston Globe*, December 28, 2000.

Daniels, Roger. *Coming to America: A History of Immigration and Ethnicity in American Life*. New York: Harper Perennial, 2002.

Easterlin, Richard A. *Population, Labor Force, and Long Swings in Economic Growth: The American Experience*. New York: National Bureau of Economic Research, 1968.

Egan, Joseph Burke. *Citizenship in Boston*. Philadelphia: The John C. Winston Co., 1925.

Erenberg, Lewis A. *Steppin' Out: New York Nightlife and the Transformation of American Culture, 1890–1930*. Chicago: University of Chicago Press, 1981.

Fischer, David Hackett. *Albion's Seed: Four British Folkways in America*. New York: Oxford University Press, 1989.

Fishman, Joshua A. *The Rise and Fall of the Ethnic Revival: Perspectives on Language and Ethnicity*. New York: Mouton Publishers, 1985.

Franklin, John Hope, Thomas F. Pettigrew, and Raymond W. Mack. *Ethnicity in American Life*. New York: Anti-Defamation League of B'nai B'rith, 1971, p. 34.

Fuchs, Lawrence H. *The American Kaleidoscope: Race, Ethnicity, and the Civic Culture*. Middletown, CT: Wesleyan University Press; Hanover, NH: University Press of New England, 1990.

Fuchs, Lawrence H. *Hawaii Pono: A Social History*. New York: Harcourt, Brace, 1961.

Galicich, Anne. *The German Americans*. New York: Chelsea House Publishers, 1989.

Gamm, Gerald H. *Urban Exodus: Why the Jews Left Boston and the Catholics Stayed*. Cambridge, MA: Harvard University Press, 1999.

Gans, Herbert J. *The Urban Villagers: Group and Class in the Life of Italian-Americans*. Glencoe, IL: The Free Press, 1966.

Garcia, Mario T. *Mexican Americans: Leadership, Ideology, and Identity, 1930–1960*. New Haven, CT: Yale University Press, 1989.

Gavit, John P. *Americans by Choice*. New York: Harper and Brothers, 1922.

Gerstle, Gary. *Working-Class Americanism: The Politics of Labor in a Textile City, 1914–1960*. New York: Cambridge University Press, 1989.

Gill, Richard, Nathan Glazer, and Stephan Thernstrom. *Our Changing Population*. Englewood Cliffs, NJ: Prentice-Hall, 1992.

Glazer, Nathan. "Ethnic Groups in America." In Morroe Berger, Theodore Abel, and Charles H. Page, eds. *Freedom and Control in Modern Society*. New York: Van Nostrand, 1954.

Glazer, Nathan. *Affirmative Discrimination: Ethnic Inequality and Public Policy*. New York: Basic Books, 1975.

Glazer, Nathan. "The Politics of a Multiethnic Society." In Lance Liebman, ed. *Ethnic Relations in America*. Englewood Cliffs, NJ: Prentice-Hall, 1982.

Glazer, Nathan. *Clamor at the Gates: The New American Immigration*. San Francisco: Institute for Contemporary Studies, 1985.

Glazer, Nathan. *We Are All Multiculturalists Now*. Cambridge, MA: Harvard University Press, 1997.

Goffman, Erving. *The Presentation of Self in Everyday Life*. Garden City, New York: Doubleday, 1959.

Gross, June. "Welcome to Somerville." *Boston Globe*, July 23, 1994.

Gutman, Herbert G. "Work, Culture, and Society in Industrializing America, 1815–1919." *American Historical Review* 78 (June 1973): 531–88.

Habakkuk, H. J., and M. Postan. *The Cambridge Economic History of Europe, The Industrial Revolutions and After: Incomes, Population and Technological Change.* Vol. VI. Cambridge: Cambridge University Press, 1965.

Handlin, Oscar. *The American People in the Twentieth Century.* Cambridge, MA: Harvard University Press, 1954.

Handlin, Oscar. *The Americans: A New History of the People of the United States.* Boston: Little, Brown, 1963.

Handlin, Oscar. *Firebell in the Night: The Crisis in Civil Rights.* Boston: Little, Brown, 1964.

Handlin, Oscar. "Historical Perspectives on the American Ethnic Group." *Daedalus* (Spring 1961).

Handlin, Oscar. *Race and Nationality in American Life.* Boston: Little, Brown, 1957.

Handlin, Oscar. *The Uprooted: The Epic Story of the Great Migrations that Made the American People.* Rev. ed. Boston: Little, Brown, [1951] 1973.

Handlin, Oscar, and Lilian Handlin. *Liberty in Expansion, 1760–1850.* Vol. 2. New York: Harper and Row, 1989.

Handlin, Oscar, and Mary Handlin. *The Dimensions of Liberty.* Cambridge, MA: Harvard University Press, 1961.

Hansen, Christine. "Die Deutsche Auswanderung im 19.Jahrhundert—ein Mittel zur Losung sozialer und sozialpolitischer Probleme?" In Gunter Moltmann, ed. *Deutsche Amerikaauswanderung im 19.Jahrhundert. Sozialgeschichtliche Beitrage.* Stuttgart: Metzler, 1976.

Hartz, Louis. *The Founding of New Societies: Africa, Canada, and Australia.* New York: Harcourt, Brace, 1964.

Higham, John. *Send These to Me: Jews and Other Immigrants in Urban America.* New York: Atheneum, 1975.

Himmelfarb, Milton. *The Jews of Modernity.* New York: Basic Books, 1973.

Hoerder, Dirk, and Jorg Nagler, eds. *People in Transit: Migrations in Comparative Perspective, 1820–1930.* Cambridge: Cambridge University Press, 2002.

Hofstadter, Richard. *The Age of Reform.* New York: Vintage Books, 1955.

Horowitz, Helen Lefkowitz. *Culture and the City: Cultural Philanthropy in Chicago from the 1880s to 1917.* Lexington: University Press of Kentucky, 1976.

Horton, John. "The Politics of Diversity in Monterey Park, California." In Louise Lamphere, ed. *Structuring Diversity: Ethnographic Perspectives on the New Immigration.* Chicago: University of Chicago Press, 1992.

Hutchinson, E. P. *Legislative History of American Immigration Policy, 1798–1965.* Philadelphia: University of Pennsylvania Press, 1981.

Isaacs, Harold R. *Idols of the Tribe: Group Identity and Political Change.* New York: Harper and Row, 1975.

Jay, John. "Federalist No. 2." In *The Federalist Papers.* New York: New American Library, 1961.

Kasson, John F. *Amusing the Million: Coney Island at the Turn of the Century.* New York: Hill and Wang, 1978.

Katznelson, Ira. *City Trenches: Urban Politics and the Patterning of Class in the United States.* New York: Pantheon, 1981.

Kennedy, John F. *A Nation of Immigrants.* Rev. ed. New York: Harper and Row, [1958] 1964.

Kessner, Thomas. *The Golden Door: Italian and Jewish Immigrant Mobility in New York City, 1880–1915.* New York: Oxford University Press, 1977.

Kinzer, Stephen. "The Neo-Nazis." *New York Times,* November 17, 1991.

Klein, Joe. "The Education of Berenice Belizaire." *Newsweek*, August 9, 1993.

Kohn, Hans. *American Nationalism: An Interpretive Essay*. New York: Macmillan, 1957.

Konvitz, Milton R. *Judaism and the American Idea*. Ithaca, NY: Cornell University Press, 1978.

Laumann, Edward O. *The Bonds of Pluralism: The Form and Substance of Urban Social Networks*. New York: John Wiley and Sons, 1973.

Levine, Lawrence W. "The Unpredictable Past: Reflections on Recent American Historiography." *American Historical Review* 94 (June 1989).

Lieberson, Stanley. *A Piece of the Pie: Blacks and White Immigrants since 1880*. Berkeley: University of California Press, 1980.

Lieberson, Stanley, and Mary C. Waters. *From Many Strands: Ethnic and Racial Groups in Contemporary America*. New York: Russell Sage, 1988.

Liebman, Lance. ed. *Ethnic Relations in America*. Englewood Cliffs, NJ: Prentice-Hall, 1982.

Lissak, Rivka Shpak. *Pluralism and Progressives: Hull House and the New Immigrants, 1890–1919*. Chicago: University of Chicago Press, 1989.

Mann, Arthur. *La Guardia: A Fighter against His Times*. Chicago: University of Chicago Press, 1959.

Mann, Arthur. *The One and the Many: Reflections on the American Identity*. Chicago: University of Chicago Press, 1979.

Masugi, Ken. "Citizens and Races: Natural Rights Versus History." In Peter Augustine Lawler and Joseph Alulis, eds. *Tocqueville's Defense of Human Liberty: Current Essays*. New York: Garland Publishers, 1993.

McDonald, Forrest, and Ellen McDonald. "The Ethnic Origins of the American People, 1790." *William and Mary Quarterly Review* 37 (April 1980): 179–99.

Moltmann, Gunter. "Auswanderung als Revolutionsersatz?" In Michael Salewski, ed. *Die Deutschen und die Revolution*. Gottingen: Muster-Schmidt, 1984.

Namias, June. *First Generation: In the Words of Twentieth Century American Immigrants*. Rev. ed. Urbana: University of Illinois Press, [1978] 1992.

Park, Robert E. "Human Migration and the Marginal Man." *American Journal of Sociology* 33 (May 1928): 881–93.

Patterson, Orlando. *Ethnic Chauvinism: The Reactionary Impulse*. New York: Stein and Day, 1977.

Peiss, Kathy. *Cheap Amusements: Working Women and Leisure in Turn-of-the-Century New York*. Philadelphia: Temple University Press, 1986.

Pettigrew, Thomas F. "Integration and Pluralism." In Phyllis A. Katz and Dalmas A. Taylor, eds. *Eliminating Racism: Profiles in Controversy*. New York: Springer Science+Business Media, 1988.

Piore, Michael. *Birds of Passage: Migrant Labor and Industrial Societies*. Cambridge: Cambridge University Press, 1979.

Portes, Alejandro, and Ruben Rumbaut. *Immigrant America: A Portrait*. Berkeley: University of California Press, 1990.

Reimers, David M. *Still the Golden Door: The Third World Comes to America*. New York: Columbia University Press, 1985.

Rieder, Jonathan. *Canarsie: The Jews and Italians of Brooklyn against Liberalism*. Cambridge, MA: Harvard University Press, 1985.

Roosevelt, Theodore. "Address to the Knights of Columbus, New York City, 1915." Reprinted in Philip Davis, ed. *Immigration and Americanization*. Boston: Ginn, 1920.

Rosenzweig, Roy. *Eight Hours for What We Will: Workers and Leisure in an Industrial City, 1870–1920*. Cambridge: Cambridge University Press, 1983.

Ruiz, Vicki L. *Cannery Women, Cannery Lives: Mexican Women, Unionization, and the California Food Processing Industry, 1930–1950*. Albuquerque: University of New Mexico Press, 1987.

Sanchez, George J. *Becoming Mexican American: Ethnicity, Culture, and Identity in Chicano Los Angeles, 1900–1945*. New York: Oxford University Press, 1993.

Saveth, Edward N. *American Historians and European Immigrants*. New York: Columbia University Press, 1948.

Smith, Ellen. "Strangers and Sojourners: The Jews of Colonial Boston" and "Israelites in Boston, 1840–1880." In Jonathan D. Sarna and Ellen Smith, eds. *The Jews of Boston: Essays on the Occasion of the Centenary 1895–1995 of the Combined Jewish Philanthropies of Greater Boston*. Boston: Combined Jewish Philanthropies of Greater Boston, 1995.

Smith, Timothy L. "Religion and Ethnicity in America." *American Historical Review* 83 (December 1978): 1155–85.

Smith, William Carlson. *Americans in Process: A Study of Our Citizens of Oriental Ancestry*. Ann Arbor, MI: Edwards Brothers, 1937.

Sontag, Deborah, and Celia W. Dugger. "The New Immigrant Tide: A Shuttle between Worlds." *New York Times*, July 19, 1998.

Sowell, Thomas. *Ethnic America: A History*. New York: Basic Books, 1981.

St. Jean de Crevecoeur, Hector. "What Is an American?" 1782. Digital History. http://www.digitalhistory.uh.edu/disp_textbook.cfm?smtID=3&psid=3644.

Strong, Josiah. *Our Country: Its Possible Future and Its Present Crisis*. 2nd ed. New York: Baker and Taylor, 1885; 1891.

Suttles, Gerald. *The Social Order of the Slum: Ethnicity and Territory in the Inner City*. Chicago: University of Chicago Press, 1968.

Taeuber, Conrad, and Irene B. Taeuber. *The Changing Population of the United States*. New York: John Wiley and Sons, 1958.

Taylor, Philip. *The Distant Magnet: European Emigration to the U.S.A.* New York: Harper, 1971.

Thernstrom, Stephan. *The Other Bostonians: Poverty and Progress in the American Metropolis*. Cambridge, MA: Harvard University Press, 1973.

Thomas, Brinley. *Migration and Economic Growth: A Study of Great Britain and the Atlantic Economy*. Cambridge: Cambridge University Press, 1973.

Thomson, Frank V. "Publisher's Note." In *Schooling of the Immigrant*. New York: Harper and Brothers, 1920.

Tocqueville, Alexis de. *Democracy in America*. Edited by Richard D. Heffner. New York: New American Library, 1956.

Ueda, Reed. *Postwar Immigrant America: A Social History*. New York: Bedford Books of St. Martin's Press, 1994.

Ueda, Reed. *West End House, 1906–1981*. Boston: West End House, 1981.

U.S. Bureau of the Census. Thirteenth U.S. Census, Washington, Vol. 1. Washington, DC: U.S. Government Printing Office, 1913.

U.S. Immigration and Naturalization Service. *1990 Statistical Yearbook*. Washington, DC: U.S. Government Printing Office, 1991.

U.S. Senate. Congressional Record, June 14, 1972. Ethnic Heritage Studies Program. House of Representatives, Ninety-First Congress, Second Session, Ethnic Heritage Studies Centers: Hearings.

Ward, David. *Cities and Immigrants: A Geography of Change in Nineteenth Century America*. New York: Oxford University Press, 1971.

Warner, Sam Bass, Jr. *Streetcar Suburbs: The Process of Growth in Boston, 1870–1900.* Cambridge, MA: Harvard University Press, 1962.

Weekly Compilation of Presidential Documents. Vol. I, no. 11. Monday, October 11, 1965.

Wieseltier, Leon. "Against Identity." *The New Republic*, November 28, 1994.

Wilentz, Sean. "Sense and Sensitivity: Multiculturalism and the Battle for America's Future." *The New Republic*, October 31, 1994, pp. 43–46.

Wilson, Woodrow. "Veto Message," January 28, 1917. In James D. Richardson, ed. *A Compilation of the Messages and Papers of the Presidents.* Vol. 16. New York: Bureau of National Literature, 1897–1925.

Winnick, Louis. *New People in Old Neighborhoods: The Role of New Immigrants in Rejuvenating New York's Communities.* New York: Russell Sage, 1990.

Wyman, Mark. *Round-Trip to America: The Immigrants Return to Europe, 1880–1930.* Ithaca, NY: Cornell University Press, 1993.

Zunz, Olivier. *The Changing Face of Inequality: Urbanization, Industrial Development, and Immigrants in Detroit, 1880–1920.* Chicago: University of Chicago Press, 1982.

STATES

ALABAMA

Capital: Montgomery
Entered Union: December 14, 1819 (22nd state)

Alabama is the 30th-most extensive and the 23rd-most populous U.S. state. Its largest and most populous city is Birmingham. The Spanish were the first Europeans to reach Alabama in the 16th century, but it was the French who founded the first European settlement in the area from 1702 to 1763. However, following the victory of the British in the Seven Years' War, Alabama became part of British West Florida until 1783. Throughout the antebellum period, Alabama was the site of many wealthy plantations and was particularly successful in cotton production. After the conclusion of the Civil War and the abolition of slavery, Alabama's economy was largely based on sharecropping, which economically disadvantaged many tenant farmers. By the mid-20th century, Alabama struggled with issues of disenfranchisement, poverty, segregation, and racism. The Civil Rights Act of 1964 and the Voting Rights Act of 1965 would produce significant change in Alabama for its African American residents, ending segregation and helping to re-enfranchise African Americans who had been historically barred from voting. Although it still contends with the legacy of its troubled past in terms of economic and race relations, Alabama remains a diverse state. The racial composition of the state's 4,779,736 residents, according to the 2010 U.S. Census, is 68.5% white, 26.2% African American, 3.9% Hispanics of any race, 1.1% Asian, 0.6% American Indian and Alaska Native, and 0.1% Native Hawaiian and other Pacific Islander.

Historical Population of Alabama

Census	Pop.	%±	Census	Pop.	%±
1800	1,250	—	1870	996,992	3.4%
1810	9,046	623.7%	1880	1,262,505	26.6%
1820	127,901	1,313.9%	1890	1,513,401	19.9%
1830	309,527	142.0%	1900	1,828,697	20.8%
1840	590,756	90.9%	1910	2,138,093	16.9%
1850	771,623	30.6%	1920	2,348,174	9.8%
1860	964,201	25.0%	1930	2,646,248	12.7%

(*continued*)

Census	Pop.	%±	Census	Pop.	%±
1940	2,832,961	7.1%	1980	3,893,888	13.1%
1950	3,061,743	8.1%	1990	4,040,587	3.8%
1960	3,266,740	6.7%	2000	4,447,100	10.1%
1970	3,444,165	5.4%	2010	4,779,745	7.5%

Source: U.S. Census Bureau.

It is estimated that a minimum of 20–23% of the population living in Alabama are of predominantly English ancestry. Additionally, there are nine officially recognized American Indian tribes in the state, which descended mostly from the Five Civilized Tribes of the American Southeast. In the past, the self-identification of Native Americans was often overlooked as the state tried to impose a white-and-black binary breakdown of the society. Today, Native American cultural identification is highly respected. The Jewish community has been present in what is now Alabama since 1763, during the colonial era of Mobile, when Sephardic Jews immigrated from London.

According to the 2008 American Religious Identification Survey, Alabamians identified as 80% Christian, 6% Catholic, 11% having no religion, 0.5% Mormon, 0.5% Jewish, 0.5% Muslim, 0.5% Buddhist, and 0.5% Hindu. Although in much smaller numbers, religious faiths such as Sikhism, the Baha'i faith, and Unitarian Universalism are represented in the state as well. It is important to note that Alabama is identified as one of the most religious states in the United States. Surveys show that approximately 58% of the population attends church regularly and 59% said they possessed a "full understanding" of their faith and needed no further learning. A majority of Alabamians identify as Evangelical Protestant. The three largest denominations in 2010 by number of adherents were the Southern Baptist Convention, The United Methodist Church, and nondenominational Evangelical Protestant. There are several Hindu temples and cultural centers in the state, which were founded by Indian immigrants and their descendants. The number of Muslims living in Alabama has been increasing recently, with 31 mosques built by 2011, many by African American converts. The majority of the residents of Alabama speak English, while approximately 2.12% of the population reported speaking Spanish.

Population by Selected Ethnic Group

	Estimate		Estimate
Total:	4,849,377	Egyptian	1,905
Afghan	0	Iraqi	249
Albanian	314	Jordanian	657
Alsatian	66	Lebanese	3,893
American	807,905	Moroccan	651
Arab:	10,775	Palestinian	440

(continued)

	Estimate		Estimate
Syrian	664	Macedonian	74
Arab	1,201	Maltese	223
Other Arab	1,610	New Zealander	111
Armenian	362	Northern European	1,242
Assyrian/Chaldean/ Syriac	76	Norwegian	16,360
		Pennsylvania German	217
Australian	1,384	Polish	24,561
Austrian	2,524	Portuguese	3,257
Basque	34	Romanian	1,869
Belgian	1,871	Russian	10,067
Brazilian	1,263	Scandinavian	4,038
British	22,071	Scotch-Irish	70,926
Bulgarian	163	Scottish	81,607
Cajun	1,526	Serbian	405
Canadian	3,688	Slavic	291
Carpatho-Rusyn	62	Slovak	1,580
Celtic	602	Slovene	364
Croatian	1,510	Sub-Saharan African:	49,261
Cypriot	0	Cape Verdean	30
Czech	3,944	Ethiopian	764
Czechoslovakian	1,614	Kenyan	152
Danish	4,538	Liberian	192
Dutch	37,916	Nigerian	2,064
Eastern European	1,709	Senegalese	45
English	368,844	Sierra Leonean	38
Estonian	243	Somali	0
European	49,868	South African	123
Finnish	1,784	Sudanese	44
French (except Basque)	72,272	Ugandan	0
French Canadian	7,779	Zimbabwean	42
German	324,970	African	44,836
German Russian	42	Other sub-Saharan African	296
Greek	6,729	Swedish	15,441
Guyanese	425	Swiss	4,140
Hungarian	5,579	Turkish	841
Icelandic	100	Ukrainian	2,859
Iranian	1,178	Welsh	16,042
Irish	439,023	West Indian	9,751
Israeli	1,536	(except Hispanic groups):	
Italian	82,032	Bahamian	530
Latvian	275	Barbadian	255
Lithuanian	1,893	Belizean	61
Luxemburger	269	Bermudan	113

(continued)

	Estimate			Estimate
British West Indian	34	West Indian		332
Dutch West Indian	761	Other West Indian		14
Haitian	3,492	Yugoslavian		902
Jamaican	3,142	Other groups		1,871,830
Trinidadian and Tobagonian	1,084	Unclassified or not reported		1,047,354
U.S. Virgin Islander	0			

Source: American Community Survey, U.S. Census Bureau, 2014.

See in Neighborhoods Section: Poarch Creek Indian Reservation (Alabama)

ALASKA

Capital: Juneau
Entered Union: January 3, 1959 (49th state)

Although the largest state by area, Alaska is the least densely populated of the United States and the fourth least populous. Prior to European arrival and settlement, indigenous peoples had occupied Alaska for thousands of years, likely arriving from Asia via the Bering land bridge. In the 18th century, the area's inhabitants began to experience substantial contact with Europeans, particularly to buy and trade exquisite Alaskan furs. Eventually, Russians colonized what would become Alaska, although the colony was largely unprofitable and unsuccessful. In 1867, the United States purchased the area from Russia and first administered it under the military, then as a district, and ultimately a state in 1959. Largely rural and sparsely populated, Alaska's economy largely runs on the oil and gas industry. According to the 2010 U.S. Census, Alaska had a population of 710,231. The U.S. Census Bureau estimates that the population of Alaska in July 2011 was 722,718, marking a 1.76% increase in population since the 2010 U.S. Census. From 2000 to July 2008, there was a population increase of 9.5%.

Historical Population of Alaska

Census	Pop.	%±	Census	Pop.	%±
1880	33,426	—	1950	128,643	77.4%
1890	32,052	−4.1%	1960	226,167	75.8%
1900	63,592	98.4%	1970	300,382	32.8%
1910	64,356	1.2%	1980	401,851	33.8%
1920	55,036	−14.5%	1990	550,043	36.9%
1930	59,278	7.7%	2000	626,932	14.0%
1940	72,524	22.3%	2010	710,231	13.3%

Source: U.S. Census Bureau.

Inuit totem lodge in Alaska. Indigenous elements remain central to Alaskan culture. (Darryl Brooks/Dreamstime.com)

The state demographic breakdown remains largely dominated by Caucasians, with a strong Native American presence. The name *Alaska* itself comes from an Aleut word that was already in use by the Russian colonial period.

Indigenous peoples inhabited Alaska long before the first Europeans settled the territory in the 17th and 18th centuries. Among these indigenous groups were the Tlingit, Haida, Tsimshian, Aleut, Yup'ik, Alutiiq, Gwich'in, and Inuit peoples. By the 18th century, Russia and Spain had sent expeditions and settlers to the Alaskan territories. These early Russian immigrants settled largely in Alaska and along the Pacific Coast. In 1867, the United States negotiated the Alaska Purchase with the Russians, but Alaskan populations remained fairly scarce for a long time. Around the turn of the 20th century, gold rushes brought thousands of settlers and miners from the continental United States (mostly from the Pacific Coast) to Alaska. Most of those in search of mining riches were not successful and many did not stay, but the rush did have lasting effects on the native peoples and on areas where boom-towns were established.

Alaska's population has remained predominantly white. The 1960 U.S. Census reported the Alaskan population to be 77.2% white, 3% black, and 18.8% American Indian and Alaska Native, while the 2010 U.S. Census reports 66.7% white (64.7% non-Hispanic white alone), 14.8% American Indian or Alaska Native, 5.4% Asian,

3.3% black or African American, 1.0% Native Hawaiian and other Pacific Islander, 1.6% from some other race, and 7.4% from two or more races. Hispanics or Latinos make up 5.5% of the population.

The linguistic and religious practices in Alaska reflect the state's cultural heritage. About 5.2% of Alaskans reportedly speak one of the state's 22 indigenous or "native" languages of either the Eskimo-Aleut or Na-Dene vein. According to the 2005–2007 American Community Survey, about 3.5% of the population speaks Spanish at home, while about 2.2% speaks another Indo-European language, and about 4.3% speaks an Asian language at home. Alaska is ranked as one of the least religious of the U.S. states, but it still has a relatively large Eastern Orthodox population as a result of early Russian colonization and missionary work. Alaska also has the largest Quaker population of any state by percentage.

Overall, while the population of Alaska has steadily increased over the course of the 20th century, the ethnic makeup of the population has remained fairly constant since its early settlement. The majority of the Alaskan population remains of white ethnicity, with a considerable American Indian and Alaska Native population. Certain areas in Anchorage, for example, contain particularly concentrated pockets of Russian and American Indian ethnic groups. There has been an increase in Alaska's Asian and Hispanic populations since the second half of the 20th century, although still rather minor in comparison to the white and American Indian populations.

Population by Selected Ethnic Group

	Estimate		Estimate
Total:	728,300	Australian	290
Afghan	134	Austrian	1,663
Albanian	330	Basque	187
Alsatian	32	Belgian	604
American	32,045	Brazilian	209
Arab:	1,267	British	4,337
Egyptian	106	Bulgarian	218
Iraqi	2	Cajun	122
Jordanian	26	Canadian	2,318
Lebanese	586	Carpatho-Rusyn	23
Moroccan	58	Celtic	361
Palestinian	127	Croatian	685
Syrian	155	Cypriot	0
Arab	61	Czech	3,893
Other Arab	222	Czechoslovakian	637
Armenian	300	Danish	6,067
Assyrian/Chaldean/Syriac	15	Dutch	12,852

(continued)

	Estimate		Estimate
Eastern European	913	Cape Verdean	12
English	60,601	Ethiopian	185
Estonian	123	Ghanaian	165
European	16,490	Kenyan	1
Finnish	4,568	Liberian	3
French (except Basque)	20,577	Nigerian	227
French Canadian	6,465	Senegalese	4
German	123,394	Sierra Leonean	0
German Russian	167	Somali	355
Greek	1,950	South African	70
Guyanese	12	Sudanese	319
Hungarian	2,781	Ugandan	6
Icelander	534	Zimbabwean	0
Iranian	279	African	1,673
Irish	77,062	Other sub-Saharan African	287
Israeli	106	Swedish	17,343
Italian	21,672	Swiss	3,914
Latvian	244	Turkish	344
Lithuanian	1,015	Ukrainian	2,561
Luxemburger	124	Welsh	6,097
Macedonian	333	West Indian (except	1,320
Maltese	4	Hispanic groups):	
New Zealander	79	Bahamian	27
Northern European	2,701	Barbadian	40
Norwegian	28,016	Belizean	54
Pennsylvania German	676	Bermudan	0
Polish	14,501	British West Indian	45
Portuguese	2,322	Dutch West Indian	58
Romanian	760	Haitian	319
Russian	10,147	Jamaican	417
Scandinavian	4,486	Trinidadian and Tobagonian	63
Scotch-Irish	8,595	U.S. Virgin Islander	3
Scottish	19,917	West Indian	267
Serbian	479	Other West Indian	27
Slavic	390	Yugoslavian	554
Slovak	842	Other groups	310,717
Slovene	313	Unclassified or not reported	87,884
Sub-Saharan African:	3,292		

Source: U.S. Census Bureau, 2010–2014, American Community Survey 5-Year Estimates.

See in Neighborhoods Section: Nikolaevsk, Russian Enclave (Alaska)

ARIZONA

Capital: Phoenix
Entered Union: February 14, 1912 (48th state)

A latecomer to U.S. statehood, Arizona did not officially become a state until 1912. It was the 48th state admitted to the United States and the last of the continental states to enter the Union. The name *Arizona* is thought to be some combination of a Spanish name from early Spanish exploration expeditions and a Native American name for the area. During World War II, Arizona served as the host of prisoner of war camps for the Italians and Germans and the internment camps for Japanese Americans. After the war these camps were abolished and migration to Arizona became a lot more popular, in part due to the invention of air conditioning, making the climate more bearable. Arizona's state population in 1910 was 204,354, but by 1970, it was 1,745,944. Arizona became the second fastest-growing state in the 1990s after Nevada. In addition, the building of retirement communities in Arizona contributed to an increase in population, as many seniors moved to the state to enjoy the warmer winter weather.

Historical Population of Arizona

Census	Pop.	%±	Census	Pop.	%±
1860	6,482	—	1940	499,261	14.6%
1870	9,658	49.0%	1950	749,587	50.1%
1880	40,440	318.7%	1960	1,302,161	73.7%
1890	88,243	118.2%	1970	1,745,944	34.1%
1900	122,931	39.3%	1980	2,718,215	55.7%
1910	204,354	66.2%	1990	3,665,228	34.8%
1920	334,162	63.5%	2000	5,130,632	40.0%
1930	435,573	30.3%	2010	6,392,017	24.6%

Source: U.S. Census Bureau.

In recent years, Arizona has come to be closely associated with the growing number of Mexican immigrants to the United States, and not without reason. Arizona shares a 389-mile international border with Mexico and has a long history of interaction with Mexico along its shared border. The 2005 American Community Survey reported the percentage distribution of languages spoken in Arizona at 72.58% English, 21.57% Spanish, and 1.54% Navajo. According to the 2010 U.S. Census, Hispanics or Latinos of any race made up 29.6% of the state's population, along with 73.0% white (57.8% non-Hispanic white), 4.1% black, 4.6% Native American and Alaska Native, 2.8% Asian, 11.9% from some other race, and 3.4% from two or more races. According to the U.S. Census Bureau, in 2009 Arizona's five largest ancestry groups were Mexican at 27.4%, German at 16.0%, Irish at 10.8%, English at 10.1%, and Italian at 4.6%. In 2010, illegal immigrants made up an estimated 7.9% of the population, the second-highest percentage of any state. In 2012, Arizona passed the harshest illegal immigration legislation in the nation: the Support Our Law Enforcement and Safe Neighborhoods Act, or Arizona SB 1070. The law triggered national and international attention and controversial debates. The law was supposed to come into effect in July 2010, but a federal judge issued a preliminary injunction against the law's most controversial specifications that to date is yet to be reversed in appeals courts.

Arizona is also home to the largest number of speakers of Native American languages in the United States, with Apache County as the largest concentration of speakers. About a quarter of Arizona federal land is home to Native American peoples of the Navajo Nation, the Hopi tribe, the Apache tribe, the Tohono O'odham, the Yaqui peoples, and the various Yuman tribes. In the late 19th century, the U.S. government created the Phoenix Indian School as an institution for distancing young Native Americans from their culture and assimilating them into Euro-American culture. These schools became controversial in later decades and were officially closed in 1990 and transformed into parkland. Today, Arizona remains one of the most populated by Native Americans in the United States and is a recognized center of Native American art.

According to a 2000 report, the largest denominational religious groups of Arizona were Roman Catholic, Evangelical Protestant, and Mainline Protestant. The significant Roman Catholic presence reflects the large Hispanic and Latino population, mostly of Roman Catholic Mexican immigrant origin. After the Roman Catholic Church, the Church of Jesus Christ of Latter-day Saints has the second highest number of adherents in Arizona, due to the large influx of Mormons to Arizona in the mid-to-late 19th century who were sent to the American Southwest by Brigham Young.

Arizona is the most populous landlocked state of the United States and one of the fastest growing states. This trend is likely to endure, especially as Arizona continues to deal with the second-largest influx of illegal immigrants of any U.S. state. With its long border with Mexico, Arizona acts as one of the most common entrances into the United States from Mexico. Arizona's tough legislative efforts against illegal immigration have not only affected immigrants within the state but also had larger national and international repercussions. These largely Republican-fueled efforts have caused a rise in Hispanic and Latino voters registering as Democrats, exemplifying some of the national implications of these state actions. Arizona's role in dealing with immigration from Mexico, both legal and illegal, has left these questions central to Arizona's agenda and reputation. However, a quarter of Arizona's federal land remains home to the largest Native American population of any U.S. state, another important population group of Arizona. Arizona's population has continued to grow and will likely continue doing so, creating problems for the state surrounding immigration law, cultural debates, and stress on the state's water supply, all issues the state will have to address in coming years.

Population by Selected Ethnic Group

	Estimate		Estimate
Total:	6,731,484	French Canadian	34,431
Afghan	2,299	German	922,464
Albanian	990	German Russian	281
Alsatian	95	Greek	21,962
American	290,369	Guyanese	366
Arab:	39,392	Hungarian	27,203
Egyptian	3,923	Icelander	1,259
Iraqi	9,787	Iranian	9,198
Jordanian	2,226	Irish	604,031
Lebanese	9,806	Israeli	1,485
Moroccan	510	Italian	279,311
Palestinian	2,576	Latvian	1,154
Syrian	2,507	Lithuanian	10,136
Arab	5,167	Luxemburger	962
Other Arab	4,253	Macedonian	468
Armenian	6,362	Maltese	747
Assyrian/Chaldean/Syriac	2,865	New Zealander	273
Australian	3,313	Northern European	4,997
Austrian	14,702	Norwegian	115,684
Basque	1,948	Pennsylvania German	2,387
Belgian	5,185	Polish	161,544
Brazilian	3,540	Portuguese	14,833
British	27,887	Romanian	11,415
Bulgarian	1,522	Russian	48,163
Cajun	495	Scandinavian	17,420
Canadian	24,208	Scotch-Irish	52,092
Carpatho-Rusyn	0	Scottish	113,773
Celtic	3,063	Serbian	5,946
Croatian	9,042	Slavic	1,820
Cypriot	0	Slovak	8,149
Czech	23,990	Slovene	3,047
Czechoslovakian	6,016	Soviet Union	46
Danish	42,058	Sub-Saharan African:	42,146
Dutch	90,532	Cape Verdean	556
Eastern European	9,426	Ethiopian	3,078
English	546,951	Ghanaian	648
Estonian	276	Kenyan	1,472
European	92,890	Liberian	498
Finnish	15,191	Nigerian	4,341
French (except Basque)	166,299	Senegalese	82

(*continued*)

	Estimate		Estimate
Sierra Leonean	58	Bahamian	221
Somali	5,047	Barbadian	65
South African	1,308	Belizean	730
Sudanese	480	Bermudan	115
Ugandan	0	British West Indian	476
Zimbabwean	150	Dutch West Indian	525
African	22,492	Haitian	1,785
Other sub-Saharan African	2,474	Jamaican	4,380
Swedish	96,930	Trinidadian and Tobagonian	727
Swiss	15,888	U.S. Virgin Islander	0
Turkish	2,903	West Indian	1,369
Ukrainian	17,370	Other West Indian	0
Welsh	41,681	Yugoslavian	8,697
West Indian	10,393	Other groups	2,976,093
(except Hispanic groups):		Unclassified or not reported	1,027,103

Source: American Community Survey, U.S. Census Bureau, 2014.

See in Neighborhoods Section: Chinatown (Phoenix, Arizona); Phoenix and Other Cities, Mexican Enclaves (Arizona); Tucson, Chinese and Southeast Asian Enclaves (Arizona)

ARKANSAS

Capital: Little Rock
Entered Union: June 15, 1836 (25th state)

Arkansas is the 32nd-most populous state, with a population of 2,915,918, according to the 2010 U.S. Census, while being the 29th largest in geographic area. Settled by the Spanish followed by the French, it was acquired by the United States in 1803 via the Louisiana Purchase. Initially part of Mississippi, after a large wave of settlers flowed into the area due to the booming cotton industry, Arkansas became part of the Union in 1836–the 25th state to do so. Arkansas's economy was largely bound to the plantation industry and the institution of slavery, and so, in the wake of the Civil War, the state experienced significant economic stagnation. The mid-20th century brought significant change to Arkansas, however. World War II spurred economic revitalization via wartime industries, and the Civil Rights Movement brought voting rights and increased political participation to long-disenfranchised African Americans. Today, Arkansas is working to counter its longstanding reputation as a poor and rural state, pointing to such famous Arkansans as former president Bill Clinton.

Historical Population of Arkansas

Census	Pop.	%±	Census	Pop.	%±
1810	1,062	—	1920	1,752,204	11.3%
1820	14,273	1,244.0%	1930	1,854,482	5.8%
1830	30,388	112.9%	1940	1,949,387	5.1%
1840	97,574	221.1%	1950	1,909,511	−2.0%
1850	209,897	115.1%	1960	1,786,272	−6.5%
1860	435,450	107.5%	1970	1,923,295	7.7%
1870	484,471	11.3%	1980	2,286,435	18.9%
1880	802,525	65.6%	1990	2,350,725	2.8%
1890	1,128,211	40.6%	2000	2,673,400	13.7%
1900	1,311,564	16.3%	2010	2,915,918	9.1%
1910	1,574,449	20.0%			

Source: U.S. Census Bureau.

According to the 2006–2008 American Community Survey, the 10 largest ancestry groups in the state are African American (15.5%), Irish (13.6%), German (12.5%), American (11.1%), English (10.3%), French (2.4%), Scotch-Irish (2.1%), Dutch (1.9%), Scottish (1.9%), and Italian (1.7%).

Furthermore, according to the 2010 U.S. Census, Arkansas had a population of 2,915,918. The racial composition of the population was as follows: 77.0% white, 15.4% black or African American, 0.8% American Indian and Alaska Native, 1.2% Asian American, 0.2% Native Hawaiian and other Pacific Islander, 3.4% from some other race, and 2.0% from two or more races, while 6.4% of the population was Hispanic or Latino of any race.

According to the 2006–2008 American Community Survey, 93.8% of Arkansas's population (over the age of five) spoke only English at home. About 4.5% of the state's population spoke Spanish at home. About 0.7% of the state's population spoke any other Indo-European language. About 0.8% of the state's population spoke an Asian language, and 0.2% spoke other languages.

According to the Association of Religion Data Archives, Arkansas, like most other Southern states, is part of the Bible Belt and is predominantly Protestant. The vast majority (86%) of the population identify as Christian, with 78% identifying as Protestant and 39% Baptist. There are also smaller Protestant denominations, Roman Catholics (7%), and Jews and Muslims less than 1%, respectively.

Population by Selected Ethnic Group

	Estimate		Estimate
Total:	2,966,369	Alsatian	0
Afghan	0	American	317,844
Albanian	0	Arab:	3,216

(continued)

	Estimate		Estimate
Egyptian	55	Irish	330,896
Iraqi	34	Israeli	111
Jordanian	152	Italian	47,407
Lebanese	632	Latvian	72
Moroccan	207	Lithuanian	1,586
Palestinian	821	Luxemburger	0
Syrian	341	Macedonian	0
Arab	431	Maltese	74
Other Arab	827	New Zealander	33
Armenian	118	Northern European	1,461
Assyrian/Chaldean/Syriac	76	Norwegian	15,979
Australian	273	Pennsylvania German	417
Austrian	2,413	Polish	24,062
Basque	75	Portuguese	3,752
Belgian	1,076	Romanian	874
Brazilian	455	Russian	6,634
British	10,512	Scandinavian	2,551
Bulgarian	265	Scotch-Irish	35,229
Cajun	3,295	Scottish	50,659
Canadian	4,075	Serbian	1,075
Carpatho-Rusyn	0	Slavic	516
Celtic	341	Slovak	988
Croatian	734	Slovene	156
Cypriot	0	Soviet Union	0
Czech	6,787	Sub-Saharan African:	9,921
Czechoslovakian	2,247	Cape Verdean	0
Danish	6,216	Ethiopian	762
Dutch	41,097	Ghanaian	0
Eastern European	414	Kenyan	41
English	284,142	Liberian	49
Estonian	56	Nigerian	362
European	45,708	Senegalese	0
Finnish	1,457	Sierra Leonean	0
French (except Basque)	56,442	Somali	0
French Canadian	8,478	South African	280
German	314,550	Sudanese	0
German Russian	0	Ugandan	0
Greek	3,531	Zimbabwean	0
Guyanese	253	African	7,925
Hungarian	2,444	Other sub-Saharan African	502
Icelander	36	Swedish	15,099
Iranian	329	Swiss	5,291

(continued)

	Estimate		Estimate
Turkish	851	Dutch West Indian	3,468
Ukrainian	1,924	Haitian	0
Welsh	11,701	Jamaican	817
West Indian	5,103	Trinidadian and Tobagonian	332
(except Hispanic groups):		U.S. Virgin Islander	0
Bahamian	0	West Indian	455
Barbadian	0	Other West Indian	0
Belizean	31	Yugoslavian	557
Bermudan	0	Other groups	1,097,589
British West Indian	0	Unclassified or not reported	718,171

Source: American Community Survey, U.S. Census Bureau, 2014.

See in Neighborhoods Section: Springdale, Marshall Islanders Enclave (Arkansas)

CALIFORNIA

Capital: Sacramento
Entered Union: September 9, 1950 (31st state)

California is the most populous of the U.S. states and the third largest in land area. If California were its own country, it would be the eighth-largest economy in the world and the 34th most populated. Los Angeles is the most populated U.S. city, and 8 of the 50 most populous cities in the United States are in California. It became the 31st state admitted to the United States in 1850 after the Mexican-American War. The Gold Rush that began in 1848 brought with it immigration on a grand scale that in turn led to dramatic social, demographic, and economic change to California. With the completion of the First Transcontinental Railroad, many U.S. citizens moved west to take advantage of the good agricultural conditions. Beginning in the early 20th century, many more began to migrate to California with the construction of transatlantic highways. From 1900 to 1965, the population of California grew from less than 1 million to being the most populous of U.S. states. Through the 20th century, California grew to be a U.S. hub of urban growth, entertainment, tourism, agriculture, and technology. Currently, California ranks as the most populated state in the United States at 37,691,912 according to the 2011 Population Estimates by the U.S. Census Bureau.

Historical Population of California

Census	Pop.	%±	Census	Pop.	%±
1850	92,597	—	1940	6,907,387	21.7%
1860	379,994	310.4%	1950	10,586,223	53.3%
1870	560,247	47.4%	1960	15,717,204	48.5%
1880	864,694	54.3%	1970	19,953,134	27.0%
1890	1,213,398	40.3%	1980	23,667,902	18.6%
1900	1,485,053	22.4%	1990	29,760,021	25.7%
1910	2,377,549	60.1%	2000	33,871,648	13.8%
1920	3,426,861	44.1%	2010	37,253,956	10.0%
1930	5,677,251	65.7%			

Source: U.S. Census Bureau.

According to the 2010 U.S. Census Bureau, California's racial breakdown is as follows: 57.6% white (40.1% non-Hispanic white), 13.0% Asian, 6.2% black or African American, 1.0% Native American, 4.9% multiracial, 0.4% Native Hawaiian or Pacific Islander, 37.6% Hispanic or Latino (of any race). As of 2009, the U.S. Census Bureau also report the principal ancestries of California's residents as being 30.6% Mexican, 9.8% German, 7.8% Irish, 6.9% English, and 4.3% Italian. These figures are certainly striking, as Mexican ancestry is far and away the clear majority in this breakdown. California still has the largest population of white Americans in the United States, the fifth-largest population of African Americans, about one-third of the nation's Asian Americans, and the highest population of Native Americans of any state, according to the U.S. Census Bureau. But the group experiencing the most current growth is the Hispanic population, which has grown from 32% of the population in 2000 to 37% in 2008 (*San Francisco Chronicle*, June 5, 2010). The U.S. Census Bureau shows that 20% of the minority populations of the United States live in California.

This growth in Hispanic populations is largely reflective of the vast influx of immigrants from Mexico, both legal and illegal. Illegal immigration is very much on the radar of California politics and society. Peter Slevin found that in 2010, illegal immigrants made up an estimated 7.3% of the population (*Washington Post*, April 30, 2010), more than half from Mexico, placing California as the U.S. state with the third highest percentage of illegal immigrants. In 2012, the California Department of Education found that the Los Angeles Unified School District, which is the largest school district in California and the second largest in the nation is 73.4% Hispanic, 9.5% African American, 9.0% non-Hispanic Caucasian, 6.2% Asian, 0.5% Native American, and 0.4% Pacific Islander.

According to a study by the Modern Language Association, 42.4% of California's population in 2005 spoke languages other than English. Historically, California is one of the most linguistically diverse areas in the world, and while the study showed that 57.6% of Californians over the age of five spoke English as a first language at home, 28.2% spoke Spanish, 2.0% spoke Filipino, 1.6% spoke Chinese, 1.4% spoke Vietnamese, and 1.1% spoke Korean as their first language. There were previously also many indigenous languages spoken in California, although now about half are no longer spoken or currently endangered.

The Pew Research Center reports that as of 2008 31% of California's population belonged to the Catholic Church, in large part as a reflection of California's Spanish history and large Hispanic population. Roman Catholic missionaries from Spain founded Los Angeles and San Francisco, along with many other missions along the California coast. The survey also reported California's population as identifying as 18% Evangelical Protestants, 14% Mainline Protestants, and 21% as unaffiliated. Overall, the Pew Research Center's studies show that California is somewhat less religious a state than many of its counterparts within the United States.

Californian culture is most certainly a Western culture, rooted in the culture of the United States, but has historically had Hispanic influences. The state shares a border with Mexico, and its coastal significance has meant that it has a long history of large immigrant populations from Europeans to Chinese. These large immigrant groups have played and continue to play a crucial role in shaping the cities and cultures of California. The state remains a very "Blue" state (strongly supportive of Democratic Party), open to alternate lifestyles and differences, and more focused on its strengths in environment, technology, agriculture, and entertainment.

As a Western state with a long coastline and a border with Mexico, California has long had a history of immigration and diversity. Roughly 20% of the nation's minority population reportedly lives in California, and its cities serve as a microcosm for the cultural diversity and integration on which the United States built its reputation as cultural melting pot. From Little Arabia or Little Gaza, from Little Tuscany to extensive Chinatowns, from Oakland to Santa Ana, California's large immigrant populations are reflected through the communities they have built and continue to create. After Brazil, California is the second most populous sub-national entity in the Western Hemisphere, a fact that brings its size and population strikingly into perspective. Its population is greater than that of all but 34 countries worldwide. Its cultural diversity and minority and immigrant populations make up a great deal of California's character and continue to influence federal politics, economics, culture, and society.

California Population by Race

Race		
One race	32,264,002	95.3
White	20,170,059	59.5
Black or African American	2,263,882	6.7
American Indian and Alaska Native	333,346	1.0
Asian	3,697,513	10.9
Asian Indian	314,819	0.9

(continued)

Race

Chinese	980,642	2.9
Filipino	918,678	2.7
Japanese	288,854	0.9
Korean	345,882	1.0
Vietnamese	447,032	1.3
Other Asian[1]	401,606	1.2
Native Hawaiian and other Pacific Islander	116,961	0.3
Native Hawaiian	20,571	0.1
Guamanian or Chamorro	20,918	0.1
Samoan	37,498	0.1
Other Pacific Islander[2]	37,974	0.1
Some other race	5,682,241	16.8
Two or more races	1,607,646	4.7

Race Alone or in Combination with One or More Other Races[3]

White	21,490,973	63.4
Black or African American	2,513,041	7.4
American Indian and Alaska Native	627,562	1.9
Asian	4,155,685	12.3
Native Hawaiian and other Pacific Islander	221,458	0.7
Some other race	6,575,625	19.4

Hispanic or Latino and Race

Total Population	**33,871,648**	**100.0**
Hispanic or Latino (of any race)	10,966,556	32.4
Mexican	8,455,926	25.0
Puerto Rican	140,570	0.4
Cuban	72,286	0.2
Other Hispanic or Latino	2,297,774	6.8
Not Hispanic or Latino	22,905,092	67.6
White alone	15,816,790	46.7

(X) Not applicable

[1] Other Asian alone or two or more Asian categories.

[2] Other Pacific Islander alone, or two or more Native Hawaiian and other Pacific Islander categories.

[3] In combination with one or more other races listed. The six numbers may add to more than the total population and the six percentages may add to more than 100% because individuals may report more than one race.

Source: U.S. Census Bureau, Census 2000 Summary File 1, Matrices P1, P3, P4, P8, P9, P12, P13, P.17, P18, P19, P20, P23, P27, P28, P33, PCT5, PCT8, PCT11, PCT15, H1, H3, H4, H5, H11, and H12.

California Population by Nativity and Place of Birth Nativity and Place of Birth

Total Population	33,871,648	100.0
Native	25,007,393	73.8
Born in United States	24,633,720	72.7
State of residence	17,019,097	50.2
Different state	7,614,623	22.5
Born outside United States	373,673	1.1
Foreign born	8,864,255	26.2
Entered 1990 to March 2000	3,270,746	9.7
Naturalized citizen	3,473,266	10.3
Not a citizen	5,390,989	15.9

Region of Birth of Foreign Born

Total (Excluding Born at Sea)	8,864,188	100.0
Europe	696,578	7.9
Asia	2,918,642	32.9
Africa	113,255	1.3
Oceania	67,131	0.8
Latin America	4,926,803	55.6
Northern America	141,779	1.6

Language Spoken at Home

Population 5 Years and Over	31,416,629	100.0
English only	19,014,873	60.5
Language other than English	12,401,756	39.5
Speak English less than "very well"	6,277,779	20.0
Spanish	8,105,505	25.8
Speak English less than "very well"	4,303,949	13.7
Other Indo-European languages	1,335,332	4.3
Speak English less than "very well"	453,589	1.4
Asian and Pacific Island languages	2,709,179	8.6
Speak English less than "very well"	1,438,588	4.6

Ancestry (Single or Multiple)

Total Population	33,871,648	100.0
Total ancestries reported	35,569,389	105.0
Arab	192,887	0.6

(continued)

Total Population	33,871,648	100.0
Czech[1]	118,889	0.4
Danish	207,030	0.6
Dutch	417,382	1.2
English	2,521,355	7.4
French (except Basque)[1]	783,576	2.3
French Canadian[1]	148,265	0.4
German	3,332,396	9.8
Greek	125,284	0.4
Hungarian	133,988	0.4
Irish[1]	2,622,089	7.7
Italian	1,450,884	4.3
Lithuanian	51,406	0.2
Norwegian	436,128	1.3
Polish	491,325	1.5
Portuguese	330,974	1.0
Russian	402,480	1.2
Scotch-Irish	410,310	1.2
Scottish	541,890	1.6
Slovak	24,535	0.1
Sub-Saharan African	184,921	0.5
Swedish	459,897	1.4
Swiss	115,485	0.3
Ukrainian	83,125	0.2
United States or American	1,140,830	3.4
Welsh	188,414	0.6
West Indian (excluding Hispanic groups)	63,639	0.2
Other ancestries	18,590,005	54.9

(X) Not applicable.

[1] The data represent a combination of two ancestries shown separately in Summary File 3. Czech includes Czechoslovakian. French includes Alsatian. French Canadian includes Acadian/Cajun. Irish includes Celtic.

Source: U.S. Census Bureau, Census 2000 Summary File 3, Matrices P18, P19, P21, P22, P24, P36, P37, P39, P42, PCT8, PCT16, PCT17, and PCT19.

Population by Selected Ethnic Group

	Estimate		Estimate
Total:	38,802,500	Egyptian	47,300
Afghan	39,732	Iraqi	25,267
Albanian	3,680	Jordanian	14,633
Alsatian	1,088	Lebanese	57,700
American	1,260,079	Moroccan	12,666
Arab:	291,524	Palestinian	22,733

(continued)

	Estimate		Estimate
Syrian	28,258	Macedonian	2,246
Arab	49,258	Maltese	8,235
Other Arab	42,498	New Zealander	4,978
Armenian	257,702	Northern European	49,566
Assyrian/Chaldean/Syriac	34,211	Norwegian	392,946
Australian	17,753	Pennsylvania German	4,812
Austrian	73,505	Polish	499,431
Basque	17,771	Portuguese	332,610
Belgian	25,430	Romanian	66,732
Brazilian	33,464	Russian	420,756
British	153,450	Scandinavian	68,630
Bulgarian	11,747	Scotch-Irish	218,324
Cajun	2,748	Scottish	504,233
Canadian	82,803	Serbian	17,074
Carpatho-Rusyn	80	Slavic	10,988
Celtic	8,216	Slovak	23,938
Croatian	50,813	Slovene	9,739
Cypriot	644	Soviet Union	500
Czech	76,949	Sub-Saharan African:	261,983
Czechoslovakian	26,612	Cape Verdean	3,874
Danish	175,366	Ethiopian	33,388
Dutch	354,484	Ghanaian	7,875
Eastern European	67,213	Kenyan	4,639
English	2,139,478	Liberian	1,940
Estonian	4,120	Nigerian	26,892
European	556,027	Senegalese	235
Finnish	57,656	Sierra Leonean	498
French (except Basque)	687,693	Somali	4,072
French Canadian	111,316	South African	9,072
German	3,133,991	Sudanese	2,158
German Russian	2,663	Ugandan	1,457
Greek	139,748	Zimbabwean	680
Guyanese	3,030	African	157,027
Hungarian	122,216	Other sub-Saharan African	9,666
Icelander	5,661	Swedish	408,739
Iranian	203,173	Swiss	104,376
Irish	2,482,084	Turkish	23,537
Israeli	32,732	Ukrainian	108,098
Italian	1,515,350	Welsh	162,542
Latvian	10,784	West Indian	86,756
Lithuanian	49,538	(except Hispanic groups):	
Luxemburger	1,992	Bahamian	505

(*continued*)

	Estimate		Estimate
Barbadian	1,988	Trinidadian and Tobagonian	6,214
Belizean	20,979	U.S. Virgin Islander	388
Bermudan	162	West Indian	11,972
British West Indian	1,111	Other West Indian	301
Dutch West Indian	2,642	Yugoslavian	30,154
Haitian	9,972	Other groups	23,183,838
Jamaican	31,638	Unclassified or not reported	4,155,040

Source: American Community Survey, U.S. Census Bureau, 2014.

See in Neighborhoods Section: Baldwin Hills (Los Angeles, California); Boyle Heights, Jewish Neighborhood (Los Angeles, California); Boyle Heights, Latino Neighborhood (Los Angeles, California); Cambodia Town (Long Beach, California); Chinatown (Los Angeles, California); Chinatown (San Francisco, California); Chinatowns (Duplicates) (San Francisco, California); East Los Angeles, Mexican American Enclave (Los Angeles, California); El Monte, Latino Enclaves (California); Fillmore District (San Francisco, California); Gardena and Torrance (South Bay Region, Los Angeles County, California); Glendale, Armenian Enclave (California); Historic Filipinotown (Los Angeles, California); Historic South Central (Los Angeles, California); Indio, Mexican and Central American Communities (California); Japantown (San Francisco, California); Kingsburg and Sveadal, Swedish Enclaves (California); Koreatown (Los Angeles, California); Little Arabia (Anaheim, California); Little Armenia (Los Angeles, California); Little Ethiopia (Los Angeles, California); Little India/Pakistan (Artesia, California); Little Italy (Los Angeles, California); Little Italy (San Diego, California); Little Italy (San Francisco, California); Little Saigon (San Francisco, California); Little Saigon (San Jose, California); Little Saigon (Westminster, California); Little Tokyo (Los Angeles, California); Logan Heights, Mexican Enclave (San Diego, California); Los Angeles, Hawaiian Enclaves (California); Los Angeles, West Side and San Fernando Valley Jewish Enclaves (California); Mayan Corner/24th and Mission (San Francisco, California); Monterey Park, First Suburban Chinatown (California); Mount Washington, Mexican Enclave (California); National City (San Diego, California); Olvera Street/La Plaza (Los Angeles, California); Pico Rivera, Latino Enclave (California); Riverside, Mexican Enclave (California); San Bernardino, Mexican Enclave (California); San Pedro, Italian and Croatian Enclaves (California); Santa Ana, Mexican Enclaves (California); Sawtelle (Los Angeles, California); Silicon Valley, Indian and South Asian Communities (Santa Clara Valley/San Jose Region, California); Sin City (Fresno, California); Solvang, Danish Community (California); Sonoma County, Italian Enclave (California); Tehrangeles (Los Angeles, California); Temescal (Oakland, California); Thai Town (Los Angeles, California); Watts (Los Angeles, California); Yuba City, Sikh Enclave (California)

COLORADO

Capital: Denver
Entered Union: August 1, 1876 (38th state)

Colorado became the 38th state to enter to Union in 1876. Silver and gold strikes lured a number of miners to the state in the late 19th century. The Dust Bowls and the Great Depression in the 1930s did not add to Colorado's population count, but after World War II, the numbers of residents and tourists started to increase. Colorado is now the 22nd most populous of the United States, and the 8th most extensive. The state's most populous city is Denver, home to about 61.90% of Colorado's residents according to the 2009 U.S. Census Bureau estimations. According to the 2010 census, Colorado had a total population of 5,029,196.

Historical Population of Colorado

Census	Pop.	%±	Census	Pop.	%±
1860	34,277	—	1940	1,123,296	8.4%
1870	39,864	16.3%	1950	1,325,089	18.0%
1880	194,327	387.5%	1960	1,753,947	32.4%
1890	413,249	112.7%	1970	2,207,259	25.8%
1900	539,700	30.6%	1980	2,889,964	30.9%
1910	799,024	48.0%	1990	3,294,394	14.0%
1920	939,629	17.6%	2000	4,301,262	30.6%
1930	1,035,791	10.2%	2010	5,029,196	16.9%

Source: U.S. Census Bureau.

The 2010 U.S. Census reported Colorado's population was 81.3% white (70.0% non-Hispanic white), 4.0% black or African American, 3.4% from two or more races, 2.8% Asian, 1.1% American Indian and Alaska Native, 0.1% Native Hawaiian and other Pacific Islander, and 7.2% from some other race. Hispanics and Latinos of any race made up 20.7% of Colorado's population. The 2000 U.S. Census reported that the largest ancestry groups in Colorado were German (including Swiss and Austrian) at 22%, Mexican at 18%, Irish at 12%, and English at 12%.

These ancestral and demographic trends are especially common in certain areas and communities. Those who identify as ancestrally German are particularly abundant in the Front Range, Rockies, and High Plains areas. There are some large African American communities in Denver, in the Montbello, Green Valley Ranch, Park Hill, Whittier, and Five Points neighborhoods, and in other East Denver areas. Colorado Springs also boasts a relatively large African American population, in the east and southeast areas of the city in particular. Asian Americans of Chinese, Japanese, Korean, Mongolian, Filipino, and Southeast Asian descent make up a considerable portion of Colorado's population as well. The highest Asian American populations

Annual National Western Stock Show Parade traveling up 17th Street in downtown Denver, 2012. (Arinahabich08/Dreamstime.com)

are found in the south and southeast parts of Denver and in some of the city's south-west side. Colorado has an especially large number of Hispanic citizens, mostly Mexican American, particularly in Denver and Colorado Springs, as well as in smaller cities and towns through the state. The 2000 U.S. Census reported the Hispanic population to be about 20% of the total state population. According to the 2010 U.S. Census, Colorado has the seventh highest percentage of Hispanics in the United States at 20.7%, after New Mexico, California, Texas, Arizona, Nevada, and Florida. And Colorado reportedly has the fourth-largest Mexican American population behind California, Texas, and Arizona.

This large Hispanic population's presence is reflected in Colorado's strong Latino culture. Hispanos, the descendants of early Mexican settlers of Spanish origins, make up a large number of the residents of Southern, Southwestern, and South-eastern Colorado. There was an early precedent for a Hispanic presence in Colo-rado due to these descendants of colonial settlers, but the prominence of Hispanic residents in Colorado has increased greatly in the past half-century or so. The 1940 U.S. Census reported Colorado's population to be 8.2% Hispanic and 90.3% non-Hispanic white, while the 2000 U.S. Census found that 10.5% of people below the age of five spoke only Spanish at home, estimating the number to be around 14% by 2009. Many of these Spanish-speaking residents are legal as Colorado has a large immigrant presence, but Colorado cities have also been referred to as "Sanctuary

Cities" for illegal immigrants. Colorado has the fourth highest percentage of undocumented immigrants in the United States behind Nevada, Arizona, and California, and tied with Texas. A 2005 study by the Colorado Alliance for Immigration Reform reported that approximately 5.5–6.0% of the state's population is composed of illegal immigrants; while over 20% of the state's prisoners are undocumented inmates.

Colorado has an above-average proportion of 25% of citizens who claim to follow no religion, while the national average is 17%. The largest religious denominations in Colorado by number of adherents in 2000 ranked at Roman Catholic first, followed by the Church of Jesus Christ of Latter-day Saints, then Baptist. The state's demographic makeup is reflected in these religious statistics. Denver and its surrounding areas are more ethnically diverse and politically liberal than much of the state concerning political and environmental issues, while Colorado Springs is typically considered a much more homogenously white. The largest population increases are expected in the Denver metropolitan area especially, the state's most populous city and state capital. Most of Colorado's population is concentrated densely in certain areas, with the center of population for the state located in Jefferson County, a little northeast of the state's center. Colorado overall is well known for its reputation of active and athletic residents, and an abundance of outdoor activities in its beautiful geographic layout of mountains and plains.

Population by Selected Ethnic Group

	Estimate		Estimate
Total:	5,355,866	Basque	2,612
Afghan	1,338	Belgian	5,647
Albanian	307	Brazilian	3,011
Alsatian	212	British	34,365
American	261,070	Bulgarian	2,324
Arab:	21,696	Cajun	723
Egyptian	803	Canadian	11,448
Iraqi	634	Carpatho-Rusyn	383
Jordanian	296	Celtic	1,613
Lebanese	7,376	Croatian	6,712
Moroccan	2,241	Cypriot	0
Palestinian	1,259	Czech	33,980
Syrian	1,718	Czechoslovakian	6,668
Arab	3,671	Danish	38,145
Other Arab	4,273	Dutch	93,188
Armenian	2,979	Eastern European	9,365
Assyrian/Chaldean/Syriac	125	English	548,014
Australian	1,964	Estonian	932
Austrian	17,960	European	87,863

(continued)

	Estimate		Estimate
Finnish	9,384	Ethiopian	9,541
French (except Basque)	146,627	Ghanaian	3,012
French Canadian	25,909	Kenyan	0
German	1,056,923	Liberian	341
German Russian	755	Nigerian	3,983
Greek	19,783	Senegalese	222
Guyanese	427	Sierra Leonean	230
Hungarian	19,398	Somali	5,718
Icelander	1,107	South African	1,389
Iranian	4,766	Sudanese	1,767
Irish	620,602	Ugandan	155
Israeli	1,081	Zimbabwean	290
Italian	254,408	African	18,425
Latvian	2,402	Other sub-Saharan African	2,246
Lithuanian	10,185	Swedish	124,984
Luxemburger	664	Swiss	23,318
Macedonian	208	Turkish	2,459
Maltese	253	Ukrainian	16,497
New Zealander	736	Welsh	49,916
Northern European	10,847	West Indian	7,692
Norwegian	114,049	(except Hispanic groups):	
Pennsylvania German	3,146	Bahamian	129
Polish	127,983	Barbadian	36
Portuguese	11,365	Belizean	351
Romanian	6,667	Bermudan	105
Russian	58,370	British West Indian	439
Scandinavian	18,640	Dutch West Indian	258
Scotch-Irish	63,208	Haitian	1,946
Scottish	133,280	Jamaican	2,059
Serbian	2,434	Trinidadian and Tobagonian	264
Slavic	5,107	U.S. Virgin Islander	0
Slovak	11,499	West Indian	2,323
Slovene	7,279	Other West Indian	0
Soviet Union	142	Yugoslavian	5,905
Sub-Saharan African:	45,980	Other groups	1,775,080
Cape Verdean	0	Unclassified or not reported	871,619

Source: American Community Survey, U.S. Census Bureau, 2014.

See in Neighborhoods Section: Little Saigon (Denver, Colorado); South Federal Boulevard (Denver, Colorado)

CONNECTICUT

Capital: Hartford
Entered Union: January 9, 1788 (5th state)

Connecticut ranks as the third-smallest state by land area and the 29th most populous state. As a result, it is one of the most densely settled of all 50 states. According to the 2010 U.S. Census, Connecticut had a population of 3,574,097.

Historical Population of Connecticut

Census	Pop.	%±	Census	Pop.	%±
1790	237,946	—	1910	1,114,756	22.7%
1800	251,002	5.5%	1920	1,380,631	23.9%
1810	261,942	4.4%	1930	1,606,903	16.4%
1820	275,248	5.1%	1940	1,709,242	6.4%
1830	297,675	8.1%	1950	2,007,280	17.4%
1840	309,978	4.1%	1960	2,535,234	26.3%
1850	370,792	19.6%	1970	3,031,709	19.6%
1860	460,147	24.1%	1980	3,107,576	2.5%
1870	537,454	16.8%	1990	3,287,116	5.8%
1880	622,700	15.9%	2000	3,405,565	3.6%
1890	746,258	19.8%	2010	3,574,097	4.9%
1900	908,420	21.7%			

Source: U.S. Census Bureau.

Connecticut's first European settlers were Dutch, and initially half of it was part of the Dutch colony, New Netherland. Connecticut was one of the first major settlements established by the English in the 1630s and was one of the 13 colonies to revolt against the British in the American Revolution. Today Connecticut is considered a wealthy state, but with an immense income gap between its urban and suburban areas. For example, New Canaan, Connecticut, has one of the highest per capita incomes in the United States, while Hartford is one of the 10 cities with the lowest per capita incomes in the country. Wealthier suburbs surround many of these less affluent urban areas of the state. Most of the southern and western area of the state is part of the New York metropolitan area, as is the majority of the state's population, an area widely referred to as the Tri-State area.

According to the 2010 U.S. Census, Connecticut ethnically broke down to 77.6% white (71.2% non-Hispanic white), 10.1% black or African American, 3.8% Asian, 0.3% American Indian and Alaska Native, 5.6% some other race, 2.6% from two or more races, with Hispanics and Latinos of any race made up 13.4% of the state's population. The percentage of non-Hispanic whites, although still Connecticut's largest ethnic group, has declined from 98% in 1940 to 84% in 1990.

A 2000 Modern Language Association study reported that 81.69% of Connecticut residents over the age of five spoke English at home, while 8.42% spoke Spanish, 1.59% Italian, 1.31% French, and 1.20% Polish. According to the U.S. Census Bureau, the state's six-largest ancestry groups rank as 19.3% Italian, 17.9% Irish, 10.7% English, 10.4% German, 8.6% Polish, and 6.6% French. Connecticut has large Italian American, Irish American, and English American populations, in addition to German American and Portuguese American populations. There is a significant Italian population across the state, as well as certain counties with large Irish American, Polish American, and French Canadian populations. African American and Hispanic populations, especially Puerto Ricans, are most common in urban areas throughout the state. Connecticut is also well known for its rather large Hungarian American population. In more recent decades, the immigrant populations' origin countries have extended more broadly beyond Western Europe to the former Soviet countries, India, the Philippines, Laos, Vietnam, Thailand, Indonesia, Mexico, Panama, Guatemala, Brazil, and Jamaica.

In terms of religious affiliation, Connecticut breaks down to about 40% Protestant, 32% Roman Catholic, 12% nonreligious, 3% Jewish, and 4% other religions according to a 2001 survey of Connecticut residents' religious self-identification. The Jewish populations are concentrated in towns near Long Island Sound between Greenwich and New Haven, Greater New Haven, and Greater Hartford. More recent immigration from more areas has brought more other non-Christian religions to Connecticut, but the numbers in these other affiliations are still relatively low.

Overall, Connecticut is a fairly homogenously white state. Its heritage as a colonial European settlement, and its position as the provider of wealthy suburbs for the Tri-State area provides for a relatively large wealthy upper-middle class, many of whom identify as white. New Canaan, Darien, Greenwich, Weston, Wilton, and Westport are ranked among some of the wealthiest towns in the state, but many of the urban areas of Connecticut rank in as some of poorest municipalities in Connecticut, Hartford being the lowest. Ethnic diversity is most often found in these urban areas of the state, particularly African American and Hispanic residents. Connecticut has a strong European-based immigrant history, but in more recent years the range of origin countries has expanded extraordinarily, and is reflected in demographic statistics of language, religion, and culture.

Population by Selected Ethnic Group

	Estimate		Estimate
Total:	3,596,677	Egyptian	2,064
Afghan	2,428	Iraqi	976
Albanian	11,758	Jordanian	77
Alsatian	129	Lebanese	7,307
American	155,634	Moroccan	2,663
Arab:	22,408	Palestinian	718

(continued)

	Estimate		Estimate
Syrian	1,970	Macedonian	1,425
Arab	3,352	Maltese	379
Other Arab	3,806	New Zealander	204
Armenian	4,498	Northern European	2,208
Assyrian/Chaldean/Syriac	425	Norwegian	19,431
Australian	1,308	Pennsylvania German	266
Austrian	12,083	Polish	264,296
Basque	98	Portuguese	48,775
Belgian	2,593	Romanian	6,605
Brazilian	18,373	Russian	61,277
British	16,160	Scandinavian	3,536
Bulgarian	1,125	Scotch-Irish	16,408
Cajun	192	Scottish	57,723
Canadian	14,782	Serbian	1,076
Carpatho-Rusyn	120	Slavic	2,700
Celtic	959	Slovak	18,477
Croatian	3,296	Slovene	1,167
Cypriot	181	Soviet Union	0
Czech	11,600	Sub-Saharan African:	37,200
Czechoslovakian	6,668	Cape Verdean	3,181
Danish	12,217	Ethiopian	531
Dutch	26,343	Ghanaian	3,152
Eastern European	10,932	Kenyan	147
English	310,677	Liberian	749
Estonian	1,046	Nigerian	3,369
European	28,600	Senegalese	315
Finnish	6,561	Sierra Leonean	0
French (except Basque)	197,527	Somali	75
French Canadian	104,241	South African	1,141
German	322,941	Sudanese	367
German Russian	71	Ugandan	908
Greek	30,304	Zimbabwean	0
Guyanese	3,856	African	21,983
Hungarian	36,839	Other sub-Saharan African	2,128
Icelander	448	Swedish	58,587
Iranian	2,275	Swiss	8,505
Irish	555,071	Turkish	3,532
Israeli	592	Ukrainian	20,707
Italian	634,102	Welsh	12,717
Latvian	1,212	West Indian	85,967
Lithuanian	24,327	(except Hispanic groups):	
Luxemburger	99	Bahamian	99

(continued)

	Estimate		Estimate
Barbadian	1,308	Trinidadian and Tobagonian	1,887
Belizean	38	U.S. Virgin Islander	1,261
Bermudan	359	West Indian	8,602
British West Indian	1,602	Other West Indian	234
Dutch West Indian	332	Yugoslavian	5,542
Haitian	20,030	Other groups	1,007,449
Jamaican	51,216	Unclassified or not reported	401,026

Source: American Community Survey, U.S. Census Bureau, 2014.

See in Neighborhoods Section: Hartford, Native American Community (Connecticut); Mashantucket (Western) Pequot Tribal Nation (Mashantucket, Connecticut)

DELAWARE

Capital: Dover
Entered Union: December 7, 1787 (1st state)

Delaware is the second smallest, sixth least populous, but sixth most densely populated U.S. state. According to the 2010 U.S. Census, Delaware's population is

The Delaware State Capitol Building in Dover, 2016. (Jon Bilous/Dreamstime.com)

897,934. Its racial composition is 68.9% white American, 21.4% African American, 0.5% American Indian and Alaska Native, and 3.2% Asian American. A total of 8.2% were Hispanics of any race. The center of population of Delaware is located in New Castle County. Its most populous city is Wilmington, measured in 2010 as having 70,851 residents.

Historical Population of Delaware

Census	Pop.	%±	Census	Pop.	%±
1790	59,096	—	1910	202,322	9.5%
1800	64,273	8.8%	1920	223,003	10.2%
1810	72,674	13.1%	1930	238,380	6.9%
1820	72,749	0.1%	1940	266,505	11.8%
1830	76,748	5.5%	1950	318,085	19.4%
1840	78,085	1.7%	1960	446,292	40.3%
1850	91,532	17.2%	1970	548,104	22.8%
1860	112,216	22.6%	1980	594,338	8.4%
1870	125,015	11.4%	1990	666,168	12.1%
1880	146,608	17.3%	2000	783,600	17.6%
1890	168,493	14.9%	2010	897,934	14.6%
1900	184,735	9.6%			

Source: U.S. Census Bureau.

Delaware has a long history of European immigration. Swedes, Finns, and Dutch were the first Europeans to settle in what is now Delaware in the 1630s. But in 1664, the area was conquered by a fleet of English ships, and Delaware became an English colony. During the 1800s, English and Irish immigrants were joined by Germans, Poles, Italians, and other European nationalities. Delaware is known as The First State because on December 7, 1787, it became the first state to ratify the Constitution of the United States.

In modern times, Delaware is known to house many corporate headquarters, likely due to the state's lenient corporate tax laws. Many immigrants have been attracted to the northern part of the state, where they found a number of job opportunities. The largest immigrant groups come from Asian- and Spanish-speaking countries. However, recent immigrants make up a relatively small portion of Delaware's population. According to a survey done in 2000, 91% of Delaware residents speak only English at home. Spanish is spoken by 5%, and French is the third most spoken language at 0.7%, followed by Chinese at 0.5%, and German at 0.5%.

The Association of Religion Data Archives reported in 2010 that the three largest denominational groups in Delaware by number of adherents are the Catholic Church, the United Methodist Church, and nondenominational Evangelical Protestant. The main religious affiliations of the people of Delaware are 20% Methodist, 19% Baptist, 17% No Religion, 9% Roman Catholic, 2% Muslim, and 1% Jewish.

A 2012 survey found that 34% of Delaware residents considered themselves "moderately religious," 33% as "very religious," and 33% as "nonreligious." To serve the religious and spiritual needs of the new immigrant populations, an Islamic mosque has been recently built in the Ogletown area, and a Hindu temple in Hockessin.

Delaware is also the name of a Native American group that was influential in the colonial period and is today headquartered in Kent County, Delaware. A band of the Nanticoke tribe of American Indians today resides in Sussex County, Delaware.

Population by Selected Ethnic Group

	Estimate		Estimate
Total:	935,614	Czechoslovakian	927
Afghan	128	Danish	2,020
Albanian	0	Dutch	8,711
Alsatian	0	Eastern European	1,043
American	53,799	English	86,625
Arab:	3,822	Estonian	38
Egyptian	446	European	7,395
Iraqi	2,043	Finnish	594
Jordanian	0	French (except Basque)	17,692
Lebanese	357	French Canadian	3,449
Moroccan	348	German	126,512
Palestinian	0	German Russian	816
Syrian	406	Greek	3,119
Arab	159	Guyanese	536
Other Arab	69	Hungarian	4,914
Armenian	272	Icelander	0
Assyrian/Chaldean/Syriac	0	Iranian	1,399
Australian	274	Irish	149,348
Austrian	2,405	Israeli	59
Basque	0	Italian	95,544
Belgian	656	Latvian	38
Brazilian	533	Lithuanian	2,829
British	3,361	Luxemburger	0
Bulgarian	262	Macedonian	0
Cajun	330	Maltese	92
Canadian	1,563	New Zealander	0
Carpatho-Rusyn	124	Northern European	548
Celtic	224	Norwegian	4,949
Croatian	259	Pennsylvania German	2,467
Cypriot	0	Polish	42,255
Czech	2,145	Portuguese	2,445

(continued)

	Estimate		Estimate
Romanian	919	African	6,095
Russian	8,355	Other sub-Saharan African	141
Scandinavian	1,933	Swedish	8,192
Scotch-Irish	6,553	Swiss	1,517
Scottish	12,196	Turkish	99
Serbian	385	Ukrainian	4,358
Slavic	164	Welsh	7,066
Slovak	1,392	West Indian	6,857
Slovene	246	(except Hispanic groups):	
Soviet Union	0	Bahamian	0
Sub-Saharan African:	9,693	Barbadian	209
Cape Verdean	97	Belizean	0
Ethiopian	36	Bermudan	45
Ghanaian	340	British West Indian	0
Kenyan	1,434	Dutch West Indian	85
Liberian	175	Haitian	2,716
Nigerian	949	Jamaican	2,173
Senegalese	0	Trinidadian and Tobagonian	318
Sierra Leonean	30	U.S. Virgin Islander	60
Somali	0	West Indian	1,251
South African	489	Other West Indian	0
Sudanese	16	Yugoslavian	418
Ugandan	0	Other groups	324,647
Zimbabwean	0	Unclassified or not reported	141,170

Source: American Community Survey, U.S. Census Bureau, 2014.

See in Neighborhoods Section: Little Italy (Wilmington, Delaware)

DISTRICT OF COLUMBIA

Capital: Washington
Creation: July 16, 1790 (signing of Residence Act, calling for creation of a federal district on the Potomac River)

The District of Columbia (i.e., Washington, D.C.) is a federal district, wherein is located the city of Washington, the capital of the United States. The District of Columbia is not a part of any U.S. state, but instead its own capital district. This wider metropolitan area has about 5.6 million residents according to the 2010 U.S. Census. Adding Baltimore, the Baltimore-Washington metropolitan area has a population above 8.5 million residents.

The District of Columbia was formed from territory ceded by Maryland and Virginia in 1788, and it was established in accordance with Acts of Congress passed in 1790 and 1791. As of the 2010 U.S. Census, the city itself is home to 601,723 people. The District of Columbia has no counties and just one city, which is a functioning government equivalent to the state level. Its constituents elect one nonvoting delegate to the House of Representatives; thus, the District of Columbia has no federal representation. Washington, D.C., borders Maryland and Virginia.

Historical Population of the District of Columbia

Census	Pop.	%±	Census	Pop.	%±
1800	8,144	—	1910	331,069	18.8%
1810	15,471	90.0%	1920	437,571	32.2%
1820	23,336	50.8%	1930	486,869	11.3%
1830	30,261	29.7%	1940	663,091	36.2%
1840	33,745	11.5%	1950	802,178	21.0%
1850	51,687	53.2%	1960	763,956	−4.8%
1860	75,080	45.3%	1970	756,510	−0.1%
1870	131,700	75.4%	1980	638,333	−15.6%
1880	177,624	34.9%	1990	606,900	−04.9%
1890	230,392	29.7%	2000	572,059	−5.7%
1900	278,718	21.0%	2010	601,723	5.2%

Source: U.S. Census Bureau.

The 2010 U.S. Census reported District of Columbia population to be 50.7% black or African American, 38.5% white (34.8% non-Hispanic white), 3.5% Asian, 0.3% Native American, 4.1% other races, 2.9% two or more races, and 9.1% Hispanics of any race. Religiously, Washington, D.C., residents break down as more than half Christian with 28% Baptist, 13% Roman Catholic, and 31% other Christian denominations. Other faiths make up 6% of the population, while 18% do not adhere to any religion, according to 2008 data from the American Religious Identification Survey.

Washington, D.C., is a very ethnically diverse city, and only just recently lost its black majority (48.3% in 2015). Since the city's founding, there has been a prominent African American population, many of whom were freed former slaves. Between 1800 and 1940, African Americans made up about 30% of the total population of the city (U.S. Census Data). The city's African American population reached a peak of 70% by 1970, earning D.C. the moniker of "Chocolate City," but the percentage has steadily declined since many African Americans left the city for the District's suburbs. Simultaneously, there has been a great deal of gentrification of many previously black-dominated areas of District of Columbia, and the city's white population has steadily increased. The black population of District of Columbia has decreased by 11.5%, while the non-Hispanic white population has increased by 31.4% since 2000 (*Washington Post*, 2011).

As of 2010, there are an estimated 81,734 foreign immigrants living in Washington, D.C. El Salvador, Vietnam, and Ethiopia make up some of the largest sources of immigrants. One potential implication of this sizable number of immigrants is its effect on the literacy rates in the District. A 2007 study from the Associated Press found that about one-third of District of Columbia residents were functionally illiterate, a finding that points partially toward immigrants who are not proficient in English.

The District does however have a fairly large divide between those who are highly educated and high earning and those who live in poverty. The U.S. Census Bureau found that 50% of District of Columbia residents have at least a four-year college degree, and in 2006 District of Columbia residents had a personal income per capita higher than any of the 50 U.S. states. Simultaneously, however, 2005 census data showed that 19% of District of Columbia residents live below in the poverty line, a higher number than any state other than Mississippi. Crime in District of Columbia is concentrated in these areas of poverty, often combined with drug abuse and gangs. A 2010 study by the District of Columbia Crime Policy Institute found that 5% of blocks in the District accounted for over one-fourth of the city's crimes, with reports of violent crime most common in the eastern side of the city. Murder rates have certainly decreased drastically since the early 1990s, and many neighborhoods such as Columbia Heights and Logan Circle are becoming safer and livelier.

Washington, D.C., places emphasis on official culture through its many museums and monuments, most of which have free entry. The city is also home to many universities, adding to the city's large youth population. Many young professionals come to the District in pursuit of careers in government and politics. This large population of young and often highly educated residents adds to the city's culture, wealth, and vibrancy. The District of Columbia Department of Employment Services found that in 2012 the federal government accounted for about 29% of the jobs in Washington, but many other organizations and industries thrive in District of Columbia, whether they are directly, indirectly, or not at all connected to the federal government. The gross product of the Washington metropolitan area put it in fourth place for largest metropolitan economy in the United States, according the U.S. Bureau of Economic Analysis. Though the demographics of the District's residents and neighborhoods has certainly been changing, and will no doubt continue to do so, the nation's capital remains a diverse and vibrant city full of history, culture, and energy.

Population by Selected Ethnic Group

	Estimate		Estimate
Total:	633,736	American	14,780
Afghan	70	Arab:	4,176
Albanian	285	Egyptian	468
Alsatian	29	Iraqi	169

(continued)

	Estimate		Estimate
Jordanian	89	Italian	22,906
Lebanese	1,121	Latvian	485
Moroccan	347	Lithuanian	1,938
Palestinian	468	Luxemburger	118
Syrian	484	Macedonian	53
Arab	441	Maltese	50
Other Arab	813	New Zealander	156
Armenian	685	Northern European	763
Assyrian/Chaldean/Syriac	105	Norwegian	3,810
Australian	511	Pennsylvania German	119
Austrian	1,918	Polish	12,605
Basque	79	Portuguese	1,197
Belgian	762	Romanian	985
Brazilian	1,260	Russian	10,693
British	4,772	Scandinavian	1,226
Bulgarian	389	Scotch-Irish	3,919
Cajun	65	Scottish	8,238
Canadian	1,028	Serbian	575
Carpatho-Rusyn	44	Slavic	168
Celtic	120	Slovak	986
Croatian	760	Slovene	331
Cypriot	39	Soviet Union	45
Czech	1,508	Sub-Saharan African:	19,800
Czechoslovakian	203	Cape Verdean	160
Danish	1,365	Ethiopian	5,870
Dutch	3,450	Ghanaian	412
Eastern European	5,308	Kenyan	205
English	32,288	Liberian	169
Estonian	124	Nigerian	2,310
European	10,300	Senegalese	123
Finnish	768	Sierra Leonean	228
French (except Basque)	9,739	Somali	121
French Canadian	2,079	South African	238
German	42,326	Sudanese	78
German Russian	14	Ugandan	15
Greek	2,232	Zimbabwean	76
Guyanese	994	African	8,809
Hungarian	2,554	Other sub-Saharan African	1,333
Icelander	76	Swedish	4,344
Iranian	1,122	Swiss	1,964
Irish	42,186	Turkish	833
Israeli	307	Ukrainian	2,491

(continued)

	Estimate		Estimate
Welsh	2,666	Haitian	937
West Indian	7,897	Jamaican	3,404
(except Hispanic groups):		Trinidadian and Tobagonian	1,582
Bahamian	136	U.S. Virgin Islander	133
Barbadian	166	West Indian	1,289
Belizean	63	Other West Indian	49
Bermudan	53	Yugoslavian	159
British West Indian	331	Other groups	344,252
Dutch West Indian	60	Unclassified or not reported	92,110

Source: U.S. Census Bureau, 2010–2014 American Community Survey 5-Year Estimates.

FLORIDA

Capital: Tallahassee
Entered Union: March 3, 1845 (27th state)

Until the middle of the 20th century, Florida was the least populous southern state. Today, it is the second most populous southern state behind Texas, the most populous state in the southeastern United States, and the fourth most populous state overall, according to data from the 2010 census. Miami is the largest metropolitan area in the southeastern United States. Florida is also the 22nd most extensive state and the 8th most densely populated. The U.S. Census Bureau estimates that the population of Florida was 19,057,542 on July 1, 2011, showing a 1.36% increase since the 2010 U.S. Census. According to recent population increases, Florida is the 30th fastest-growing U.S. state. The 2010 U.S. Census reported Florida's population at 18,801,310.

Historical Population of Florida

Census	Pop.	%±	Census	Pop.	%±
1830	34,730	—	1930	1,468,211	51.6%
1840	54,477	56.9%	1940	1,897,414	29.2%
1850	87,445	60.5%	1950	2,771,305	46.1%
1860	140,424	60.6%	1960	4,951,560	78.7%
1870	187,748	33.7%	1970	6,789,443	37.1%
1880	269,493	43.5%	1980	9,746,324	43.6%
1890	391,422	45.2%	1990	12,937,926	32.7%
1900	528,542	35.0%	2000	15,982,378	23.5%
1910	752,619	42.4%	2010	18,801,310	17.6%
1920	968,470	28.7%			

Source: U.S. Census Bureau.

Prior to European arrival, Florida was heavily settled by Native American tribes. First, it was settled by the Spanish, until the area was traded to Britain in 1763. In 1819, Florida became part of the United States. The U.S. government passed the Indian Removal Act in 1830, and in 1832 the United States signed the Treaty of Payne's Landing with some of the Seminole chiefs, giving them land west of the Mississippi if they left Florida willingly. Many did leave voluntarily, but others chose to stay. By the end of 1835, the Second Seminole War had begun as the U.S. Army arrived to enforce the treaty. The U.S. Army fought the guerrilla tactics of the Seminole Indian warriors until 1842. After Florida's induction as the 27th U.S. state in 1845, the Third Seminole War began in 1855, removing most of the remaining Seminoles out of Florida through 1858. Some Seminoles did remain however, especially in the region of the Everglades, where their descendants still reside today.

Even as more settlers began to build cotton plantation in Florida, the state's population increased at a rather slow speed. And due to the plantations' demand for slave labor, slaves made up 44% of Florida's population by 1860. Florida declared its succession from the United States in January 1861 and became the founding member of the Confederate States of America. Even after the Civil War, the state's constitution and statutes disenfranchised most blacks and many poor whites with provisions such as poll taxes, literacy tests, and residency requirements. This disenfranchisement for African Americans lasted until the Civil Rights Movement of the 1960s. Before the Civil War and during the Reconstruction era, blacks made up nearly half the state's population, but early 20th-century racial violence caused a record number of African Americans to leave Florida in the Great Migration to the northern and midwestern states.

Florida is a diverse state, with the population made up of 75% white (57.9% non-Hispanic), 16.0% black or African American, 0.4% American Indian or Alaska Native, 2.4% Asian, 0.1% Native Hawaiian or other Pacific Islander, 3.6% from some other race, and 2.5% from two or more races. Hispanics and Latinos of any race made up 22.5% of the population. The largest reported ancestry groups in the 2000 U.S. Census were German at 11.8%, Irish at 10.3%, English at 9.2%, American at 8%, Italian at 6.3%, Cuban at 5.2%, Puerto Rican at 3.0%, French at 2.8%, Polish at 2.7%, and Scottish at 1.8%. Although Florida's black population vastly decreased in the early 20th century with the Great Migration, it has begun to rise again in more recent years. Florida's Hispanic population has continued to grow in affluence and mobility, as well as in size.

About two-thirds of the population was born in another state, a partial reflection of Florida's considerable elderly and immigrant populations. In 2010, illegal immigrants made up an estimated 5.7% of the population, the sixth highest percentage of any state, with an estimated 675,000 illegal immigrants. Florida often gets media attention for its large illegal immigrant populations, most commonly from the islands not far from Florida's coast such as Cuba, Haiti, the Dominican Republic, and Puerto Rico. Cuba particularly has a complex history of U.S. immigration. Before the 1980s, all refugees from Cuba were welcomed as political refugees, but in the 1990s, this changed to only those who reached U.S. soil. But Cuban refugees are often seen as having an advantage over other Latino U.S. immigrants. As Cuba is only about

90 miles from Florida's shore, Miami (not shockingly) has an extremely prominent Cuban American community, in part due to this proximity.

Florida's culture reflects the deep influences of its various heritages: European, Native American, African American, and most recently and prominently, Hispanic. As of a 2005 study by the Modern Language Association, 74.54% of Florida residents over the age of five spoke English at home as their first language, while 18.65% spoke Spanish, and 1.73% spoke French Creole (almost entirely Haitian Creole). As of 2000, the three largest religious denominational groups in Florida were Catholic, Evangelical Protestant, and Mainline Protestant. Florida is mostly Protestant, but Roman Catholicism is the largest single denomination in the state. There is also a rather considerable Jewish community, located mostly in South Florida, constituting the largest Jewish population in the South and the third largest in the country behind New York and California. The state's growing population and increasing environmental worries are of central concern today, while its economy relies mostly on tourism and agriculture. Florida's heritage of European Americans, American Indians, African Americans, and Hispanics is displayed across the state through architecture, cuisine, and cultural events.

Population by Selected Ethnic Group

	Estimate		Estimate
Total:	19,893,297	Brazilian	68,287
Afghan	1,821	British	97,161
Albanian	12,680	Bulgarian	4,674
Alsatian	481	Cajun	3,228
American	1,872,736	Canadian	63,333
Arab:	116,199	Carpatho-Rusyn	254
Egyptian	14,394	Celtic	2,616
Iraqi	3,762	Croatian	21,637
Jordanian	4,533	Cypriot	342
Lebanese	40,635	Czech	54,156
Moroccan	11,312	Czechoslovakian	15,200
Palestinian	6,347	Danish	40,100
Syrian	10,429	Dutch	184,646
Arab	17,785	Eastern European	28,587
Other Arab	11,209	English	1,401,315
Armenian	8,849	Estonian	1,678
Assyrian/Chaldean/Syriac	457	European	194,994
Australian	4,336	Finnish	25,831
Austrian	50,608	French (except Basque)	467,042
Basque	1,405	French Canadian	106,563
Belgian	15,737	German	1,952,960

(continued)

	Estimate		Estimate
German Russian	1,169	Kenyan	1,345
Greek	89,933	Liberian	143
Guyanese	25,847	Nigerian	10,427
Hungarian	98,823	Senegalese	273
Icelander	1,518	Sierra Leonean	92
Iranian	11,299	Somali	0
Irish	1,740,312	South African	6,277
Israeli	14,109	Sudanese	2,167
Italian	1,171,607	Ugandan	182
Latvian	5,116	Zimbabwean	757
Lithuanian	40,637	African	83,286
Luxemburger	944	Other sub-Saharan African	3,165
Macedonian	2,283	Swedish	147,358
Maltese	1,586	Swiss	36,632
New Zealander	462	Turkish	17,618
Northern European	9,959	Ukrainian	48,375
Norwegian	115,824	Welsh	93,292
Pennsylvania German	7,387	West Indian	890,583
Polish	456,749	(except Hispanic groups):	
Portuguese	71,684	Bahamian	28,945
Romanian	32,049	Barbadian	7,775
Russian	201,273	Belizean	5,265
Scandinavian	21,749	Bermudan	984
Scotch-Irish	145,679	British West Indian	17,293
Scottish	302,430	Dutch West Indian	1,165
Serbian	12,740	Haitian	472,073
Slavic	6,233	Jamaican	288,158
Slovak	26,509	Trinidadian and Tobagonian	32,894
Slovene	6,160	U.S. Virgin Islander	4,345
Soviet Union	0	West Indian	43,092
Sub-Saharan African:	116,156	Other West Indian	2,299
Cape Verdean	4,093	Yugoslavian	18,161
Ethiopian	3,460	Other groups	7,980,082
Ghanaian	1,817	Unclassified or not reported	2,864,125

Source: American Community Survey, U.S. Census Bureau, 2014.

See in Neighborhoods Section: Little Haiti ("La Petite Haiti"/Lemon City) (Miami, Florida); Little Havana (Miami, Florida); Tarpon Springs, Greek Enclaves (Florida); Ybor City (Tampa, Florida)

GEORGIA

Capital: Atlanta
Entered Union: January 2, 1788 (4th state)

Georgia is the 8th most populous state, with a population of 9,687,653 according to the 2010 U.S. Census. Somewhat densely populated, Georgia is the 24th-largest state in terms of land area. Georgia displayed a diverse racial makeup of 59.7% white (55.9% non-Hispanic white alone), 30.5% black or African American, 0.3% American Indian and Alaska Native, 3.2% Asian, 0.1% Native Hawaiian or other Pacific Islander, 4.0% from some other race, and 2.1% from two or more races. Hispanics and Latinos of any race accounted for 8.8% of the population.

Historical Population of Georgia

Census	Pop.	%±	Census	Pop.	%±
1790	82,548	—	1910	2,609,121	17.7%
1800	162,686	97.1%	1920	2,895,832	11.0%
1810	251,407	54.5%	1930	2,908,506	0.4%
1820	340,989	35.6%	1940	3,123,723	7.4%
1830	516,823	51.6%	1950	3,444,578	10.3%
1840	691,392	33.8%	1960	3,943,116	14.5%
1850	906,185	31.1%	1970	4,589,575	16.4%
1860	1,057,286	16.7%	1980	5,463,105	19.0%
1870	1,184,109	12.0%	1990	6,478,216	18.6%
1880	1,542,181	30.2%	2000	8,186,453	26.4%
1890	1,837,353	19.1%	2010	9,687,653	18.3%
1900	2,216,331	20.6%			

Source: U.S. Census Bureau.

Georgia was founded as one of the original 13 British colonies in 1733 and was the fourth state to ratify the U.S. constitution. In the early 19th century, gold mining in the state prompted a surge of white settlement and immigration. As a result, tensions between European settlers and the Cherokee nation increased, and the U.S. government looked to absorb additional Cherokee territory. The 1830 Indian Removal Act resulted in the forcible removal of thousands of Cherokees in what would become known as the "Trail of Tears," witnessing the death of some 4,000 Cherokee citizens.

Georgia was a major site for Civil War battles. After the war's conclusion and the abolition of slavery, Georgia continued to experience troubled race relations. In 1877, the state passed a poll tax, and in 1908 established a white primary, effectively removing African Americans from the political process. The so-called Great Migration saw a considerable outward movement of African Americans from Georgia to industrial cities in the north, seeking more job opportunities and better treatment. The Civil Rights Era, including the Civil Rights Act of 1965 and the Voting Rights Act of 1964, helped to alleviate this political and social disenfranchisement somewhat for African Americans who remained in Georgia.

As of 2011, statistics show that 58.8% of Georgia's population under the age of one were minorities. As of 2005, 90% of Georgia residents over the age of five speak only English at home and 5.6% speak Spanish, with French as the third most popular language at 0.9%, followed by German at 0.8%, and Vietnamese at 0.6%. Georgia had the second fastest-growing Asian population growth in the United States from 1990 to 2000, according to the Census Bureau's Population Estimates. Like most other Southern U.S. states, Georgia is largely Protestant at 70% of the population, breaking down into 24% Baptist, 12% Methodist, 3% Presbyterian, and 3% Pentecostal. The remaining 30% breaks down to 12% Catholic, 13% nonreligious, and 3% other.

As of 2004, African Americans made up approximately 29.6% of the population. Historically, about half of Georgia's population was made up of African Americans who were almost entirely enslaved before the Civil War, although the African American population was greatly reduced during the period of the Great Migration between 1914 and 1970. According to census data estimates, Georgia ranks third among states in total African American population, behind Mississippi and Alabama. Georgia had the third-largest black population after New York and Florida, and it was the state with the largest increase in black population from 2006 to 2007.

Georgia's state culture of food, language, and music has been greatly influenced by its colonial settlements in the mountains and piedmont by large numbers of Scottish American, English American, and Scotch-Irish Americans, and the coastal settlement of English Americans and African Americans. There is a specific language and culture in the Low Country among African Americans due to the concentration of West Africans imported to the coastal areas, which carries on African traditions of food, religion, and culture. Many of their food traditions have become a central part of Southern cooking in the Low Country.

Population by Selected Ethnic Group

	Estimate		Estimate
Total:	10,097,343	Lebanese	8,412
Afghan	3,241	Moroccan	1,885
Albanian	1,056	Palestinian	1,184
Alsatian	58	Syrian	2,187
American	1,210,429	Arab	3,861
Arab:	23,797	Other Arab	3,756
Egyptian	1,890	Armenian	2,782
Iraqi	825	Assyrian/Chaldean/Syriac	196
Jordanian	485	Australian	2,763

(continued)

	Estimate		Estimate
Austrian	11,610	Polish	112,980
Basque	409	Portuguese	12,039
Belgian	3,684	Romanian	16,503
Brazilian	7,919	Russian	43,901
British	46,861	Scandinavian	9,288
Bulgarian	2,359	Scotch-Irish	118,359
Cajun	2,737	Scottish	174,595
Canadian	15,988	Serbian	1,427
Carpatho-Rusyn	47	Slavic	1,792
Celtic	1,526	Slovak	7,790
Croatian	4,778	Slovene	2,536
Cypriot	6	Soviet Union	208
Czech	12,973	Sub-Saharan African:	190,665
Czechoslovakian	4,603	Cape Verdean	1,658
Danish	13,133	Ethiopian	16,429
Dutch	70,953	Ghanaian	3,797
Eastern European	9,552	Kenyan	4,350
English	815,421	Liberian	2,392
Estonian	1,107	Nigerian	23,611
European	110,612	Senegalese	218
Finnish	6,027	Sierra Leonean	417
French (except Basque)	137,654	Somali	4,886
French Canadian	25,948	South African	2,608
German	713,676	Sudanese	742
German Russian	431	Ugandan	213
Greek	18,618	Zimbabwean	157
Guyanese	6,624	African	120,808
Hungarian	19,999	Other sub-Saharan African	10,565
Icelander	604	Swedish	47,377
Iranian	8,871	Swiss	12,586
Irish	810,190	Turkish	3,486
Israeli	3,225	Ukrainian	10,860
Italian	239,916	Welsh	39,252
Latvian	1,676	West Indian	122,950
Lithuanian	6,481	(except Hispanic groups):	
Luxemburger	381	Bahamian	2,632
Macedonian	358	Barbadian	3,593
Maltese	262	Belizean	1,108
New Zealander	619	Bermudan	781
Northern European	4,791	British West Indian	5,677
Norwegian	36,139	Dutch West Indian	455
Pennsylvania German	1,006	Haitian	27,698

(continued)

	Estimate		Estimate
Jamaican	61,568	Other West Indian	551
Trinidadian and Tobagonian	6,624	Yugoslavian	6,970
U.S. Virgin Islander	1,873	Other groups	4,543,532
West Indian	12,996	Unclassified or not reported	1,621,240

Source: American Community Survey, U.S. Census Bureau, 2014.

See in Neighborhoods Section: Sweet Auburn (Atlanta, Georgia)

HAWAII

Capital: Honolulu
Entered Union: August 21, 1959 (50th state)

Hawaii is the most recent of the 50 U.S. states, admitted in 1959. The Kingdom of Hawaii was sovereign from 1810 until 1893, when the monarchy was overthrown. It was an independent republic from 1894 until 1898, when it was annexed by the United States as a territory. When it achieved statehood, Hawaii became the 11th most populous, the 13th most densely populated, and 8th smallest in land area of the 50 U.S. states.

The 2010 U.S. Census reports Hawaii's population of 1,360,301, with the state being 38.6% Asian, 24.7% white (22.7% non-Hispanic white alone), 23.6% from two or more races, 10.0% Native Hawaiian and other Pacific Islanders, 8.9% Hispanics and Latinos of any race, 1.6% black or African American, 1.2% from some other race, and 0.3% American Indian and Alaska Native.

A Hula dancer performing in a traditional luau in Maui, Hawaii, 2013. (Ivansabo/Dreamstime.com)

Historical Population of Hawaii

Census	Pop.	%±	Census	Pop.	%±
1900	154,001	—	1960	632,772	26.6%
1910	191,874	24.6%	1970	769,913	21.7%
1920	255,881	33.4%	1980	964,691	25.3%
1930	368,300	43.9%	1990	1,108,229	14.9%
1940	422,770	14.8%	2000	1,211,537	9.3%
1950	499,794	18.2%	2010	1,360,301	12.3%

Source: U.S. Census Bureau.

Hawaii has the highest percentage of Asian Americans and multiracial Americans, as well as the lowest percentage of white Americans of any state. The 2010 U.S. Census reported Hawaii's population as 1,360,301, with the state being 38.6% Asian, 24.7% white (22.7% non-Hispanic white alone), 23.6% from two or more races, 10.0% Native Hawaiian and other Pacific Islanders, 8.9% Hispanics and Latinos of any race, 1.6% black or African American, 1.2% from some other race, and 0.3% American Indian and Alaska Native. Hawaii's Asian population consists of 14.6% Filipino Americans and 13.6% Japanese Americans. Additionally, there are 4.0% Chinese Americans and 1.8% Korean Americans. There is also a significant number of Hispanic and Latino Americans living in Hawaii, among whom Mexicans number more than 35,000 (2.6%) and Puerto Ricans 44,000 (3.2%).

According to the 2010 U.S. Census, Hawaii had a population of 1,360,301. Due to a large military presence and tourist population, Hawaii had a de facto population of over 1.3 million. Approximately 1.3% of the population in the islands is made up of U.S. military personnel.

The largest denominations by number of adherents are the Catholic Church and the Church of Jesus Christ of Latter-day Saints. According to data provided by religious establishments in 2010, Hawaiians identified as 28.9% Christian, 9% Buddhist, 0.8% Jewish, 0.5% Muslim, 10% other, and 52% unaffiliated. The group "other" includes Baha'i faith, Confucianism, Daoism, the Hawaiian religion, Hinduism, Islam, Sikhism, Shintoism, and Zoroastrianism. According to 2009 data from the state's religious establishments, religion in Hawaii broke down into the following categories: 37.8% Protestant/other Christian, 22.8% Roman Catholic, 3.3% Mormonism, 0.7% Judaism, and 21.0% irreligious, agnostic, or atheist.

Indigenous Hawaiians make up 5.9% of the population, while 8.8% are Hispanic and Latino Americans, 2.6% are Mexicans, and 3.2% are Puerto Ricans. The non-Hispanic white population form just over one-fifth of the population, while multiracial Americans form almost one-quarter of Hawaii's population, and Eurasian Americans form about 4.9%. About 82.2% of Hawaii's residents were born in the United States, while roughly 75% of the foreign-born residents are from Asia. In 1970, by comparison, the Census Bureau reported Hawaii's population to be 38.8% white and 57.7% Asian and Pacific Islander.

According to the Census Bureau, the largest ancestry groups in Hawaii as of 2008 were Filipino at 13.6%, Japanese 12.6%, Polynesian 9.0%, German 7.4%, Irish 5.2%, English 4.6%, Portuguese 4.3%, Chinese 4.1%, Korean 3.1%, Mexican 2.9%, Puerto Rican 2.8%, Italian 2,7%, African 2.4%, French 1.7%, and Scottish 1.2%. A large proportion of Hawaii's population is now of Asian ancestry, as many are descendants of the mostly Chinese and Japanese immigrants who were recruited to work on sugar plantations in the 1850s and after. In addition to these immigrants, many Portuguese and Puerto Ricans came to work and settle on the islands as well.

The state of Hawaii has two official languages recognized in its state constitution: English and Hawaiian. According to the 2008 American Community Survey, 74.6% of Hawaii's residents over the age of five speak only English at home. Additionally, however, 2.6% of the population speaks Spanish, 1.6% speaks other Indo-European languages, 21.0% speaks an Asian language, and 0.2% speaks a different language at home. The Hawaiian language has about 2,000 native speakers, less than 0.1% of the total population. Some locals also speak Hawaii Creole English, often called "pidgin," which derives mostly from English but also has words from Hawaiian, Chinese, Japanese, Portuguese, Ilocano, and Tagalog.

Population by Selected Ethnic Group

	Estimate		Estimate
Total:	1,419,561	Brazilian	1,046
Afghan	0	British	4,150
Albanian	0	Bulgarian	99
Alsatian	36	Cajun	299
American	18,452	Canadian	1,940
Arab:	2,729	Carpatho-Rusyn	26
Egyptian	53	Celtic	20
Iraqi	0	Croatian	443
Jordanian	0	Cypriot	0
Lebanese	483	Czech	2,091
Moroccan	4	Czechoslovakian	629
Palestinian	216	Danish	2,783
Syrian	998	Dutch	8,581
Arab	371	Eastern European	1,046
Other Arab	604	English	60,641
Armenian	266	Estonian	396
Assyrian/Chaldean/Syriac	43	European	9,018
Australian	160	Finnish	1,259
Austrian	1,358	French (except Basque)	18,651
Basque	64	French Canadian	2,381
Belgian	513	German	86,329

(continued)

	Estimate		Estimate
German Russian	0	Kenyan	0
Greek	3,692	Liberian	0
Guyanese	0	Nigerian	145
Hungarian	2,676	Senegalese	0
Icelander	88	Sierra Leonean	0
Iranian	264	Somali	0
Irish	61,084	South African	265
Israeli	350	Sudanese	0
Italian	32,598	Ugandan	0
Latvian	571	Zimbabwean	0
Lithuanian	1,095	African	2,512
Luxemburger	82	Other sub-Saharan African	101
Macedonian	36	Swedish	8,623
Maltese	0	Swiss	2,802
New Zealander	0	Turkish	1,228
Northern European	1,128	Ukrainian	1,550
Norwegian	8,495	Welsh	3,543
Pennsylvania German	46	West Indian	2,476
Polish	13,188	(except Hispanic groups):	
Portuguese	48,015	Bahamian	0
Romanian	729	Barbadian	50
Russian	4,414	Belizean	0
Scandinavian	1,303	Bermudan	0
Scotch-Irish	6,907	British West Indian	353
Scottish	16,308	Dutch West Indian	0
Serbian	63	Haitian	451
Slavic	184	Jamaican	1,172
Slovak	1,121	Trinidadian and Tobagonian	368
Slovene	295	U.S. Virgin Islander	0
Soviet Union	0	West Indian	113
Sub-Saharan African:	3,023	Other West Indian	0
Cape Verdean	0	Yugoslavian	406
Ethiopian	0	Other groups	1,046,867
Ghanaian	0	Unclassified or not reported	132,177

Source: American Community Survey, U.S. Census Bureau, 2014.

See in Neighborhoods Section: Chinatown Historic District/Aʻala (Honolulu, Hawaii); Kakaʻako (Honolulu, Hawaii); Los Angeles, Hawaiian Enclaves (California)

IDAHO

Capital: Boise
Entered Union: July 3, 1890 (43rd state)

Idaho is the 14th-largest, the 39th most populous, and the 7th least densely populated U.S. state. Idaho's population center is in Custer County. The state's largest city and capital is Boise. As part of the Oregon Country, Idaho was claimed by both the United States and Great Britain until the United States gained undisputed jurisdiction in 1846.

According to the 2010 U.S. Census, Idaho's racial composition is 89.1% white American, 11.2% Hispanic, 0.6% African American, 1.4% American Indian and Alaska Native, 1.2% Asian American, and 0.1% Native Hawaiian and other Pacific Islander.

Historical Population of Idaho

Census	Pop.	%±	Census	Pop.	%±
1870	14,999	—	1950	588,637	12.1%
1880	32,610	117.4%	1960	667,191	13.3%
1890	88,548	171.5%	1970	712,567	6.8%
1900	161,772	82.7%	1980	943,935	32.5%
1910	325,594	101.3%	1990	1,006,749	6.7%
1920	431,866	32.6%	2000	1,293,953	28.5%
1930	445,032	3.0%	2010	1,567,582	21.1%
1940	524,873	17.9%			

Source: U.S. Census Bureau.

Although its population is overwhelmingly white, Idaho is home to several ethnic minority communities. Notably, there are five Native American reservations in Idaho, the most extensive being that of the Nez Percé in northern Idaho. Hispanic or Latino residents make up the largest minority group in the state. Otherwise, there is a very small population of black Americans and a larger number of Asians. Of the Asian population in Idaho, 2,642 are Japanese. In a sense, ethnic heterogeneity has been preserved in Idaho because it was a frontier society, and so many ethnic groups did not readily blend into the society at large.

The first Chinese came to Idaho in 1864 to mine the Oro Fino gold fields. They were brought from California to alleviate a shortage of labor, and soon every mining town in the territory had an ethnic Chinese community. The Japanese first came to Idaho in the decade following statehood in 1890. Since then, they have constituted the state's largest ethnic group. By the end of the 1890s, Japanese settlements were common features along the length of the Oregon Short Line Railroad. In addition, there is a very visible Basque community in the Boise area. Basques came to the

Boise Valley in their greatest numbers between 1900 and 1920. Today, there are several organizations in Idaho devoted to preserving the Basque language and culture.

According to a 2008 report produced by the Pew Forum on Religion & Public Life, Idahoans identify as 23% the Church of Jesus Christ of Latter-day Saints, 22% Evangelical, 18% Catholic, 16% Mainline Protestant, 1% Jehovah's Witnesses, Muslim<0.5%, Jewish<0.5%, Buddhist<0.5%, Hindu<0.5%. The largest denominations by number of members are the Church of Jesus Christ of Latter-day Saints, the Catholic Church, the nondenominational Evangelical Protestants, and the Assemblies of God. Eastern Idaho was overwhelmingly part of the Mormon intermountain empire, made up mostly of Mormon converts from England and Scandinavia.

On the whole, Idaho is growing as a state. In 2005, Idaho saw a population increase of 2.4% from 2004, or a 10.4% increase from 2000. In fact, it is the sixth fastest-growing state after Arizona, Nevada, Florida, Georgia, and Utah. From 2004 to 2005, Idaho grew at the third fastest rate of any state. Furthermore, Idaho's minority population is expanding. As of 2011, 27.2% of Idaho's children under the age of one belonged to minority groups.

The most frequent reported ancestries in Idaho are German 18.9%, English 18.1% Irish 10%, American 8.4%, Norwegian 3.6%, and Swedish 3.5%. There are large numbers of Americans of English and German ancestry in Idaho due to past waves of immigration.

Population by Selected Ethnic Group

	Estimate		Estimate
Total:	1,634,464	Australian	508
Afghan	1,046	Austrian	3,829
Albanian	56	Basque	6,704
Alsatian	72	Belgian	918
American	129,082	Brazilian	181
Arab:	3,904	British	8,122
Egyptian	59	Bulgarian	310
Iraqi	1,088	Cajun	491
Jordanian	0	Canadian	5,613
Lebanese	854	Carpatho-Rusyn	65
Moroccan	0	Celtic	586
Palestinian	65	Croatian	1,835
Syrian	426	Cypriot	0
Arab	502	Czech	8,157
Other Arab	910	Czechoslovakian	1,340
Armenian	1,122	Danish	30,757
Assyrian/Chaldean/Syriac	141	Dutch	30,736

(continued)

	Estimate		Estimate
Eastern European	1,273	Sub-Saharan African:	4,115
English	268,600	Cape Verdean	0
Estonian	11	Ethiopian	272
European	33,536	Ghanaian	52
Finnish	6,820	Kenyan	0
French (except Basque)	39,697	Liberian	0
French Canadian	8,625	Nigerian	591
German	287,026	Senegalese	374
German Russian	66	Sierra Leonean	0
Greek	3,559	Somali	0
Guyanese	0	South African	0
Hungarian	2,806	Sudanese	58
Icelander	857	Ugandan	0
Iranian	305	Zimbabwean	0
Irish	150,596	African	1,644
Israeli	194	Other sub-Saharan African	1,212
Italian	47,472	Swedish	47,831
Latvian	994	Swiss	15,337
Lithuanian	2,139	Turkish	68
Luxemburger	162	Ukrainian	2,902
Macedonian	32	Welsh	20,176
Maltese	0	West Indian	458
New Zealander	79	(except Hispanic groups):	
Northern European	3,723	Bahamian	0
Norwegian	49,708	Barbadian	0
Pennsylvania German	582	Belizean	99
Polish	19,196	Bermudan	0
Portuguese	6,004	British West Indian	0
Romanian	521	Dutch West Indian	0
Russian	6,673	Haitian	174
Scandinavian	9,193	Jamaican	284
Scotch-Irish	16,010	Trinidadian and Tobagonian	0
Scottish	48,560	U.S. Virgin Islander	0
Serbian	496	West Indian	0
Slavic	189	Other West Indian	0
Slovak	777	Yugoslavian	1,712
Slovene	902	Other groups	394,951
Soviet Union	14	Unclassified or not reported	324,447

Source: American Community Survey, U.S. Census Bureau, 2014.

See in Neighborhoods Section: Malad City, Welsh Enclave (Idaho)

ILLINOIS

Capital: Springfield
Entered Union: December 3, 1818 (21st state)

It is the 5th most populous and 25th most extensive U.S. state, and it is sometimes referred to as a microcosm of the entire country. The state's largest population center encompasses Chicago, which is the 3rd most populous city in the United States. Illinois was part of the French empire of La Louisiane until 1763, when it passed to the British with their defeat of France in the Seven Years' War. In 1818, Illinois became the 21st U.S. state.

According to the 2010 U.S. Census, the racial composition of the state is 71.5% white American, 15.8% Hispanic, 14.5% African American, 0.3% American Indian and Alaska Native, and 4.6% Asian American. The Indian population of Illinois had disappeared by 1832 as a result of warfare and emigration. However, American Indian migration, mainly from Wisconsin and Minnesota, had brought the Native American population to 31,006, concentrated in Chicago.

Historical Population of Illinois

Census	Pop.	%±	Census	Pop.	%±
1800	2,458	—	1910	5,638,591	16.9%
1810	12,282	399.7%	1920	6,485,280	15.0%
1820	55,211	349.5%	1930	7,630,654	17.7%
1830	157,445	185.2%	1940	7,897,241	3.5%
1840	476,183	202.4%	1950	8,712,176	10.3%
1850	851,470	78.8%	1960	10,081,158	15.7%
1860	1,711,951	101.1%	1970	11,113,976	10.2%
1870	2,539,891	48.4%	1980	11,426,518	2.8%
1880	3,077,871	21.2%	1990	11,430,602	0.0%
1890	3,826,352	24.3%	2000	12,419,293	8.6%
1900	4,821,550	26.0%	2010	12,830,632	3.3%

Source: U.S. Census Bureau.

The official language of Illinois is English. Approximately 80% of Illinoisans speak English natively, and most of the rest speak it fluently as a second language. Illinois is home to speakers of many other immigrant languages, of which Spanish is the most widespread.

In terms of religion in Illinois, Roman Catholics constitute the single largest religious denomination in the state; they are heavily concentrated in and around Chicago and account for nearly 30% of the state's population. However, taken together as a group, the various Protestant denominations comprise a greater percentage of the state's population compared to Catholics. The largest Protestant denominations are the United Methodist Church and the Southern Baptist Convention. In addition, Muslims constitute the largest non-Christian group in Illinois. Chicago and its suburbs are also home to a large and growing population of Hindus, Baha'is, and Buddhists. Most ethnic groups in Illinois maintain their own newspapers, clubs, festivals, and houses of worship.

Illinois Population by Race

Race		
One race	12,184,277	98.1
White	9,125,471	73.5
Black or African American	1,876,875	15.1
American Indian and Alaska Native	31,006	0.2
Asian	423,603	3.4
Asian Indian	124,723	1.0
Chinese	76,725	0.6
Filipino	86,298	0.7
Japanese	20,379	0.2
Korean	51,453	0.4
Vietnamese	19,101	0.2
Other Asian[1]	44,924	0.4
Native Hawaiian and other Pacific Islander	4,610	0.0
Native Hawaiian	1,003	0.0
Guamanian or Chamorro	988	0.0
Samoan	1,062	0.0
Other Pacific Islander[2]	1,557	0.0
Some other race	722,712	5.8
Two or more races	235,016	1.9

Race Alone or in Combination with One or More Other Races[3]

White	9,322,831	75.1
Black or African American	1,937,671	15.6
American Indian and Alaska Native	73,161	0.6
Asian	473,649	3.8
Native Hawaiian and other Pacific Islander	11,848	0.1
Some other race	847,369	6.8

Hispanic or Latino and Race

Total Population	12,419,293	100.0
Hispanic or Latino (of any race)	1,530,262	12.3
Mexican	1,144,390	9.2
Puerto Rican	157,851	1.3
Cuban	18,438	0.1
Other Hispanic or Latino	209,583	1.7
Not Hispanic or Latino	10,889,031	87.7
White alone	8,424,140	67.8

(X) Not applicable
[1] Other Asian alone, or two or more Asian categories.
[2] Other Pacific Islander alone, or two or more Native Hawaiian and other Pacific Islander categories.
[3] In combination with one or more other races listed. The six numbers may add to more than the total population and the six percentages may add to more than 100% because individuals may report more than one race.
Source: U.S. Census Bureau, Census 2000 Summary File 1, Matrices P1, P3, P4, P8, P9, P12, P13, P,17, P18, P19, P20, P23, P27, P28, P33, PCT5, PCT8, PCT11, PCT15, H1, H3, H4, H5, H11, and H12.

Illinois Population by Nativity and Place of Birth Nativity and Place of Birth

Total Population	12,419,293	100.0
Native	10,890,235	87.7
Born in United States	10,768,063	86.7
State of residence	8,335,553	67.1
Different state	2,432,510	19.6
Born outside United States	122,172	1.0
Foreign born	1,529,058	12.3
Entered 1990 to March 2000	687,564	5.5
Naturalized citizen	603,521	4.9
Not a citizen	925,537	7.5

Region of Birth of Foreign Born

Total (Excluding Born at Sea)	1,529,058	100.0
Europe	389,928	25.5
Asia	359,812	23.5
Africa	26,158	1.7
Oceania	2,553	0.2
Latin America	731,397	47.8
Northern America	19,210	1.3

Language Spoken at Home

Population 5 Years and Over	11,547,505	100.0
English only	9,326,786	80.8
Language other than English	2,220,719	19.2
Speak English less than "very well"	1,054,722	9.1
Spanish	1,253,676	10.9
Speak English less than "very well"	665,995	5.8
Other Indo-European languages	640,237	5.5
Speak English less than "very well"	253,352	2.2
Asian and Pacific Island languages	248,800	2.2
Speak English less than "very well"	111,065	1.0

Ancestry (Single or Multiple)

Total Population	12,419,293	100.0
Total ancestries reported	13,248,253	106.7
Arab	52,798	0.4
Czech[1]	152,461	1.2
Danish	59,632	0.5
Dutch	195,847	1.6
English	831,820	6.7
French (except Basque)[1]	267,850	2.2
French Canadian[1]	45,664	0.4
German	2,440,549	19.7
Greek	95,064	0.8
Hungarian	55,971	0.5
Irish[1]	1,513,005	12.2
Italian	744,274	6.0
Lithuanian	87,294	0.7
Norwegian	178,923	1.4
Polish	932,996	7.5
Portuguese	7,593	0.1
Russian	121,397	1.0
Scotch-Irish	126,963	1.0
Scottish	150,255	1.2
Slovak	42,966	0.3
Sub-Saharan African	73,194	0.6
Swedish	303,044	2.4
Swiss	37,505	0.3
Ukrainian	47,623	0.4
United States or American	569,102	4.6

(*continued*)

Total Population	12,419,293	100.0
Welsh	51,769	0.4
West Indian (excluding Hispanic groups)	27,286	0.2
Other ancestries	4,035,408	32.5

(X) Not applicable.

[1] The data represent a combination of two ancestries shown separately in Summary File 3. Czech includes Czechoslovakian. French includes Alsatian. French Canadian includes Acadian/Cajun. Irish includes Celtic.

Source: U.S. Census Bureau, Census 2000 Summary File 3, Matrices P18, P19, P21, P22, P24, P36, P37, P39, P42, PCT8, PCT16, PCT17, and PCT19.

Population by Selected Ethnic Group

	Estimate		Estimate
Total:	12,880,580	Cypriot	438
Afghan	873	Czech	107,310
Albanian	14,582	Czechoslovakian	18,486
Alsatian	210	Danish	47,032
American	618,224	Dutch	170,195
Arab:	104,570	Eastern European	15,783
Egyptian	5,840	English	736,037
Iraqi	9,459	Estonian	649
Jordanian	11,086	European	103,266
Lebanese	12,243	Finnish	15,969
Moroccan	4,379	French (except Basque)	231,974
Palestinian	16,085	French Canadian	34,344
Syrian	7,783	German	2,392,885
Arab	28,997	German Russian	773
Other Arab	10,281	Greek	100,717
Armenian	10,498	Guyanese	1,089
Assyrian/Chaldean/Syriac	14,319	Hungarian	49,970
Australian	2,748	Icelander	1,100
Austrian	38,527	Iranian	11,918
Basque	590	Irish	1,489,662
Belgian	27,963	Israeli	5,273
Brazilian	5,906	Italian	749,579
British	32,638	Latvian	5,130
Bulgarian	9,824	Lithuanian	84,935
Cajun	248	Luxemburger	5,928
Canadian	14,736	Macedonian	3,405
Carpatho-Rusyn	191	Maltese	737
Celtic	1,214	New Zealander	122
Croatian	38,934	Northern European	7,560

(continued)

	Estimate		Estimate
Norwegian	159,866	Ugandan	759
Pennsylvania German	4,710	Zimbabwean	134
Polish	890,174	African	52,246
Portuguese	10,442	Other sub-Saharan African	4,495
Romanian	31,640	Swedish	268,344
Russian	116,565	Swiss	34,808
Scandinavian	17,252	Turkish	8,443
Scotch-Irish	71,309	Ukrainian	51,339
Scottish	149,495	Welsh	46,551
Serbian	23,217	West Indian	32,219
Slavic	3,936	(except Hispanic groups):	
Slovak	34,705	Bahamian	368
Slovene	13,965	Barbadian	370
Soviet Union	131	Belizean	5,738
Sub-Saharan African:	90,566	Bermudan	18
Cape Verdean	0	British West Indian	370
Ethiopian	3,881	Dutch West Indian	329
Ghanaian	3,761	Haitian	6,991
Kenyan	1,728	Jamaican	16,202
Liberian	1,046	Trinidadian and Tobagonian	1,465
Nigerian	18,943	U.S. Virgin Islander	0
Senegalese	675	West Indian	1,267
Sierra Leonean	30	Other West Indian	0
Somali	821	Yugoslavian	16,323
South African	1,281	Other groups	4,862,532
Sudanese	1,494	Unclassified or not reported	1,756,594

Source: American Community Survey, U.S. Census Bureau, 2014.

See in Neighborhoods Section: Andersonville (Chicago, Illinois); Bridgeport (Chicago, Illinois); Bronzeville (Chicago, Illinois); Chicago, Mexican and Puerto Rican Enclaves (Illinois); Little India (Chicago, Illinois); Pilsen (Chicago, Illinois)

INDIANA

Capital: Indianapolis
Entered Union: December 11, 1816 (19th state)

Indiana is the 38th largest by area and the 16th most populous of the 50 United States. It was admitted to the United States as the 19th state in 1816, and its capital and largest city is Indianapolis.

Historical Population of Indiana

Census	Pop.	%±	Census	Pop.	%±
1800	2,632	—	1910	2,700,876	7.3%
1810	24,520	831.6%	1920	2,930,390	8.5%
1820	147,178	500.2%	1930	3,238,503	10.5%
1830	343,031	133.1%	1940	3,427,796	5.8%
1840	685,866	99.9%	1950	3,934,224	14.8%
1850	988,416	44.1%	1960	4,662,498	18.5%
1860	1,350,428	36.6%	1970	5,193,669	11.4%
1870	1,680,637	24.5%	1980	5,490,224	5.7%
1880	1,978,301	17.7%	1990	5,544,159	1.0%
1890	2,192,404	10.8%	2000	6,080,485	9.7%
1900	2,516,462	14.8%	2010	6,483,802	6.6%

Source: U.S. Census Bureau.

Before it became a territory, varying cultures of indigenous peoples and historic Native Americans inhabited Indiana for thousands of years. After it became a territory, it experienced regional cultural segmentation: the state's northernmost tier was settled primarily by people from New England and New York, Central Indiana by migrants from the Mid-Atlantic states and from adjacent Ohio, and Southern Indiana by settlers from the Southern states, particularly Kentucky and Tennessee. The Hispanic population is the state's fastest-growing minority, and blacks have long been present. The populations of Asians and Pacific Islanders have also increased in recent decades. As a result, 28.2% of Indiana's children under the age of one year belonged to minority groups.

German is the largest ancestry reported in Indiana, with 22.7% of the population reporting that ancestry in the Census. Persons citing American (12.0%) and English ancestry (8.9%) are also numerous, as are Irish (10.8%) and Polish (3.0%). European immigration largely occurred in the 19th century, as Indiana transitioned from a largely agrarian to increasingly industrial economy. The Indiana Gas Boom of the mid-19th century, for example, saw Indiana become a local source of natural gas, a highly valuable resource. As the 20th century began, Indiana grew to become a major figure in the production of automobiles and the development of the automotive industry.

However, even through all of Indiana's industrialization and development of some local industry, it did not attract many non-white residents by the middle of the 20th century. The 1950 census reported the state as over 95% white. The oil crises of the 1970s did not help attract non-white residents, as major Indiana businesses faced closure and downsizing until the 1980s brought some economic resurgence. Currently, major sporting teams and industry have helped to revitalize Indiana's economy and increasingly attract new, diverse settlers.

Although racial diversity in Indiana is limited overall, the state has witnessed other types of population diversity. For example, Indiana is religiously diverse.

The largest single religious denomination in the state is Catholic (747,706 members). Members of various Protestant denominations make up a large portion of the population. The largest Protestant denomination by number of adherents in 2010 was the United Methodist Church with 355,043. A study by the Graduate Center found that 20% are Roman Catholic, 14% belong to different Baptist churches, 10% are other Christians, 9% are Methodist, and 6% are Lutheran. The study found that 16% of Indiana is affiliated with no religion. Indiana is home to the St. Meinrad Archabbey (one of 11 in the world), to the largest branch of American Quakerism (based in Richmond), and to the headquarters of the Islamic Society of North America (in Plainfield).

Except for the dialect mixture in the industrial northwest corner and for the Northern-dialect fringe of counties along the Michigan border, Indiana speech is essentially that of the South Midland pioneers from south of the Ohio River, with a transition zone toward North Midland north of Indianapolis. In 2000, 93.5% of all Hoosiers (residents of Indiana) five years old and older spoke only English at home, down from 95.2% in 1990.

Population by Selected Ethnic Group

	Estimate		Estimate
Total:	6,596,855	British	25,536
Afghan	545	Bulgarian	1,188
Albanian	2,107	Cajun	234
Alsatian	99	Canadian	7,301
American	634,735	Carpatho-Rusyn	79
Arab:	20,934	Celtic	1,008
Egyptian	3,329	Croatian	12,165
Iraqi	226	Cypriot	41
Jordanian	381	Czech	19,929
Lebanese	3,718	Czechoslovakian	6,418
Moroccan	980	Danish	11,157
Palestinian	1,257	Dutch	127,630
Syrian	2,172	Eastern European	3,202
Arab	5,899	English	554,443
Other Arab	3,319	Estonian	503
Armenian	1,069	European	62,593
Assyrian/Chaldean/Syriac	318	Finnish	5,735
Australian	1,227	French (except Basque)	148,729
Austrian	8,724	French Canadian	15,420
Basque	97	German	1,586,217
Belgian	11,149	German Russian	287
Brazilian	1,289	Greek	18,437

(*continued*)

	Estimate		Estimate
Guyanese	41	Liberian	263
Hungarian	34,126	Nigerian	3,703
Icelander	146	Senegalese	81
Iranian	1,841	Sierra Leonean	41
Irish	783,128	Somali	0
Israeli	485	South African	189
Italian	185,002	Sudanese	224
Latvian	1,204	Ugandan	319
Lithuanian	8,968	Zimbabwean	52
Luxemburger	486	African	31,032
Macedonian	5,739	Other sub-Saharan African	1,357
Maltese	298	Swedish	58,252
New Zealander	361	Swiss	40,018
Northern European	3,838	Turkish	1,871
Norwegian	39,954	Ukrainian	10,791
Pennsylvania German	15,443	Welsh	38,279
Polish	217,428	West Indian	7,052
Portuguese	4,471	(except Hispanic groups):	
Romanian	7,302	Bahamian	437
Russian	22,372	Barbadian	0
Scandinavian	6,862	Belizean	36
Scotch-Irish	56,282	Bermudan	0
Scottish	118,364	British West Indian	112
Serbian	7,799	Dutch West Indian	69
Slavic	1,405	Haitian	2,052
Slovak	20,147	Jamaican	3,136
Slovene	3,529	Trinidadian and Tobagonian	213
Soviet Union	77	U.S. Virgin Islander	0
Sub-Saharan African:	40,591	West Indian	997
Cape Verdean	16	Other West Indian	0
Ethiopian	585	Yugoslavian	3,957
Ghanaian	1,603	Other groups	1,598,053
Kenyan	1,869	Unclassified or not reported	1,493,197

Source: American Community Survey, U.S. Census Bureau, 2014.

IOWA

Capital: Des Moines
Entered Union: December 28, 1846 (29th state)

Iowa ranks 26th among all states in land area and is the 30th most populous. The state's population is most concentrated in the Des Moines metropolitan area, with Des Moines being the state's capital and biggest city. Of the residents of Iowa,

72.2% were born in Iowa, 23.2% were born in a different U.S. state, 0.5% were born in Puerto Rico, U.S. Island areas, or born abroad to American parent(s), and 4.1% were foreign born. According to the 2010 U.S. Census, Iowa had a population of 3,046,355.

Historical Population of Iowa

Census	Pop.	%±	Census	Pop.	%±
1840	43,112	—	1930	2,470,939	2.8%
1850	192,214	345.8%	1940	2,538,268	2.7%
1860	674,913	251.1%	1950	2,621,073	3.3%
1870	1,194,020	76.9%	1960	2,757,537	5.2%
1880	1,624,615	36.1%	1970	2,824,376	2.4%
1890	1,912,297	17.7%	1980	2,913,808	3.2%
1900	2,231,853	16.7%	1990	2,776,755	−4.7%
1910	2,224,771	−0.3%	2000	2,926,324	5.4%
1920	2,404,021	8.1%	2010	3,046,355	4.1%

Source: U.S. Census Bureau.

The United States acquired Iowa via the Louisiana Purchase in 1803. Its population was sparse until after the Civil War, when railroad construction facilitated the state's transition to become a major agricultural producer. While farm-related industry was the first to develop in Iowa, increased industrialization resulted as a byproduct of economic growth. As a result, both European immigrants, largely German, and migrants from within the United States moved to Iowa.

Since Iowa's great economic boom following the Civil War, it has not experienced a tremendous population shift. As a result, it remains a largely white state. As of 2010, 91.3% of the state's population was white (88.7% non-Hispanic white), 2.9% was black or African American, 0.4% American Indian and Alaska Native, 1.7% Asian, 0.1% Native Hawaiian and other Pacific Islander, and 1.8% from two or more races; in

Teenagers in 4-H showing swine at the Iowa State Fair, Des Moines, Iowa, 2014. (Scott Griessel/Dreamstime .com)

addition, 5% of the total population was of Hispanic or Latino origin. Iowans are mostly of Western European descent. The five largest ancestry groups in Iowa are German (35.7%), Irish (13.5%), English (9.5%), American (6.6%), and Norwegian (5.7%).

Reflecting mixed European origins, some religious diversity in Iowa does exist. A 2001 survey from the City University of New York found that 52% of Iowans are Protestant, while 23% are Catholic, and other religions made up 6%. Thirteen percent responded with nonreligious, and 5% did not answer. A study called Religious Congregations & Membership: 2000 found that in the southernmost two tiers of Iowa counties, and in other counties in the center of the state, the largest religious group was the United Methodist Church; in the northeast part of the state, including Dubuque and Linn counties (where Cedar Rapids is located), the Catholic Church was the largest; and in 10 counties, including three in the northern tier, the Evangelical Lutheran Church in America was the largest. Historically, religious sects and orders who desired to live apart from the rest of society established themselves in Iowa, such as the Amish and German Pietists.

English is the most common language in Iowa, used by 94% of the population. Despite Iowa having been a French colony as part of the French Louisiana, Spanish is the second most common language spoken in Iowa. The third most common language is German, spoken by 17,000 people in the state. No other language is spoken by more than 0.5% of the Iowa population. The only indigenous language used regularly in Iowa is Meskwaki, spoken by members of the Sac and Fox tribe.

Presently, Iowa is shifting from a rural to an urban state, as currently over half of Iowans live in urban areas. While demographic shifts are slow, Iowa's increasingly mixed economy foreshadows that the state might come to attract more diverse residents in coming years.

Population by Selected Ethnic Group

	Estimate		Estimate
Total:	3,107,126	Arab	1,691
Afghan	0	Other Arab	1,261
Albanian	257	Armenian	482
Alsatian	0	Assyrian/Chaldean/Syriac	0
American	176,384	Australian	447
Arab:	9,583	Austrian	4,118
Egyptian	466	Basque	59
Iraqi	1,594	Belgian	7,371
Jordanian	0	Brazilian	851
Lebanese	3,379	British	8,005
Moroccan	751	Bulgarian	954
Palestinian	116	Cajun	164
Syrian	434	Canadian	1,946

(continued)

	Estimate		Estimate
Carpatho-Rusyn	28	Slavic	900
Celtic	262	Slovak	1,690
Croatian	2,268	Slovene	785
Cypriot	21	Soviet Union	0
Czech	57,408	Sub-Saharan African:	16,489
Czechoslovakian	6,286	Cape Verdean	0
Danish	51,920	Ethiopian	363
Dutch	133,310	Ghanaian	400
Eastern European	713	Kenyan	210
English	256,620	Liberian	2,052
Estonian	314	Nigerian	523
European	30,895	Senegalese	0
Finnish	3,356	Sierra Leonean	93
French (except Basque)	66,724	Somali	3,162
French Canadian	7,262	South African	111
German	1,108,232	Sudanese	1,203
German Russian	291	Ugandan	67
Greek	5,095	Zimbabwean	214
Guyanese	0	African	7,519
Hungarian	4,506	Other sub-Saharan African	1,094
Icelander	183	Swedish	80,409
Iranian	280	Swiss	14,298
Irish	415,806	Turkish	695
Israeli	789	Ukrainian	2,635
Italian	62,144	Welsh	22,177
Latvian	673	West Indian	2,260
Lithuanian	2,783	(except Hispanic groups):	
Luxemburger	3,927	Bahamian	0
Macedonian	421	Barbadian	49
Maltese	252	Belizean	0
New Zealander	119	Bermudan	0
Northern European	3,958	British West Indian	0
Norwegian	152,514	Dutch West Indian	95
Pennsylvania German	4,695	Haitian	1,198
Polish	38,250	Jamaican	367
Portuguese	2,486	Trinidadian and Tobagonian	40
Romanian	1,132	U.S. Virgin Islander	0
Russian	9,275	West Indian	511
Scandinavian	8,175	Other West Indian	0
Scotch-Irish	23,714	Yugoslavian	8,144
Scottish	46,910	Other groups	473,700
Serbian	1,574	Unclassified or not reported	644,306

Source: American Community Survey, U.S. Census Bureau, 2014.

See in Neighborhoods Section: Amana Colonies (Iowa); Elk Horn, Danish Enclaves (Iowa)

KANSAS

Capital: Topeka
Entered Union: January 29, 1861 (34th state)

Kansas is the 15th most extensive in land area and the 34th most populous of the 50 United States. The state's capital is Topeka, but the biggest city is Wichita. The largest metropolitan area is located around Kansas City. In 2010, the racial makeup of the population of Kansas was as follows: 83.8% of the population was white American (77.5% non-Hispanic white), 5.9% was black or African American, 1.0% American Indian and Alaska Native, 2.4% Asian American, 0.1% Native Hawaiian and other Pacific Islander, and 3.0% from two or more races.

Historical Population of Kansas

Census	Pop.	%±	Census	Pop.	%±
1860	107,206	—	1940	1,801,028	−4.3%
1870	364,399	239.9%	1950	1,905,299	5.8%
1880	996,096	173.4%	1960	2,178,611	14.3%
1890	1,428,108	43.4%	1970	2,246,578	3.1%
1900	1,470,495	3.0%	1980	2,363,679	5.2%
1910	1,690,949	15.0%	1990	2,477,574	4.8%
1920	1,769,257	4.6%	2000	2,688,418	8.5%
1930	1,880,999	6.3%	2010	2,853,118	6.1%

Source: U.S. Census Bureau.

Immigration from outside the United States resulted in a net increase for the population of Kansas, part of a 0.7% population increase from 2006 to 2007, and a 3.3% increase since the year 2000. As of 2004, foreign-born immigrants made up 5.5% of the state's population. The 10 largest reported ancestry groups in Kansas, which make up over 85% of the population, are German at 33.75%, Irish at 14.4%, English at 14.1%, American at 7.5%, French at 4.4%, Scottish at 4.2%, Dutch at 2.5%, Swedish at 2.4%, Italian at 1.8%, and Polish at 1.5%. Different areas within the state show slightly different demographic concentrations. The northwest area of the state has an especially strong number of people of German ancestry.

Kansas remains a predominantly white state, although it has seen a growth in its Hispanic, black, and Asian populations over the past several decades. The southeast area shows an especially large number of those of English ancestry and descendants of white Americans from other states. Mexicans are present in the southwest and make up nearly half of the population in certain counties. In the southwest regions of the state for example, Mexicans make up nearly half the population in certain counties. There is also a continued history of European immigration and migration of newly freed African Americans from the South after the end of the Civil War. Many of the residents of Kansas today descend from these ancestral lineages. Although much of the last few decades has been marked by patterns of population shifts from rural Kansas to metropolitan cities, and many rural communities have been declining, some of the communities of metropolitan Kansas City are among the fastest growing in the country. And it is in these areas in particular that immigrant communities have flourished.

According to the 2010 U.S. Census, the racial makeup of the population was as follows: 83.8% of the population was white American (77.5% non-Hispanic white), 5.9% was black or African American, 1.0% American Indian and Alaska Native, 2.4% Asian American, 0.1% Native Hawaiian and other Pacific Islander, and 3.0% from two or more races, while 10.5% of the total population was of Hispanic or Latino origin. In 2004, it was estimated that 5.5% of the state's population was foreign-born.

The 10 largest reported ancestry groups, which account for over 85% of the population, are German (33.75%), Irish (14.4%), English (14.1%), American (7.5%), French (4.4%), Scottish (4.2%), Dutch (2.5%), Swedish (2.4%), Italian (1.8%), and Polish (1.5%). German descendants are especially present in the northwest, English descendants especially present in the southeast, and Mexicans especially present in the southwest. Many African Americans in Kansas are descended from the Exodusters, newly freed blacks who fled the South for land in Kansas following the Civil War.

The 2008 Pew Religious Landscape Survey showed the religious makeup of Kansas was as follows: Christian 86%, Protestant 53.7%, Roman Catholic 29%, Latter-day Saints/Mormons 2%, Jehovah's Witness 2%, nondenominational 1%, nonreligious 9%, Jewish 2%, Muslim 0.5%, Buddhist 0.5%, and Hindu 0.5%. As of the year 2010, the Association of Religion Data Archives (ARDA) reported that the three largest denominational groups in Kansas are the Roman Catholic Church, the United Methodist Church, and the Southern Baptist Convention.

English is the predominant language, with 91.3% of the population five years or older speaking only English. Of the population, 5.5% speaks Spanish, and 0.7% speaks German. No other language is spoken by more than 0.4% of the state's population.

Population by Selected Ethnic Group

	Estimate		Estimate
Total:	2,904,021	Alsatian	85
Afghan	709	American	213,926
Albanian	0	Arab:	9,346

(continued)

	Estimate		Estimate
Egyptian	280	Irish	345,174
Iraqi	1,645	Israeli	137
Jordanian	408	Italian	64,447
Lebanese	2,865	Latvian	382
Moroccan	818	Lithuanian	3,208
Palestinian	255	Luxemburger	685
Syrian	535	Macedonian	45
Arab	1,441	Maltese	30
Other Arab	1,259	New Zealander	7
Armenian	747	Northern European	1,785
Assyrian/Chaldean/Syriac	0	Norwegian	33,534
Australian	879	Pennsylvania German	2,907
Austrian	7,446	Polish	42,209
Basque	0	Portuguese	3,288
Belgian	4,470	Romanian	1,323
Brazilian	1,012	Russian	18,078
British	9,370	Scandinavian	6,266
Bulgarian	436	Scotch-Irish	35,605
Cajun	407	Scottish	59,905
Canadian	2,864	Serbian	543
Carpatho-Rusyn	73	Slavic	813
Celtic	31	Slovak	1,681
Croatian	5,903	Slovene	698
Cypriot	90	Soviet Union	0
Czech	24,137	Sub-Saharan African:	27,342
Czechoslovakian	4,116	Cape Verdean	0
Danish	14,255	Ethiopian	1,284
Dutch	56,394	Ghanaian	931
Eastern European	1,987	Kenyan	1,653
English	264,947	Liberian	0
Estonian	7	Nigerian	2,249
European	58,825	Senegalese	44
Finnish	1,745	Sierra Leonean	53
French (except Basque)	78,873	Somali	2,589
French Canadian	11,347	South African	355
German	786,373	Sudanese	70
German Russian	1,249	Ugandan	0
Greek	5,020	Zimbabwean	0
Guyanese	0	African	17,618
Hungarian	6,512	Other sub-Saharan African	684
Icelander	179	Swedish	69,310
Iranian	4,368	Swiss	15,053

(continued)

	Estimate		Estimate
Turkish	776	Dutch West Indian	412
Ukrainian	2,472	Haitian	596
Welsh	19,846	Jamaican	2,297
West Indian	3,892	Trinidadian and Tobagonian	74
(except Hispanic groups):		U.S. Virgin Islander	36
Bahamian	0	West Indian	488
Barbadian	116	Other West Indian	0
Belizean	24	Yugoslavian	509
Bermudan	0	Other groups	788,511
British West Indian	19	Unclassified or not reported	528,486

Source: American Community Survey, U.S. Census Bureau, 2014.

See in Neighborhoods Section: Lindsborg, Swedish Enclave (Kansas)

KENTUCKY

Capital: Frankfort
Entered Union: June 1, 1792 (15th state)

Kentucky ranked 37th in land area and 26th in population among all states. Frankfort is the state's capital, but the largest city is Louisville. According to the 2010 U.S. Census, the racial composition of Kentucky was 86.3% white, non-Hispanic, 7.8% black or African American, 3.1% Hispanic or Latino, 1.1% Asian, 0.2% American Indian or Alaska Native, and 0.1% Pacific Islander.

Historical Population of Kentucky

Census	Pop.	%±	Census	Pop.	%±
1790	73,677	—	1910	2,289,905	6.6%
1800	220,955	199.9%	1920	2,416,630	5.5%
1810	406,511	84.0%	1930	2,614,589	8.2%
1820	564,317	38.8%	1940	2,845,627	8.8%
1830	687,917	21.9%	1950	2,944,806	3.5%
1840	779,828	13.4%	1960	3,038,156	3.2%
1850	982,405	26.0%	1970	3,218,706	5.9%
1860	1,155,684	17.6%	1980	3,660,777	13.7%
1870	1,321,011	14.3%	1990	3,685,296	0.7%
1880	1,648,690	24.8%	2000	4,041,769	9.7%
1890	1,858,635	12.7%	2010	4,339,367	7.4%
1900	2,147,174	15.5%			

Source: U.S. Census Bureau.

Originally a part of Virginia, Kentucky became the 15th state to join the Union in 1792. Before European settlement, the area that is today Kentucky was inhabited by two main Native American groups: the Southern Cherokees and the Ridgetop Shawnees. Awareness of Native Americans in Kentucky has been raised and advocated by groups such as the Ridgetop Shawnee. Central Kentucky was the center of the greatest slaveholding in the early 19th century, with Louisville becoming a major slave market. African Americans made up roughly 25% of Kentucky's population prior to the Civil War, but their population decreased during the 20th century primarily as a result of their massive migration in search of jobs in developing northern industrial cities. During the 20th century, one of Kentucky's main economic activities was the tobacco industry, which led to the Black Patch Tobacco Wars. Finally, in the 1960s, successful local civil rights sit-ins helped end practices of segregation.

Currently, the largest ancestries of Kentuckians are English (30.6%), German (12.7%), Irish (10.5%), and African (7.8%). In 2010, the Association of Religion Data Archives reported that out of the state's population, 48% is not affiliated with any religious group, 33% is Evangelical Protestant, 23% adheres to the Southern Baptist Convention, 8% follows the Catholic Church, 4% belongs to the United Methodist Church, and 1% is affiliated with other theologies.

Population by Selected Ethnic Group

	Estimate		Estimate
Total:	4,413,457	Belgian	1,984
Afghan	150	Brazilian	1,034
Albanian	1,083	British	19,817
Alsatian	46	Bulgarian	25
American	832,800	Cajun	658
Arab:	13,940	Canadian	3,079
Egyptian	1,083	Carpatho-Rusyn	0
Iraqi	1,331	Celtic	388
Jordanian	83	Croatian	873
Lebanese	2,990	Cypriot	78
Moroccan	661	Czech	4,849
Palestinian	716	Czechoslovakian	1,266
Syrian	364	Danish	4,374
Arab	4,068	Dutch	43,152
Other Arab	2,826	Eastern European	971
Armenian	940	English	425,531
Assyrian/Chaldean/Syriac	444	Estonian	0
Australian	395	European	42,262
Austrian	2,756	Finnish	2,041
Basque	142	French (except Basque)	70,291

(continued)

	Estimate		Estimate
French Canadian	6,035	Ghanaian	604
German	643,012	Kenyan	442
German Russian	450	Liberian	801
Greek	8,723	Nigerian	869
Guyanese	935	Senegalese	0
Hungarian	6,438	Sierra Leonean	256
Icelander	290	Somali	5,830
Iranian	2,574	South African	537
Irish	544,961	Sudanese	0
Israeli	523	Ugandan	48
Italian	87,867	Zimbabwean	0
Latvian	74	African	28,011
Lithuanian	1,947	Other sub-Saharan African	2,232
Luxemburger	142	Swedish	19,242
Macedonian	214	Swiss	10,974
Maltese	147	Turkish	888
New Zealander	0	Ukrainian	3,536
Northern European	1,783	Welsh	22,808
Norwegian	16,668	West Indian	6,663
Pennsylvania German	2,420	(except Hispanic groups):	
Polish	37,593	Bahamian	435
Portuguese	2,044	Barbadian	0
Romanian	2,959	Belizean	0
Russian	8,752	Bermudan	0
Scandinavian	3,074	British West Indian	24
Scotch-Irish	60,903	Dutch West Indian	175
Scottish	88,765	Haitian	2,177
Serbian	1,011	Jamaican	1,949
Slavic	589	Trinidadian and Tobagonian	153
Slovak	2,421	U.S. Virgin Islander	93
Slovene	317	West Indian	1,553
Soviet Union	0	Other West Indian	128
Sub-Saharan African:	40,169	Yugoslavian	5,179
Cape Verdean	49	Other groups	935,482
Ethiopian	646	Unclassified or not reported	1,163,825

Source: American Community Survey, U.S. Census Bureau, 2014.

See in Neighborhoods Section: Irish Hill (Louisville, Kentucky)

LOUISIANA

Capital: Baton Rouge
Entered Union: April 30, 1812 (18th state)

Louisiana is the 31st largest and the 25th most populous of the 50 states. Baton Rouge is its capital, but the largest city is New Orleans. As reported in the 2010 U.S. Census, the population of Louisiana was 63.7% white American, 32.4% black or African American, 1.7% Asian, 1.4% multiracial American, 0.7% Native American, 0.1% some other race, and 5.6% of the population is Hispanic or Latino of any race.

Historical Population of Louisiana

Census	Pop.	%±	Census	Pop.	%±
1810	76,556	—	1920	1,798,509	8.6%
1820	153,407	100.4%	1930	2,101,593	16.9%
1830	215,739	40.6%	1940	2,363,516	12.5%
1840	352,411	63.4%	1950	2,683,516	13.5%
1850	517,762	46.9%	1960	3,257,022	21.4%
1860	708,002	36.7%	1970	3,641,306	11.8%
1870	726,915	2.7%	1980	4,205,900	15.5%
1880	939,946	29.3%	1990	4,219,973	0.3%
1890	1,118,588	19.0%	2000	4,468,976	5.9%
1900	1,381,625	23.5%	2010	4,533,372	1.4%
1910	1,656,388	19.9%			

Source: U.S. Census Bureau.

Before the arrival of Europeans in the 16th century, Louisiana was inhabited by Native Americans. The first Europeans to arrive to Louisiana were the Spaniards in 1528, and later came the French in the 17th century. These European colonies were built with sovereign, religious, and commercial aims, and it was during colonial times when the first black slaves were brought into the state. Starting in the 1790s, waves of immigration from Haiti took place. The new immigrants increased the French-speaking population and reinforced the African culture in many parts of the state. The Louisiana territory, which included the area of the present-day state of Louisiana, was purchased by the United States in 1803.

Thus, Louisiana has had a very diverse mix of national origins and cultural influences over the past four hundred years. Additionally, Louisiana was a slave state until the Civil War, resulting in a considerable African American population that still exists within the state today. However, that population was reduced during the early 20th century, as thousands of African Americans left the state and migrated north in search of better jobs and better education in growing northern industrial centers.

Jazz musicians performing in the French Quarter at Mardis Gras, New Orleans. (Americanspirit/ Dreamstime.com)

Migration to Louisiana persists to the present day, and the state remains ethnically and culturally diverse. Some urban environments across the state have a multicultural, multilingual heritage with influences from French, Spanish, Native American, and African cultures. The major ancestry groups of Louisiana are French (16.8%), American (9.5%), German (8.3%), Irish (7.5%), English (6.6%), Italian (4.8%), and Scottish (1.1%). Today, Louisiana is the southern state with the most Native American tribes. As of 2011, 49% of Louisiana's population younger than age one was a minority.

According to the 2010 U.S. Census, 3.5% of the population aged five and older spoke Spanish at home, and 4.5% spoke French. The largest religious denominations by number of adherents in 2010 were the Roman Catholic Church, the Southern Baptist Convention, and the United Methodist Church. It is estimated that 60% of the adult population is Protestant. Because Catholics constitute a majority of Louisiana's population, Catholics have continued to be influential in state politics.

Population by Selected Ethnic Group

	Estimate		Estimate
Total:	4,649,676	Alsatian	181
Afghan	0	American	422,793
Albanian	251	Arab:	23,625

(continued)

	Estimate		Estimate
Egyptian	1,815	Iranian	1,240
Iraqi	1,187	Irish	338,263
Jordanian	629	Israeli	877
Lebanese	6,053	Italian	221,093
Moroccan	427	Latvian	572
Palestinian	3,621	Lithuanian	1,199
Syrian	1,568	Luxemburger	61
Arab	6,508	Macedonian	10
Other Arab	2,324	Maltese	34
Armenian	363	New Zealander	0
Assyrian/Chaldean/Syriac	36	Northern European	645
Australian	299	Norwegian	11,760
Austrian	2,430	Pennsylvania German	258
Basque	147	Polish	24,241
Belgian	3,768	Portuguese	3,788
Brazilian	3,495	Romanian	1,573
British	13,785	Russian	8,313
Bulgarian	789	Scandinavian	4,112
Cajun	51,259	Scotch-Irish	37,161
Canadian	3,938	Scottish	47,686
Carpatho-Rusyn	0	Serbian	729
Celtic	789	Slavic	418
Croatian	2,004	Slovak	1,463
Cypriot	0	Slovene	599
Czech	4,947	Soviet Union	0
Czechoslovakian	871	Sub-Saharan African:	51,271
Danish	3,247	Cape Verdean	0
Dutch	25,703	Ethiopian	621
Eastern European	1,564	Ghanaian	59
English	261,701	Kenyan	0
Estonian	14	Liberian	0
European	21,069	Nigerian	2,744
Finnish	869	Senegalese	0
French (except Basque)	586,826	Sierra Leonean	0
French Canadian	149,127	Somali	0
German	345,510	South African	899
German Russian	0	Sudanese	64
Greek	7,222	Ugandan	200
Guyanese	36	Zimbabwean	131
Hungarian	5,540	African	45,847
Icelander	170	Other sub-Saharan African	950

(continued)

	Estimate		Estimate
Swedish	11,751	British West Indian	113
Swiss	2,647	Dutch West Indian	210
Turkish	618	Haitian	5,652
Ukrainian	2,082	Jamaican	2,995
Welsh	10,247	Trinidadian and Tobagonian	365
West Indian	11,739	U.S. Virgin Islander	134
(except Hispanic groups):		West Indian	1,175
Bahamian	342	Other West Indian	0
Barbadian	40	Yugoslavian	1,139
Belizean	926	Other groups	2,010,073
Bermudan	0	Unclassified or not reported	691,625

Source: American Community Survey, U.S. Census Bureau, 2014.

See in Neighborhoods Section: French Quarter (New Orleans, Louisiana); Lower Ninth Ward (New Orleans, Louisiana); Spanish Town (Baton Rouge, Louisiana); Tremé (New Orleans, Louisiana)

MAINE

Capital: Augusta
Entered Union: March 15, 1820 (23rd state)

Maine is the 39th most extensive and the 41st most populous state in the country. Maine is the least densely populated state east of the Mississippi River. Nearly 40% of the state's population lives within the greater Portland metropolitan area. At the 2010 U.S. Census, 94.4% of the population was non-Hispanic white, 1.1% non-Hispanic black or African American, 0.6% American Indian and Alaska Native, 1.0% Asian, 0.1% from some other race and 1.4% of two or more races. In addition, 1.3% of Maine's population was of Hispanic, Latino, or Spanish origin.

Historical Population of Maine

Census	Pop.	%±	Census	Pop.	%±
1790	96,540	—	1850	583,169	16.2%
1800	151,719	57.2%	1860	628,279	7.7%
1810	228,705	50.7%	1870	626,915	−0.2%
1820	298,335	30.4%	1880	648,936	3.5%
1830	399,455	33.9%	1890	661,086	1.9%
1840	501,793	25.6%	1900	694,466	5.0%

(*continued*)

Census	Pop.	%±	Census	Pop.	%±
1910	742,371	6.9%	1970	992,048	2.4%
1920	768,014	3.5%	1980	1,124,660	13.4%
1930	797,423	3.8%	1990	1,227,928	9.2%
1940	847,226	6.2%	2000	1,274,923	3.8%
1950	913,774	7.9%	2010	1,328,361	4.2%
1960	969,265	6.1%			

Source: U.S. Census Bureau.

The first European settlement in Maine was by the French in 1604. Only three years later, the English set up a colony of their own. What is now Maine was made a part of the Massachusetts Bay Colony in 1652. Contentions arose over the state's ownership and governance: the French and British, as well as local Native American tribes, fought with each other repeatedly over territory disputes. During the American Revolution and during the War of 1812, Maine's territory was contended by the Patriot and the Loyalist forces. In 1820, Maine separated from Massachusetts and became an independent state. As a result of its history of French settlement, as well as its proximity to French-speaking Canada, Maine is the state with the highest percentage of people speaking French at home (5.28%).

Compared to many other states, Maine is an overwhelmingly white state with a high percentage of European descendants. As estimated in 2011, the largest ancestries were French or French Canadian (23.9%), English (21.6%), Irish (17.8%), American (9.4%), German (8.5%), Italian (5.8%), Scottish (5.5%), Polish (2.1%), Swedish (1.8%), and Scots-Irish (1.7%). Even those who identify as Americans are overwhelmingly of European descent but have ancestry that has been in the region for several generations.

According to the Association of Religion Data Archives, the major religious affiliations in Maine in 2011 were Catholic Church (28%), Protestant (7%), Evangelical Protestant (4%), other religions (1.7%). The low overall percentage of religious practitioners makes evident why, in 2010, a study named Maine as the least religious state in the United States. With respect to crime rates, Maine is also often considered the safest state in the United States.

Population by Selected Ethnic Group

	Estimate		Estimate
Total:	1,330,089	Arab:	5,057
Afghan	206	Egyptian	381
Albanian	1,015	Iraqi	1,131
Alsatian	145	Jordanian	0
American	97,984	Lebanese	1,652

(continued)

	Estimate		Estimate
Moroccan	402	Lithuanian	6,478
Palestinian	48	Luxemburger	0
Syrian	423	Macedonian	0
Arab	1,089	Maltese	0
Other Arab	340	New Zealander	0
Armenian	2,156	Northern European	1,584
Assyrian/Chaldean/Syriac	0	Norwegian	10,370
Australian	439	Pennsylvania German	447
Austrian	2,339	Polish	31,018
Basque	22	Portuguese	8,696
Belgian	882	Romanian	565
Brazilian	359	Russian	10,577
British	8,450	Scandinavian	2,846
Bulgarian	374	Scotch-Irish	18,549
Cajun	816	Scottish	67,883
Canadian	14,818	Serbian	160
Carpatho-Rusyn	0	Slavic	1,283
Celtic	195	Slovak	1,547
Croatian	612	Slovene	276
Cypriot	0	Soviet Union	0
Czech	1,806	Sub-Saharan African:	10,276
Czechoslovakian	761	Cape Verdean	123
Danish	6,827	Ethiopian	106
Dutch	13,212	Ghanaian	88
Eastern European	3,078	Kenyan	547
English	272,386	Liberian	0
Estonian	156	Nigerian	423
European	14,121	Senegalese	0
Finnish	5,082	Sierra Leonean	86
French (except Basque)	204,018	Somali	3,890
French Canadian	106,463	South African	110
German	115,052	Sudanese	830
German Russian	0	Ugandan	7
Greek	7,145	Zimbabwean	0
Guyanese	25	African	3,046
Hungarian	3,831	Other sub-Saharan African	1,490
Icelander	433		
Iranian	83	Swedish	25,456
Irish	232,233	Swiss	2,720
Israeli	127	Turkish	207
Italian	80,027	Ukrainian	1,978
Latvian	426	Welsh	10,154

(continued)

	Estimate		Estimate
West Indian	1,952	Jamaican	1,078
(except Hispanic groups):		Trinidadian and Tobagonian	112
Bahamian	0	U.S. Virgin Islander	0
Barbadian	4	West Indian	314
Belizean	0	Other West Indian	14
Bermudan	87	Yugoslavian	552
British West Indian	22	Other groups	167,700
Dutch West Indian	0	Unclassified or not reported	203,123
Haitian	321		

Source: American Community Survey, U.S. Census Bureau, 2014.

See in Neighborhoods Section: Lewiston and Portland, Somali and Bantu Enclaves (Maine)

MARYLAND

Capital: Annapolis
Entered Union: April 28, 1788 (7th state)

Maryland is one of the smallest states in terms of area, as well as one of the most densely populated states. It is the country's 42nd largest state in land area and the 19th most populous. The state's capital is Annapolis, but the largest city is Baltimore, around which most of the population lives. According to the 2010 census, the racial breakdown of the population of Maryland was white (60.8%), black (29.8%), Asian (5.5%), Native (0.3%), Hawaiian or Pacific Islander (0.1%), other race (3.6%), two or more races (2.9%). Most African Americans in the state are descendants from slaves brought from West Africa, and many are of mixed race, including European and Native American ancestry.

Historical Population of Maryland

Census	Pop.	%±	Census	Pop.	%±
1790	319,728	—	1860	687,049	17.8%
1800	341,548	6.8%	1870	780,894	13.7%
1810	380,546	11.4%	1880	934,943	19.7%
1820	407,350	7.0%	1890	1,042,390	11.5%
1830	447,040	9.7%	1900	1,188,044	14.0%
1840	470,019	5.1%	1910	1,295,346	9.0%
1850	583,034	24.0%	1920	1,449,661	11.9%

(continued)

Census	Pop.	%±	Census	Pop.	%±
1930	1,631,526	12.5%	1980	4,216,975	7.5%
1940	1,821,244	11.6%	1990	4,781,468	13.4%
1950	2,343,001	28.6%	2000	5,296,486	10.8%
1960	3,100,689	32.3%	2010	5,773,552	9.0%
1970	3,922,399	26.5%			

Source: U.S. Census Bureau.

Maryland was established as a safe haven for England's minority Roman Catholics, who were the first major group to migrate into the state. Chartered in 1632, Maryland's early history was fraught with disputes between Catholics and Protestants, who were present in large majorities in surrounding colonies. Given its original mission, Maryland is often considered to be the birthplace of religious freedom in the United States.

Maryland's ethnic diversity began early on as well. Most of Maryland's early arrivals from Europe came to the state as indentured servants. These white migrants often worked alongside black laborers, and interracial unions and mixed-race children were not unknown. Mixed-race children born to white mothers and slave fathers were granted freedom, and so the state had a longstanding population of free blacks. In the years following the American revolution, abolitionist sentiments caught on in Maryland as plantation owners freed slaves, and so the state had a relatively high population of free blacks.

In the modern era, ethnic and cultural diversity persists in Maryland. Large ethnic minorities include Eastern Europeans include Croatians, Russians, and Ukrainians. Following the dissolution of the Soviet Union, Yugoslavia, and Czechoslovakia, many immigrants from Eastern Europe came to the United States (12% of whom currently reside in Maryland). New residents of African descent include 20th-century and later immigrants from Nigeria, particularly of the Igbo and Yoruba tribes. Irish American populations can be found throughout the Baltimore area, and the Northern and Eastern suburbs of Washington, D.C., in Maryland as well as Western Maryland, where Irish immigrant laborers helped to build the C & O Railroad. A large percentage of the population of the Eastern Shore and Southern Maryland are descendants of British American ancestry. Western and northern Maryland have large German American populations. The top reported ancestries by Maryland residents in 2010 were German (15.6%), Irish (11.8%), English (8.4%), Italian (5.3%), American (4.8%), Polish (3.4%), sub-Saharan African (3.2%), and Salvadorian (2.1%).

Religious diversity is similarly present. Jews of European American descent are numerous throughout Montgomery County and in Pikesville and Owings Mills northwest of Baltimore.

In 2010, the Association of Religion Data Archives (ARDA) reported that the largest religious groups in Maryland are the Catholic Church, nondenominational Evangelical Protestant, and the United Methodist Church. Judaism is the largest non-Christian religion in Maryland, making up 4.3% of the total population. Furthermore, because Maryland has the country's highest median household income, it is considered to be the wealthiest state in the nation.

Population by Selected Ethnic Group

	Estimate		Estimate
Total:	5,976,407	English	437,053
Afghan	1,961	Estonian	1,075
Albanian	1,968	European	64,716
Alsatian	472	Finnish	4,407
American	299,102	French (except Basque)	90,069
Arab:	27,524	French Canadian	18,397
Egyptian	4,129	German	825,840
Iraqi	2,012	German Russian	913
Jordanian	621	Greek	32,363
Lebanese	6,130	Guyanese	7,009
Moroccan	3,065	Hungarian	24,151
Palestinian	2,367	Icelander	272
Syrian	1,194	Iranian	15,591
Arab	4,127	Irish	632,738
Other Arab	4,546	Israeli	2,277
Armenian	5,262	Italian	291,125
Assyrian/Chaldean/Syriac	182	Latvian	2,311
Australian	1,910	Lithuanian	20,506
Austrian	12,854	Luxemburger	40
Basque	338	Macedonian	624
Belgian	4,282	Maltese	63
Brazilian	8,188	New Zealander	77
British	28,789	Northern European	4,877
Bulgarian	1,500	Norwegian	29,250
Cajun	535	Pennsylvania German	2,392
Canadian	9,512	Polish	190,191
Carpatho-Rusyn	176	Portuguese	11,626
Celtic	1,119	Romanian	8,292
Croatian	4,918	Russian	74,620
Cypriot	443	Scandinavian	5,072
Czech	21,540	Scotch-Irish	41,030
Czechoslovakian	6,886	Scottish	90,237
Danish	8,620	Serbian	2,260
Dutch	46,475	Slavic	4,033
Eastern European	21,649	Slovak	12,799

(*continued*)

	Estimate			Estimate
Slovene	1,685		Turkish	5,920
Soviet Union	270		Ukrainian	19,810
Sub-Saharan African:	257,907		Welsh	34,264
Cape Verdean	572		West Indian	79,822
Ethiopian	24,756		(except Hispanic groups):	
Ghanaian	7,512		Bahamian	436
Kenyan	2,247		Barbadian	1,520
Liberian	5,663		Belizean	286
Nigerian	34,405		Bermudan	175
Senegalese	190		British West Indian	3,666
Sierra Leonean	6,269		Dutch West Indian	0
Somali	2,394		Haitian	15,378
South African	2,022		Jamaican	40,423
Sudanese	181		Trinidadian and Tobagonian	9,815
Ugandan	1,637		U.S. Virgin Islander	496
Zimbabwean	531		West Indian	9,610
African	147,754		Other West Indian	75
Other sub-Saharan African	23,268		Yugoslavian	1,955
Swedish	30,591		Other groups	2,432,676
Swiss	12,374		Unclassified or not reported	910,758

Source: American Community Survey, U.S. Census Bureau, 2014.

See in Neighborhoods Section: Langley Park, Latino Enclaves (Maryland); Upper Fells Point (Spanish Town) (Baltimore, Maryland)

MASSACHUSETTS

Capital: Boston
Entered Union: February 6, 1788 (6th state)

Massachusetts is the 7th smallest, but the 14th most populous, and the 3rd most densely populated state in the United States. Approximately two-thirds of the state's population lives in the greater Boston metropolitan area, and the state has the nation's sixth highest GDP per capita. As of 2010, the racial composition of the population of Massachusetts was white (80.4%), black (6.6%), Asian (5.3%), Native (0.3%), other race (4.7%), and two or more races (2.6%)

A group of runners in the 113th annual Boston Marathon, a quintessential tradition, on April, 20, 2009. (Teconley/Dreamstime.com)

Historical Population of Massachusetts

Census	Pop.	%±	Census	Pop.	%±
1790	378,787	—	1910	3,366,416	20.0%
1800	422,845	11.6%	1920	3,852,356	14.4%
1810	472,040	11.6%	1930	4,249,614	10.3%
1820	523,287	10.9%	1940	4,316,721	1.6%
1830	610,408	16.6%	1950	4,690,514	8.7%
1840	737,699	20.9%	1960	5,148,578	9.8%
1850	994,514	34.8%	1970	5,689,170	10.5%
1860	1,231,066	23.8%	1980	5,737,037	0.8%
1870	1,457,351	18.4%	1990	6,016,425	4.9%
1880	1,783,085	22.4%	2000	6,349,097	5.5%
1890	2,238,947	25.6%	2010	6,547,629	3.1%
1900	2,805,346	25.3%			

Source: U.S. Census Bureau.

As late as 1795, the population of Massachusetts was nearly 95% of English ancestry. During the early and mid-19th century, immigrant groups began arriving in Massachusetts in large numbers; first from Ireland in the 1840s; today the Irish and part-Irish are the largest ancestry group in the state at nearly 25% of the total population. Others arrived later from Quebec as well as European countries such as Italy and Poland. In the early 20th century, a number of African Americans migrated to Massachusetts, although in somewhat fewer numbers than many other Northern states. Later in the 20th century, immigration from Latin America, Africa, and East Asia increased considerably. Massachusetts has the third-largest population of Haitians in the United States.

As of 2010, 78.93% of Massachusetts residents aged five and older spoke English at home as a primary language, 7.50% spoke Spanish, 2.97% spoke Portuguese, 1.59% spoke Chinese, 1.11% spoke French, 0.89% spoke French Creole, 0.72% spoke Italian, 0.62% spoke Russian, and 0.58% spoke Vietnamese. In 2005, a study found that 40% of foreign immigrants were from Central or South America.

In addition to ethnic diversity, Massachusetts is religiously diverse as well. Massachusetts was founded and settled by the Puritans in 1628. Today, the descendants of the Puritans belong to many different churches. Currently, Protestants make up less than one-quarter of the state's population. Roman Catholics now predominate because of massive Catholic immigration from Ireland as well as Italy, Portugal, Quebec, and Latin America. A large Jewish population came to the Boston and Springfield areas in the years between 1880–1920. Buddhists, Pagans, Hindus, Seventh-day Adventists, Muslims, and Mormons also can be found in the state. The religious affiliations of the people of Massachusetts, according to a 2001 survey, were Catholic (44%), Protestant (25%), Jewish (3%), Muslim (1%), other (7%), no religion (15%), and refused to answer (7%).

Population by Selected Ethnic Group

	Estimate		Estimate
Total:	6,745,408	Assyrian/Chaldean/Syriac	314
Afghan	2,032	Australian	3,348
Albanian	18,846	Austrian	16,964
Alsatian	623	Basque	310
American	280,412	Belgian	5,927
Arab:	82,426	Brazilian	63,013
Egyptian	5,684	British	32,467
Iraqi	4,004	Bulgarian	4,310
Jordanian	601	Cajun	856
Lebanese	36,492	Canadian	52,530
Moroccan	7,875	Carpatho-Rusyn	46
Palestinian	2,598	Celtic	769
Syrian	7,526	Croatian	3,097
Arab	9,818	Cypriot	134
Other Arab	10,216	Czech	13,741
Armenian	25,370	Czechoslovakian	3,409

(continued)

	Estimate		Estimate
Danish	13,574	Soviet Union	11
Dutch	39,525	Sub-Saharan African:	129,789
Eastern European	25,836	Cape Verdean	62,094
English	654,651	Ethiopian	6,676
Estonian	1,381	Ghanaian	5,761
European	83,214	Kenyan	2,868
Finnish	23,732	Liberian	1,566
French (except Basque)	444,304	Nigerian	8,069
French Canadian	259,901	Senegalese	561
German	401,771	Sierra Leonean	109
German Russian	0	Somali	7,423
Greek	85,798	South African	1,111
Guyanese	1,907	Sudanese	1,547
Hungarian	18,191	Ugandan	4,478
Icelander	674	Zimbabwean	730
Iranian	7,604	African	21,554
Irish	1,452,985	Other sub-Saharan African	6,661
Israeli	3,367	Swedish	111,148
Italian	899,979	Swiss	10,431
Latvian	3,570	Turkish	8,548
Lithuanian	40,657	Ukrainian	23,831
Luxemburger	169	Welsh	24,168
Macedonian	437	West Indian	126,115
Maltese	315	(except Hispanic groups):	
New Zealander	586	Bahamian	75
Northern European	7,894	Barbadian	6,087
Norwegian	33,876	Belizean	450
Pennsylvania German	904	Bermudan	306
Polish	300,317	British West Indian	3,958
Portuguese	294,631	Dutch West Indian	408
Romanian	9,422	Haitian	70,805
Russian	103,597	Jamaican	27,604
Scandinavian	7,067	Trinidadian and Tobagonian	6,694
Scotch-Irish	41,197	U.S. Virgin Islander	481
Scottish	144,123	West Indian	12,047
Serbian	1,969	Other West Indian	176
Slavic	1,298	Yugoslavian	2,268
Slovak	6,006	Other groups	1,606,424
Slovene	1,647	Unclassified or not reported	803,791

Source: American Community Survey, U.S. Census Bureau, 2014.

See in Neighborhoods Section: Cambodia Town (Lowell, Massachusetts); Chinatown (Boston, Massachusetts); Fall River, Portuguese Enclave (Massachusetts); Framingham, Brazilian Enclave (Massachusetts); Holyoke, Puerto Rican Enclaves (Massachusetts); Lawrence, Latino Enclaves (Massachusetts); Lower Roxbury, African American Enclave (Massachusetts); Mattapan (Boston, Massachusetts); North End (Boston, Massachusetts); Quincy, Asian Enclaves (Massachusetts); Roxbury, African American Enclave (Massachusetts); Salem, French Canadian Enclave (Massachusetts); South Boston/Southie (Boston Massachusetts); South End (Boston, Massachusetts); Watertown, Armenian Capital (Massachusetts); West End (Boston, Massachusetts)

MICHIGAN

Capital: Lansing
Entered Union: January 26, 1837 (26th state)

Michigan is the 11th most extensive state and the 9th most populous state. Its capital is Lansing, but the largest city is Detroit. The 2010 U.S. Census also reported that the racial breakdown was as follows: white (79.0%), black (14.2%), Asian (2.4%), Native (0.6%), other race (1.5%), and two or more races (2.3%).

Historical Population of Michigan

Census	Pop.	%±	Census	Pop.	%±
1800	3,757	—	1910	2,810,173	16.1%
1810	4,762	26.8%	1920	3,668,412	30.5%
1820	7,452	56.5%	1930	4,842,325	32.0%
1830	28,004	275.8%	1940	5,256,106	8.5%
1840	212,267	658.0%	1950	6,371,766	21.2%
1850	397,654	87.3%	1960	7,823,194	22.8%
1860	749,113	88.4%	1970	8,875,083	13.4%
1870	1,184,059	58.1%	1980	9,262,078	4.4%
1880	1,636,937	38.2%	1990	9,295,297	0.4%
1890	2,093,890	27.9%	2000	9,938,444	6.9%
1900	2,420,982	15.6%	2010	9,883,640	−0.6%

Source: U.S. Census Bureau.

What is now Michigan was first settled by various Native American tribes. It was then colonized by French explorers in the 17th century and became a part of New France. After the defeat of France in the French and Indian War in 1763 the region came under British rule, and it was finally ceded to the newly independent United States after the British defeat in the American Revolutionary War.

In 1825, the Erie Canal opened and created substantial opportunity for farming and trading the area's abundant natural resources. As a result, settlers of European descent poured into the area. In the late 19th and early 20th centuries, the state received an additional influx of French Canadian settlers coming to work in the lumber industry. As a result of these migratory patterns, Michigan continues to reflect considerable European ancestry today. As of 2010, the 10 largest reported ancestries in the state are German (21.8%), Irish (11.6%), English (9.9%), Polish (8.9%), French or French Canadian (6.5%), American (5.3%), Dutch (5.0%), Italian (4.8%), Scottish (2.4%), and Swedish (1.7%). Additionally, Michigan has the largest Dutch, Finnish, and Macedonian populations in the United States.

Modern migration in Michigan reflects a different collection of national origins than its early history. Michigan developed as a major industrial center during the 20th century, with immigrants, as well as largely African American migrants from elsewhere in the United States, came to work in its booming automotive industry. The past several decades have also seen a heavy influx of settlers from the Middle East. As of 2010, the top 10 non-English languages spoken in Michigan are Spanish (2.93%), Arabic (1.04%), German (0.44%), Chinese (0.36%), French (0.31%), Polish (0.29%), Syriac languages (0.25%), Italian (0.21%), Albanian (0.19%), and Hindi, Tagalog, Vietnamese, Japanese, and Korean (0.16%). As of 2010, 6% of the state's population was foreign-born.

Religious diversity exists in the state as well. The breakdown of religious adherence in Michigan, based on a 2007 survey, was Catholic (23%), Protestant (53%), Mormon (1%), Jehovah's Witness (1%), Jewish (1%), Muslim (1%), Buddhist (1%), and Orthodox (0.5%).

Population by Selected Ethnic Group

	Estimate		Estimate
Total:	9,909,877	Other Arab	29,304
Afghan	129	Armenian	15,125
Albanian	24,290	Assyrian/Chaldean/Syriac	47,020
Alsatian	133	Australian	2,929
American	608,536	Austrian	23,285
Arab:	184,994	Basque	392
Egyptian	4,498	Belgian	48,065
Iraqi	26,624	Brazilian	3,560
Jordanian	4,619	British	35,502
Lebanese	61,391	Bulgarian	2,687
Moroccan	2,163	Cajun	739
Palestinian	6,056	Canadian	44,714
Syrian	12,673	Carpatho-Rusyn	228
Arab	43,688	Celtic	1,237

(continued)

	Estimate		Estimate
Croatian	19,957	Slovak	25,154
Cypriot	91	Slovene	4,341
Czech	41,253	Soviet Union	16
Czechoslovakian	13,921	Sub-Saharan African:	53,556
Danish	33,912	Cape Verdean	91
Dutch	457,992	Ethiopian	1,664
Eastern European	10,719	Ghanaian	868
English	868,554	Kenyan	919
Estonian	827	Liberian	908
European	100,118	Nigerian	6,082
Finnish	97,634	Senegalese	269
French (except Basque)	402,794	Sierra Leonean	618
French Canadian	163,945	Somali	2,399
German	2,025,617	South African	2,162
German Russian	803	Sudanese	238
Greek	45,549	Ugandan	276
Guyanese	273	Zimbabwean	193
Hungarian	89,540	African	34,935
Icelander	1,007	Other sub-Saharan African	2,437
Iranian	4,372	Swedish	147,031
Irish	1,068,515	Swiss	21,389
Israeli	1,143	Turkish	2,292
Italian	463,307	Ukrainian	38,225
Latvian	5,262	Welsh	42,854
Lithuanian	26,138	West Indian	15,590
Luxemburger	675	(except Hispanic groups):	
Macedonian	7,830	Bahamian	206
Maltese	12,025	Barbadian	260
New Zealander	592	Belizean	1,041
Northern European	6,290	Bermudan	25
Norwegian	71,601	British West Indian	132
Pennsylvania German	8,282	Dutch West Indian	143
Polish	835,480	Haitian	3,337
Portuguese	7,162	Jamaican	7,609
Romanian	29,297	Trinidadian and Tobagonian	1,478
Russian	70,207	U.S. Virgin Islander	0
Scandinavian	14,615	West Indian	1,443
Scotch-Irish	67,551	Other West Indian	0
Scottish	213,611	Yugoslavian	13,881
Serbian	8,755	Other groups	2,562,694
Slavic	7,034	Unclassified or not reported	1,574,644

Source: American Community Survey, U.S. Census Bureau, 2014.

See in Neighborhoods Section: Dearborn and Detroit, Middle Eastern Enclaves (Michigan); Little Poland (Hamtramck, Michigan); Mexicantown (Detroit, Michigan)

MINNESOTA

Capital: Saint Paul
Entered Union: May 11, 1858 (32nd state)

Minnesota is the 12th-largest and the 21st most populous state in the United States. Nearly 60% of its residents live in the Minneapolis-Saint Paul metropolitan area (known as the "Twin Cities").

Minnesota is known for its relatively mixed social and political orientations. The large majority of residents are of Scandinavian and German descent. The state is known as a center of Scandinavian American culture. The principal ancestries of Minnesota's residents in 2010 were surveyed to be the following: 37.9% German, 32.1% from the Nordic countries, 11.7% Irish, 6.3% English, 5.1% Polish, 4.2% French, and 3.7% Czech.

Historical Population of Minnesota

Census	Pop.	%±	Census	Pop.	%±
1850	6,077	—	1940	2,792,300	8.9%
1860	172,023	2,730.7%	1950	2,982,483	6.8%
1870	439,706	155.6%	1960	3,413,864	14.5%
1880	780,773	77.6%	1970	3,804,971	11.5%
1890	1,310,283	67.8%	1980	4,075,970	7.1%
1900	1,751,394	33.7%	1990	4,375,099	7.3%
1910	2,075,708	18.5%	2000	4,919,479	12.4%
1920	2,387,125	15.0%	2010	5,303,925	7.8%
1930	2,563,953	7.4%			

Source: U.S. Census Bureau.

Minnesota's early inhabitants were members of the Dakota, Ojibwe, and Ho-Chunk Native American tribes. The region became part of Spanish Louisiana in 1762, and it was sold to the United States as part of the Louisiana Purchase in 1803. By the middle of the 19th century, Minnesota had a substantial population that had arrived to work in its abundant timber and farming industries. Many of these residents were of European descent, and a great portion were migrants from New England. As a result, the state was often nicknamed "the New England of the West."

The discovery of iron in the state in the late 19th century created rapid industrialization and population growth in Minnesota. Although its agrarian sector was hit hard during the Great Depression, wartime industries during World War II helped to revitalize Minnesota's economy. Today, it is a bustling business hub, largely

Weisman Art Museum in Minneapolis, home to a thriving arts scene. (Aliaksandr Nikitsin/ Dreamstime.com)

transformed from its agrarian origins. Its strong economy has provided employment opportunities and attractions for migrants: in recent decades, substantial influxes of Asian, African, and Latin American immigrants have joined the descendants of European settlers. Minnesota's growing minority groups, however, still form a smaller percentage of the population than in the nation as a whole.

The majority of Minnesotans are Protestants, including a significant Lutheran contingent, owing to the state's largely Northern European ethnic makeup, but Roman Catholics (of largely German, Irish, and Slavic descent) make up the largest single Christian denomination. A 2010 survey by the Pew Forum on Religion and Public Life showed that 32.0% of Minnesotans were affiliated with Mainline Protestant traditions, 21.0% were Evangelical Protestants, 28.0% were Roman Catholic, 1.0% each were Jewish, Muslim, Buddhist, and black Protestant, and smaller amounts were of other faiths, with 13.0% unaffiliated.

Population by Selected Ethnic Group

	Estimate		Estimate
Total:	5,457,173	Alsatian	41
Afghan	276	American	188,536
Albanian	149	Arab:	20,780

(continued)

	Estimate		Estimate
Egyptian	2,599	Irish	566,406
Iraqi	1,241	Israeli	1,265
Jordanian	1,318	Italian	133,149
Lebanese	7,148	Latvian	2,504
Moroccan	597	Lithuanian	4,891
Palestinian	976	Luxemburger	5,082
Syrian	1,700	Macedonian	417
Arab	2,440	Maltese	114
Other Arab	3,248	New Zealander	245
Armenian	1,418	Northern European	8,993
Assyrian/Chaldean/Syriac	130	Norwegian	837,098
Australian	1,175	Pennsylvania German	2,344
Austrian	17,799	Polish	250,059
Basque	84	Portuguese	3,660
Belgian	13,910	Romanian	6,331
Brazilian	2,986	Russian	44,374
British	14,103	Scandinavian	73,276
Bulgarian	2,045	Scotch-Irish	27,286
Cajun	363	Scottish	65,467
Canadian	8,054	Serbian	4,317
Carpatho-Rusyn	89	Slavic	3,366
Celtic	327	Slovak	8,697
Croatian	10,784	Slovene	10,570
Cypriot	78	Soviet Union	0
Czech	87,162	Sub-Saharan African:	124,965
Czechoslovakian	11,603	Cape Verdean	115
Danish	71,384	Ethiopian	19,286
Dutch	94,070	Ghanaian	1,028
Eastern European	6,260	Kenyan	3,472
English	289,487	Liberian	11,708
Estonian	350	Nigerian	6,939
European	61,938	Senegalese	237
Finnish	96,418	Sierra Leonean	178
French (except Basque)	179,372	Somali	48,536
French Canadian	50,673	South African	532
German	1,853,401	Sudanese	3,282
German Russian	951	Ugandan	44
Greek	11,525	Zimbabwean	159
Guyanese	2,208	African	26,503
Hungarian	14,118	Other sub-Saharan African	5,730
Icelander	3,301	Swedish	435,163
Iranian	2,712	Swiss	21,453

(continued)

	Estimate		Estimate
Turkish	1,994	Dutch West Indian	0
Ukrainian	14,973	Haitian	1,503
Welsh	23,129	Jamaican	3,225
West Indian	6,298	Trinidadian and Tobagonian	644
(except Hispanic groups):		U.S. Virgin Islander	0
Bahamian	34	West Indian	384
Barbadian	134	Other West Indian	72
Belizean	89	Yugoslavian	7,692
Bermudan	57	Other groups	950,761
British West Indian	156	Unclassified or not reported	718,740

Source: American Community Survey, U.S. Census Bureau, 2014.

See in Neighborhoods Section: Minneapolis-St. Paul, Twin Cities Hmong Community (Minnesota)

MISSISSIPPI

Capital: Jackson
Entered Union: December 10, 1817 (20th state)

Jackson, Mississippi skyline over the Capitol Building, 2016. (Sean Pavone/Dreamstime.com)

Mississippi is the 32nd most extensive state and the 31st most populous. However, the state ranks last in health, educational attainment, and median household income. The state's capital, Jackson, is also its largest city. The 2010 U.S. Census reported the population of Mississippi as being 59.1% white American, 37.0% African American, 0.5% American Indian, 0.9% Asian American, 1.1% multiracial American, and 1.4% other. Ethnically, 2.7% of the total population, among all racial groups, was of Hispanic or Latino origin. As of 2011, 53.8% of Mississippi's population younger than age one belonged to a minority group.

Historical Population of Mississippi

Census	Pop.	%±	Census	Pop.	%±
1800	7,600	—	1910	1,797,114	15.8%
1810	31,306	311.9%	1920	1,790,618	−0.4%
1820	75,448	141.0%	1930	2,009,821	12.2%
1830	136,621	81.1%	1940	2,183,796	8.7%
1840	375,651	175.0%	1950	2,178,914	−0.2%
1850	606,526	61.5%	1960	2,178,141	0.0%
1860	791,305	30.5%	1970	2,216,912	1.8%
1870	827,922	4.6%	1980	2,520,638	13.7%
1880	1,131,597	36.7%	1990	2,573,216	2.1%
1890	1,289,600	14.0%	2000	2,844,658	10.5%
1900	1,551,270	20.3%	2010	2,967,297	4.3%

Source: U.S. Census Bureau.

Before the arrival of Europeans, Mississippi was heavily settled with Native American tribes such as the Choctaw. Under French and Spanish rule beginning in the 17th century, the few Europeans in what is now Mississippi were Roman Catholics. The growth of the cotton industry after 1815 brought in tens of thousands of Anglo-American settlers each year, most of whom were Protestants from Southeastern states. Due to such migration, there was rapid growth in Protestant churches, especially Methodist, Presbyterian and Baptist. Americans of Scots-Irish, English and Scottish ancestry are present throughout the state. Additionally, plantation farming resulted in a significant African American population in Mississippi.

After the Civil War, Mississippi underwent significant demographic transformation. Some 400,000 African Americans left Mississippi in the first half of the 20th century to seek work in northern industrial cities as part of the so-called Great Migration. Additionally, between 1910 and 1930 Chinese settlers were recruited as farm laborers. Largely working as sharecroppers upon arrival, Chinese settlers often left farming after several years to find work as small merchants or grocers. The fishing industry also brought significant immigrants from Vietnam in the early 1980s.

In the post–Civil War years, religion became even more influential, as the South became known as the "Bible Belt." Freedmen withdrew from white-run churches in favor of setting up their own. The majority of blacks left the Southern Baptist Church, and by 1895 had established numerous black Baptist state associations and the National Baptist Convention of black churches. African American Baptist churches grew to total twice as many members as their white Baptist counterparts. The end of legal segregation and Jim Crow led to the integration of some churches, but most today remain divided along racial lines. Public opinion polls have consistently ranked Mississippi as the most religious state in the United States, with 59% of Mississippians considering themselves "very religious." The same survey also found that 11% of the population was nonreligious.

The U.S. Census Bureau reported that in the last decade, Mississippi had the highest rate of increase in mixed-race population. This change reflects new births among a young population, but also people who have chosen to identify as multiracial who in earlier years may have identified as only one ethnicity, a carryover from days of racial segregation. After having comprised a majority of the state's population since well before the Civil War and through the 1930s, today African Americans comprise approximately 37% of the population, with most having ancestors who were enslaved and forcibly transported from Africa and the Upper South in the 19th century to labor on the area's new plantations.

Population by Selected Ethnic Group

	Estimate		Estimate
Total:	2,984,345	Belgian	693
Afghan	37	Brazilian	204
Albanian	0	British	7,563
Alsatian	81	Bulgarian	35
American	351,566	Cajun	2,316
Arab:	5,805	Canadian	1,571
Egyptian	56	Carpatho-Rusyn	0
Iraqi	46	Celtic	234
Jordanian	165	Croatian	1,014
Lebanese	3,185	Cypriot	0
Moroccan	144	Czech	1,958
Palestinian	216	Czechoslovakian	475
Syrian	311	Danish	2,495
Arab	1,217	Dutch	18,389
Other Arab	539	Eastern European	416
Armenian	246	English	226,278
Assyrian/Chaldean/Syriac	35	Estonian	73
Australian	268	European	22,537
Austrian	1,639	Finnish	826
Basque	22	French (except Basque)	73,018

(continued)

	Estimate		Estimate
French Canadian	7,147	Ghanaian	87
German	165,484	Kenyan	0
German Russian	70	Liberian	81
Greek	3,062	Nigerian	495
Guyanese	64	Senegalese	12
Hungarian	2,181	Sierra Leonean	13
Icelander	196	Somali	6
Iranian	623	South African	224
Irish	251,855	Sudanese	51
Israeli	121	Ugandan	0
Italian	55,954	Zimbabwean	11
Latvian	152	African	17,189
Lithuanian	666	Other sub-Saharan African	107
Luxemburger	5	Swedish	8,178
Macedonian	0	Swiss	2,107
Maltese	126	Turkish	514
New Zealander	40	Ukrainian	916
Northern European	1,938	Welsh	8,314
Norwegian	6,098	West Indian	3,042
Pennsylvania German	347	(except Hispanic groups):	
Polish	13,000	Bahamian	72
Portuguese	1,654	Barbadian	10
Romanian	373	Belizean	53
Russian	3,987	Bermudan	5
Scandinavian	1,532	British West Indian	110
Scotch-Irish	47,006	Dutch West Indian	414
Scottish	43,684	Haitian	621
Serbian	181	Jamaican	1,196
Slavic	687	Trinidadian and Tobagonian	132
Slovak	764	U.S. Virgin Islander	0
Slovene	292	West Indian	412
Soviet Union	0	Other West Indian	21
Sub-Saharan African:	18,434	Yugoslavian	1,148
Cape Verdean	47	Other groups	1,422,697
Ethiopian	172	Unclassified or not reported	536,851

Source: U.S. Census Bureau, 2010–2014 American Community Survey 5-Year Estimates.

See in Neighborhoods Section: Point Cadet (Biloxi, Mississippi)

MISSOURI

Capital: Jefferson City
Entered Union: August 10, 1821 (24th state)

Missouri is the 21st most extensive and 18th most populous U.S. state. Over half of Missouri's residents live within two of the state's largest metropolitan areas—St. Louis and Kansas City.

Historical Population of Missouri

Census	Pop.	%±	Census	Pop.	%±
1810	19,783	—	1920	3,404,055	3.4%
1820	66,586	236.6%	1930	3,629,367	6.6%
1830	140,455	110.9%	1940	3,784,664	4.3%
1840	383,702	173.2%	1950	3,954,653	4.5%
1850	682,044	77.8%	1960	4,319,813	9.2%
1860	1,182,012	73.3%	1970	4,676,501	8.3%
1870	1,721,295	45.6%	1980	4,916,686	5.1%
1880	2,168,380	26.0%	1990	5,117,073	4.1%
1890	2,679,185	23.6%	2000	5,595,211	9.3%
1900	3,106,665	16.0%	2010	5,988,927	7.0%
1910	3,293,335	6.0%			

Source: U.S. Census Bureau.

The land that is now the state of Missouri was part of the Louisiana Purchase territory that the United States acquired from France in 1803. Missouri became a major departure point for expeditions and settlers that were heading west, and St. Louis became a major supply point for these parties. As early American settlers moved into Missouri from the South, many brought enslaved African Americans with them. In the 1821 Missouri Compromise, the territory was admitted as a slave state. In the early 1830s, Mormons began to migrate down from northern states and Canada and settle in Missouri. These groups came into conflict with the earlier settlers over religion and slavery before the Mormons were forcibly expelled from the state. As migration increased from the 1830s to 1860s, Missouri's population almost doubled every decade. While most of the new residents were American-born, there were significant Irish and German populations that arrived in the late 1840s and 1850s. These populations were largely Catholic and opposed slavery.

Missouri did not have an especially large enslaved population (in 1860 enslaved African Americans made up less than 10% of the state's population), but there were tensions over slavery within the state and region due to concerns about the future of the state and nation. After the secession of many of the Southern states, the Missouri legislature held a special convention that voted decisively to remain within the Union, but there remained however, still a decent amount of Confederate support within the state.

Over the past century, Missouri has had to adjust to different economies and demographic changes. Moving from a rural economy to an industrial-service-agricultural economy, to 1950s and 1960s deindustrialization, Missouri has had to combat the same economic problems that have faced much of the Midwest.

The five largest ancestry groups in Missouri are German at 27.4%, Irish at 14.8%, English 10.2%, American 8.5%, and French 3.7%. Those who were identified as American included some who reported as Native American or African American, but also European Americans with a long ancestral history in the United States. German Americans have a particularly large presence throughout the state, as do African Americans, particularly in areas were plantation agriculture was once an important part of the region's economy. Kansas City is currently home to a range of large and growing immigrant communities from Latin America, Africa, Southeast Asia, and Eastern Europe. There are particularly large Mexican, Sudanese, Somali, Nigerian, Chinese, Filipino, and Bosnian populations in Missouri in addition to a notable Cherokee Indian population.

The majority of residents of Missouri speak English, while approximately 5.1% of the population reported speaking a language other than English at home. In certain small Latino communities in the St. Louis and Kansas City areas, Spanish is spoken. Missouri is also home to an endangered dialect of French known as Missouri French, spoken by descendants of the French pioneers who settled the area in the late 17th century. Although once very popular in the area, the dialect is quite different from the varieties of Canadian French and Louisiana Creole French and is nearly extinct now, only spoken by a few elderly speakers who call themselves Creoles.

Of those who identify with a religion, three of five Missouri residents are Protestant, and about one of five is Roman Catholic. Certain areas have especially large Catholic communities, dating back to the large influxes of Catholic Irish and German immigrants. In addition to these larges Catholic populations, the St. Louis and Kansas City areas also have important Jewish communities, as well as Hindu and Muslim congregations built by the large numbers of Indian and Pakistani immigrants. According to the American Religious Identification Survey, Missourians identified as 77% Christian, divided into 4% Anglican, 4% Episcopal, 45% Protestant (combined), 19% Roman Catholic, 1% Latter-day Saint, 8% other or unspecified Christian, 2% other religions, 15% not religious, and 5% no answer. The largest denominations in 2000 by number of adherents were the Roman Catholic Church, followed by the Southern Baptist Convention, and the United Methodist Church.

While Missouri retains a relatively large white percentage of its population, the state has a long history of immigrants. From enslaved African Americans who were brought in Missouri, to the Germans and Irish who came to escape famine, oppression, and violence in the 19th century, to the large immigrant populations today from across the continents, Missouri has a history of diverse immigrant populations. Over half of Missouri's population lives within the St. Louis and Kansas City metropolitan areas, and these areas in particular play host to the most lively and dynamic immigrant communities. Migration within the country produced a net increase of 37,638 people.

Population by Selected Ethnic Group

	Estimate		Estimate
Total:	6,063,589	German	1,464,596
Afghan	623	German Russian	488
Albanian	1,898	Greek	12,887
Alsatian	274	Guyanese	347
American	588,873	Hungarian	16,777
Arab:	18,560	Icelander	114
Egyptian	2,079	Iranian	2,323
Iraqi	607	Irish	794,232
Jordanian	314	Israeli	1,498
Lebanese	6,532	Italian	216,503
Moroccan	735	Latvian	426
Palestinian	806	Lithuanian	7,298
Syrian	1,139	Luxemburger	410
Arab	3,341	Macedonian	138
Other Arab	3,038	Maltese	33
Armenian	2,399	New Zealander	91
Assyrian/Chaldean/Syriac	335	Northern European	6,363
Australian	998	Norwegian	41,729
Austrian	12,059	Pennsylvania German	2,052
Basque	113	Polish	110,914
Belgian	6,301	Portuguese	6,428
Brazilian	1,837	Romanian	7,351
British	25,299	Russian	29,816
Bulgarian	1,303	Scandinavian	10,311
Cajun	1,122	Scotch-Irish	63,455
Canadian	6,099	Scottish	102,653
Carpatho-Rusyn	0	Serbian	1,421
Celtic	705	Slavic	1,553
Croatian	11,005	Slovak	4,812
Cypriot	0	Slovene	1,844
Czech	26,754	Soviet Union	110
Czechoslovakian	4,564	Sub-Saharan African:	38,364
Danish	18,297	Cape Verdean	0
Dutch	90,252	Ethiopian	4,186
Eastern European	4,907	Ghanaian	1,139
English	540,499	Kenyan	3,537
Estonian	186	Liberian	1,025
European	79,956	Nigerian	2,124
Finnish	2,481	Senegalese	57
French (except Basque)	183,744	Sierra Leonean	0
French Canadian	16,960	Somali	2,284

(*continued*)

	Estimate			Estimate
South African	274	Belizean		161
Sudanese	1,187	Bermudan		0
Ugandan	187	British West Indian		49
Zimbabwean	63	Dutch West Indian		883
African	21,436	Haitian		1,729
Other sub-Saharan African	1,444	Jamaican		2,625
Swedish	61,110	Trinidadian and Tobagonian		179
Swiss	22,826	U.S. Virgin Islander		8
Turkish	1,052	West Indian		397
Ukrainian	6,493	Other West Indian		184
Welsh	37,906	Yugoslavian		11,563
West Indian	6,811	Other groups		1,583,175
(except Hispanic groups):		Unclassified or not reported		1,289,042
Bahamian	173			
Barbadian	494			

Source: American Community Survey, U.S. Census Bureau, 2014.

See in Neighborhoods Section: The Hill (St. Louis, Missouri); Old Mines, French Enclave (Missouri); St. Louis, German Enclaves (Missouri)

MONTANA

Capital: Helena
Entered Union: November 8, 1889 (41st state)

Montana is the fourth most extensive state by land area but the 44th most populous, with a total population of 989,415. At 6.8 persons per square mile, Montana has the third-lowest population density in the nation. The United States acquired part of the area of Montana from France as part of the Louisiana Purchase in 1803, and it obtained the rest through a treaty with Great Britain in 1846. Montana Territory was organized in 1864 with more or less the present state boundaries and became the 44th state on November 8, 1889. Its capital is Helena. Montana has one congressional district, 50 state senate districts, and 100 state house districts. It borders North and South Dakota to the east, Idaho to the west, and Canada to the north. Portions of Yellowstone National Park are located in southern Montana along the state's border with Wyoming.

According to the 2010 U.S. Census, 89.4% of the population was white (87.8% non-Hispanic white), 6.3% American Indian and Alaska Native, 2.9% Hispanics and Latinos of any race, 0.6% Asian, 0.4% black or African American, 0.1% Native Hawaiian and other Pacific Islander, 0.6% from some other race, and 2.5% from two or more races. The largest European ancestry groups in Montana as of 2010 are German (27.0%), Irish (14.8%), English (12.6%), and Norwegian (10.9%). Montana has a larger Native American population numerically and percentage-wise than most U.S. states. Native people constitute 6.5% of the state's total population, the sixth highest percentage of all 50 states. Montana is home to eight federally recognized American Indian areas.

Historical Population of Montana

Census	Pop.	%±	Census	Pop.	%±
1870	20,595	—	1950	591,024	5.6%
1880	39,159	90.1%	1960	674,767	14.2%
1890	142,924	265.0%	1970	694,409	2.9%
1900	243,329	70.3%	1980	786,690	13.3%
1910	376,053	54.5%	1990	799,065	1.6%
1920	548,889	46.0%	2000	902,195	12.9%
1930	537,606	−2.1%	2010	989,415	9.7%
1940	559,456	4.1%			

Source: U.S. Census Bureau.

While the largest European American population in Montana overall is German, pockets of significant Scandinavian ancestry are prevalent in some of the farming-dominated northern and eastern prairie regions. Many of Montana's historic logging communities originally attracted people of Scottish, Scandinavian, Slavic, English and Scots-Irish descent. The Hutterites, an Anabaptist sect originally from Switzerland, settled here, and today Montana is second only to South Dakota in U.S. Hutterite population, with several colonies spread across the state. Beginning in the mid-1990s, the state also saw an influx of Amish, who relocated to Montana from the increasingly urbanized areas of Ohio and Pennsylvania. Montana's Hispanic population is concentrated around the Billings area in south-central Montana, and Great Falls has the highest percentage of African Americans. The Chinese in Montana, while a low percentage today, have historically been an important presence. At least 2,000 Chinese miners were in the mining areas of Montana by 1870, and 2,500 in 1890. However, public opinion grew increasingly negative toward them in the 1890s, and nearly half of the state's Asian population left by 1900.

According to the 2000 U.S. Census, 94.8% of the population aged five and older speaks English at home. Spanish is the language most commonly spoken at home other than English. There were about 13,040 Spanish-language speakers in the state (1.4% of the population) in 2011. There were also 15,438 (1.7% of the state population) speakers of Indo-European languages other than English or Spanish, 10,154 (1.1%) speakers of a Native American language, and 4,052 (0.4%) speakers of an Asian or Pacific Islander language.

According to the Pew Forum, the religious affiliations of the people of Montana are as follows: Protestant 47%, Catholic 23%, Mormon 5%, Jewish 0.5%, Jehovah's Witness 2%, Muslim 0.5%, Buddhist 1%, Hindu 0.5%, and nonreligious at 20%.

Population by Selected Ethnic Group

	Estimate		Estimate
Total:	1,023,579	French Canadian	7,665
Afghan	0	German	265,797
Albanian	0	German Russian	16
Alsatian	0	Greek	1,594
American	71,395	Guyanese	33
Arab:	2,042	Hungarian	3,825
Egyptian	256	Icelander	338
Iraqi	163	Iranian	625
Jordanian	0	Irish	134,761
Lebanese	1,144	Israeli	157
Moroccan	0	Italian	33,546
Palestinian	29	Latvian	111
Syrian	58	Lithuanian	690
Arab	236	Luxemburger	172
Other Arab	156	Macedonian	249
Armenian	295	Maltese	0
Assyrian/Chaldean/Syriac	0	New Zealander	74
Australian	61	Northern European	2,421
Austrian	4,264	Norwegian	95,271
Basque	1,339	Pennsylvania German	474
Belgian	1,726	Polish	16,159
Brazilian	298	Portuguese	2,204
British	3,607	Romanian	828
Bulgarian	116	Russian	11,080
Cajun	246	Scandinavian	5,858
Canadian	1,991	Scotch-Irish	15,495
Carpatho-Rusyn	0	Scottish	29,794
Celtic	370	Serbian	1,177
Croatian	2,635	Slavic	1,022
Cypriot	0	Slovak	2,023
Czech	9,331	Slovene	641
Czechoslovakian	1,058	Soviet Union	12
Danish	13,306	Sub-Saharan African:	1,345
Dutch	22,188	Cape Verdean	0
Eastern European	760	Ethiopian	97
English	112,967	Ghanaian	0
Estonian	189	Kenyan	132
European	17,809	Liberian	0
Finnish	6,160	Nigerian	80
French (except Basque)	33,982	Senegalese	0

(continued)

	Estimate		Estimate
Sierra Leonean	0	Bahamian	0
Somali	0	Barbadian	0
South African	163	Belizean	191
Sudanese	0	Bermudan	0
Ugandan	0	British West Indian	0
Zimbabwean	0	Dutch West Indian	0
African	851	Haitian	0
Other sub-Saharan African	22	Jamaican	152
Swedish	27,086	Trinidadian and Tobagonian	0
Swiss	4,163	U.S. Virgin Islander	0
Turkish	448	West Indian	400
Ukrainian	2,192	Other West Indian	0
Welsh	7,826	Yugoslavian	2,035
West Indian (except Hispanic groups):	743	Other groups	186,184
		Unclassified or not reported	179,488

Source: American Community Survey, U.S. Census Bureau, 2014.

See in Neighborhoods Section: Butte, Irish Americans (Montana)

NEBRASKA

Capital: Lincoln
Entered Union: March 1, 1867 (37th state)

Nebraska is the 15th-largest state by land area and the 38th most populous. The state capital is Lincoln, and it continues to grow as the state experiences a "rural flight" phenomenon. The United States acquired the area of Nebraska from France as part of the Louisiana Purchase in 1803. A portion of the large Missouri Territory was organized into the Nebraska Territory in 1854. At the time, Nebraska Territory included almost all of present-day Nebraska and parts of Colorado, Montana, North Dakota, and South Dakota. When Colorado and Dakota territories were organized in 1861, the size of Nebraska Territory shrank significantly. Nebraska became the 37th state on March 1, 1867. It has three congressional districts, seven federally recognized American Indian areas, and a unicameral state legislature with 49 state senate districts. Nebraska borders six other states: Colorado, Iowa, Kansas, Missouri, South Dakota, and Wyoming.

As of the 2010 U.S. Census, Nebraska's total population is 1,826,341. It is the eighth most sparsely populated state in the nation, with 23.8 persons per square mile. Nebraska's most populated city is Omaha, which has 408,958 inhabitants. According to same census, 86.1% of the population is white (82.1% non-Hispanic white), 4.5% is black or African American, 1.0% American Indian and Alaska Native,

1.8% Asian, 0.1% Native Hawaiian and other Pacific Islander, and 2.2% identify with two or more races, while 9.2% of the total population is of Hispanic or Latino origin.

Historical Population of Nebraska

Census	Pop.	%±	Census	Pop.	%±
1860	28,841	—	1940	1,315,834	−4.5%
1870	122,993	326.5%	1950	1,325,510	0.7%
1880	452,402	267.8%	1960	1,411,330	6.5%
1890	1,062,656	134.9%	1970	1,483,493	5.1%
1900	1,066,300	0.3%	1980	1,569,825	5.8%
1910	1,192,214	11.8%	1990	1,578,385	0.5%
1920	1,296,372	8.7%	2000	1,711,263	8.4%
1930	1,377,963	6.3%	2010	1,826,341	6.7%

Source: U.S. Census Bureau.

Ethnically, the largest group of Nebraskans is the German American population. The state also has the largest per capita population of Czech Americans among U.S. states. More specifically, the five largest ancestry groups in Nebraska are German (38.6%), Irish (12.4%), English (9.6%), Mexican (8.7%), and Czech (5.5%). As of 2004, 4.8% of the population of Nebraska was foreign-born.

The religious affiliations of the people of Nebraska are Catholic (28%), Lutheran (16%), Methodist (11%), Baptist (9%), Presbyterian (4%), other Protestant (21%), other Christian (1%), nonreligious (9%), and other religions (1%). The largest denominations by number of adherents in 2010 were the Roman Catholic Church (372,838), the Lutheran Church—Missouri Synod (112,585), the Evangelical Lutheran Church in America (110,110), and the United Methodist Church (109,283).

The 2000 U.S. Census found that the population of Nebraska that was five years or older spoke the following languages at home: English (92.1%), Spanish (4.9%), German (0.6%), Vietnamese (0.4%), other Slavic languages (0.3%), French (0.2%), Chinese (0.2%), Arabic (0.1%), Russian (0.1%), African languages (0.1%), Polish (0.1%), Italian (0.1%), Tagalog (0.1%), and Japanese (0.1%).

Population by Selected Ethnic Group

	Estimate		Estimate
Total:	1,881,503	Arab:	7,773
Afghan	450	Egyptian	367
Albanian	151	Iraqi	1,423
Alsatian	23	Jordanian	0
American	74,796	Lebanese	1,724

(continued)

	Estimate		Estimate
Moroccan	47	Latvian	650
Palestinian	156	Lithuanian	3,452
Syrian	753	Luxemburger	1,239
Arab	2,478	Macedonian	25
Other Arab	865	Maltese	65
Armenian	415	New Zealander	0
Assyrian/Chaldean/Syriac	0	Northern European	2,016
Australian	464	Norwegian	34,633
Austrian	3,549	Pennsylvania German	1,163
Basque	0	Polish	67,456
Belgian	2,241	Portuguese	1,392
Brazilian	770	Romanian	972
British	4,849	Russian	12,122
Bulgarian	40	Scandinavian	4,103
Cajun	334	Scotch-Irish	13,580
Canadian	1,806	Scottish	24,337
Carpatho-Rusyn	183	Serbian	845
Celtic	171	Slavic	607
Croatian	1,829	Slovak	1,291
Cypriot	73	Slovene	472
Czech	91,814	Soviet Union	0
Czechoslovakian	6,264	Sub-Saharan African:	17,002
Danish	37,631	Cape Verdean	0
Dutch	37,311	Ethiopian	369
Eastern European	717	Ghanaian	177
English	137,905	Kenyan	284
Estonian	127	Liberian	0
European	15,287	Nigerian	1,081
Finnish	1,487	Senegalese	58
French (except Basque)	43,023	Sierra Leonean	0
French Canadian	4,656	Somali	2,376
German	676,834	South African	185
German Russian	541	Sudanese	3,202
Greek	3,375	Ugandan	42
Guyanese	0	Zimbabwean	56
Hungarian	2,234	African	8,689
Icelander	230	Other sub-Saharan African	631
Iranian	867	Swedish	75,488
Irish	259,783	Swiss	6,472
Israeli	198	Turkish	795
Italian	51,221	Ukrainian	2,246

(continued)

	Estimate		Estimate
Welsh	10,407	Haitian	206
West Indian	1,409	Jamaican	738
(except Hispanic groups):		Trinidadian and Tobagonian	32
Bahamian	0	U.S. Virgin Islander	0
Barbadian	0	West Indian	301
Belizean	9	Other West Indian	0
Bermudan	58	Yugoslavian	1,916
British West Indian	65	Other groups	392,982
Dutch West Indian	0	Unclassified or not reported	310,540

Source: American Community Survey, U.S. Census Bureau, 2014.

See in Neighborhoods Section: Greek Town (Omaha, Nebraska); Little Bohemia (Omaha, Nebraska); Little Italy (Omaha, Nebraska); Sheeley Town and Little Poland (Omaha, Nebraska)

NEVADA

Capital: Carson City
Entered Union: October 31, 1864 (36th state)

While the Navajo Nation is spread primarily through Arizona, New Mexico, and Utah, there are populations in Nevada as well. (Feije Riemersma/Dreamstime.com)

Nevada is the seventh-largest state by area, and the 35th most populous with 2,700,551 total inhabitants. At 24.6 persons per square mile, it is the ninth least densely populated state. Prior to European contact, Native Americans of the Paiute, Shoshone, and Washoe tribes inhabited the area that is now Nevada. The first Europeans who explored the region were the Spaniards, who gave it the name of Nevada. The United States acquired the area from Mexico in 1848 under the Treaty of Guadalupe Hidalgo at the end of the Mexican-American War. Nevada Territory was organized from the western part of Utah Territory in 1861, with further additions in 1862. In the midst of the Civil War, Nevada was admitted to the Union on October 31, 1864, as the 36th state. In 1866, additional territory was cobbled from Utah and Arizona territories, at which point Nevada more or less assumed its modern boundaries. The capital of Nevada is Carson City, located in the west near the California border. Nevada has four congressional districts, 19 senatorial districts, and 42 assembly districts. There are 28 federally recognized American Indian areas in the state.

Nevada is known for its libertarian laws. Establishment of legalized gambling and lenient marriage and divorce proceedings in the 20th century transformed Nevada into a major tourist destination. From about the 1940s until 2003, Nevada was the fastest-growing state in the United States. Today, nearly three-quarters of the state's 2,700,551 inhabitants live in Clark County, which contains the Las Vegas–Paradise metropolitan area.

Historical Population of Nevada

Census	Pop.	%±	Census	Pop.	%±
1860	6,857	—	1940	110,247	21.1%
1870	42,941	526.2%	1950	160,083	45.2%
1880	62,266	45.0%	1960	285,278	78.2%
1890	47,355	23.9%	1970	488,738	71.3%
1900	42,335	10.6%	1980	800,493	63.8%
1910	81,875	93.4%	1990	1,201,833	50.1%
1920	77,407	5.5%	2000	1,998,257	66.3%
1930	91,058	17.6%	2010	2,700,551	35.1%

Source: U.S. Census Bureau.

People in rural counties tend to be native Nevada residents, unlike in the Las Vegas and Reno areas, where the vast majority of the population was born in another state. The rural population is also less diverse in terms of race and ethnicity. According to the 2010 U.S. Census, racial distribution is as follows: 66.2% white American, 8.1% African American, 1.2% American Indian and Alaska Native, 7.2% Asian American, 0.6% Native Hawaiian and other Pacific Islander, 4.7% multiracial American, and 12.0% some other race. Hispanics or Latinos of any race constitute 26.5% of the population.

The principal ancestries of Nevada's residents in 2009 were 20.8% Mexican, 13.3% German, 10.0% Irish, 9.2% English, 6.3% Italian, 3.8% American, and 3.6% Scandinavian (1.4% Norwegian, 1.4% Swedish, and 0.8% Danish). Nevada is home to many cultures and nationalities. As of 2011, 63.6% of Nevadans under age one were minorities, and Las Vegas is now a minority majority city. In the 1990s and the early 20th century, Las Vegas was a major destination for immigrants from South Asia and Latin America seeking employment in the gaming and hospitality industries, but farming and construction are the biggest employers of immigrant labor.

According to the 2000 U.S. Census, 16.19% of Nevada's population aged five and older speaks Spanish at home, while 1.59% speaks Tagalog and 1% speaks Chinese languages.

Church attendance in Nevada is among the lowest of all U.S. states. Major religious affiliations of the people of Nevada are Roman Catholic 27%, Protestant 26%, Latter-day Saint/ Mormon 11%, Muslim 2%, Jewish 1%, Hindu 1%, and Buddhist 0.5%. The unaffiliated category accounts for 20%.

Population by Selected Ethnic Group

	Estimate		Estimate
Total:	2,839,099	Bulgarian	3,670
Afghan	481	Cajun	177
Albanian	437	Canadian	7,810
Alsatian	0	Carpatho-Rusyn	0
American	143,522	Celtic	786
Arab:	16,972	Croatian	2,399
Egyptian	2,055	Cypriot	109
Iraqi	433	Czech	8,342
Jordanian	1,946	Czechoslovakian	2,408
Lebanese	6,455	Danish	17,073
Moroccan	853	Dutch	33,021
Palestinian	127	Eastern European	2,813
Syrian	1,312	English	189,486
Arab	1,425	Estonian	217
Other Arab	2,502	European	35,327
Armenian	4,221	Finnish	4,832
Assyrian/Chaldean/Syriac	226	French (except Basque)	55,953
Australian	865	French Canadian	12,627
Austrian	5,441	German	321,866
Basque	3,588	German Russian	122
Belgian	1,663	Greek	11,253
Brazilian	3,130	Guyanese	87
British	10,762	Hungarian	10,425

(*continued*)

	Estimate		Estimate
Icelander	1,286	Nigerian	497
Iranian	7,083	Senegalese	0
Irish	254,390	Sierra Leonean	0
Israeli	1,525	Somali	369
Italian	167,174	South African	530
Latvian	122	Sudanese	0
Lithuanian	6,225	Ugandan	412
Luxemburger	424	Zimbabwean	40
Macedonian	125	African	14,326
Maltese	216	Other sub-Saharan African	885
New Zealander	154	Swedish	33,696
Northern European	1,410	Swiss	8,248
Norwegian	37,853	Turkish	2,172
Pennsylvania German	631	Ukrainian	5,488
Polish	62,796	Welsh	15,609
Portuguese	13,613	West Indian	6,318
Romanian	4,225	(except Hispanic groups):	
Russian	25,869	Bahamian	0
Scandinavian	5,152	Barbadian	364
Scotch-Irish	16,022	Belizean	484
Scottish	44,760	Bermudan	208
Serbian	2,721	British West Indian	247
Slavic	608	Dutch West Indian	165
Slovak	2,889	Haitian	717
Slovene	950	Jamaican	3,099
Soviet Union	0	Trinidadian and Tobagonian	291
Sub-Saharan African:	25,215	U.S. Virgin Islander	57
Cape Verdean	55	West Indian	849
Ethiopian	7,434	Other West Indian	40
Ghanaian	301	Yugoslavian	3,138
Kenyan	390	Other groups	1,413,033
Liberian	307	Unclassified or not reported	347,787

Source: American Community Survey, U.S. Census Bureau, 2014.

NEW HAMPSHIRE

Capital: Concord
Entered Union: June 21, 1788 (9th state)

Prior to European settlement, various Algonquian (Abenaki and Pennacook) tribes inhabited the area of New Hampshire. English and French explorers visited

New Hampshire in 1600–1605, and English fishermen settled at Odiorne's Point in present-day Rye in 1623. The area of New Hampshire was originally included in the Charter of New England in 1620, and a separate grant established the colony of New Hampshire in 1629. In 1641, the area reunited with Massachusetts, and it separated and reunited several times until it assumed a separate provincial government in 1741. New Hampshire ratified the U.S. Constitution on June 21, 1788; it was the ninth of the original 13 states to join the Union. The state's boundary with Canada was formally established in 1842, when New Hampshire assumed generally the same boundary as the present state. New Hampshire also borders Maine, Massachusetts, and Vermont.

New Hampshire has a total population of 1,316,470 and has the ninth-smallest population of any state. Concord is the capital, while Manchester is the largest city, with 109,565 inhabitants. New Hampshire has two congressional districts, 24 state senate districts, and 103 state house districts. It is the seventh-smallest state by land area.

Historical Population of New Hampshire

Census	Pop.	%±	Census	Pop.	%±
1790	141,885	—	1910	430,572	4.6%
1800	183,858	29.6%	1920	443,083	2.9%
1810	214,460	16.6%	1930	465,293	5.0%
1820	244,155	13.8%	1940	491,524	5.6%
1830	269,328	10.3%	1950	533,242	8.5%
1840	284,574	5.7%	1960	606,921	13.8%
1850	317,976	11.7%	1970	737,681	21.5%
1860	326,073	2.5%	1980	920,610	24.8%
1870	318,300	−2.4%	1990	1,109,252	20.5%
1880	346,991	9.0%	2000	1,235,786	11.4%
1890	376,530	8.5%	2010	1,316,470	6.5%
1900	411,588	9.3%			

Source: U.S. Census Bureau.

According to the 2010 U.S. Census, the racial makeup of New Hampshire is as follows: 93.9% white American (92.3% non-Hispanic white, 1.6% white Hispanic), 2.2% Asian American, 1.1% black or African American, 0.2% Native American/American Indian, 1.6% two or more races, 1.0% some other race. Hispanic and Latino Americans of any race made up 2.8% of the population in 2010. The largest ancestry groups in New Hampshire are, per 2011 U.S. Census Bureau estimates: 23.2% French and French Canadian, 21.5% Irish, 17.9% English, 9.9% Italian, 9.3% German, 6.1% American, 4.6% Scottish, 4.5% Polish, 2.1% Swedish, 1.4% Greek, 1.3% Portuguese, 1.1% Scots-Irish, and 1.0% Dutch. The large Irish American and French Canadian populations are descended largely from mill workers, and many still live in the former mill towns, like Manchester.

Of the population five years of age and older, 3.41% speaks French at home, while 1.60% speaks Spanish. In Coös County, 16% of the population speaks French at home.

A Pew survey showed that the religious affiliations of the people of New Hampshire are Protestant 34%, Catholic 29%, LDS (Mormon) 1%, Jewish 1%, Jehovah's Witness 0.5%, Muslim 0.5%, Buddhist 1%, Hindu 0.5%, and nonreligious 26%. In 2012, 23% of New Hampshire residents responding to a Gallup poll considered themselves "very religious," while 52% considered themselves "nonreligious." According to the Association of Religion Data Archives (ARDA), the largest denominations are the Roman Catholic Church with 311,028 members; the United Church of Christ with 26,321 members; and the United Methodist Church with 18,029 members.

Population by Selected Ethnic Group

	Estimate		Estimate
Total:	1,326,813	Carpatho-Rusyn	0
Afghan	0	Celtic	554
Albanian	442	Croatian	656
Alsatian	113	Cypriot	50
American	70,542	Czech	2,345
Arab:	9,640	Czechoslovakian	1,284
Egyptian	773	Danish	3,793
Iraqi	537	Dutch	14,738
Jordanian	0	Eastern European	1,519
Lebanese	5,744	English	226,643
Moroccan	741	Estonian	380
Palestinian	68	European	16,218
Syrian	631	Finnish	8,166
Arab	601	French (except Basque)	200,065
Other Arab	687	French Canadian	113,227
Armenian	3,696	German	124,394
Assyrian/Chaldean/Syriac	0	German Russian	0
Australian	624	Greek	18,585
Austrian	3,286	Guyanese	0
Basque	0	Hungarian	4,167
Belgian	2,119	Icelander	44
Brazilian	2,973	Iranian	798
British	6,846	Irish	277,088
Bulgarian	455	Israeli	0
Cajun	65	Italian	143,017
Canadian	17,046	Latvian	338

(continued)

	Estimate		Estimate
Lithuanian	7,495	Somali	4
Luxemburger	147	South African	447
Macedonian	90	Sudanese	133
Maltese	545	Ugandan	0
New Zealander	107	Zimbabwean	634
Northern European	682	African	1,973
Norwegian	10,608	Other sub-Saharan African	2,129
Pennsylvania German	577	Swedish	24,523
Polish	56,118	Swiss	4,075
Portuguese	19,390	Turkish	1,414
Romanian	2,962	Ukrainian	3,852
Russian	10,784	Welsh	9,665
Scandinavian	2,486	West Indian	2,535
Scotch-Irish	14,322	(except Hispanic groups):	
Scottish	52,799	Bahamian	0
Serbian	251	Barbadian	47
Slavic	291	Belizean	79
Slovak	1,510	Bermudan	44
Slovene	246	British West Indian	0
Soviet Union	0	Dutch West Indian	0
Sub-Saharan African:	6,923	Haitian	1,307
Cape Verdean	294	Jamaican	942
Ethiopian	314	Trinidadian and Tobagonian	5
Ghanaian	48	U.S. Virgin Islander	0
Kenyan	583	West Indian	158
Liberian	117	Other West Indian	0
Nigerian	596	Yugoslavian	1,918
Senegalese	0	Other groups	172,340
Sierra Leonean	0	Unclassified or not reported	167,869

Source: American Community Survey, U.S. Census Bureau, 2014.

See in Neighborhoods Section: Manchester, French Canadian Enclave (New Hampshire)

NEW JERSEY

Capital: Trenton
Entered Union: December 18, 1787 (3rd state)

New Jersey is the fourth-smallest state, but the 11th most populous, and it is the most densely populated state. It is also the second wealthiest U.S. state by median household income, according to the 2008–2012 American Community Survey. Trenton is the state capital, while Newark is its largest city, and New York City is its largest metropolitan area. New Jersey has 12 congressional districts and borders Delaware, New York, and Pennsylvania.

Native Americans inhabited the area for more than 2,800 years, with historical tribes such as the Lenape along the coast. In the early 17th century, the Dutch and the Swedes made the first European settlements. The English later seized control of the region, naming it the Province of New Jersey. On December 18, 1787, it became the third state to ratify the U.S. Constitution. New Jersey's geographic location at the center of the Northeast megalopolis, between Boston and New York City to the northeast, and Philadelphia, Baltimore, and Washington, D.C., to the southwest, fueled its rapid growth through the process of suburbanization in the 1950s and beyond.

Historical Population of New Jersey

Census	Pop.	%±	Census	Pop.	%±
1790	184,139	—	1910	2,537,167	34.7%
1800	211,149	14.7%	1920	3,155,900	24.4%
1810	245,562	16.3%	1930	4,041,334	28.1%
1820	277,575	13.0%	1940	4,160,165	2.9%
1830	320,823	15.6%	1950	4,835,329	16.2%
1840	373,306	16.4%	1960	6,066,782	25.5%
1850	489,555	31.1%	1970	7,168,164	18.2%
1860	672,035	37.3%	1980	7,364,823	2.7%
1870	906,096	34.8%	1990	7,730,188	5.0%
1880	1,131,116	24.8%	2000	8,414,350	8.9%
1890	1,444,933	27.7%	2010	8,791,894	4.5%
1900	1,883,669	30.4%			

Source: U.S. Census Bureau.

According to the 2010 U.S. Census, there are 8,791,894 people residing in the state, of which 68.6% are white American, 13.7% African American, 0.3% Native American, 8.3% Asian American, 6.4% from other races, and 2.7% identifying as multiracial. Hispanics or Latinos (of any race) comprise 17.7% of the population. Non-Hispanic whites were 58.9% of the population in 2011, down from 85% in 1970, and in 2010, undocumented immigrants constituted an estimated 6.4% of the population. As of 2005, 19.2% of the population was foreign-born. New Jersey is one of the most ethnically and religiously diverse states in the country. It has been alleged to have more scientists and engineers per square mile than anywhere else in the world.

According to the 2000 U.S. Census, New Jersey has the second-largest Jewish population by percentage (after New York); the second-largest Muslim population by percentage (after Michigan); the largest population of Peruvian Americans in the United States; the largest population of Cubans outside of Florida; the third highest Asian population by percentage; and the third highest Italian population by percentage. African Americans, Hispanics, Arabs, and Brazilian and Portuguese Americans are also numerous. The five largest ethnic groups in 2000 were Italian (17.9%), Irish (15.9%), African (13.6%), German (12.6%), and Polish (6.9%).

As of 2010, 71.31% of New Jersey residents age five and older spoke English at home as a primary language, while 14.59% spoke Spanish, 1.23% Chinese (which includes Cantonese and Mandarin), 1.06% Italian, 1.06% Portuguese, 0.96% Tagalog, and 0.89% Korean.

In 2001, the distribution of religions in New Jersey was 37% Catholic, 15% none, 8% Baptist, 6% Methodist, 5% refused to identify, 2% Jewish (5.7% in 2012), 4% other, 4% Presbyterian, 3% Lutheran, 2% Episcopalian/Anglican, 2% other Protestant, 1% Jehovah's Witnesses, 1% Mormon, and 1% Muslim/Islamic. In 2010, the largest denominations in New Jersey were the Roman Catholic Church with 3,235,290; Islam with 160,666; and the United Methodist Church with 138,052, according to the Association of Religion Data Archives.

Population by Selected Ethnic Group

	Estimate		Estimate
Total:	8,938,175	Brazilian	33,867
Afghan	2,273	British	20,618
Albanian	12,703	Bulgarian	3,513
Alsatian	687	Cajun	205
American	367,425	Canadian	14,027
Arab:	97,357	Carpatho-Rusyn	511
Egyptian	40,285	Celtic	992
Iraqi	661	Croatian	11,179
Jordanian	7,359	Cypriot	602
Lebanese	9,767	Czech	27,154
Moroccan	5,756	Czechoslovakian	11,255
Palestinian	7,347	Danish	17,003
Syrian	11,967	Dutch	96,890
Arab	10,572	Eastern European	32,221
Other Arab	6,897	English	430,333
Armenian	15,284	Estonian	1,543
Assyrian/Chaldean/Syriac	1,744	European	47,746
Australian	4,044	Finnish	5,646
Austrian	36,521	French (except Basque)	108,638
Basque	581	French Canadian	20,210
Belgian	5,949	German	937,219

(continued)

	Estimate			Estimate
German Russian	579		Kenyan	3,249
Greek	67,953		Liberian	4,864
Guyanese	18,311		Nigerian	16,708
Hungarian	90,087		Senegalese	827
Icelander	769		Sierra Leonean	1,114
Iranian	11,383		Somali	0
Irish	1,243,989		South African	1,629
Israeli	11,707		Sudanese	51
Italian	1,424,568		Ugandan	1,025
Latvian	5,154		Zimbabwean	0
Lithuanian	31,611		African	38,429
Luxemburger	160		Other sub-Saharan African	5,895
Macedonian	8,215		Swedish	50,952
Maltese	1,059		Swiss	16,058
New Zealander	368		Turkish	23,268
Northern European	2,920		Ukrainian	73,018
Norwegian	43,241		Welsh	30,545
Pennsylvania German	6,342		West Indian	159,341
Polish	509,388		(except Hispanic groups):	
Portuguese	72,824		Bahamian	1,891
Romanian	16,821		Barbadian	2,726
Russian	163,542		Belizean	1,247
Scandinavian	5,515		Bermudan	227
Scotch-Irish	35,402		British West Indian	5,466
Scottish	86,211		Dutch West Indian	298
Serbian	4,440		Haitian	59,731
Slavic	6,581		Jamaican	64,365
Slovak	36,438		Trinidadian and Tobagonian	14,533
Slovene	1,983		U.S. Virgin Islander	197
Soviet Union	480		West Indian	10,510
Sub-Saharan African:	86,315		Other West Indian	132
Cape Verdean	1,254		Yugoslavian	6,577
Ethiopian	1,587		Other groups	3,515,504
Ghanaian	11,420		Unclassified or not reported	931,597

Source: American Community Survey, U.S. Census Bureau, 2014.

See in Neighborhoods Section: Bergen County, Korean Enclaves (New Jersey); Ironbound and the Wards (Newark, New Jersey); Little Havana on the Hudson (North Hudson, New Jersey); Little India, Newark Avenue (Jersey City, New Jersey); Little Lima (Paterson, New Jersey)

NEW MEXICO

Capital: Santa Fe
Entered Union: January 6, 1912 (47th state)

New Mexico is the fifth most extensive and the 36th most populous state, with a total population of 2,059,179. At 17 persons per square mile, it is the sixth least densely populated of the 50 U.S. states. The state capital is Santa Fe, and the largest city is Albuquerque, with 545,852 inhabitants. Indigenous peoples of the Americas populated the area for many centuries before European exploration. New Mexico subsequently became part of the Imperial Spanish Viceroyalty of New Spain and then part of Mexico. The United States acquired most of the area of New Mexico in 1848 at the end of the Mexican-American War. New Mexico Territory was organized from the acquired area in 1850 and included most of present-day Arizona and New Mexico as well as parts of Colorado and Nevada. The territory was reduced with the organization of Colorado Territory in 1861 and Arizona Territory in 1863, at which point New Mexico assumed generally the same boundary as the present state. New Mexico became the 47th U.S. state in 1912. It has three congressional districts and 23 federally recognized American Indian reservations.

Historical Population of New Mexico

Census	Pop.	%±	Census	Pop.	%±
1850	61,547	—	1940	531,818	25.6%
1860	93,516	51.9%	1950	681,187	28.1%
1870	91,874	−1,87	1960	951,023	39.6%
1880	119,565	30.1%	1970	1,017,055	6.9%
1890	160,282	34.1%	1980	1,303,302	28.1%
1900	195,310	21.9%	1990	1,515,069	16.2%
1910	327,301	67.6%	2000	1,819,046	20.1%
1920	360,350	10.1%	2010	2,059,179	13.2%
1930	423,317	17.5%			

Source: U.S. Census Bureau.

Among U.S. states, New Mexico has the highest percentage of Hispanics, including descendants of Spanish colonists and recent immigrants from Latin America. It also has the second highest percentage of Native Americans, including the Navajo, Puebloan, and Apache peoples. For these reasons, the state's demographics and culture are unique for their strong Hispanic and Native American influences, both of which are reflected in the state flag.

Of the people residing in New Mexico, 51.4% were born in New Mexico, 37.9% were born in a different U.S. state, 1.1% were born in Puerto Rico, U.S. Island areas, or born abroad to American parent(s), and 9.7% were foreign-born. The U.S.

The mission-style Catholic churches of New Mexico are testaments to the lasting influence of Spanish culture. (Bryan Busovicki/Dreamstime.com)

Census Bureau estimates the racial composition of the population in 2012 was 83.2% white American, 2.4% black or African American, 10.2% American Indian and Alaska Native, 1.6% Asian, 0.2% Native Hawaiian and other Pacific Islander, and 2.4% two or more races. Ethnically, 47.0% of the total population was of Hispanic or Latino descent.

According to the 2000 U.S. Census, the most commonly claimed ancestry groups in New Mexico were Mexican (16.3%), American Indian (10.3%), German (9.8%), Spanish (9.3%), and English (7.2%).

According the 2000 U.S. Census, 28.76% of the population aged five and older speak Spanish at home, while 4.07% speak Navajo. Speakers of New Mexican Spanish dialect are mainly descendants of Spanish colonists who arrived in New Mexico in the 16th, 17th, and 18th centuries. The original state constitution of 1912 provided for a bilingual government with laws published in both English and Spanish; this requirement was renewed twice, in 1931 and 1943. Nonetheless, the constitution does not declare any language as "official."

According to Association of Religion Data Archives (ARDA), the largest denominations in 2010 were the Catholic Church, the Southern Baptist Convention, the Church of Jesus Christ of Latter-day Saints, and the United Methodist Church. According to a 2008 survey by the Pew Research Center, the most common self-reported religious affiliation of New Mexico residents are Roman Catholic (42%), Protestant (30%), Mormon (3%), Jewish (2%), Buddhist (2%), other religion (3%), and unaffiliated (22%).

Population by Selected Ethnic Group

	Estimate		Estimate
Total:	2,085,572	French Canadian	7,357
Afghan	957	German	184,253
Albanian	71	German Russian	0
Alsatian	65	Greek	5,859
American	89,182	Guyanese	62
Arab:	7,522	Hungarian	4,541
Egyptian	1,161	Icelander	84
Iraqi	2,178	Iranian	630
Jordanian	263	Irish	131,833
Lebanese	2,395	Israeli	167
Moroccan	0	Italian	48,387
Palestinian	84	Latvian	393
Syrian	193	Lithuanian	1,892
Arab	813	Luxemburger	116
Other Arab	435	Macedonian	180
Armenian	1,660	Maltese	0
Assyrian/Chaldean/Syriac	0	New Zealander	336
Australian	639	Northern European	3,318
Austrian	3,600	Norwegian	18,340
Basque	2,032	Pennsylvania German	685
Belgian	1,523	Polish	24,833
Brazilian	967	Portuguese	1,741
British	7,916	Romanian	981
Bulgarian	511	Russian	7,701
Cajun	1,378	Scandinavian	4,414
Canadian	1,495	Scotch-Irish	15,220
Carpatho-Rusyn	77	Scottish	31,634
Celtic	1,335	Serbian	653
Croatian	1,112	Slavic	527
Cypriot	76	Slovak	1,092
Czech	4,306	Slovene	536
Czechoslovakian	1,439	Soviet Union	0
Danish	6,911	Sub-Saharan African:	5,521
Dutch	17,921	Cape Verdean	0
Eastern European	2,688	Ethiopian	225
English	117,720	Ghanaian	589
Estonian	0	Kenyan	174
European	33,617	Liberian	90
Finnish	1,201	Nigerian	1,433
French (except Basque)	31,029	Senegalese	0

(continued)

	Estimate		Estimate
Sierra Leonean	0	Bahamian	0
Somali	0	Barbadian	0
South African	168	Belizean	20
Sudanese	57	Bermudan	92
Ugandan	240	British West Indian	0
Zimbabwean	0	Dutch West Indian	441
African	2,364	Haitian	26
Other sub-Saharan African	181	Jamaican	1,299
Swedish	15,589	Trinidadian and Tobagonian	0
Swiss	4,289	U.S. Virgin Islander	0
Turkish	472	West Indian	260
Ukrainian	1,726	Other West Indian	0
Welsh	11,737	Yugoslavian	960
West Indian (except Hispanic groups):	2,138	Other groups	1,267,319
		Unclassified or not reported	257,580

Source: American Community Survey, U.S. Census Bureau, 2014.

See in Neighborhoods Section: Gallup, Palestinian Enclave (New Mexico)

NEW YORK

Capital: Albany
Entered Union: July 26, 1788 (11th state)

The state of New York has a total population of 19,378,102, the third largest in the nation. With 411.2 persons per square mile, it is the seventh most densely populated state. New York was much larger when originally chartered in 1664. Over the years, portions have been ceded to create the Northwest Territory, New Jersey, Delaware, and Pennsylvania. New York ratified the U.S. Constitution on July 26, 1788, becoming the 11th of the original 13 states. New York has 27 congressional districts, 62 state senate districts, and 150 assembly districts. In addition to an international border with Canada, it borders six states: Connecticut, Massachusetts, New Jersey, Pennsylvania, Rhode Island, and Vermont.

New York has the second-largest foreign-born population behind California. According to a 2008 estimate, over 4 million immigrants lived in or near New York City. The non-Hispanic white population, which was 94.6% in 1940, has declined dramatically to 58.3% in 2010. As of 2011, 55.6% of children under age one were born to minorities.

Historical Population of New York

Census	Pop.	%±	Census	Pop.	%±
1790	340,120	—	1910	9,113,614	25.4%
1800	589,051	73.2%	1920	10,385,227	14.0%
1810	959,049	62.8%	1930	12,588,066	21.2%
1820	1,372,812	43.1%	1940	13,479,142	7.1%
1830	1,918,608	39.8%	1950	14,830,192	10.0%
1840	2,428,921	26.6%	1960	16,782,304	13.2%
1850	3,097,394	27.5%	1970	18,236,967	8.7%
1860	3,880,735	25.3%	1980	17,558,072	−3.7%
1870	4,382,759	12.9%	1990	17,990,455	2.5%
1880	5,082,871	16.0%	2000	18,976,457	5.5%
1890	6,003,174	18.1%	2010	19,378,102	2.1%
1900	7,268,894	21.1%			

Source: U.S. Census Bureau.

New York City has registered the highest population of any city in the United States since 1790. It was estimated that in 2012, New York City had grown to a record high of 8.4 million people.

To a large extent, the arrival of multiple and diverse immigrant groups has driven its growth. New York City has the greatest metropolitan population of Chinese in the U.S., as well as the largest populations of Puerto Ricans, Dominicans, and Jamaicans in the United States.

The New York City neighborhood of Harlem has been the historic African American cultural capital and is exceeded in the size of its black population only by Bedford-Stuyvesant in Brooklyn and the south side of Chicago.

New York City has large populations of white ancestry groups. Large concentrations of Italian Americans are in Brooklyn, Staten Island, and the Bronx. Descendants of Irish immigrants who came after the Irish Potato Famine of the 1840s can be found throughout New York City. Jews descended primarily from Eastern European and Russian immigrants are in Manhattan and Brooklyn. The Jewish population, historically the largest in any state, is on the rise. This growth has been driven by the arrival of Orthodox Jews who have congregated in Brooklyn and on the fringes of Greater New York City.

New Yorkers tend to migrate to other regions of the country. After World War II, a large wave of New Yorkers, particularly from Brooklyn, moved to Los Angeles and other parts of California. More people from New York move to Florida than from any other state.

The Jackson Heights neighborhood in the borough of Queens in New York City has grown into one of the most culturally and racially diverse areas in the United States, and indeed the whole world. East Asian (Chinese and Korean), South Asian (Indian and Pakistani), and South American (Columbian, Peruvian, Ecuadorian, Bolivian, and Chilean) immigrants have settled thickly in Jackson Heights. These groups have been very active in the small business economy, setting up retail stores and restaurants that sustain a vibrant, multicultural urban life.

Population by Selected Ethnic Group

	Estimate		Estimate
Total:	19,746,227	European	169,956
Afghan	7,536	Finnish	19,672
Albanian	47,146	French (except Basque)	418,513
Alsatian	1,369	French Canadian	134,946
American	1,091,853	German	1,967,176
Arab:	176,150	German Russian	1,147
Egyptian	34,801	Greek	149,418
Iraqi	5,467	Guyanese	143,397
Jordanian	5,716	Hungarian	143,289
Lebanese	31,451	Icelander	1,733
Moroccan	11,013	Iranian	27,655
Palestinian	8,843	Irish	2,293,263
Syrian	17,966	Israeli	37,120
Arab	25,644	Italian	2,529,668
Other Arab	39,850	Latvian	9,179
Armenian	25,319	Lithuanian	47,259
Assyrian/Chaldean/Syriac	640	Luxemburger	866
Australian	8,738	Macedonian	13,040
Austrian	79,942	Maltese	3,977
Basque	1,399	New Zealander	1,265
Belgian	11,625	Northern European	9,558
Brazilian	29,105	Norwegian	83,297
British	63,677	Pennsylvania German	14,365
Bulgarian	6,517	Polish	904,157
Cajun	410	Portuguese	51,893
Canadian	43,724	Romanian	49,149
Carpatho-Rusyn	1,403	Russian	385,114
Celtic	2,813	Scandinavian	10,768
Croatian	21,196	Scotch-Irish	58,518
Cypriot	2,205	Scottish	206,216
Czech	53,521	Serbian	8,436
Czechoslovakian	19,026	Slavic	9,133
Danish	35,291	Slovak	35,037
Dutch	227,938	Slovene	4,319
Eastern European	97,995	Soviet Union	125
English	992,153	Sub-Saharan African:	259,729
Estonian	4,578	Cape Verdean	1,171

(continued)

	Estimate			Estimate
Ethiopian	8,373		Welsh	78,817
Ghanaian	22,653		West Indian	812,905
Kenyan	849		(except Hispanic groups):	
Liberian	3,746		Bahamian	1,414
Nigerian	32,226		Barbadian	27,122
Senegalese	4,761		Belizean	8,373
Sierra Leonean	1,814		Bermudan	497
Somali	3,456		British West Indian	59,652
South African	3,683		Dutch West Indian	2,359
Sudanese	3,364		Haitian	198,219
Ugandan	2,031		Jamaican	329,428
Zimbabwean	326		Trinidadian and Tobagonian	93,082
African	146,652		U.S. Virgin Islander	3,535
Other sub-Saharan African	27,524		West Indian	103,264
Swedish	120,630		Other West Indian	1,930
Swiss	34,957		Yugoslavian	22,322
Turkish	31,063		Other groups	7,384,097
Ukrainian	142,510		Unclassified or not reported	2,408,168

Source: American Community Survey, U.S. Census Bureau, 2014.

See in Neighborhoods Section: Bedford-Stuyvesant (Brooklyn, New York); Borough Park/Williamsburg/Crown Heights, Jewish Enclaves (Brooklyn, New York); Brighton Beach-Sheepshead Bay (Brooklyn, New York); Brooklyn, West Indian Enclave (New York); Chinatowns (Manhattan; Sunset Park East, Brooklyn; Flushing, Queens) (New York City); Coney Island (Brooklyn, New York); Crown Heights, Jamaican Enclave (Brooklyn, New York); Five Points (New York City); Greenpoint (Brooklyn, New York); Greenwich Village (New York City); Harlem (New York City); Harlem, Senegalese Enclave (New York City); Hell's Kitchen (New York City); Jackson Heights (Queens, New York); Jackson Heights, South Asian Enclave (Queens, New York); Little Brazil Street (Manhattan, New York); Little India, Jackson Heights (Queens, New York); Little Italy (Manhattan, New York); Lower East Side (New York City); Sleepy Hollow, Ecuadorian Enclave (New York); Staten Island, Sri Lankan Enclave (New York City); Sunset Park West and North Corona (New York City); Washington Heights (New York City); Yorkville, German Enclave (New York City)

NORTH CAROLINA

Capital: Raleigh
Entered Union: November 21, 1789 (12th state)

North Carolina is the 29th most extensive and the 10th most populous U.S. state, with 9,535,483 total inhabitants. In the 16th century, Spanish colonial forces were

Skyline view of North Carolina's capital city, Raleigh, 2015. (Sean Pavone/Dreamstime.com)

the first to establish a stable European settlement in what is now North Carolina. Both North Carolina and South Carolina were included in the charter that established Carolina as an English colony in 1663. The two areas separated in 1712, which was finalized in the formal dissolution of the Carolina Colony in 1729. At that point, North and South Carolina assumed generally the same shared boundary as the present states. North Carolina ratified the U.S. Constitution on November 21, 1789, becoming the 12th of the original 13 states. In 1790, North Carolina ceded its territory westward to the Mississippi River, comprising present-day Tennessee, to the United States. North Carolina has 13 congressional districts, 50 state senate districts, and 120 state house districts. Raleigh is the state capital, while Charlotte is the most populous city, with 731,424 residents. North Carolina borders four states: Georgia, South Carolina, Tennessee, and Virginia.

Historical Population of North Carolina

Census	Pop.	%±	Census	Pop.	%±
1790	393,751	—	1850	869,039	15.3%
1800	478,103	21.4%	1860	992,622	14.2%
1810	556,526	16.4%	1870	1,071,361	7.9%
1820	638,829	14.8%	1880	1,399,750	30.7%
1830	737,987	15.5%	1890	1,617,949	15.6%
1840	753,419	2.1%	1900	1,893,810	17.1%

(continued)

Census	Pop.	%±	Census	Pop.	%±
1910	2,206,287	16.5%	1970	5,082,059	11.5%
1920	2,559,123	16.0%	1980	5,881,766	15.7%
1930	3,170,276	23.9%	1990	6,628,637	12.7%
1940	3,571,623	12.7%	2000	8,049,313	21.4%
1950	4,061,929	13.7%	2010	9,535,471	18.5%
1960	4,556,155	12.2%			

Source: U.S. Census Bureau.

According to the 2010 U.S. Census, the state's racial composition is 68.5% white, 21.5 African American, 2.2% Asian American, 0.1% Native Hawaiian and other Pacific Islander, and 8.4% Hispanic American of any race. Surveys from the same year indicate that 89.66% of North Carolina residents age five and older speak English at home as their primary language, while 6.93% spoke Spanish, 0.32% French, 0.27% German, and 0.27% spoke Chinese as a main language by 0.27%. In total, 10.34% of North Carolinians speak a mother language other than English. In addition, a small portion of the population speaks Arabic, Russian, or Italian.

Since the colonial era, North Carolinians, like the residents of other Southern states, have been overwhelmingly Protestant. By the late 19th century, the largest Protestant denomination was the Baptist Church. After the Civil War, black Baptists left white churches to set up their own independent congregations. While the Baptists in total have maintained the majority in this part of the country, the population in North Carolina practices a wide variety of faiths, such as Judaism, Islam, Hinduism, Buddhism, and Baha'i. As of 2010, the four biggest denominations in North Carolina are the Southern Baptist Church, the United Methodist Church, the Roman Catholic Church, and the Presbyterian Church (USA), which Scotch-Irish immigrants brought to the Carolinas in the colonial era. The rapid influx of northerners and immigrants from Latin America is steadily increasing the ethnic and religious diversity in North Carolina. The number of Roman Catholics and Jews in the state has increased, as well as general religious diversity.

Population by Selected Ethnic Group

	Estimate		Estimate
Total:	9,943,964	Egyptian	4,445
Afghan	501	Iraqi	1,098
Albanian	1,496	Jordanian	2,827
Alsatian	255	Lebanese	12,134
American	1,223,727	Moroccan	4,559
Arab:	42,940	Palestinian	2,738

(continued)

	Estimate		Estimate
Syrian	3,493	Luxemburger	30
Arab	5,362	Macedonian	1,580
Other Arab	7,117	Maltese	1,063
Armenian	3,599	New Zealander	237
Assyrian/Chaldean/Syriac	176	Northern European	5,699
Australian	2,527	Norwegian	45,207
Austrian	14,838	Pennsylvania German	2,792
Basque	323	Polish	135,482
Belgian	4,693	Portuguese	16,680
Brazilian	4,781	Romanian	6,875
British	53,257	Russian	39,731
Bulgarian	2,584	Scandinavian	7,822
Cajun	2,122	Scotch-Irish	252,989
Canadian	18,198	Scottish	230,086
Carpatho-Rusyn	248	Serbian	2,706
Celtic	1,533	Slavic	2,609
Croatian	5,732	Slovak	9,149
Cypriot	0	Slovene	1,707
Czech	15,672	Soviet Union	0
Czechoslovakian	4,601	Sub-Saharan African:	108,867
Danish	13,246	Cape Verdean	469
Dutch	97,300	Ethiopian	4,961
Eastern European	8,687	Ghanaian	4,722
English	938,408	Kenyan	1,955
Estonian	498	Liberian	4,181
European	114,024	Nigerian	6,148
Finnish	6,844	Senegalese	70
French (except Basque)	168,976	Sierra Leonean	95
French Canadian	31,450	Somali	70
German	1,069,106	South African	2,856
German Russian	1,131	Sudanese	562
Greek	29,395	Ugandan	0
Guyanese	2,205	Zimbabwean	309
Hungarian	23,606	African	79,200
Icelander	661	Other sub-Saharan	5,534
Iranian	5,258	African	
Irish	868,346	Swedish	52,967
Israeli	3,583	Swiss	14,527
Italian	328,503	Turkish	6,500
Latvian	1,054	Ukrainian	17,433
Lithuanian	10,052	Welsh	51,380

(continued)

	Estimate		Estimate
West Indian	43,058	Jamaican	17,778
(except Hispanic groups):		Trinidadian and	4,022
Bahamian	918	Tobagonian	
Barbadian	1,067	U.S. Virgin Islander	887
Belizean	614	West Indian	7,337
Bermudan	56	Other West Indian	28
British West Indian	1,168	Yugoslavian	4,915
Dutch West Indian	971	Other groups	3,792,570
Haitian	9,430	Unclassified or not reported	1,716,788

Source: American Community Survey, U.S. Census Bureau, 2014.

See in Neighborhoods Section: Little India, Chatham Street (Cary, North Carolina)

NORTH DAKOTA

Capital: Bismarck
Entered Union: November 2, 1889 (39th state)

North Dakota is the 17th-largest state by land area but the third least populous, with only 672,591 residents. At 9.7 persons per square mile, North Dakota is the fourth most sparsely populated U.S. state. The first European to reach the area was a French Canadian trader in 1738. Throughout the latter half of the 19th century and into the 20th century, North Dakota was a popular destination for immigrant farmers and general laborers and their families, mostly from Norway, Sweden, Germany, and the United Kingdom.

The United States acquired most of the area of North Dakota from France in 1803 as part of the Louisiana Purchase. Dakota Territory was organized on March 2, 1861 from administratively unorganized areas formerly within Minnesota Territory and part of Nebraska Territory. Dakota Territory included all of the present-day states of North Dakota and South Dakota, most of Montana, the northern half of Wyoming, and a small part of Nebraska. The territory was reduced in 1863 with the organization of Idaho Territory, enlarged in 1864 with the addition of most of the remainder of present-day Wyoming, and again reduced with the organization of Wyoming Territory in 1868. North Dakota was admitted to the Union simultaneously with South Dakota on November 2, 1889, as the 39th and 40th states respectively, with generally the same boundaries as the present states. Bismarck is the state capital. Fargo is the largest city, with 105,549 residents. North Dakota has five federally recognized American Indian areas. The state has 1 congressional district, 47 state senate districts, and 47 state house districts. North Dakota borders Minnesota, Montana, South Dakota, and Canada. The town of Rugby, North Dakota, is the geographical center of North America.

Historical Population of North Dakota

Census	Pop.	%±	Census	Pop.	%±
1870	2,405	—	1950	619,636	−3.5%
1880	36,909	1,434.7%	1960	632,446	2.1%
1890	190,983	417.4%	1970	617,761	−2.3%
1900	319,146	67.1%	1980	652,717	5.7%
1910	577,056	80.8%	1990	638,800	−2.1%
1920	646,872	12.1%	2000	641,298	0.4%
1930	680,845	5.3%	2010	672,591	4.9%
1940	641,935	−5.7%			

Source: U.S. Census Bureau.

According to the 2010 U.S. Census, the racial and ethnic composition of North Dakota is 90.0% white American, 5.4% Native American, 1.2% African American, 1.0% Asian, and 0.1% Pacific Islander. As of 2009, the six largest ancestry groups in North Dakota are German (47.2%), Norwegian (30.8%), Irish (7.7%), Swedish (4.7%), Russian (4.1%), and French (4.1%). North Dakota has a great number of Native Americans. Social gatherings called "powwows" are an important aspect of Native American culture and occur regularly throughout the State. In addition, ethnic Germans who came from Russia constitute a significant portion of the population in North Dakota. About 100,000 Germans who were dissatisfied with the Russian economy immigrated to the United States by 1900, settling primarily in North Dakota. This is why the south-central part of North Dakota is known as "the German-Russian triangle."

In 2010, 94.86% of North Dakotans spoke English as their primary language, while 5.14% of the population spoke a language other than English: 1.39% spoke German, 1.37% spoke Spanish, and 0.30% spoke Norwegian. Other languages spoken included Serbo-Croatian, Chinese, Japanese, Native American languages, and French.

North Dakota has the most churches per capita of any state. The total Christian population of the state is 86%. According to a 2001 survey, 35% of North Dakotans are Lutheran, and 30% are Catholic. Other religious groups and faiths represented in North Dakota are Methodists (7%), Baptists (6%), and the Assemblies of God (3%). Judaism, Islam, Buddhism, and Hinduism make up 4% of the population all together.

Population by Selected Ethnic Group

	Estimate		Estimate
Total:	704,925	Alsatian	0
Afghan	0	American	22,422
Albanian	49	Arab:	1,428

(continued)

	Estimate		Estimate
Egyptian	149	Irish	55,815
Iraqi	230	Israeli	8
Jordanian	55	Italian	8,813
Lebanese	298	Latvian	111
Moroccan	0	Lithuanian	255
Palestinian	17	Luxemburger	303
Syrian	194	Macedonian	15
Arab	224	Maltese	0
Other Arab	289	New Zealander	39
Armenian	233	Northern European	448
Assyrian/Chaldean/Syriac	0	Norwegian	193,489
Australian	64	Pennsylvania German	192
Austrian	971	Polish	17,871
Basque	91	Portuguese	355
Belgian	994	Romanian	473
Brazilian	78	Russian	22,436
British	1,059	Scandinavian	9,867
Bulgarian	281	Scotch-Irish	4,464
Cajun	55	Scottish	8,414
Canadian	1,403	Serbian	188
Carpatho-Rusyn	11	Slavic	179
Celtic	101	Slovak	308
Croatian	321	Slovene	167
Cypriot	0	Soviet Union	0
Czech	12,494	Sub-Saharan African:	4,434
Czechoslovakian	1,356	Cape Verdean	5
Danish	7,386	Ethiopian	357
Dutch	9,471	Ghanaian	13
Eastern European	54	Kenyan	48
English	31,569	Liberian	174
Estonian	16	Nigerian	152
European	3,409	Senegalese	0
Finnish	3,832	Sierra Leonean	18
French (except Basque)	30,702	Somali	936
French Canadian	6,696	South African	75
German	306,055	Sudanese	179
German Russian	1,766	Ugandan	373
Greek	639	Zimbabwean	2
Guyanese	14	African	1,614
Hungarian	2,788	Other sub-Saharan African	566
Icelander	3,027	Swedish	31,308
Iranian	111	Swiss	1,743

(continued)

	Estimate			Estimate
Turkish	168		Dutch West Indian	0
Ukrainian	4,205		Haitian	31
Welsh	1,959		Jamaican	124
West Indian	331		Trinidadian and Tobagonian	36
(except Hispanic groups):			U.S. Virgin Islander	0
Bahamian	29		West Indian	83
Barbadian	5		Other West Indian	0
Belizean	0		Yugoslavian	1,292
Bermudan	0		Other groups	87,609
British West Indian	23		Unclassified or not reported	66,742

Source: U.S. Census Bureau, 2010–2014 American Community Survey 5-Year Estimates.

See in Neighborhoods Section: Minot and Other Cities, Norwegian Enclaves (North Dakota); Warsaw, Polish Enclave (North Dakota)

OHIO

Capital: Columbus
Entered Union: March 1, 1803 (17th state)

Ohio is the 35th-largest state by area and the 7th most populous, with a total of 11,536,504 inhabitants. At 282.3 persons per square mile, Ohio is the 10th most densely populated U.S. state. The capital and largest city is Columbus, home to 787,033 people. During the 18th century, the French set up a system of trading posts to control the fur trade in the region. In 1754, as a result of the Seven Years' War, the French ceded control of Ohio and the remainder of the Old Northwest to Great Britain. The area of Ohio subsequently was an original territory of the United States, designated the "Territory northwest of the River Ohio" in 1787. Ohio Territory was organized on April 30, 1802, from the Northwest Territory, with generally the same boundary as the present state. Ohio was admitted to the Union on March 1, 1803, as the 17th state. Ohio has 16 congressional districts, 33 state senate districts, and 99 state house districts. In addition to an international border with Canada, Ohio borders five states: Indiana, Kentucky, Michigan, Pennsylvania, and West Virginia.

Historical Population of Ohio

Census	Pop.	%±	Census	Pop.	%±
1800	45,365	—	1830	937,903	61.3%
1810	230,760	408.7%	1840	1,519,467	62.0%
1820	581,434	152.0%	1850	1,980,329	30.3%

(continued)

Census	Pop.	%±	Census	Pop.	%±
1860	2,339,511	18.1%	1940	6,907,612	3.9%
1870	2,665,260	13.9%	1950	7,946,627	15.0%
1880	3,198,062	20.0%	1960	9,706,397	22.1%
1890	3,672,329	14.8%	1970	10,652,017	9.7%
1900	4,157,545	13.2%	1980	10,797,630	1.4%
1910	4,767,121	14.7%	1990	10,847,115	0.5%
1920	5,759,394	20.8%	2000	11,353,140	4.7%
1930	6,646,697	15.4%	2010	11,536,504	1.6%

Source: U.S. Census Bureau.

According to the 2010 U.S. Census, the racial composition of Ohio is 82.7% white, 12.2% African American, 0.2% Native American, 1.7% Asian (0.6% Indian, 0.4% Chinese, 0.1% Filipino, 0.1% Korean, 0.1% Vietnamese, 0.1% Japanese), 0.03% Pacific Islander, and 3.1% Hispanic of any race. Migrants from the eastern United States, the British Isles, and Northern Europe, especially Germany, were the first Europeans to settle Ohio. Cincinnati had such a large German population that its public schools were bilingual until World War I. With the coming of the railroads and the development of industry, Slavic and other south Europeans were recruited in large numbers. As of 2000, 11.5% of the population is black or African American. Most African Americans in Ohio live in the larger cities, particularly Cleveland, where 51.0% of residents were African American in 2000. Ohio was very active in the abolition movement. Oberlin College, established in 1833 by dissident theological students, has admitted black students since its founding.

As a first language, 6.7% of the Ohioans speak a language other than English, with 2.2% of the population speaking Spanish, 2.6% speaking other Indo-European languages, and 1.1% speaking Asian and Austronesian languages. Ohio also has the nation's largest population of Slovene speakers, the second-largest populations of Slovak and Pennsylvania Dutch (German) speakers, and the third-largest population of Serbian speakers.

According to a 2008 Pew Forum poll, 76% of Ohioans identified as Christian. Specifically, 26% of Ohioans identified as Evangelical Protestant, 22% as Mainline Protestant, and 21% as Roman Catholic. According to the Association of Religion Data Archives, the largest denominations in Ohio in 2010 were the Roman Catholic Church, the United Methodist Church, and the Evangelical Lutheran Church in America. In addition, 17% of the population is unaffiliated with any religious body, and 1.3% are Jewish. There are also small minorities of Jehovah's Witnesses, Muslims (1%), Hindus, Buddhists, and Mormons.

Population by Selected Ethnic Group

	Estimate		Estimate
Total:	11,594,163	French Canadian	32,493
Afghan	1,184	German	2,989,278
Albanian	1,610	German Russian	265
Alsatian	229	Greek	51,063
American	898,449	Guyanese	688
Arab:	82,399	Hungarian	183,593
Egyptian	4,329	Icelander	579
Iraqi	1,266	Iranian	5,851
Jordanian	4,223	Irish	1,604,196
Lebanese	30,567	Israeli	1,835
Moroccan	3,082	Italian	732,372
Palestinian	7,130	Latvian	3,170
Syrian	6,655	Lithuanian	20,057
Arab	11,415	Luxemburger	671
Other Arab	14,761	Macedonian	5,226
Armenian	4,630	Maltese	54
Assyrian/Chaldean/Syriac	163	New Zealander	487
Australian	1,860	Northern European	4,973
Austrian	26,353	Norwegian	40,154
Basque	220	Pennsylvania German	28,215
Belgian	9,576	Polish	420,149
Brazilian	3,805	Portuguese	7,756
British	42,573	Romanian	28,851
Bulgarian	2,715	Russian	76,547
Cajun	762	Scandinavian	8,663
Canadian	15,928	Scotch-Irish	108,748
Carpatho-Rusyn	1,500	Scottish	206,103
Celtic	1,401	Serbian	16,569
Croatian	37,505	Slavic	5,747
Cypriot	107	Slovak	118,975
Czech	60,377	Slovene	52,143
Czechoslovakian	21,351	Soviet Union	71
Danish	16,578	Sub-Saharan African:	97,954
Dutch	178,162	Cape Verdean	335
Eastern European	14,617	Ethiopian	5,378
English	967,683	Ghanaian	5,290
Estonian	482	Kenyan	1,507
European	106,201	Liberian	1,075
Finnish	17,877	Nigerian	6,833
French (except Basque)	258,255	Senegalese	545

(*continued*)

188   OKLAHOMA

	Estimate		Estimate
Sierra Leonean	538	Bahamian	199
Somali	12,938	Barbadian	353
South African	605	Belizean	195
Sudanese	0	Bermudan	96
Ugandan	968	British West Indian	397
Zimbabwean	260	Dutch West Indian	251
African	56,067	Haitian	3,128
Other sub-Saharan African	7,320	Jamaican	9,957
Swedish	68,909	Trinidadian and Tobagonian	1,173
Swiss	74,679	U.S. Virgin Islander	25
Turkish	6,776	West Indian	1,867
Ukrainian	40,742	Other West Indian	26
Welsh	115,956	Yugoslavian	8,215
West Indian	17,442	Other groups	2,766,870
(except Hispanic groups):		Unclassified or not reported	2,145,726

Source: American Community Survey, U.S. Census Bureau, 2014.

See in Neighborhoods Section: German Village (Columbus, Ohio); Over-the-Rhine (Cincinnati, Ohio); Slavic Village (Cleveland, Ohio)

OKLAHOMA

Capital: Oklahoma City
Entered Union: November 16, 1907 (46th state)

Oklahoma is the 19th-largest state and is home to 3,751,351 people, making it the 28th most populous state. French explorers claimed what is now Oklahoma in the 1700s, and it remained under French rule until 1803, when the United States acquired it in the Louisiana Purchase. The area of Oklahoma was part of unorganized territory and designated as Indian Country or Indian Territory in 1834, although this conflicted with territory already included within Missouri Territory. Oklahoma Territory was organized in 1890 from the western part of Indian Territory and the Public Land Strip (the Panhandle, which Texas sold to the United States), and resulted in a split territory. The Cherokee Outlet was added, which merged Oklahoma Territory into a single area. Oklahoma Territory and the remaining Indian Territory were combined, and Oklahoma was admitted to the Union on November 16, 1907, as the 46th state, with generally the same boundary as the present state.

Oklahoma has one federally recognized American Indian area reservation, 25 Oklahoma tribal statistical areas (OTSAs), and four joint-use OTSAs. The state has five congressional districts, 48 state senate districts, and 101 state house

The iconic Golden Driller monument of an oil worker in Tulsa, Oklahoma. (Wiktor Wojtas/
Dreamstime.com)

districts. The capital, Oklahoma City, is also its largest city with 579,999 inhabitants. Oklahoma borders six states: Arkansas, Colorado, Kansas, Missouri, New
Mexico, and Texas.

Historical Population of Oklahoma

Census	Pop.	%±	Census	Pop.	%±
1890	258,657	—	1960	2,328,284	4.3%
1900	790,391	205.6%	1970	2,559,229	9.9%
1910	1,657,155	109.7%	1980	3,025,290	18.2%
1920	2,028,283	22.4%	1990	3,145,585	4.0%
1930	2,396,040	18.1%	2000	3,450,654	9.7%
1940	2,336,434	−2.5%	2010	3,751,351	8.7%
1950	2,233,351	−4.4%			

Source: U.S. Census Bureau.

According to the 2010 U.S. Census, 68.7% of the population is white, 7.3%
African American, 8.2% American Indian and Alaska Native, 1.7% Asian, 0.1%
Native Hawaiian and other Pacific Islander, and 8.9% Hispanic of any race. During
the 19th century, thousands of Native Americans were expelled from their ancestral homelands from across North America and were relocated to present-day

Oklahoma and the surrounding areas. Today, Oklahoma is home to some of the nation's largest Indian reservations, including those of the Creek, Cherokee, Chickasaw, and Choctaw Indians.

Beginning in 1889, Oklahoma held a series of land rushes that facilitated mass migration into the territory. In 1893, an estimated 100,000 people participated in the fourth land rush when the government opened the Cherokee Outlet to settlement. It was the largest such event in American history.

Mexicans came to Oklahoma during the 19th century as laborers on railroads, ranches, and in coalmines. Today, most first- and second-generation Mexicans live in Oklahoma City, Tulsa, and Lawton. In 2000, Oklahomans who were classified as Hispanics or Latinos represented 5.2% of the state's total population. Italians, Czechs, Germans, Poles, Britons, and Irish also came to Oklahoma during the 19th century. Foreign immigration has slowed since that time. In 2000, less than 4% of the population was foreign-born.

Oklahoma is part of the Bible Belt, a geographical region characterized by its conservatism and Evangelical Christianity. According to the Pew Research Center, the majority of Oklahoma's religious adherents are Christian, accounting for about 80% of the population. The percentage of Oklahomans affiliated with Catholicism is half of the national average, while the percentage affiliated with Evangelical Protestantism is more than twice the national average. In 2010, the state's largest church memberships were in the Southern Baptist Convention, the United Methodist Church, the Roman Catholic Church, and the Assemblies of God. Buddhism, Hinduism, and Islam are among other religions represented in the state.

Oklahomans speaking only English at home make up 92.6% of the population. Spanish is the second most commonly spoken language in the state, followed by Cherokee, German, and Vietnamese. There are roughly 22,000 Cherokee speakers living within the Cherokee Nation tribal jurisdiction area of eastern Oklahoma.

See in Neighborhoods Section: Asian District (Oklahoma City, Oklahoma); Greenwood (Tulsa, Oklahoma)

Population by Selected Ethnic Group

	Estimate		Estimate
Total:	3,878,051	Lebanese	4,000
Afghan	0	Moroccan	633
Albanian	290	Palestinian	47
Alsatian	70	Syrian	1,131
American	358,141	Arab	2,452
Arab:	12,549	Other Arab	2,031
Egyptian	921	Armenian	786
Iraqi	1,277	Assyrian/Chaldean/Syriac	0
Jordanian	333	Australian	1,295

(*continued*)

	Estimate		Estimate
Austrian	4,422	Polish	35,709
Basque	337	Portuguese	4,328
Belgian	2,054	Romanian	1,622
Brazilian	722	Russian	11,775
British	17,947	Scandinavian	4,735
Bulgarian	571	Scotch-Irish	40,709
Cajun	1,039	Scottish	61,820
Canadian	3,580	Serbian	959
Carpatho-Rusyn	115	Slavic	601
Celtic	440	Slovak	1,530
Croatian	1,498	Slovene	586
Cypriot	81	Soviet Union	0
Czech	13,168	Sub-Saharan African:	18,890
Czechoslovakian	2,553	Cape Verdean	109
Danish	8,285	Ethiopian	1,160
Dutch	66,166	Ghanaian	937
Eastern European	748	Kenyan	843
English	293,889	Liberian	85
Estonian	263	Nigerian	2,218
European	44,576	Senegalese	83
Finnish	3,490	Sierra Leonean	0
French (except Basque)	83,012	Somali	20
French Canadian	8,625	South African	107
German	547,115	Sudanese	298
German Russian	1,678	Ugandan	0
Greek	5,321	Zimbabwean	226
Guyanese	37	African	12,231
Hungarian	4,871	Other sub-Saharan African	573
Icelander	566	Swedish	28,426
Iranian	3,632	Swiss	5,975
Irish	429,860	Turkish	748
Israeli	550	Ukrainian	3,478
Italian	73,135	Welsh	18,269
Latvian	59	West Indian	23,449
Lithuanian	2,154	(except Hispanic groups):	
Luxemburger	23	Bahamian	428
Macedonian	70	Barbadian	85
Maltese	0	Belizean	70
New Zealander	197	Bermudan	77
Northern European	1,903	British West Indian	225
Norwegian	25,530	Dutch West Indian	19,769
Pennsylvania German	975	Haitian	748

(continued)

	Estimate		Estimate
Jamaican	1,487	Other West Indian	0
Trinidadian and Tobagonian	327	Yugoslavian	786
U.S. Virgin Islander	0	Other groups	1,556,611
West Indian	289	Unclassified or not reported	812,872

Source: American Community Survey, U.S. Census Bureau, 2014.

See in Neighborhoods Section: Asian District (Oklahoma City, Oklahoma); Greenwood (Tulsa, Oklahoma)

OREGON

Capital: Salem
Entered Union: February 14, 1859 (33rd state)

Oregon is the 10th largest and 27th most populous state, home to 3,831,074 people. More than 46% of the state's population lives in the Oregon portion of the Portland metropolitan area. The first Europeans to visit Oregon were Spanish explorers who spotted southern Oregon off the Pacific Coast in 1543. The United States acquired the area of Oregon through a treaty with Great Britain in 1846. Oregon Territory was organized in 1848, and included all of present-day Oregon, Idaho, and Washington and part of western Montana and Wyoming. The territory was reduced in 1853 when Washington Territory was organized. In 1859, additional territory was transferred to Washington Territory, leaving Oregon with generally the same boundary as the present state. Oregon was admitted to the Union on February 14, 1859, as the 33rd state. Today, it has 5 congressional districts, 30 state senate districts, and 60 state house districts. Oregon borders four states: California, Idaho, Nevada, and Washington.

In 2000, an estimated 45,211 American Indians were living in Oregon, with most of the population residing in urban areas. The state's four reservations are the Umatilla, Siletz, Spokane, and Kalispel. French Canadians have lived in Oregon since the opening of the territory, and they have continued to come in a small but steady migration. As of 2000, 31,354 Oregonians reported French Canadian ancestry. French Canadian presence can be found in the numerous names of French origin in different parts of the state.

Historical Population of Oregon

Census	Pop.	%±	Census	Pop.	%±
1850	12,093	—	1870	90,923	73.3%
1860	52,465	333.8%	1880	174,768	92.2%

(continued)

Census	Pop.	%±	Census	Pop.	%±
1890	317,704	81.8%	1960	1,768,687	16.3%
1900	413,536	30.2%	1970	2,091,533	18.3%
1910	672,765	62.7%	1980	2,633,156	25.9%
1920	783,389	16.4%	1990	2,842,321	7.9%
1930	953,786	21.8%	2000	3,421,399	20.4%
1940	1,089,684	14.2%	2010	3,831,074	12.0%
1950	1,521,341	39.6%			

Source: U.S. Census Bureau.

The non-Hispanic white percentage of Oregon's population has declined from 95.8% in 1970 to 77.8% in 2012. In 2011, 38.7% of Oregon children under one year of age belonged to minority groups. In 2004, 309,700 Oregon residents were foreign-born (accounting for 8.7% of the state population).

The largest reported ancestry groups in Oregon are as follows: German (22.5%), English (14.0%), Irish (13.2%), Scandinavian (8.4%), and American (5.0%). Approximately 62% of Oregon residents are wholly or partly of English, Welsh, Irish, or Scottish ancestry. Mexican Americans are concentrated in Malheur and Jefferson counties, proximate to the urbanized areas of Portland, Eugene, and Salem. Russians constitute only 1.4% of the population, but Russian is the third most spoken language in Oregon after English and Spanish.

Major religious affiliations of the people of Oregon are 67% Christian, divided into 47% Protestant, 14% Roman Catholic, 5% Latter-day Saints/Mormon, and 1% other Christian traditions. The largest denominations by number of adherents in 2010 were the Roman Catholic Church, the Church of Jesus Christ of Latter-day Saints, and the Assemblies of God. Two percent of the population is Buddhist, while 1% is Jewish, and 0.5% is Muslim. Oregon also contains the largest community of Russian Old Believers in the United States. Additionally, the Northwest Tibetan Cultural Association is headquartered in Portland.

Population by Selected Ethnic Group

	Estimate		Estimate
Total:	3,970,239	Lebanese	3,838
Afghan	2,988	Moroccan	378
Albanian	632	Palestinian	567
Alsatian	165	Syrian	1,819
American	220,136	Arab	2,309
Arab:	13,842	Other Arab	1,931
Egyptian	2,377	Armenian	3,037
Iraqi	825	Assyrian/Chaldean/Syriac	116
Jordanian	785	Australian	2,330

(continued)

	Estimate		Estimate
Austrian	11,890	Portuguese	22,826
Basque	2,642	Romanian	10,864
Belgian	5,976	Russian	52,520
Brazilian	2,528	Scandinavian	22,493
British	33,226	Scotch-Irish	59,252
Bulgarian	1,477	Scottish	124,858
Cajun	178	Serbian	1,248
Canadian	11,805	Slavic	1,846
Carpatho-Rusyn	0	Slovak	2,848
Celtic	1,320	Slovene	1,572
Croatian	6,570	Soviet Union	0
Cypriot	84	Sub-Saharan African:	25,013
Czech	21,561	Cape Verdean	100
Czechoslovakian	5,228	Ethiopian	4,878
Danish	43,832	Ghanaian	240
Dutch	80,929	Kenyan	1,079
Eastern European	6,228	Liberian	234
English	453,080	Nigerian	1,217
Estonian	642	Senegalese	0
European	98,928	Sierra Leonean	29
Finnish	21,795	Somali	3,843
French (except Basque)	126,921	South African	888
French Canadian	25,641	Sudanese	1,256
German	762,620	Ugandan	47
German Russian	85	Zimbabwean	9
Greek	14,535	African	11,327
Guyanese	0	Other sub-Saharan African	432
Hungarian	13,488	Swedish	111,178
Icelander	1,852	Swiss	29,508
Iranian	4,264	Turkish	1,597
Irish	460,425	Ukrainian	18,976
Israeli	1,659	Welsh	40,117
Italian	150,980	West Indian	6,380
Latvian	1,496	(except Hispanic groups):	
Lithuanian	6,440	Bahamian	0
Luxemburger	758	Barbadian	0
Macedonian	143	Belizean	17
Maltese	434	Bermudan	40
New Zealander	529	British West Indian	50
Northern European	9,973	Dutch West Indian	2,442
Norwegian	148,892	Haitian	913
Pennsylvania German	1,856	Jamaican	872
Polish	70,340	Trinidadian and Tobagonian	1,309

(continued)

	Estimate		Estimate
U.S. Virgin Islander	103	Yugoslavian	3,400
West Indian	634	Other groups	1,155,845
Other West Indian	0	Unclassified or not reported	674,178

Source: American Community Survey, U.S. Census Bureau, 2014.

See in Neighborhoods Section: New Chinatown (Portland, Oregon)

PENNSYLVANIA

Capital: Harrisburg
Entered Union: December 12, 1787 (2nd state)

Pennsylvania is the sixth most populous state and the 32nd-largest state by land area. Claimed by the English, Swedes, and Dutch in the 16th century, the English won the territory in 1664 after the capture of New York. In 1681, King Charles II granted Pennsylvania to William Penn, a Quaker. It was chartered in 1681, although New York did not relinquish its claim to the area until the following year. The southern boundary was resolved with the survey of the Mason-Dixon Line in the 1760s. Pennsylvania ratified the U.S. Constitution on December 12, 1787, becoming the second of the original 13 states. Pennsylvania assumed generally the same boundary as the present state with the acquisition of the Erie Triangle from New York in 1792. Pennsylvania is one of four states legally described as a commonwealth, which denotes that it is a political community founded for the common good, and a social compact into which the individuals of the commonwealth enter with one another.

Pennsylvania has 18 congressional districts, 50 state senate districts, and 203 state house districts. In addition to an international border with Canada, Pennsylvania borders six states: Delaware, Maryland, New Jersey, New York, Ohio, and West Virginia. Harrisburg is the capital.

Philadelphia was the seat of the federal government almost continuously from 1776 to 1800; the Declaration of Independence was signed there in 1776, as was the U.S. Constitution in 1787. The Liberty Bell is located in a glass pavilion across from Independence Hall. Today, Philadelphia is Pennsylvania's largest city, home to 1,526,006 people.

Historical Population of Pennsylvania

Census	Pop.	%±		Census	Pop.	%±
1790	434,373	—		1820	1,049,458	29.5%
1800	602,365	38.7%		1830	1,348,233	28.5%
1810	810,091	34.5%		1840	1,724,033	27.9%

(continued)

Census	Pop.	%±	Census	Pop.	%±
1850	2,311,786	34.1%	1940	9,900,180	2.8%
1860	2,906,215	25.7%	1950	10,498,012	6.0%
1870	3,521,951	21.2%	1960	11,319,366	7.8%
1880	4,282,891	21.6%	1970	11,793,909	4.2%
1890	5,258,113	22.8%	1980	11,863,895	0.6%
1900	6,302,115	19.9%	1990	11,881,643	0.1%
1910	7,665,111	21.6%	2000	12,281,054	3.4%
1920	8,720,017	13.8%	2010	12,702,379	3.4%
1930	9,631,350	10.5%			

Source: U.S. Census Bureau.

As of the 2010 U.S. Census, the total population of Pennsylvania was 12,702,379. The racial composition of the state is as follows: 81.9% white (79.2% non-Hispanic white), 11.3% black or African American, 0.3% American Indian and Alaska Native, 2.9% Asian, and 1.9% from two or more races. Individuals of Hispanic or Latino origin of any race comprise 5.9% of the total population.

Of the people residing in Pennsylvania, 74.5% were born in Pennsylvania, 18.4% were born in a different US state, 1.5% were born in Puerto Rico, in the U.S. Island areas, or abroad to American parent(s), and 5.6% were foreign born.

As of 2010, 90.15% of Pennsylvania residents aged five and older speak English at home as a primary language, while 4.09% speak Spanish, 0.87% German (including Pennsylvania Dutch) and 0.47% Chinese. In total, 9.85% of Pennsylvania's population aged five and older speaks a mother language other than English.

According to the Pew Research Center, 73% of Pennsylvanians are Christian. Evangelical Protestants, Mainline Protestants, and Catholics comprise the three largest subgroups, while 6% of Pennsylvanians follow non-Christian faiths (Judaism, Islam, Buddhism, Hinduism, and others). A total of 35% of the population consider themselves unaffiliated or nothing in particular.

Population by Selected Ethnic Group

	Estimate		Estimate
Total:	12,787,209	Jordanian	357
Afghan	2,491	Lebanese	19,697
Albanian	8,506	Moroccan	4,918
Alsatian	593	Palestinian	1,818
American	646,582	Syrian	14,010
Arab:	62,984	Arab	7,338
Egyptian	5,847	Other Arab	7,884
Iraqi	2,607	Armenian	9,860

(continued)

	Estimate		Estimate
Assyrian/Chaldean/Syriac	409	Norwegian	37,449
Australian	2,840	Pennsylvania German	145,242
Austrian	54,422	Polish	816,218
Basque	477	Portuguese	18,201
Belgian	9,536	Romanian	16,782
Brazilian	13,331	Russian	178,302
British	38,885	Scandinavian	7,638
Bulgarian	2,449	Scotch-Irish	133,016
Cajun	884	Scottish	186,482
Canadian	15,978	Serbian	16,349
Carpatho-Rusyn	2,339	Slavic	12,108
Celtic	1,491	Slovak	204,923
Croatian	49,457	Slovene	14,280
Cypriot	161	Soviet Union	125
Czech	44,522	Sub-Saharan African:	100,004
Czechoslovakian	21,684	Cape Verdean	108
Danish	17,667	Ethiopian	4,941
Dutch	206,896	Ghanaian	2,359
Eastern European	25,961	Kenyan	1,571
English	889,663	Liberian	8,564
Estonian	456	Nigerian	8,594
European	83,189	Senegalese	654
Finnish	8,610	Sierra Leonean	1,044
French (except Basque)	198,206	Somali	1,277
French Canadian	29,036	South African	1,573
German	3,239,286	Sudanese	1,028
German Russian	966	Ugandan	1,048
Greek	60,910	Zimbabwean	114
Guyanese	5,149	African	61,083
Hungarian	127,231	Other sub-Saharan African	7,054
Icelander	261	Swedish	101,966
Iranian	5,589	Swiss	62,912
Irish	2,100,315	Turkish	8,021
Israeli	4,359	Ukrainian	106,440
Italian	1,557,027	Welsh	158,600
Latvian	3,632	West Indian	80,618
Lithuanian	75,176	(except Hispanic groups):	
Luxemburger	540	Bahamian	363
Macedonian	1,321	Barbadian	2,863
Maltese	130	Belizean	960
New Zealander	131	Bermudan	695
Northern European	7,210	British West Indian	2,101

(continued)

	Estimate		Estimate
Dutch West Indian	416	West Indian	8,463
Haitian	26,627	Other West Indian	31
Jamaican	31,401	Yugoslavian	11,090
Trinidadian and Tobagonian	7,055	Other groups	2,834,503
U.S. Virgin Islander	1,183	Unclassified or not reported	1,952,396

Source: American Community Survey, U.S. Census Bureau, 2014.

See in Neighborhoods Section: Black Bottom (Philadelphia, Pennsylvania); Germantown (Philadelphia, Pennsylvania)

RHODE ISLAND

Capital: Providence
Entered Union: May 29, 1790 (13th state)

Rhode Island is the smallest state by land area and has the eighth-smallest population. An original patent was granted for the Providence Plantations in 1643, and a charter was granted for the Colony of Rhode Island and Providence Plantations in 1663. Rhode Island was the first of the original 13 colonies to declare independence from British rule, declaring itself independent on May 4, 1776, two months before any other colony. Rhode Island ratified the Constitution on May 29, 1790, the last of the original 13 states to do so. The official name of the state is "State of Rhode Island and Providence Plantations."

Providence is both the capital and the state's largest city, home to 178,042 residents. Given its diminutive size, Rhode Island is actually the second most densely populated state, with 1,081.1 persons per square mile. Rhode Island has 2 congressional districts, 38 state senate districts, and 75 state house districts. It borders Connecticut, Massachusetts, and New York.

Historical Population of Rhode Island

Census	Pop.	%±	Census	Pop.	%±
1790	68,825	—	1860	174,620	18.4%
1800	69,122	0.4%	1870	217,353	24.5%
1810	76,931	11.3%	1880	276,531	27.2%
1820	83,059	8.0%	1890	345,506	24.9%
1830	97,199	17.0%	1900	428,556	24.0%
1840	108,830	12.0%	1910	542,610	26.6%
1850	147,545	35.6%	1920	604,397	11.4%

(continued)

Census	Pop.	%±		Census	Pop.	%±
1930	687,497	13.7%		1980	947,154	0.0%
1940	713,346	3.8%		1990	1,003,464	5.9%
1950	791,896	11.0%		2000	1,048,319	4.5%
1960	859,488	8.5%		2010	1,052,567	0.4%
1970	946,725	10.1%				

Source: U.S. Census Bureau.

According to the 2010 U.S. Census, 81.4% of the population was white, 5.7% African American, 0.6% American Indian and Alaska Native, 2.9% Asian, and 0.1% Native Hawaiian and other Pacific Islander. Hispanics or Latinos of any race comprised 12.8% of the population, and they predominantly claim Dominican, Puerto Rican, and Guatemalan roots. According to the 2000 U.S. Census, 84% of the population speaks only American English, while 8.07% speaks Spanish at home, 3.80% speaks Portuguese, 1.96% speaks French, and 1.39% speaks Italian.

Rhode Island has a higher percentage of Americans of Portuguese ancestry, including Portuguese Americans and Cape Verdean Americans, than any other state in the nation. Additionally, the state also has the highest percentage of Liberian immigrants, with more than 15,000 residing in the state. Italian Americans make up a plurality in central and southern Providence County and French Canadians form a large part of northern Providence County. Irish Americans have a strong presence in Newport and Kent counties. People of English ancestry still have a presence in the state as well, especially in Washington County, and they are often referred to as "Swamp Yankees." African immigrants, including Cape Verdean Americans, Liberian Americans, Nigerian Americans, and Ghanaian Americans, form significant and growing communities in Rhode Island.

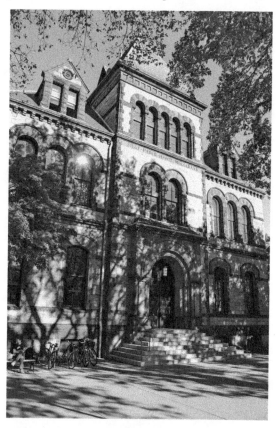

Sayles Hall at Brown University. Brown is one of the oldest colleges in the United States and was founded before the American Revolution. (Kevin Ruck/Dreamstime.com)

A Pew survey of Rhode Islanders' religious self-identification shows that 43% of residents are Roman Catholic, 27% Protestant, 23% nonreligious, 0.5% Mormon, 1% Jewish, 1% Orthodox, 1% Jehovah's Witness, 0.5% Hindu, 1% Buddhist, and 0.5% Muslim. The largest denominations are the Roman Catholic Church, the Episcopal Church, and the American Baptist Churches. Rhode Island has one of the highest percentages of Roman Catholics in the nation mainly due to large Irish, Italian, and French Canadian immigration in the past. The Jewish community of Rhode Island is centered in the Providence area. It emerged during a wave of Jewish immigration between 1880 and 1920. The presence of the Touro Synagogue in Newport, the oldest existing synagogue in the United States, emphasizes that these second-wave immigrants did not create Rhode Island's first Jewish community; a comparatively smaller wave of Portuguese Jews immigrated to Newport during the colonial era.

Population by Selected Ethnic Group

	Estimate		Estimate
Total:	1,055,173	Carpatho-Rusyn	39
Afghan	0	Celtic	208
Albanian	576	Croatian	314
Alsatian	0	Cypriot	0
American	41,200	Czech	1,643
Arab:	8,793	Czechoslovakian	411
Egyptian	771	Danish	1,733
Iraqi	69	Dutch	6,651
Jordanian	181	Eastern European	1,882
Lebanese	4,052	English	103,234
Moroccan	208	Estonian	0
Palestinian	217	European	5,380
Syrian	2,138	Finnish	1,018
Arab	783	French (except Basque)	103,610
Other Arab	549	French Canadian	53,122
Armenian	4,757	German	54,858
Assyrian/Chaldean/Syriac	0	German Russian	0
Australian	136	Greek	6,685
Austrian	1,577	Guyanese	94
Basque	1,056	Hungarian	2,882
Belgian	440	Icelander	155
Brazilian	2,252	Iranian	479
British	2,991	Irish	189,587
Bulgarian	63	Israeli	0
Cajun	0	Italian	194,168
Canadian	2,747	Latvian	420

(continued)

	Estimate		Estimate
Lithuanian	4,116	Somali	0
Luxemburger	0	South African	101
Macedonian	55	Sudanese	0
Maltese	4	Ugandan	0
New Zealander	120	Zimbabwean	0
Northern European	1,265	African	3,777
Norwegian	4,876	Other sub-Saharan African	279
Pennsylvania German	0	Swedish	17,152
Polish	42,737	Swiss	1,733
Portuguese	93,973	Turkish	421
Romanian	1,017	Ukrainian	2,687
Russian	11,405	Welsh	3,528
Scandinavian	370	West Indian	6,854
Scotch-Irish	5,133	(except Hispanic groups):	
Scottish	18,309	Bahamian	0
Serbian	30	Barbadian	168
Slavic	299	Belizean	56
Slovak	815	Bermudan	42
Slovene	95	British West Indian	0
Soviet Union	160	Dutch West Indian	0
Sub-Saharan African:	34,319	Haitian	4,239
Cape Verdean	23,529	Jamaican	1,642
Ethiopian	220	Trinidadian and Tobagonian	518
Ghanaian	1,375	U.S. Virgin Islander	0
Kenyan	0	West Indian	541
Liberian	3,116	Other West Indian	0
Nigerian	2,390	Yugoslavian	62
Senegalese	267	Other groups	252,942
Sierra Leonean	0	Unclassified or not reported	106,951

Source: American Community Survey, U.S. Census Bureau, 2014.

See in Neighborhoods Section: Federal Hill (Providence, Rhode Island); Pawtucket, Cape Verdean Enclave (Rhode Island); Woonsocket, French Canadian Enclave (Rhode Island)

SOUTH CAROLINA

Capital: Columbia
Entered Union: May 23, 1788 (8th state)

South Carolina is the 40th most extensive and the 24th most populous U.S. state. Columbia is its most populous city. The Spanish and the French claimed the area that is now South Carolina during the 16th century. Both North Carolina and South Carolina were included in the charter that established Carolina as an English colony in 1663. The two areas formally separated in 1729, with generally the same shared boundary as the present states. In 1802, South Carolina ceded area to the United States that became part of the Georgia and Mississippi Territory. At that point, South Carolina assumed more or less its modern boundaries. South Carolina ratified the U.S. Constitution on May 23, 1788, to become the eighth of the original 13 states. In 1860, South Carolina was the first state to secede from the United States and ratify the Constitution of the Confederate States of America. On April 12, 1861, Confederate artillery fired upon the Union garrison at Fort Sumter in the Charleston harbor, thus initiating the American Civil War.

As of the 2010 U.S. Census, South Carolina is home to 4,625,364 people. The capital is Columbia, which has a total of 129,272 residents. South Carolina has seven congressional districts, 46 state senate districts, and 124 state house districts. It borders North Carolina and Georgia.

Historical Population of South Carolina

Census	Pop.	%±	Census	Pop.	%±
1790	249,073	—	1910	1,515,400	13.1%
1800	345,591	38.8%	1920	1,683,724	11.1%
1810	415,115	20.1%	1930	1,738,765	3.3%
1820	502,741	21.1%	1940	1,899,804	9.3%
1830	581,185	15.6%	1950	2,117,027	11.4%
1840	594,398	2.3%	1960	2,382,594	12.5%
1850	668,507	12.5%	1970	2,590,516	8.7%
1860	703,708	5.3%	1980	3,121,820	20.5%
1870	705,606	0.3%	1990	3,486,703	11.7%
1880	995,577	41.1%	2000	4,012,012	15.1%
1890	1,151,149	15.6%	2010	4,625,364	15.3%
1900	1,340,316	16.4%			

Source: U.S. Census Bureau.

According to the 2010 census, the racial makeup of South Carolina is 66.2% white, 27.9% African American, 0.4% American Indian and Alaska Native, 1.3% Asian, 0.1% Native Hawaiian and other Pacific Islander, and 5.1% Hispanic. The white population of South Carolina is mainly of Northern European stock; the great migratory wave from Southern and Eastern Europe during the late 19th century left South Carolina nearly untouched. In 2000, the black population made up 29.5% of the state's population (the third highest percentage in the nation). In the coastal regions and offshore islands of South Carolina, some vestiges of African heritage can still be found, notably the Gullah dialect. South Carolina has always had an urban black elite, much of it of mixed racial heritage. After 1954, racial integration proceeded relatively peacefully, with careful planning by both black leaders and white leaders.

The religious makeup of the state is 85% Christian, roughly divided into 41% Baptist, 15% Methodist, 7% Catholic, 5% Presbyterian, 3% Pentecostal, 2% Episcopal, and 2% Lutheran, while 7% of residents reported having no religious affiliation. According to the Association of Religion Data Archives (ARDA), in 2010 the largest denominations in South Carolina by number of adherents were the Southern Baptist Convention, the United Methodist Church, the Roman Catholic Church, and the African Methodist Episcopal Church.

Population by Selected Ethnic Group

	Estimate		Estimate
Total:	4,832,482	Cypriot	48
Afghan	49	Czech	7,564
Albanian	244	Czechoslovakian	2,612
Alsatian	0	Danish	7,370
American	548,709	Dutch	45,133
Arab:	12,772	Eastern European	1,190
Egyptian	3,044	English	473,860
Iraqi	843	Estonian	0
Jordanian	0	European	53,819
Lebanese	4,747	Finnish	3,471
Moroccan	472	French (except Basque)	91,851
Palestinian	456	French Canadian	15,222
Syrian	699	German	487,169
Arab	1,612	German Russian	103
Other Arab	1,177	Greek	16,588
Armenian	1,211	Guyanese	467
Assyrian/Chaldean/Syriac	263	Hungarian	14,647
Australian	751	Icelander	166
Austrian	6,585	Iranian	1,097
Basque	255	Irish	463,727
Belgian	2,116	Israeli	827
Brazilian	2,714	Italian	141,735
British	23,091	Latvian	617
Bulgarian	791	Lithuanian	5,522
Cajun	562	Luxemburger	157
Canadian	6,126	Macedonian	449
Carpatho-Rusyn	56	Maltese	508
Celtic	1,128	New Zealander	44
Croatian	1,750	Northern European	1,678

(continued)

	Estimate		Estimate
Norwegian	18,417	Ugandan	45
Pennsylvania German	1,832	Zimbabwean	55
Polish	69,016	African	27,634
Portuguese	6,614	Other sub-Saharan African	990
Romanian	2,856	Swedish	23,156
Russian	16,273	Swiss	7,506
Scandinavian	5,111	Turkish	1,832
Scotch-Irish	117,031	Ukrainian	11,455
Scottish	110,374	Welsh	23,179
Serbian	491	West Indian	14,883
Slavic	862	(except Hispanic groups):	
Slovak	4,633	Bahamian	835
Slovene	1,073	Barbadian	202
Soviet Union	0	Belizean	651
Sub-Saharan African:	36,535	Bermudan	0
Cape Verdean	53	British West Indian	518
Ethiopian	1,198	Dutch West Indian	122
Ghanaian	363	Haitian	2,176
Kenyan	841	Jamaican	8,310
Liberian	325	Trinidadian and Tobagonian	823
Nigerian	3,761	U.S. Virgin Islander	115
Senegalese	99	West Indian	1,507
Sierra Leonean	968	Other West Indian	69
Somali	0	Yugoslavian	428
South African	662	Other groups	1,823,504
Sudanese	0	Unclassified or not reported	862,795

Source: American Community Survey, U.S. Census Bureau, 2014.

SOUTH DAKOTA

Capital: Pierre
Entered Union: November 2, 1889 (40th state)

South Dakota is the 16th most extensive by land area but the fifth least populous and the fifth least densely populated U.S. state. South Dakota became the 39th state on November 2, 1889, simultaneously with North Dakota. The first European contact with the area was in 1743, when the LaVerendrye brothers explored the region and claimed it for France. In 1803, the United States purchased the Louisiana Territory, an area that included most of South Dakota, from Napoleon Bonaparte.

South Dakota has a total population of 814,180. Pierre is the state capital. Sioux Falls, with a population of 153,888, is South Dakota's largest city. There are nine American Indian reservations, one congressional district, 35 state senate districts, and 37 state house districts. South Dakota borders six states: Iowa, Minnesota, Montana, Nebraska, North Dakota, and Wyoming.

Historical Population of South Dakota

Census	Pop.	%±	Census	Pop.	%±
1860	4,837	—	1940	642,961	−42,9
1870	11,776	143.5%	1950	652,740	1.5%
1880	98,268	734.5%	1960	680,514	4.3%
1890	348,600	254.7%	1970	665,507	−65,5
1900	401,570	15.2%	1980	690,768	3.8%
1910	583,888	45.4%	1990	696,004	0.8%
1920	636,547	9.0%	2000	754,844	8.5%
1930	692,849	8.8%	2010	814,180	7.9%

Source: U.S. Census Bureau.

According to the 2010 U.S. Census, the racial composition of the population was 84.7% white, 8.5% American Indian and Alaska Native, 2.7% Hispanic, 1.2% African American, and 0.9% Asian American. The five largest ancestry groups in South Dakota are German (40.7%), Norwegian (15.3%), Irish (10.4%), Native American (8.3%), and English (7.1%). German Americans are the largest ancestry group in most parts of the state, although there are also large Scandinavian-descended populations in some counties. South Dakota has the nation's largest population of Hutterites, a communal Anabaptist group that emigrated from Europe in 1874. South Dakota has the third highest proportion of Native Americans of any state, behind Alaska and New Mexico. Unfortunately, living standards on many South Dakota reservations are often far below the national average. Ziebach County, for example, ranked as the poorest county in the nation in 2009.

English is specified by law as the "common language" of the state. According to the 2010 census, 93.46% of the residents speak English as their primary language, 1.37% speak German at home, while 1.39% speak Dakota, and 2.06% Spanish.

The largest religious denominations by number of adherents in 2010 were the Roman Catholic Church, the Evangelical Lutheran Church in America, and the United Methodist Church. According to a 2001 survey, 61% of South Dakotans identify their religion as Protestant, 25% as Roman Catholic, 8% as not religious, and 3% as other religions.

Population by Selected Ethnic Group

	Estimate		Estimate
Total:	834,708	Albanian	56
Afghan	121	Alsatian	17

(continued)

	Estimate		Estimate
American	32,065	Icelander	165
Arab:	1,637	Iranian	44
Egyptian	36	Irish	90,660
Iraqi	117	Israeli	11
Jordanian	0	Italian	11,202
Lebanese	502	Latvian	187
Moroccan	10	Lithuanian	349
Palestinian	13	Luxemburger	855
Syrian	514	Macedonian	34
Arab	334	Maltese	0
Other Arab	119	New Zealander	22
Armenian	350	Northern European	681
Assyrian/Chaldean/Syriac	2	Norwegian	115,664
Australian	155	Pennsylvania German	353
Austrian	1,071	Polish	13,152
Basque	33	Portuguese	661
Belgian	1,582	Romanian	338
Brazilian	212	Russian	10,916
British	1,811	Scandinavian	5,899
Bulgarian	130	Scotch-Irish	4,852
Cajun	27	Scottish	9,802
Canadian	645	Serbian	231
Carpatho-Rusyn	7	Slavic	97
Celtic	103	Slovak	340
Croatian	306	Slovene	158
Cypriot	0	Soviet Union	0
Czech	18,188	Sub-Saharan African:	4,883
Czechoslovakian	1,629	Cape Verdean	10
Danish	16,890	Ethiopian	1,567
Dutch	39,720	Ghanaian	0
Eastern European	72	Kenyan	49
English	49,245	Liberian	332
Estonian	0	Nigerian	91
European	6,719	Senegalese	3
Finnish	3,993	Sierra Leonean	0
French (except Basque)	20,572	Somali	210
French Canadian	4,069	South African	80
German	335,407	Sudanese	349
German Russian	197	Ugandan	42
Greek	1,084	Zimbabwean	29
Guyanese	11	African	2,008
Hungarian	1,115	Other sub-Saharan African	183

(continued)

	Estimate		Estimate
Swedish	28,379	British West Indian	11
Swiss	3,248	Dutch West Indian	5
Turkish	171	Haitian	31
Ukrainian	1,417	Jamaican	165
Welsh	4,303	Trinidadian and Tobagonian	62
West Indian	369	U.S. Virgin Islander	3
(except Hispanic groups):		West Indian	62
Bahamian	0	Other West Indian	0
Barbadian	34	Yugoslavian	1,154
Belizean	24	Other groups	156,767
Bermudan	0	Unclassified or not reported	101,359

Source: American Community Survey, U.S. Census Bureau, 2014.

See in Neighborhoods Section: Tabor, Czech Enclave (South Dakota)

TENNESSEE

Capital: Nashville
Entered Union: June 1, 1796 (16th state)

The world famous Country Music Hall of Fame in Nashville, Tennessee, 2016. (Brenda Kean/ Dreamstime.com)

Tennessee is the 34th most extensive and the 17th most populous U.S. state. It supposedly earned its nickname, "The Volunteer State," during the War of 1812, thanks to the prominent role of its volunteer soldiers. Tennessee's capital and second largest city is Nashville, and Memphis is the state's largest city with 646,889 residents. The first recorded European excursions into what is now called Tennessee were three expeditions led by Spanish explorers in 1540, 1559, and 1567. The first British settlement in the region that is now Tennessee was built in 1756. The area of Tennessee was originally part of North Carolina, who ceded it to the United States in 1790. Tennessee was admitted to the Union on June 1, 1796, as the 16th state. Upon resolution of a boundary dispute with Kentucky in 1820, Tennessee assumed generally the same boundary as the present state. It was the last state to leave the Union and join the Confederacy during the Civil War, and was the first to be admitted upon the war's conclusion.

Tennessee has nine congressional districts, 33 state senate districts, and 99 state house districts. Tennessee borders eight states: Alabama, Arkansas, Georgia, Kentucky, Mississippi, Missouri, North Carolina, and Virginia.

Historical Population of Tennessee

Census	Pop.	%±	Census	Pop.	%±
1790	35,691	—	1910	2,184,789	8.1%
1800	105,602	195.9%	1920	2,337,885	7.0%
1810	261,727	147.8%	1930	2,616,556	11.9%
1820	422,823	61.6%	1940	2,915,841	11.4%
1830	681,904	61.3%	1950	3,291,718	12.9%
1840	829,210	21.6%	1960	3,567,089	8.4%
1850	1,002,717	20.9%	1970	3,923,687	10.0%
1860	1,109,801	10.7%	1980	4,591,120	17.0%
1870	1,258,520	13.4%	1990	4,877,185	6.2%
1880	1,542,359	22.6%	2000	5,689,283	16.7%
1890	1,767,518	14.6%	2010	6,346,105	11.5%
1900	2,020,616	14.3%			

Source: U.S. Census Bureau.

According to the 2010 U.S. Census, the racial composition of the state is 77.6% white, 16.7% African American, 1.4% Asian, 0.3% Native American, and 0.1% Native Hawaiian and other Pacific Islander. Most Tennesseans who self-identify as having American ancestry are of English and Scotch-Irish descent. An estimated 21–24% of Tennesseans are of predominantly English ancestry. Africans, originally brought into the state as slaves to labor in the cotton fields of West Tennessee, made up about 10% of the population in 1790. White Tennesseans were divided on the issue of slavery. The small farmers of the eastern region were against it, and in the late 1820s and 1830s there were more antislavery societies in Tennessee than in any other southern state except North Carolina.

The religious affiliations of the residents of Tennessee are 82% Christian, which is divided into 70% Protestants, 6% Church of Christ, 6% Roman Catholic, and 12% other Christian. One percent of Tennesseans identified as Muslim, 9% as nonreligious and 2% as other religions. The largest denominations by number of adherents in 2010 were the Southern Baptist Convention, the United Methodist Church, the Roman Catholic Church, and the Churches of Christ.

Population by Selected Ethnic Group

	Estimate		Estimate
Total:	6,549,352	Danish	8,381
Afghan	490	Dutch	74,221
Albanian	694	Eastern European	3,762
Alsatian	98	English	589,823
American	1,082,731	Estonian	193
Arab:	35,553	European	72,550
Egyptian	7,919	Finnish	3,991
Iraqi	2,340	French (except Basque)	108,467
Jordanian	2,013	French Canadian	18,885
Lebanese	3,889	German	636,742
Moroccan	1,328	German Russian	259
Palestinian	514	Greek	10,292
Syrian	706	Guyanese	980
Arab	7,107	Hungarian	11,618
Other Arab	10,068	Icelander	148
Armenian	2,153	Iranian	6,529
Assyrian/Chaldean/Syriac	229	Irish	678,182
Australian	1,003	Israeli	449
Austrian	5,499	Italian	147,032
Basque	0	Latvian	300
Belgian	2,530	Lithuanian	6,036
Brazilian	2,988	Luxemburger	237
British	27,038	Macedonian	93
Bulgarian	710	Maltese	540
Cajun	2,107	New Zealander	86
Canadian	5,622	Northern European	2,718
Carpatho-Rusyn	0	Norwegian	29,362
Celtic	858	Pennsylvania German	4,218
Croatian	1,929	Polish	64,821
Cypriot	0	Portuguese	5,458
Czech	8,637	Romanian	4,101
Czechoslovakian	2,337	Russian	17,511

(*continued*)

	Estimate		Estimate
Scandinavian	5,653	Other sub-Saharan African	2,779
Scotch-Irish	135,220	Swedish	31,722
Scottish	140,754	Swiss	9,526
Serbian	1,479	Turkish	1,224
Slavic	1,742	Ukrainian	7,150
Slovak	3,216	Welsh	31,415
Slovene	804	West Indian	11,968
Soviet Union	0	(except Hispanic groups):	
Sub-Saharan African:	78,748	Bahamian	487
Cape Verdean	0	Barbadian	337
Ethiopian	2,301	Belizean	471
Ghanaian	629	Bermudan	60
Kenyan	507	British West Indian	470
Liberian	1,824	Dutch West Indian	1,499
Nigerian	2,578	Haitian	2,289
Senegalese	557	Jamaican	3,846
Sierra Leonean	158	Trinidadian and Tobagonian	152
Somali	2,903	U.S. Virgin Islander	0
South African	1,318	West Indian	2,748
Sudanese	1,708	Other West Indian	42
Ugandan	68	Yugoslavian	1,981
Zimbabwean	192	Other groups	2,052,510
African	61,634	Unclassified or not reported	1,417,166

Source: American Community Survey, U.S. Census Bureau, 2014.

See in Neighborhoods Section: Orange Mound (Memphis, Tennessee)

TEXAS

Capital: Austin
Entered Union: December 29, 1845 (28th state)

Texas is the second most populous state and also the second-largest state by size. Texas was settled by the Spanish in the 16th century and, to a much smaller extent, the French in the 18th century. American settlers began to arrive in the 19th century. Texas was originally part of Mexico, achieving independence as the Republic of Texas in 1836. The United States acquired the area of Texas through annexation, and Texas was admitted to the Union on March 1, 1845, as the 28th state. At the time of statehood, Texas included part of present-day Colorado, Kansas, New Mexico, Oklahoma, and Wyoming. This annexation and the subsequent border dispute with Mexico led to the Mexican-American War of 1846–1848. Texas sold territory to the United States in 1850 to assume generally the same boundary as the present state. As the Rio Grande has changed its course, the United States and the Republic of Mexico have made periodic adjustments to their boundary that have affected the boundary of Texas. Much of the population resides in Dallas, Houston, San Antonio, Fort Worth, Austin, and El Paso.

Austin is the capital, while Houston is its largest city with 2,099,451 inhabitants. Texas has 36 congressional districts, 31 state senate districts, and 150 state house districts. It borders Arkansas, Louisiana, New Mexico, and Oklahoma, in addition to its international border with Mexico.

Historical Population of Texas

Census	Pop.	%±	Census	Pop.	%±
1850	212,592	—	1940	6,414,824	10.1%
1860	604,215	184.2%	1950	7,711,194	20.2%
1870	818,579	35.5%	1960	9,579,677	24.2%
1880	1,591,749	94.5%	1970	11,196,730	16.9%
1890	2,235,527	40.4%	1980	14,229,191	27.1%
1900	3,048,710	36.4%	1990	16,986,510	19.4%
1910	3,896,542	27.8%	2000	20,851,820	22.8%
1920	4,663,228	19.7%	2010	25,145,561	20.6%
1930	5,824,715	24.9%			

Source: U.S. Census Bureau.

The 2010 U.S. Census recorded Texas as having a population of 25.1 million—an increase of 4.3 million since the year 2000, involving an increase in population in all three subcategories of population growth: natural increase (births minus deaths), net immigration, and net migration. The state passed New York in the 1990s to become the second-largest U.S. state in population, after California.

As of 2012, the state has an estimated 4.1 million foreign-born residents, constituting approximately 15% of the state population. An estimated 1.7 million people are illegal immigrants.

According to the 2010 U.S. Census, the racial distribution in Texas is as follows: 70.4% white American; 11.8% African American; 3.8% Asian American; 0.7% American Indian; 0.1% Native Hawaiian or Pacific Islander; 10.5% some other race; and 2.7% two or more races. Hispanics (of any race) were 37.6% of the population, while non-Hispanic whites composed 45.3%. Furthermore, as of 2010, 45% of Texas residents have Hispanic ancestry; these include recent immigrants from Mexico, Central America, and South America, as well as Tejanos, whose ancestors have lived in Texas as early as the 1700s.

Latinos are the second-largest group in Texas. Over 8.5 million people claim Latino ethnicity, comprising 36% of Texas's population. People of Mexican descent are the most numerous, over 7.3 million, and comprise 30.7% of the population. Over

104,000 Puerto Ricans live in the state, as do roughly 38,000 Cubans. A further 1.1 million people (4.7% of the population) are of varying Hispanic and Latino ancestries, such as Costa Rican, Venezuelan, and Argentine. Texas is home to 6,304,207 white Hispanics and 2,594,206 Hispanics of "some other race," which is usually mestizo (mixed white and Indian).

Multiracial residents constitute 1.9% of the population, over 448,000 people. Nearly 80,000 Texans claim mixed African and European heritage and make up 0.3% of the population. Persons of mixed European and Native American heritage form a population of 108,800 (close to the number of Native Americans), and make up 0.5% of the population. The population of European and Asian heritage is 57,600, 0.2% of the Texas population. The population of mixed African and Native American heritage is 15,300, or 0.1% of the total population.

The largest European ancestry group in Texas is English, which makes up nearly a third of the state total. Other major European ancestry groups in Texas include German Americans (11.3%) and Irish Americans (8.2%). About 600,000 French Americans and 472,000 Italian Americans form 2.5% and 2.0% of the Texas population, respectively.

According to the Modern Language Association, as of 2010, 65.8% of Texas residents age five and older speak English at home as a primary language, while 29.21% speak Spanish, 0.75% Vietnamese, and 0.56% Chinese (Cantonese and Mandarin). Other languages spoken include German (including Texas German) at 0.33%, Tagalog with 0.29%, and French (including Cajun French) at 0.25%.

According to the Pew Research Center, 77% of adult Texans identify as Christian, with Evangelical Protestants, Catholics, and Mainline Protestants as the three largest subgroups. Evangelical Protestant Christian influence has had a strong social, cultural, and political impact in Texas throughout its history. Non-Christian faiths, including Islam, Buddhism, Hinduism, Judaism, and others, make up 4% of the Texas population, while 31% of Texans consider themselves unaffiliated or nothing in particular.

Population by Selected Ethnic Group

	Estimate		Estimate
Total:	26,956,958	Lebanese	33,655
Afghan	2,532	Moroccan	2,948
Albanian	5,771	Palestinian	11,574
Alsatian	3,027	Syrian	7,764
American	1,504,038	Arab	20,701
Arab:	117,930	Other Arab	14,633
Egyptian	6,900	Armenian	7,718
Iraqi	15,044	Assyrian/Chaldean/Syriac	100
Jordanian	7,832	Australian	5,958

(continued)

	Estimate		Estimate
Austrian	26,431	Polish	291,514
Basque	2,512	Portuguese	28,636
Belgian	12,102	Romanian	14,640
Brazilian	16,903	Russian	85,053
British	104,347	Scandinavian	24,275
Bulgarian	4,365	Scotch-Irish	266,528
Cajun	22,556	Scottish	385,310
Canadian	33,102	Serbian	4,280
Carpatho-Rusyn	71	Slavic	3,429
Celtic	4,226	Slovak	12,541
Croatian	11,671	Slovene	6,378
Cypriot	132	Soviet Union	0
Czech	203,962	Sub-Saharan African:	304,508
Czechoslovakian	22,430	Cape Verdean	531
Danish	43,808	Ethiopian	24,383
Dutch	218,208	Ghanaian	5,585
Eastern European	12,260	Kenyan	10,121
English	1,681,167	Liberian	2,549
Estonian	977	Nigerian	59,431
European	233,684	Senegalese	83
Finnish	17,070	Sierra Leonean	713
French (except Basque)	539,035	Somali	8,386
French Canadian	71,150	South African	6,497
German	2,599,555	Sudanese	6,563
German Russian	1,460	Ugandan	412
Greek	48,046	Zimbabwean	674
Guyanese	2,854	African	163,843
Hungarian	41,115	Other sub-Saharan African	18,742
Icelander	2,828	Swedish	144,947
Iranian	32,538	Swiss	37,364
Irish	1,857,861	Turkish	12,147
Israeli	3,262	Ukrainian	21,168
Italian	514,367	Welsh	99,639
Latvian	3,027	West Indian	69,931
Lithuanian	16,539	(except Hispanic groups):	
Luxemburger	983	Bahamian	1,053
Macedonian	1,486	Barbadian	1,813
Maltese	1,317	Belizean	2,931
New Zealander	1,277	Bermudan	121
Northern European	13,979	British West Indian	3,629
Norwegian	140,198	Dutch West Indian	12,091
Pennsylvania German	4,469	Haitian	8,722

(continued)

	Estimate		Estimate
Jamaican	23,750	Other West Indian	246
Trinidadian and Tobagonian	7,006	Yugoslavian	11,000
U.S. Virgin Islander	550	Other groups	15,325,721
West Indian	8,958	Unclassified or not reported	3,616,196

Source: American Community Survey, U.S. Census Bureau, 2014.

See in Neighborhoods Section: Dallas, Mexican Enclaves (Texas); Houston, Mexican Enclaves (Texas); Little India, Hillcroft (Houston, Texas); Little Saigon (Houston, Texas); Muenster, German Enclave (Texas); New Braunfels, German Enclave (Texas); Serbin, German Enclave (Texas)

UTAH

Capital: Salt Lake City
Entered Union: January 4, 1896 (45th state)

Utah is the 12th-largest and the 34th most populous state. With 33.6 persons per square mile, Utah is the 10th least densely populated U.S. state. The Spanish first explored the southern Utah region in 1540. The Spanish made further explorations in the region, but they were not interested in colonizing the area because of its desert climate. In 1821, the year Mexico achieved its independence from Spain, the region of Utah became part of Mexico. The first band of Mormon pioneers came to the Salt Lake Valley, Utah, on July 24, 1847. Over the next 22 years, more than 70,000 pioneers crossed the plains and settled in the region, where they could practice their religion without harassment. Utah became the 45th state admitted to the Union on January 4, 1896. Utah has three congressional districts, 29 state senate districts, and 75 state house districts. Salt Lake City is the capital, which is also its largest city with 186,440 residents. Utah borders six other states: Arizona, Colorado, Idaho, Nevada, New Mexico, and Wyoming.

Historical Population of Utah

Census	Pop.	%±	Census	Pop.	%±
1850	11,380	—	1900	276,749	31.3%
1860	40,273	253.9%	1910	373,351	34.9%
1870	86,336	114.4%	1920	449,396	20.4%
1880	143,963	66.7%	1930	507,847	13.0%
1890	210,779	46.4%	1940	550,310	8.4%

(continued)

Census	Pop.	%±	Census	Pop.	%±
1950	688,862	25.2%	1990	1,722,850	17.9%
1960	890,627	29.3%	2000	2,233,169	29.6%
1970	1,059,273	18.9%	2010	2,763,885	23.8%
1980	1,461,037	37.9%			

Source: U.S. Census Bureau.

According to the 2010 U.S. Census, 80.4% of the population in Utah is white, 13.0% Hispanic, 0.9% African American, 1% American Indian and Alaska Native, 2% Asian, and 0.9% Native Hawaiian and other Pacific Islander. Most Utahans are of Northern European descent. Hispanics and Latinos constitute the largest ethnic minority in Utah, with an estimated 9% of the total population, up from 6.8% in 1990. American Indians are the third-largest minority group in Utah, numbering an estimated 29,684 in 2000. The Uintah and Ouray Indian reservation in the northeast and the Navaho Indian reservation in the southeast are the largest reservations in Utah.

According to a report produced by the Pew Forum on Religion & Public Life, the self-identified religious affiliations of Utahans other than the Church of Jesus Christ of Latter-day Saints are 16% unaffiliated, 10% Catholic, 7% Evangelicals, 6% Mainline Protestants, Islam < 0.8%, Buddhism < 0.5%, and Eastern Orthodox < 0.5%. Utah is the most religiously homogeneous state in the Union. Approximately 62% of Utahans are reported to be members of the Church of Jesus Christ of Latter-day Saints (Mormons), which greatly influences Utah culture and daily life. The world headquarters of the Church of Jesus Christ of Latter-day Saints (LDS Church) is located in Utah's state capital, Salt Lake City. Mormons now make up about 34–41% of Salt Lake City, while rural and suburban areas tend to be overwhelmingly Mormon. Although the LDS Church officially maintains a policy of neutrality in regards to political parties, the church's doctrine has a strong regional influence on politics. LDS doctrine's influence is seen in Utah's high birth rate, which is 25% higher than the national average.

Population by Selected Ethnic Group

	Estimate		Estimate
Total:	2,942,902	Egyptian	374
Afghan	1,710	Iraqi	2,676
Albanian	689	Jordanian	50
Alsatian	0	Lebanese	2,231
American	175,860	Moroccan	0
Arab:	10,130	Palestinian	400

(continued)

	Estimate		Estimate
Syrian	413	Macedonian	0
Arab	596	Maltese	127
Other Arab	3,476	New Zealander	735
Armenian	2,974	Northern European	6,286
Assyrian/Chaldean/Syriac	0	Norwegian	69,209
Australian	2,119	Pennsylvania German	122
Austrian	4,464	Polish	22,967
Basque	1,608	Portuguese	4,543
Belgian	1,902	Romanian	1,700
Brazilian	3,107	Russian	10,404
British	40,849	Scandinavian	33,050
Bulgarian	450	Scotch-Irish	21,122
Cajun	77	Scottish	129,611
Canadian	10,700	Serbian	2,184
Carpatho-Rusyn	0	Slavic	1,192
Celtic	320	Slovak	1,434
Croatian	3,626	Slovene	971
Cypriot	0	Soviet Union	0
Czech	5,956	Sub-Saharan African:	12,111
Czechoslovakian	895	Cape Verdean	0
Danish	147,403	Ethiopian	481
Dutch	67,382	Ghanaian	112
Eastern European	2,015	Kenyan	732
English	732,758	Liberian	27
Estonian	237	Nigerian	178
European	129,138	Senegalese	0
Finnish	5,997	Sierra Leonean	116
French (except Basque)	58,444	Somali	2,134
French Canadian	8,175	South African	1,196
German	333,283	Sudanese	784
German Russian	256	Ugandan	367
Greek	17,006	Zimbabwean	0
Guyanese	0	African	5,665
Hungarian	5,611	Other sub-Saharan African	356
Icelander	4,051	Swedish	108,547
Iranian	2,186	Swiss	42,398
Irish	166,385	Turkish	960
Israeli	410	Ukrainian	2,896
Italian	84,655	Welsh	58,472
Latvian	717	West Indian	2,291
Lithuanian	1,582	(except Hispanic groups):	
Luxemburger	224	Bahamian	20

(continued)

	Estimate		Estimate
Barbadian	0	Trinidadian and Tobagonian	0
Belizean	33	U.S. Virgin Islander	0
Bermudan	0	West Indian	804
British West Indian	85	Other West Indian	0
Dutch West Indian	32	Yugoslavian	3,400
Haitian	949	Other groups	741,171
Jamaican	368	Unclassified or not reported	456,603

Source: American Community Survey, U.S. Census Bureau, 2014.

See in Neighborhood Section: Iosepa, Pacific Islander Enclave (Utah); Old Greektown (Salt Lake City, Utah)

VERMONT

Capital: Montpelier
Entered Union: March 4, 1791 (14th state)

Vermont is the sixth smallest in area and the second least populous U.S. state. In 1666, French settlers erected the first European settlement in Vermont. From 1731 to 1734, the French constructed Fort St. Frédéric and kept the control of the

Milk cow on a Vermont dairy farm, one of the state's biggest industries. (Chee-onn Leong/Dreamstime.com)

New France/Vermont frontier region in their hands. Following France's defeat in
the French and Indian War and the 1763 Treaty of Paris, the French ceded the control of the land to the British. The area of Vermont was part of the original territory
of the United States. It was included in the Charter of New England in 1620, but
was later included in grants creating New York in 1664 and 1674. Representatives
of 51 towns in the present area declared an independent state of "New Connecticut
alias Vermont" in 1777, but also referred to the area as the "New Hampshire Grants."
New York consented to the statehood separation of Vermont, which was admitted
to the Union on February 18, 1791 as the 14th state, with generally the same boundary as the present state.

The state capital, Montpelier, is the least populous state capital in the country,
with just 7,855 inhabitants as of the 2010 U.S. Census. Vermont's most populous
city is Burlington, with a 2010 population of 42,417. Vermont has one congressional district, 13 state senate districts, and 108 state house districts. Vermont borders
the states of Massachusetts, New Hampshire, and New York, in addition to an international border with Canada.

Historical Population of Vermont

Census	Pop.	%±	Census	Pop.	%±
1790	85,425	—	1910	355,956	3.6%
1800	154,465	80.8%	1920	352,428	−52,4
1810	217,895	41.1%	1930	359,611	2.0%
1820	235,981	8.3%	1940	359,231	−59,2
1830	280,652	18.9%	1950	377,747	5.2%
1840	291,948	4.0%	1960	389,881	3.2%
1850	314,120	7.6%	1970	444,330	14.0%
1860	315,098	0.3%	1980	511,456	15.1%
1870	330,551	4.9%	1990	562,758	10.0%
1880	332,286	0.5%	2000	608,827	8.2%
1890	332,422	0.0%	2010	625,741	2.8%
1900	343,641	3.4%			

Source: U.S. Census Bureau.

In 2010, Vermont was rated the "second whitest" state in the nation. Vermont's
racial composition is 94.3% white, 1.3% Asian, 1.5% Hispanic, 1.0% African American, and 0.4% Native American.

The largest ancestry groups in Vermont are French or French Canadian at 23.9%,
English at 18.6%, and Irish at 17.9%. The northern part of the state in particular is
home to a significant percentage of people of French Canadian ancestry. According
to the 2000 U.S. Census, 2.54% of the population aged five and older speaks French
at home, while 1% speaks Spanish.

As of 2012, Vermont is considered the least religious state in the United States,
with 23% of the residents considering themselves "very religious." The largest single

religious body in the state is the Roman Catholic Church. According to the ARDA in 2010, the Catholic Church had 128,293 members. Almost one-third of Vermonters were self-identified Protestants. The Congregational United Church of Christ is the largest Protestant denomination in Vermont. The second-largest Protestant denomination is the United Methodist Church, followed by the Baptists. In 2008, 34% of Vermonters reported having no religious affiliation, which is the highest percentage in the nation. Vermont may have the highest concentration of western-convert Buddhists in the country. Several Buddhist retreat centers are located in the state.

Population by Selected Ethnic Group

	Estimate		Estimate
Total:	626,358	Czech	2,106
Afghan	11	Czechoslovakian	458
Albanian	84	Danish	2,243
Alsatian	26	Dutch	8,238
American	51,927	Eastern European	1,975
Arab:	2,421	English	106,558
Egyptian	129	Estonian	124
Iraqi	153	European	15,973
Jordanian	23	Finnish	2,276
Lebanese	1,646	French (except Basque)	85,785
Moroccan	41	French Canadian	51,549
Palestinian	147	German	65,436
Syrian	179	German Russian	31
Arab	103	Greek	2,699
Other Arab	59	Guyanese	115
Armenian	652	Hungarian	3,422
Assyrian/Chaldean/Syriac	33	Icelander	48
Australian	115	Iranian	215
Austrian	2,397	Irish	112,215
Basque	64	Israeli	95
Belgian	505	Italian	45,920
Brazilian	225	Latvian	224
British	4,698	Lithuanian	2,196
Bulgarian	36	Luxemburger	29
Cajun	50	Macedonian	24
Canadian	5,818	Maltese	29
Carpatho-Rusyn	0	New Zealander	23
Celtic	293	Northern European	1,764
Croatian	236	Norwegian	5,346
Cypriot	13	Pennsylvania German	276

(*continued*)

	Estimate		Estimate
Polish	23,043	Zimbabwean	0
Portuguese	2,398	African	806
Romanian	868	Other sub-Saharan African	369
Russian	8,574	Swedish	9,970
Scandinavian	1,215	Swiss	2,232
Scotch-Irish	7,007	Turkish	138
Scottish	27,282	Ukrainian	1,712
Serbian	348	Welsh	6,599
Slavic	254	West Indian	1,016
Slovak	1,063	(except Hispanic groups):	
Slovene	322	Bahamian	1
Soviet Union	0	Barbadian	58
Sub-Saharan African:	2,244	Belizean	0
Cape Verdean	103	Bermudan	3
Ethiopian	186	British West Indian	5
Ghanaian	128	Dutch West Indian	0
Kenyan	2	Haitian	214
Liberian	3	Jamaican	446
Nigerian	50	Trinidadian and Tobagonian	76
Senegalese	5	U.S. Virgin Islander	68
Sierra Leonean	0	West Indian	146
Somali	449	Other West Indian	5
South African	113	Yugoslavian	1,292
Sudanese	46	Other groups	86,763
Ugandan	12	Unclassified or not reported	85,371

Source: U.S. Census Bureau, 2010–2014 American Community Survey 5-Year Estimates.

See in Neighborhoods Section: Burlington/Winooski/Derby Line and Other Cities, French Canadian Enclaves (Vermont)

VIRGINIA

Capital: Richmond
Entered Union: June 25, 1788 (10th state)

In 1607, the London Company established the Colony of Virginia as the first permanent New World English colony. The London Company was incorporated as a joint stock company by the proprietary Charter of 1606, which granted land rights to this area. The company financed the first permanent English settlement in the "New World," Jamestown. Named for King James I, it was founded in May 1607 by Christopher Newport. On June 25, 1788, Virginia was admitted to the Union as the 10th state.

Virginia is the 12th most populated and the 36th-largest state by area. The capital is Richmond, which was also the capital of the Confederacy during the American Civil War. Virginia Beach is the state's biggest city, with 437,994 inhabitants. Virginia has 11 congressional districts, 40 state senate districts, and 100 state house districts. It borders five other states: Kentucky, Maryland, North Carolina, Tennessee, and West Virginia, in addition to the District of Columbia. Virginia is one of four states legally described as a commonwealth, which denotes that it is a political community founded for the common good, and a social compact into which the individuals of the commonwealth enter with one another.

Those who self-identify as having American ethnicity are predominantly of English descent. Of the English immigrants to Virginia in the 1600s, 75% came as indentured servants. The western mountains have many settlements that were founded by Scots-Irish immigrants before the American Revolution. The largest minority group in Virginia is African American, at 19.7% as of 2013. Most African American Virginians are descendants of enslaved Africans from west-central Africa, primarily Angola and the Bight of Biafra, who worked on hemp, tobacco, and cotton plantations. According to the Pew Research Center, the state has the highest concentration of black and white interracial marriages. More recent immigration in the late 20th century and early 21st century has fueled new communities of Hispanics and Asians. As of 2013, 8.6% of Virginians are Hispanic, and 6.1% are Asian. The state's Hispanic population rose by 92% from 2000 to 2010, with two-thirds of Hispanics living in Northern Virginia. Northern Virginia also has a significant population of Vietnamese Americans, whose major wave of immigration followed the Vietnam War, and Korean Americans, whose migration has been more recent and was induced in part by the quality school system. Additionally, 0.5% of Virginians are American Indian or Alaska Native, and 0.1% are Native Hawaiian or other Pacific Islander. Virginia has extended state recognition to eight Native American tribes in the state, though all lack federal recognition status.

Historical Population of Virginia

Census	Pop.	%±	Census	Pop.	%±
1790	691,737	—	1870	1,225,163	0.5%
1800	807,557	16.7%	1880	1,512,565	23.5%
1810	877,683	8.7%	1890	1,655,980	9.5%
1820	938,261	6.9%	1900	1,854,184	12.0%
1830	1,044,054	11.3%	1910	2,061,612	11.2%
1840	1,025,227	−1.8%	1920	2,309,187	12.0%
1850	1,119,348	9.2%	1930	2,421,851	4.9%
1860	1,219,630	9.0%	1940	2,677,773	10.6%

(continued)

Census	Pop.	%±	Census	Pop.	%±
1950	3,318,680	23.9%	1990	6,187,358	15.7%
1960	3,966,949	19.5%	2000	7,078,515	14.4%
1970	4,648,494	17.2%	2010	8,001,024	13.0%
1980	5,346,818	15.0%			

Source: U.S. Census Bureau.

According to a 2010 survey, 85.87% of Virginia residents speak English at home as their primary language, while 6.41% speak Spanish, 0.77% Korean, 0.63% Vietnamese, 0.57% Chinese, and 0.56% speak Tagalog.

Virginia is predominantly Christian and Protestant. Baptists are the largest single group, with 27% of the population as of 2008. Roman Catholics are the second-largest religious group with 673,853 members. Among other religions, adherents of the Church of Jesus Christ of Latter-day Saints constitute 1% of the population. While the state's Jewish population is small, organized Jewish sites date to 1789. In addition, Muslims are a growing religious group throughout the Commonwealth through immigration.

Population by Selected Ethnic Group

	Estimate		Estimate
Total:	8,326,289	Belgian	6,919
Afghan	13,394	Brazilian	6,832
Albanian	1,768	British	54,836
Alsatian	448	Bulgarian	3,504
American	845,516	Cajun	1,014
Arab:	78,682	Canadian	15,982
Egyptian	11,950	Carpatho-Rusyn	231
Iraqi	4,849	Celtic	1,316
Jordanian	2,171	Croatian	8,589
Lebanese	16,508	Cypriot	235
Moroccan	5,965	Czech	20,155
Palestinian	5,066	Czechoslovakian	4,539
Syrian	4,315	Danish	21,908
Arab	10,600	Dutch	82,574
Other Arab	18,737	Eastern European	12,487
Armenian	4,539	English	843,336
Assyrian/Chaldean/Syriac	987	Estonian	797
Australian	2,578	European	135,342
Austrian	14,968	Finnish	6,818
Basque	575	French (except Basque)	150,431

(continued)

	Estimate		Estimate
French Canadian	36,198	Ghanaian	14,464
German	982,537	Kenyan	1,603
German Russian	398	Liberian	1,599
Greek	32,712	Nigerian	5,103
Guyanese	1,774	Senegalese	150
Hungarian	31,454	Sierra Leonean	5,064
Icelander	1,040	Somali	3,311
Iranian	23,366	South African	1,767
Irish	810,784	Sudanese	5,145
Israeli	3,900	Ugandan	654
Italian	327,652	Zimbabwean	117
Latvian	2,119	African	104,832
Lithuanian	16,912	Other sub-Saharan African	7,531
Luxemburger	999	Swedish	54,152
Macedonian	345	Swiss	17,438
Maltese	668	Turkish	8,844
New Zealander	534	Ukrainian	21,740
Northern European	8,507	Welsh	54,108
Norwegian	46,676	West Indian	42,656
Pennsylvania German	3,210	(except Hispanic groups):	
Polish	157,873	Bahamian	477
Portuguese	15,968	Barbadian	1,472
Romanian	11,408	Belizean	710
Russian	58,801	Bermudan	189
Scandinavian	11,595	British West Indian	1,541
Scotch-Irish	142,980	Dutch West Indian	84
Scottish	172,367	Haitian	6,837
Serbian	3,832	Jamaican	17,902
Slavic	4,712	Trinidadian and Tobagonian	6,037
Slovak	17,345	U.S. Virgin Islander	257
Slovene	3,782	West Indian	7,505
Soviet Union	126	Other West Indian	303
Sub-Saharan African:	178,029	Yugoslavian	3,282
Cape Verdean	891	Other groups	3,005,189
Ethiopian	27,597	Unclassified or not reported	1,397,892

Source: American Community Survey, U.S. Census Bureau, 2014.

See in Neighborhoods Section: Annandale, Latino and Asian Enclaves (Virginia)

WASHINGTON, DC. *See* District of Columbia

WASHINGTON

Capital: Olympia
Entered Union: November 11, 1889 (42nd state)

Washington is the 20th-largest state by land area, and the 13th most populated. Before European contact, the area was home to a number of established tribes, best known today for their totem poles and ornate canoes and masks. The Kennewick Man, one of the oldest and most complete skeletons ever found in North America, was discovered in Washington.

The first Europeans to venture into the area were the Spanish in 1775, followed by the British in 1778. The Nootka Convention in 1790 ended Spanish exclusivity along the Northwest coast and opened the region up to other traders and settlers. The United States acquired the area of Washington through a treaty with Great Britain in 1846. Washington Territory was organized from part of Oregon Territory on March 2, 1853; it included all of present-day Washington, northern Idaho, and northwestern Montana. In 1859, when Oregon was admitted as a state, the remainder of Oregon Territory, the rest of Idaho, additional area of Montana, and part of Wyoming was added to Washington Territory. Washington Territory assumed generally the same boundary as the present state when Idaho Territory was organized

A hiker stops to view the mountains in North Cascades National Park, Washington. Hiking is one of the most popular outdoor activities in a state that's populated by outdoorsmen and women. (Roy E Farr/Dreamstime.com)

in 1863. Washington was admitted to the Union on November 11, 1889, as the 42nd state.

Olympia is the state capital, while Seattle is Washington's largest city, with 608,660 inhabitants as of the 2010 U.S. Census. Washington has 10 congressional districts, 49 state senate districts, and 49 state house districts. In addition to its international border with Canada, Washington borders Oregon to the south, Idaho to the east, and the Pacific Ocean to the west. Washington makes up the northwestern corner of the contiguous United States.

Historical Population of Washington

Census	Pop.	%±	Census	Pop.	%±
1850	1,201	—	1940	1,736,191	11.1%
1860	11,594	865.4%	1950	2,378,963	37.0%
1870	23,955	106.6%	1960	2,853,214	19.9%
1880	75,116	213.6%	1970	3,409,169	19.5%
1890	357,232	375.6%	1980	4,132,156	21.2%
1900	518,103	45.0%	1990	4,866,692	17.8%
1910	1,141,990	120.4%	2000	5,894,121	21.1%
1920	1,356,621	18.8%	2010	6,724,540	14.1%
1930	1,563,396	15.2%			

Source: U.S. Census Bureau.

As of the 2010 U.S. Census, Washington is home to 6,724,540 people. The racial composition is as follows: 77.3% white, 7.2% Asian, 3.6% black or African American, 1.5% Native American, 0.4% Pacific Islander, 4.7% two or more races, and 5.1% other races. Hispanics or Latinos of any race comprise 11.2% of the population and mainly claim Mexican (8.9%) heritage. Asian Americans and Pacific Islanders primarily reside in the Seattle-Tacoma metropolitan area, while African Americans are concentrated in the South End and Central Districts of Seattle and inner Tacoma. The six largest self-identified ancestry groups are 20.7% German, 12.6% Irish, 12.3% English, 8.2% Hispanic, 6.2% Norwegian, and 3.9% French.

According to the same census, 82% of Washington residents age five and older speak English at home, while 7.79% speak Spanish, 1.19% Chinese, 0.94% Vietnamese, 0.84% Tagalog, 0.83% Korean, 0.80% Russian, and 0.55% German.

The Pew Research Center's 2014 Religious and Public Life survey found that 61% of Washington residents identify as Christian, with Evangelical Protestants (25%), Catholics (17%), and Mainline Protestants (13%) as the three largest subgroups. Six percent follow non-Christian faiths, and 32% are unaffiliated. A full 10% of Washingtonians identify as Agnostic or Atheist.

Population by Selected Ethnic Group

	Estimate		Estimate
Total:	7,061,530	French Canadian	54,788
Afghan	187	German	1,272,636
Albanian	466	German Russian	1,672
Alsatian	299	Greek	29,421
American	316,200	Guyanese	219
Arab:	33,031	Hungarian	21,523
Egyptian	3,349	Icelander	6,991
Iraqi	3,316	Iranian	8,219
Jordanian	493	Irish	759,507
Lebanese	8,510	Israeli	2,149
Moroccan	882	Italian	236,536
Palestinian	2,166	Latvian	2,255
Syrian	2,177	Lithuanian	8,832
Arab	5,729	Luxemburger	939
Other Arab	8,017	Macedonian	635
Armenian	6,838	Maltese	187
Assyrian/Chaldean/Syriac	76	New Zealander	1,836
Australian	4,911	Northern European	22,057
Austrian	17,345	Norwegian	379,028
Basque	3,701	Pennsylvania German	3,203
Belgian	6,735	Polish	134,483
Brazilian	2,413	Portuguese	24,054
British	45,994	Romanian	21,579
Bulgarian	4,014	Russian	86,928
Cajun	833	Scandinavian	49,188
Canadian	28,345	Scotch-Irish	85,489
Carpatho-Rusyn	89	Scottish	201,479
Celtic	4,085	Serbian	3,046
Croatian	15,097	Slavic	3,067
Cypriot	63	Slovak	6,245
Czech	31,300	Slovene	3,640
Czechoslovakian	6,959	Soviet Union	40
Danish	68,714	Sub-Saharan African:	72,634
Dutch	143,159	Cape Verdean	192
Eastern European	6,269	Ethiopian	19,592
English	736,754	Ghanaian	190
Estonian	918	Kenyan	2,032
European	166,099	Liberian	652
Finnish	46,256	Nigerian	2,611
French (except Basque)	221,991	Senegalese	0

(continued)

	Estimate		Estimate
Sierra Leonean	326	Bahamian	578
Somali	9,394	Barbadian	66
South African	1,597	Belizean	398
Sudanese	1,003	Bermudan	0
Ugandan	222	British West Indian	197
Zimbabwean	279	Dutch West Indian	454
African	32,679	Haitian	2,605
Other sub-Saharan African	3,715	Jamaican	4,432
Swedish	229,659	Trinidadian and Tobagonian	1,150
Swiss	38,431	U.S. Virgin Islander	87
Turkish	4,375	West Indian	971
Ukrainian	56,672	Other West Indian	0
Welsh	68,460	Yugoslavian	15,069
West Indian	10,752	Other groups	2,292,485
(except Hispanic groups):		Unclassified or not reported	1,045,260

Source: American Community Survey, U.S. Census Bureau, 2014.

See in Neighborhoods Section: Ballard (Seattle Washington); International District (Seattle, Washington)

WEST VIRGINIA

Capital: Charleston
Entered Union: June 20, 1863 (35th state)

West Virginia is the 41st-largest by area and the 37th most populous U.S. state. In 1669, King Charles II granted land patents, including the eastern part of the present state of West Virginia, to supporters of his family. Over the next two decades, England granted other large tracts of property to various land companies, but the Native Americans, French, and scattered settlers complicated their efforts. It would take many years to establish British control over the region. West Virginia became a state following the Wheeling Conventions of 1861, in which 50 northwestern counties of Virginia decided to break away from Virginia during the American Civil War. The new state was admitted to the Union on June 20, 1863 as the 35th state, and was a key Civil War border state.

Charleston is the state's capital and largest city, with 51,400 inhabitants. West Virginia has 3 congressional districts, 16 state senate districts, and 58 state house districts. It borders five states: Kentucky, Maryland, Ohio, Pennsylvania, and Virginia.

Historical Population of West Virginia

Census	Pop.	%±	Census	Pop.	%±
1790	55,873	—	1910	1,221,119	27.4%
1800	78,592	40.7%	1920	1,463,701	19.9%
1810	105,469	34.2%	1930	1,729,205	18.1%
1820	136,808	29.7%	1940	1,901,974	10.0%
1830	176,924	29.3%	1950	2,005,552	5.4%
1840	224,537	26.9%	1960	1,860,421	−7.2%
1850	302,313	34.6%	1970	1,744,237	−6.2%
1860	376,688	24.6%	1980	1,949,644	11.8%
1870	442,014	17.3%	1990	1,793,477	−8.0%
1880	618,457	39.9%	2000	1,808,344	0.8%
1890	762,794	23.3%	2010	1,852,994	2.5%
1900	958,800	25.7%			

Source: U.S. Census Bureau.

According to the 2010 U.S. Census, the racial composition of the state's population was 93.2% white, 3.4% African American, 1.2% Hispanic, 0.2% American Indian and Alaska Native, and 0.7% Asian American. The five largest ancestry groups in West Virginia are English (35.2%), German (17.2%), Irish (8%), Scots-Irish (5%), and Italian (4.8%). Large numbers of people of German ancestry are present in the northeastern counties of the state. Only 1.1% of the state's residents were foreign-born, placing West Virginia last among the 50 states in that statistic. It also has the lowest percentage of residents that speak a language other than English in the home (2.7%).

According to the Pew Forum on Religion and Public Life's 2014 survey, 78% of West Virginians identify as Christian, with Evangelical Protestants (39%), Mainline Protestants (29%), and Catholics (6%) forming the largest subgroups. Roughly 18% are unaffiliated, while just 3% follow non-Christian faiths.

Population by Selected Ethnic Group

	Estimate		Estimate
Total:	1,850,326	Iraqi	99
Afghan	0	Jordanian	152
Albanian	0	Lebanese	3,337
Alsatian	34	Moroccan	255
American	236,373	Palestinian	0
Arab:	6,135	Syrian	1,029
Egyptian	260	Arab	516

(continued)

	Estimate		Estimate
Other Arab	675	New Zealander	0
Armenian	404	Northern European	801
Assyrian/Chaldean/Syriac	0	Norwegian	3,915
Australian	313	Pennsylvania German	1,232
Austrian	1,496	Polish	35,790
Basque	0	Portuguese	925
Belgian	1,246	Romanian	477
Brazilian	526	Russian	6,122
British	6,516	Scandinavian	1,005
Bulgarian	126	Scotch-Irish	39,604
Cajun	318	Scottish	36,062
Canadian	1,466	Serbian	2,040
Carpatho-Rusyn	34	Slavic	1,285
Celtic	340	Slovak	4,163
Croatian	1,152	Slovene	896
Cypriot	0	Soviet Union	0
Czech	3,643	Sub-Saharan African:	5,544
Czechoslovakian	2,625	Cape Verdean	26
Danish	685	Ethiopian	266
Dutch	32,058	Ghanaian	0
Eastern European	1,071	Kenyan	0
English	192,543	Liberian	380
Estonian	60	Nigerian	239
European	16,941	Senegalese	51
Finnish	888	Sierra Leonean	30
French (except Basque)	26,413	Somali	0
French Canadian	2,312	South African	0
German	307,350	Sudanese	134
German Russian	0	Ugandan	0
Greek	5,609	Zimbabwean	0
Guyanese	112	African	4,418
Hungarian	8,110	Other sub-Saharan African	0
Icelander	220	Swedish	8,330
Iranian	1,222	Swiss	3,336
Irish	262,051	Turkish	699
Israeli	166	Ukrainian	2,160
Italian	85,976	Welsh	13,548
Latvian	187	West Indian	2,135
Lithuanian	870	(except Hispanic groups):	
Luxemburger	253	Bahamian	127
Macedonian	0	Barbadian	93
Maltese	0	Belizean	0

(continued)

	Estimate		Estimate
Bermudan	0	U.S. Virgin Islander	0
British West Indian	250	West Indian	50
Dutch West Indian	48	Other West Indian	0
Haitian	725	Yugoslavian	1,550
Jamaican	844	Other groups	311,480
Trinidadian and Tobagonian	98	Unclassified or not reported	569,573

Source: American Community Survey, U.S. Census Bureau, 2014.

See in Neighborhoods Section: Adamston (Clarksburg, West Virginia)

WISCONSIN

Capital: Madison
Entered Union: May 29, 1848 (30th state)

Wisconsin is the 25th state by total area and the 20th most populous U.S. state. Wisconsin is known as "America's Dairyland" because it is one of the nation's leading dairy producers, particularly famous for cheese.

The first Europeans to visit what is today Wisconsin were the French, who continued to ply the fur trade across Wisconsin through the 17th and 18th centuries. No permanent settlements existed in Wisconsin until Great Britain won control of the region following the French and Indian War in 1763. Following American

Wisconsin's largest city Milwaukee, seen here at dusk. (Benkrut/Dreamstime.com)

Independence, Wisconsin subsequently became a territorial possession of the United States in 1783. In 1787, the area was deemed the "Territory northwest of the River Ohio." However, the British remained in control until after the War of 1812, the outcome of which finally established an American presence in the area. It became the 30th state on May 29, 1848.

Wisconsin's largest city, with a total population of 594,833, is Milwaukee, located on the western shore of Lake Michigan. The state has 8 congressional districts, 33 state senate districts, and 99 assembly districts. Wisconsin borders Illinois, Iowa, the Michigan Upper Peninsula, and Minnesota. To the east of Wisconsin is Lake Michigan and to the north is Lake Superior.

Since its founding, Wisconsin has been ethnically heterogeneous. Following the period of French fur traders, the next wave of settlers were miners, many of whom were Cornish. They settled in the southwestern area of the state. The next wave was the "Yankees," who were migrants of English descent from New England and upstate New York. In the early years of statehood, they dominated the state's heavy industry, finance, politics, and education. Between 1850 and 1900, large numbers of European immigrants came to Wisconsin, including Germans, Scandinavians, and smaller groups of Belgians, Dutch, Swiss, Finns, Irish, Poles, and so on. In the 20th century, large numbers of Mexicans and African Americans arrived, settling mainly in Milwaukee. And finally, after the end of the Vietnam War, an influx of Hmong people settled in Wisconsin.

Historical Population of Wisconsin

Census	Pop.	%±	Census	Pop.	%±
1820	1,444	—	1920	2,632,067	12.8%
1830	3,635	151.7%	1930	2,939,006	11.7%
1840	30,945	751.3%	1940	3,137,587	6.8%
1850	305,391	886.9%	1950	3,434,575	9.5%
1860	775,881	154.1%	1960	3,951,777	15.1%
1870	1,054,670	35.9%	1970	4,417,731	11.8%
1880	1,315,457	24.7%	1980	4,705,767	6.5%
1890	1,693,330	28.7%	1990	4,891,769	4.0%
1900	2,069,042	22.2%	2000	5,363,675	9.6%
1910	2,333,860	12.8%	2010	5,686,986	6.0%

Source: U.S. Census Bureau.

According to the 2010 U.S. Census, the racial composition of Wisconsin is 86.2% white, 6.3% African American, 5.9% Hispanic, 1.0% American Indian and Alaska Native, and 2.3% Asian American.

Christianity is the predominant religion of Wisconsin. According to the Pew Research Center's 2014 survey, 71% of Wisconsinites identify as Christian. The three largest subgroups are Catholic (25%), Evangelical Protestant (22%), and Mainline Protestant (18%). Roughly 4% follow non-Christian faiths, and 25% are unaffiliated.

Population by Selected Ethnic Group

	Estimate		Estimate
Total:	5,757,564	Estonian	587
Afghan	373	European	51,237
Albanian	3,922	Finnish	38,372
Alsatian	139	French (except Basque)	172,979
American	210,648	French Canadian	56,914
Arab:	12,926	German	2,333,895
Egyptian	887	German Russian	926
Iraqi	213	Greek	13,322
Jordanian	190	Guyanese	23
Lebanese	4,500	Hungarian	24,935
Moroccan	935	Icelander	1,513
Palestinian	1,412	Iranian	1,290
Syrian	738	Irish	615,178
Arab	2,690	Israeli	279
Other Arab	1,514	Italian	195,501
Armenian	4,028	Latvian	3,732
Assyrian/Chaldean/Syriac	91	Lithuanian	12,794
Australian	1,338	Luxemburger	6,542
Austrian	23,439	Macedonian	458
Basque	304	Maltese	76
Belgian	52,192	New Zealander	93
Brazilian	1,504	Northern European	5,445
British	11,790	Norwegian	436,204
Bulgarian	1,312	Pennsylvania German	6,906
Cajun	270	Polish	498,076
Canadian	7,143	Portuguese	3,005
Carpatho-Rusyn	255	Romanian	4,070
Celtic	548	Russian	38,841
Croatian	16,913	Scandinavian	20,161
Cypriot	55	Scotch-Irish	26,006
Czech	95,224	Scottish	61,070
Czechoslovakian	8,798	Serbian	8,458
Danish	53,865	Slavic	3,542
Dutch	141,215	Slovak	11,408
Eastern European	5,355	Slovene	7,875
English	325,419	Soviet Union	111

(continued)

	Estimate		Estimate
Sub-Saharan African:	33,257	Ukrainian	10,640
Cape Verdean	23	Welsh	28,814
Ethiopian	594	West Indian	5,124
Ghanaian	119	(except Hispanic groups):	
Kenyan	676	Bahamian	80
Liberian	1,168	Barbadian	0
Nigerian	1,451	Belizean	170
Senegalese	205	Bermudan	0
Sierra Leonean	109	British West Indian	320
Somali	557	Dutch West Indian	76
South African	312	Haitian	581
Sudanese	52	Jamaican	2,717
Ugandan	420	Trinidadian and Tobagonian	282
Zimbabwean	0	U.S. Virgin Islander	352
African	26,780	West Indian	766
Other sub-Saharan African	1,441	Other West Indian	0
Swedish	147,297	Yugoslavian	3,718
Swiss	57,963	Other groups	1,103,020
Turkish	847	Unclassified or not reported	741,981

Source: American Community Survey, U.S. Census Bureau, 2014.

See in Neighborhoods Section: Appleton (Fox Cities), Hmong Community (Wisconsin); Milwaukee, German Enclaves (Wisconsin)

WYOMING

Capital: Cheyenne
Entered Union: July 10, 1890 (44th state)

Wyoming is the ninth most extensive state has the smallest population, rendering it the second least densely populated state in the United States (5.8 persons per square mile). It is a state of scenic contrast, featuring the Rocky Mountains in the west and the High Plains in the east. Wyoming is best known as the home of Yellowstone National Park. Cheyenne is the state's capital and largest city, with 59,466 residents.

Several groups of Native Americans originally inhabited the region that is now known as Wyoming. These included the Crow, Arapaho, Lakota, and Shoshone, amongst others. What is today the southwestern part of the state was once part of the Spanish Empire and was later part of the Mexican Territory of Alta California. Despite this early Spanish influence, the state today does not show signs of retaining much of this influence. In the late 18th century, French Canadian explorers

Silhouette of a cowboy with a lasso at small-town Wyoming rodeo. Rodeos remain a vital element of the culture in Wyoming. (Alptraum/Dreamstime.com)

arrived, but their only lasting contributions are the names of a handful of toponyms such as Téton and La Ramie. Finally, the territory became part of the United States in 1848 at the end of the Mexican-American War. It did not become a state until July 10, 1890, when it joined the Union as the 44th state. It has 1 congressional district, 30 state senate districts, and 60 state house districts. Wyoming borders six states: Colorado, Idaho, Montana, Nebraska, South Dakota, and Utah.

Historical Population of Wyoming

Census	Pop.	%±	Census	Pop.	%±
1870	9,118	—	1950	290,529	15.9%
1880	20,789	128.0%	1960	330,066	13.6%
1890	62,555	200.9%	1970	332,416	0.7%
1900	92,531	47.9%	1980	469,557	41.3%
1910	145,965	57.7%	1990	453,588	−3.4%
1920	194,402	33.2%	2000	493,782	8.9%
1930	225,565	16.0%	2010	563,626	14.1%
1940	250,742	11.2%			

Source: U.S. Census Bureau.

Wyoming was nearly homogeneously white in 2000, with the proportion of the white population at 92.1%. The largest ancestry groups in Wyoming are as follows: German (26.0%), English (16.0%), Irish (13.3%), American (6.5%), Norwegian (4.3%), and Swedish (3.5%).

The racial composition of the population in 2010 was 90.7% white American, 0.8% black or African American, 2.4% American Indian and Alaska Native, 0.8% Asian American, 0.1% Native Hawaiian and other Pacific Islander, 2.2% from two or more races, and 3.0% from some other race. The Hispanic proportion of the total population grew to 8.9%. In 2004, the foreign-born population was 11,000 (2.2%). In 2011, 24.9% of Wyoming's population younger than one year of age belonged to a minority group.

In 2010, 93.39% of Wyomingites over the age of five spoke English as their primary language, 4.47% spoke Spanish, 0.35% spoke German, and 0.28% spoke French. Other non-English languages included Algonquian (0.18%), Russian (0.10%), Tagalog, and Greek (both 0.09%).

The religious affiliations of the people of Wyoming are as follows: Protestant 47%, Catholic 23%, Mormon 9%, Jewish < 0.5%, Jehovah's Witness 2%, Muslim < 0.5%, Buddhist 1%, Hindu < 0.5%, and nonreligious at 18%.

Population by Selected Ethnic Group

	Estimate		Estimate
Total:	575,251	Bulgarian	120
Afghan	0	Cajun	60
Albanian	51	Canadian	746
Alsatian	0	Carpatho-Rusyn	0
American	48,982	Celtic	178
Arab:	740	Croatian	344
Egyptian	88	Cypriot	0
Iraqi	0	Czech	4,377
Jordanian	0	Czechoslovakian	726
Lebanese	327	Danish	8,389
Moroccan	0	Dutch	12,142
Palestinian	81	Eastern European	221
Syrian	103	English	76,080
Arab	76	Estonian	99
Other Arab	83	European	9,540
Armenian	70	Finnish	2,254
Assyrian/Chaldean/Syriac	9	French (except Basque)	17,668
Australian	174	French Canadian	2,599
Austrian	1,206	German	146,532
Basque	1,060	German Russian	80
Belgian	683	Greek	1,775
Brazilian	131	Guyanese	6
British	2,402	Hungarian	1,959

(*continued*)

	Estimate		Estimate
Icelander	283	Nigerian	40
Iranian	253	Senegalese	0
Irish	72,849	Sierra Leonean	2
Israeli	78	Somali	61
Italian	18,667	South African	44
Latvian	94	Sudanese	0
Lithuanian	482	Ugandan	0
Luxemburger	18	Zimbabwean	0
Macedonian	36	African	733
Maltese	12	Other sub-Saharan African	36
New Zealander	79	Swedish	16,780
Northern European	611	Swiss	3,141
Norwegian	19,777	Turkish	56
Pennsylvania German	571	Ukrainian	811
Polish	11,462	Welsh	6,039
Portuguese	1,049	West Indian	254
Romanian	302	(except Hispanic groups):	
Russian	4,519	Bahamian	2
Scandinavian	2,448	Barbadian	0
Scotch-Irish	9,329	Belizean	0
Scottish	17,829	Bermudan	0
Serbian	359	British West Indian	0
Slavic	507	Dutch West Indian	66
Slovak	569	Haitian	82
Slovene	347	Jamaican	43
Soviet Union	0	Trinidadian and Tobagonian	12
Sub-Saharan African:	1,023	U.S. Virgin Islander	0
Cape Verdean	0	West Indian	62
Ethiopian	74	Other West Indian	0
Ghanaian	4	Yugoslavian	858
Kenyan	46	Other groups	128,258
Liberian	0	Unclassified or not reported	96,044

Source: American Community Survey, U.S. Census Bureau, 2014.

See in Neighborhoods Section: Volga German Enclaves (Wyoming)

NEIGHBORHOODS

ADAMSTON (CLARKSBURG, WEST VIRGINIA)

Adamston was a community in Clarksburg, West Virginia, that was the destination of a large number of Belgian immigrants in the late 19th and early 20th centuries. These French-speaking Belgians were primarily glassworkers and their families who were recruited by the glassmaking industry.

In the late 1800s, the glass business in Belgium was failing, in part due to conditions inhospitable to the trade guilds (unions). In the United States, the glass-working industry was being restructured as new technology emerged, only to find a dearth of skilled workers. In order to pursue greater growth, the American glass industry recruited skilled glassworkers from France and Belgium. These immigrants and their families settled in boomtowns in West Virginia, Pennsylvania, and Indiana. In 1885, the national trade union Knights of Labor, Local Assembly 300, recruited up to 700 Belgian glassworkers to West Virginia in order to operate glass factories. These French-speaking Belgians settled in various communities in the state, such as South Charleston, Clarksburg, and Salem.

A large number of Belgians originally from the Charleroi region of Wallonia, Belgium, relocated to Adamston, a small town north of Clarksburg that later became part of the Clarksburg city proper. In 1904, with inexpensive fuel and real estate to attract new factories, these workers established the Clarksburg Cooperative Window Glass Company. In control of the production, the glassworkers themselves were able to create what has been called a "glassmaker's paradise." By 1909, the town had five active glass plants that employed a large number of Belgian and French workers.

The Belgian inhabitants of Adamston had initially been either apolitical or supporters of the local Republican leaders. Belgian immigrants noticed the social unrest that was leading to negative perceptions of Poles and Italians and worked hard to ensure their community was pleasant and peaceful. They wanted to do nothing their neighbors could complain about. Indeed, the Belgians were seen as skilled and productive workers. However, as the economy favored the Belgian and French cooperative-owned businesses and drove up costs for nonimmigrant-led factories, local newspapers began portraying the Belgians as enemies that were taking work from Americans. In the years leading up to World War I, this animosity, as well as demographic and economic concerns, advanced the Belgians' involvement in the socialist movement in Adamston and Clarksburg.

The advent of World War I and a high demand for glass negated the economic troubles that had appeared in the industry. It also served to redirect Belgian immigrants' political will to the relief effort for their war-torn kin back in the old country. The absorption of Adamston and North View into Clarksburg and other administrative restructuring further reduced the political power of the Belgian minority.

The decade following World War I saw drastic technological developments that changed the face of the glassworking industry. Processes were automated, putting many hand-blown crafters out of work. However, in Clarksburg, many of them adroitly transferred their skills to the flat-window glassworking business, which had replaced the entire handcrafted glassworking industry by the end of the 1920s.

During the heyday of glass production in Clarksburg, French was heard regularly in the streets. Belgian immigrants formed theater clubs that put on French-language plays and musical groups that played for activities and parades. They attended Catholic church services. They held summer festivals and put on sporting events such as bowling, bicycle racing, and pigeon racing. In particular, Belgian immigrants had a unique community-building tradition: To celebrate the new year, the youngest couple would visit the next youngest couple to share a toast. Then the older couple would visit the next oldest couple, until the second-oldest couple had visited the oldest couple in the community. This and the predilection of the European immigrants to drink much more wine and beer than their soberer neighbors occasionally created friction between communities, particularly in the early years.

Belgian Glass Workers in South Charleston

The story of Belgian immigrants in South Charleston, West Virginia, closely parallels the history of Adamston. In 1907, three Belgian glassworkers of the cooperative-owned Banner Window Glass company in Shirley, Indiana, relocated to South Charleston in response to an offer of free natural gas for two years and free land. The new Banner Window Glass factory produced its first piece of glass on December 12, 1907, but it burned down the next day due to the high temperatures. The reconstructed factory opened several months later.

Belgian immigrants settled near the factory to provide it with a skilled workforce. For the first winter, many new residents lived in primitive shelters with no civic services. Permanent dwellings were not constructed until the spring thaw. Most children attended school in other areas of the city, but after the eighth grade the boys were expected to learn the family's glassblowing trade and the girls were expected to become ready for marriage. Many families saved up their money to travel back to Belgium during the summer, when the factories temporarily shut down.

In 1917, Libbey-Owens in nearby Kanawha City opened a flat-glass plant that became the world's largest. They also used a new and patented automated process that quickly put Banner Window Glass out of business. Some of the glassworkers went to work for Libbey-Owens, while others found jobs outside of the glass industry. Over time, the unique Belgian culture in South Charleston melded with local traditions and eventually disappeared.

As the years progressed, the second- and third-generation immigrants lost their regional Belgian identities (such as Walloons from Wallonia) so that they merged under a single national "Belgian" identity. They then successively melded into American culture. Few remnants of Belgian heritage remain in West Virginia today, although the Museum of South Charleston sponsors a Belgian Days festival and opened an exhibit in 2009 that features Belgian glassworkers.

Julianne Long

Further Reading

Barkey, Frederick A. *Cinder Heads in the Hills: The Belgian Window Glass Workers of West Virginia.* Charleston: Humanities Foundation of West Virginia, 1988.

Bumgardner, Stan. "In the Beginning: South Charleston's Belgian Roots." *Goldenseal* (Winter 2011): 16–21.

Fones-Wolf, Ken. *Glass Towns: Industry, Labor and Political Economy in Appalachia, 1890–1930s.* Champaign: University of Illinois Press, 2007.

Fones-Wolf, Ken. "Immigrants, Labor and Capital in a Transnational Context: Belgian Glass Workers in America, 1880–1925." *Journal of American Ethnic History* 21, no. 2 (2002): 59–80.

Nash, Betty Joyce. "Economic History: West Virginia Glass Houses." *Region Focus* 13, no. 1 (Winter 2009): 43–46.

AFRICAN AMERICAN ENCLAVES. *See* Baldwin Hills (Los Angeles, California; Bedford-Stuyvesant (Brooklyn, New York); Black Bottom (Philadelphia, Pennsylvania); Bronzeville (Chicago, Illinois); Greenwood (Tulsa, Oklahoma); Harlem (New York City); Harlem, Senegalese Enclave (New York City); Historic South Central (Los Angeles, California); Ironbound and the Wards (Newark, New Jersey); Lewiston and Portland, Somali and Bantu Enclaves (Maine); Little Ethiopia (Los Angeles, California); Lower Ninth Ward (New Orleans, Louisiana); Lower Roxbury, African American Enclave (Massachusetts); Mattapan (Boston, Massachusetts); Orange Mound (Memphis, Tennessee); Roxbury, African American Enclave (Massachusetts); Sweet Auburn (Atlanta, Georgia); Tremé (New Orleans, Louisiana); Watts (Los Angeles, California)

AFRICAN ENCLAVES. *See* Harlem, Senegalese Enclave (New York City); Lewiston and Portland, Somali and Bantu Enclaves (Maine); Little Ethiopia (Los Angeles, California)

AMANA COLONIES (IOWA)

The Amana Colonies in Iowa are one of the more unique ethnic enclaves in the United States, because they are both a planned community that has lasted, in some form, since the mid-19th century, and a religious separatist group that has adjusted

View of the Amana Colonies village in Iowa. The Amana people have much in common with Mennonites and other groups that avoid modern intrusions, but they have their own traditions and origin. (Dustin88/Dreamstime.com)

to sustaining itself through cultural and heritage tourism. The Amana people have much in common with Mennonites, the Amish, and other groups that avoid modern intrusions, but they have their own traditions and origin. Similarly, the group was originally German, but their language and culture is distinct from German American culture.

The German settlers of the Amana colonies originated, generations before they came to the United States, as a group within the Lutheran dissident strain known as Pietism. The most radical Pietists formed separatist groups; the one that eventually emigrated to Iowa called themselves the Community of True Inspiration. Formed in 1714, the Inspirationists believed that their leaders, or "Werkzeuge" (instruments) of God, were receiving divine inspiration. Members of the Community of True Inspiration were persecuted in Prussia because of their differences from mainstream Lutheranism. Inspirationists had different baptism practices, meaning their baptisms were not recognized by the church, and some were fined for not baptizing their children properly. They wanted their own schools rather than the state schools, and they refused to participate in the military for religious reasons, both of which caused friction with the government.

In 1842, a group of Inspirationists moved to an area near Buffalo, New York, where they were to settle on a section of 5,000 acres of land acquired from the Seneca Indian Reservation. However, the Senecas were hostile because of disputes over the legitimacy of how the land was sold and purchased. After three years of negotiating and a state court ruling, the Inspirationists were able to settle the Ebenezer colonies in what is now West Seneca, New York. However, by then the community was growing rapidly, facing scarcity of land and fearing growing influence from the nearby city of Buffalo. They decided to move.

A committee journeyed to Iowa to determine whether it would be appropriate for a settlement. In 1854, the community members purchased 25,000 acres from the government in eastern Iowa, not far from the Iowa River. This area had been used by a variety of Algonquian-speaking peoples, such as the Sauk and Meskwaki (Fox) who hunted and trapped in the area. There were also some Native Americans from the eastern United States in Iowa because of forced relocation. However, according to the U.S. government, the Native claims to the land expired in 1843 as part of a larger agreement. Soon after the community purchased the land, Christian Metz, the leading Werkzeuge at the time, directed his followers to move to the new settlement. By 1865, all of the Inspirationists had left New York.

The community was organized much the same way it had been in the Ebenezer Colonies, with several villages which were designed to be self-supporting. They deliberately avoided influences from the outside world, so the settlement was located a several-day's trip from the nearest train station. Settlers dug a six-mile canal from the Iowa River to Amana to provide water power for mills. Members of the first generation were quite successful in avoiding contact with outsiders or "worldly minded people" as they called them (Neubauer 1993, p. 10). In the decades following settlement, other small waves of European immigration introduced more diversity to the area. For example, in the 1860s, Czechs began settling Cedar Rapids, which was to become one of the biggest towns nearby. While the Inspirationists had not lived in a communal system in Europe, in order to remain self-sufficient and to orient their community around the church, they organized their new colonies as socialist communes. Eventually, their deliberate insulation led to the language they spoke morphing into their own local dialect, known as Amana German.

Because it was not known whether each generation would have leaders they considered divinely inspired, the community created a Great Council or board of trustees and a system of village elders. Elders of the community were appointed by the Werkzeuge. Elders were all male, and most of the Werkzeuge were as well, but one of the spiritual leaders who co-founded the colonies was a woman, Barbara Landmann. After the founding generation in the colonies, the Great Council chose the Elders from among those they considered the most spiritual of each village. The village churches had their own leadership, who were semi-autonomous on local matters. While some elections and other decisions were put to a popular vote (adult men and unmarried or widowed women over 30 were allowed to vote) many were handled solely by the Great Council. From the time of settlement until the socialist system was abandoned in 1932, wealth was distributed by a system of credits that were redeemable at the general store.

The 19th-century Inspirationists divided the faithful into three "spiritual orders," from lowest to highest. Sunday worship was segregated by gender and with the lowest order worshipping separately, so the church in each village was built with space for four services to take place simultaneously. However, Sunday services were just one of many religious meetings held at the church each week, some segregated and some not. The Inspirationists believe in simple and unadorned spaces for worship and consider ornamented church furniture and architecture to be inappropriately worldly. Most restrictions regarding the church, such as the ban on musical instruments, applied to the daily lives of the Amana people as well.

The Amana colonists of the 19th and early 20th centuries lived in plain, square houses with gable roofs, decorated only with grapevines on trellises. The houses were unpainted, in part because paint was expensive but lumber was plentiful, so it was economical to leave wood untreated and replace it when needed. Plain unadorned clothes were available at the general store for men and sewn at home for women, and they stayed more or less unchanged in style between the settlement of the community and the 1930s. Amana clothing is often compared to Amish clothing, although the particulars of the restrictions are different. In the 19th century, photographs and gift-giving were both banned, but these regulations were loosened by around the turn of the century. Reading for pleasure rather than religious study or work was also discouraged.

The seven villages of the Amana Colonies, Amana (or Main Amana), East Amana, High Amana, Middle Amana, South Amana, West Amana, and Homestead, are each a few miles apart. Each village is divided into village and factory sites, vegetable gardens, timberland, cultivated fields, and grazing lands. Houses were arranged like a 19th-century German village, with one long street and several smaller streets branching off from it. Barns, factories, and gardens were arranged around this main street in planned groupings. Each village had its own church, school, bakery, dairy, wine cellar, post office, general store, and sawmill. All women worked in the community kitchen, which included farm work and other outdoor labor as well as cooking and cleaning. Men worked at a trade assigned to them by the village elders. The Amana colonists developed a strong tradition of handicrafts and artisanal production, largely because, in their determination to avoid worldly influences, they avoided technological innovations and commercial goods from the outside. Some also attribute Amana interest in craftsmanship to German cultural heritage.

Local doctors and pharmacists were educated outside of Amana at communal expense. Like many other communities in the late 19th-century, the Amanas typically sent away seriously disabled family members to state institutions and cared for people with mild disabilities at home. The schools in Amana have technically been public schools since the 19th century. Each township in Iowa is responsible for levying school taxes and administering school districts, so Amana township's schools were run in a manner that was congruent with both society and state requirements. Teachers were another category of professional who were educated outside of the community, these at county-wide teacher institutes.

Immigration to the colonies tapered off in the 1880s. While there were local politics and cultural changes, for the most part the culture, religion, and government of the Inspirationists stayed constant from the 1850s through the first decades of the 20th century. Generally, colonists refused to participate in worldly politics, including state and national elections. They were generally a pacifist society. During the Civil War, the community paid the army recruiters for substitutes rather

---

The Amana Population: 1864–2010

The population of Amana has remained small but stable since the first village was laid out in 1855. By 1864, all of Amana's 1,200 residents had arrived from New York. Amana reached its peak population of 1,813 in 1881, and it hovered around 1,800 into the twentieth century.

As of the 2010 Census, there are 1,636 residents among Amana's seven villages. The largest is Middle Amana with a population of 581, and the smallest is East Amana with 56. The Amana Colonies remain ethnically homogenous; 1.7% of Amana residents identified as Hispanic or Latino. A handful of others identify as African American, Asian, or two or more races, but combined, these individuals constitute less than 1% of the population.

---

than send their own men to war. Some outsiders have joined the society; however, in the late 19th and early 20th centuries, a number of outsiders came because they were interested in socialism but were asked to leave when they were not found to demonstrate full faith in the church. As agriculture was a staple of self-sufficiency, the community often hired field hands from the outside, with Amana colony members acting as overseers.

In the first decades of the 20th century, the Amana colonies had a somewhat troubled relationship with the outside world. They survived civil actions that accused the society of being a for-profit operation and of land monopoly. Then, during World War I, they were dealt a cultural blow, as it became problematic to use the German language because of anti-German sentiment. While the colonies had always used English for financial records to facilitate necessary trade with the outside, English was a second language for most colonists. Beginning with the war, English became the primary language used in Amana schools, and by the 1930s, it was the dominant language in the colonies.

Despite difficulties, the Amana colonists held onto their cultural traditions, including their talent at handicrafts. While hotels were not a part of the original village plan, they were constructed because hundreds of outsiders visited the village each year. However, while cultural traditions remained intact, the structure of Amana society and government did not. Between the World War I, the Great Depression, and a major fire that affected Amana mills, the colonies struggled financially in the early 20th century. They saw many of the younger generation leave permanently in search of a way of life that allowed them to participate in the growing consumer culture of the United States. The stresses on the society culminated in 1932 with the hotly contested decision that became known as the Great Change.

The Great Change was the formal separation of church and state in the Amana colonies and the end of their socialist commune structure. The first Amana Society, formed in 1859, was the legal incorporation of the colonies. The society owned all of the land, means of production, and schools. It was governed by the church elders, who decided who lived where, provided for education, and assigned adults work tasks in addition to running the church. The second Amana Society, created in 1932, is the parent company of many, but not all, 20th-century Amana businesses. The people retained some communal ownership of certain industries, but they structured this ownership in corporate terms as shareholders. Amana colonists now own their own homes and property.

While the community had always partially supported itself through exports, especially woolen products, after the Great Change the Amana Society began participating more in the national market. The most notable example of this is Amana Refrigeration, one of the early producers of refrigerators. They began by borrowing space from woodworking areas and woolen mills in the society and eventually splintered off into a separate entity, which won a contract to provide freezers for the army in World War II. In 1965, the company became a subsidiary of the national corporation Raytheon, based in Massachusetts. Amana Refrigeration was still headquartered on its original site through the late 20th century. Apart from these industries, the biggest businesses in the area were farming—mostly beef, dairy, and feed products such as corn and soybeans.

Cultural tourism is one of the staples of the modern Amana economy. Tourists come not so much for the German heritage as for the remnants of pre-industrialized life, such as artisan textiles and bread from an open-hearth bakery reminiscent of the former communal kitchens. However, traditionally made German foods are also a local specialty and a part of the tourist industry. Wine was originally communally made and distributed by ration. The Amana Colonies made grape wine as well as "piestengel," or rhubarb wine. Today, there are a number of small wineries in the Amanas, all of which produce grape as well as rhubarb and other specialty small-batch wines. Modern businesses, including national chains, conform to the Old World aesthetic of the area; for example, a Holiday Inn sells local products. Tourism has actually introduced some non-Inspirationist expressions of German heritage to the area, such as an annual Oktoberfest. Inspirationists are not abstinent from alcohol but did not celebrate this festival prior to its introduction via tourism.

The church of the Community of True Inspiration exists to this day. Many Amana colonists practice more traditional lifestyle elements, such as wearing traditional Amana clothing and speaking Amana German on Sundays for church services. While the communities have gone through one major transformation and many smaller, more gradual changes, they have also retained some of the character and goals of the original German settlers.

Notable people from Amana history include Christian Metz, who directed his followers to settle in the area, and Barbara Landmann, another cofounder of the colonies. William Henry Prestele was a child when his family moved from Germany to New York State and then to Iowa as part of the community's pilgrimage; he grew up to be a prominent botanical illustrator. Several other famous Amana residents lived around the time of the Great Change, including George Foerstner, who founded Amana Refrigeration. Bill Zuber, a major league baseball player, began learning the sport in the tumultuous years in which more and more people from Amana began to accept worldly outside influences, including the national pastime.

See also in Iowa: Elk Horn, Danish Enclaves (Iowa)

Tegan Kehoe

Further Reading

Amana Colonies in Iowa: Three Articles from the Palimpsest. Des Moines, IA: State Historical Society of Iowa, 1988.

Bourret, Joan Liffring-Zug, and John Zug. *The Amana Colonies: Seven Villages in Iowa: New World Home of the True Inspirationists.* Monticello, IA.: Julian Print. Co., 1977.

"The History of Amana." Amana Heritage Society. Accessed June 8, 2016. http://www .amanaheritage.org/history.html.

Neubauer, Allyn, Joan Liffring-Zug Bourret, and John Zug. *The Amana Colonies: Seven Historic Villages.* Monticello, IA: Julian Printing Co., 1993.

Shambaugh, Bertha, and Maude Horack. *Amana: The Community of True Inspiration.* Iowa City, IA: The State Historical Society of Iowa, 1908.

Shoup, Don, Joan Liffring-Zug Bourret, and John Zug. *The Amana Colonies.* Monticello, IA: Julian Print. Co., 1988.

Wall, Joseph Frazier. *The WPA Guide to 1930s Iowa.* Iowa City, IA: University of Iowa Press, 2010.

ANDERSONVILLE (CHICAGO, ILLINOIS)

Andersonville is a neighborhood of Chicago, lying north of the city's downtown area. Part of the larger neighborhood of Edgewater, it is anchored by the vibrant business district along Clark Street and celebrates its vibrant immigrant past and enduring Swedish culture. The Clark Street business district is listed on the National Register of Historic Places and is notable for its loyalty to locally owned businesses— there are no national chains in Andersonville. The modern demographics of the neighborhood are increasingly diverse, including Chicago's second-largest lesbian, gay, bisexual, transgender (LGBT) community, but the Swedish origins of the area are celebrated by Swedish businesses and cultural institutions such as the Swedish American Museum. Its unique atmosphere of small businesses gives the neighborhood a small-town feel, and Andersonville has become an increasingly attractive area of residence and a "hot" real estate market to watch.

In the 19th century, the area that would eventually become the neighborhood of Andersonville was a remote, undeveloped area near the rapidly growing city of Chicago. In 1848, the area became a township called Ridgeville, which was quickly altered in 1854 when a new township of Lakeview was formed. Early platting maps of Ridgeville labeled a small area in the center of the township as Andersonville, marking the first time the area was called by that name. Farmers, mostly immigrants, began settling in the area in the mid-19th century, but population was sparse until after the Great Chicago Fire of 1871. In the fire's aftermath, the city banned all construction of wooden structures within city limits. Many new immigrant communities could not afford to build in brick or stone and moved outside of the city;

Interior of a Scandinavian grocery store, Andersonville, Chicago, Illinois, 1977. (Library of Congress)

the growing Swedish population of Chicago migrated north and began settling in Andersonville in large numbers.

As the area's population grew, a vibrant business corridor developed along the main artery of Clark Street, with Swedish shops and businesses propelling economic development. Even the churches that were built along the center artery were all Swedish. The neighborhood quickly became a "little Sweden" of sorts, and it reflected Sweden's religious diversity—Ebenezer Lutheran Church, Bethany Methodist Episcopal Church, and St. Gregory's Roman Catholic Church were all built in the late 1800s to serve Swedish denominations. The neighborhood's commitment to its commercial core was demonstrated by the quality of the craftsmanship of the buildings. Due to the commercial district's distinct late-19th and early-20th century architecture, it was added to the National Register of Historic Places in 2010. One of the best examples of this turn-of-the-century commercial building style is the Temple Theatre building on Clark Street, now home to the feminist bookstore Women and Children First Books. The neighborhood's appeal to Swedish immigrants increasingly attracted Swedes to Chicago. In 1890, Swedes were the third-largest immigrant group in the city, behind Germans and Irish; in 1900, Chicago was the second-largest Swedish city in the world, behind only Stockholm; and 10% of the Swedish population in the United States in 1910 lived within Chicago's city limits.

As the 20th century progressed, Andersonville, like many urban neighborhoods, experienced a population shift. Many Swedish families that had lived in the area for decades abandoned the urban neighborhood to purchase larger homes in the suburbs. With the departure of these residents, the neighborhood experienced a period of decline in the mid-20th century. Fearing the loss of the neighborhood's cultural identity, business owners rallied to prevent continued decline. The Uptown Clark Street Business Association renamed itself the Andersonville Chamber of Commerce, which adopted as part of its mission a commitment to preserving the neighborhood's Swedish heritage. In this spirit, the 1960s became a time of intentional revival of the area. Andersonville revived some Swedish traditions, in particular the celebration of the summer solstice; this celebration evolved into Midsommerfest, which remains one of Chicago's most popular annual street festivals. In 1964, the neighborhood was rededicated by Mayor Richard Daley. As Andersonville's revival continued, the businesses and residents of the area, Swedish or not, embraced the area's Swedish heritage. This energetic revival culminated in 1976, when the Swedish American Museum opened in Andersonville after five decades of planning. The museum's dedication was celebrated with an elaborate ceremony that was attended by King Carl XVI Gustaf of Sweden. The museum, now located on Clark Street, remains a cornerstone of the cultural life of the neighborhood.

Although conscious attempts were made in the second half of the 20th century to preserve Andersonville's Swedish identity, the neighborhood changed and evolved in many ways. As some Swedish businesses closed or moved, the neighborhood saw the arrival of some owned by new immigrant groups: Korean, Lebanese, Mexican, and others. A vibrant Hispanic commercial area in the northern part of the neighborhood, above Catalpa Avenue, sprouted up and continues to thrive. While the Swedish bakeries are certainly the more prominent and well known in the area, Andersonville has also acquired a large collection of Middle Eastern bakeries. The diversity of residents has continued to grow, as the last three decades of the 20th century saw the migration of many professionals to the neighborhood; they were (and continue to be) drawn to Andersonville for the good housing stock and close proximity both to downtown Chicago and also the Lake Michigan lakefront. Some residents also seek out Andersonville for its reputation of maintaining a thriving local and independent business culture; the resulting small-town atmosphere and economic vitality have made living in Andersonville appealing for an increasingly diverse collection of residents.

Perhaps most notable in the developing diversity in Andersonville has been the growth of a prominent and thriving LGBT community. In the 1970s and 1980s, Chicago's gay and lesbian residents began moving to the Near North and Near South sides of the city, where there were concentrations of lodging houses that provided accommodation for single residents. The LGBT population in Chicago especially clustered in Boystown, a neighborhood north of downtown near Wrigley Field, and Andersonville; both of these areas saw the rise of gay and lesbian activism in the 1970s and 1980s. After Andersonville hosted its first gay pride parade in 1970, the area became known for its growing organized efforts to fight for LGBT rights and protest police action and discrimination. In 1996, the community reached a significant political milestone when Larry McKeon was elected to the Illinois state legislature for the district that includes Andersonville; McKeon was the first openly gay state legislator in Illinois and advocated for gay rights during his 10 years in the state legislature. The neighborhood's annual Gay Pride parade remains among the largest and most popular Pride events in the city.

Twenty-first century Andersonville reflects the various stages of its past and is rising in popularity as a "hot" neighborhood for entertainment and real estate. Real estate brokers tout the neighborhood's charming local businesses along the Clark Street commercial corridor and the frequency of neighborhood celebrations and street festivals; in 2015, real estate website Redfin named Andersonville the top neighborhood in Chicago and one of the top ten neighborhoods in the entire country to watch for rising popularity. Andersonville residents have developed a reputation for pride in their neighborhood and continue the legacy of dedication to neighborhood preservation left by the 20th-century Swedish community.

Andersonville's Swedish heritage remains visible and celebrated. Neighborhood institutions—such as Svea Restaurant, serving Swedish food—continue to draw Swedish residents from the city and surrounding areas to find authentic cuisine and goods. Midsommerfest remains the neighborhood's premiere street festival, and the Swedish American Museum organizes events and rotating exhibitions of Swedish history and heritage. In the 1990s, the museum, almost by accident, gave Andersonville its most celebrated and recognizable Swedish symbol when it painted the water tower that sits atop its building with the Swedish flag. The water tower was built in 1927 and for almost 90 years provided the water for the fire suppression system of the building on Clark Street that now houses the museum. In the 1990s, the wooden water tower was painted in the bold blue and yellow pattern of the Swedish flag. The change in the paint job made the water tower an iconic landmark for the neighborhood. In the winter of 2014, record cold temperatures in Chicago damaged the structure of the water tower, so the museum removed it from its roof to consider repairs. The landmark's removal was widely covered in the Chicago press, as was the museum's subsequent decision to replace the structure, which could not be safely and effectively repaired, with a new structure that would also be painted with the Swedish flag. The significance of the landmark to the neighborhood is clear: the museum has raised over $100,000 to fund the construction of a new water tower, much of it from the generous support of Andersonville local businesses.

Much of the current vibrancy and popularity of Andersonville can be attributed to its close-knit culture, anchored by the independent businesses along Clark Street. Owners seeking to grow their independent businesses intentionally choose Andersonville, with its strong chamber of commerce and local resistance to national chains. Alma Gutierrez, an immigrant from Honduras who owns a furniture store on Clark Street, says that she moved her shop to Andersonville for the lingering European feel from its Swedish origins and that now there is a "melting pot of people from all over, and it keeps getting better and better" (CBS Chicago 2012).

Locals Supporting Locals

The Great Chicago Fire of 1871 led to a rebuilding process that produced a neighborhood known for ethnic loyalties. After the fire destroyed much of the city's residential homes, city officials banned wood construction within the city limits. Many new immigrants could not afford to build in stone or brick and thus moved outside of the city. The new town became known as Andersonville and was settled primarily by Swedish immigrants. As the town's population grew, a vibrant corridor developed along the main artery of Clark Street. The Swedish community was most responsible for the area's economic development. Furthermore, the Clark Street business district also became known for its resistance to national chains and its fostering of local and independent businesses. In recent years, the Andersonville Chamber of Commerce launched the "LoLo" program—Locals Supporting Locals—which rewards consumers who register with the program with 5% rewards on all money spent at local businesses. The Clark Street business district is listed on the National Register of Historic Places and is notable for its loyalty to locally owned businesses. Andersonville (through its chamber of commerce) identifies itself as a "quaint neighborhood in the middle of a world-class city," and its celebration of that unique identity makes it a model for a diverse and successful modern urban neighborhood.

The Andersonville Chamber of Commerce works tirelessly to support independent businesses, exemplified by their launching of LoLo—"Locals Supporting Locals"—which rewards consumers who register with the program with 5% rewards on all money spent at local businesses. The Chamber of Commerce also supports the "Eco-Andersonville" program, which facilitates recycling in the commercial district and offers a sustainable business certification for qualifying establishments in the neighborhood. They have also been successful in lobbying for the creation of "People Spots," parking spaces throughout Andersonville that have been converted to small green spaces intended to encourage gathering and conversations, While some of the neighborhood's independent businesses, such as Svea Restaurant and Women and Children First Books, have been around for decades, programs like LoLo and Eco-Andersonville, along with the strength of the neighborhood's independent reputation, ensure that local businesses will continue to shape the commercial culture of Andersonville for the foreseeable future.

In a city of vibrant and interesting neighborhoods, Andersonville stands out. While the Swedish population has declined, the neighborhood remains one of the most concentrated areas of Swedish culture in the United States. The Swedish atmosphere of the neighborhood has evolved to embrace new diversity, including a large and active LGBT community, and the resulting mix of history and progressive spirit has made Andersonville increasingly popular and perpetually vibrant. Andersonville (through its chamber of commerce) identifies itself as a "quaint neighborhood in the middle of a world-class city," and its celebration of that unique identity makes it a model for a diverse and successful modern urban neighborhood.

See also in Illinois: Bridgeport (Chicago, Illinois); Bronzeville (Chicago, Illinois); Chicago, Mexican and Puerto Rican Enclaves (Illinois); Little India (Chicago, Illinois); Pilsen (Chicago, Illinois)

See also Swedish Enclaves: Kingsburg and Sveadal, Swedish Enclaves (California); Lindsborg, Swedish Enclave (Kansas)

Molly Uppenkamp

Further Reading

Andersonville Chamber of Commerce. "The Neighborhood—History." Accessed October 13, 2016. http://www.andersonville.org/the-neighborhood/history.

Barton, H. Arnold. "Chicago: a Door for Swedish Americans." Review of Philip J. Anderson and Dag Blanck, eds. *Swedish-American Life in Chicago: Cultural and Urban Aspects of an Immigrant People, 1850–1930* in *Illinois Issues* (July 1993): Summer Book Section. http://www.lib.niu.edu/1993/ii930731.html.

CBS Chicago. "Your Chicago: Andersonville, a Swedish Holdover." September 14, 2012. Accessed October 13, 2016. http://chicago.cbslocal.com/2012/09/14/your-chicago-andersonville-a-swedish-holdover.

Choose Chicago. "About Andersonville." Accessed October 13, 2016. http://www.choosechicago.com/neighborhoods-and-communities/andersonville.

Curbed. "Andersonville: The Nation's 7th Hottest 'Hood for 2015." January 22, 2015. Accessed October 13, 2016. http://chicago.curbed.com/archives/2015/01/22/andersonville-the-nations-7th-hottest-neighborhood.php.

Edgewater Historical Society. "Early Andersonville: Ante Fire (1871)." *Scrapbook* 18, no. 3 (2007). Accessed October 13, 2016. http://www.edgewaterhistory.org/ehs/articles/v18-3-2.

Gellman, Erik. "Andersonville." *The Electronic Encyclopedia of Chicago* (2005). Accessed October 13, 2016. http://encyclopedia.chicagohistory.org/pages/2466.html.

Gustafson, Anita Olson. "Swedes." *The Electronic Encyclopedia of Chicago* (2005). Accessed October 13, 2016. http://encyclopedia.chicagohistory.org/pages/1222.html.

Heap, Chad. "Gays and Lesbians." *The Electronic Encyclopedia of Chicago* (2005). Accessed October 13, 2016. http://encyclopedia.chicagohistory.org/pages/509.html.

Swedish American Museum. "Andersonville Water Tower." Accessed October 13, 2016. http://www.swedishamericanmuseum.org/andersonville-water-tower.

ANNANDALE, LATINO AND ASIAN ENCLAVES (VIRGINIA)

Annandale is a Census Designated Place (CDP) in Fairfax County in northern Virginia. As a CDP, it has no separate government, but it has a shared social history and has boundaries known well to locals. Located about 13 miles southwest of Washington, D.C., Annandale is a second-ring suburb, home to people in a range of socioeconomic statuses. Its total area is just less than eight square miles, sliced by the Capital Beltway (I-495) and Little River Pike (Rt. 236). According to the 2010

U.S. Census, Annandale has a current population of 41,008, 36.5% of whom are non-Hispanic white, 27.6 % Latino, 24.6% Asian, and 8.6% African American. Some of this ethnic diversity is relatively recent, compared to some other parts of the state and the county. Furthermore, Annandale serves as a commercial and cultural center for the metropolitan region's Korean population, even while the majority of Korean Americans live in other areas.

The land now comprising Annandale was first developed by William Fitzhugh, who, in 1685, purchased nearly 22,000 acres directly from the Jamestown, Virginia, government. He brought the first enslaved Africans to the land and built one of the largest tobacco plantations in Northern Virginia, calling it "Ravensworth," for which a central road in Annandale is named today. The land passed through several generations and was continuously divided. By 1850, the area was called Annandale and included a post office and several commercial establishments. Plantations were replaced by small farms, and a community of European American farmers began to populate the area.

The agricultural community grew through the next century, until after World War II, when Annandale grew into a suburb, although it retained farm area. In the 1950s, veterans returning to the United States bought tracts in Annandale and built small, single-family homes surrounded by land. The development of subdivisions began in earnest in the 1960s and ended in the early 1970s, including many existing neighborhoods today, such as Winterset and Varsity Park, where multiple generations of Annandale residents now live. So-called "redlining" policies that prevented African Americans from purchasing homes in new suburbs kept these communities almost exclusively white. While Annandale High School was built in 1954, the same year as the landmark Supreme Court case *Brown v. Board of Education* that delegitimized racial segregation in education, Fairfax County schools would not begin racial integration until 1960. They would not completely end blatant segregationist policies until 1966–1967.

International immigration soon began in the region, complicating racial and ethnic dynamics further. Some of the first immigrants were from Vietnam, fleeing the violence of civil war. The Vietnamese population in Annandale is relatively small compared to that in neighboring Arlington; however, a sizeable community developed and by the late 1970s comprised a noticeable contingent of the population. In 1975, the Catholic Vietnamese community in Northern Virginia began holding masses in Vietnamese at various churches in the area but sought a church of their own. In 1979, 25 families put up their personal homes as collateral to help finance a building for their own church, which they found in a former Salvation Army location in Annandale, where they established the first Vietnamese Catholic parish in country. The church quickly grew, although the first year was marred by repeated acts of harassment and vandalism. Blaming local teens and young adults, the pastor reported that people drove around the parking lot yelling "fake Chinese" during the opening ceremonies, conduct that was followed by multiple instances of vandalism on the property (Bernhard 1979). In 1985, the church moved to its current location in Arlington, where it has an active congregation of nearly 7,000 parishioners.

Korean Americans make up the most visible and prominent immigration group in Annandale today. Koreans began moving to the area in the 1970s, starting small businesses and building community resources. In the 1990s, Korean immigration began to increase dramatically. "Koreatown," as downtown Annandale quickly came to be called, consists largely of a series of strip malls and shopping centers along Little River Turnpike and through the heart of Annandale. Toward the end of the century, Korean business became especially visible, as entire commercial lots transformed shopping centers catering almost exclusively to Koreans. In 1999, prominent businessman and Korean immigrant Steven Choi bought Seoul Plaza in Annandale, eventually opening up three more shopping centers. Other Korean Americans bought the Great World Plaza in 2001, and in 2011, Annandale's largest shopping center was bought by a Korean American group headed by a local Korean American. The area is now home to nearly a thousand businesses catering to Koreans, including restaurants, clothing stores, cafés, lawyers and doctors. Korean businesses grew, along with an entire independent media industry, including several daily and weekly newspapers, TV channels, and a radio station, many based in Annandale.

This growth has been controversial in the larger community. Many local residents complain that Koreatown is not welcoming to non-Koreans, especially businesses with signs and menus only in Korean, or with Korean-only speaking employees. Long-time white residents are particularly resentful because, as they point out, a relatively small portion of Koreatown customers actually live in Annandale. Rather, the majority of Korean Americans live elsewhere in the country, traveling to Annandale to eat, shop, and socialize. This has caused a rift with the established, white leadership of the area, including the chamber of commerce. Almost none of the Korean businesses belong to the chamber, nor are they likely to attend meetings of local civic associations. Many Korean business owners say they work long hours all week and don't have time for evening meetings. Furthermore, they say their businesses are profitable the way they are—catering to fellow Korean Americans. While some locals reject the name *Koreatown*, arguing that the Korean community does not define Annandale, Koreans often point out that their business has been responsible for rejuvenating the Annandale economy, which was faltering dangerously before Korean businesses arrived.

The immigrants who reside directly in Annandale have also been a source of contention for some long-term residents. Latino immigrants, many from El Salvador and Bolivia, began moving to Annandale in the 1980s and 1990s. Between 2000 and 2010, this population doubled, going from just over 6,000 to over 11,000, although these estimates are likely low, given that the Census undercounts immigrants, English language learners, the poor, and the less educated, all of which characterizes much of this population (U.S. Census Bureau). New immigrants in Annandale are far more likely to live with multiple families or roommates in houses and apartments, or to run businesses out of their homes, arrangements that old Annandale residents claim create a visual blight and drive down housing prices. In response, Fairfax County instituted a complaint line in order to systematically address resident concerns. However, some residents report feeling harassed. For example, one Annandale resident, a Vietnamese immigrant, has established a Buddhist Temple in his home and doesn't understand why other residents are bothered by this. Another resident lives in a 6-bedroom home with 13 other members of his extended family, who immigrated to Annandale from Colombia and Ecuador 15 years ago. Although he understands the complaints about apartments being turned into boarding houses, he reports that his family's home has been investigated for complaints seven times in 5 years, only one resulting in a citation for overcrowding. One local politician warns that this system threatens the civil liberties of area residents.

However, as Annandale has become increasingly international, many institutions in the area have embraced this newfound diversity. For example, Annandale High School, once intentionally all-white, now has students from over 90 countries and native speakers of more than 50 different languages. The school has won substantial recognition for implementing effective programs embracing diversity, including widespread enrollment in college-level courses and multicultural parent workshops.

Notable residents from Annandale include *Star Wars* actor Mark Hamill.

See also Asian Enclaves: Appleton (Fox Cities), Hmong Community (Wisconsin); Asian District (Oklahoma City, Oklahoma); Bergen County, Korean Enclaves (New Jersey); Bridgeport (Chicago, Illinois); Cambodia Town (Long Beach, California); Cambodia Town (Lowell, Massachusetts); Chinatown (Los Angeles, California); Chinatown (Phoenix, Arizona); Chinatown (San Francisco, California); Chinatown Historic District/A'ala (Honolulu, Hawaii); Chinatowns (Duplicates) (San Francisco, California); Chinatowns (Manhattan; Sunset Park East, Brooklyn; Flushing, Queens) (New York City); Historic Filipinotown (Los Angeles, California); International District (Seattle, Washington); Ironbound and the Wards (Newark, New Jersey); Jackson Heights (Queens, New York); Jackson Heights, South Asian Enclave (Queens, New York); Japantown (San Francisco, California); Koreatown (Los Angeles, California); Little India (Chicago, Illinois); Little India, Chatham Street (Cary, North Carolina); Little India, Hillcroft (Houston, Texas); Little India, Jackson Heights (Queens, New York); Little India, Newark Avenue (Jersey City, New Jersey); Little India/Pakistan (Artesia, California); Little Saigon (Denver, Colorado); Little Saigon (Houston, Texas); Little Saigon (San Francisco, California); Little Saigon (San Jose, California); Little Saigon (Westminster, California); Little Tokyo (Los Angeles, California); Minneapolis-St. Paul, Twin Cities Hmong Community (Minnesota); Monterey Park, First Suburban Chinatown (California); New Chinatown (Portland, Oregon); Quincy, Asian Enclaves (Massachusetts); Silicon Valley, Indian and South Asian Communities (Santa Clara Valley/San Jose Region, California); Sin City (Fresno, California); Staten Island, Sri Lankan Enclave (New York City); Thai Town (Los Angeles, California); Tucson, Chinese and Southeast Asian Enclaves (Arizona); Yuba City, Sikh Enclave (California)

See also Hispanic Enclaves: Boyle Heights, Latino Neighborhood (Los Angeles, California); Bridgeport (Chicago, Illinois); Chicago, Mexican and Puerto Rican Enclaves (Illinois); Dallas, Mexican Enclaves (Texas); East Los Angeles, Mexican American Enclave (Los Angeles, California); El Monte, Latino Enclaves (California); Historic South Central (Los Angeles, California); Holyoke, Puerto Rican Enclaves (Massachusetts); Houston, Mexican Enclaves (Texas); Indio, Mexican and Central American Communities (California); Jackson Heights (Queens, New York); Langley Park, Latino Enclaves (Maryland); Lawrence, Latino Enclaves (Massachusetts); Little Havana (Miami, Florida); Little Havana on the Hudson (North Hudson, New Jersey); Little Lima (Paterson, New Jersey); Logan Heights, Mexican Enclave (San Diego, California); Mayan Corner/24th and Mission (San Francisco, California); Mexicantown (Detroit, Michigan); Mount Washington, Mexican Enclave (California); Olvera Street/La Plaza (Los Angeles, California); Phoenix and Other Cities, Mexican Enclaves (Arizona); Pico Rivera, Latino Enclave (California); Riverside, Mexican Enclave (California); San Bernardino, Mexican Enclave (California); Santa Ana, Mexican Enclaves (California); Sleepy Hollow, Ecuadorian Enclave (New York); South Federal Boulevard (Denver, Colorado); Sunset Park West and North Corona (New York City); Upper Fells Point (Spanish Town) (Baltimore, Maryland); Washington Heights (New York City); Watts (Los Angeles, California)

Elizabeth Anne Yates

Further Reading

Bernhard, Marianne. "Vietnamese Church in Annandale Vandalized." *Washington Post*, November 3, 1979. http://www.washingtonpost.com/archive/local/1979/11/03/vietnamese-church-in-annandale-vandalized/e2ff8d6c-2f02-44d0-9a41-1f31267126d9.

Capone, Audrey B. "Ravensworth, a Short History of Annandale, VA." 1985. Accessed October 13, 2016. http://annandale.va.us/history.html.

Cho, David. "'Koreatown' Image Divides a Changing Annandale." *Washington Post*, March 14, 2005. http://www.washingtonpost.com/wp-dyn/articles/A32442-2005Mar13_2.html.

Collins, Katie. Parish Profile: Arlington Holy Martyrs of Vietnam—A Multiplicity of Stories, One Faith: Vietnamese Community Brought Together by Heritage, Bound Together by Love for Church." *Arlington Catholic Herald*, February 2, 2011. http://catholicherald.com/stories/A-multiplicity-of-stories-one-faith,14878.

Connection Newspapers. "Fairfax's Long Road to Integration: Fairfax Museum Looks at Desegregation within Fairfax County Public Schools While Commemorating History of *Brown v. Board of Education*." March 3, 2004. Accessed October 13, 2016. http://www.connectionnewspapers.com/news/2004/mar/03/fairfaxs-long-road-to-integration.

Festa, Elizabeth. "In Annandale, a Place of Many Happy Returns." *Washington Post*, June 3, 2006. http://www.washingtonpost.com/wpdyn/content/article/2006/06/02/AR2006060200712.html.

Olivo, Antonio. "In Fairfax, Housing-Code Complaints Stir Up Tensions As Some Immigrants Feel Targeted." *Washington Post*, March 29, 2014. http://www.washingtonpost.com/local/virginia-news/2014/03/29/88e6dc96-b5e1-11e3-8cb6-284052554d74_story.html.

Seminara, Dave. "Koreans Make Their Mark in Fairfax: Direct Flights, Outstanding Schools Cited as Reasons for Growth in Past Decade." *Fairfax Times*, October 5, 2011. http://www.fairfaxtimes.com/article/20111005/NEWS/710059373/koreans-make-their-mark-in-fairfax&template=fairfaxTimes.

APPLETON (FOX CITIES), HMONG COMMUNITY (WISCONSIN)

After California and Minnesota, Wisconsin has the third-largest Hmong population in the United States. Founded by French explorers in the 1840s, Appleton is the biggest of the "Fox Cities," made up of towns located along the Fox River. Appleton was also an unlikely location for a Hmong cultural center.

Prior to the 1970s, Wisconsin had relatively few Asian immigrants, and the state as a whole was one of the whitest in the nation. At this point, there were only 408 Hmong living in Appleton. By 1990, Wisconsin's Hmong population had swelled to 16,980. And, by 2010, the census counted 49,240 people of Hmong ancestry, making up 0.9% of the population of Wisconsin. Of the nearly 50,000 Hmong living in Wisconsin, 4,082 were living in Appleton.

This first wave of refugees had spent recent years in Thailand's refugee camps. They often lacked formal education, and many of them spoke little to no English. The Hmong's written language only goes as far back as the 1950s, which made it even more difficult for refugees to learn English. The Hmong also tended to have large families, although the average family size has shrunk in recent years. Educational and financial difficulties initially caused some growing pains in the community. As of 1998, 74% of the Hmong population was below the federal poverty level. This caused some strain on local budgets, creating tensions between the Hmong population and the rest of the town. Many of the new arrivals also had difficulty adjusting, as the schools weren't initially equipped to help them learn English, and their sponsors didn't always understand the culture shock that they were dealing with.

In 1994, *The Atlantic* published an article by Roy Beck that lamented the toll that the Hmong population had taken on the economy in nearby Wasau (about an hour's drive away). Beck's article was followed by a piece on *60 Minutes*. Local tempers flared, partially over the semi-national controversy, but also about a regional busing plan designed to better integrate the Hmong population into the local school systems. After the initial clash, the community calmed down, and the Hmong began, over time, to integrate themselves into the local fabric. Appleton continues to welcome refugees from around the world to the city.

In the intervening years, the Hmong population has been able to improve its socioeconomic position. From 1987 to 1997, Hmong welfare participation went from 77% to just 12%. This did not, unfortunately, immediately contribute to the upward mobility among the Hmong, who still suffered as a result of their lower level of formal education. Most who left the welfare rolls did not see an increase in their annual income, and many of them saw their annual earnings actually decrease. It was a point of pride among many in the community to be working for an hourly wage, even if this didn't always translate to greater household income. The Hmong in Appleton have steadily built themselves up, with a majority of them now owning their own homes and nearly all of the adult population holding full-time jobs. As their children have been able to take advantage of educational opportunities, the community has further thrived.

As the local Hmong community has grown, the area has become a locus for more recent Hmong immigrants, as well as first-wave immigrants who were originally settled elsewhere. Many Hmong who were originally settled in California eventually made their way to Wisconsin. Family members who were initially placed around the country were motivated by strong family ties to move in order to live closer to each other. Appleton's original Hmong population also sponsored their relatives in the Thai refugee camps, bringing an influx of new immigrants to the area.

Starting in 1997, Appleton hired a diversity coordinator for the town. The library also has a Hmong resource center. The school system, which originally struggled to educate Hmong children who didn't speak much English, has also greatly expanded its English Language Learners (ELL) program. The Appleton police department has made efforts to hire a more diverse police force. The police department is now considered to be one of the more diverse departments in the area, with one African American officer, three Hispanic officers, and four Asian officers, including Hmong officer Kevin Lee.

The local Hmong medical clinic has also made great strides in reaching out to the community. Its director, Cha Lee, speaks English, Thai, and Hmong. After receiving his medical degree and completing his residency, he returned to nearby Sheboygan to work with the Hmong community. He told a reporter in 2014 that the Hmong are often difficult patients to work with—they tend to be suspicious of Western medicine and often prefer the use of herbs, under the auspices of family members or shamans. Family bonds play a large role in the Hmong culture, so doctors often have to contend with well-meaning family members who end up contradicting their advice.

The Hmong have traditionally been subsistence farmers and foragers. After immigrating, many Hmong cultivated their own local gardens in Wisconsin. They use the food that they grow to supplement their family's food budgets, as well as selling some surplus at local farmers markets. Foraging is not something that they've found to be socially acceptable in the United States, so they tend to practice it in secret. The Hmong are often deeply aware of how they are perceived outside their community, and so they have made great efforts to fit in. Many Hmong have embraced the local culture of hunting and fishing as a socially acceptable way to provide extra food for their families. While the Hmong tend to hunt and fish more for the meat that it provides and less for social or relaxation aspects, these outdoor sports have allowed them to more fully integrate with the local culture.

Most Hmong adults have found work in local factories, but there are also a handful of Hmong-owned businesses in the area, including grocery stores and restaurants. Mai's Deli began as proprietor Mai Lee's side business, when she sold chicken wings stuffed with cabbage, noodles, and vegetables at local farmers markets. Her wings proved to be so popular that she opened her own restaurant in 2010.

Because Hmong culture tends toward familiar socialization, with strong kinship ties, they tend to associate most frequently with family members, not necessarily their immediate neighbors. Nevertheless, several Hmong cultural institutions have sprung up in Appleton. Appleton has its own Internet-based Hmong radio station, Hmong Wisconsin Radio, which broadcasts talk radio in Hmong 24 hours a day, 7 days a week. Hmong citizens who need assistance can get help from the Hmong American

From Anticommunist Guerrillas to Evangelical Lutherans

In the mid- to late 1970s, after an unsuccessful fight against Communists in Laos and facing recrimination for their aid to the Americans during the Vietnam War, an influx of Hmong refugees made their way to the United States, mostly by way of over-crowded refugee camps in Thailand. The U. S. government's policy at this time was to disperse these refugees throughout the United States, so that no one community would be overwhelmed by their presence. This first wave of immigrants also needed to find local American sponsors. In 1976, the Appleton community, as well as the larger Wisconsin community, began sponsoring Hmong families. This was primarily the effort of local religious groups: Lutherans as well as Catholic social services. Many of these refugees ultimately settled in Appleton. Furthermore, upon their arrival many Hmong converted to the Evangelical sect of Lutheran Christianity. The Hmong Central Lutheran Church in St. Paul, Minnesota, is the largest Hmong Lutheran congregation, with nearly 500 members (Mooch 2008).

Partnership Fox Valley, Inc. (HAP), which works to integrate Hmong immigrants into the local community. English language learners (ELL) classes offer an opportunity for students both to work on their English and to socialize with their fellow Hmong. Many Hmong are also active participants in their church communities.

Many Hmong can also be found playing and enjoying the outdoors with their families in local parks. Children play a traditional game that involves tossing small stones, while men might play kickball (*kotaw*) and women socialize. There are also informal kickball and volleyball leagues.

The biggest event of the year is the Hmong New Year celebration, held annually in late November or early December at the local high school, Appleton East High School. The event draws about 1,500 attendants, many of them wearing traditional Hmong garb. Hmong dresses often feature elaborate beading and can take a year to construct. The new year was traditionally a time for young people to court one another, but it has taken a decidedly more modern turn in Appleton. Teens still play Pov Pob, a traditional game that involves tossing a ball back and forth. But these days it's mostly just for fun, not necessarily an opportunity to let someone know that you like them. The New Year's celebration also features performances of traditional dancing and singing, as well as talent and fashion shows.

See also Wisconsin: Milwaukee, German Enclaves (Wisconsin)

See also Hmong Enclaves: Minneapolis-St. Paul, Twin Cities Hmong Community (Minnesota); Sin City (Fresno, California)

Hope Roth

Further Reading

2010 Census Hmong Populations of Wisconsin Metro and Micro Areas. Accessed October 13, 2016. http://www.hmong.org/page334104652.aspx.

20th-Century Immigration. Accessed October 13, 2016. http://www.wisconsinhistory.org.

Higgins, D. "Mai's Deli Drawing Admirers with Stuffed Wings." August 26, 2014. Accessed October 13, 2016. http://www.postcrescent.com/story/life/2014/08/26/mais-deli-wings /14614439.

Jones, T. "In Wausau, Hmong at Another Crossroads." *Chicago Tribune*, June 16, 2003.

Koltyk, J. *New Pioneers in the Heartland: Hmong Life in Wisconsin.* Boston: Allyn and Bacon, 1998.

Mentzer, R. "How Wausau's Immigration Fears Failed to Come True." *Wausau Daily Herald*, December 7, 2014.

Mooch, Katie. "Lutheran and Hmong in Minnesota." *Twin Cities Daily Planet*, November 12, 2008. Accessed June 24, 2016. http://www.tcdailyplanet.net/lutheran-and-hmong -minnesota.

Pabst, G. "Report Shows Growth in Hmong Community." *Milwaukee Wisconsin Journal Sentinel*, January 6, 2013.

Penzenstadler, N. "Fox Valley Expects 150 More Refugees in 2015." *The Post-Crescent* (Appleton), August 11, 2014. http://www.postcrescent.com/story/news/local/2014/08 /10/appleton-expects-refugees/13867343.

Van Berkel, J. "Hmong New Year Celebration Bridges Old, New Generations." *The Post-Crescent* (Appleton), November 27, 2011.

Zettel, J. "Appleton Schools Expected to Get More Diverse." *The Post-Crescent* (Appleton), October 22, 2014. http://www.postcrescent.com/story/news/local/2014/10/22/appleton -schools-expected-get-diverse/17692495.

ARMENIAN ENCLAVES. *See* Glendale, Armenian Enclave (California); Little Armenia (Los Angeles, California); Watertown, Armenian Capital (Massachusetts)

ASIAN DISTRICT (OKLAHOMA CITY, OKLAHOMA)

The Asian District (also sometimes referred to as Asia district) in Oklahoma City, Oklahoma, is regarded by many as a center for Asian culture and food, not only in Oklahoma but also for the entire region of south central United States.

The Asian District is home to one of the largest groupings of Asian Americans and Asian descendants. The first people of Asian descent to arrive in Oklahoma were Chinese workers in the 1880s. It is unknown what brought these men to the area. They may have been railroad workers, but it has also been speculated that they worked as cooks and launderers for the U.S. Army. The first Asian-owned businesses in Oklahoma City were laundries. By 1889, there were five such establishments, and an estimated Chinese population of 18. The number of Chinese residents in Oklahoma roughly doubled each year that the census was taken, but these Chinese Americans (mostly men) were mostly dispersed throughout the state. The precursor to Oklahoma City's Asian District was a small "Chinatown," located downtown. This community, made up almost entirely of men, provided labor for local businesses, as well as a few small restaurants and shops geared toward the Chinese community. Most residents resided in basements or sub-basements, creating a local legend that

The Asian District sign in Oklahoma City. (Justin Brotton/Dreamstime.com)

told of a secret series of tunnels. While the Chinese remained Oklahoma's largest Asian group until the 1950s, they mostly left the area during the Great Depression.

The next Asian group to move to the area was Japanese immigrants who came to the United States starting in the 1890s. Many Japanese men were drawn to Oklahoma because of the relatively easy availability of farm work. Japanese workers also found jobs as gardeners and domestic servants. Japanese settlers began arriving in earnest in the 1920s. Many of the area's wealthy elite, newly rich from Oklahoma oil money, hired Japanese men to tend to their gardens and to look after their estates. The advent of World War II brought some initial tensions, but the governor of Oklahoma, Leon Phillips, made it clear that he would countenance no violence against the state's Japanese population. Between 110,000 and 120,000 people of Japanese descent living in the United States were placed in internment camps, but none of them was interned from Oklahoma.

Oklahoma City's Asian District began as Little Saigon in 1975, a destination for the thousands of refugees fleeing Vietnam. A large number of the first wave of Vietnamese refugees was quartered at Fort Chaffee in nearby Arkansas. At the time, leaving the base required a local sponsor. While most of the refugees ultimately ended up dispersed throughout the country, many of them were resettled in Oklahoma City. A smaller coterie of activists in Oklahoma City worked to help these Vietnamese immigrants. Catholic Charities sponsored many refugees, helping them to move into the Central Park neighborhood. The neighborhood, which began as a working-class neighborhood of Irish, Polish, and German immigrants, had fallen into decline. Many of its original inhabitants had recently left for the suburbs. The infusion of Vietnamese immigrants helped revitalize the area. The district is now home to Chinese, Japanese, Thai, and Korean descendants, as well as its original Vietnamese population. As of the 2010 Census, people of Asian descent made up 3.5% of the population of Oklahoma City.

The defining building of the Asian District is the "Milk Bottle Building" on Classen Boulevard. Built in 1930, the triangle-shaped building originally functioned as a restaurant for streetcar riders. Starting in the late 1980s, the building was home to the Saigon Baguette store, also sometimes called Bale Banh Mi, which sold banh mi along with other sandwiches. The store closed in 2014. The building is currently being renovated and restored. The Milk Bottle Building serves as an unofficial border to the Asian District. The other borders are generally considered to be Oklahoma City University and the Paseo Arts District. The bulk of the Asian District is located on Classen Boulevard, and it encompasses about an eight-block stretch of the street.

The Asian District had humble beginnings. In 1975, there were just three Asian restaurants and no supermarkets or other businesses. The first wave of refugees had difficulties with English. Many of them had worked professional jobs in Vietnam, but they were often relegated to menial labor upon arrival. Over time, the community pursued educational opportunities, and the Asian District now houses a large professional class. Many of these newly minted doctors and lawyers have started their own businesses in the district, which sports doctors and lawyers' offices along with other businesses like nail salons, travel agents, video stores, nightclubs, and supermarkets.

In 2000, the city of Oklahoma City officially designated the area as the "Asian District," putting the area under the supervision of the city's Urban Design Committee and providing funds for improvements. There have been some attempts to rename nearby Military Avenue to Saigon Avenue, but those proposals have all been controversial, and the city has stated that it has no plans for a name change.

Oklahoma City has one of the largest per capita populations of Vietnamese Americans. Only San Jose, Honolulu, and Oakland have more. As of the 2000 U.S. Census, Oklahoma ranked third in the country for the number of its Vietnamese students pursuing higher education. The Asian District has built on its own success. Starting in the 1980s, refugees who had originally been placed in other parts of the countries began flocking to the district. And then, in the 1990s, as diplomatic relations between the United States and Vietnam improved, local residents were able to sponsor their relatives back in Vietnam. With this second wave of immigration, the districts' Asian population grew further.

While still primarily Vietnamese, the district is now home to immigrants from many other Asian nations. Along with banh mi and Vietnamese coffee, visitors and residents can now purchase Hong Kong dim sum at restaurants and Taiwanese bubble teas at cafés. The clientele includes Asian locals, but has also become a tourist draw in recent years. The Vietnamese soup dish pho tends to be a specialty, but a multitude of restaurants also serve Asian fusion, sushi, Szechuan-style Chinese food, and Pad Thai. In a region that isn't known for its fresh produce or spices, the Asian District has become a draw for hungry travelers looking for that extra kick.

The Asian District is home to the Super Cao Nguyen, one of the largest Asian supermarkets in the region. The store opened as the Cao Nguyen in 1979, a small family-owned market, but it has grown and expanded over time. After it moved into its current location, the family added the word *Super* to the store's name. The grocery store is now one of the biggest supermarkets of any type in Oklahoma City, and people drive from all across the state to shop there. The store features fresh produce and seafood, and quality is paramount. The store includes a bakery, kimchee bar, and sushi bar.

The Asian District hosts many yearly events, including a combined Chinese and Vietnamese New Year celebration in late January/early February. Because the traditions of both cultures share many similarities, the celebration has been merged. Revelers light fireworks in the parking lot of the Super Cao Nguyen to start the celebration. The store has been the official host since it opened. They now set off a million firecrackers each year. A parade of Chinese lion dancers, mostly local teens, make their way down the store's aisles before dancing their way down the districts' streets. Musicians play drums and cymbals. Residents thank the dancers for their service with red envelopes containing small amounts of money. There are also evening dances and parties.

The district gets a small economic boost during the New Year celebrations, as residents traditionally buy new clothes for good luck. There is also heavy demand for candy, nuts, and red envelopes. Local hair salons do a brisk business with residents who get haircuts for good luck.

Another big event is the Asian moon festival, held during the eighth lunar month of the Vietnamese calendar, generally around the end of September. The moon festival features lion dancing as well, along with performances of traditional Vietnamese music. The moon festival tends to focus around children, who receive gifts of candy and school supplies at its conclusion.

The district also hosts a yearly Asian Festival in the spring, celebrating cultures from Vietnam, China, India, Indonesia, Japan, Korea, Laos, the Philippines, and Taiwan. The festival includes crafts and cultural displays, as well as a beauty pageant.

After an initial period of rapid growth, the Asian District has slowly but steadily improved. Its residents have reinvested profits in the area, revitalizing blighted buildings and shoring up property values. Nearby neighborhoods suffered from empty buildings and blight during the recent economic downturn, but the Asian District continued to thrive. Often, when their family members were unable to secure bank loans, established Asian District merchants would provide the initial financial outlay for new businesses. Members of the Asian District community have been praised for preserving the district's original buildings, like the Milk Bottle Building and a golden-domed building, keeping the early Americana architectural elements and giving the neighborhood some of its distinct character.

In some ways, the Asian District has been a victim of its own success. As its population ages and becomes wealthier, many of them have moved from the district to the wealthier areas in the suburbs. There are also smaller enclaves in the

Oklahoma City metro area where Asian shops and restaurants have sprung up in older strip malls. The Asian District still remains central, however, and business continues briskly apace.

See also in Oklahoma: Greenwood (Tulsa, Oklahoma)

See also Asian Enclaves: Annandale, Latino and Asian Enclaves (Virginia); Appleton (Fox Cities), Hmong Community (Wisconsin); Bergen County, Korean Enclaves (New Jersey); Bridgeport (Chicago, Illinois); Cambodia Town (Long Beach, California); Cambodia Town (Lowell, Massachusetts); Chinatown (Los Angeles, California); Chinatown (Phoenix, Arizona); Chinatown (San Francisco, California); Chinatown Historic District/A'ala (Honolulu, Hawaii); Chinatowns (Duplicates) (San Francisco, California); Chinatowns (Manhattan; Sunset Park East, Brooklyn; Flushing, Queens) (New York City); Historic Filipinotown (Los Angeles, California); International District (Seattle, Washington); Ironbound and the Wards (Newark, New Jersey); Jackson Heights (Queens, New York); Jackson Heights, South Asian Enclave (Queens, New York); Japantown (San Francisco, California); Koreatown (Los Angeles, California); Little India (Chicago, Illinois); Little India, Chatham Street (Cary, North Carolina); Little India, Hillcroft (Houston, Texas); Little India, Jackson Heights (Queens, New York); Little India, Newark Avenue (Jersey City, New Jersey); Little India/Pakistan (Artesia, California); Little Saigon (Denver, Colorado); Little Saigon (Houston, Texas); Little Saigon (San Francisco, California); Little Saigon (San Jose, California); Little Saigon (Westminster, California); Little Tokyo (Los Angeles, California); Minneapolis-St. Paul, Twin Cities Hmong Community (Minnesota); Monterey Park, First Suburban Chinatown (California); New Chinatown (Portland, Oregon); Quincy, Asian Enclaves (Massachusetts); Silicon Valley, Indian and South Asian Communities (Santa Clara Valley/San Jose Region, California); Sin City (Fresno, California); Staten Island, Sri Lankan Enclave (New York City); Thai Town (Los Angeles, California); Tucson, Chinese and Southeast Asian Enclaves (Arizona); Yuba City, Sikh Enclave (California)

Hope Roth

Further Reading

Allen, S. "Oklahoma City's Chinese New Year Festival Draws a Crowd." *The Oklahoman*, February 21, 2015.

Brianna, B. "Oklahoma City's Milk Bottle Building Is Being Restored to Its Original Appearance." *The Oklahoman*, August 19, 2014.

Cathey, D. "Eateries Come, Go, Evolve and Grow in Oklahoma City-Area." *The Oklahoman*, July 9, 2013.

Cathey, D. "Family Owns Super Cao Nguyen Market, Lives American Dream in Oklahoma City." *The Oklahoman*, July 1, 2009.

Christopher, D. "Vietnamese Culture in Oklahoma: Oklahoma City's Asian District, Asian Festival, Vietnamese Food and Vietnamese Students." *The Oklahoman*, June 24, 2010.

Dean, B. "City's Asian Pearl." *The Oklahoman*, May 18, 2004.

Everett, D. "Asians." *Encyclopedia of Oklahoma History and Culture*. Accessed November 2, 2016. http://www.okhistory.org/publications/enc/entry.php?entry=AS006.

Gibbs Robinson, J. "Preparation Begins for Lunar New Year Traditions Include Cleaning, Haircuts." *The Oklahoman*, January 30, 2005.

Gross, M. "Good Morning, Vietnam . . . er, Oklahoma." *The New York Times*, July 4, 2007.

Hussain, S. "Annual Moon and Children Festival Brings Great Turnout in Oklahoma City." *The Oklahoman*, October 1, 2013.

Johnstonbaugh, K. "Cao Nguyen Asian Market and How to Find Your Way Around." October 20, 2010. Accessed November 2, 2016. http://www.dishinanddishes.com/how-to -find-your-way-around-an-asian-market.

Knittle, A. "Vietnamese Have Strong Presence in Oklahoma City's Asian District." *The Oklahoman*, October 9, 2011.

Lackmeyer, S., and J. Money. "Council Designates Section of Classen as Asian district." *The Oklahoman*, June 28, 2000.

"Oklahoma City's Vibrant Asian Food Scene Revealed." Accessed November 2. 2016. http:// www.travelok.com/article_page/oklahoma-citys-vibrant-asian-food-scene-revealed

Slipke, D. "Dancers Bring Good Luck to Asian District." *The Oklahoman*, February 6, 2011.

ASIAN ENCLAVES. *See* Annandale, Latino and Asian Enclaves (Virginia); Appleton (Fox Cities), Hmong Community (Wisconsin); Asian District (Oklahoma City, Oklahoma); Bergen County, Korean Enclaves (New Jersey); Bridgeport (Chicago, Illinois); Cambodia Town (Long Beach, California); Cambodia Town (Lowell, Massachusetts); Chinatown (Los Angeles, California); Chinatown (Phoenix, Arizona); Chinatown (San Francisco, California); Chinatown Historic District/A'ala (Honolulu, Hawaii); Chinatowns (Duplicates) (San Francisco, California); Chinatowns (Manhattan; Sunset Park East, Brooklyn; Flushing, Queens) (New York City); Historic Filipinotown (Los Angeles, California); International District (Seattle, Washington); Ironbound and the Wards (Newark, New Jersey); Jackson Heights (Queens, New York); Jackson Heights, South Asian Enclave (Queens, New York); Japantown (San Francisco, California); Koreatown (Los Angeles, California); Little India (Chicago, Illinois); Little India, Chatham Street (Cary, North Carolina); Little India, Hillcroft (Houston, Texas); Little India, Jackson Heights (Queens, New York); Little India, Newark Avenue (Jersey City, New Jersey); Little India/Pakistan (Artesia, California); Little Saigon (Denver, Colorado); Little Saigon (Houston, Texas); Little Saigon (San Francisco, California); Little Saigon (San Jose, California); Little Saigon (Westminster, California); Little Tokyo (Los Angeles, California); Minneapolis-St. Paul, Twin Cities Hmong Community (Minnesota); Monterey Park, First Suburban Chinatown (California); New Chinatown (Portland, Oregon); Quincy, Asian Enclaves (Massachusetts); Silicon Valley, Indian and South Asian Communities (Santa Clara Valley/San Jose Region, California); Sin City (Fresno, California); Staten Island, Sri Lankan Enclave (New York City); Thai Town (Los Angeles, California); Tucson, Chinese and Southeast Asian Enclaves (Arizona); Yuba City, Sikh Enclave (California)

BALDWIN HILLS (LOS ANGELES, CALIFORNIA)

Baldwin Hills is a neighborhood in the northwest region of South Los Angeles. Known as "The Black Beverly Hills," the area is an affluent and majority African

American community. According to the 2010 U.S. Census, Baldwin Hills has a population of 26,303 and more than 65% is African American (LA Almanac 2010). Baldwin Hills has seen significant changes over the past century and a half, transforming from empty grazing land to the site of the world's first Olympic Village to the desired home of Los Angeles's white upper middle class and most recently to the "Black Beverly Hills," a moniker that remains to this day, although it is being challenged due to recent growing demographic changes.

The area that is now Baldwin Hills was initially part of *Rancho La Ciénega o Paso de la Tijera,* a land grant given to Vicente Sánchez (1785–1846) in 1843 from the Mexican government. The dual name was derived from the marshlands and natural springs in the area (*La Ciénega*) and two valleys forming a narrow pass in the shape of pair of scissors (*Paso de la Tijera*). Sánchez was the *alcalde,* or local magistrate (also translated as mayor) for the area. Because his local duties required him to live in Los Angeles and the ranch was nearly a day's journey from the city at the time, Sánchez used the ranch mostly for cattle grazing and remained in town. In about 1846, upon Sánchez's death, his properties were divided among his heirs. Sánchez's grandson Tomás A. Sánchez (the sheriff of Los Angeles for nearly 10 years) received Rancho La Ciénega. Upon the younger Sánchez's marriage in 1875, he moved with his wife to property she had inherited near Glendale and sold Rancho Ciénega.

Sánchez sold the ranch to a group of business partners led by banker Francisco P. F. Temple (1827–1880), a prominent banker, oilman, rancher, and real estate speculator who had cofounded the Temple Workman Bank with his father-in-law, William Workman, in 1871. Unfortunately for Temple, he was swept up in a statewide panic that hit the banking industry in 1875, sending scores of customers to withdraw their savings from his bank and forcing him to seek out a loan. Temple went to Elias "Lucky" Baldwin (1828–1909), a millionaire recently arrived from San Francisco, for his loan. Baldwin gave Temple the loan, but with the condition that if Temple was unable to repay, Baldwin would foreclose on the bank's real estate holdings. The Temple Workman Bank failed soon after. By 1880, Baldwin had cashed in on his agreement with Temple and taken ownership of nearly all of San Gabriel Valley, including Rancho La Ciénega.

"Lucky" Baldwin was a colorful character, a transplant to California from the Midwest who earned his nickname from more than one instance in his exciting life. Baldwin was born in Ohio in 1828 and moved to Indiana with his family in 1834. He lived there until 1853, when he and his wife and young daughter joined a wagon train heading west. On his journey to California, Baldwin managed to get separated from his wagon train and nearly starved to death before being rescued by friendly Native Americans. His wagon train was later attacked outside Salt Lake City by a less friendly group of Native Americans, and Baldwin's group barely escaped with their lives. Baldwin did not set out to California to take part in the Gold Rush. Already a successful grocer and saloon owner, Baldwin instead packed his wagons with provisions to sell when he arrived in the West. Once in Salt Lake City, Baldwin sold the contents of his wagons for a handsome profit, which he in turn used to buy extra horses for the journey to California. Baldwin then sold the horses for an even greater profit, more than doubling his initial investment by the time he reached San Francisco.

Baldwin's luck continued through the years. In San Francisco, he purchased a brick foundry that supplied the materials for Alcatraz federal prison as well as a successful hotel. His investments in the silver market and the Comstock Lode paid off. By 1873, Baldwin was soon an extremely wealthy man, with a fortune estimated at $5 million. His other ventures soon grew to include other hotels, more mining investments, and large tracts of land in Southern California. It was his investments in Los Angeles that put him in contact with Temple and positioned him to become the owner of nearly all of San Gabriel Valley.

After Lucky Baldwin's death in 1909, his real estate holdings were divided between his daughters, Clara and Anita. Baldwin's land eventually came to be developed into cities and neighborhoods well known to residents of the Los Angeles area, including Arcadia, Monrovia, Temple City, Sierra Madre, the Montebello Oil Fields, and parts of West Covina, Bassett and La Puente among others. It was the hills in the west of Rancho La Ciénega, however, that retained Lucky's name and came to be known as Baldwin Hills.

The Baldwin family initially leased Rancho La Ciénega to the Sunset Golf Corporation, who used it as an extension of their club. Clara Baldwin soon after sold the land to William H. Leimert, a developer from Oakland, in 1927. Leimert's name would eventually come to be used on a smaller, adjacent neighborhood, Leimert Park. Soon after buying the property, Leimert used the land to take advantage of the Olympics being hosted in Los Angeles in 1932, and the first ever purpose-built Olympic Village was erected in the Baldwin Hills area. The Village was comprised of 600 two-room dwellings for the male athletes competing in the games, as well as a telegraph office, hospital, amphitheater, fire station, post office, and bank. The buildings were removed after the games were finished, with the only remaining indication of the area's history being street names such as Athenian Way and Olympiad Drive.

The Baldwin Hills of today was developed in the post–1932 Olympics era. After the Olympic Village was torn down, the area was further developed for homes. Baldwin Hills is currently bordered to the north by Rodeo Road and Martin Luther King Boulevard, with Slauson Avenue forming its southern border. The eastern edge of the neighborhood is marked by Crenshaw Boulevard, with La Cienega Boulevard forming the western edge of Baldwin Hills. Baldwin Hills is frequently combined with the nearby, smaller area of Crenshaw for census and city planning purposes. As Leimert began developing the former Rancho La Ciénega, the neighborhood soon gained a different name, Pill Hill, as it was the prime choice of the city's physicians and medical professionals through the 1960s for its affordability in comparison to other neighborhoods with similarly striking views of downtown Los Angeles.

Another major event to occur in the neighborhood was the disastrous break in the Baldwin Hills Dam, which held back nearly 300 million gallons of water in the Baldwin Hills Reservoir. The reservoir, built on a low hilltop in Baldwin Hills in the early 1950s, developed a small crack in its side on December 14, 1963. An alert reservoir caretaker, Revere G. Wells, notified the maintenance team and authorities to the danger of the growing crack, giving police time to begin the evacuation of the hillside community beneath the reservoir. Wells noticed the pencil-sized crack at approximately 11:15 a.m., and in just over four hours the crack grew to a 75-foot-wide gash. At 3:38 p.m., the dam burst and sent a 50-foot high wall of water into the houses below. In just over 75 minutes, 292 million gallons of water emptied from the reservoir, coating the entire hillside in thick mud. Five people were killed, 65 homes were completely obliterated, and another 210 were heavily damaged. The cause was initially thought to be a minor earthquake, but a 1976 study by federal geologists concluded that the actual cause was overexploitation of the nearby Inglewood Oil Field, which caused land under the reservoir to shift and sink, stressing the walls of the dam. The reservoir was never rebuilt, and the land was instead used as the beginning of a system of parks. County Supervisor Kenneth Hahn (1920–1997) proposed using the land once occupied by the reservoir and land used for oil drilling to begin a large green space. The park, now known as the Kenneth Hahn State Recreation Area, began as a 50-acre plot and has grown to more than 300 acres. As old oil wells run dry, lands acquired by the county are added to the parks system, and now more than one-third of Baldwin Hills is taken up by park land.

Another development of the early 1960s, shortly before the Baldwin Hills reservoir disaster, was the beginning of the shift in the demographics of Baldwin Hills. Long the home of affluent white professionals, Baldwin Hills experienced an influx of African Americans as a result of the easing of restrictive housing covenants in the city. Unlike areas like Watts, which experienced a growth in the number of working class African Americans moving into the neighborhood, Baldwin Hills instead attracted black entertainers, musicians, and actors who were still unable to move into the typical star-studded neighborhoods of Los Angeles. Soon, Baldwin Hills' nickname became "Black Beverly Hills" for the large number of well-known African Americans who lived in the area. The neighborhood attracted stars such as Ray Charles, Ike and Tina Turner, Loretta Devine, and former mayor of Los Angeles Tom Bradley. Bradley was a five-term mayor, serving from 1973 to 1993, and held the distinction of being the first African American mayor of a major American city with an overwhelmingly white population.

Baldwin Hills

BET (Black Entertainment Television) aired *Baldwin Hills*, a reality television series following the lives of African American teens from the neighborhood. The show aired for three seasons, from July 2007 to March 2009, and was considered the African American version of other reality television shows, such as MTV's *Laguna Beach: The Real Orange County*.

As racist housing policies continued to decline in the decades following the 1960s, prominent African Americans began moving into other neighborhoods and away from Baldwin Hills. Rather than becoming a more diverse neighborhood, however, Baldwin Hills continued to be a predominantly black community. As black celebrities moved out, middle-class African Americans moved in, allowing Baldwin Hills to continue on as a more well-to-do area than some of the nearby neighborhoods. The 2010 U.S. Census shows that more than 40 years later, after African Americans began to move into Baldwin Hills in large numbers, they are still the majority population in the neighborhood, making up nearly 66% of the residents.

Baldwin Hills today remains an affluent and majority African American neighborhood, although it faces an increasing number of non-black new residents. It and the nearby areas of View Park, Ladera Heights, and Windsor Hills have faced a growing demographic shift in the past several years as increasing real estate prices in Los Angeles push whites back into neighborhoods that have been majority black for decades. Despite this, the area still retains its status as representative of African American success in Los Angeles, and the name "Black Beverly Hills" has strong connections with the area well known outside Los Angeles.

See also in California: Boyle Heights, Jewish Neighborhood (Los Angeles, California); Boyle Heights, Latino Neighborhood (Los Angeles, California); Cambodia Town (Long Beach, California); Chinatown (Los Angeles, California); Chinatown (San Francisco, California); Chinatowns (Duplicates) (San Francisco, California); East Los Angeles, Mexican American Enclave (Los Angeles, California); El Monte, Latino Enclaves (California); Fillmore District (San Francisco, California); Gardena and Torrance (South Bay Region, Los Angeles County, California); Glendale, Armenian Enclave (California); Historic Filipinotown (Los Angeles, California); Historic South Central (Los Angeles, California); Indio, Mexican and Central American Communities (California); Japantown (San Francisco, California); Kingsburg and Sveadal, Swedish Enclaves (California); Koreatown (Los Angeles, California); Little Arabia (Anaheim, California); Little Armenia (Los Angeles, California); Little Ethiopia (Los Angeles, California); Little India/Pakistan (Artesia, California); Little Italy (Los Angeles, California); Little Italy (San Diego, California); Little Italy (San Francisco, California); Little Saigon (San Francisco, California); Little Saigon (San Jose, California); Little Saigon (Westminster, California); Little Tokyo (Los Angeles, California); Logan Heights, Mexican Enclave (San Diego, California); Los Angeles, Hawaiian Enclaves (California); Los Angeles, West Side and San Fernando Valley Jewish Enclaves (California); Mayan Corner/24th and Mission (San Francisco, California); Monterey Park, First Suburban Chinatown (California); Mount Washington, Mexican Enclave (California); National City (San Diego, California); Olvera Street/La Plaza (Los Angeles, California); Pico Rivera, Latino Enclave (California); Riverside, Mexican Enclave (California); San Bernardino, Mexican Enclave (California); San Pedro, Italian and Croatian Enclaves (California); Santa Ana, Mexican Enclaves (California); Sawtelle (Los Angeles, California); Silicon Valley, Indian and South Asian Communities (Santa Clara Valley/San Jose Region, California); Sin City

(Fresno, California); Solvang, Danish Community (California); Sonoma County, Italian Enclave (California); Tehrangeles (Los Angeles, California); Temescal (Oakland, California); Thai Town (Los Angeles, California); Watts (Los Angeles, California); Yuba City, Sikh Enclave (California)

See also African American Enclaves: Bedford-Stuyvesant (Brooklyn, New York); Black Bottom (Philadelphia, Pennsylvania); Bronzeville (Chicago, Illinois); Greenwood (Tulsa, Oklahoma); Harlem (New York City); Harlem, Senegalese Enclave (New York City); Historic South Central (Los Angeles, California); Ironbound and the Wards (Newark, New Jersey); Lewiston and Portland, Somali and Bantu Enclaves (Maine); Little Ethiopia (Los Angeles, California); Lower Ninth Ward (New Orleans, Louisiana); Lower Roxbury, African American Enclave (Massachusetts); Mattapan (Boston, Massachusetts); Orange Mound (Memphis, Tennessee); Roxbury, African-American Enclave (Massachusetts); Sweet Auburn (Atlanta, Georgia); Tremé (New Orleans, Louisiana); Watts (Los Angeles, California)

Jake DeSousa

Further Reading

Bridging the Divide. "Biography of Tom Bradley." *Tom Bradley and the Politics of Race.* 2009. Accessed May 15, 2016. http://www.mayortombradley.com/biography.

Hale, Mike. "Posh Princes and Princesses of the Hill." *The New York Times*, August 7, 2007. Accessed May 15, 2016. http://www.nytimes.com/2007/08/07/arts/television/07hale.html?_r=0.

Hoover, Mildred Brooke, et al. *Historic Spots in California.* 5th ed. Revised by Douglas Kyle. Stanford, CA: Stanford University Press, 2002.

Jennings, Angel. "'Black Beverly Hills' Debates Historic Status vs. White Gentrification." *Los Angeles Times*, July 18, 2015. Accessed May 15, 2016. http://www.latimes.com/local/la-me-adv-view-park-20150719-story.html.

Los Angeles Almanac. *Neighborhoods of the City of Los Angeles—Population and Race, 2010 Census.* Given Place Media. Accessed May 15, 2016. http://www.laalmanac.com/population/po24la.htm.

Los Angeles County Department of Parks and Recreation. "Baldwin Hills Info." Accessed May 15, 2016. http://www.baldwinhills.info/.

Los Angeles Times. "Baldwin Hills/Crenshaw." *Mapping LA.* Accessed May 15, 2016. http://maps.latimes.com/neighborhoods/neighborhood/baldwin-hillscrenshaw.

Losee, Edgar F. "Elias Jackson Lucky Baldwin." Redlands Fortnightly Literary Club. October 2006. Accessed May 15, 2016. http://www.redlandsfortnightly.org/papers/losee06.htm.

Parra, Alvaro. *Elias "Lucky" Baldwin: Land Baron of Southern California.* KCET History and Society Series. 2013. Accessed May 15, 2016. https://www.KCET.org/shows/de"partures/elias-lucky-baldwin-land-baron-of-southern-california.

Pool, Bob. "The 1963 Baldwin Hills Dam Collapse." *Los Angeles Times.* 2003. Accessed May 15, 2016. http://framework.latimes.com/2013/12/13/the-1963-baldwin-hills-dam-collapse/#/0.

Powers, Kemp. "The Neighborhood Project: Baldwin Hills." LAist.com. August 2007. Accessed May 15, 2016. http://laist.com/2007/08/17/baldwin_hills_los_angeles.php.

BALLARD (SEATTLE, WASHINGTON)

Ballard is a neighborhood in Seattle, Washington, north of the city's downtown area. The neighborhood is bordered to the south by the Lake Washington Ship Canal, which connects the lake to the Pacific Ocean's Puget Sound, and to the west by the Sound's Shilshole Bay. This waterfront location has long defined the character of the neighborhood. Since the area was populated entirely by American Indian tribes, fishing and boating have been defining industries for Ballard. In the 19th century, Scandinavian and Nordic immigrants were drawn to the entire Puget Sound region for the economic opportunities that came with close proximity to the Pacific for shipping. As the population of Seattle and its surrounding regions grew and the immigrant population of the area continued to rise, Ballard became the center of Nordic population and culture in the area. Ballard long held onto its identity as a sleepy Scandinavian fishing village, even as Seattle grew and changed throughout the 20th century. In recent decades, the neighborhood's character has begun to shift as more young, hip residents are making Ballard home; however, the Norwegian and Nordic heritage continues to be celebrated by all residents, old and new.

Ballard was first settled in the 1860s as the population of the Pacific Northwest was beginning to grow. The land that eventually became Ballard was near the large American Indian village known as Shilshole, for the tribe that was prominent in the area; while the tribe (and village) lent its name to the modern Shilshole Bay,

Fishermen at the docks at Ballard Locks, Seattle. (Denise P. Lett/Dreamstime.com)

the native population in the area was quickly decimated after the arrival of large numbers of white settlers. The city of Seattle was formally settled in 1852 by a young man named Arthur Denny, and that prompted adventurous settlers making their way to Oregon territory to explore opportunities further north. The area was particularly appealing for settlers because of its abundant timber resources and opportunities for fishing; these two industries disproportionately drew Scandinavian and Nordic immigrants, and these communities quickly defined the character of the area. Some of the earliest landholders, ship captains William Ballard and J. A. Hatfield, reluctantly ended up owning large swaths of land near Salmon Bay, which feeds into Puget Sound, as payment for another business deal. Neither man wanted responsibility for the land, so they flipped a coin to see who would be stuck with it. Ballard lost the toss, and the land fell to him to develop. He encouraged the construction of the area's first lumber mill in 1888, followed by a shingle mill the following year. As fate would have it, the great fire Seattle suffered in 1889 created enormous demand for new construction materials and the now abundant jobs available in the mills drew immigrant laborers to Ballard.

With the foundation of the thriving lumber and shingle mills, as well as a rising commercial district along Ballard Avenue, the city of Ballard was established in 1889. The new city's population continued to grow thanks to the construction of electric streetcars that linked Ballard to nearby Seattle. Many of the new residents were Scandinavian immigrants, and the popularity of chewing tobacco among that population earned Ballard the nickname "Snoose Junction" ("snoose" is slang for chewing tobacco) throughout the Pacific Northwest. The city's government sought to ensure a balance of vice and virtue, and according to legend the number of saloon licenses within the city was limited to exactly the number of churches. Ballard continued to grow as the turn of the century approached, and a large and decorative city hall was built in 1899. However, the fledgling city government struggled to deliver basic services, in particular an adequate supply of potable water, to its residents. In 1906 Ballard requested annexation by the city of Seattle. When the process was completed in 1907 and Ballard officially became a neighborhood of the much larger city, the residents demonstrated their mixed feelings by donning black armbands. Despite annexation, Ballard continued to maintain its "city within a city" reputation and atmosphere for decades into the 20th century (Ballard Historical Society 2015).

Economically, Ballard was booming at the time of annexation. The success of the shingle mills earned the neighborhood a reputation as the "Shingle Capital of the World." By 1905, more red cedar shingles were made in the 10 mills in Ballard than in any other area in the entire country. In 1911, construction began on a ship canal to link Lake Washington with Puget Sound and the Pacific Ocean; in 1912, the project's scope expanded to include a complex of locks to prevent intrusion of the Sound's saltwater into the freshwater lake and canal and to help ships navigate the nearly 20-foot difference in water levels between Lake Washington and the ocean. The locks, operated by the U.S. Army Corps of Engineers and eventually named after lead engineer Hiram M. Chittenden, officially opened in 1917. They drastically improved Ballard's industrial prospects, thanks to the greatly improved opportunity for shipping. In 1914, the Fisherman's Terminal was established on the south shore of Shilshole Bay and became the cornerstone of a growing fishing fleet. As prospects for shipping and the rise of a massive commercial fishing industry helped facilitate economic growth in the area, a commercial district also grew along Ballard Avenue, and new commercial buildings continued to be built along that corridor up until the 1930s. The significance of the Ballard Avenue commercial area led to the district's addition to the National Register of Historic Places in the 1970s. Scandinavian immigrants, especially Norwegians, were at the heart of the growth and success of Ballard in the early 20th century, and Ballard's unique economy and culture reflected their influence.

The Nordic immigrants who moved to Ballard to fill jobs in the mills and in the fishing industry brought vibrant cultural institutions with them. The commercial district that grew along Ballard Avenue was home to restaurants and shops that catered to the immigrant population, and a variety of religious and secular Nordic organizations and businesses peppered the neighborhood. The residential areas of Ballard are home to dozens of churches with roots in the Protestant traditions of the Scandinavian countries who had many immigrants that moved to the area; today, there remain over 10 Lutheran churches in the neighborhood, just one sign of the legacy of the Nordic influence. Just after the turn of the 20th century, the Leif Erikson Lodge of the Sons of Norway was established in the area and quickly became part of the cultural core of the neighborhood; today it is the largest chapter of the Sons of Norway in the country. The Lodge, along with other neighborhood cultural institutions, celebrates Norwegian Constitution Day (*Syttende Mai*) every May 17th. The celebrations began in 1889 and have been held annually each year since; in 1974 Ballard began a large community parade in conjunction with the celebrations that is the largest *Syttende Mai* parade outside of Norway.

A renewed interest in celebrating and preserving Nordic heritage began in Seattle in the mid-20th century, and Ballard was at the heart of those efforts. In 1962, a prominent statue of Leif Erikson was erected at the Shilshole Bay Marina as part of cultural improvements for the Seattle World's Fair that year. In 1967, Seattle established a sister city relationship with Bergen, Norway. In 1975, Bergen Place Park was constructed to commemorate the relationship, and the new park was dedicated by King Olaf V of Norway. The following year, King Carl XVI Gustaf of Sweden participated in celebrations dedicating the Ballard Avenue Historic District by reading a proclamation in support of the area's commercial historical value. In 1980, Ballard ensured that the neighborhood's connections to its Nordic heritage would be preserved when the Nordic Heritage Museum opened its doors on NW Sixty-Seventh Street.

Throughout the 20th century, many of the original Nordic families that settled in Ballard in the late 19th century continued to live there. This tendency for the immigrant families to age in place, rather than move to more suburban communities or warmer climates, meant that the population of Ballard remained largely Nordic and also increasingly comprised of senior citizens. This earned Ballard a reputation of feeling like a sleepy fishing village in the midst of Seattle's vibrant urban growth. Ballard resident Ethan Van Eck, who served as the neighborhood's

A City Within a City

By 1907, the population of the city of Ballard was 17,000, and it was the second-largest city in King County, just after Seattle. It was a growing town, mostly settled by immigrations from Scandinavian countries. However, by the turn of the 20th century, like other smaller cities near Seattle, Ballard was affected by growing water problems. The city's rapid population growth made it difficult for city officials to provide safe drinking water and to facilitate an efficient sewage system. They contemplated asking Seattle to annex the town, and in 1905 a referendum was held. The annexation plan was rejected by voters, and the city continued to be plagued by water problems. Moreover, in 1906, the U.S. Supreme Court ruled that Seattle was not required to share water with surrounding communities. Following the ruling by the U.S. Supreme Court, a second referendum was held on the question, and annexation was reluctantly approved by the voters. "On May 29, 1907 at 3:45 pm the city of Ballard officially became part of Seattle. On that day Ballard residents showed their mixed feelings about the handover by draping their city hall with black crepe and flying the flag at half mast" (City of Seattle, "Ballard") Some of the citizens even wore black armbands to show their dissatisfaction over the annexation. Despite annexation, Ballard continued to maintain its "city within a city" reputation and atmosphere for decades into the 20th century.

land use and planning chairperson, noted, "When I moved here in the mid-1990s, there were hardly any children; there were a lot of older Scandinavian people" (Ogburn 2013). The most prominent businesses in the area also remained rooted in the manufacturing and fishing industries that had facilitated the original economic boom in the area in the late 1800s. These unique population and economic trends, along with the prominent Nordic cultural institutions, ensured that Ballard maintained its own unique ethnic and working-class identity and remained a kind of city-within-a-city for a full century.

Since about 2000, the character and population of Ballard have been changing drastically. A boom of new development in the neighborhood has come mostly in the form of large-format retail buildings and apartment and condominium residential construction, which has drawn new residents to the area and made Ballard one of the 10 most rapidly growing areas of Seattle. Between 2000 and 2010, there was a nearly 40% increase in the number of housing units in the neighborhood and the overall population grew by 24%, and in the same time period the population over age 65 dropped by 22.7%. The area of Ballard around Salmon Bay and including Ballard Avenue and Market Street has been designated by the City of Seattle as one of six "Hub Urban Villages" in its comprehensive plan, and is experiencing a boom in redevelopment and renewal projects. While the demographics have been changing rapidly in age and occupation of Ballard residents—most of the employment growth since 2000 has come in service industries as manufacturing has experienced a decline—other varieties of diversity that have been seen in other parts of Seattle have not been found in Ballard. The population has persistently been less racially diverse than Seattle as a whole, with only 10.6% of Ballard residents being non-white in 2010, compared to 33.7% in the city overall (City of Seattle 2015). The median housing price and median income in Ballard are higher than in the city as a whole, which coincides with lower rates of poverty and unemployment than sur-rounding areas. These changes have, to a certain extent, pushed out some of the old businesses in Ballard, including many marine industry–related businesses that have shut their doors. As the aging Nordic population declines, some businesses that long catered to them, such as Olsen's Scandinavian Foods on Market Street, have also closed and been replaced by new businesses catering to a younger popu-lation; Ballard, for instance, has the highest concentration of craft breweries in the city and is home to the city's first food truck park and beer garden. The young and hip urban vibe rising in the neighborhood has overshadowed the historic Scandi-navian fishing village feel that defined Ballard for generations, and the rate of growth and change shows no signs of slowing.

Visitors to Ballard today, of which there are many, cannot miss the enduring land-marks of the city's Nordic heritage, from the Nordic Heritage Museum and the Leif Erikson statue to the architecture and businesses that hold onto Scandinavian roots. However, future Ballard residents will face the challenge of preserving elements of the neighborhood's ethnic heritage in light of continuing transformation to a young and hip urban village.

See also in Washington: International District (Seattle, Washington)

See also Norwegian and Swedish Enclaves: Andersonville (Chicago, Illinois); Kings-burg and Sveadal, Swedish Enclaves (California); Lindsborg, Swedish Enclave (Kansas); Minot and Other Cities, Norwegian Enclaves (North Dakota)

Molly Uppenkamp

Further Reading

Ballard Chamber of Commerce. "Welcome to Ballard." Accessed February 18, 2016. http://www.ballardchamber.com.

Ballard Historical Society. "A Concise History of the City of Ballard." Accessed February 22, 2016. http://www.ballardhistory.org/ballardhistory.html.

Ballard Partnership for Smart Growth. *Ballard Existing Conditions Report: In support of the Bal-lard Urban Design Framework.* March 2014. Accessed March 1, 2016. http://www.seattle.gov/dpd/cs/groups/pan/@pan/documents/web_informational/s048045.pdf.

City of Seattle. "Ballard." Accessed June 23, 2016. http://www.seattle.gov/cityarchives/exhibits-and-education/online-exhibits/annexed-cities/ballard.

City of Seattle. "Seattle Department of Neighborhoods: Ballard District." Accessed Febru-ary 19, 2016. http://www.seattle.gov/neighborhoods/districts/ballard.htm.

City of Seattle. "Seattle Historic Tours—Ballard." June 2001. Accessed February 19, 2016. http://www.seattle.gov/tour/historicdistricts/ballard.

MacIntosh, Heather. "Preservation in the Ballard Neighborhood." *Preservation Seattle,* March 2003. Accessed February 22, 2016. https://web.archive.org/web/20090805030325; http://www.historicseattle.org/preservationseattle/neighborhoods/default mar.htm.

National Park Service, United States Department of the Interior. "Ballard Avenue Historic District—Seattle: A National Register of Historic Places Travel Itinerary." Accessed February 18, 2016. http://www.nps.gov/nr/travel/seattle/s1.htm.

Nelson, Gerald B. *Seattle: The Life and Times of an American City*. New York: Alfred A. Knopf, 1977.

Ogburn, Ian. "The Two Faces of Ballard." *City Living Seattle*, April 19, 2013. Accessed February 28, 2016. http://citylivingseattle.com/Content/News/City-News/Article/The-two-faces-of-Ballard/22/167/89211.

Visit Seattle. "Ballard Neighborhood." Accessed February 18, 2016. http://www.visitseattle.org/Visitors/Discover/Heritage/Nordic-American-Heritage/Ballard-Neighborhood.aspx.

Visit Seattle. "Seattle Neighborhoods: Ballard." Accessed February 19, 2016. http://www.visitseattle.org/Visitors/Discover/Neighborhoods/Ballard.aspx.

BEDFORD-STUYVESANT (BROOKLYN, NEW YORK)

Bedford-Stuyvesant occupies 653 city blocks in the northeastern section of Brooklyn, New York City's largest borough. It shares borders with Williamsburg to the north, Clinton Hill and Fort Greene to the west, Crown Heights and Brownsville to the south, and Bushwick to the east. Often referred to as "Bed-Stuy," since the mid-20th century it has been the largest black neighborhood in New York City and one of the most significant hubs of African American culture in the United States.

Dutch settlers during the 17th century first called the region "Bedford," and it remained primarily agricultural throughout the 18th century. During the 19th century, waves of German, Irish, and Jewish immigrants settled the area, while an African American community, Weeksville—named for the areas first black property owners, also developed. The region's growth intensified after the completion of the Brooklyn Bridge in 1883 and the elevated railroad in 1885, which facilitated travel and commerce between Manhattan and Brooklyn. A flurry of construction followed as developers erected numerous landmarks, such as the Romanesque Revival St. Bartholomew's Church, along with the neighborhood's iconic brownstone homes. With their ornate brick- and ironwork, stately bay windows, and rich brown and terra cotta exteriors, the brownstones remain closely associated with Bedford-Stuyvesant and Brooklyn as a whole. The growing population also demanded more local services, which led to the creation of Boys and Girls high schools. The schools remained segregated by gender until the 1970s, when they unified as Boys and Girls High School. Counting the segregated period, Boys and Girls High School is the oldest public school in New York City and counts among its alumni Lena Horne, Norman Mailer, and Isaac Asimov.

By 1920, the area's population had reached 45,000 and was rising rapidly. The Great Black Migration, which brought thousands of African Americans from the South to northern cities, transformed Bedford-Stuyvesant, where the Southern migrants joined a burgeoning community of European and West Indian residents. It was also was during these years that neighbors began referring to Bedford and nearby Stuyvesant Heights as a single neighborhood with the combined name of

Bedford-Stuyvesant, which is often shortened to Bed-Stuy. Two factors contributed to the growth of Bedford-Stuyvesant, and particularly its black community, during the 1930s and 1940s. The A train line, completed in 1930, connected Bedford-Stuyvesant and Harlem by subway, thus providing Harlemites access to Bed-Stuy's numerous housing and job opportunities. For the first time, numerous families from Harlem and other parts of Manhattan could move to an outer borough while remaining connected to the old neighborhood. Second, World War II stimulated production at the Brooklyn Navy Yard, attracting a significant number of black workers who flocked to the area and settled their families in nearby Bed-Stuy.

In addition to migration from other parts of New York, many of Bed-Stuy's new residents came from West Indian islands such as St. Kitts, Grenada, and Jamaica. Among them was the family of Paule Marshall, a novelist born in Bedford-Stuyvesant to parents who had emigrated from Barbados. After graduating from Girls High School and Brooklyn College, Marshall went on to publish a number of critically acclaimed works. Her 1959 novel *Brown Girl, Brownstones* depicts her experiences growing up in Bed-Stuy's West Indian community during the 1930s. That community's influence remains an indelible aspect of Bed-Stuy's culture. Walking along Fulton Street, Marshall writes, "I have to remind myself that I'm in Brooklyn and not in the middle of a teeming outdoor market in St. George's, Grenada, or Kingston, Jamaica. . . . Because there, suddenly, are all the sights and sounds, colors, smells, and textures of the entire Caribbean archipelago, transplanted intact to the sidewalks of New York" (Marshall 1985, p. 67). Indeed, the West Indian presence in Bedford-Stuyvesant makes terms such as *black* and *African American* highly ambiguous: they can refer to people who trace their lineage to the American South, to other parts of the north, as well as to the West Indies, islands such as Haiti and the Dominican Republic, and Africa. "Black" thus serves as a catchall used by outside observers and obscures the neighborhood's linguistic, ethnic, and cultural diversity.

Between 1940 and 1960, migration to Bedford-Stuyvesant quadrupled, and the neighborhood's population grew to 450,000 by 1965. One particularly acute consequence of this growth was a shortage of living space, with more families squeezed into fewer available housing units and many homes that were zoned for one or two families actually sheltering three or more. As the population rose, racial demographics changed as well. In 1950, Bed-Stuy remained 50% white, but by the 1960s that number had dropped to less than 10%. This demographic evolution made Bedford-Stuyvesant, by 1965, "America's second largest ghetto" after the South Side of Chicago (Davies 2013, pp. 744–45).

To understand how Bedford-Stuyvesant changed so dramatically in such a short period, one must consider the impact of government policies implemented between the 1930s and 1950s. The most obvious for a visitor to Bed-Stuy is public housing: between the construction of the Kingsborough Homes in 1941 and Weeksville Gardens in 1974, the New York City Housing Authority and various federal agencies oversaw the construction of nearly a dozen massive apartment complexes in Bed-Stuy. From the Marcy Houses complex of 27 buildings to the 16-story highrises in the Tompkins Houses, public housing projects remain a prominent component of the neighborhood's landscape.

Upon construction, these projects were an answer to a pressing need for affordable housing in New York and intended as a temporary solution for low-income families. Yet their emergence coincided with another process, in which government programs attracted white residents out of neighborhoods like Bedford-Stuyvesant to underdeveloped areas of Brooklyn, Queens, and suburban Long Island and New Jersey. Beginning in the 1930s, the Home Owners Loan Corporation (HOLC), a federal agency, assigned qualitative values to neighborhoods throughout the United States in an effort to standardize real estate practices. Among factors considered in this process were the condition of buildings in the neighborhood, the age of its homes, and its racial composition. This process, referred to as "redlining," was particularly deleterious in Bed-Stuy, where a racially diverse population meant a low HOLC grade and declining property values. Following the war, redlining and the promise of low-interest, guaranteed loans from the Veterans Housing Administration drove white families to the suburbs, while a series of restrictive measures in the new neighborhoods prohibited black families from joining them. Nor did these practices simply draw people out of Bedford-Stuyvesant: businesses and investment capital followed as well, enervating the local economy. The impact of these policies was impossible to ignore: in 1960, 85% of Brooklynites identified as white, yet Bedford-Stuyvesant was more than 80% black. Meanwhile, a series of federal restrictions degraded the quality of public housing and transformed the once temporary solution into a permanent residence for thousands of families.

The lack of opportunities in Bed-Stuy coupled with the extraordinary concentration of low-income families in public housing to display "all the classic indicators of extreme social and economic deprivation" (Davies 2013, p. 745). The high population density joined poorly performing schools, a lack of medical services, high infant mortality, and joblessness to earn Bedford-Stuyvesant a reputation as a "slum" and "ghetto." The deterioration of the neighborhood's landscape fueled these perceptions: a 1964 survey conducted by the Central Brooklyn Coordinating Council and the Pratt Institute (located in nearby Clinton Hill) noted that Bed-Stuy contained 346 abandoned buildings, "which are dangerous and hazardous for the children who get great joy playing in them because of inadequate play areas in the community" (Purnell 2012, p. 223). In addition to abandonment, the neighborhood's 378 vacant lots had become de facto garbage dumps as city services to the area declined.

Despite the severity of these conditions, not all was lost in Bedford-Stuyvesant. Indeed, the neighborhood also contained a significant population of homeowners, whose number had actually grown between 1945 and 1960. Many residents had lived in Bed-Stuy for decades and felt a deep personal connection to the neighborhood. They viewed problems such as deteriorating architecture and accumulating refuse as consequences of discriminatory practices on the part of negligent landlords and municipal authorities. Leaders in the neighborhood compared their situation with that of less populated, whiter neighborhoods elsewhere in New York and found that the city invested as much or more in those places as it did for Bed-Stuy's half million residents. There was little question that Bedford-Stuyvesant was falling behind white, well-connected neighborhoods.

In 1962, members of the Brooklyn Congress of Racial Equality (CORE) articulated their concerns in a letter to the mayor's office, noting the overcrowding and segregation of their schools, the poor condition of streets and sidewalks, and the city's unwillingness to punish negligent landlords. They also called the mayor's attention to Bed-Stuy's shortage of playgrounds, parks, and adequate transportation compared with other Brooklyn neighborhoods. A lack of genuine congressional representation compounded these problems. Gerrymandering had divided Bed-Stuy between two other districts. Officeholders, aware of the area's high poverty rate, exerted little energy toward improvements that could be spent in more influential areas of their district.

A riot in 1964 illustrated the depths of Bedford-Stuyvesant's frustration with this state of affairs. Following a New York City police officer's killing of a black teen in Manhattan, charges of epidemic police brutality swelled into visceral rage in both Harlem and Bed-Stuy. For days, people filled Bedford-Stuyvesant's main thoroughfares to express despair over the killing while protesting the police department's aggressive tactics. The event served as a dramatic example of tensions that had existed before, and would continue long after, in Bed-Stuy and New York's other prominent black neighborhoods.

The severity of the situation was not lost on national civil rights organizations such as the Congress of Racial Equality (CORE), the National Association for the Advancement of Colored People (NAACP), and the National Urban League. As leaders such as Martin Luther King Jr., Roy Wilkins, and James Farmer were leading the Civil Rights Movement in the American South, they also offered a sharp critique of racial inequality in northern cities. In addition to police brutality, activists targeted New York City's heavily segregated school system and, with the support of local grassroots movements, developed tactics to combat the problem. In 1964, for instance, thousands of Bedford-Stuyvesant parents kept their children out of school, forcing New York officials to take their calls for educational equality more seriously.

Another notable repudiation of the city's discrimination came in 1962 with CORE's "Operation Clean Sweep." A direct-action protest of the accumulation of garbage in the neighborhood, Operation Clean Sweep saw Bed-Stuy residents collecting garbage from their streets and driving it to Brooklyn's Borough Hall. There they dumped discarded furniture, appliances, and piles of trash on the building's steps while imploring leaders to take the condition of Bedford-Stuyvesant more seriously. While some city officials rejected CORE's actions, blaming the Bed-Stuy's state of affairs on an abstract "culture of poverty," the protest apparently worked, as trash collection steadily increased throughout the 1960s (Purnell 2013, p. 155). Operation Clean Sweep symbolized Bed-Stuy's long tradition of grassroots activism even in the face of difficult circumstances and official indifference. It also revealed a commitment to community that made Bedford-Stuyvesant unique in an age of increasingly fragmented suburbs and high-rise condos.

Community investment took a variety of forms in Bedford-Stuyvesant. Numerous churches, block associations, and tenant activists joined CORE and other organizations to develop social capital that compensated for their neighborhood's challenges. The Central Brooklyn Coordinating Council spent much of the 1960s bringing together community organizations across Bed-Stuy and lobbying the city for improvements. In other words, for years Bed-Stuy residents "spent most, if not all, of their free time in community organizations trying to make the area a more habitable place to live, work, and raise children" (Purnell 2012, p. 217). Those efforts converged later in the 1960s with the creation of the Bedford-Stuyvesant Restoration Corporation (Restoration), the first and most notable community development corporation (CDC) in the United States. CDCs became popular during the 1960s and 1970s as an anti-poverty strategy that combined government funding with support from businesses and nonprofits.

Restoration's story began in 1966 when then-Senator from New York Robert F. Kennedy visited Bed-Stuy. In the wake of the 1964 riot, as well as the devastating Watts riot in Los Angeles, Kennedy came to believe that ghettoization was the most serious crisis facing the United States. Inspired by the organizational prowess of the Central Brooklyn Coordinating Council, Kennedy also recognized that simply pouring money into the problem would not suffice. Following his tour of the neighborhood, Kennedy assembled leaders from Bedford-Stuyvesant and beyond. Among early supporters were New York's other senator, Jacob Javits, as well as Mayor John Lindsay and the leaders of several major corporations and nonprofits. With the organizational structure in place, Kennedy proclaimed that the combination of government, business, and local leadership would make Bedford-Stuyvesant a beacon for similar communities around the country. "[I]t is Bedford-Stuyvesant that is the vanguard," he said. "Bedford-Stuyvesant . . . can take the lead. If we here can meet and master our problems; if this community can become an avenue of opportunity and a place of pleasure . . . for its people, then others will take heart" (Rusk 1999, p. 26).

Known to many residents simply as "Restoration," the organization remains a powerful force for its founders' ideals. Restoration aimed to build Bed-Stuy's already notable middle class by improving or demolishing decaying buildings, attracting outside investment, promoting local entrepreneurship, and providing affordable loans for homebuyers. It also sought to target the root causes of urban poverty, including redlining, unemployment, and the paucity of available bank credit. To that end, in 1967 Restoration organized a consortium of 80 financial institutions to create a mortgage pool of $65 million in federally insured loans for homebuyers. In 1968, Restoration convinced IBM, one of the largest corporations in the United States, to construct a plant in Bed-Stuy. The plant grew quickly and remained critical to IBM's operation until the 1990s, when a primarily black- and Puerto Rican–owned company called Advanced Technological Systems purchased it. Restoration's support of entrepreneurship led to a number of new small businesses in the neighborhood as well, including New York State's first black-owned car dealership and the nation's first black-owned McDonald's. Additionally, a Restoration-produced television show, *Inside Bedford Stuyvesant*, focused exclusively on issues important to the neighborhood while providing a forum for residents to air their perspectives.

During the early 1970s, Restoration set up its headquarters, "Restoration Plaza," in a former milk bottling plant on Fulton Street. The building's art galleries, office space, and the famous Billie Holiday Theatre have promoted creativity and local cooperation ever since. Likewise, Restoration played a critical role in the founding of Medgar Evers College, a branch of the City University of New York system and Bedford-Stuyvesant's only institution of higher learning. Thus, while Restoration could not eliminate continued struggles in the neighborhood, it has almost certainly mitigated them. Its production of homegrown leaders has been particularly benefi-cial, with several going on to represent Bedford-Stuyvesant on the national stage. For example, Franklin Thomas, born in Bed-Stuy to a mother from Barbados, was Restoration's first president. A graduate of Columbia Law School, he later became president of the Ford Foundation—the first African American man to lead a major national social welfare organization.

Another prominent leader to emerge from Bedford-Stuyvesant in the 1960s was Shirley Chisholm. Born in 1924, she graduated from Girls High School in 1942 and Brooklyn College in 1946. She became a teacher—one of the few job oppor-tunities open to black women during the period—and in 1953 helped found the Bedford-Stuyvesant Political League. Although the League eventually dissolved, it paved the way for groups like Restoration by challenging housing discrimination and campaigning for improved services to the neighborhood. In 1964, Bed-Stuy elected Chisholm to the New York State Assembly, where she supported the elimi-nation of racial discrimination in banking as well as the creation of civil rights train-ing for New York police officers. Following a successful lawsuit to alter Bed-Stuy's congressional representation, Chisholm campaigned for the newly created seat and won, becoming the first black woman elected to the U.S. Congress. Her career also included a notable run for president in 1972 and decades of effort on behalf of Bedford-Stuyvesant and communities like it throughout the United States.

Despite the positive changes wrought by Bedford-Stuyvesant's leaders, the last decades of the 20th century posed a series of significant challenges. Racial segrega-tion persisted throughout the greater New York area and particularly in Bed-Stuy, where 85% of the population was black, accounting for 60% of all African Ameri-cans in Brooklyn. The Puerto Rican population grew as well, to as much as 12% of the neighborhood's total during the 1970s (Manoni 1973, p. 12). At the same time, racist attitudes mixed with sensational newspaper headlines to create a popular image of Bed-Stuy as seedy, violent, and frightening. For example, a *New York Times* article conjured images from Charles Dickens when it described Bedford-Stuyvesant as a place "of decay and degradation—of drug dens, crumbling tenements and ragged urchins romping in rubbish strewn lots" (Holmes 1989, p. B1).

While outsiders' fears often exaggerated the "slum" reputation, many locals agreed that things had declined by the 1980s. Organizations like Restoration persevered, but numerous factors made their work more difficult. The rise of anti-welfare poli-tics and the 1980 election of President Ronald Reagan meant massive budget cuts for social programs like Restoration. In its earliest days, Restoration had employed 300 people; by the end of the 1980s, that number had plummeted to 36. Other organizations emerged to lend a hand, such as the Volunteer Ambulance Corp, which sought to supplement New York's overwhelmed Emergency Medical Services. Donning berets of red, green, and black—the colors of the Black Liberation Flag—ambulance volunteers responded to fires, births, and incidents of violence while providing neighborhood residents an opportunity to gain medical training. Yet homegrown voluntarism was not enough. Some critics, while praising Restoration, nonetheless pointed out that its tremendous efforts let responsible parties off the hook. To many it seemed that powerful leaders in government, big business, and philanthropy had made peace with inner-city discrimination and poverty.

Adding to the unfavorable political scene, a scourge of crack cocaine descended on New York City during the mid-1980s and created particularly harsh consequences for Bedford-Stuyvesant. Cheap and addictive, crack exacerbated the circumstances of poverty as it derailed young lives and promoted criminal activity. The situation further damned Bed-Stuy's reputation, with media outlets projecting an image of a neighborhood at war with itself. Nor were they totally wrong: the parents of slain children spoke to journalists about the lasting effects of violence, and anecdotes of murdered business owners and elderly homeowners imprinted themselves on readers' imaginations. The neighborhood's violent crime rate drastically exceeded the rest of New York: in 1983, for example, the murder rate in Bed-Stuy was more than twice that of New York as a whole (Gill 2005, p. R1). Meanwhile, owners abandoned thousands of residential properties, leaving them empty or providing shelter to squatters. Although poverty dropped in the New York region between 1970 and 1990, in Bedford-Stuyvesant it actually increased from 27.5% to 34% in the same period (Rusk 1999, p. 33).

Nonetheless, the problem with Bed-Stuy's negative reputation was its ability to make the ghastly seem commonplace. Newspaper coverage followed police cruisers and ambulances but ignored other aspects of Bedford-Stuyvesant: the community's willingness to band together, to form anti-drug and anti-violence alliances, to watch out for one another's children. For some, media depictions simply bashed Bedford-Stuyvesant without the context that made it a total community. In particular, they tended to ignore Bed-Stuy's prominent population of professionals—teachers, secretaries, lawyers, and professors—who had long called the neighborhood home. And Bed-Stuy's middle class was not merely composed of older hangers-on: while the overall population dropped by nearly 100,000 in the two decades after 1970, the loss would have been greater were it not for an influx of black professionals. Those people, as well as many who had spent their lives in Bedford-Stuyvesant, agreed with the perspective of Basketball Hall of Famer Lenny Wilkens, who grew up in the neighborhood, when he said, "Bed-Stuy wasn't as bad as people make it out to be. Maybe it was to people who didn't live there. But it wasn't a ghetto to me. It was where I lived" (Manoni 1973, p. 9).

This balance between a reputation for crime and community pride contributed to the abundant artistic culture that emerged during the 1980s and 1990s. The generation of Bedford-Stuyvesant residents raised in those years included numerous notable figures, such as the rappers Jay-Z, Lil' Kim, Mos Def, and Notorious B.I.G. Their music often discussed the travails of growing up in Bed-Stuy, detailing their experiences with family, religion, drugs, and violence. Comedian Chris Rock also grew up in Bed-Stuy and set his sitcom *Everybody Hates Chris* there. The show emphasized the humorous aspects of life in the neighborhood, and Rock pointed out that while Bedford-Stuyvesant was not an easy place to grow up, "if you're like me and had the two parents and rules and regulations in your house, it wasn't as tough" (Gill 2005, p. R1).

Perhaps the most famous depiction of Bedford-Stuyvesant came not from newspapers, rap music, or television, but from Spike Lee's 1989 film *Do The Right Thing*. Lee also set his first film, *Joe's Bed-Stuy Barbershop: We Cut Heads*, in the neighborhood, anticipating a number of his later work's themes. Set on the hottest day of the year, *Do The Right Thing* begins with the routine of an ordinary morning and ends in the aftermath of police brutality and a riot; it explores the complex politics of ethnic diversity, economic self-sufficiency, and police violence that have shaped Bedford-Stuyvesant since the end of World War II. It remains a powerful depiction of a fragile community in which resources are scarce and seemingly trivial forces—a heat wave, the volume of a stereo—can expose tensions and invite disaster. *Do The Right Thing* also revealed, however, the fierce determination of Bed-Stuy's residents to preserve their neighborhood's culture. The motto "Bed-Stuy, Do or Die," which was popularized by the film, reflects that resolve.

A number of neighborhood traditions demonstrate this preservationist ethos. The African Arts Festival, once known as the Afrikan Street Carnival and later the African Street Festival, is a five-day event that began at the Uhuru Sasa School during the 1970s. The festival has attracted thousands of people while promoting traditional African arts, crafts, and food. Likewise, the Fulton Street Fair, held each summer on Bed-Stuy's central thoroughfare, brings together hundreds of vendors dealing in African arts while celebrating the diversity of heritages found in the neighborhood.

Although Bed-Stuy remains one of the major hubs of black culture in the United States, since the late 1980s new groups have begun calling the neighborhood home. In addition to the prominent Puerto Rican population, Bed-Stuy has witnessed an influx of Korean residents, a number of whom have opened businesses, such as grocery and convenience stores. During the late 1990s, skyrocketing real estate prices in Manhattan sent many wealthier New Yorkers in search of cheaper housing in Brooklyn, which initiated the process of gentrification. Change came rapidly for nearby neighborhoods, such as Williamsburg and Fort Greene, where newcomers spent millions of dollars for homes. Residents worried that gentrification would soon come to Bedford-Stuyvesant, with its preponderance of beautiful Victorian architecture, spacious brownstone homes, and subway access. Perhaps because of its reputation, however, gentrification has not occurred as rapidly or as thoroughly in Bedford-Stuyvesant as it did in other parts of Brooklyn. Nonetheless, the past decade has seen steadily rising home prices and rents drive longtime businesses out of Bed-Stuy. For the first time since the 1960s, the population has actually risen, from 143,000 in 2000 to 153,000 in 2010; at the same time, the black population's percentage of the total has dropped from 77% to 64% (Population Division—NYC Department of City Planning 2011).

Gentrification has posed a series of difficult questions for Bed-Stuy. On the one hand, new restaurants, clothing boutiques, and other businesses have opened. Longtime residents, whose families purchased homes in the neighborhood years ago, have seen the value of those homes rise rapidly. City services, from police presence to sanitation, have improved. On the other hand, those changes have not necessarily benefited the significant low-income population that still calls Bed-Stuy home. With monthly rents averaging more than $1,000, many people have been priced out of the neighborhood after decades of calling it home. The new businesses are mostly small and can do little to alleviate what remains an unemployment crisis for many in Bedford-Stuyvesant. Many worry that the diversity of identities often associated with their neighborhood—as a hub of African and Caribbean culture, as well as a tight-knit community dedicated to improvement—will be lost.

Despite these developments, Bedford-Stuyvesant continues to evade easy categorization. Home prices can reach the millions, but in 2010 more than 30% of the population lived below the poverty line. For children, 47% of whom live in poverty, the situation is particularly challenging. According to one survey, as many as 60% of Bed-Stuy's children read below their grade levels, and the schools are failing to meet state standards. Boys and Girls High School, for generations of beacon of pride in the neighborhood, has struggled through low rates of attendance and graduation. While crime has plummeted since the 1990s, Bed-Stuy's rates of assault and murder still outpace nearby areas (Hymowitz 2013).

Meanwhile, the determination to make Bedford-Stuyvesant work, to persevere, continues. Natives who left during the 1990s have returned, joined by the children of former residents. They have brought with them the investment capital necessary to improve Bed-Stuy along with a commitment to preserving the neighborhood's cultural character. Restoration continues to support various local endeavors, but today it is joined by organizations such as the Coalition for the Improvement of Bedford-Stuyvesant, which promotes business vitality, health and wellness, and

---

Bed Stuy, Do-or-Die

A number of rappers were born and raised in Bed-Stuy. Many of these artists reference their old neighborhood, reflecting the broader trend of pride and solidarity within the black community of Bedford-Stuyvesant. Songs that mention Bed-Stuy include:

"Empire State of Mind" and "Brooklyn's Finest"—Jay-Z
"Whatchu Want" and "Guaranteed Raw"—Biggie Smalls
"Astronomy (Eighth Light)"—Black Star (Talib Kweli and Mos Def)
"Get By"—Talib Kweli
"Bed-Stuy Parade and Funeral March"—Mos Def
"Brooklyn"—Fabolous (feat. Jay-Z, Uncle Murda)
"Lighters Up" and "Who Shot Ya"—Lil' Kim
"Gettin' High"—Ol' Dirty Bastard

Bed-Stuy artists continue to cultivate and push the genre. Established in 2005, the Brooklyn Hip-Hop Festival highlights hip-hop's legacy as an "agent of artistic progression, community building, and social change." Bed-Stuy artists Fabolous and Talib Kweli performed at the festival in 2016.

affordable housing in the neighborhood. Indeed, while Bedford-Stuyvesant has experienced many changes over the years, continuity exists in the communitarian ethos of its residents. That dedication will remain critical as Bedford-Stuyvesant balances its heritage with the opportunities of the future.

See also in New York: Borough Park/Williamsburg/Crown Heights, Jewish Enclaves (Brooklyn, New York); Brighton Beach-Sheepshead Bay (Brooklyn, New York); Brooklyn, West Indian Enclave (New York); Chinatowns (Manhattan; Sunset Park East, Brooklyn; Flushing, Queens) (New York City); Coney Island (Brooklyn, New York); Crown Heights, Jamaican Enclave (Brooklyn, New York); Five Points (New York City); Greenpoint (Brooklyn, New York); Greenwich Village (New York City); Harlem (New York City); Harlem, Senegalese Enclave (New York City); Hell's Kitchen (New York City); Jackson Heights (Queens, New York); Jackson Heights, South Asian Enclave (Queens, New York); Little Brazil Street (Manhattan, New York); Little India, Jackson Heights (Queens, New York); Little Italy (Manhattan, New York); Lower East Side (New York City); Sleepy Hollow, Ecuadorian Enclave (New York); Staten Island, Sri Lankan Enclave (New York City); Sunset Park West and North Corona (New York City); Washington Heights (New York City); Yorkville, German Enclave (New York City)

See also African American Enclaves: Baldwin Hills (Los Angeles, California; Black Bottom (Philadelphia, Pennsylvania); Bronzeville (Chicago, Illinois); Greenwood (Tulsa, Oklahoma); Harlem (New York City); Harlem, Senegalese Enclave (New York City); Historic South Central (Los Angeles, California); Ironbound and the Wards (Newark, New Jersey); Lewiston and Portland, Somali and Bantu Enclaves (Maine); Little Ethiopia (Los Angeles, California); Lower Ninth Ward (New Orleans, Louisiana); Lower Roxbury, African American Enclave (Massachusetts); Mattapan (Boston, Massachusetts); Orange Mound (Memphis, Tennessee); Roxbury, African American Enclave (Massachusetts); Sweet Auburn (Atlanta, Georgia); Tremé (New Orleans, Louisiana); Watts (Los Angeles, California)

Patrick Mulford O'Connor

Further Reading

Abu-Lughod, Janet L., *Race, Space, and Riots in Chicago, New York, and Los Angeles*. New York: Oxford University Press, 2007.

Brooklyn Hip-Hop Festival Website. Accessed June 15, 2016. http://www.bkhiphopfestival .com.

Davies, Tom Adam. "Black Power in Action: The Bedford-Stuyvesant Restoration Corporation, Robert F. Kennedy, and the Politics of the Urban Crisis." *Journal of American History* 100 (December 2013): 736–60.

Gallagher, Julie. "Waging 'The Good Fight': The Political Career of Shirley Chisholm, 1953–1982." *The Journal of African American History* 92 (Summer 2007): 392–416.

Gill, John Freeman. "'Wonder Years,' By Way of Bed-Stuy." *New York Times*, December 4, 2005, R1.

Holmes, Steven A. "Community Shrinks from Crack's Embrace." *New York Times*, November 15, 1989, B1.

Hymowitz, Kay S. "Bed-Stuy's (Unfinished) Revival." *City Journal* (Summer 2013). http://www.city-journal.org/2013/23_3_bed-stuy.html.

Jackson, Kenneth, and John B. Manbeck, eds. *The Neighborhoods of Brooklyn*. New Haven, CT: Yale University Press, 2004.

Manoni, Mary H. *Bedford-Stuyvesant: The Anatomy of a Central City Community*. New York: Quadrangle/The New York Times Book Co., 1973.

Marshall, Paule. "Rising Islanders of Bed-Stuy." *New York Times Magazine*, November 3, 1985, 67.

Martin, Douglas. "Bed-Stuy, Do or Die. For Real. 911." *New York Times*, December 8, 1990, L27.

New York City Housing Authority. "NYCHA Housing Developments." Accessed October 13, 2016. http://www.nyc.gov.

Population Division—NYC Department of City Planning. "Demographic Profile—New York City Community Districts 1990 to 2010: Brooklyn Community District 3." July 2011. Accessed October 13, 2016. http://www.nyc.gov/html/dcp/html/neigh_info/bk03_info.shtml.

Purnell, Brian. "What We Need Is Brick and Mortar': Race, Gender, and Early Leadership of the Bedford-Stuyvesant Restoration Corporation." In Laura Warren Hill and Julia Rabig, eds. *The Business of Black Power: Community Development, Capitalism, and Corporate Responsibility in Postwar America*. Rochester, NY: University of Rochester Press, 2012.

Purnell, Brian. *Fighting Jim Crow in the County of Kings: The Congress of Racial Equality in Brooklyn*. Lexington: University Press of Kentucky, 2013.

Rusk, David. *Inside Game/Outside Game: Winning Strategies for Saving Urban American*. Washington, DC: Brookings Institution, 1999.

Sharif, Pamela D. "Rebirth in Bed-Stuy." *New York Times*, May 31, 1992, F8.

Sugrue, Thomas J. *Sweet Land of Liberty: The Forgotten Struggle for Civil Rights in the North*. New York: Random House, 2008.

BELGIAN ENCLAVES. *See* Adamston (Clarksburg, West Virginia)

BERGEN COUNTY, KOREAN ENCLAVES (NEW JERSEY)

New Jersey has become the state with the third-largest settlement of the Korean population (93,697), following California (451,891) and New York (140,994) (U.S. Census Bureau 2010). Historically, the influx of Korean immigrants to New Jersey has been closely linked to its proximity to New York City, with most northern and middle counties of New Jersey included in the New York metropolitan area. The proportion of Korean immigrants in New Jersey has continued to increase since the late 1980s, with a concomitant decrease in the proportion in New York State. This is mainly due to the maturation of decentralization in U.S. metropolitan areas and the increasing suburbanization of Korean immigrants as a growing number of affluent Koreans directly settle in the suburbs. New Jersey has emerged as the most rapidly growing suburban destination for Korean immigrants in the New York-New Jersey metropolitan area. The continuous increase in the critical mass of suburban Koreans has led to the development of Korean enclaves in northern New Jersey.

Table 1   Korean Immigrants Admitted to the United States (1970–2009)

Five-Year Period	The United States	New York State	New Jersey
1970–1974	92,745	11,129	3,710
1975–1979	148,645	13,378	4,459
1980–1984	162,178	16,218	6,487
1985–1989	175,803	19,338	10,548
1990–1994	112,215	15,710	8,977
1995–1999	75,579	9,069	5,291
2000–2004	89,871	8,088	7,190
2005–2009	125,878	12,588	10,702

Sources: Reconstructed from Table 6 in Min (2013, p. 149). Min's original sources were Immigration and Naturalization Service, Annual Reports, 1965–1978; Statistical Yearbooks, 1979–2001; Office of Immigration and Statistics, Yearbook of Immigration Statistics, 2002–2009.

More than half of the state's Korean population lives in Bergen County. Just across the Hudson River from Manhattan, Bergen County, consisting of 70 municipalities, hosts the largest suburban Korean enclaves in the New York-New Jersey metropolitan area with 21% of the metropolitan Korean population in 2000 and 27% in 2010 (U.S. Census Bureau 2000 and 2010). Bergen County is one of most affluent suburban counties in the nation, with increasing multiethnic neighborhoods. In 2000, 72% of the county population was non-Hispanic white, and 25% of the population was foreign-born (U.S. Census Bureau 2000). In 2010, the percent of non-Hispanic white population significantly decreased to 63% with an increase in the foreign-born population (30%) (U.S. Census Bureau 2010).

The Korean population in Bergen County remarkably grew over the past few decades, from 3,087 in 1980, 16,073 in 1990, and 36,075 in 2000 to 56,773 in 2010 (U.S. Census Bureau 1990, 2000, and 2010). This increase in the Korean population resulted in spatial clustering of the Korean population, affirming the development of Korean enclaves. For example, in 1990, the highest percentage of Koreans per census tract in Bergen County was 19%, and no census tracts had more than 20% Koreans. As of 2000, the highest percentage of Koreans per census tract was 38%, and seven census tracts had more than 20% Koreans (U.S. Census Bureau 1990 and 2000). In 2010, the highest percentage of Koreans per census tract was 59%, and 19 census tracts had more than 20% of Koreans. Out of 19 census tracts, 6 tracts had more than 30% of Koreans. These statistics reinforce the maturation of Korean enclaves over the past three decades.

The growth of the Korean suburban enclaves in Bergen County can be explained by a few factors. First, once Koreans saved enough money to become upwardly mobile, they moved out of the urban Korean enclave in New York City in pursuit of a better living environment and better public schools for their children. Bergen County, due to its relatively affluent residential neighborhoods, lower crime and traffic congestion, and good public schools, became a popular suburban relocation area. Indeed, Bergen County is quite an affluent suburban residential area, with higher median household income ($83,794), homeownership rates (66%), and median housing values ($451,400) than Korean urban enclaves in Queens (U.S. Census Bureau 2009–2013). In addition, 60% of residents in Bergen County are non-Hispanic white (60%), compared to Queens where only 27% of the residents is non-Hispanic white as of 2010 (U.S. Census Bureau 2010).

This comparison is important, because the entry of Koreans into the suburbs signifies higher residential status. Although Queens, as an outer borough of New York City, may possess some suburban-like amenities, it is apparent that Bergen County is a more predominantly white suburb with lower population density and better residential status than Queens. Not surprisingly, Koreans who choose to live in Bergen County have more school-age children than their urban counterparts in Queens County, New York City.

Many Korean real estate agents remarked that having school options was the clear priority for most of their clients. Korean clients are willing to move to a good school district even if they have to sacrifice housing quality at a given location. Some clients may choose a three-bedroom house in a good school district over a four- or five- bedroom house in another location. Moreover, when housing stock was unavailable in a good school district at the time of purchase, many were willing to rent a house or townhouse within that school district rather than buy a house somewhere else.

When it comes to good public schools, Tenafly township has been considered the most popular school district in Bergen County. The appeal of Tenafly for Korean immigrants lay in the fact that Tenafly High School was recognized as the best public high school in the state. The school had a broad range of advanced placements (AP) and honors courses, as well as a noteworthy music program. More than 95% of the graduates entered a four-year college, compared to the state average of 53% (www.greatschools.net). Korean immigrant parents also tend to encourage their children to enter specialized high schools, if possible. Bergen Academies, a comparable school to Stuyvesant High School and Bronx High School of Science in New York City, enrolls many Asian students (40% of total number of students). Korean parents believe that specialized high schools' heavy emphasis on academic-oriented curriculum and association with high-performing peers assist their children in entering elite universities. The prolific establishment of education-related businesses further confirms why Bergen County has an attractive infrastructure to many Koreans with school-age children. There were approximately 100 or more private afterschool institutions, including college preparatory academies, in Bergen County in 2015 (www.koreadaily.com).

The proportion of recent immigrants does not significantly differ between Bergen and Queens Counties. This fact implies that many recently arrived Koreans now bypass the urban enclave and choose Bergen County as their initial destination, perhaps due to the presence of a more developed ethnic infrastructure. As of 2000, 21% of the Korean residents in Bergen County migrated from New York City, while more than 30% of them directly immigrated from abroad (U.S. Census Bureau 2000). Many "geese families," consisting of mothers and school-aged children whose husbands and fathers stay and work in their home country, as well as temporary employees of Korean government agencies working in Manhattan and visiting scholars, represent a significant proportion of those who directly settled in Bergen County.

In addition, Bergen County's accessibility to Manhattan makes it an attractive suburban area for not only local Korean merchants but also Koreans with businesses and jobs in New York City. Around 38% of Korean residents of Bergen County commute to New York City, and two-thirds of these commuters take daily trips to Manhattan (Public Use Micro Sample 1990). Many Korean-specialized small businesses, such as dry cleaners, delis and grocery stores, and beauty and nail salons, are widespread throughout the New York metropolitan area. These Korean-owned businesses usually serve a variety of consumers and are not limited to the Korean ethnic community. As a result, their locations are dispersed, allowing for easy separation between the workplace and the residence.

Third, from the mid-1980s, many branches of Korean multinational corporations, including Samsung (Ridgefield Park) and LG (Englewood Cliffs), have moved into the Fort Lee area in Bergen County. This relocation has attracted many corporate managers and their families who receive generous rent subsidies from their corporate headquarters so that the high rents do not hinder them from temporarily residing in affluent communities. These suburban dwellers constitute a demand for a wide assortment of ethnic goods and services and thereby promote the suburbanization of Korean small businesses in retail and personal services, grocery stores, video rental shops, and real estate agencies.

Fourth, for many immigrants, where one lives depends on who one knows. The reliance on family members and friends has a direct effect on the concentration of Korean immigrants. Recently arrived immigrants frequently settle outside old ethnic concentrations; chain migration leads many of them toward partially assimilated friends and relatives who are living elsewhere. Ethnic realtors also play an important role in the choice of residential location. Coethnic realtors not only help newcomers and immigrants to purchase housing by communicating in Korean but also implicitly steer them into particular neighborhoods. The fact that there are more than 390 Korean realtors in 2015 operating businesses throughout Bergen County signifies their role in residential choice (www.koreadaily.com).

Palisades Park Enclave

Palisades Park, located in southeastern Bergen County, became the epicenter of the Korean enclaves in Bergen County and includes the census tract with 59% Koreans. It is a relatively small suburban township, numbering 17,073 residents in 2010. Palisades Park has been a traditionally Italian community, consisting of blue-collar Italian and some Irish immigrants who replaced the original Dutch settlers. In 2000, 36% of Palisades Park's residents were Korean (6,065) (U.S. Census Bureau 2010). By 2010, they grew to be 52%, (10,115 Koreans) achieving demographic dominance (U.S. Census Bureau 2010). Indeed, Palisades Park has the largest Korean concentration among U.S. cities. It also has experienced the out-migration of whites and in-migration of Koreans over time, consisting of mainly Asians (58%) with

Korean dominance, whites (22%), and Hispanics (18%) as of 2010. In 1990, Palisades Park's non-Hispanic white population was 76% (U.S. Census Bureau 1990).

Historically, Korean communities made their initial appearance in Fort Lee and Palisades Park. Palisades Park, Fort Lee, and adjacent boroughs such as Ridgefield, Cliffside Park, and Leonia, were major municipalities with the largest Korean populations in Bergen County. Of the Korean residents in Bergen County, 46% were spatially clustered there in 2000. In addition to the five municipalities mentioned, Tenafly, a relatively more affluent township in northeast Bergen County, has had a steady increase in the Korean population due to its well-known superior public schools, which send many graduates to highly ranked universities.

Koreans have given rise to ethnic enclave businesses in Palisades Park and Fort Lee. In 1990, there were only 20 Korean businesses on the main commercial street (Broad Avenue of Palisades Park and Main Street of Fort Lee); there were more than 350 businesses in 2012 counted by Min (Min 2012a). Koreans operate 95% of all businesses around the mile-long commercial strip along Broad Avenue. Prior to 1980, Palisades Park had been a stable but economically declining community. During the 1980s, a recession and increased competition from big malls forced many of the retail shops to close. There were many abandoned storefronts, signifiers of a declining town center, and Koreans saw this as an opportunity to establish their businesses. Longtime residents acknowledge that Koreans have revived the dying local economy. About more than half of municipal business tax revenues come from Korean business owners.

While Korean Americans' political representation in Palisades Park lagged behind their demographic and economic dominance, Korean Americans, as the majority of the township population in 2010, have gained political representation over time. For instance, Jason Kim, a Korean-born Korean American, was elected to the school board in 1994 and to the city council in 2004. He was also appointed Deputy Major of Palisades Park in 2011. Two other Korean Americans, Jong Chul Lee and Christopher Chung, are currently serving as borough council members (out of six members). Reflecting the growing Korean population, in 2012 the county mandated the provision of voting ballots in the Korean language as Palisades Park's Korean population makes up more than 5% of the voting-age population, or at least 10,000 citizens.

Fort Lee Enclave

Fort Lee, adjacent to Palisades Park, Bergen County's first and largest concentration of Koreans (2,537) in 1990, is now the second largest (5,978 and 8,318 Koreans in 2000 and 2010 respectively), where Koreans make up 24% of the municipality population (U.S. Census Bureau 2000 and 2010). Until the early 1980s, Fort Lee was a popular suburban relocation area for many Japanese Americans. The decline of Japanese population, influenced by the closing of many Japanese companies in Manhattan during the 1990s and 2000s, contributed to the succession of Korean Americans in the Borough of Fort Lee. The influx of large numbers of Koreans from Korea and New York City gradually replaced Japanese residents. The Japanese population decreased 23%, while the Korean population increased 23% in the 1990s. Fort Lee, compared to Palisades Park, is characterized by multiethnic neighborhoods with a considerable number of Latinos, Chinese, and Japanese, and other ethnic groups. However, with no other numerically dominant minority groups, Korean Americans in Fort Lee have been able to exercise empowerment in local politics. At present, three of the nine school board members in Fort Lee are Korean Americans. In Fort Lee's downtown, there are 150 Korean businesses on Main Street and on Lemoine Avenue.

In sum, Palisades Park and Fort Lee are the ethnic centers for suburban Koreans in New Jersey. In their downtowns, there are hundreds of Korean stores and organizations featuring Korean-language signs. Their downtowns are made up mostly of Korean spas, restaurants, financial institutions, and other Korean-owned businesses. These Korean stores serve mostly both Koreans in the neighboring townships and a dispersed Korean population from northern and central New Jersey to upstate New York. Among Korean-owned businesses, H-Mart, a chain of large Korean grocery stores and a strong indicator of ethnic concentration, has four locations in Bergen County only. Now H-Mart markets to broader Asian American populations, serving not only Korean foods and recipe ingredients but also major Chinese and South Asian foods and recipe ingredients. Another kind of business that it is worth noting is the Korean-style spa sauna. The most famous one, the King Spa Sauna located in Palisades Park, is open 24/7, attracting a wide range of spa-loving customers, both Korean and non-Korean. Even the *New York Times* featured the detox and therapeutic advantages of Korean-style saunas (*jjimjilbang*). They are popular social gathering places for many Koreans who desire to relax and spend some time with family and friends. A Korean *jjimjilbang* typically has a big open sitting place for gathering and relaxing and serves meals and snacks, including famous baked eggs.

Bergen County's established Korean enclaves have a level of institutional completeness similar to that of urban Korean enclaves, implying that Koreans have developed the full array of ethnic institutions that make an autonomous community possible in the suburbs. The church is the most visible and significant social organization for the institutional completeness of Korean immigrants. It has been noted that Korean churches focus not only on religious activities but also on building social networks among coethnics: immigration orientation, job and business information networks, cultural events and a Korean language program for the second generation. Koreans in Bergen County have comparable rates of church affiliation and attendance as their urban counterparts.

The majority of Korean churches rent their sanctuaries from non-Korean American churches on Sunday afternoons. Often, easily observable notes at the bottom of the signboards alert one that a Korean congregation is also worshiping there. Korean churches, since the beginning of Korean immigration, have been the key mechanism for Korean immigrants and their children to preserve their culture, customs, and identity. They also tend to confine social interaction within the ethnic social boundary. Generally speaking, Korean churches are not associated with the broader community through interethnic contacts, although a few Korean churches recently have begun to become more involved in community affairs by providing free breakfast to the poor and the homeless. The growth of Korean churches often results in tensions with native non-Hispanic white residents because of a lack of cross-cultural understanding and an erosion of white residents' sense of place and identity.

The growth of suburban Korean enclaves in Bergen County has altered the landscape of host communities. Certain sections of the township have taken on a new cultural character. Admittedly, Korean immigrants have played a key role in revitalizing many neighborhoods that had fallen on hard times. Yet at the same time, their transactions and interactions within the boundary of coethnic members and institutions in the suburban enclaves have created a strain in relations between Koreans and longtime members of the host communities. In particular, tensions between Koreans (mainly Korean merchants) and city officials and council members had been rising concerning the regulation of the operation of small businesses and the new construction of big Korean churches in residential areas. Opposition to the rapid growth of Korean community from longtime residents has also risen.

This sentiment was reflected on national television when, in July 1999, ABC News's *Nightline* aired an episode about Palisades Park, titled "New Faces on Main Street: The Melting Pot That Isn't" (Ahn 2005). A rally was held in Palisades Park in 1999 to protest a series of the local ordinances enacted and discriminatory incidents (e.g., anti-Korean graffiti) against Korean merchants and students. The borough council approved revisions that set a uniform 9 p.m. closing time for retail stores and 3 a.m. closing time for all nighttime businesses. However, hundreds of protestors comprised of Korean residents, merchants, college students, and members of the Chamber of Commerce from New York, New Jersey, and Pennsylvania, supported Korean merchants who complained of racist policies and unfair ordinances. The mayor of Palisades Park argued at the time that "the rally was misguided because the conflict, in his opinion, was about greedy merchants who wanted to keep their businesses open 24 hours daily and were playing up the race card for gain, while protestors thought differently" (Ahn 2005, p. 31).

Another source of conflict with the host community frequently is the presence of large Korean churches or ongoing construction of large-scale Korean church facilities. After a period of renting a church building from an established local church that is typically declining in congregation and attendance, growing Korean churches often need to acquire or construct a bigger church space. However, suburban townships in Bergen County do not always look favorably on hosting a big ethnic church, citing the likelihood of problematic environmental impacts such as the traffic and noise. Proposals for new construction of Korean church buildings often meet a hostile reaction from current residents concerned with maintaining the status quo.

For example, New Jersey Chodae Church met resistance from Norwood township government when it proposed a new 54,000-square-foot church building. Several community hearings, community board meetings, and planning board meetings were held to decide the case. Although the site was legally zoned for a community facility, the final decision was to disallow its construction due to the existing residents' opposition. After appealing to the court, the church won the case. However, the church had to revise the proposal to reduce the size (to 40,000 square feet) and arrange for substantial contributions to the community. These contributions included paying the wages of police officers who would work on Sundays around the church, making a contribution of $25,000 in lieu of taxes, reimbursing the city for the pavement costs for neighboring streets, and providing the free use of church space for community events. These indications of tension pose a challenge to the integration of rapidly growing suburban ethnic enclaves into their host communities. Through these experiences, both Koreans and non-Korean residents have sought to move forward by seeking mutual understanding of cultural differences.

Korean Cuisine and Shops

Famous venues for local Korean cuisine in Bergen County's Korean enclaves include Parisienne Bakery, serving Korean-style baked goods to a mostly Korean American clientele; Yiga, offering authentic traditional Korean dishes; Chicken BonChon, serving fried chicken coated with or without a spicy sauce; and Palisadium attracting customers with its dazzling view of Manhattan. Broad Avenue in Palisades Park is called a Korean food walk of fame. Store signs in both Korean and English mark the location of bars, bakeries, groceries, noodle houses, and table barbecue restaurants. Among these, So Moon Nan Jib serves Korean food in a rather old-fashioned way. Muk Eun Ji is a restaurant specializing seafood noodles and bean paste stew

---

The First "Hollywood"

Fort Lee, now a Korean American enclave, was once the film capital of the world before the studios migrated to Southern California. Hundreds of films were produced in Fort Lee. There were seven major film studios, and 21 others shot on location there. Douglas Fairbanks, the Marx Brothers, D. W. Griffith, the Barrymores, Dorothy and Lillian Gish, Charlie Chaplin, and Will Rogers all made films in the New Jersey suburb. Fort Lee was also the site of Mary Pickford's first films, as well as Theda Bara's vamp movies.

Fort Lee was perfect for filming; it had the Hudson River, the rolling hills and fields of the adjacent Palisades Park, and was just a short drive from the New York homes of the silent film stars. The term "cliffhanger," or a suspenseful, unresolved ending, was invented in Fort Lee to describe the nail-biting endings of Paula White films, where the actress would dangle precariously over the cliff in the Palisades. By 1916, all of the major studios had moved west, and Fort Lee descended into obscurity. Though the film history of Fort Lee has been largely forgotten, some are working to bring that history into the light. The Fort Lee Film Commission works to promote the film industry's New Jersey roots, tracking down rare film prints and securing them for screenings. Not only is the Commission reviving Fort Lee's legacy, it is actively uncovering and preserving film history itself.

with generous portions and side dishes (banchan). Myung Dong serves noodle soups and dumplings, and Shilla Bakery serves cookies and pastries.

Recently, many Korean franchise companies and businesses such as Kumkang (a large Korean shoe company), Face Shop (body products and cosmetics company), Café Bene, and Paris Baguette (a Korean bakery and coffeehouse) opened their branches in Palisades Park and further shaped its Korean landscape.

Notable Individuals

Seo Kwang Bum

Historically, in the 19th century, a notable Korean American from New Jersey is Seo Kwang Bum, a political refugee during the end of Chosun dynasty and the Japanese colonial period. He was the first Korean to graduate from New Brunswick Seminary in New Jersey. He became a naturalized U.S. citizen in 1892.

Jason Kim

More recently, there have emerged a few Korean American public figures in the realm of politics. As mentioned previously, Palisades Park Councilman Jason Kim started his political career in 1994 as the first Korean American school board trustee of Palisades Park after the third trial. In 2004, he became the first Korean American councilman in the township. Recently, he took another step up and was elected as deputy mayor of Palisades Park. Jason Kim, along with Mayor James Rotundo, contributed to standing a memorial outside the public library on Broad Avenue to the thousands of comfort women from Korea and other Asian countries who were sexually exploited by the Japanese military during World War II.

Jun Choi (1971–)

Jun Choi is the former mayor of Edison, New Jersey, a community of over 100,000 residents. He was elected as the youngest mayor in Edison in 2006, as well as the first Asian American mayor of a major city in New Jersey. Prior to becoming mayor, he served as a senior official on education policy at the New Jersey Department of Education and also served in the White House Office of Management and Budget. Choi grew up in Elizabeth, New Jersey, and earned a bachelor of science from the Massachusetts Institute of Technology and a master's degree in public policy and administration from Columbia University.

See also in New Jersey: Ironbound and the Wards (Newark, New Jersey); Little Havana on the Hudson (North Hudson, New Jersey); Little India, Newark Avenue (Jersey City, New Jersey); Little Lima (Paterson, New Jersey)

See also Korean Enclaves: Koreatown (Los Angeles, California)

Sookhee Oh

Further Reading

Ahn, Eumi. "Two Worlds, One Town: The Case of Palisades Park." Thesis for the Degree of Master of Science in Urban Planning, Columbia University, 2005.

Cho, Jong Moo. *Anchoring in the Hudson River.* New York: Korea-America Heritage Foundation, 2011.

Hillinger, Charles. "Hooray Fort Lee, N.J., Birthplace of Film: Thomas Edison, D. W. Griffith and Other Pioneers Made It the Hollywood of the Pre-WWI Movie Industry." *Los Angeles Times,* July 3, 1986. Accessed November 14, 2016. http://articles.latimes.com/1986 -07-03/entertainment/ca-1189_1_film-capital.

Korea Daily (JoongAng Ilbo). Online Directories of Korean Business. Accessed October 19, 2016. http://www.koreadaily.com/index.html?branch=HOME.

Lee, James. "In Suburban N.J., Let Off Steam the Traditional Korean Way." *The Washington Post,* December 31, 2014. Accessed October 19, 2016. http://www.washingtonpost.com /lifestyle/travel/a-taste-of-korea-in-new-jersey/2014/12/31/b0619018-87b9-11e4 -9534-f79a23c40e6c_story.html.

Min, Pyong Gap. *Caught in the Middle: Korean Communities in New York and Los Angeles.* Los Angeles: University of California Press, 1996.

Min, Pyong Gap. Koreans: "An Institutionally Complete Community in New York." In Nancy Foner, ed. *New Immigrant in New York.* New York: Columbia University Press, 2001.

Min, Pyong Gap. *Population Growth and Racial Composition in Korean Enclaves in the New York-New Jersey Area, 1980–2010.* Research Center for the Korean Community. Queens College of City University of New York. Research Report 5 (2012a): 1–21.

Min, Pyong Gap. "The Korean Community in the New York-New Jersey Area in the 1980s." *Journal of Chung-Ang Historical Studies* 36 (2012b): 573–640.

Moreno, Manuel. "Out of the Shadows." *New Jersey Monthly,* June 9, 2008. Accessed November 14, 2016. http://njmonthly.com/articles/jersey-living/out-of-the-shadows.

Oh, Sookhee. "Spatial Assimilation and Ethnic Church Linkages: Suburban Koreans in Bergen County, New Jersey." *Journal of Studies of Koreans Abroad* 29 (2013): 45–78.

U.S. Census Bureau. *American Community Survey 2009–2013.*

U.S. Census Bureau. Decennial Censuses, 1990, 2000, and 2010.

U.S. Census Bureau. *Public Use Micro Sample 1990 and 2000.*

BLACK BOTTOM (PHILADELPHIA, PENNSYLVANIA)

Black Bottom, Philadelphia, was a formerly African American neighborhood in West Philadelphia, now called University City, surrounding the University of Pennsylvania. Also previously known as Area 3, Black Bottom lay roughly between Thirty-Third and Fortieth Streets from east to west and between Lancaster/Powelton Avenue and University Avenue from north to south. Today, the neighborhood is almost entirely subsumed by campuses of the University of Pennsylvania, Drexel University, and the University of Sciences in Philadelphia, as well as transformed by the student housing that arose to meet this new demand. While some residential areas remain on the fringes of Black Bottom, by and large the once thriving community members that existed there have been scattered to other areas of the City of Brotherly Love.

During the 19th century, the cheap housing available in the neighborhood—especially in light of discriminatory housing practices in other, more wealthy neighborhoods—led to a concentration of African Americans that had moved north throughout the Great Migration starting in the early 20th century. At its height before World War II, Black Bottom was a thriving working-class neighborhood. Densely constructed rowhomes housed African American families working in area hospitals, local factories, and on the railroads, as well, given the neighborhood's proximity to Thirtieth Street Station, which linked the city to the other East Coast metropolises.

Although originally founded in Center City, the University of Pennsylvania had moved into the Black Bottom area in the 1870s and, since then, has driven the transformation of the neighborhood. The university's exponential growth after World War II was at least partly the result of rising enrollment because of the GI Bill and partly the result of the overall postwar economic boom. As the University of Pennsylvania expanded, the neighborhood was also reshaped by the resulting influx of faculty and students, compounded by the founding of other institutions such as Drexel University, the University of the Sciences in Philadelphia, and the Presbyterian Hospital. Together, these institutions formed the West Philadelphia Corporation in 1959.

As in other large urban areas, the Housing Act of 1954 would be one of the first of numerous waves of "slum clearance" in the area, as federal funds were used to relocate Black Bottom residents into public housing. Under the auspices of the Philadelphia Redevelopment Authority, and with the heavy influence of the West Philadelphia Corporation, eminent domain was leveraged to take over the neighborhood for "urban renewal." What is remembered by residents as a thriving, active, and safe neighborhood was turned into a "redevelopment zone" and razed to the ground. Although residents organized the Black Bottom Association in 1976 to respond to these challenges, ultimately, they were unable to halt the unceasing expansion of vested institutional interests, which continued to transform West Philadelphia, including the Powelton Village neighborhood to the north of Black Bottom. Approximately 5,000 residents were displaced.

In the course of this expansion, the very topography of the neighborhood was completely erased. Where once were small residential streets, now stand massive commercial and institutional "superblocks," as portions of some streets, such as Thirty-Seventh Street or Cuthbert Street, were literally erased from the map. As a result, these large "superblocks" changed traffic patterns, both vehicular and pedestrian, and further consolidated the hold of large institutions on the landscape of West Philadelphia. To the south, in 1974, the Children's Hospital of Philadelphia moved to its current location near the Veterans Administration Hospital. Even today, these hospital campuses continue to develop the southern fringes of what was once Black Bottom, while the University of Pennsylvania has aggressively encroached west since its arrival in the neighborhood.

However, the community of Black Bottom could never had expanded beyond its borders or be transferred easily to adjacent neighborhoods because the entire area is hemmed in by the Schuylkill River, which separates the downtown core of

Center City from West Philadelphia. The border created by how the river curves to the north and south practically encloses this eastern-most part of West Philadelphia on three sides. As a result, whenever one of the large institutions expands, it pushes neighborhoods further and further against the edge of the river.

Today, former residents fondly remember their once thriving community and gather in Fairmount Park with some regularity in the summer. In the meantime, the institutions that destroyed the neighborhood have engaged in some forms of community outreach in recent years. For example, at the University of Pennsylvania, one project in the late 1990s, the Black Bottom Performance Project, tried to capture and dramatize the spirit of the neighborhood, while college courses conducted by former Black Bottom resident Dr. Walter Palmer and others have looked at the politics of displacement and "urban renewal" in the area. However, by and large, the institutions that destroyed the neighborhood are now long-entrenched features of the local urban landscape, and whatever displacement occurred over the decades has no hope of being reversed.

With the more recent wave of gentrification in the new millennium, and its companion influx of largely middle-class whites, both student and nonstudent, into the urban center that previous white generations had abandoned, the neighborhood continues to experience change in what few residential streets are left in Black Bottom, as well as into the adjacent neighborhoods of Kingsessing, Cobbs Creek, and Mantua to the southwest, west, and northwest, respectively. However, the original neighborhood has largely been obliterated by the institutions that now form the economic backbone of the area, not only because of physical displacement to accommodate the large hospital and university campuses but also because of the resulting rise of mostly white residents as gentrification takes hold.

See also in Pennsylvania: Germantown (Philadelphia, Pennsylvania)

See also African American Enclaves: Baldwin Hills (Los Angeles, California); Bedford-Stuyvesant (Brooklyn, New York); Bronzeville (Chicago, Illinois); Greenwood (Tulsa, Oklahoma); Harlem (New York City); Harlem, Senegalese Enclave (New York City); Historic South Central (Los Angeles, California); Ironbound and the Wards (Newark, New Jersey); Lewiston and Portland, Somali and Bantu Enclaves (Maine); Little Ethiopia (Los Angeles, California); Lower Ninth Ward (New Orleans, Louisiana); Lower Roxbury, African American Enclave (Massachusetts); Mattapan (Boston, Massachusetts); Orange Mound (Memphis, Tennessee); Sweet Auburn (Atlanta, Georgia); Tremé (New Orleans, Louisiana); Watts (Los Angeles, California)

Yvette M. Chin

Further Reading

Becher, Debbie. *Private Property and Public Power: Eminent Domain in Philadelphia.* New York: Oxford University Press, 2014.

O'Mara, Margaret Pugh. *Cities of Knowledge.* PhD Dissertation, University of Pennsylvania, 2002.

Puckett, John L., and Mark Frazier Lloyd. *Becoming Penn: The Pragmatic American University.* Philadelphia: University of Pennsylvania Press, 2015.

BOROUGH PARK/WILLIAMSBURG/CROWN HEIGHTS, JEWISH ENCLAVES (BROOKLYN, NEW YORK)

Borough Park, Williamsburg, and Crown Heights are neighborhoods in Brooklyn with the most prominent Orthodox and Hasidic Jewish communities. The majority of Hasidim in the United States reside in Brooklyn.

Jews began immigrating to New York City as early as 1654, with the Sephardic Jews' immigration from Spain. In the 1870s, Jews made up a mere 9% of New York City's population, a number that ballooned to 28% by 1915. Early waves of Jewish immigrants settled in the Lower East Side section of Manhattan. Many worked in sweatshops, with future generations becoming small business owners. Soda fountains and candy stores were among the businesses Jews owned, and each was a staple of their community, serving as type of community center. According to legend, the famous New York egg cream beverage was invented by a Jewish Lower East Side resident in his soda shop.

By the 1890s, Jewish migration to the outer boroughs of New York City had taken off. In the latter half of the decade, Jewish immigrants were pouring in at 1,000 per week. The Lower East Side reached its peak density in 1910, with 542,061

The Williamsburg area of Brooklyn is an enclave of Hassidic Jews who dress in traditional clothing, and many of the area outdoor advertisements are written in Yiddish lettering. (Peter Spirer/Dreamstime.com)

residents in an area that is just under two-thirds of a square mile. Lower East Side crowding, along with displacement from bridge and park construction, lower living costs, and improved public transportation contributed to Jewish migration to Brooklyn. Xenophobic attitudes that developed after World War I and the Immigration Act of 1924 slowed Jewish immigration to the United States tremendously. It did not pick up again until World War II, and many Eastern and Central European Jews immigrated directly to Brooklyn. Although the Orthodox communities vary in some ways, they share many similarities, such as modest dress, moderate to intense segregation from mainstream society, and their own school systems.

Borough Park, also written as Boro Park, is one of six original colonial Brooklyn towns. Until the early 1800s, the land was used for commercial horticulture. In the early 1900s, then State Senator William H. Reynolds, who also developed Coney Island's Dreamland Amusement Park, purchased the land known today as Borough Park and subdivided it for house construction. In 1904, the neighborhood's first synagogue was built, and Russian Jews residing in the Lower East Side began migrating to Borough Park, earning the neighborhood the nickname "New Jerusalem." They lived initially in a community just south of Borough Park, called Blytheborne, which by 1920 had been absorbed into Borough Park.

The elevated New Utrecht train line, built after World War I and now the D line in New York's subway system, further enabled the neighborhood's growth. Today, it has the highest overall concentration of Jews in all of New York City, with 78% of households identifying as Jewish. It is home to several Hasidic sects, but the Bobvers, Polish Jews who arrived around the time of the Great Depression, are the largest. Hungarian Hasidim came to the neighborhood due to the Hungarian uprising of 1956, as did displaced Crown Heights and Williamsburg Jews after the construction of the Brooklyn-Queens Expressway in 1957. Most non-Hasidic Jews have left the neighborhood. Borough Park's city councilman, David G. Greenfield, referred to the neighborhood as the "Jewish capital of the United States."

Borough Park consists of roughly 200 city blocks and has a population of 100,000 to 130,000 people. The neighborhood's median household income is $35,508, the average household size is 4.35, and the majority of residents are politically conservative. Despite the fact that nearly 30% of the community lives below the poverty line, 79% of voters favored Republican policies of John McCain in 2008. Overall, property values in the area are strong, however, with the average cost of a single-family home being $772,810 in 2009.

Thirteenth Avenue, roughly a mile in length, is Borough Park's commercial center. Packed with grocery stores, restaurants, and banks, as well as merchandise like clothing and Judaica, it is famous for its delis, bakeries, and the popular Amnon Kosher Pizza restaurant. The street shuts down each week in observance of the Sabbath. During Purim, a holiday that celebrates the Jews' rescue from their ancient Persian enemy Haman, the children of Borough Park parade the streets dressed as royalty, villains, and clowns. Several street parties take place during the holiday and attract visitors from all over New York City.

Maimonides Medical Center on Tenth Avenue, originally the New Utrecht Dispensary Clinic founded in 1911 by the women of Borough Park, was known for its polio rehabilitation service and advanced surgical techniques. Recently, Asian Americans have been purchasing property in Borough Park, although the neighborhood remains dominated by Orthodox Jews.

Williamsburg is home to the New York's largest Satmar Hasidic Jewish population, a sect known for isolating itself from mainstream society. Williamsburg was a playground for the rich until the Williamsburg Bridge opened in 1853, enabling Lower East Side Jews to escape their crowded conditions. Williamsburg Jews inhabit the neighborhood's south side, just northeast of Brooklyn's Navy Yard. Lee Avenue is their main commercial zone.

Williamsburg is home to the largest network of Jewish schools in the United States. More than 30% of men are unemployed, and 78% of Jewish households reported making less than $50,000 a year. New York's overall Jewish population has increased over the past decade by 9%. Two-thirds of that increase is attributed to the high birthrates of the Williamsburg and Borough Park neighborhoods.

Crown Heights was once called Crow Hill, after the crows that filled the trees on the neighborhood's tallest hill. In 1873, the *Brooklyn Eagle* speculated that the name actually referenced the African American settlement there, as whites called blacks by the pejorative term *crows*. Others contend that "crow" is a reference to the inmates of Kings County Penitentiary, which was located in Crown Heights from 1846 to 1907. Today, Crown Heights is home to the Chabad-Lubavitch Hasidic movement and the Lubavitch world headquarters, located on Frederick Law Olmstead and Calvert Vaux-designed Eastern Parkway. The Lubavitch are known for their outreach programs, for which they travel to major U.S. cities in "Mitzvah Tanks," offering free religious kits to nonobservant Jews to promote religious practice. Crown Heights is home to the first children's museum in the United States, built in 1899. Most of the museum is underground. Since 1969, the renowned West Indian Carnival parade has taken place each Labor Day in Crown Heights. It draws more than two million attendees to celebrate the community's prominent Afro-Caribbean population and enjoy an elaborate parade with festive costumes, floats, and food.

What historian Edward Shapiro referred to as the most serious anti-Semitic event in American history occurred in Crown Heights from August 19 to 22, 1991. A car accident involving the Lubavitch leader Rabbi Menachem Mendel Schneerson's police-escorted motorcade killed a seven-year-old Guyanese boy named Gavin Cato and injured his cousin Angela. A car behind Rabbi Schneerson's car collided with another vehicle at an intersection, careened onto the sidewalk where the children were playing, and knocked a 600-pound stone slab onto them. The black community, fueled by a number of rumors—including Hetzolah's (a Hasidic volunteer EMT organization) supposed refusal to assist the black children and comments by Reverend Al Sharpton—responded to the tragic event by looting several stores and killing one Jewish doctoral candidate from Australia named Yankel Rosenbaum as he walked home from YIVO, a Jewish research center. Tensions and violence on behalf of both the blacks and Jews continued, prompted in part by Mayor David Dinkins' seemingly diffident response to the riots and Rabbi Schneerson's refusal to address the incident at all.

From the incident, however, grew several anti-bias initiatives in the community, headed by black and Jewish organizers. Project CURE (Commission on Urgent Relief and Equipment), for instance, coalesced young men of different ethnic backgrounds, promoting tolerance and cultural understanding. The 71st Precinct Community Council instituted Unity Day, which gathers more than 10,000 people each June to celebrate cultural traditions, differences, and progressive movement toward a more unified future. Rabbi Schneerson died in 1994, leaving no successor to lead the Chabad-Lubavitch. The sect has expanded by more than 30% since his death.

Other areas in Brooklyn with significant Jewish populations include Flatbush, which is home to a large Syrian Jewish community, Midwood, Kensington, Russian Jew–dominated Brighton Beach, as well Manhattan's Upper West Side and the Upper East Side, which has seen declines in its Orthodox Jewish community in recent years. Brownsville, adjacent to Crown Heights, was once the most populous Jewish community in Brooklyn, albeit of secular Jews. In 1925, 95% of its residents were Jewish. Today, it is predominantly black and Hispanic.

Brooklyn's Jewish communities produced several notable figures in acting, politics, and the arts: comedienne Joan Rivers, actor Richard Dreyfus, Lou Reed of the Velvet Underground band, film director and actor Woody Allen. Producer and film director Mel Brooks was raised in Williamsburg, as was singer Barry Manilow. Betty Smith's 1943 classic coming of age novel, *A Tree Grows in Brooklyn,* was set in Williamsburg.

See also in New York: Bedford-Stuyvesant (Brooklyn, New York); Brighton Beach-Sheepshead Bay (Brooklyn, New York); Brooklyn, West Indian Enclave (New York); Chinatowns (Manhattan; Sunset Park East, Brooklyn; Flushing, Queens) (New York City); Coney Island (Brooklyn, New York); Crown Heights, Jamaican Enclave (Brooklyn, New York); Five Points (New York City); Greenpoint (Brooklyn, New York); Greenwich Village (New York City); Harlem (New York City); Harlem, Senegalese Enclave (New York City); Hell's Kitchen (New York City); Jackson Heights (Queens, New York); Jackson Heights, South Asian Enclave (Queens, New York); Little Brazil Street (Manhattan, New York); Little India, Jackson Heights (Queens, New York); Little Italy (Manhattan, New York); Lower East Side (New York City); Sleepy Hollow, Ecuadorian Enclave (New York); Staten Island, Sri Lankan Enclave (New York City); Sunset Park West and North Corona (New York City); Washington Heights (New York City); Yorkville, German Enclave (New York City)

See also Jewish Enclaves: Boyle Heights, Jewish Neighborhood (Los Angeles, California); Los Angeles, West Side and San Fernando Valley Jewish Enclaves (California); Lower East Side (New York City); South End (Boston, Massachusetts); West End (Boston, Massachusetts)

Meridith Roy

Further Reading

Abramovitch, Ilana, and Seán Galvin, eds. *Jews of Brooklyn*. Hanover, NH: Brandeis University Press, 2002.

Beyer, Gregory. "Borough Park, Brooklyn." *New York Times Real Estate*, October 8, 2010.

Blasina, Niki. "Orthodox Jews Defy Conventions of Low Income Voters." *Brooklyn Campaign*, November 3, 2012.

Epstein, Lawrence J. *At the Edge of a Dream: The Story of Jewish Immigrants in New York's Lower East Side 1880–1820*. San Francisco: Jossey-Bass, 2007.

Jackson, Kenneth T., ed. *The Neighborhoods of Brooklyn*. New Haven, CT: Yale University Press, 1998.

Jackson, Sharyn. "Passed Over: Borough Park Gets a Census Recount." *The Brooklyn Ink*, July 11, 2010.

Logan, John R., et al., "Immigrant Enclaves and Ethnics Communities in New York and Los Angeles." *American Sociological Review* 2 (2002): 299–322.

Otterman, Sharon. "Jewish Population Is Up in the New York Region." *New York Times*, January 17, 2013.

Shapiro, Edward S. *Crown Heights: Blacks, Jews, and the 1991 Brooklyn Riot*. Lebanon, NH: Brandeis University Press, 2006.

Rischin, Moses. *The Promised City: New York Jews*. Cambridge, MA: Harvard University Press, 1977.

BOYLE HEIGHTS, JEWISH NEIGHBORHOOD (LOS ANGELES, CALIFORNIA)

Like all great American cites, Los Angeles is defined by its immigrants. Immigrants from around the world have shaped LA into the thoroughly multicultural place it is today. Jews form an important part of LA, and the Jewish experience in the city is strongly connected to two particular neighborhoods: Boyle Heights and the Fairfax District. Today, Jews are dispersed across the city and the broader Southern California region. The Fairfax district has a dwindling population of Jews and Boyle Heights has even fewer. Even so, these two neighborhoods have traditionally defined what it means to be Jewish in LA. Broadly put, Boyle Heights was home to Jewish life in the first half of the 20th century, and Fairfax home for the second. The story of the Jews in these two particular neighborhoods reflects upon both the changing fabric of the city around them and the changing fortunes of Jews in the United States.

Jews have been present in Los Angeles since its days as a Mexican outpost. In 1841, Jacob Frankfurt arrived in a party of pioneers to the Puebla de Los Angeles. He was a tailor, born in Germany, who came first to New York and gradually made his way west. His journey, from Europe to the East Coast to California, has an oracular tint to it. Over the next hundred years, the two-part trip would be repeated by thousands of Jews just like him. However, in this era, migration stories like Frankfurt's were quite rare. In 1850, when California was admitted as a state, the census reported that just eight Jews were living in Los Angeles. They were all unmarried men, six from Germany and two from Poland. That same year,

Morris Goodman, age 24, joined the first ever Los Angeles City Council, beginning a long tradition of Jewish activity in LA politics. By 1854, the rabbi Joseph Newmark was holding informal shabbat services for the dozen or so Jewish men in the town.

Even though it was small and heavily male, the Jewish community established itself during the years between California's admission to the union and the coming of the railroad. By 1870, there were 330 Jews in a city of 5,728. They accounted for 5.7% of the population, a figure remarkably close to the percentage today. About 85% of them were born in Europe, like Jacob Frankfurt, but a small number were coming from other American cities. The merchant brothers Samuel and Joseph Labatt were the first American born Jews to reside in Los Angeles. They arrived from New Orleans in 1853 and set up a dry goods store. Their wives joined them a year later. American-born Jews, with their fluent English and better understanding of American culture, came to dominate Jewish life in 19th-century Los Angeles. Louis Lewin and Charles Jacoby, migrants from New Jersey, ran a powerful real estate company and developed much of what would become downtown LA. They also created a corporation of their own, the Pioneer Lot Association, which began to build houses in the area that would become Boyle Heights.

Boyle Heights took a long time to develop, and an even longer time to become Jewish. Named after Andrew Boyle, a vintner, it was primarily a farming community for several decades. By 1877, the area had just 40 residents, almost all of them members of Boyle's extended family. Boyle Heights was, at the time, relatively far from the urban core of the city and a less than convenient place to live for new arrivals. Jewish life in this era clustered around the northern portion of downtown, which was home to the most important Jewish institutions in the city. The first synagogue in Los Angeles, Congregation B'nai B'rith, was built on Broadway in 1872. In 1877, Emil Harris started the Los Angeles Turnverein, a social and sporting club for German-Jewish men. His brother, Leopold Harris, owned the first kosher meat market. The neighborhood was also home to important Jewish-owned businesses, like the White House Hotel. By the time the railroad came in 1887, Jews had established a strong presence in the young city.

The Southern Pacific railroad transformed Los Angeles from a sleepy frontier outpost into a bustling metropolis. New arrivals, mostly white Protestants from the Midwest, came in droves. Joining them was a small number of Jews. These Jews were different from those already living in Los Angeles. They were, for the most part, from Eastern Europe and not Germany. Throughout America's cities, the new wave of Eastern European Jews clashed with the more established German Jews. The former were poor, old fashioned, and very religious. By the time they arrived, many German Jews had become quite prosperous and taken up Reform Judaism, which was far more liberal than the orthodoxy of the Eastern Europeans. German Jews were embarrassed by the Eastern Europeans, who they feared would bring about anti-Semitism and interrupt the progress they had made in assimilating. The epicenter of this clash in LA was at the B'nai B'rith Synagogue. In 1890, 42 Eastern European children tried to sign up for Sunday School, prompting an outcry from the congregation's older members. After several days of discussion, representatives from the Ladies' Hebrew Benevolent Society were able to grant the children admission. This was certainly a progressive development, but only a few months later, in 1891, 100 German Jewish families founded the Concordia Club, a social club modeled on gentile country clubs. The Club was highly exclusive and intended to preserve the elite status of the original Jewish settlers. As the 1890s progressed, Eastern European Jews built more Orthodox synagogues and lived in homes clustered around them. For the most part, they lived north of the older areas of Jewish settlement. The community was segregating itself along religious lines, but it had grown significantly. By 1900, the Jewish population in LA numbered 2500. Boyle Heights had just three Jewish families and only a few hundred total residents, but it would soon develop as a neighborhood thanks to influxes of very different types of immigrants.

In 1904, 2,000 Russian Molokans settled in Boyle Heights. The Molokans are a separatist sect of Russian Christians who were persecuted by the Czar and fled Russia en masse. Most went into the Caucasus Mountains, but a handful of Molokans already living in Boyle Heights encouraged resettlement in California (Japanese American National Museum, p. 12). In Boyle Heights, they found abundant land to practice their preferred trade, dairy farming. By the time the Molokans arrived, Boyle Heights had already begun diversifying. Breed Street was home to a collection of shops owned by Armenian and Lebanese settlers, who had come to America seeking refuge from the Ottoman massacres of the late 19th century. They worked as grocers and merchants and lived in homes rented from the descendants of Andrew Boyle. African Americans had also begun to migrate to Los Angeles in the mid-1890s. They were excluded, by discriminatory housing covenants, from living downtown, so they settled in the eastern and southern parts of the city, which included Boyle Heights. Boyle Heights received another population boost from the San Francisco earthquake of 1906, which drove many of San Francisco's Japanese residents to Los Angeles. They tended to settle in Little Tokyo, which rapidly expanded along First Street into Boyle Heights. In addition to these other groups, Boyle Heights also had a large Mexican population that had lived there for generations. Despite all of these different groups, in 1910 the overall population of the neighborhood was still under 10,000 and had not grown nearly as rapidly as Downtown. However, by that point several pivotal developments were already underway to turn the area into a much larger and much more Jewish neighborhood.

The year 1908 was key for Boyle Heights. The Los Angeles City Council banned industrial development on the Westside, a move intended to protect its wealthier, predominantly white residents from air and water pollution. From that year on, new factories had to be built on the eastern side of the Los Angeles River. The law brought thousands of new jobs to eastern Los Angeles. Boyle Heights heavily industrialized over the next few years. By 1920, a quarter of its land was occupied by industrial developments (Boyle Heights Timeline). In 1910, perhaps anticipating the increase in trade between east and west LA that the zoning law would cause, the city built two new bridges over the river between Downtown and Boyle Heights. The bridge building proved to be a decades-long project; by 1933, four more would be built. The bridges played an essential role in making Boyle Heights a more attractive place to live. It was no longer a rural village making its living from grape growing and cattle ranching. As the area industrialized, many farmers left and took their herds into the Valley. The Molokans switched from milk production to milk wholesaling. Also in 1910, the Mexican Revolution sparked a mass exodus of Mexican peasants from the northern regions of Mexico. Although almost all of them had been farmers in their home country, they quickly settled down in East LA neighborhoods like Boyle Heights, and many worked in the expanding garment and food processing factories.

The emerging industrialization of Boyle Heights caught the attention of Jews on a national level. In 1909, the Workman's Circle established their Los Angeles headquarters on Breed Street. The Workman's Circle (or Arbeiter Ring, in Yiddish) was a national organization of Jewish unionists and labor activists. They encouraged Eastern European Jews to leave an increasingly expensive Downtown and get new jobs in the factories. Their efforts were less than successful. Downtown Jews were comfortable and enjoyed their proximity to the German Jewish and gentile elites. The Workman's Circle instead took on a more ambitious project—resettling Eastern European immigrants living in the northeast.

To populate Boyle Heights with a class of industrious Jews, The Workman's Circle worked with Industrial Removal Offices from New York, Philadelphia, Baltimore, and Boston. The stated goal of these groups was to find Jewish immigrants work and assimilate them into communities across America. However, they had an ulterior motive. Industrial Removal Offices (IROs) were funded and staffed by German American Jews, who had been living in northeastern cities since the 1830s and felt that droves of Jewish peasants would undo the work they had done to normalize American perceptions of Jewishness. When the IROs were founded, from 1900 to 1903, established Jews were embarrassed by the thousands of Eastern European new arrivals, whose dress, diet, and religious customs represented everything they were trying to move away from in their modern American lives. Nevertheless, IROs did an excellent job of hiding their true intentions from the new immigrants. Offices were typically swarmed with applicants, who badly wanted jobs and felt no attachment to whatever city they were living in at the time (Center for Jewish History). The Panic of 1907 and ensuing economic crash intensified operations at the IROs. They had previously sent most of their clientele to cities in the Midwest, like Cincinnati, Chicago, and Milwaukee. However, the recession hit these places hard, and they quickly had even fewer jobs than there were in northeastern cities (Center for Jewish History). As a result, they sent their applicants further away, to the South, the Rocky Mountains, and the Pacific Coast, especially Los Angeles. During the 1910s, thousands of IRO workers arrived in Boyle Heights. The IRO system was designed to produce chain reactions. An IRO would send one worker to a city, and then, if he was successful, correspond with him and put him in charge of coordinating jobs and housing for subsequent workers. In this way, IROs could delegate responsibility and successfully resettle thousands of Jews with only a few staff members.

The 1910s were a time of enormous growth for Boyle Heights, which had become the preferred destination for IROs across the Eastern Seaboard. By 1920, Boyle Heights had 1,826 Jewish families. Boyle Heights had always been receptive to immigrants, and thousands of Jews were able to move into the neighborhood without causing a stir. The International Institute of Los Angeles, founded in 1914 by the Young Women's Christian Association, helped the wives of recent arrivals make homes for themselves and socialize. They also helped young women find work in the booming garment industry. Los Angeles developed an international reputation as a welcoming place for Jews ready to work. By the early 1920s, a small but significant portion of Eastern Europeans were coming directly to Los Angeles with only a brief stopover on the East Coast.

At the same time, a parallel community of Sephardic Jews was putting down roots in Boyle Heights. Sephardic Jews flocked to LA because the climate reminded them of their Mediterranean homeland. By 1912, there was a Sephardic synagogue on Whittier Street, Congregation Avat Shalom. In 1917, Sephardic Jews from the Greek island of Rhodes founded the Sephardic Peace and Progress Society, a benevolent aid group for new Sephardic arrivals. In 1920, the organization changed its name to La Communidad, a reminder to all that the Sephardic Jews were culturally different from their Ashkenazi (European) neighbors. They spoke Spanish or Ladino instead of Yiddish, wore different clothing, and sang their prayers with different melodies. There does not appear to have been significant conflict between the two Jewish communities, and today intermarriage has blurred the lines between Sephardic and Ashkenazi. However, in Boyle Heights's early years as a Jewish enclave, the two cultures existed side by side.

The 1920s saw the greatest yet influx of Jews to Los Angeles. Many of them settled in Boyle Heights, which by 1920 was home to 40% of the city's Jews (Romo 1983, p. 95). By 1930, Boyle Heights had over 10,000 Jewish families. Brooklyn Avenue and Temple Street resembled the Lower East Side, but with more palm trees. Peddlers sold produce and trinkets, boys played stickball and dodged trolley cars, and kosher restaurants and markets could be found on every corner. Two lavish synagogues anchored the neighborhood. The Breed Street Shul was home to the Orthodox Congregation Talmud Torah, who called it "Queen of the Shuls" (Reft 2013). Designed by architect Abram Edelman at a then extravagant cost of $75,000, it featured elaborately carved pews, vibrant murals, and stained glass, as well as polychromatic stonework inside and out. On New Hampshire Avenue, the Sinai Temple, completed in 1925, served Boyle Heights's growing Conservative community. The Conservative movement sought to reconcile what they viewed as overly traditional Orthodox practice with overly secular Reform practice. Boyle Heights was home to one of the biggest Conservative populations in the world, and Sinai Temple was their home. Its architects took a heavy-handed approach to temple architecture. Enormous carved stone menorahs and slabs bearing the Ten Commandments adorn the facade of the building, still visible today despite the purchase of Temple Sinai by a Korean Presbyterian church. The synagogues signaled to new arrivals in Boyle Heights that the neighborhood was home to a well-established Jewish community.

The population expanded in spite of the Immigration Act of 1924, which drastically limited migration from Southern and Eastern Europe. The racially focused quota system was specifically designed to keep out all immigrants except those hailing from Northern Europe (the United Kingdom, Scandinavia, and Germany). After 1924, many Jewish enclaves on the East Coast began to slowly depopulate as older immigrants dispersed across their cities. Without a supply of new arrivals to replenish those departing, enclaves such as Plum Street in Cincinnati and Bolton Street in Baltimore lost the bulk of their Jewish residents. Los Angeles, however, was immune to this issue because most of its settlers had always come from within the United States. Jewish Americans kept coming to Boyle Heights, which by 1931 had 35,000 Jews. Despite this high number, Boyle Heights was still quite diverse. Little Tokyo had shifted over the years, and greater numbers of Japanese now lived along First Street than earlier in the 20th century. The Molokans were by now quite well established, and photographs from the era show them driving new cars and living in large houses. For the most part, they still practiced their distinctive religion, but many Molokans joined the Azusa Street Revival movement, an early Pentecostal church founded by the charismatic African American preacher William Seymour. This cultural mixing is characteristic of the history of Los Angles in the early 20th century, when multiethnic neighborhoods thrived. A major blow to diversity in Boyle Heights came in 1931. The federal government, under pressure to create more jobs for American citizens, began to aggressively deport Mexican Americans. Around one million Mexicans were deported, and the scholar Abraham Hoffman estimates that about 60% of them were American citizens.

The Repatriation Program, as it was called by the U.S. government, hit Los Angeles particularly hard. About a third of its Mexican American population was deported from 1931 to 1933. Boyle Heights witnessed the violence brought by repatriation. Los Angeles police, California state troopers, and federal agents swarmed the Mexican blocks of the neighborhood. Wearing military garb, they physically and verbally abused thousands of Mexican Americans, some of whom had been living in the neighborhood for decades. Their rights to due process and equal protection were summarily ignored as they were taken to jail and forced to leave the country. Deportations tore families apart. Broadcasting from his radio show at the eastern edge of Boyle Heights, Jose David Orozco described women crying in the streets, unable to find their husbands (Balderrama 1995, p. 70). This was clearly a deeply traumatic episode for the neighborhood. Students at Theodore Roosevelt High School, in the heart of Boyle Heights, published scathing criticism of the repatriation program in an independent newspaper. When they refused to redact the controversial articles, the school suspended the authors.

Mass deportation made Boyle Heights less diverse and more Jewish. The same year, 1931, saw the construction of the biggest Jewish community center yet seen in the city: the Menorah Center. Up to 150 different Jewish groups used its facility on Wabash Avenue, which was also home to an expansive Hebrew school, a daycare center, and a large kosher kitchen. Throughout the 1930s, it averaged 15,000 visitors each month. The community built more synagogues, both Sephardic and Ashkenazi: Congregation Haim Vahessed in 1932, and the Sephardic Hebrew

Center in 1935. Boyle Heights in the 1930s was also the site of community activism against the treatment of Jews in Nazi Germany. In 1934, Congregation Talmud Torah and the Sephardic brotherhood led a mass rally at the Philharmonic to spread awareness of the Nazi boycott of Jewish businesses. The rally reflected Jewish uneasiness about mounting anti-Semitism in the United States as well, where radio host Charles Coughlin was agitating for an American boycott of Jewish businesses. This was the beginning of Los Angeles Jews' activism against Nazism, which would grow throughout the 1930s and intensify as knowledge of the Holocaust began to escape Europe.

As Boyle Heights continued to surge in population to 14,000 Jewish families by 1938, Jews gradually began moving out to other areas of Los Angeles. As was the case in other cities, when immigrants became prosperous, they left their neighborhood of first settlement. West LA, which traditionally had virtually zero Jews, quietly became a popular destination for those ready to leave Boyle Heights. On the eve of World War II, Wilshire had 2,410 Jewish families, and West Adams had 1,534. Hollywood, since the 1910s home to many Jews who worked in the movie industry, had 3,827 Jewish families. Compared to Boyle Heights, Jewish residents of these West LA communities were of higher social and economic status than their eastern counterparts, according to census data on education, rent, and occupation. World War II would dramatically intensify the westward movement for LA's Jews.

The war was a seismic event for Los Angeles. Before the war, the city was a patchwork of different towns separated by farmland. In 1940, Los Angeles County was the most agriculturally productive county in the nation and a leader in citrus and tree nuts. Downtown was small and bereft of tall buildings, thanks to a law that made it illegal to build taller than 150 feet, which wouldn't be repealed until 1956. Visiting the city in 1940, Jean-Paul Sartre wrote that Los Angeles was like "a big earthworm that might be chopped into twenty pieces without being killed. If you go through this enormous urban cluster, you come upon twenty juxtaposed cities, strictly identical, each with its poor section, its business streets, night-clubs and smart suburb." Thanks in part to the still-flowing Los Angeles River, Boyle Heights was traditionally isolated from the other towns in the county. By the end of the 1940s, it would be a transportation hub.

World War II filled in the gaps between LA's separate towns, which became neighborhoods in the greater city of Los Angeles. Factories shot up on the farmland in the outskirts of neighborhoods. The U.S. Navy brought thousands of jobs to the ports of Long Beach and Los Angeles, and areas further inland soon housed facilities producing a wealth of goods for the war effort. The war replaced citrus and tree nuts with munitions and aircraft. Migrants from all over the country, primarily the South and Midwest, flocked to Los Angeles to get jobs in those factories. Black workers, barred from living in the center of the city, for the most part settled in South-Central LA. However, a significant number made their homes in Boyle Heights, just as Jews were beginning to move westward. Meanwhile, Mexican Americans were returning to Los Angeles en masse to work in the same factories, and many settled in the traditionally Mexican area of Boyle Heights. By the late 1940s, Boyle Heights was a majority Mexican neighborhood.

The relationship between Mexican Americans, African Americans, and Jews in Boyle Heights is complicated. The relevant correlation is that as more African Americans and Mexican Americans lived in Boyle Heights, fewer Jews remained in Boyle Heights. Many historical observers have called upon the traditional narrative of "white flight" to describe this demographic shift. In this framing, Jews no longer wanted to live in an area that was becoming less white and, by their reasoning, less safe and less prosperous. The reality is more interesting. Up until World War II, Los Angeles was segregated into white and non-white neighborhoods. At this point in time, the term "non-white" included Jews, Italians, Slavs, as well as those of Asian, African, and Latin American descent. Non-white neighborhoods, like Boyle Heights, were traditionally very diverse and home to people of various backgrounds living in adjacent lots. White neighborhoods were homogenous, composed of Protestant families who had emigrated from the Midwest. The institution that powered segregation in LA (and across the country) was the housing covenant. Housing covenants prohibited home owners and realtors from selling to, depending on the contract, "alien races," "non-Caucasians," or specific groups like "Chinese" or "Irish." After the war, because of the influx of African and Mexican Americans, white Protestants began to look upon all those of European descent as white. Gradually, housing covenants allowed for Jews to buy homes throughout Los Angeles,

---

Holocaust Remembrance in Fairfax

In 1961, a group of Holocaust survivors studying English at Hollywood High School banded together and discovered they all had objects, such as concentration camp uniforms and photographs, related to the Holocaust. In an effort to preserve these objects and the story of the Holocaust in perpetuity, they founded the Los Angeles Museum of the Holocaust (LAMOTH), the first Holocaust museum in the United States. Their mission statement lays out two concurrent purposes: commemoration and education. With the largest collection of Holocaust-related objects and archival material on the West Coast, LAMOTH aims to memorialize the dead and educate the world so that no one will forget.

The Jewish Federation of Greater Los Angeles had supported the museum until 2005, but LAMOTH had shuttled from place to place since losing its building in a 1994 earthquake. In 2010, LAMOTH found a new permanent home, a $15.5 million building in the Fairfax District. Among its permanent exhibits, visitors will find a wealth of photographs, documents, newspapers, and personal items from survivors. Current and past temporary exhibitions have explored the Kindertransport, the recovery of the painting *Portrait of Adele Bloch-Bauer*, and objects on loan from the State Museum of Auschwitz-Birkenau. High-tech interactive exhibits supplement the visitor experience. Admission has always been free, as the founders insisted on, so that no one would ever be turned away from learning about the Holocaust.

which accelerated the movement of prosperous Jews to West LA. Certainly, then, the demographic shift in Boyle Heights was driven in part by racism. "White flight" is too reductive a term, but Jews benefited from a racist system of housing discrimination.

For those Jews who stayed after the war, freeway construction made leaving Boyle Heights a necessity. This construction completely remade the built environment of Los Angeles. It connected all of Sartre's "twenty juxtaposed cities" and made a metropolis, but it also demolished thousands of homes. In 1946, Los Angeles built the San Bernardino Freeway on several residential blocks between Aliso and Indiana Streets. In 1948, it built the Santa Ana Freeway nearby, on Soto Street. It is estimated that freeway construction demolished 10,000 Boyle Heights homes, most of them Jewish. Even as freeways destroyed the old community in Boyle Heights, they opened up other areas for settlement by making them accessible for the first time.

See also in California: Baldwin Hills (Los Angeles, California); Boyle Heights, Latino Neighborhood (Los Angeles, California); Cambodia Town (Long Beach, California); Chinatown (Los Angeles, California); Chinatown (San Francisco, California); Chinatowns (Duplicates) (San Francisco, California); East Los Angeles, Mexican American Enclave (Los Angeles, California); El Monte, Latino Enclaves (California); Fillmore District (San Francisco, California); Gardena and Torrance (South Bay Region, Los Angeles County, California); Glendale, Armenian Enclave (California); Historic Filipinotown (Los Angeles, California); Historic South Central (Los Angeles, California); Indio, Mexican and Central American Communities (California); Japantown (San Francisco, California); Kingsburg and Sveadal, Swedish Enclaves (California); Koreatown (Los Angeles, California); Little Arabia (Anaheim, California); Little Armenia (Los Angeles, California); Little Ethiopia (Los Angeles, California); Little India/Pakistan (Artesia, California); Little Italy (Los Angeles, California); Little Italy (San Diego, California); Little Italy (San Francisco, California); Little Saigon (San Francisco, California); Little Saigon (San Jose, California); Little Saigon (Westminster, California); Little Tokyo (Los Angeles, California); Logan Heights, Mexican Enclave (San Diego, California); Los Angeles, Hawaiian Enclaves (California); Los Angeles, West Side and San Fernando Valley Jewish Enclaves (California); Mayan Corner/24th and Mission (San Francisco, California); Monterey Park, First Suburban Chinatown (California); Mount Washington, Mexican Enclave (California); National City (San Diego, California); Olvera Street/La Plaza (Los Angeles, California); Pico Rivera, Latino Enclave (California); Riverside, Mexican Enclave (California); San Bernardino, Mexican Enclave (California); San Pedro, Italian and Croatian Enclaves (California); Santa Ana, Mexican Enclaves (California); Sawtelle (Los Angeles, California); Silicon Valley, Indian and South Asian Communities (Santa Clara Valley/San Jose Region, California); Sin City (Fresno, California); Solvang, Danish Community (California); Sonoma County, Italian Enclave (California); Tehrangeles (Los Angeles, California); Temescal (Oakland, California); Thai Town (Los Angeles, California); Watts (Los Angeles, California); Yuba City, Sikh Enclave (California)

See also Jewish Enclaves: Borough Park/Williamsburg/Crown Heights, Jewish Enclaves (Brooklyn, New York); Los Angeles, West Side and San Fernando Valley Jewish Enclaves (California); Lower East Side (New York City); South End (Boston, Massachusetts); West End (Boston, Massachusetts)

Daniel Katter

Further Reading

Balderrama, Francisco E., and Raymond Rodriguez. *Decade of Betrayal: Mexican Repatriation in the 1930s.* Albuquerque, NM: University of New Mexico, 1995.

Boyle Heights Project: Power of Place. "Boyle Heights Timeline." Japanese American National Museum. Accessed October 14, 2016. http://www.janm.org/exhibits/bh/exhibition/timeline.htm.

Center for Jewish History. "Guide to the Records of the Industrial Removal Office, 1899–1922." American Jewish Historical Society. Accessed October 14, 2016. http://findingaids.cjh.org/?pID=109188.

Hoffman, Abraham. *Unwanted Mexican Americans in the Great Depression: Repatriation Pressures, 1929–1939.* Tucson, AZ: University of Arizona Press, 1974.

Japanese American National Museum. *Los Angeles's Boyle Heights: An Illustrated History.* Charleston, SC: Arcadia, 2005.

Los Angeles Museum of the Holocaust Website. Accessed June 15, 2016. http://www.lamoth.org/.

Newmark, Harris, Maurice Harris Newmark, Marco Ross Newmark, and J. Perry Worden. *Sixty Years in Southern California, 1853–1913, Containing the Reminiscences of Harris Newmark.* Boston, MA: Houghton Mifflin, 1930.

Reft, Ryan. "The Shifting Cultures of Multiracial Boyle Heights." KCET Community Television. August 9, 2013. Accessed October 14, 2016. https://www.kcet.org/departures-columns/the-shifting-cultures-of-multiracial-boyle-heights.

Romo, Ricardo. *East Los Angeles: History of a Barrio.* Austin: University of Texas Press, 1983.

Rothstein, Edward. "Bearing Witness Beyond the Witnesses." *The New York Times,* March 23, 2011. Accessed November 14, 2016. http://www.nytimes.com/2011/03/24/arts/design/holocaust-museum-in-los-angeles-makes-hard-choices-review.html?_r=0.

BOYLE HEIGHTS, LATINO NEIGHBORHOOD (LOS ANGELES, CALIFORNIA)

Boyle Heights is a densely populated, majority Latino neighborhood of Los Angeles, California. Located just to the east of downtown Los Angeles, Boyle Heights had an estimated population of 99,243 in 2008. Over half of Boyle Heights' residents are foreign born, and 94% are ethnically Latino. With a median resident age of 25 years, Boyle Heights is a youthful neighborhood with a storied ethnic past.

In the 19th century, when Los Angeles was still a part of Mexico, the area that has since become Boyle Heights was known as Paredon Blanco, Spanish for "white bluffs" (Vigeland 2013). In the wake of the Mexican American War, an Irish immigrant paid $4,000 for 22 acres of Paredon Blanco land. The buyer, Andrew Boyle, remains the area's namesake today. In the first years after its purchase, Boyle Heights was home to farmsteads and sheepherding, owned and operated by Basque, Mexican, and Irish settlers.

The early decades of the 20th century saw a boom in Boyle Heights's population, and, as a result, in its ethnic diversity as well. In the 1920s, Jews made up the largest ethnic subgroup in working-class Boyle Heights. In 1923, the Breed Street Shul opened to serve Congregation Talmud Torah, which eventually became the largest Jewish congregation in Los Angeles. The Shul, parts of which date back to 1915, was declared a historic-cultural monument by the City of Los Angeles in 1988 (The City Project). By the 1930s, some 35,000 Jews lived in Boyle Heights.

However, Jews did not make up the entirety of Boyle Heights' prewar ethnic diversity. Other groups in the area included Mexicans, Armenians, Japanese, and Eastern Europeans. Much of the early ethnic diversity in Boyle Heights resulted inadvertently from attempts at segregation in Los Angeles. As the city's white, majority Protestant residents worked to keep immigrants and non-whites from settling in their delineated residential areas, ethnic minorities were relegated to separate neighborhoods, such as Boyle Heights. Thus, attempts at preserving ethnic homogeneity elsewhere in Los Angeles ultimately contributed significantly to Boyle Heights's ethnic heterogeneity.

Eventually, the Jewish community of Boyle Heights gradually left the area. World War II brought about new housing developments, as well as increased industrial employment opportunity, in the nearby San Gabriel Valley. Subsequently, new planned neighborhoods such as North Hollywood and Panorama City became attractive residential destinations for Boyle Heights Jews.

Yet, the gradual decline of the area's Jewish population hardly resulted in an empty Boyle Heights. In the war's immediate aftermath, overcrowding became an overwhelmingly prominent feature of the working-class neighborhood. After World War II, Mexican Americans became the dominant ethnic group in Boyle Heights. During World War II, the U.S. government had allowed for the legal immigration of Mexican agricultural workers to compensate for labor shortages (National Museum for American History). Many of these workers, known as *braceros*, drifted into urban areas such as Boyle Heights in the war's aftermath. These new residents, along with returning veterans of all ethnic backgrounds, resulted in unprecedented levels of population density throughout Boyle Heights and nearby working-class neighborhoods.

Gradually, Mexican immigrants gained increased voice and visibility within Boyle Heights. In 1945, the Casa del Mexicano was dedicated as a community center for the town's Mexican population. In 1949, Edward R. Roybal, a Mexican American resident of Boyle Heights, was elected to the Los Angeles city council, providing the community with more visibility and voice in municipal politics. This became vital in 1950, when postwar anxieties about the potential for immigrants to facilitate communist infiltration led to a push for deportation of residents. In response, Jewish and Mexican residents together formed a local chapter for the Los Angeles Committee for the Protection of the Foreign Born, which communicated with residents to address experiences of discrimination.

For the next several decades, both problems and progress came to characterize Boyle Heights. As the area's remaining Jews were increasingly seen as desirable white residents, Mexicans, as well as Asian and black residents, were increasingly prevented from purchasing homes and real estate. While not as frequently discriminated against as black residents, Mexicans in Boyle Heights and throughout East Los Angeles experienced marginalization in terms of access to housing opportunities. But in 1963, the California state legislature passed the Rumford Act to prohibit discriminatory practices in housing sales and rentals. Although the eventual version of the act signed into law was a less vehement defense of minority rights than the originally drafted bill, it nonetheless was a symbolic victory for ethnic and racial equality.

But while rights to equal housing remained theoretically attainable for Boyle Heights residents, inadequate housing continued to plague the neighborhood. Crime, unemployment, and drug use also continued to trouble Boyle Heights. In 1967, federal funding allowed for the establishment of the Boyle Heights Narcotics Prevention Project, which provided a means for recovered addicts to mentor those struggling with addiction.

Yet through the 1980s and 1990s, violent crime continued to persist in Boyle Heights. Gang activity, graffiti, and a general climate of fear became familiar to neighborhood residents. However, concerns about violence and neighborhood disrepair did not go unaddressed by citizens. In 1986, area residents formed Proyecto Pastoral, a local organization to provide services toward strengthening community ties. Local police forces have worked to gain residents' trust, trying to address issues of inadequate diversity among officers and encourage community activism such as anonymous crime reporting. While street violence remains a reality in Boyle Heights today, rates of violent crime have plummeted since the 1980s and 1990s).

In fact, the pacification of Boyle Heights has gone so far in recent years as to spark concerns over neighborhood gentrification. Nicknamed "gentefication" (a play on the Spanish word *gente*), Boyle Heights has recently witnessed a trend of young Mexican American residents returning to the neighborhood that their parents left in a hurry a generation ago. Although young and financially stable residents have brought with them opportunities for local economic development, they have also caused tension with longtime residents who stand to be priced out of the neighborhood.

Overall, Boyle Heights today is a predominantly Mexican community in transition. With a storied history of ethnic diversity and civil strife, the neighborhood as it exists today appears a model of tranquility compared to its past. While the precise features of the community's future remain uncertain, it is hard to imagine that ethnic pride and investment in community will ever become relics of the past in Boyle Heights.

See also in California: Baldwin Hills (Los Angeles, California); Boyle Heights, Jewish Neighborhood (Los Angeles, California); Cambodia Town (Long Beach, California); Chinatown (Los Angeles, California); Chinatown (San Francisco, California); Chinatowns (Duplicates) (San Francisco, California); East Los Angeles, Mexican American Enclave (Los Angeles, California); El Monte, Latino Enclaves (California); Fillmore

District (San Francisco, California); Gardena and Torrance (South Bay Region, Los Angeles County, California); Glendale, Armenian Enclave (California); Historic Filipinotown (Los Angeles, California); Historic South Central (Los Angeles, California); Indio, Mexican and Central American Communities (California); Japantown (San Francisco, California); Kingsburg and Sveadal, Swedish Enclaves (California); Koreatown (Los Angeles, California); Little Arabia (Anaheim, California); Little Armenia (Los Angeles, California); Little Ethiopia (Los Angeles, California); Little India/Pakistan (Artesia, California); Little Italy (Los Angeles, California); Little Italy (San Diego, California); Little Italy (San Francisco, California); Little Saigon (San Francisco, California); Little Saigon (San Jose, California); Little Saigon (Westminster, California); Little Tokyo (Los Angeles, California); Logan Heights, Mexican Enclave (San Diego, California); Los Angeles, Hawaiian Enclaves (California); Los Angeles, West Side and San Fernando Valley Jewish Enclaves (California); Mayan Corner/24th and Mission (San Francisco, California); Monterey Park, First Suburban Chinatown (California); Mount Washington, Mexican Enclave (California); National City (San Diego, California); Olvera Street/La Plaza (Los Angeles, California); Pico Rivera, Latino Enclave (California); Riverside, Mexican Enclave (California); San Bernardino, Mexican Enclave (California); San Pedro, Italian and Croatian Enclaves (California); Santa Ana, Mexican Enclaves (California); Sawtelle (Los Angeles, California); Silicon Valley, Indian and South Asian Communities (Santa Clara Valley/San Jose Region, California); Sin City (Fresno, California); Solvang, Danish Community (California); Sonoma County, Italian Enclave (California); Tehrangeles (Los Angeles, California); Temescal (Oakland, California); Thai Town (Los Angeles, California); Watts (Los Angeles, California); Yuba City, Sikh Enclave (California)

See also Hispanic Enclaves: Annandale, Latino and Asian Enclaves (Virginia); Bridgeport (Chicago, Illinois); Chicago, Mexican and Puerto Rican Enclaves (Illinois); Dallas, Mexican Enclaves (Texas); East Los Angeles, Mexican American Enclave (Los Angeles, California); El Monte, Latino Enclaves (California); Historic South Central (Los Angeles, California); Holyoke, Puerto Rican Enclaves (Massachusetts); Houston, Mexican Enclaves (Texas); Indio, Mexican and Central American Communities (California); Jackson Heights (Queens, New York); Langley Park, Latino Enclaves (Maryland); Lawrence, Latino Enclaves (Massachusetts); Little Havana (Miami, Florida); Little Havana on the Hudson (North Hudson, New Jersey); Little Lima (Paterson, New Jersey); Logan Heights, Mexican Enclave (San Diego, California); Mayan Corner/24th and Mission (San Francisco, California); Mexicantown (Detroit, Michigan); Mount Washington, Mexican Enclave (California); Olvera Street/La Plaza (Los Angeles, California); Phoenix and Other Cities, Mexican Enclaves (Arizona); Pico Rivera, Latino Enclave (California); Riverside, Mexican Enclave (California); San Bernardino, Mexican Enclave (California); Santa Ana, Mexican Enclaves (California); Sleepy Hollow, Ecuadorian Enclave (New York); South Federal Boulevard (Denver, Colorado); Sunset Park West and North Corona (New York City); Upper Fells Point (Spanish Town) (Baltimore, Maryland); Washington Heights (New York City); Watts (Los Angeles, California)

Marena Cole

Further Reading

Bermudez, Esmeralda. "New Life for an Old Gem in Boyle Heights." *Los Angeles Times*, July 31, 2008. Accessed February 15, 2016. http://www.latimes.com/local/la-me-casa31 -2008jul31-story.html.

"Boyle Heights Profile—Mapping Los Angeles." *Los Angeles Times*, February 15, 2016. http:// maps.latimes.com/neighborhoods/neighborhood/boyle-heights.

Bullington, Bruce, John Munns, and Gilbert Geis. "Purchase of Conformity: Ex-Narcotic Addicts Among the Bourgeoisie." *Social Problems* 16, no. 4(1969): 456–63.

Burns, Sean. "Archie Green: The Making of a Working-Class Hero." Urbana, IL: University of Illinois Press, 2011.

Felker-Kantor, Max. "Fighting Many Battles: Max Mont, Labor, and Interracial Civil Rights Activism in Los Angeles, 1950–1970." In Bruce Zuckerman, ed. *Beyond Alliances: The Jewish Role in Reshaping the Racial Landscape of Southern California.* West Lafayette, IN: Purdue University Press, 2012.

"Historic—Cultural Monuments (HCM) Listing." The City Project. Accessed February 5, 2016. http://www.cityprojectca.org/ourwork/documents/HCMDatabase090707.pdf.

Medina, Jennifer. "Los Angeles Neighborhood Tries to Change, but Avoid the Pitfalls." *Los Angeles Times*, August 17, 2013. Accessed February 15, 2016. http://www.nytimes.com /2013/08/18/us/los-angeles-neighborhood-tries-to-change-but-avoid-the-pitfalls.html ?_r=0.

"Opportunity or Exploitation: The Bracero Program." National Museum of American History. Accessed February 15, 2016. http://amhistory.si.edu/onthemove/themes/story_51 _5.html.

Patiño, Charley. "Boyle Heights Beat: Reclaiming the Streets as Residents and Police Cooperate to Make Boyle Heights Safer." *Huffpost Latino Voices*, December 14, 2011. Accessed February 15, 2016. http://www.huffingtonpost.com/2011/12/13/boyle-heights-violence -safety_n_1146400.html.

Reft, Ryan. The Shifting Cultures of Multiracial Boyle Heights." KCET.org. August 9, 2013. Accessed February 5, 2016. http://www.kcet.org/socal/departures/columns/intersections /the-shifting-cultures-of-multiracial-boyle-heights.html.

Sánchez, George J. "'What's Good for Boyle Heights Is Good for the Jews': Creating Multiracialism on the Eastside During the 1950s." *Los Angeles and the Future of Urban Cultures* 56, no. 3 (2004): 633–61.

Vigeland, Tess. "Neighborhoods: Exploring the Rich History and Culture of Boyle Heights." Southern California Public Radio, March 14, 2013. Accessed February 5, 2016. http:// www.scpr.org/programs/take-two/2013/03/14/30909/exploring-new-neighborhoods -in-los-angeles.

BRAZILIAN ENCLAVES. *See* Framingham, Brazilian Enclave (Massachusetts); Little Brazil Street (Manhattan, New York)

BRIDGEPORT (CHICAGO, ILLINOIS)

Bridgeport is a neighborhood on Chicago's southside, bounded by the South Branch of the Chicago River, Bubbly Creek, Pershing Road, and the Union Pacific railroad tracks. Traditionally an Irish enclave, today it is one of Chicago's most diverse neighborhoods. While slightly more than half of the neighborhood's population of 34,483, as of 2011, is white, Bridgeport is also home to a large number of first- and second-generation Chinese and Mexican immigrants. Foreign-born residents number 41.5% (Urban Mapping 2011). Bridgeport has a long history as a working-class neighborhood and as a center for Democratic politics.

Its history as an Irish enclave began in the 1830s. Since the late 17th century, Bridgeport served as a portage for French and British explorers. It soon became a fur-trading outpost for Indians, French, and French-Indians. In the early 19th century, with an influx of American settlers, it became known as Hardscrabble. A quarry opened in 1833. Soon after, construction on a canal to connect the post with Lake Michigan commenced. Irish immigrants, some of whom had worked on the digging of the Erie Canal, moved to the area for work. Construction on the Illinois and Michigan Canal slowed in 1839 and stopped in 1841. Workers either moved on or found other occupations. Some purchased land along the canal route; others, unable to afford property, squatted on federal land. When construction recommenced in 1845 and the canal opened in 1848, Irish and German immigration increased as the area established its status as an industrial hub. By 1850, 66% of Chicago's men were immigrants, 21% were German, and 26% were Irish. Packing houses operated during the winter to provide off-season work for lumberyard, canal, road, and railroad workers. Some immigrants raised farm animals and grew cabbages to supplement their income. The Illinois state legislature created a South Chicago school district in 1847, and the Irish residents soon established the Bridgeport school in 1847. Bridgeport's population increased in the 1850s as the cholera epidemic of 1849, as well as concerns about pollution from slaughterhouses further up the South Branch of the Chicago River, pushed many laborers south to Bridgeport. The openings of the Union Stock Yard and Union Rolling Mill in 1865 prompted an influx Czech, Lithuanian, and Polish immigrants (Chicago Historical Society 2005). Each ethnic group established churches, most of which were Catholic. One of the first churches in the area was the Irish Saint Patrick church, built in 1846. Germans built Lutheran and Catholic churches in the 1860s, and Czechs had a Catholic parish by the early 1870s. While Bridgeport's Irish residents were the neighborhood's most prominent ethnic group for much of the 19th century, by the latter years of the century, Poles dominated much of Bridgeport. Gangs became very active, with feuding between Germans, Irish, and Poles. These conflicts increased in the years following World War I.

The ethnic composition began to shift around the turn of the century. Mexicans began migrating to Chicago in the first decades of the 20th century as a result of the social unrest and economic crises caused by the Mexican Revolution of the 1910s. Many found work in the city's steel plants or at the Central Manufacturing District, an industrial park that opened in 1905 in the western section of Bridgeport. It was the nation's first planned manufacturing district, and, by 1915, it employed 40,000 people (Chicago Historical Society 2005). Bridgeport also became home to Chinese immigrants, who had begun moving to the city with the completion of the Transcontinental Railroad in the 1870s, but whose numbers remained small until the 1950s. As a result of relaxed immigration laws in the United States and revolutionary unrest in China, the Chinese population in Chicago doubled from 7,000 to 14,000 during the 1950s and 1960s. The existence of the Ling Shen Ching Tze Buddhist Temple, our Lady of Guadalupe, and many other places of worship, along with Irish pubs, Mexican eateries, and Chinese restaurants, are testament to Bridgeport's diversity today. But while Bridgeport has long been a center for immigrants, its residents have often been hostile to African Americans. During the Civil Rights Movement, Bridgeport residents resisted "black intrusion" and racial violence discouraged integration. The Chicago Housing Authority in fact reserved public housing projects in Bridgeport for whites in the 1950s (Hirsch 2009, pp. 65, 24, 230). Even in the first decades of the 21st century, African Americans are less than 2% of Bridgeport's population, and the neighborhood remains a cog in Chicago's political machine historically controlled by whites (Einhorn 2001, p. xv).

In the first decades of the 21st century, Bridgeport retains its identity as an Irish enclave. Despite increasing diversity, the neighborhood continues to be associated with Irish heritage and was a prime location for the annual South Side Irish St. Patrick' Day Parade until the parade was discontinued in 2010. Bridgeport has a long history as a center for Irish-Democratic political organizing, even as the city as a whole was fairly hostile to Irish immigrants. By the mid-19th century, Democrats claimed to champion the working class; the majority of the male Irish population were laborers, with 28% percent of the population skilled workers and 57% unskilled workers. Chicago's labor movement won its first victory with the 1870 election of Mark Sheridan, a Democratic alderman in Bridgeport who had been an Irish revolutionary. During the 20th century, five of Chicago's mayors came from Bridgeport, four of whom were Irish. Long associated with the working class, Bridgeport's population may become more white-collar as a result of its proximity to the Loop, Chicago's central business district. As the 21st century progresses, it seems likely that Bridgeport will become increasingly diverse, while also maintaining its identity as a residential community that preserves its cultural history.

See also in Illinois: Andersonville (Chicago, Illinois); Bronzeville (Chicago, Illinois); Chicago, Mexican and Puerto Rican Enclaves (Illinois); Little India (Chicago, Illinois); Pilsen (Chicago, Illinois)

See also Hispanic Enclaves: Annandale, Latino and Asian Enclaves (Virginia); Boyle Heights, Latino Neighborhood (Los Angeles, California); Chicago, Mexican and Puerto Rican Enclaves (Illinois); Dallas, Mexican Enclaves (Texas); East Los Angeles, Mexican American Enclave (Los Angeles, California); El Monte, Latino Enclaves (California); Historic South Central (Los Angeles, California); Holyoke, Puerto Rican Enclaves (Massachusetts); Houston, Mexican Enclaves (Texas); Indio, Mexican and Central American Communities (California); Jackson Heights (Queens, New York); Langley Park, Latino Enclaves (Maryland); Lawrence, Latino Enclaves (Massachusetts); Little Havana (Miami, Florida); Little Havana on the Hudson (North Hudson, New Jersey); Little Lima (Paterson, New Jersey); Logan Heights, Mexican Enclave (San Diego, California); Mayan Corner/24th and Mission (San Francisco, California); Mexicantown (Detroit, Michigan); Mount Washington, Mexican Enclave (California); Olvera Street/La Plaza (Los Angeles, California); Phoenix and Other

Cities, Mexican Enclaves (Arizona); Pico Rivera, Latino Enclave (California); Riverside, Mexican Enclave (California); San Bernardino, Mexican Enclave (California); Santa Ana, Mexican Enclaves (California); Sleepy Hollow, Ecuadorian Enclave (New York); South Federal Boulevard (Denver, Colorado); Sunset Park West and North Corona (New York City); Upper Fells Point (Spanish Town) (Baltimore, Maryland); Washington Heights (New York City); Watts (Los Angeles, California)

Lindsay Schakenbach Regele

Further Reading

Electronic Encyclopedia of Chicago. "Bridgeport." Chicago, IL: Chicago Historical Society, 2005. Accessed November 4, 2016. http://www.encyclopedia.chicagohistory.org/pages/165 .html.

Cohen, Adam, and Elizabeth Taylor. *American Pharaoh: Mayor Richard J. Daley—His Battle for Chicago and the Nation.* New York: Hachette Digital, 2001.

Cohen, Lizabeth. *Making a New Deal: Industrial Workers in Chicago, 1919–1939.* New York: Cambridge University Press, 1991.

Einhorn, Robin L. *Property Rules: Political Economy in Chicago, 1833–1872.* Chicago, IL: University of Chicago Press, 2001.

Electronic Encyclopedia of Chicago. "Multicentered Chicago." Chicago, IL: Historical Society, 2005. Accessed November 4, 2016. http://www.encyclopedia.chicagohistory.org/pages /854.html.

Hirsch, Arnold R. *Making the Second Ghetto: Race and Housing in Chicago 1940–1960.* Chicago, IL: University of Chicago Press, 2009.

Pacyga, Dominic. *Chicago: A Biography.* Chicago, IL: University of Chicago Press, 2011.

Pacyga, Dominic, and Ellen Skerrett. *Chicago, City of Neighborhoods: Histories and Tours.* Chicago, IL: Loyola Press, 1986.

Thrasher, Frederic Milton. *The Gang: A Study of 1,313 Gangs in Chicago.* Chicago, IL: University of Chicago Press, 1963.

BRIGHTON BEACH-SHEEPSHEAD BAY (BROOKLYN, NEW YORK)

Russians ranked last among the top-10 largest immigrant groups in New York City in 2010. The Brighton Beach-Sheepshead Bay area, also known as "Little Odessa," includes the neighborhoods of West Brighton, Brighton Beach, Sheepshead Bay-Gerritsen Beach-Manhattan Beach, is a well-established Russian community in New York City. Today, these neighborhoods are home to 20,066 Russian immigrants, or over a quarter of the total Russian immigrants in the city as of 2011, boasting the largest concentration of Russians and vibrant co-ethnic institutions.

History of Brighton Beach-Sheepshead Bay

Developed by William Engemann in the late 1870s, Brighton Beach-Sheepshead Bay area was designed as a seaside resort. Although not intended to attract Jewish

The Little Odessa enclave in Brooklyn, New York, also known as the Brighton Beach-Sheepshead Bay area, is a community made up of Russian immigrants. (Hohlfeld/ullstein bild via Getty Images)

residents, it became a popular residential neighborhood among Jews who moved into the area when the housing facilities and public transportation infrastructures were built. However, after World War II, especially during the economic downturn in the 1970s, a lot of young Jews moved out of the neighborhood. During the same time, an influx from the third wave of Jews from Russia began, including those escaping the hostile atmosphere toward Jews from the former Soviet Union. (The first wave was between the 1880s and 1910s; the second wave occurred right after World War II.) The fourth and most recent wave of Soviet Jews came afterwards, driven by their desire to reunify with their family here and also avoid the detrimental impact after Chernobyl nuclear power plant accident drove them away from Russia.

Upon their arrival, Brighton Beach-Sheepshead Bay became these new immigrants' first choice because the majority of them settled in New York City with the aid of New York Association for New Americans (NYANA), which listed Brighton Beach-Sheepshead Bay as one of their top housing recommendations based on its affordable price, proximity to the sea, and convenient access to transportation and the well-established Eastern European Jewish community. Since the 1980s, Brighton Beach-Sheepshead Bay became the largest Russian community, often called "Little Odessa." Brighton Beach Avenue is the main commercial strip and lies at the heart of this ethnic community.

Demographic Profiles

Brighton Beach-Sheepshead Bay is predominantly white. In 2010, the white population accounted for 73% of the total population, followed by Asians and Hispanics (another 20%), whereas the black population was fewer than 5%. Across the three neighborhoods, West Brighton had the largest share of Russians as a percentage of the overall population (31.4%) in 2010, followed by Brighton Beach and Sheepshead Bay. Except for Brighton Beach, the other two neighborhoods witnessed an increase in the share of Russians in overall population, which implies the expansion of Russian Jewish community into these adjacent neighborhoods. In 2010, nearly 40% of total residents in Brighton Beach-Sheepshead Bay area held a bachelor's degree or higher, which is higher than the city average, and only 13.4% reported not having a high school education. These statistics reflect Russian immigrants' relatively high level of education. In terms of income, Brighton Beach-Sheepshead Bay is a middle-class neighborhood. Specifically, 31.6% of the total households reported an annual household income between $20,000 and $49,999 in 2010, whereas another 29.1% reported earning between $50,000 and $99,999.

Culture and Religion

Brighton Beach is an oceanside neighborhood with easy access to the beach. Jewish culture began to take over Brighton Beach-Sheepshead Bay with the arrival of Jewish immigrants at the turn of the 20th century. A Yiddish theater, vibrant restaurants, a dance hall, and a horse-racing track represented this area's entertainment offerings. Among local residents, catering to visitors escaping the hot weather as a summer resort also became a popular business. The main synagogue did not exist until 1923, when residents raised funds to create the Hebrew Alliance of Brighton by the Sea.

The arrival of formerly Soviet newcomers brought Russian cultural elements to this area in the 1990s. Grocery stores sold packaged goods in Russian style. An array of specialty Russian desserts, such as *smetannik* (a Russian sour cream cake) and *korolevsky* cake (a three-layer cake with each layer a different flavor—chopped walnuts, poppy seeds, and cocoa powder), are available in Russian bakeries. Russian restaurants along the beach provide a unique dining experience, mixing seaside scenery with delicate Russian cuisine, such as borscht soup and chicken cutlet with roasted vegetables. Ukrainian food is perhaps the most common fare representative of Russian identity in nightclubs in this neighborhood. For example, meat-, cheese-, and potato-filled dumplings are served everywhere despite the different names reflecting diverse origins given to this dish (Orleck 2013, p. 109). Despite the geographically different origins, these restaurants are quite similar in terms of decoration, which often features "groaning banquet tables covered with zakuski (appetizers) flowers and elaborate place settings" (Orleck 2013, p.109). Vodka is indispensable during the meal. Finally, nightclubs are another important feature of Russian community life in Brighton Beach-Sheepshead Bay.

Little Odessa

Little Odessa's fabled mafia activity was depicted in the 1995 film *Little Odessa*, a crime drama which follows the activity of the Shapira family. Actor Tim Roth plays Joshua Shapira, a hit man who has been disowned from his family for committing murder. However, in the film, Joshua decides to return to his home neighborhood of Little Odessa for another hit job. There, he is confronted by his abusive father, works to make amends with his dying mother, and reconnects with his younger brother. Surrounding the drama are references to the larger immigrant culture of Odessa, such as a score with Russian music and comments about the Shapiras' Jewish upbringing.

The film received mixed reviews. Film critic Roger Ebert commented that the family drama aspect of the film's plot seemed an awkward afterthought, implemented as a device to distinguish an otherwise banal crime drama. While the film had some bright spots and good performances, Ebert wrote in his review that an inexperienced director likely contributed to the film feeling overdone and forced (Ebert 1995). In contrast, Caryn James, writing for the *New York Times*, found the film superbly acted and well-shot overall. While the film's reception was mixed, a common theme from reviewers was an appreciation of the character and interest Little Odessa's setting lent to the film.

Marena Cole

However, these Soviet Jews also had a hard time integrating with the existing traditional Jews here at the beginning, as the presence of their Jewish tradition was quite scarce largely due to the repression of Jews in Russia, where practicing Judaism was strictly forbidden. This disparity often gave rise to the argument among these two groups about "authenticity" of Jewish practices.

Political Life

Russian Jews have a long history of participating in American politics. Although they are regarded as rather conservative in terms of political views, most are registered as Democrats, and they remain a swing voting bloc. The economy and Israel tend to be their two biggest concerns when making political decisions. For example, in the 2011 special election for the 9th Congressional District in New York (Brooklyn-Queens), Republican candidate Bob Turner won the seat largely due to support from local Russian Jews who believed that Republicans would do a better job in boosting the economy in the aftermath of a major recession. Similarly, Russian Jews are emotionally affected by Israel-related affairs, as more than 80% of them have relatives or distant relatives in Israel. Among local organizations, the American Jewish Committee, established in 1906, is one of the most active Jewish political associations. It initially launched a lot of programs to protect Russian Jews from anti-Semitism. Its firm support of Israel's security and well-being is respected among Russian Jews.

See also in New York: Bedford-Stuyvesant (Brooklyn, New York); Borough Park/ Williamsburg/Crown Heights, Jewish Enclaves (Brooklyn, New York); Brooklyn, West Indian Enclave (New York); Chinatowns (Manhattan; Sunset Park East, Brooklyn; Flushing, Queens) (New York City); Coney Island (Brooklyn, New York); Crown Heights, Jamaican Enclave (Brooklyn, New York); Five Points (New York City); Greenpoint (Brooklyn, New York); Greenwich Village (New York City); Harlem (New York City); Harlem, Senegalese Enclave (New York City); Hell's Kitchen (New York City); Jackson Heights (Queens, New York); Jackson Heights, South Asian Enclave (Queens, New York); Little Brazil Street (Manhattan, New York); Little India, Jackson Heights (Queens, New York); Little Italy (Manhattan, New York); Lower East Side (New York City); Sleepy Hollow, Ecuadorian Enclave (New York); Staten Island, Sri Lankan Enclave (New York City); Sunset Park West and North Corona (New York City); Washington Heights (New York City); Yorkville, German Enclave (New York City)

See also Russian/Ukrainian Enclaves: Coney Island (Brooklyn, New York); Nikolaevsk, Russian Enclave (Alaska)

Van C. Tran and Mengying Li

Further Reading

Ebert, Roger. "Little Odessa." *Rogerebert.com*, June 2 1995. Accessed November 6, 2016. http://www.rogerebert.com/reviews/little-odessa-1995.

James, Caryn. "FILM REVIEW; Russian Emigre Family With a Son in the Mob." *The New York Times,* May 19 1995. Accessed November 6, 2016. http://www.nytimes.com/movie /review?res=990CE5D6143EF93AA25756C0A963958260.

Kasinitz, Philip, John H. Mollenkopf, Mary C. Waters, and Jennifer Holdaway. *Inheriting the City: The Children of Immigrants Come of Age.* Cambridge, MA: Harvard University Press and the Russell Sage Foundation, 2008.

Kliger, S. "Russian-Jewish Immigrants in the U.S.: Social Portrait, Challenges, and AJC Involvement." American Jewish Committee, 1995. Accessed November 1, 2016. http:// www.ajcrussian.org/site/apps/nlnet/content2.aspx?c=chLMK3PKLsF&b=7718799&ct =11713359.

Lobo, A. P., and J. J. Salvo. *The Newest New Yorkers: Characteristics of the City's Foreign-born Population.* New York: New York City Department of City Planning, 2013.

Orleck, A. "The Continuing Russification of Jewish New York." In Nancy Foner, ed. *One Out of Three: Immigrants in New York in the Twenty-first Century.* New York: Columbia University Press, 2013.

BRONZEVILLE (CHICAGO, ILLINOIS)

Bronzeville is the name given to a historically African American neighborhood on Chicago's South Side. For much of the mid-20th century, Bronzeville was one of the most important centers of African American literature, music, and culture in the United States. Like many urban centers and many African American neighborhoods,

The Forum, an entertainment venue in the Bronzeville neighborhood of Chicago. Bronzeville was one of the most important centers of African American literature, music, and culture in the United States. It suffered from decay and poverty in the latter part of the century, but in recent decades a revitalization effort has begun to bring Bronzeville back. (Jim Roberts/Dreams time.com)

it suffered from decay and poverty in the latter part of the century, but in recent decades a revitalization effort has begun to bring Bronzeville back, in large part through a focus on the neighborhood's vibrant historical legacy.

Bronzeville's story begins in the late 1800s, with a small African American community known as the Black Belt. Like most northern cities before the World War I, Chicago's African American population was relatively small; only around 30,000 by 1900. Among its most notable early residents was the crusading journalist and anti-lynching activist Ida B. Wells-Barnett, who moved to Chicago from Memphis to escape threats on her life. Her activism during Chicago's Columbian Exposition of 1893 showed the growing consciousness of Chicago's black community as it protested the lack of inclusion of African American culture and history in the Exposition's exhibits.

The Black Belt, as it was known in the early decades of the 20th century, resembled a "city within a city." In part due to the intentional marginalization of black Chicagoans by the rest of the city, the Black Belt developed its own institutions quickly; in 1908, Jesse Binga opened the city's first African American–owned bank, which invested in black businesses throughout the neighborhood. The most notable publication of the period was the *Chicago Defender* newspaper, founded in 1905 by Robert S. Abbott. It was in part Abbott's regular reporting on the horrors of Southern life that helped set the stage for one of Chicago's greatest demographic shifts.

During and after World War I, African Americans by the hundreds of thousands began an exodus out of the South to escape the violence and terror of Jim Crow racial segregation and find better opportunities for themselves and their children. This exodus, often referred to as the Great Migration, eventually brought nearly half of the nation's African American population north of the Mason-Dixon line, with most migrants settling in urban centers as they sought manufacturing and industrial jobs in a booming wartime market. Chicago was one of the cities whose black population grew most dramatically, due to its geographical position at the end of the Illinois Central Railroad, a line that stretched from Chicago along the Mississippi River into Mississippi and Louisiana, as well as its growing industrial sector. As a result of this migration, by 1920 the city's black population stood at nearly 110,000, a jump of over 350% over the course of 20 years.

This rapid influx of African American workers and families exacerbated racial tension within Chicago, as indeed it did throughout the country. In 1919, just after the end of the World War I, racial violence struck cities across the United States, the deadly result of renewed xenophobia and isolationism that grew after the war, mixed with the demographic changes of African Americans leaving the South. In places as far from each other as Omaha, Washington, D.C., and Chicago, black migrants found themselves under attack.

Chicago's riot—the most destructive and deadly of that "Red Summer" of 1919—began with a small mistake: Eugene Williams, a young boy swimming in Lake Michigan near the Twenty-Fifth Street Beach, accidentally crossed the invisible line separating the unofficially segregated lakefront. As he swam into the "white" area, a man on shore began throwing rocks in his direction. One rock struck Williams in the head, knocking him unconscious and drowning him. When the Chicago police refused to arrest the culprit, local African Americans began to protest and were then attacked by white mobs, primarily drawn from the city's large Irish working class, with whom racial tensions were already high. In the violence that followed, 38 Chicago citizens, 23 of whom were black, were killed. The riots only ended with the arrival of 6,000 members of the National Guard.

The riots reflected a larger unease in Chicago over the influx of African Americans. In 1917, only a decision by the U.S. Supreme Court kept Chicago's Real Estate Board from seeking zoning laws that would have created race-based housing areas; when that effort failed, "restrictive covenants"—contractual agreements between homeowners that prevented them from leasing or selling to African Americans—were often put in place. Violence, too, was used to prevent African American settlement outside of the South Side. The 1919 riots were an outgrowth of that tension: black growth in a city that viewed such a migration as an invasion of sorts. Reacting to the wave of violence and repression, Illinois Governor Robert Lowden created a commission to examine the issue of race in Chicago. The Commission's report made specific, community-level suggestions—more equitable policing, encouragement toward white homeowners to accept integrated neighborhoods, better resources in

African American neighborhood schools—but was unable to offer any larger structural solutions. The report praised public organizations that had been helping African American migrants such as the Chicago Urban League. However, it also cautioned black Chicagoans on putting too much attention on issues of race publically, exhibiting a strong bias toward quiet assimilation and integration.

Despite the riot, and the residual tension, black Chicago continued to grow rapidly. During the 1920s, Bronzeville acquired its name; although its origins are often disputed, the term refers to the skin color of the area's residents and was meant to evoke a more respectable identity than "Black Belt" often implied. African Americans in Chicago had begun to gain a modicum of political power; Oscar DePriest, who in 1915 became Chicago's first black alderman, was elected to the House of Representatives in 1928, the first African American to ever serve in that chamber. At the University of Chicago, sociologist Robert Park gathered a school of young social investigators to study the growing black center of Bronzeville from the ground. Their investigation of the social, economic, and political realities of life in black Chicago forms the foundation of much modern understanding of race and racial policy in America's cities.

The flow of migration from the south continued during the 1920s, and Bronzeville also become a center of culture; jazz took root in Chicago during the Prohibition years, as organized crime—funded by illegal liquor smuggling and sales—also funded some of the great jazz musicians of the time. Louis Armstrong was perhaps the greatest, having made his way to Chicago from New Orleans in 1922, following "King" Oliver, a jazz pioneer. Once in Chicago, Armstrong made the form his own, becoming a legendary bandleader. Because of Armstrong, as well as other important bandleaders such as Earl Hines, Bronzeville became, in the late 1920s, one of the most vibrant jazz neighborhoods in the north, on par with New York's scene.

Jazz was not the only form of artistic expression among Bronzeville's African American community during the 1920s: visual, performance, and literary artists flocked to Chicago's South Side. The Cube Theater created a window into the African American experience—both Northern and Southern—with a series of dance and performance pieces from the late 1920s to the mid-1930s. Archibald Motley, the famed portrait artist, was the biggest name in Bronzeville's growing art scene. Chicago's vibrant literary scene included Bronzeville poets and writers, such as Fenton Johnson, whose poems built a vision of ancient African wonders as a means of modern social commentary. In 1927, a young migrant by the name of Richard Wright arrived in Chicago; he too would leave his imprint on the city through his own powerful writing.

The growth of Chicago's black community meant economic opportunity as well. Bronzeville was able to develop a community economic structure that promoted black wealth and enterprise. Over the course of the 1920s, black-owned business grew; according to St. Clair Drake and Horace Cayton's groundbreaking study *Black Metropolis*, retail establishments owned by African Americans nearly doubled between 1921 and 1930, outpacing even the growth of the area's African American population. However, with the end of the 1920s came the Great Depression, spelling economic disaster for vulnerable populations such as Chicago's African Americans.

The Great Depression struck Chicago hard, but it struck Bronzeville even harder. In 1931, almost 60% of black Chicagoans were unemployed. Businesses were shuttered, and the jazz and swing opulence that had begun to take root was destroyed. Poverty and crime rose hand in hand. The center of pre-Depression Bronzeville, the intersection of Thirty-Fifth and State, emptied out, with one writer referring to it as "Bronzeville's Skid Row" as late as 1950. In large part, this was due to increasingly restrictive housing opportunities for Chicago's black population. Although African Americans had largely been restricted to the South Side before the 1930s, this had been due more to societal racism than clear structural policies. This changed with the creation of the Federal Housing Administration (FHA) in 1934. The FHA was created to attempt to alleviate the housing crisis of the early Depression by guaranteeing mortgage loans in certain situations. They created a system of lending in which banks, now dependent on federal standards for their loans, were discouraged from lending in areas characterized as "lacking homogeneity" or suffering from "an influx of a lower grade population," language clearly designed to evoke racial classification. The result of this was to threaten the ability of black Chicagoans to move up in social status. The connection between homogeneity and property value only increased white Chicago's reliance on restrictive covenants to enforce racial segregation, and black Chicago became more and more densely populated, crime-ridden, and poor; by the 1940s, population density in black Chicago stood at 90,000 per square mile, according to Drake and Cayton, while density in neighboring white areas was only 20,000 per square mile. All of these indicators only worsened in the opening years of the Depression.

However, although many modern accounts of Bronzeville's history suggest an irreversible decline following the 1929 stock market crash, historians Robert Bone and Richard A. Courage make the clear case that Bronzeville's greatest contributions to African American culture came during and after the Depression. In their book *The Muse in Bronzeville*, they point especially to the naturalist writings of black Chicago authors like Richard Wright, whose *Black Boy* and *Native Son* depict the struggles of black migrants in an inhospitable city. Wright became the center of an active literary movement in Chicago and contributed as well to sociological research conducted by the University of Chicago, helping to cement 1930s and 1940s Bronzeville as—as Bone and Courage call it—"comparable in historical significance to the Harlem Renaissance."

Much of this "Bronzeville Renaissance" was spurred on by Franklin Roosevelt's New Deal legislation. The Works Progress Administration and other employment programs provided jobs for much of Bronzeville's previously jobless population; in particular, the WPA's artistic programs—The Federal Writers Project, Federal Theater Project, and others—funded African American cultural expression throughout the latter half of the 1930s. It was in this atmosphere that Wright extended his writing, from the semi-autobiographical novels that made him famous to the ambitious works of sociological art that examined the migrant experience in documentary detail. It was also in this atmosphere that poets such as Gwendolyn Brooks used

Bronzeville as inspiration. Her most famous collection, *A Street in Bronzeville*, was published in 1945 and was praised for its high-minded yet realistic portrayals of daily struggle.

Just two years before Brooks published *A Street in Bronzeville*, a young blues musician named Muddy Waters arrived in Chicago hoping to hit it big in the city's burgeoning recording industry. Waters was far from the first blues musician to come to Chicago; the best known before him was "Big Bill" Broonzy, a star of the late 1920s and 1930s. Broonzy helped Waters get his start on the Chicago club circuit. Once Waters had established himself—in part through the adoption of the electric guitar, a relatively new invention—he signed on to Chess Records. Chess soon became the center of Chicago's music world, as well as the beating heart of electric blues, R&B, and eventually rock and roll.

Outside of the rollicking blues scene, Chicago itself experienced a boom after World War II, as did so many American cities. Bronzeville, however, received little of that prosperity. The slums created by the Great Depression persisted, and as urban renewal swept the country, some of Bronzeville's oldest areas were bulldozed to make way for large housing projects. The largest of these was the Robert Taylor Homes, built in 1962 and named for one of Chicago's most prominent black citizens. The Taylor Homes became notorious for unemployment, crime, and narcotics usage.

As the Taylor Homes were being built, Bronzeville became the center of battles over racial integration in Chicago housing. Redlining (the denial of financial services) and its legacy continued to restrict African Americans in Chicago (and in other major U.S. cities) to tracts of land suffering from high degrees of poverty, density, and crime; however, any attempt to move out of those areas—either into neighboring areas of Chicago itself or into the booming post–World War II suburbs (most of which were entirely white by practice and custom if not law) was met with fierce resistance. In 1965, Martin Luther King Jr. visited Chicago in an attempt to bring his nonviolent Civil Rights approach to bear on Chicago's housing issues. Upon his arrival, he was shocked at the vitriol leveled at him by white citizens of Chicago, remarking later that it was the worst treatment he'd received anywhere, including the South. His visit, and the reaction to it, showed the deep divisions in Chicago's patterns of settlement, many of which persist today.

Rising crime and poverty in Bronzeville's housing projects reversed Bronzeville's status as a center of black culture in the United States after 1950. In the last several decades of the 20th century, Bronzeville gained a reputation as one of Chicago's most troubled neighborhoods. Gang activity increased steadily in the 1980s, as occupancy rates declined throughout the area. In 1986, the area was declared a National Historic Place due to its contributions to African American culture, but it was not until the 1990s that serious efforts to rehabilitate the area began.

In 1998, the City of Chicago published plans to redevelop the Bronzeville area. Many of the largest housing projects, including the Robert Taylor Homes and the Ida Wells Homes, were demolished in favor of smaller townhouses and mixed-use facilities meant to spur investment and settlement. There have been signs of success; affluent residents have been moving back to Bronzeville, and unlike participants in other urban revitalization projects, many of those moving in are African

American rather than white, allowing Bronzeville to avoid the sometimes problematic racial elements of gentrification. However, as a recent study in Urban Affairs Review points out, Bronzeville's redevelopment has not been proceeding as quickly as those in neighboring areas, in part due to the neighborhood's lingering reputation for being crime-ridden and impoverished. Still, efforts continue to promote Bronzeville as an area rich in historical legacy and business potential. Many of the neighborhood's landmark buildings have been restored. Tourism, especially for those interested in the musical and artistic legacy of Bronzeville, is bringing in money to the area.

See also in Illinois: Andersonville (Chicago, Illinois); Bridgeport (Chicago, Illinois); Chicago, Mexican and Puerto Rican Enclaves (Illinois); Little India (Chicago, Illinois); Pilsen (Chicago, Illinois)

See also African American Enclaves: Baldwin Hills (Los Angeles, California; Bedford-Stuyvesant (Brooklyn, New York); Black Bottom (Philadelphia, Pennsylvania); Greenwood (Tulsa, Oklahoma); Harlem (New York City); Harlem, Senegalese Enclave (New York City); Historic South Central (Los Angeles, California); Ironbound and the Wards (Newark, New Jersey); Lewiston and Portland, Somali and Bantu Enclaves (Maine); Little Ethiopia (Los Angeles, California); Lower Ninth Ward (New Orleans, Louisiana); Lower Roxbury, African American Enclave (Massachusetts); Mattapan (Boston, Massachusetts); Orange Mound (Memphis, Tennessee); Roxbury, African-American Enclave (Massachusetts); Sweet Auburn (Atlanta, Georgia); Tremé (New Orleans, Louisiana); Watts (Los Angeles, California)

Andrew Lipsett

Further Reading

Anderson, M. B., and C. Sternberg. ""Non-White" Gentrification in Chicago's Bronzeville and Pilsen: Racial Economy and the Intraurban Contingency of Urban Redevelopment." *Urban Affairs Review* 49, no. 3 (December 2013): 435–67. doi:10.1177/1078087412465590.

Bone, Robert, and Richard A. Courage. *The Muse in Bronzeville: African American Creative Expression in Chicago, 1932–1950.* New Brunswick, NJ: Rutgers University Press, 2011.

"Bronzeville Area Residents' and Commerce Council." Bronzeville Area Residents' and Commerce Council. Accessed October 14, 2016. http://www.thebarcc.org/history.php.

Chicago Magazine. "Why Are Pilsen and Bronzeville Redeveloping at Different Speeds?" Chicago Magazine Real Estate Neighborhoods. Accessed October 14, 2016. http://www.chicagomag.com/Radar/Deal-Estate/January-2013/Why-Are-Pilsen-and-Bronzeville-Redeveloping-at-Different-Speeds.

"Chicago's Bronzeville Keeps Fighting for Revitalization—Next City." Accessed October 14, 2016. http://nextcity.org/daily/entry/gentrification-revitalization-chicago-bronzeville-progress.

City of Chicago, Bronzeville Redevelopment Plan and Project, June 9, 1998.

Commission on Chicago Landmarks, "The Black Metropolis-Bronzeville District." Submitted March 1984; recommended August 1997.

Drake, St. Clair, and Horace R. Cayton. *Black Metropolis; a Study of Negro Life in a Northern City.* New York: Harper & Row, 1962.

Dyja, Tom. *The Third Coast: When Chicago Built the American Dream*. Reprint ed. New York: Penguin Books, 2014.

United States National Park Service. "Chicago's Black Metropolis—Reading: National Register Nomination." Accessed October 14, 2016. http://www.nps.gov/nr/twhp/wwwlps/lessons/53black/53factsr.htm.

Wilkerson, Isabel. *The Warmth of Other Suns: The Epic Story of America's Great Migration*. New York: Random House, 2010.

BROOKLYN, WEST INDIAN ENCLAVE (NEW YORK)

Central Brooklyn, including the neighborhoods of Flatbush, East Flatbush, Crown Heights, Canarsie, Rugby-Remsen Village, Prospect Lefferts Gardens-Wingate, Flatlands and Erasmus, accommodates the greatest concentration of West Indians in New York City. Specifically, Crown Heights is the home to the largest population of foreign-born immigrants from Trinidad and Tobago; Flatbush is the home to the largest population of foreign-born Haitians; and Canarsie is the home to the second-largest population of persons born in Jamaica. Taken together, Central Brooklyn provides a unique window into the social lives of these ethnic groups and how their presence has reshaped race relations in inner-city neighborhoods. More so than any other post-1965 immigrant groups, West Indian immigrants and their children not only complicate our conceptions of race, but also highlight the significant diversity that exists within the black community.

History of Central Brooklyn

West Indians have a long history of migration to both the United States and the United Kingdom. This tradition is largely due to the economic situation in their home countries, which are scarce in natural resources and notorious for unstable social and political environment. For example, countries like Haiti are plagued by corruption. The United States is at the top of their migration destination list because of its proximity to their homelands and is also widely acknowledged as a "promising" land among West Indian communities. New York City has long been a favored destination among West Indians because it is home to the largest concentration of West Indians in the country (Kasinitz 1992).

As a former European colony, Central Brooklyn used to be a predominantly white community and saw the subsequent waves of Dutch and Jewish immigrants arriving prior to the 1900s. The first West Indian immigrants came to New York City in the early 20th century. Due to racial segregation, the West Indian first generation mainly settled in Central Harlem and the Bedford-Stuyvesant section of Brooklyn. These were traditionally African American neighborhoods and West Indians were subjected to similar social discrimination against blacks. Since 1965, West Indians began to develop their own ethnic community in Central Brooklyn, where housing became affordable and available for West Indians despite the prevalent discriminant housing policy against blacks in New York City. West Indians maintained their traditional emphasis on family ties by bringing their family and relatives into the United States, which further enhanced the dominance of West Indians in these neighborhoods. Similar to many other neighborhoods, the post-1965 influx of immigrants in Central Brooklyn accompanied the exodus of white residents to the suburbs. However, Crown Heights, the earliest and most diverse West Indian neighborhood in New York City, also saw the increase in the Orthodox Jewish community. The neighborhood's image as a West Indian enclave was further strengthened when "Flatbush U.S.," a radio station sponsored by West Indian merchants, was set up to broadcast news and experiences of local West Indian immigrants.

Since 2014, Central Brooklyn has been undergoing another rapid wave of gentrification and renewal. In addition to West Indians, significant numbers of young professionals have also come to the neighborhood in search of better housing as the more established and gentrified areas of Williamsburg and Green Point in Brooklyn became increasingly unaffordable.

Beyond Central Brooklyn, significant numbers of West Indians also live in Queens Village, St. Albans, and Cambria Heights, middle-class neighborhoods in Queens. In addition, they are also found in Woodlawn, Wakefield, Williamsbridge, and Eastchester, lower-middle-class neighborhoods in the North Bronx.

Demographic Profiles

Central Brooklyn is a predominantly black area; its overall racial composition has not changed significantly over the last decade. In 2010, the black population, including both West Indians and African Americans, made up 69.7% of the total population, followed by whites (10.7%) and Hispanics (10.3%). Across the eight neighborhoods of Central Brooklyn, there was significant variation in the concentration of West Indians in 2010, ranging from a high of 51.4% in East Flatbush to a low of 26.3% in Crown Heights. Over the last decade, the share of the West Indian population has significantly increased, with the exception of Crown Heights South and Prospect Lefferts Gardens. The most dramatic growth was in Canarsie, where the West Indian population increased by 150% from 33% in 2000 to 46.7% of the total population in 2010.

The majority of the population of Central Brooklyn in 2010 reported having a high school education or less, although about a quarter also reported having a bachelor's degree or more. More generally, West Indians are well known for their focus on education, which is often pointed to as evidence for their relative success and advantage over African Americans. West Indian parents tend to be more involved in their children's education, providing both parental support and supervision. In 2010, about a quarter of Central Brooklyn residents reported annual household income below $20,000, whereas only 15.4% reported household income above $100,000.

Culture and Religion

The Western Indian Parade, also called West Indian Carnival, is held annually, on the first Monday of September, in Crown Heights. It enjoys a reputation as one of the largest ethnic festivals in the New York City. It aims to pay homage to traditional culture and show the pride in achievements abroad. Almost one million revelers dressed up in outrageous costumes decorated with colorfully glazed features wore the traditional ghost masks, proudly waved their national flags, and danced to loud traditional music along Eastern Parkway all the way from Schenectady Avenue to Grand Army Plaza to celebrate the 2013 parade. There were also extraordinary pre-parade events held on the weekends before the parade. For example, J'ouvert featured thousands of revelers covered in mud, oil, paint, and fancy costumes dancing all night and into the morning.

Street vendors and restaurants lining the streets sell traditional West Indian food. One of the most popular foods is a Jamaican patty with a thin flaky crust encasing a flavor-filled interior of spicy ground beef. Doubles is another common street food in Trinidad and Tobago. It is a sandwich made with turmeric-hued fry filled with curried chick peas. Calypso and soca, the traditional form of West Indian music, played with a mix of instruments, including a piano, a small orchestra, and sometimes a drum and hand clapping, are known for their fast beat, heavy percussion, and social expression.

Entertainment is also a large part of West Indians' life in New York. Cricket and soccer enjoy the most popularity among West Indians. Tim Hector, an Antiguan politician, once said that "Cricket and cricket alone provided the medium in popular sports, through which we could take an English institution and transform it, recreate it in our own image and likeness, and stamp our personality on it." Soccer is especially attractive to Haitians. They conduct championship games against Latin American and American games on weekends in Brooklyn that attract a big Haitian audience. Another important entertainment for Haitian Americans is Saturday evening dancing, either private or public, providing a great platform for networking and reinforcing ethnic identity (Laguerre 1984).

West Indians are also well known for their strong attachment to their homeland. For example, barrel shipping is a common business in Central Brooklyn. It serves the West Indian community's need to ship goods (usually packed in barrels) home. Besides the physical remittance, monetary transfers are also an important way for West Indians to be supportive of their families in their homelands. For example, remittances account for nearly 15% of GDP in Jamaica in 2011 (Forbes 2013).

Ethnic Economy

Similar to other groups, a small portion of West Indians lack legal status and are locked out of jobs in the formal sector. Instead, they rely on underground and off-the-book jobs such as dishwashing, and they endure seedy working conditions and lower-than-average wages. It is also common for West Indians to seek work through the ethnic network, that is, their family and friends, who are often willing to assist new immigrants in preparing for job interviews or to act as references.

A lot of West Indian families are "matrifocal," and women play an important role in supporting the family. West Indian women are prominent in the job market, and most of them have jobs in education, health care, and domestics. They are popular among the professional fields because of their professional skills, cultural background, language familiarity, and their motivation to pursue a high educational degree to further qualify them in these areas. Among those without professional credentials, West Indian women are concentrated in domestic work either as maids or nannies for other professional, often white, families.

In contrast, West Indian men are concentrated both in construction and security guards, along with other professional occupations. In addition, they are also known for their jitney van business (also known as commuter van or dollar van). The business is developed to make up for the slow and inconvenient New York public transportation system and is also deeply rooted in their culture from the islands. Although met with objection in the beginning, this business was eventually legalized due to the lobbying efforts of West Indian politicians.

Political Life

According to Henke (2001), there are three types of political leading powers among West Indian community: one is mainly comprised of the middle class; one is represented by ethnicity entrepreneurs; and one is made up of young, radical politicians enthusiastically pursuing political careers.

Dr. Lamuel Stanislaus, arriving in the United States in the early 1900s, is one of the representative politicians from the middle class. Though not deliberately taking the leadership in West Indian politics in Brooklyn, he devoted himself to uniting the conflicted ethnic organizations to focus on the welfare of West Indian communities. He also did a lot of work in support of West Indian candidates in political campaigns. His political influence was exerted in two ways: one is the U.S. political realm regarding West Indian immigrants; the other is the political impact of West Indian migrants on their home countries. Due to his friendship with Herbert Blaize, the former prime minister in Grenada, he was nominated ambassador of Grenada to the United Nations.

Dr. Roy A. Hastick Sr. is a prominent member in business and civic politics from the working class. As a founder of Caribbean American Chamber of Commerce and Industry, (CACCI), he tirelessly advocated for the development of small businesses run by West Indian immigrants and also actively supported two-way trade between West Indian countries and the United States, especially when he was elected as a delegate to the 1995 White House Conference on Small Business. He was devoted to addressing racial harmony and to Brooklyn's Crown Heights community where he serves as First Vice Chairman of Community Board #9. He also emphasized the power of media in promoting West Indian businesses. He once published the West Indian Tribune and made public speeches over the "Business and You," a business radio. In 1986, he received the Immigrant of the Year Award from Brooklyn Borough President Honorable Howard Golden, the West Indian American Achievers Award for contributions to the growth and development of West Indians in the United States and in the Caribbean region, and the Ron Brown Leadership Award for business development.

The third type of political power is relatively loose and its members are devoted to the idea of black empowerment. Compared to the other two political groups, these radial activists only seemed to have strong leadership in West Indian political community when certain events affected their society. Colin Moore, a Guyana-born lawyer, used to live in Crown Heights and was the cofounder of Caribbean Action lobby, an organization aiming at making the voice of their community heard. He is also passionate about politics and once ran for a city council seat representing the East Flatbush neighborhood.

Social Problems

Jews and West Indians often exist in harmony despite the fact that most West Indians are still wary of the "black-Jewish difference" (Goldschmidt 2006, p. 6). Periodically, this difference has been aggravated in racial riots and violence. The most infamous incident was the Crown Heights riot in 1991, which was the peak of conflicts between the black and Jewish communities. This three-day riot began after a car, owned by the leader of Lubavitch community, killed a Guyanese immigrant in a controversial accident and an Australian orthodox Jewish was stabbed intentionally by a young black man. Although the tension has been much eased two decades after the incident, Crown Heights today is still infamous for its racial integration problem.

Racial conflict with West Indians is not limited to Jews, but also among whites in general. To many white Americans, West Indians are often visible as "blacks" but invisible as "immigrants," despite the effort to declare their ethnicity to distinguish themselves from African Americans (Waters 1999). Similarly, Vickerman (2013) attributes this situation to the disparity between how West Indians regard themselves, in an ethnic sense, and how the society treats them, in a racial sense.

Gang violence and mugging are two other challenges that Crown Heights residents still face. For example, the day of the Western Indian Parade has often been under the shadow of shootings and street crime. In 2003, one person was shot and one other was stabbed; in 2005, one person was shot; in 2006, one person was shot and another was stabbed; in 2007, one person was shot in the leg, and the other was fatally shot; in 2011, four people were shot during the parade; in 2012, three people were shot and two were fatally stabbed; in 2013, two people were murdered and three were injured in several shootings. Teen gangs are a serious concern for parents in Crown Heights, too. Some of these gangs, organized by West Indian or African American teens, mainly target the Jewish population. For example, several muggings targeting Jews turned out to be connected with these gangs. Brower Park has turned into a headquarters for gang activities.

Poverty and health are two other concerns. Bedford Stuyvesant-Crown Heights have rather high rates of poverty. Similarly, Flatbush-East Flatbush, with a moderate poverty rate, reported the second highest elevated blood lead levels in New York City and the fifth highest severe crowding rate (Furman Center 2012). Flatbush also suffers from severe health problems: more than 1 in 4 adults in Flatbush are obese, and more than half of adults report that they do no physical activity at all (New York City Department of Health and Mental Hygiene 2006).

Make Futbol, Not Riots

Racial tensions in Crown Heights were running high and eventually imploded in summer of 1991. A motorcade carrying the grand rabbi of the Lubavitch Hasidic movement, Menachem M. Schneerson, "accidently struck a 7-year old son of Guyanese immigrants, Gavin Cato" (Berger 2014). The anger quickly turned into riots as Americans of Caribbean descent rampage through the streets, attacking Hasidic Jews. Yankel Rosenbaum, a Hasidic Jew, was stabbed and killed during the Crown Heights riots. Black residents claimed that the police and government service officials gave preferential treatment to Hasidim residents.

However, in 2014, just as the World Cup was beginning, an informal soccer match took place between the two communities. The match was sponsored by the local police precinct. According to the *New York Times*, "Hasidic women with strollers watched a brass band, the Brooklyn Legion of Sound Marching Band, perform boisterous tunes while a few yards away Hasidic men grilled glatt kosher hot dogs and hamburgers for a line of black and Hasidic children."

Furthermore, the *New York Times* reported that Tony Wright, 48, a Jamaican soccer player who during the week paints apartments for a Hasidic landlord, said that the game demonstrated how "we try to get along. Some of them are skeptical of us," he said of the Hasidim. "But we cool eventually" (Berger 2014).

Notable People

Edwidge Danticat is a Haitian American author and grew up in Flatbush. Her first novel *Breath, Eyes, Memory* was selected for Oprah's Book Club and was featured in the *New York Times Magazine* as one of the "30 under 30" people to watch. Al Roker, whose parents are of West Indian origins, is a television weather forecaster on NBC's *Today* and lives in Canarsie.

See also in New York: Bedford-Stuyvesant (Brooklyn, New York); Borough Park/Williamsburg/Crown Heights, Jewish Enclaves (Brooklyn, New York); Brighton Beach-Sheepshead Bay (Brooklyn, New York); Chinatowns (Manhattan; Sunset Park East, Brooklyn; Flushing, Queens) (New York City); Coney Island (Brooklyn, New York); Crown Heights, Jamaican Enclave (Brooklyn, New York); Five Points (New York City); Greenpoint (Brooklyn, New York); Greenwich Village (New York City); Harlem (New York City); Harlem, Senegalese Enclave (New York City); Hell's Kitchen (New York City); Jackson Heights (Queens, New York); Jackson Heights, South Asian Enclave (Queens, New York); Little Brazil Street (Manhattan, New York); Little India, Jackson Heights (Queens, New York); Little Italy (Manhattan, New York); Lower East Side (New York City); Sleepy Hollow, Ecuadorian Enclave (New York); Staten Island, Sri Lankan Enclave (New York City); Sunset Park West and North Corona (New York City); Washington Heights (New York City); Yorkville, German Enclave (New York City)

See also West Indian/Jamaican Enclaves: Chicago, Mexican and Puerto Rican Enclaves (Illinois); Crown Heights, Jamaican Enclave (Brooklyn, New York); Holyoke,

Puerto Rican Enclaves (Massachusetts); Little Haiti ("La Petite Haiti"/Lemon City) (Miami, Florida); Little Havana (Miami, Florida); Little Havana on the Hudson (North Hudson, New Jersey); Washington Heights (New York City); Ybor City (Tampa, Florida)

Van C. Tran and Mengying Li

Further Reading

Berger, Joseph. "In Crown Heights, Once Torn by Race Riots, a Friendly Game of Soccer." *The New York Times*, June 8, 2014. Accessed June 24, 2016. http://www.nytimes.com /2014/06/09/nyregion/once-torn-by-riots-crown-heights-finds-harmony-in-soccer .html.

Forbes. "Best Countries for Business—Jamaica." 2013. Accessed November 2, 2016. http:// www.forbes.com/places/jamaica.

Furman Center. State of New York City's Housing and Neighborhoods. 2012. Accessed November 2, 2016. http://furmancenter.org/files/sotc/SOC2012.pdf.

Goldschmidt, H. *Race and Religion among the Chosen Peoples of Crown Heights*. New Brunswick, NJ: Rutgers University Press, 2006.

Henke, H. *The West Indian Americans*. Westport, CT: Greenwood, 2001.

Kasinitz, P. *Caribbean New York: Black Immigrants and the Politics of Race*. Ithaca, NY: Cornell University Press, 1992.

Laguerre, M. S. *American Odyssey: Haitians in New York City*. Ithaca, NY: Cornell University Press, 1984.

Lobo, A. P., and J. J. Salvo. *The Newest New Yorkers: Characteristics of the City's Foreign-born Population*. New York City Department of City Planning, 2013.

New York City Department of Health and Mental Hygiene. The Community Health Profile (Flatbush). 2006. Accessed November 2, 2016. http://www.nyc.gov/html/doh/down loads/pdf/data/2006chp-207.pdf.

Vickerman, M. "Jamaicans: Balancing Race and Ethnicity." In Nancy Foner, ed. *One Out of Three: Immigrants in New York in the Twenty-first Century*. New York: Columbia University Press, 2013.

Waters, Mary C. *Black Identities: West Indian Immigrant Dreams and American Reality*. Cambridge, MA: Harvard University Press, 1999.

BURLINGTON/WINOOSKI/DERBY LINE AND OTHER CITIES, FRENCH CANADIAN ENCLAVES (VERMONT)

Vermont has longtime close connections with French Canada. Franco-Americans—descendants of French Canadians, who were themselves descendants of French immigrants—make up the largest ethnic group in Vermont (22% in 2011) and the third-largest ethnic group (14%) in New England, after Irish Americans and Italian Americans.

After the Revolutionary War ended in 1783, French Canadians began settling in Vermont, on the shores of Lake Champlain, in small numbers. Larger groups of French Canadians fled Quebec in 1837 and 1838 in the wake of the Upper and Lower Canada Rebellions. By 1840, approximately 5,000 French Canadians lived in Vermont. Immigration continued over the next century, but as better transportation links were developed, the proportion of French Canadians remaining in Vermont fell as they migrated to larger cities in New England. Throughout the 19th century, economic pressures in Quebec, including overpopulation and lack of fertile land, continued to lead many young French Canadians to emigrate. The Industrial Revolution led to higher wages and more job opportunities in the United States, and factories in New England often actively recruited French Canadian laborers by sending agents to rural parishes in Quebec. The majority of Vermont's French Canadian immigrants worked as laborers and farmers, but in the cities a good portion worked in the trades of blacksmithing, masonry, carpentry, and shoemaking.

Like many other immigrant groups, French Canadians tended to congregate in areas where other French Canadians had already settled. This tendency and the physical proximity of Quebec preserved the immigrants' culture and language for quite some time. Local residents saw Franco-Americans in stereotypes. They were said to have great *joie de vivre* but no interest in operating outside of the Franco-American community. They valued their families and their Catholic faith. However, generations of immersion in American culture have left their impact on Franco-Americans in Vermont, only 5% of which speak another language at all. Franco-Americans have for the most part integrated into the local community.

Yet remnants of French Canadian heritage remain, as do connections to modern Quebec. Burlington, some 40 miles from the Canadian border on the shore of Lake Champlain, has long been a hub for French Canadians, both visitors and permanent residents. In recent years, Burlington has been adding French signs to its downtown area. Neighboring Winooski, once a major hub for French Canadian textile workers, began celebrating the annual French Heritage Day festival in 2006. And Derby Line, Vermont, sits right on the Canadian border, with its Canadian counterpart Rock Island across the border. The international boundary cuts right through

Beaudoin Family

For generations, the Beaudoin family has been involved in music, passing along their musical talent from generation to generation and creating one of the best-known names in French Canadian music. Louis Beaudoin, known as "one of the great Quebeçois fiddlers," was born in Lowell, Massachusetts, to a family of musicians (Chadbourne). In 1937, they moved to Burlington, Vermont, where Louis lived most of his life. After serving in World War II, Louis returned to Burlington, first as a police officer and then as the manager of an automobile repair shop—which quickly became the local hangout for fiddlers. Louis's daughter Lisa also inherited the Beaudoin talent, and the two, along with Louis's brother, performed a square dance for the Smithsonian for the inauguration of President Jimmy Carter. Throughout his life, Louis supported younger musicians and played a role in community organizations that supported the arts. His name lives on in the Beaudoin Legacy, a group of fiddlers who were inspired by Beaudoin's music.

the middle of the Haskell Free Library and Opera House; one can watch a performance on the stage on the Canadian side from the audience on the American side.

See also French Canadian Enclaves: Manchester, French Canadian Enclave (New Hampshire); Salem, French Canadian Enclave (Massachusetts); Woonsocket, French Canadian Enclave (Rhode Island)

Julianne Long

Further Reading

Beattie, Betsy. "Migrants and Millworkers: The French Canadian Population of Burlington and Colchester, 1860–1870." *Vermont History: The Proceedings of the Vermont Historical Society* 60, no. 2 (Spring 1992): 95–117.

Bélanger, Claude. "French Canadian Emigration to the United States." *Levasseur Newsletter* 14, no. 2 (July 2002): 26–30.

Chadbourne, Eugene. "Louis Beaudoin Biography & History." *AllMusic.* Accessed December 7, 2016. http://www.allmusic.com/artist/louis-beaudoin-mn0001552148.

Myall, James. "Franco-Americans in New England: Statistics from the American Community Survey." October 24, 2012. Accessed December 8, 2016. https://usm.maine.edu/sites/default/files/franco/Francoamericansinnewengland.pdf.

Resnik, Robert J. "The Beaudoin Family's Legacy." In *Legendary Locals of Burlington, Vermont*, 84. Charleston, SC: Arcadia, 2013.

Stout, Marilyn. "Where Vermont and Quebec Meld." *New York Times*, September 20, 1989, sec. Travel.

Vicero, Ralph D. "French-Canadian Settlement in Vermont Prior to the Civil War." *The Professional Geographer* 23, no. 4 (October 1971): 290–94. doi:10.1111/j.0033-0124.1971.00290.x.

Woolfson, Peter A. "The Franco-Americans of Northern Vermont: Cultural Factors for Consideration by Health and Social Services Providers." In Peter A. Woolfson and André Senécal, eds. *The French in Vermont: Some Current Views.* Burlington, VT: Center for Research on Vermont, University of Vermont, 1983.

BUTTE, IRISH AMERICANS (MONTANA)

Butte, Montana, is the nation's most Irish American city, according to the 2010 U.S. Census. As a percentage, more residents of Butte claim Irish heritage than any other city, including Boston. Out of 33,922 residents, 23.6% identify as Irish American. While historical research and popular culture has fixated on the Irish in East Coast cities like Boston and New York City, the most Irish city in America has often been overlooked.

The Great Potato Famine of 1845–1849 triggered mass migration to the United States. By 1854, more than 1.2 million Irish immigrated to the United States to escape the blight. During those years, the Irish constituted 40% of all immigrants to the United States. These new immigrants were usually Catholic and Gaelic-speaking people from rural, impoverished families. Irish immigration, however, was not merely a result of famine, as the Irish continued to make their way to the

Portrait of Irish immigrant John Hogan, a retired miner, Butte, Montana. (Library of Congress)

United States in large numbers until stricter laws halted immigration from all over Europe. Between 1856 and 1921, long after the famine's effects had worn off, roughly 3.1 million Irish had immigrated to the United States. It was these post-famine Irish immigrants who constituted Butte's Irish community.

By the late 19th century, Butte was a thriving industrial city, unrivaled for hundreds of miles in all directions. A host of immigrant groups arrived in Butte to work in the city's economic backbone, mining. Arrivals were mainly Irish and German, but Cornish, Welsh, Lebanese, Canadian, Finnish, Austrian, Serbian, Italian, Croatian, Syrian, and Chinese immigrants also settled there in significant numbers. They mined gold and silver, and later copper, to meet the growing demand for electricity.

Butte's Irish character was distinctly apparent by 1900, especially in the mines. By this time, about one-quarter of Butte's residents were Irish born or second generation Irish Americans. The Anaconda Mines alone employed 1,250 Irish-born men. It was perfectly normal to hear Gaelic in the deep copper mines. In all, a staggering 90% of the Irish in Butte worked in the mines by the turn of the century. Tracing the most common last names at this time, many of these Irishmen hailed from Beara Peninsula, in Cork County, which had a mining community. Even so, nearly all of Catholic Ireland had at least some representation in Butte. Indeed, the Irish made their homes in a number of mining cities from the coalfields of Pennsylvania to the gold mines of California.

Many of Butte's Irish lived in an enclave known as Dublin Gulch, with additional Irish settlement in adjacent areas known as Hungry Hill and Corktown, all reflective of the origins of the recent arrivals. The religious organizations also illustrated these roots; the patrons of the first two churches there were St. Patrick and St. Lawrence O'Toole. Within these communities, Irish women were crucial to the formation and perpetuation of these enclaves. In addition to caring for children, Irish women ran boarding houses, sustained Catholic churches, and raised fund for Ireland and the Irish. These communities sprang up in close proximity to the mines themselves, so even with the introduction of a street-railway system in 1887, neighborhood patterns remained largely unchanged.

By World War I, the intact Butte Irish community faced serious internal and external threats. The Butte Irish and Germans cultivated a relationship based on anti-English sentiment, and the Irish organizations opposed the growing alliance between Britain and the United States. Additionally, Butte Irish groups consistently sent funds to Ireland in order to support the independence movement. Finally, Irish strikes in 1917 left other groups suspicious of Irish patriotism, and deeply divided the Butte Irish over issues such as Irish nationalism. After the war, a depressed copper market fueled a mass exodus of miners from Butte, many of them Irish.

Though the town is no longer a thriving economic center, its ethnic and economic legacy remains. The Ancient Order of the Hibernians, an Irish fraternal organization, still operates a chapter out of Butte. There is a Tiernan Irish dancing school in Butte, as well as an Irish studies program at the nearby University of Montana-Missoula. Many Butte residents still maintain links to Irish politics and culture; the president of Ireland even visited Butte in 2006.

Butte's annual St. Patrick's Day Parade draws in about 30,000 visitors, nearly doubling the town's population for the day. The parade runs through the Uptown District and features music venues along the way. Butte is one of the few U.S. cities with lenient open-container laws, which visiting revelers take advantage of during the festivities. The Montana Gaelic Cultural Society hosts the annual An Ri Ra Music Festival in celebration of Irish music, dance, and heritage. There is even a popular local band called Dublin Gulch in homage to the original Irish enclave. The World Museum of Mining houses perhaps the largest trove of documents related to Irish America, preserving the Irish legacy in the Midwest for posterity.

See also Irish Enclaves: Hell's Kitchen (New York City); Irish Hill (Louisville, Kentucky); South Boston/Southie (Boston Massachusetts); South End (Boston, Massachusetts); West End (Boston, Massachusetts)

Katherine Anderson

Further Reading

Curran, Francis. "The Most Irish Town in America?" *The Irish Times*, March 16, 2011. Accessed December 1, 2016. http://www.irishtimes.com/news/the-most-irish-town-in-america -1.573655.

Emmons, David M. *The Butte Irish: Class and Ethnicity in an American Mining Town, 1875–1925.* Vol. 42. Champaign: University of Illinois Press, 1990.

Montana Gaelic Cultural Society. "An Ri Ra Montana Irish Festival." Accessed November 26, 2016. http://www.mtgaelic.org/an-ri-ra-montana-irish-festival.

Thomas, G. Scott. Montana City Is Unlikely Center of Irish-American Culture." *The Business Journals*, July 31, 2012. Accessed December 1, 2016. http://www.bizjournals.com/bizjournals/on-numbers/scott-thomas/2012/07/montana-city-is-unlikely-center-of.html.

CAMBODIA TOWN (LONG BEACH, CALIFORNIA)

As a part of the multicultural landscape of southern California, Cambodia Town sits on the east side of Long Beach, California, on a one-mile business corridor of Anaheim Street, between Atlantic and Juniper Avenues, south of Pacific Coast Highway and north of East Seventh Street. Long Beach is the second-largest city in Greater Los Angeles (Los Angeles is the first). Located on the Pacific Coast just south of Los Angeles, the city is the seventh largest in California, with a 2010 population of 462, 257 (U.S. Census Bureau 2010) and contains one of the busiest ports on the West Coast. Since the 1980s, Cambodia Town has developed in the eastern part of the city, bounded by Bixby Knolls and the Long Beach Airport to the north, Los Alamitos to the east, and Lomita to the west. The strip between Atlantic and Juniper contains Cambodian restaurants, grocery stores, clothing stores, jewelry stores, gift shops, auto repair shops, as well as temples, offices, creative firms, and nonprofit organizations catering to the Cambodian community. Unlike other Asian ethnic enclaves determined primarily by changing immigration laws throughout the course of the 20th century, the Cambodian American diaspora was created directly through

An art and video rental shop that features Cambodian culture on Anaheim Street in Long Beach, which has been newly designated Cambodia Town. (Luis Sinco/Los Angeles Times via Getty Images)

the policies related to the Vietnam War from 1961 to 1975, marking a parallel to many Vietnamese, Hmong, and Lao communities in the United States.

Most Cambodians arrived in the United States in the 1970s, particularly from 1975 onward. In 1975, at the end of the Vietnam War, thousands of Cambodians arrived as refugees to the United States through the Indochina Migration and Refugee Assistance Act of 1975 that resettled nearly 150,000 Vietnamese, Laotian, and Cambodian refugees. Previous to the 1975 formal end of the Vietnam War, the U.S. policy for Southeast Asian refugees featured resettlement close to their homes, but as the war ended in 1975, the United States under President Gerald Ford authorized evacuation of up to 200,000 refugees to the United States. The next large wave of migration began in 1979 with the overthrow of the Khmer Rouge. The first migrants of this generation entered through Florida, Pennsylvania, and New York, but quickly established residences and businesses in California near other Asian populations, such as Long Beach, Stockton, and Fresno, California, Lowell, Massachusetts, and other locations in Ohio, Washington, and Portland.

The total population of Cambodian Americans as of 2010 was 231, 616 (U.S. Census Bureau 2010), with the highest concentration in Long Beach and other significant populations in Lowell, Massachusetts, the Twin Cities region of Minnesota, Providence, Rhode Island, and Philadelphia, Pennsylvania. The Long Beach community is among the largest enclaves of Cambodians in the country, with 10,410 Cambodian Americans as of 2010. Since the initial waves of migration in the late

---

Problems with the 1990 U.S. Census

When results were collated and published, the 1990 U.S. Census revealed a surprisingly low amount of Cambodian residents living in Long Beach. Immediately, suspicions arose that the area had experienced an undercount. To discover why this undercount had occurred, and to generate more accurate statistics on the area's Cambodian residents, a Joint Statistical Agreement formed between the U.S. Census Bureau and the United Cambodian Community.

Researchers selected two blocks of Cambodia Town to work with. First, they spent a week and a half observing the neighborhood and gathering information about its population. Next, they spent about a month attempting to speak to all of the neighborhood's residents. Throughout this fieldwork, researchers found several difficulties endemic to surveying both Cambodian and Hispanic neighborhood residents.

Illiteracy in English on the part of adults and a heavy reliance on young people and other informal translators negatively affected the accuracy of the count. Unusual and complicated household arrangements sometimes led to confusion and inaccuracy. Fear of local criminal activity and fear of how information would be used also contributed to difficulties in conducting the census. The study concluded that these problems led to a reluctance on the part of many people in Long Beach's Cambodian and Hispanic communities to comply with census takers. Researchers used this study to suggest that these barriers be retained when collecting future censuses.

Marena Cole

1970s, family members have reunited with their relatives and local residents have integrated into local service, oil, and aerospace industries in the region. An array of community organizations, such as the Cambodian Association of America (begun in Long Beach in 1975), the Cambodian Community of Long Beach, and the Cambodian Community History and Archive Project, serve the community's needs and document its particular history. Since 2001, the idea of naming the area "Cambodia Town" was debated by city council members. It finally passed in 2007. In 2012, freeway signs listing "Cambodia Town" for the 710 thoroughfare were installed, after a naming ceremony presided over by Buddhist monks and other community leaders at the *Watt Khmer Samaki Buddhist Temple*, one of many religious and cultural organizations in the region.

See also in California: Baldwin Hills (Los Angeles, California); Boyle Heights, Jewish Neighborhood (Los Angeles, California); Boyle Heights, Latino Neighborhood (Los Angeles, California); Chinatown (Los Angeles, California); Chinatown (San Francisco, California); Chinatowns (Duplicates) (San Francisco, California); East Los Angeles, Mexican American Enclave (Los Angeles, California); El Monte, Latino Enclaves (California); Fillmore District (San Francisco, California); Gardena and Torrance (South Bay Region, Los Angeles County, California); Glendale, Armenian Enclave (California); Historic Filipinotown (Los Angeles, California); Historic South Central (Los Angeles, California); Indio, Mexican and Central American Communities (California); Japantown (San Francisco, California); Kingsburg and Sveadal, Swedish Enclaves (California); Koreatown (Los Angeles, California); Little Arabia (Anaheim, California); Little Armenia (Los Angeles, California); Little Ethiopia (Los Angeles, California); Little India/Pakistan (Artesia, California); Little Italy (Los Angeles, California); Little Italy (San Diego, California); Little Italy (San Francisco, California); Little Saigon (San Francisco, California); Little Saigon (San Jose, California); Little Saigon (Westminster, California); Little Tokyo (Los Angeles, California); Logan Heights, Mexican Enclave (San Diego, California); Los Angeles, Hawaiian Enclaves (California); Los Angeles, West Side and San Fernando Valley Jewish Enclaves (California); Mayan Corner/24th and Mission (San Francisco, California); Monterey Park, First Suburban Chinatown (California); Mount Washington, Mexican Enclave (California); National City (San Diego, California); Olvera Street/La Plaza (Los Angeles, California); Pico Rivera, Latino Enclave (California); Riverside, Mexican Enclave (California); San Bernardino, Mexican Enclave (California); San Pedro, Italian and Croatian Enclaves (California); Santa Ana, Mexican Enclaves (California); Sawtelle (Los Angeles, California); Silicon Valley, Indian and South Asian Communities (Santa Clara Valley/San Jose Region, California); Sin City (Fresno, California); Solvang, Danish Community (California); Sonoma County, Italian Enclave (California); Tehrangeles (Los Angeles, California); Temescal (Oakland, California); Thai Town (Los Angeles, California); Watts (Los Angeles, California); Yuba City, Sikh Enclave (California)

See also Cambodian Enclaves: Cambodia Town (Lowell, Massachusetts)

Neilesh Bose

Further Reading

Adebiyi, Alemat, et al. "The State of Cambodia Town." Accessed 15 July 2016. http://www
.aasc.ucla.edu/research/pdfs/cambodiatown.pdf.

Bunte, Pamela A., and Rebecca M. Joseph. "The Cambodian Community of Long Beach:
An Ethnographic Analysis of Factors Leading to Census Undercount." *Ethnographic Eval-
uation of the 1990 Decennial Census Report Series*. Long Beach, CA: United Cambodian
Community.

"Cambodia Town." Accessed July 15, 2016. http://www.cambodiatown.com/.

Lee, Jonathan H.vX. *Cambodian American Experiences: Histories, Communities, and Identities*.
Dubuque, IA: Kendall Hunt, 2010.

Mortland, Carol A. "Cambodian Resettlement in America." In Jonathan H. X. Lee, ed. *Cambodian Experiences: Histories, Communities, Cultures, and Identities*. Dubuque, IA: Kendall Hunt, 2010, pp. 76–102.

U.S. Census Bureau. "Asian Population 2010." Accessed July 15, 2016. https://www.census
.gov/prod/cen2010/briefs/c2010br-11.pdf.

U.S. Census Bureau. 2010 Decennial Census. "Long Beach, CA." Accessed 15 July 2016.
http://www.census.gov/quickfacts/table/PST045215/0643000.

CAMBODIA TOWN (LOWELL, MASSACHUSETTS)

As a part of the industrial and historic landscape of Massachusetts, Cambodia
Town sits across two square miles just below the historic Merrimack River and the
University of Massachusetts-Lowell, from Chelmsford Street west of the Lowell
Train Station, eastward to the convergence of Middlesex and Branch Streets. At a
2010 population of 108,000, Lowell is the fourth-largest city in Massachusetts,
after Boston, Worcester, and Springfield. Since the 1980s, the section between
Chelmsford and Middlesex/Branch contains Cambodian restaurants, grocery stores,
clothing stores, jewelry stores, gift shops, as well as temples, community organizations, and nonprofit organizations catering to the Cambodian community. Unlike
other Asian ethnic enclaves determined primarily by changing immigration laws
throughout the course of the 20th century, the Cambodian American diaspora
was created directly through the policies related to the Vietnam War from 1961 to
1975, marking a parallel to many Vietnamese, Hmong, and Lao communities in the
United States.

The total population of Cambodian Americans in 2010 is 276,667, with the
highest concentrations in Long Beach and in Lowell, Massachusetts, the Twin Cities region of Minnesota, Providence, Rhode Island, and Philadelphia, Pennsylvania. The Lowell population is among the largest enclaves of Cambodians in the
United States, with over 22,000 Cambodian Americans as of 2010. Since the initial waves of migration in the late 1970s, family members have reunited with their
relatives and local residents have integrated into local businesses and work in and
universities, retail, and related occupations in the region.

Founded in 1820 as a center for the industrial production of textiles, the city
became the leading center for textile production until the U.S. Civil War, but
began to decline from the early 20th century through the 1980s due to the Great

Actors in a rehearsal hall in Lowell, Massachusetts prepare for *Year Zero,* a play about the Khmer Rouge takeover of Cambodia and the subsequent refugee experience of Cambodian-Americans. (Jim Davis/The Boston Globe via Getty Images)

Depression and the loss of manufacturing to the South and other regions of the world. In the 1980s, however, with the rise of electronics industries and high-tech manufacturing, Lowell's economy bounced back, partially through the presence of diverse groups of immigrants. The city's long immigration history features communities of German, French, Swedish, Polish, and other Eastern European migrants seeking work in the cotton textile industries of the 19th centuries and early 20th centuries. But with the Great Depression and restrictive immigration policies in the early to mid-20th centuries, many of these European American communities declined severely in population. The first wave of Cambodian migrants, refugees from the Khmer Rouge regime, arrived in 1979, and consisted of 160 families. This first group of migrants created the basis for further migration in the 1980s and 1990s, as relatives of the first group joined their families. In addition, Cambodian migrants began to work in low-skill manufacturing jobs and to start businesses, as well as establish places of worship, such as the Theravada Buddhist Triraratnam Temple. By the 1980s, there were Cambodian-run video stores, grocery stores, auto repair shops, restaurants, and community organizations, such as the Cambodian Mutual Assistance Association. At the same time, many new migrants worked in the emergent fields of electronics and technology manufacturing, as well as plastics manufacturing in Lowell.

Fire Shows Community Strength, Spirit

Lowell, Massachusetts, is a densely populated city with many tightly spaced buildings and multistory apartments. Such were contributing factors to a massive fire in July 2014 that killed seven and displaced 50 residents, mostly Cambodian. Five of the victims were a family—Torn Sak, his partner Ellen Vuong, and three of their children. Two children survived.

Many local residents and members of the Cambodian community in Lowell were shaken to the core after the fire. Voop de Vulpillieres, deputy director of the Cambodian Mutual Assistance Association of Lowell, explained to the *Boston Globe* that to many Cambodian immigrants, the United States represents a safe haven once it is finally reached. It was therefore devastating for something as tragic as this fire to occur.

Yet despite anxiety and uneasiness, the community rallied to show support, incorporating Cambodian traditions into the mourning and relief process. Various well-wishers donated money to the Cambodian Mutual Assistance Association—even those who had never met and had no connection to those affected by the blaze.

The Glory Buddhist Temple organized a service and fund-raiser the Sunday after the fire, and Buddhist monks also visited the site after the blaze in order to support those who looked to spirituality to carry them through the time of crisis. In addition, the Cambodian Mutual Assistance Association worked to increase education for Cambodian residents as to how to properly maintain smoke detectors. Because electricity is not a regular feature of many Cambodian homes, Cambodian immigrants often arrive to the United States without much knowledge of household appliances, which can be a frustration within the community.

Marena Cole

As of 2010, there are approximately 200 Cambodian American businesses servicing the needs of the community as well as the broader Lowell population. Restaurants serving the spectrum of Cambodian and broader Southeast Asian cuisine, jewelry stores, clothing stores, and specialty gift shops dot the landscape from Chelmsford to Middlesex. Three Buddhist temples offer religious services in Lowell. A variety of organizations serve the community at large, such as the Cambodian Mutual Assistance Association, offering culturally appropriate social services, Metta Health Clinic of Lowell Community Health Center, featuring culturally competent healthcare, and the Angkor Dance Troupe, performing classical and folk dances for the broader community.

In 2010, the city of Lowell designated a Cambodia Town in order to officially recognize the Cambodian American community's contribution over the past three decades to Lowell. This ethnic enclave bears a history deeply connected to industrialization and de-industrialization in during the American Revolution and early America, and it continues the tradition of immigrant settlement in the region begun over a century ago.

See also in Massachusetts: Chinatown (Boston, Massachusetts); Fall River, Portuguese Enclave (Massachusetts); Framingham, Brazilian Enclave (Massachusetts);

Holyoke, Puerto Rican Enclaves (Massachusetts); Lawrence, Latino Enclaves (Massachusetts); Lower Roxbury, African American Enclave (Massachusetts); Mattapan (Boston, Massachusetts); North End (Boston, Massachusetts); Quincy, Asian Enclaves (Massachusetts); Roxbury, African American Enclave (Massachusetts); Salem, French Canadian Enclave (Massachusetts); South Boston/Southie (Boston Massachusetts); South End (Boston, Massachusetts); Watertown, Armenian Capital (Massachusetts); West End (Boston, Massachusetts)

See also Cambodian Enclaves: Cambodia Town (Long Beach, California)

Neilesh Bose

Further Reading

Crane, Brent. "At Home in Lowell." *The Phnom Penh Post*, May 23, 2015. Accessed October 2, 2016. http://www.phnompenhpost.com/post-weekend/home-lowell.

Kong, Sengla. "Cambodia Town of Lowell." *Khmer Post USA*, August 23, 2013. Accessed October 2, 2016. http://www.richardhowe.com/2013/08/23/cambodia-town-of-lowell-by-dr-sengly-kong.

Lee, Jonathan H. X. *Cambodian American Experiences: Histories, Communities, and Identities.* Dubuque, IA: Kendall Hunt, 2010.

Mortland, Carol A. "Cambodian Resettlement in America." In Jonathan H. X. Lee, ed. *Cambodian Experiences: Histories, Communities, Cultures, and Identities.* Dubuque, IA: Kendall Hunt, 2010, pp. 76–102.

U.S. Census Bureau. 2010 Decennial Census. "Lowell City, Massachusetts." Accessed October 2, 2016. http://www.census.gov/quickfacts/table/RHI425215/2537000.

U.S. Census Bureau. "Asian Population 2010." Accessed October 2, 2016. https://www.census.gov/prod/cen2010/briefs/c2010br-11.pdf.

CAMBODIAN ENCLAVES. *See* Cambodia Town (Long Beach, California); Cambodia Town (Lowell, Massachusetts)

CAPE VERDEAN/CANARY ISLANDER ENCLAVES. See Pawtucket, Cape Verdean Enclave (Rhode Island); Spanish Town (Baton Rouge, Louisiana)

CHICAGO, MEXICAN AND PUERTO RICAN ENCLAVES (ILLINOIS)

Chicago is, by almost any measure, one of the great U.S. cities—in terms of population, importance in industry and commerce, cultural offerings in the fine and popular arts, history of labor organization and struggle, and as a lodestone for migration from elsewhere in the United States and the world. With the 1890 U.S. Census, Chicago became the country's second most populous city, and would remain the "Second City" for most of the 20th century. By the time Los Angeles officially surpassed it for the second spot, with the 1990 U.S. Census, Chicago had grown from just over 1 million people to just over 3 million. To the present, it remains the third most populous city in the United States (U.S. Census Bureau 1998; U.S. Census Bureau 2010–2014).

Today, Chicago has the second-largest Hispanic/Latino population of any U.S. city outside the Southwest, surpassed only by New York City. It has the highest Mexican American population outside the Southwest, bar none. Chicago is a highly diverse city, and its Hispanic/Latino population reflects this. The city is home to thousands of Mexicans, Puerto Ricans, Cubans, and Dominicans, as well as Guatemalans, Hondurans, Salvadorans, Ecuadorians, Colombians, and Peruvians. Mexicans are by far the largest group—accounting for some three-quarters of the Hispanic/Latino population—followed by Puerto Ricans—accounting for about half the balance (U.S. Census Bureau 2009–2013).

Chicago is at the confluence of two great rivers of Latin American migration to the continental United States, from Mexico and from the Caribbean. (Note that the latter includes migration of Puerto Ricans, who are legal citizens of the United States and therefore not immigrants.) Immigrants from Mexico, and the broader population of Mexican ancestry, are concentrated in the western United States. Of the top 10 states ranked by percentage of population of Mexican heritage (by official census count), nine are in the West. The only exception is Illinois, which ranks seventh among all states. Meanwhile, migrants from the Caribbean and the broader population of Caribbean heritage are largely centered in the East. Of the top 10 states by percentage of the population from the top three Caribbean nationalities in the United States—Puerto Rican, Dominican, or Cuban—nine are in the East. (Nevada is the sole exception.) Illinois comes in 11th among all states (U.S. Census Bureau 2009–2013).

The Mexican and Puerto Rican communities in Chicago have been historically separated by their distinct national origins, the differences in the timing of their migration, the spatial patterns of their settlement in distinct neighborhoods on opposite sides of the city, and the differences in their migratory status. Against these centrifugal forces, activists have attempted to forge a broader, pan-Latino/a identity and politics of solidarity uniting Mexicans, Puerto Ricans, and other Latin Americans.

Industry, Migration, and Struggle

Chicago's growth was fueled by its role as the linchpin connecting the American West with the East. The rail lines from the West converged on Chicago, carrying the corn, wheat, cattle, and hogs from western agriculture that would be the grist for the growing industrial cities of the East. In the words of historian William Cronon, Chicago became "Nature's Metropolis": "gathering the resources and the energies of the Great West—the region stretching from the Appalachians and Great Lakes to the Rockies and the Pacific—and concentrating them in a single favored spot at the southwest corner of Lake Michigan" (Cronon 1991, p. 9). The city became a financial center, where contracts on the great flow of commodities from the West were traded. It also became an industrial center in its own right. Some of that industry grew directly out of the city's role as the entrepôt for western commodities. American poet Carl Sandburg's paean to the city begins with the words "Hog Butcher for the World." Chicago became the country's leading meatpacking center in the late 19th century, spawning industrial giants like Swift and Armour, both of which ranked among the very largest U.S. industrial companies through the 1960s (*Fortune 500*). Chicago also became (along with neighboring Gary, Indiana) one of the country's—and the world's—leading centers of steel production.

The city's industrial growth attracted migrants from the rest of the United States and the world. After the Civil War, Germany was the leading country of origin for the city's immigrants. By the end of the 19th century, immigrants were increasingly coming from Italy, Poland, Russia, and elsewhere in southern and eastern Europe (PBS, *American Experience*, "Chicago: City of the Century, Decades of Immigrants"). With the beginning of the First Great Migration, Chicago became a leading destination for African American migrants from the South. The city's African American population rose from about 40,000 in 1910 to over 800,000 in 1960 (*Encyclopedia of Chicago*, "African Americans").

Industry drew migrants into its vast and often brutal gears, provoking intense labor struggles. The battle for the eight-hour workday in the United States was centered in Chicago. The Haymarket affair—the May 4, 1886, bombing at an eight-hours rally and the subsequent trial of eight labor activists and radicals for alleged involvement—attracted worldwide attention. Seven were executed, five of them German immigrants, part of a broader "red scare." In the late 19th century, the city emerged, in the words of historian Mike Davis, as the "national center of the experiment of uniting Populism and the new labor radicalism" (Davis 1986, p. 36). It was the scene of triumphant union organizing in meatpacking during World War I, and of a historic defeat in steel organizing in the immediate wake of the war. As Davis (1986) put it, the crushing of the 1919 steel strike was the "failed test of native labor's ability to unite with the immigrant proletariat" (Davis 1986, p. 50), postponing the organization of America's key mass production industries for another generation.

Mexican and Puerto Rican Settlement in Chicago

For Chicago, as for the United States as a whole, the places of origin for new immigrants has shifted over time. The shifts from the British Isles to northwestern continental Europe to Southern and Eastern Europe have been followed—especially after the 1960s immigration reforms—by non-European countries. In Chicago, this has meant growing migrant populations from Latin America and the Caribbean.

In absolute numbers, Chicago stands out among U.S. cities in its combination of a large population of Mexican heritage and a large population of Puerto Rican heritage. Only two U.S. cities rank among the top 25 on both lists, New York City and Chicago. (Certainly, the large overall populations of both cities are contributing factors. Nonetheless, other giant cities like Los Angeles and Houston do not make the cut, since they are largely outside the stream of Caribbean immigration.) Chicago ranks fourth in Mexican population (one of only five cities over 500,000);

third in Puerto Rican population (one of only three cities over 100,000) (U.S. Census Bureau 2009–2013).

Small-scale Mexican migration to Chicago and the surrounding area began at the start of the 20th century. By World War I, Mexicans were a "notable" presence in the Chicago labor force, as labor recruiters sought out Mexican workers as a "reserve labor supply for large industry," sometimes to break strikes and sometimes to cope with peak labor requirements on a "temporary" basis (De Genova and Ramos-Zayas 2003, p. 34; Padilla 1985, pp. 24–25). By the 1920s, they represented upwards of a tenth of the labor force in the large meatpacking and steel plants (much more than that, notably, at Inland Steel, in the outskirts of Chicago), and upwards of a third of laborer positions with the railroads. Nonetheless, Mexicans still represented a disposable labor population for employers and authorities. Economic downturns brought disproportionately high unemployment for Mexican workers; the onset of the Great Depression, mass deportations—"forced removals of Mexican immigrants and their U.S. citizen children"—and a dramatic drop of the area's Mexican population (De Genova and Ramos-Zayas 2003, p. 35; Padilla 1985, pp. 26–27). The Mexican population in the Chicago area started to recover again in the 1940s—due in part to the need for wartime labor in the railroad industry, drawing on Mexicans as a "reserve labor supply," once again, through a guest-worker (*bracero*) program (De Genova and Ramos-Zayas 2003, p. 35; Padilla 1985, pp. 31–32). After 1960, it grew dramatically, from just over 50,000 to over half a million (*Encyclopedia of Chicago,* "Mexicans").

Large-scale Puerto Rican migration came to Chicago later, after the World War II. The disruptions of Puerto Rico's agricultural economy, first by the transition from diversity to monoculture, and then the transition from agriculture to industry, left the island with a serious unemployment problem. In response, the Puerto Rican government pushed migration to the continental United States. Felix M. Padilla notes two key factors drawing Puerto Ricans to Chicago, in particular. The first, as for Mexican workers a generation earlier, was labor recruitment, primarily for domestic labor and work in foundries. The second was word about economic conditions in the United States from earlier migrants. The twist on the familiar story of migrants sending news about job opportunities, encouraging others to follow, is that it was *negative* news about job opportunities in New York City—an earlier destination for large-scale Puerto Rican migration—that encouraged migration to alternative destinations in the continental United States, including Chicago (Padilla 1985, p. 58). Puerto Rican migration to the metropolitan area accelerated during the 1950s and 1960s, fueling the increase in the Puerto Rican population, by official census count, from just a few hundred in 1940 to nearly 80,000 in 1970.

Mexicans and Puerto Ricans, by and large, have not settled in the same Chicago neighborhoods. Mexicans originally settled in the neighborhoods near the industrial sites where they worked—railroads, meatpacking plants, and steel mills. This may have been due both to the convenience of proximity to work and the low cost of housing in neighborhoods exposed to disamenities from nearby industry. Nicholas De Genova and Ana Y. Ramos-Zayas, for example, describe Mexicans being "relegated to the most foul-smelling area" near the stockyards and slaughterhouses

(De Genova and Ramos-Zayas 2003, p. 36). The borders of the Mexican barrios shifted over time. "Urban renewal" projects pushed Mexicans out of some areas, mainly to adjacent ones. The arrival of later migrants pushed out the boundaries of dense Mexican settlement. Overall, however, the original areas of settlement anchored Mexican neighborhoods on the city's South Side. An important caveat is that, as industry moved out of the city to industrial suburbs, Mexican workers moved with them, so that there is a "significant Mexican presence through much of the metropolitan area that renders anachronistic . . . any effort to circumscribe Chicago's Mexican communities within the original barrios of the South Side" (De Genova and Ramos-Zayas 2003, p. 39).

By the time Puerto Ricans arrived in large numbers in the 1950s, Mexicans were already well established on the South Side of the city. Local and Puerto Rican authorities attempted to "keep the newly arrived Puerto Ricans separate from the Mexican community," pushing them to settle instead in predominantly white-Anglo neighborhoods (De Genova and Ramos-Zayas 2003, p. 43). In one sense, this project succeeded and in another it did not. In the long run, Puerto Ricans did not end up settling in the historic Mexican South Side barrios. On the other hand, they did not remain dispersed in white neighborhoods. By the 1970s, predominantly Puerto Rican neighborhoods had formed on the city's North Side.

Urban renewal programs and gentrification pushed Puerto Ricans out of some of their original North Side barrios early on, in the 1950s and 1960s. Some other Puerto Rican barrios saw an influx of non-Puerto Ricans, including large numbers of Mexicans, in the 1970s and 1980s. Nonetheless, the geographic division between South Side and North Side still symbolizes the division between these two distinct Latino communities in Chicago. De Genova and Ramos-Zayas note, for example, how a prominent Latino/a community organization chose its downtown office location: "If we were located on the North Side, Mexicans would complain that we are too Puerto Rican. If we were located on the South Side, Puerto Ricans would complain that we are too Mexican" (De Genova and Ramos-Zayas 2003, p. 33).

Latino Politics in Chicago

Latino politics in Chicago have been driven by the economic marginality and political disempowerment of Mexicans, Puerto Ricans, and other Latino groups in the city. Mexicans in Chicago have faced conditions of low-paid and precarious employment, police abuses, harassment by immigration authorities (and, sometimes, large-scale deportations), racial stereotyping, housing discrimination, inadequate public services, and so on. Mexican civic organizations emerged soon after the first arrivals of Mexicans in Chicago, many of them "voluntary associations . . . of the mutual-benefit type so common among immigrant groups" (Padilla 1985, p. 29). Over the years, varied types of organizations—churches, settlement houses, the Mexican government, labor unions, community-organizing groups—would all play a role in Chicago-area Mexicans' "organizational response[s] to their conditions in urban America" (Padilla 1985, pp. 29–31, 34–35). Padilla argues, however, that Mexicans' efforts at collective organization were hampered by divisions between Mexicans long-established in Chicago and more recent arrivals, and civic organizations' lack of commitment to incorporate the latter. He points to their lack of response to 1950s mass immigration sweeps and deportations as a case in point (Padilla 1985, pp. 32–33). Both Padilla (1985) and De Genova and Ramos-Zayas (2003) point to the South Side's Pilsen neighborhood, the epicenter of Mexican Chicago, as the crucible of a more unified Mexican politics in the city in the late 1960s and 1970s (Padilla 1985, p. 37; De Genova and Ramos-Zayas 2003, pp. 39–40).

Padilla identifies housing discrimination and police abuses as two galvanizing issues for Puerto Rican political activism beginning in the 1950s and 1960s (Padilla 1985, p. 45). These grievances gave rise to assimilationist civic organizations— aimed, according to the director of one, at the "adjustment of an essentially rural population to the conditions . . . of modern life"—as well as to more militant oppo- sitional politics, including the rise of the Young Lords organization in the late 1960s (Padilla 1985, pp. 48–49, 52–53).

Both Mexicans and Puerto Ricans were excluded from the Democratic machine politics for which Chicago was known into the 1970s. De Genova and Ramos-Zayas point to the lack of Latinos in full-time city jobs and city political districting that made it well-nigh impossible for Latinos to win elected office (De Genova and Ramos-Zayas 2003, p. 54). Puerto Rican challenges to the Democratic machine in the 1970s were not successful, at least in narrow electoral terms. In the 1980s, how- ever, large-scale Latino support would play a crucial role in then-U.S. representa- tive Harold Washington's successful bid to become the city's first African American mayor. In the years since then, several Latinos have been elected to major public office in the Chicago area.

Immigration Politics in Chicago

Mexicans in Chicago, as in the United States generally, have been caught between two tendencies—their usefulness as an exploitable source of cheap labor and their marginalization as a disposable population. They have been at the epicenter of immi- gration politics, singled out by nativists/restrictionists as a menace. "An ever grow- ing, already significant and effectively indispensable segment of the working class" in the United States, De Genova writes, "Mexican/migrant labor is ubiquitously stigmatized as 'illegal,' subjected to excessive and extraordinary forms of policing, denied fundamental human rights, and thus consigned to an always uncertain social predicament" (De Genova 2005, p. 229).

The threat of expulsion, never far away, has periodically erupted in spasms of raids and deportations—especially during economic downturns. During the Great Depression of the 1930s, De Genova explains, "Mexicans were targeted nationally for mass expulsion," and disproportionately so in Illinois. The state had been home to about 2% of the country's Mexican population but accounted for over 5% of those deported. Chicago's Mexican population plummeted by over one-third during the 1930s, under the blow of "forced removals of both Mexican migrants and their U.S. citizen children" (De Genova 2005, p. 115).

Mass immigration from Mexico resumed in the 1940s, continued through the 1950s, and accelerated in the 1960s. As the Mexican population rose in the late

1960s, so did immigration enforcement targeting undocumented Mexican immigrants. In the Chicago area, a nativist scare about the "illegal Mexican alien problem" (as put by an "alarmist" report from a commission of the Illinois state legislature) led to a dramatic rise in deportations, overwhelmingly focused on Mexicans (De Genova 2005, p. 126). The U.S. economic crisis of the 1970s further raised the "campaign of mass apprehensions" in Chicago. "This period has become notorious not only for raids in factories," notes De Genova, "but also for neighborhood round-ups in public parks, Spanish-language movie theaters, and . . . in front of Mexican grocery stores" (De Genova 2005, p. 127). The mass raids sparked mass protest against the "racial profiling of the Mexican community in particular, and Latinos in general" (De Genova 2005, p. 127). However, two decades later, immigration raids still "almost exclusively targeted Mexicans" (De Genova 2005, p. 127) far out of proportion to their numbers among undocumented immigrants.

In the mid-to-late 2000s, immigration activism surged across the United States, nowhere more intensely than in Chicago—the place of the "first [immigrant-rights] megamarch of 2006 and the largest marches of 2007 and 2008" (Pallares 2010, p. 37). Amalia Pallares describes growing Latino immigrant-rights organizing in Chicago in the mid-to-late 1990s, interrupted by the xenophobic reaction after the September 11, 2001, attacks, and then building back up to the mass mobilizations of the mid-2000s (Pallares 2010, pp. 44–47). The Chicago immigrant-rights movement drew together multiple forces, including Latino and immigrant-rights advocacy, social service, and community organizing groups; the city's Mexican hometown associations; and the labor movement. The movement was galvanized by the rise of anti-immigrant politics, especially legislation that would have made felons out of "undocumented immigrants and anyone who assisted them" (Flores-Gonzáles and Gutiérrez 2010, pp. 5, 47; Bada 2010, pp. 146, 156).

The hometown associations, "immigrant membership organizations formed by people from the same community of origin"—previously focused on assistance to the towns from which their members originated—became increasingly active on immigrant-rights issues in the United States in the years preceding the mobilization. Their participation in the mid-2000s mobilization, inspired by the threatening legislation, can be seen as a culmination of this shift (Bada 2010, pp. 146, 152, 156). Labor unions also became important participants in the immigrant-rights coalition. Some unions (e.g., SEIU, UNITE-HERE, and UFCW), realizing that anti-immigrant policies only made immigrant workers more vulnerable and hampered organizing efforts in industries with many immigrant workers, "had already formed positive connections with the new immigrant and especially Latino communities" (Fink 2010, p. 111). Fink argues that, in this regard, Chicago was "likely ahead of the curve . . . [as] an active alliance . . . emerged between unions and the new immigrant activism" (Fink 2010, p. 111).

The immigrant-rights mobilization, in addition, spanned different groups within the Chicago Latino community—by generation, citizenship status, and national origin. The protests, for example, included large numbers of high-school students, despite school-administration threats of punishment for those skipping or walking out of school. "U.S.-born [or 'second generation'] Latino youth," Flores-Gonzáles notes, participated in the mobilization regardless of their own status as U.S. citizens, and even regardless of whether they had family members who were non-citizens (Flores-Gonzáles 2010, p. 199). Many "consider themselves immigrants even though they were born in the United States," in part as an expression of their ethnic heritage and in part because all people of Mexican ancestry are labeled—and stigmatized—as "immigrants." Some viewed their own secure status as carrying with it an obligation to advocate on behalf of others (Flores-Gonzáles 2010, pp. 202–06).

The participation of Puerto Ricans in the immigrant-rights mobilization spanned differences in both national origin and citizenship status. Puerto Ricans (whether born in the United States or, since 1941, in Puerto Rico) are natural-born U.S. citizens and so mostly do not face the insecurity of status or the immigration enforcement targeting that Latino/a communities do, including large numbers of immigrants, many of them undocumented. (Surely there are some exceptions, such as Puerto Ricans married to immigrants from Mexico or other countries.) Previous researchers on Latino/a identity and political action, Michael Rodríguez-Muñiz notes, "argue that the uneven application of U.S. citizenship to Puerto Ricans and Mexicans prevents the development of a popular pan-Latino/a identity" (Rodríguez-Muñiz 2010, p. 240).

The role of Puerto Ricans in the immigrant-rights movement in Chicago at least partially belies this analysis. "Grassroots organizations, activists, religious leaders, and elected officials," Rodríguez-Muñiz argues, "have consistently advocated progressive immigration reform and have stood in defense of the human rights of their undocumented 'brothers and sisters'" (Rodríguez-Muñiz 2010, p. 238). Chicago's pro-independence/anticolonialist Puerto Rican Cultural Center (PRCC) worked closely with Mexican immigrant-rights organizations, organized contingents and feeder marches for the megamarches, and put pressure on Puerto Rican elected officials to take up the issue. Rodríguez-Muñiz describes how, despite the differences in citizenship status between Puerto Ricans and Mexicans, the PRCC articulated a shared concept of Latinidad based on "similar histories of colonialism, conquest, and racial domination" (Rodríguez-Muñiz 2010, pp. 247–49).

See also in Illinois: Andersonville (Chicago, Illinois); Bridgeport (Chicago, Illinois); Bronzeville (Chicago, Illinois); Little India (Chicago, Illinois); Pilsen (Chicago, Illinois)

See also Hispanic Enclaves: Annandale, Latino and Asian Enclaves (Virginia); Boyle Heights, Latino Neighborhood (Los Angeles, California); Bridgeport (Chicago, Illinois); Dallas, Mexican Enclaves (Texas); East Los Angeles, Mexican American Enclave (Los Angeles, California); El Monte, Latino Enclaves (California); Historic South Central (Los Angeles, California); Holyoke, Puerto Rican Enclaves (Massachusetts); Houston, Mexican Enclaves (Texas); Indio, Mexican and Central American Communities (California); Jackson Heights (Queens, New York); Langley Park, Latino Enclaves (Maryland); Lawrence, Latino Enclaves (Massachusetts); Little Havana (Miami, Florida); Little Havana on the Hudson (North Hudson, New Jersey); Little Lima (Paterson, New Jersey); Logan Heights, Mexican Enclave (San Diego,

California); Mayan Corner/24th and Mission (San Francisco, California); Mexican-town (Detroit, Michigan); Mount Washington, Mexican Enclave (California); Olvera Street/La Plaza (Los Angeles, California); Phoenix and Other Cities, Mexican Enclaves (Arizona); Pico Rivera, Latino Enclave (California); Riverside, Mexican Enclave (California); San Bernardino, Mexican Enclave (California); Santa Ana, Mexican Enclaves (California); Sleepy Hollow, Ecuadorian Enclave (New York); South Federal Boulevard (Denver, Colorado); Sunset Park West and North Corona (New York City); Upper Fells Point (Spanish Town) (Baltimore, Maryland); Washington Heights (New York City); Watts (Los Angeles, California)

Alejandro Reuss

Further Reading

Bada, Xóchitl. "Mexican Hometown Associations in Chicago: The Newest Agents of Civic Participation." In *¡Marcha! Latino Chicago and the Immigrant Rights Movement*. Urbana, IL: University of Illinois Press, 2010.

Cronon, William. *Nature's Metropolis: Chicago and the Great West*. New York: W. W. Norton, 1991.

Davis, Mike. *Prisoners of the American Dream*. New York: Verso, 1986.

De Genova, Nicholas. *Working the Boundaries: Race, Space, and "Illegality" in Mexican Chicago*. Durham, NC: Duke University Press, 2005.

De Genova, Nicholas, and Ana Y. Ramos-Zayas. *Latino Crossings: Mexicans, Puerto Ricans, and the Politics of Race and Citizenship*. New York: Routledge, 2003.

Encyclopedia of Chicago. "African Americans." Accessed October 14, 2016. www.encyclopedia.chicagohistory.org/pages/27.html.

Encyclopedia of Chicago. "Mexicans." Accessed October 14, 2016. www.encyclopedia.chicagohistory.org/pages/824.html.

Fink, Leon. "Labor Joins La Marcha: How New Immigrant Activists Restored the Meaning of May Day." In *¡Marcha! Latino Chicago and the Immigrant Rights Movement*. Urbana, IL: University of Illinois Press, 2010.

Flores-Gonzáles, Nilda. "Immigrants, Citizens, or Both? The Second Generation in the Immigrant Rights Marches." In *¡Marcha! Latino Chicago and the Immigrant Rights Movement*. Urbana, IL: University of Illinois Press, 2010.

Oliva, Sonia. "Permission to March? High School Youth Participation in the Immigrant Rights Movement." In *¡Marcha! Latino Chicago and the Immigrant Rights Movement*. Urbana, IL: University of Illinois Press, 2010.

Padilla, Felix M. *Puerto Rican Chicago*. Notre Dame, IN: University of Notre Dame Press, 1985.

Pallares, Amalia. "The Chicago Context." In *¡Marcha! Latino Chicago and the Immigrant Rights Movement*. Urbana: University of Illinois Press, 2010.

PBS, American Experience. "Chicago: City of the Century, Decades of Immigrants." Accessed October 14, 2016. www.pbslearningmedia.org/resource/arct14.soc.amexchidec/chicago-city-of-the-century-decades-of-immigrants.

Rodríguez-Muñiz, Michael. "Grappling with *Latinidad*: Puerto Rican Activism in Chicago's Pro-Immigrant Rights Movement." In *¡Marcha! Latino Chicago and the Immigrant Rights Movement*. Urbana: University of Illinois Press, 2010.

U.S. Census Bureau, American Community Survey, B03001: Hispanic or Latino Origin by Specific Origin, 2009–2013.

U.S. Census Bureau, American Fact Finder, Annual Estimates of the Resident Population for Incorporated Places of 50,000 or More, Ranked by July 1, 2014 Population: April 1, 2010 to July 1, 2014.

U.S. Census Bureau, Population of the 100 Largest Cities and Other Urban Places in the United States: 1790 to 1990, June 1998.

CHINATOWN (BOSTON, MASSACHUSETTS)

Boston's Chinatown is the fifth-largest Chinatown in the United States. It covers 137 acres in central Boston, nestled between the business district, the cultural district, and the Boston Common. It is convenient to rail, subway, and bus lines. Population estimates for 2010 were 9,275 (47% Asian). As a distinct urban area inhabited by Chinese that dates to the 1880s, it is one of the oldest Chinatowns in the United States—older even than many West Coast Chinatowns, including Seattle and Vancouver. Unlike many mid-sized Chinatowns in the United States that today are largely symbolic spaces and touristic destinations following the dispersal of Chinese residents to suburban locations, Boston's Chinatown has a substantial residential population and significant social service networks in addition to thriving businesses, markets, and restaurants. It serves as the regional hub for Chinese (and other Asian) residents not only in Greater Boston but also throughout the Northeast, who make use of the area's many Chinese-language resources. This is particularly the case for working-class Chinese who live in Chinatown's satellite communities of Quincy and Malden.

There are few accurate accounts of Boston's first Chinese residents, although historians agree that a cluster of Chinese residents and businesses grew steadily throughout the latter decades of the 19th century. Longstanding mercantile connections existed between the Northeast United States and China through tea trade routes that were already well established in the 18th century. However, the first group of about 75 Chinese workers arrived in Massachusetts overland from San Francisco in 1870 on the newly completed Pacific Railroad. Hired by Calvin T. Sampson as strikebreakers for his shoe factory in North Adams, Massachusetts, the majority of the workers were under 20 years old; the foreman was 22. All were from the Pearl River Delta region of Guangdong Province in China. Although Chinese continued to work at the factory until 1880, in 1873 the original Chinese strikebreakers went on strike themselves, and many were dismissed. While it is likely that some of them returned to California, it is also assumed that some of them relocated to Boston from North Adams, since Boston's first Chinese residents are also documented around this time. Other Chinese arrived in Boston as groups of Chinese moved across the United States fleeing violence in California. The first Chinese-run business, a tea shop already established in Boston by 1865, predates the arrival of these groups of Chinese by several years.

In the latter decades of the 19th century, more Chinese lived scattered across Boston outside Chinatown than in it, as they established laundries throughout the region. In 1875, there were five laundries in Boston; by 1900, there were at least

The fifth largest Chinatown district in the United States, Boston's Chinatown district, 2013. (Tupungato/Dreamstime.com)

500 laundries. On Sundays, when laundrymen had the day off, they came to Chinatown to meet with friends, gamble, and send money home. Chinatown initially grew as a service area to support these early Chinese residents of Boston. By 1900, there were numerous Chinese businesses, including several grocery stores, drugstores, and restaurants, along Harrison Avenue, Oxford Place, and Oxford Street between Beach Street and Essex Street. The Chinese residential population in Chinatown had grown to several hundred individuals.

When the Chinese settled in this area of Boston, although centrally located, its residential stock had already declined significantly in value from when it had been originally built in the early 1800s. Known as the South Cove landfill area, it was, like much of central Boston today, land reclaimed from the tidal flats that lay between Beacon Hill (part of the original Shawmut Peninsula) and Roxbury. Close enough to the core city areas for convenience, but far enough away to provide ample residential space, the newly built area was initially attractive to middle-income, native-born families. By 1850, however, those families had begun to move out of South Cove to other areas of Boston. The residential value of the area was first depressed by the construction in 1840 of Boston's railway terminus, South Station, and its railway yard, which continued to be expanded over the next 20 years. By the 1850s, the area was also bordered by numerous leather factories, built in close proximity to both the railway and port to facilitate transportation of leather hides. The area was further industrialized with the establishment of garment factories during the 1860s. In 1899, an elevated railway was built through Chinatown along Harrison Avenue, subjecting businesses and residents to the shadow and noise of the elevated train for the next 40 years.

While the neighborhood's proximity to the train station, railway yard, and factories made it undesirable for the white, middle-income Americans who were South Cove's original residents, these factors contributed to the subsequent waves of residents who moved in to the area in their place. As a relatively low-rent area that was also near railway transportation, it was a convenient residential destination for different groups of immigrants who arrived in Boston from the 1850s onwards. Between the 1850s and 1880s, the Irish were the primary inhabitants of the area. Following the Irish, the area was settled by Central European Jews and Italians. By 1900, the neighborhood's residents were primarily Arabic-speaking Syrian and Lebanese, who remained prominent until the 1950s. Initially, the Syrians lived alongside the Chinese north of Kneeland Street; later Kneeland Street became the dividing line between Syrian and Chinese populations, with Syrians resident south of Kneeland St. and Chinese resident north of Kneeland St. When the Syrians began to leave South Cove, as first generation immigrants died and the second generation began moving to suburban areas, the Chinese continued to expand into the residential area south of Kneeland Street. Syrian families (as well as some Chinese families) who remained in the area were forced out when several South Cove residential streets were razed in the 1950s and 1960s to build the Central Artery and the Massachusetts Turnpike, two major expressways linking Boston's growing suburbs to downtown.

Chinese who grew up in South Cove during the first half of the 20th century point out the tight-knit neighborhood focus and community fabric of Boston's Chinatown in its early years. Despite living alongside Syrians and other ethnic groups, there was little social interaction across ethnic lines. Boston's early Chinese residents were the subject of both fascination and derision by Boston's white population; nonetheless, they appear to have had less strained racial relationships than Chinese on the West Coast of the United States, where the Chinese were repeated targets of violence. This situation was aided in part by Boston's community of abolitionists, who also took up the cause of Chinese when they did become targets of violence. In 1903, Boston police raided Boston's Chinatown and arrested 250–300 Chinese men following a shooting that took place in the area. Fifty of those arrested were found to have incomplete papers and were repatriated to China; the community also suffered from the collective identification of all Chinese in Boston with negative qualities associated with the illegal actions of a few individuals.

Because of the Chinese exclusion laws in effect from 1882 until 1943, the Chinese population of Chinatown remained relatively small well into the 20th century. Nonetheless, businesses thrived, as Chinese who worked in laundries throughout the area continued to make weekend trips to Chinatown to socialize and make purchases. After World War I, the economy of Chinatown shifted, as laundries diminished throughout the region and Chinese turned to opening restaurants instead. In Chinatown, restaurants attracted non-Chinese patrons with large, bright signs, combining Chinese characters and easily remembered English names or figures. A substantial mercantile infrastructure grew in Chinatown to support the restaurant industry, supplying key ingredients like noodles, bean sprouts, and tofu. Additional businesses supported Chinese residents and weekly visitors with services. The garment industry also continued to expand next to Chinatown during the 1930s, replacing housing stock with industrial space. Surrounded by the railway yard, leather, and garment industries, as well as Boston's theater district, Chinatown continued to be a low-rent neighborhood.

As with other Chinatowns across the nation, the first generation of Chinese residents in Boston's Chinatown were referred to as a "bachelor society," because restrictive immigration laws made it virtually impossible for ordinary Chinese laborers in the United States to bring brides with them from China. Chinese who could document merchant status did have the right to bring brides from China, but there were only a few marriages between Chinese grooms and brides in Boston up until 1910. Some Chinese men married interracially: census data indicates that the majority of these brides were native-born white Americans, primarily of Irish, English, and Scottish descent. By the 1920s, although there were still large numbers of single males in Chinatown, there was a growing presence of families in Boston's Chinatown, resulting primarily from the emergence of the "paper son" generation in the early decades of the 20th century. Chinese men with American citizenship were able to bring their Chinese children from China, who were also U.S. citizens, to the United States despite the Chinese Exclusion Act. The destruction of public records following the San Francisco earthquake of 1906 allowed additional Chinese immigrants to gain citizenship and bring family from China, through claims that their birth records had been lost. This second generation of Chinese American children grew up speaking both English and Toisanese, the Chinese dialect spoken by most early Chinese immigrants to the United States, in Boston and elsewhere. By the 1940s, families predominated in Chinatown.

Chinese American children who grew up in South Cove—like the Irish, Italian, and Jewish immigrant children who lived in the area before them, and the neighboring Syrian and Lebanese children who grew up alongside them—all attended the Quincy School, first established in 1847 on Tyler Street and lauded as the first school in the country with graded classrooms and separate seats for each student. Chinese American children were also taught about Chinese language and culture at the Quong (Kwong) Kow School, established by the Chinese Merchants Associated in 1916 on Oxford Street. Using Toisanese as the primary language of instruction, children learned to read and write Chinese and were awarded diplomas for completing programs of study through sixth and ninth grades.

The Quong Kow School was just one of many community-based organizations that provided financial and social support to the Chinese workers and families living in Boston. Numerous Chinatown institutions created important infrastructures that were otherwise lacking for the Chinese, such as helping immigrants adapt to American business practices and facilitating communication with Chinese residents in other parts of the nation and in China. Surname Associations (also known as *huiguan*) allowed individuals with the same surname to socialize together and create pseudo-familial relationships of support otherwise lacking for single male immigrants; they also often provided translation services, helped men write letters home to their families, and (through the collection of annual subscription fees) helped pay for funeral expenses or ensure that men's bodies would be shipped back to China after death. Community governance and local representation were provided through Boston's Chinese Consolidated Benevolent Association of New England and the Chinese Merchant's Association. These organizations also sponsored annual banquets and other Chinese cultural events for the community.

Boston's South Cove residents also benefitted from the services of organizations initially external to the Chinese community, including the YMCA and the Boy Scouts. Christian missionary groups were active in South Cove and were instrumental in developing strong organizational support for the Chinese American girls and women in Boston's Chinatown through the Chinese Mission, Denison House, and the Catholic Maryknoll Sisters Center. In the 1930s and 1940s, girls and women participated in Chinese music and dance troops, played in local marching bands, and organized their own basketball team. As the political situation in China became more contentious throughout the 1930s and 1940s—with the Japanese invasion of China, World War II, and Republican and Communist factions fighting for control—male and female residents of Boston's Chinatown sought to educate the American public about the turmoil and orchestrate support for the Chinese cause with frequent demonstrations and parades. Chinese Americans from Boston's Chinatown served in the military, including the 14th Air Service Group. Rose Lok, the first Chinese American female pilot in Boston, joined the Chinese Patriotic Flying Corps.

World War II served as a turning point for Boston's Chinese. Following World War II, Chinatown's population began to grow. Between 1940 and 1950, there was a 60% increase in Chinatown's residential population. Chinese brides and children were able to join their fathers or other family members in Boston through changes in federal legislation, including the repeal of the Chinese Exclusion Act in 1943 and the 1945 War Brides Act, which allowed Chinese veterans to return to China and get married. Employment opportunities opened up for both men and women, and veterans as well as young, college-educated Chinese Americans entered the workforce. Chinatown's residents remained a close-knit group of families who all knew each other and had access to each other's homes; children played on the street or at the Quincy School playground. Housing conditions were poor and cramped, but the community as a whole had potential for continued growth and social mobility given its stable family structure, increased employment opportunities, and the rise of a postwar generation of young adult leaders.

In the mid-1950s, Chinatown's physical space was threatened with major urban development projects. The New England Medical Center purchased half of a city block (bounded by Oak, Harrison, Posner, and Tyler Streets) in the center of residential Chinatown and demolished housing. Additional streets were razed because of the Central Artery and the Massachusetts Turnpike. One-third of the area's residents were forced to relocate with no compensation and only 60 days' notice. These projects also changed the character of the urban neighborhood, contributing significant traffic, air, and noise pollution. The newly built Chinese Merchant's Association Building, a structure designed by a Chinese architect for community use, was cut in half to make space for the freeway. Although the Chinese American community had mobilized enough support to prevent the building's complete demolition, its space was so compromised that the building was unable to serve its original community functions.

In the mid-1960s, important changes reinvigorated South Cove and enabled the area to maintain its viability as a residential community for Chinese families at a time when many other urban Chinatowns in the country lost their residential communities through urban renewal projects and exodus of urban Chinese populations to suburban communities. One of those changes was the Hart Cellar Immigration Act, which repealed the restrictive quota system that had been in place since 1924 and also established provisions for refugees and individuals with professional skills to immigrate to the United States. The Hart Cellar Act benefitted Chinese across the nation who, for the first time, were able to sponsor their relatives in China to immigrate to the United States. Boston's Chinatown—aided by its central location, convenience to public transportation, low rents, and community infrastructure—was an attractive destination for new immigrants, who moved to the area throughout the 1960s and 1970s. Women worked in nearby garment factories; both men and women worked in local restaurants and shops. Cantonese replaced Toisanese as the predominant spoken language.

At the same time, the postwar generation of educated Chinese Americans who had grown up in Chinatown stepped up as leaders for Chinatown's continued social and economic development. Spurred by the Civil Rights Movement, in the late 1960s Chinese Americans began establishing new social service organizations aimed at supporting Chinese immigrants and Asian Americans in Chinatown and the greater Boston area. These new service organizations included the Chinese American Civic Association (now known as the Asian American Civic Association), founded in 1967; the Greater Boston Chinese Golden Age Center, founded in 1972; and the Chinese Progressive Association, founded in 1977. These and other institutions supplemented the support available through the surname, regional, and other traditional associations already well-established in Chinatown through new forms of expanded service provision. Traditional associations continued to attract new members; however, the new organizations were open to all immigrants; they were also oriented toward advocacy, increasing rights' access, and improving the living conditions of Chinatown's Asian and low-income populations. These organizations have been crucial in maintaining services for Chinatown's low-income immigrant residents and expanding community infrastructure despite additional social and spatial challenges to South Cove over the past 40 years.

In addition, although the urban renewal projects of the 1950s and 1960 had previously led to the degradation and loss of housing stock in South Cove, they also allowed for the reorganization of urban space that resulted in the expansion of Chinatown's residential area. By the mid-1960s, the public reaction in Boston to the massive demolition caused by urban renewal was substantial; as a result, Mayor John Collins and the Boston Redevelopment Authority (BRA) implemented new plans to work with urban communities and improve living conditions, including the South Cove Redevelopment Plan of 1965. This plan created several hundred affordable housing units in Chinatown, including the high-density residential developments of Tai Tung Village and Mass Pike Towers. Although not built specifically for Chinese residents, the subsidized units attracted low-income Chinese immigrants. Together with Castle Square, another subsidized housing complex built in the 1960s in Boston's South End, these buildings continue to house much of the residential core of Chinatown today.

In the mid-1970s, an adult entertainment district known as the "Combat Zone" developed along Washington Street bordering Chinatown. Although the zoned area was established by the city of Boston in order to confine adult entertainment to a limited urban area, the problems with drugs, gang violence, and prostitution that were endemic to the area spilled over the into Chinatown, leading to higher crime and making it dangerous for families and other residents to live there. By the mid-1980s, following a dive in profitability from sex shops and growing awareness of property values in the area, economic and zoning pressures reduced the Combat Zone to just two blocks along Washington Street. Around the same time, Vietnamese immigrants, many of whom were of Chinese descent, spoke Cantonese, and had entered the country following the Refugee Act of 1980, also began establishing small shops along Washington Street. The Vietnamese presence added a new constituency to Chinatown's Asian American community, and the predominance of Vietnamese restaurants and other businesses worked to extend Chinatown's border to include Washington Street.

Chinatown's residential and service organizations contributed to a significant community victory in the 1990s over the use of an important parcel of land situated in the heart of residential Chinatown. This site, known as "parcel C," was identified by the Tufts-New England Medical Center as the location for an eight-story parking garage. Chinatown residents protested the proposed development plan and were able to retain land rights over parcel C, where the Metropolitan, a mixed-use 23-story high-rise, was built instead. With help from the Asian Community Development Corporation, a Chinatown NGO, the building was designed to benefit and strengthen the Chinatown residential community in which it is situated. It includes both low-income and full rent housing units as well as four NGOs, community spaces, and below-ground parking. This success created a foundation for Chinatown organizations and residents to work together to achieve positive benefits for improving the community in the face of continuing environmental challenges.

Today, the community infrastructure of Chinatown is thriving. The boundaries of Chinatown extend well beyond the two blocks along Harrison Avenue and Oxford Place first settled by Chinese 140 years ago. The core business district, comprised of restaurants, grocery stores, fresh food markets, teahouses, travel agents, and specialty stores, remains north of Kneeland Street, in the area originally settled by the area's first Chinese residents. The core residential area and most of Chinatown's service infrastructure—now 75 agencies strong—is south of Kneeland Street. Residential Chinatown extends across the Massachusetts Turnpike into the neighborhood known as the South End, where Castle Square is located, along with an Asian supermarket. South Cove is not only a substantial residential community but also a lively business district, with a multidimensional economic and social base serving Chinese, Asian, and other Boston residents.

Chinatown's residential base and community structures will continue to change in coming decades. Because of its central location and development value, Chinatown has experienced considerable numbers of high income residents moving into the area over the past two decades. The site of upscale hotels and luxury high rises, Chinatown's residential community now includes much greater racial and socioeconomic diversity than in the past. NGOs continue to successfully advocate for the inclusion of as many subsidized housing units as possible within newly built developments, so that the area's low-income, non–English speaking residential population will also continue to thrive and take advantage of the rich resource infrastructures within a walkable radius. Chinatown's businesses and service organizations also serve as important resources for Chinese immigrants who settle outside Chinatown in the greater Boston area, particularly in the cities of Quincy and Malden, which are both directly connected to Chinatown by subway lines. This ease of access to Chinatown for residents living outside the area, particularly working-class Asian Americans and newly arrived non-English-speaking immigrants, combined with the area's significant subsidized housing stock, indicate that Chinatown's role as a regional hub and center for service provision is likely to continue in the future.

The non-English-speaking population in Chinatown, including elderly residents who have lived there for decades, remains high, and will continue to grow in coming years through the continued desirability of Chinatown as a residential location. A number of initiatives in recent years has benefitted Chinatown's residents, including the successful advocacy for bilingual (Chinese/English) election ballots and the creation of a public park—part of the Rose Greenway Conservancy—when the Central Artery was moved underground. Ongoing efforts by residents and community development organizations continue to strive for increased access to high quality, affordable housing and additional improvements to South Cove's physical area,

---

Boston's Dark History with Its Chinese Community

Chinese who grew up in South Cove during the first half of the 20th century point out the tight-knit neighborhood focus and community fabric of Boston's Chinatown in its early years. Despite living alongside Syrians and other ethnic groups, there was little social interaction across ethnic lines. Boston's early Chinese residents were the subject of both fascination and derision by Boston's white population; nonetheless, they appear to have had less strained racial relationships than Chinese on the nation's West Coast, where the Chinese were repeated targets of violence. This situation was aided in part by Boston's community of abolitionists, who also took up the cause of Chinese when they did become targets of violence. In 1903, Boston police raided Boston's Chinatown and arrested 250–300 Chinese men following a shooting that took place in the area. Fifty of those arrested were found to have incomplete papers and were repatriated to China; the community also suffered from the collective identification of all Chinese in Boston with negative qualities associated with the illegal actions of a few individuals. Some of those who were wrongly detained by the police had their Caucasian spouses and African American friends vouch for them and produce papers. It was a show of multiracial solidarity within the community. Today, Boston's Chinatown is the fifth-largest Chinatown in the United States. It spans 137 acres in central Boston, nestled between the business district, the cultural district, and the Boston Common and it is convenient to rail, subway, and bus lines.

including additional green spaces and modernization of decrepit building structures that date to the early 1800s.

Between 1900 and 2000, Massachusetts's Chinese population grew from 2,000 residents to 122,000. Boston's Chinatown has been centrally important to the support of Massachusetts's Chinese population throughout that time. Despite repeated actions that threatened the continued existence of the neighborhood—from the Exclusion Acts, the 1903 raid, the building of the elevated train, urban renewal projects, the establishment of the Combat Zone, and so on—the Chinese have thrived and, with each setback, grown stronger. Chinatown, a socio-economically diverse and vibrant urban community, has proven its resilience—theirs is a legacy to carry into the future, even as South Cove continues to change in the decades to come.

See also in Massachusetts: Cambodia Town (Lowell, Massachusetts); Fall River, Portuguese Enclave (Massachusetts); Framingham, Brazilian Enclave (Massachusetts); Holyoke, Puerto Rican Enclaves (Massachusetts); Lawrence, Latino Enclaves (Massachusetts); Lower Roxbury, African American Enclave (Massachusetts); Mattapan (Boston, Massachusetts); North End (Boston, Massachusetts); Quincy, Asian Enclaves (Massachusetts); Roxbury, African-American Enclave (Massachusetts); Salem, French Canadian Enclave (Massachusetts); South Boston/Southie (Boston Massachusetts); South End (Boston, Massachusetts); Watertown, Armenian Capital (Massachusetts); West End (Boston, Massachusetts)

See also Chinese/Taiwanese Enclaves: Bridgeport (Chicago, Illinois); Chinatown (Los Angeles, California); Chinatown (Phoenix, Arizona); Chinatown (San Francisco, California); Chinatown Historic District/A'ala (Honolulu, Hawaii); Chinatowns (Duplicates) (San Francisco, California); Chinatowns (Manhattan; Sunset Park East, Brooklyn; Flushing, Queens) (New York City); International District (Seattle, Washington); Monterey Park, First Suburban Chinatown (California); New Chinatown (Portland, Oregon); Tucson, Chinese and Southeast Asian Enclaves (Arizona)

Nicole Newendorp

Further Reading

Asian Community Development Corporation. "Metropolitan." Accessed October 14, 2016. http://www.asiancdc.org/content/metropolitan-0.

A Chinatown Banquet: Exploring Boston Chinatown. Boston, MA: Mike Blockstein and the Asian Community Development Corporation, 2006.

Boston Redevelopment Authority Research Division. "Chinatown 2010 Census Population." Accessed October 14, 2016. https://data.cityofboston.gov/dataset/Chinatown-Neighborhood-2010-Census-Population/ff3a-vq2d.

Chen, Thomas C. *Remaking Boston's Chinatown: Race, Space, and Urban Development, 1943–1994.* PhD dissertation, Brown University, 2014.

Chinatown Masterplan 2010: Community Vision for the Future. Boston, MA: Chinatown Masterplan Oversight Committee, 2010.

Chinese Progressive Association for Justice, Democracy, and Equality. "About Us." Accessed October 14, 2016. http://cpaboston.org/en/about-us.

Chu, Doris C. J. *Chinese in Massachusetts: Their Experiences and Contributions*. Boston, MA: Chinese Culture Institute, 1987.

Lee, Anthony W. *A Shoemaker's Story: Being Chiefly about French Canadian Immigrants, Enterprising Photographers, Rascal Yankees, and Chinese Cobblers in a Nineteenth-Century Factory Town*. Princeton, NJ: Princeton University Press, 2008.

Lee, Tunney. "Chinatown Then and Now: Beach Street El Demolition." *Sampan*, April 10, 2013.

Liang, Kye. "MIT150 Exhibit Celebrates Faculty, Alumni, and Students' Role in Shaping Chinatown's Future." *Sampan*, February 25, 2011.

Liu, Michael, and Kim Geron. "Changing Neighborhood: Ethnic Enclave and the Struggle for Social Justice." *Social Justice* 35, no. 2 (112), Asian American & Pacific Islander Population Struggles for Social Justice (2008): 18–35.

Liu, Michael, and Shauna Lo. "Insights Into Early Chinese American Community Development in Massachusetts through the U.S. Census." Institute for Asian American Studies, University of Massachusetts, Boston, March 2014. Accessed October 14, 2016. http://cdn.umb.edu/images/centers_institutes/institute_asian_american_studies/Early_Chinese_in_MA_w_maps.pdf.

Lo, Shauna, and Laura Wai Ng. "Beyond Bachelorhood: Chinese American Interracial Marriage in Massachusetts During the Exclusion Era." *Chinese America: History and Perspectives* (2013): 29–37.

Murphey, Rhoads. "Boston's Chinatown." *Economic Geography* 28, no. 3 (July 1952): 244–55.

To, Wing-kai, and The Chinese Historical Society of New England. *Chinese in Boston: 1870–1965*. Charleston, SC: Arcadia, 2008.

Wong, K. Scott. "The Eagle Seeks a Helpless Quarry: The 1903 Boston Chinatown Raid Revisited." *Amerasia Journal* 22, no. 3, (1996): 81–103.

CHINATOWN (LOS ANGELES, CALIFORNIA)

Early Chinese Immigration to Los Angeles

Chinese immigrants first came to California in significant numbers during the California Gold Rush of 1848–1855, only a few years after Great Britain's triumph in the First Opium War in 1842, which legalized Chinese emigration. Chinese laborers were able to command much higher wages in America than they were able to back home, saving enough to send a portion of their earnings back to their families and communities in China.

Who were these Chinese immigrants? Often, they were young male workers who were sent by their families to find better economic opportunities abroad. Many immigrants planned to return to China after working and saving up money for a number of years but changed their minds and settled permanently in America. If immigrants had wives and children back in China, those who became citizens were able to bring their families over to the United States. Chinese immigrants in Los Angeles worked primarily as unskilled laborers on construction projects such as the First Transcontinental Railroad, as road builders, laundry workers, market gardeners, and agricultural and ranch workers.

Over time, racial tensions arose from nativists who feared that Chinese immigrants were lowering average wages and taking away jobs from white workers. Nativists believed that Chinese immigrants were doing little to integrate into American society, which in part resulted from laws that prevented Chinese immigrants from intermarrying with Americans and starting families of their own. Tension and violence built to a climax in the Chinese massacre of 1871, one of the largest mass lynchings in American history. A mob of 500 Los Angeles citizens systematically assaulted, robbed, and murdered local Chinese, killing 18 and wounding countless others.

A little more than a decade later, in 1882, the Chinese Exclusion Act was passed, which prohibited Chinese immigration into California. There were loopholes, however, that allowed Chinese students, businesspeople, and other commercial professionals, along with their spouses and children, to enter the states.

Old Chinatown (1880–1938)

In 1880, Chinese immigrants formed what we will refer to as "Old Chinatown" in one of the roughest neighborhoods of Los Angeles. The determination to save a large portion of their earnings to later send or bring back to China led Chinese immigrants to find the cheapest accommodations possible. Old Chinatown formed in a low-rent neighborhood formerly popular with Mexican immigrants, centered on Calle de los Negroes ("Negro Alley"), a short unpaved alley about 13 feet wide and 500 feet in length, located between El Pueblo Plaza and Old Arcadia Street. As Chinese immigrants settled in the area, it grew to include about 15 streets and alleys containing approximately 200 buildings, including a Chinese opera theater, three temples, a newspaper business and a telephone exchange. Slowly, the number of Chinese women increased and families with children formed.

Despite the rapid growth, there were several developments that would prevent Old Chinatown from succeeding. Laws prohibiting Chinese immigrants from obtaining citizenship also prevented them from owning property, sowing seeds of trouble for the future. Population growth issues stemmed from the low number of females and families in combination with the Chinese Exclusion Act, which was not repealed until 1943. Economic issues caused Old Chinatown to decline in the early 1910s as rumors of seedy gambling houses, opium dens, and fierce tong warfare between competing Chinese merchant associations (wars which were often started over women) greatly reduced business and tourism in the area. The lack of property ownership by Chinese Americans led to disrepair and poor building conditions in Old Chinatown as rumors of redevelopment led landlords to spend very little, if anything, on property upkeep.

Old Chinatown became entangled in a series of lawsuits between different estates and property owners that culminated in a California Supreme Court decision on May 19, 1931, to condemn the land. Old Chinatown was approved to be demolished to make room for the construction of Los Angeles's new Union Station. Chinese Americans needed to find somewhere new to move, quickly.

China City (1938–1949)

Fortunately, two new competing areas formed for the displaced Chinese population. The first was made primarily by the efforts of Christine Sterling, a prominent local Los Angeles civic leader and socialite, who was also the force behind the Mexican-themed Olvera Street. Sterling raised funds and worked with Hollywood set designers, including Paramount set designer William Puntke, on an area called "China City."

In 1938, China City, a walled district with Chinese-style architecture, shops, restaurants, rickshaw rides, a temple, and a lotus pond opened. In China City, costumed workers greeted tourists, and a Chinese opera troupe performed live shows in front of the shops. China City residents, perhaps mistaken for employees, were often asked to pose for photos for tourists and were frequently recruited to be actors in films such as *The Good Earth*. Some replica buildings from the film remained in the city. In Lisa See's novel *On Gold Mountain: The One-Hundred-Year Odyssey of my Chinese-American Family*, she vividly describes the experiences her family had owning an antique shop in China City. Movie studios would rent vases, clothing, and all kinds of things from her family's store to dress sets, and her family made a decent living.

China City received mixed support from the community. While it gave many a place to live, it was seen as an enterprise corrupted by Hollywood influences, not especially honest and true to Chinese culture. China City did not last for very long. It was destroyed by fires and rebuilt numerous times during its 11-year lifespan. In 1949, an act of arson destroyed China City for the final time and it would not be rebuilt.

New Chinatown (1938–)

While the Chinese American community faced the harsh realities of eviction from Old Chinatown, which was soon to be demolished and turned into Union Station, parallel to Sterling's efforts in the 1930s about 28 prominent Chinese Americans, many of them business owners, formed the Los Angeles Chinatown Project Association to raise funds to acquire land, design, and construct what is referred to as "New Chinatown." Community leader Peter Soo Hoo, a Chinese American born and raised in Old Chinatown, was an important member of the association and architect of New Chinatown. Soo Hoo, a USC graduate, was fluent in both English and Cantonese and worked as an engineer for the Department of Water and Power. Soo Hoo met with railway agent Herbert Lapham, a man who was sensitive to the Chinese plight, and negotiated the sale of a vacant railroad yard in Los Angeles' (now nonexistent) Little Italy to the Los Angeles Chinatown Project Association for 75 cents a square foot.

On June 25, 1938, New Chinatown officially opened to the public. Its central plaza contained many restaurants and shops, as well as a Chinese grocery store and an herbal medicine store. Several Chinese organizations, including the Hop Sing Tong Society and the Chinese Consolidated Benevolent Association, moved to the New Chinatown. These "Family Associations," also known as "Benevolent

Associations," were originally founded by the Chinese who lived in Old China-town and served immigrants by helping them find housing and work. Each Family Association was set up to service Chinese immigrants from the same family name as the organization (e.g., a "Huang" would go to the Huang Benevolent Association for help upon arriving in Los Angeles). For the next several decades, New China-town would grow in size and population.

New citizenship laws around this time started to make it easier for Chinese immi-grants to become true, legally recognized Chinese Americans. The 1930s and 1940s served as an opportunity for Chinese to fight in the army and become Amer-ican citizens. After World War II began, a California law allowed Chinese immi-grants who were in the country illegally to turn themselves in and become citizens. Changes in immigration law in 1965 also made it much easier for Asian immigrants to come to America.

During the 1980s, many shopping centers and mini-malls appeared in New Chi-natown. A large Chinese gateway was completed at the intersection of Broadway and Cesar Chavez Avenue. New Chinatown grew in size to its current borders in today's downtown Los Angeles between Beaudry Avenue, Stadium Way, North Broadway, Cesar Chavez Avenue, and the Los Angeles River. New Chinatown became situated between Elysian Park and Dodger Stadium to the north, Echo Park to the west, Lincoln Heights to the east, and Olvera Street, Union Station, and Little Tokyo to the south.

Filming in Chinatown

Hollywood's interest in China City extended into New Chinatown, and a multitude of productions occurred in Chinatown over the years. Some of the many films shot in Chinatown include *Rush Hour, Lethal Weapon 4, Primal Fear, Beverly Hills Ninja, Mystery Men, Freaky Friday, Chinatown, Gangster Squad, Balls of Fury, Anchorman,* and *Collateral.* A few of the episodic television productions in Chinatown include *Melrose Place, Beverly Hills 90210, JAG, The A Team, Beauty and the Beast, Murder She Wrote, Baywatch, Charmed* and *Angel.* Chinatown is also a popular commercial pro-duction spot. Clients such as Land Rover, Sprint PCS, Diet Coke, UPS, Conoco, AT&T, McGraw-Hill, and McDonald's have shot there. Additionally, artists such as Enrique Iglesias, Natalie Cole, Nellie Furtado, and Kelly Rowland have filmed music videos in Chinatown (Hummer).

Decline of New Chinatown (1970s–)

By the 1980s and 1990s, living conditions had begun to noticeably decline. A series of crimes exemplified the decline in safety and living conditions in New China-town. In 1983, two Los Angeles Police officers died in the line of duty when their patrol car was hit by a speeding vehicle driven by suspects who were allegedly escap-ing from a failed drug deal. In 1984, a jewelry store shootout resulted in the death of a police officer. A shooting occurred in 1985 in the First Chinese Baptist Church in which a pastor and a deacon were killed by a man who was a former member of the church and who suffered from mental illness. An off-duty law enforcement officer returned fire and killed the gunman. In 1996, an Academy Award–winning Cambodian refugee, physician and actor Haing S. Ngor, was killed during a failed robbery attempt by members of an Asian gang in a Chinatown residential area. Chinese Triad groups grew in size and became responsible for a number of illegal activities, including gambling, extortion, prostitution, robbery, corruption of government officials, and murder. Chinese organized crime was a paramount concern to the FBI in the mid-1980s.

While it was a primary goal of the Los Angeles Chinatown Project Association for Chinese residents to own their own property to prevent getting stuck as tenants to negligent landlords, over the years people living outside of Chinatown have bought property, and business owners and residents found themselves renters yet again. Residents found themselves at the mercy of landlords for building improvements and modernization.

Another factor prohibiting the growth and affecting the decline of New Chinatown is the geography of Los Angeles. Los Angeles is not a pedestrian-friendly city, with people often living several miles away from their place of work and facing long commutes. Public transportation systems lag behind other Chinatowns in cities like San Francisco and New York. On the positive side, New Chinatown became accessible by the Gold Line of Los Angeles's Metro Rail in 2003. As construction and other jobs typically held by the early Chinese laborers began to disappear or went to a growing number of Mexican immigrants, Chinese and other Asian immigrants saw higher education as the answer for their children to get employment. As a result, their children tended to move away from Chinatown.

New immigration trends and a population drain greatly affected the demographics and prosperity of Chinatown. Many Chinese Americans, particularly middle class families and more affluent Chinese (including new immigrants), began moving from Chinatown to suburban areas like the city of Monterey Park, located in the San Gabriel Valley just eight miles east of Chinatown. This was in part due to the efforts of Chinese real estate agent Frederic Hsieh, who in the 1970s began buying and selling large amounts of property, marketing Monterey Park as a "Chinese Beverly Hills" (Fong, p. 30). New Chinese immigrants as well as Chinese Americans with growing families moved to other Southern California cities like Walnut, Diamond Bar, Rowland Heights, Whittier, Pasadena, Arcadia, Cerritos, and Irvine for better schools and safer neighborhoods. The 1980 U.S. Census shows that the Chinese population in Monterey Park outnumbered the Japanese at 8,082 to 7,533. In the 1990 U.S. Census, the Chinese population had grown to 21,971 compared to the 6,081 Japanese still living in the area (Fong, pp. 27, 31). In 2012, only 15,000 of Los Angeles County's 400,000-plus Chinese Americans still lived in Chinatown. Chinese university students, after attending universities in the area such as the University of California Los Angeles (UCLA) and the University of Southern California (USC), had job opportunities in safer areas to live and work in than what Chinatown could offer them.

As Chinese immigrants with better education and jobs began to arrive, family associations started losing their financial support and shifted their focus to helping residents that were already living there. They currently cater to Chinese residents of Chinatown age 50 and older.

Los Angeles Chinatown in 2015

Chinatown in the present day looks very old, very culturally Chinese, and feels abandoned. It contains many elderly Chinese Americans who have lived there for most of their lives as well as a notably large minority Mexican population. A possible perception problem is that Chinatown today only serves to help newly arrived immigrants who are seeking entry-level work and elderly Chinese with poor English skills who can't drive. Several low-income senior citizens who were originally Chinese immigrants live in the area, as do young college graduates and hipsters in nearby condominiums. There was a large influx of Taiwanese and Hong Kong immigrants in the 1960s and 1970s, as well as many Chinese Vietnamese. Chinatown is still located in what is considered a lower-income, fairly urban area of Los Angeles. The Los Angeles County Jail is located adjacent to Chinatown, Union Station, and the Los Angeles River.

Per the 2000 U.S. Census, Chinatown was the neighborhood in Los Angeles with the highest proportion of residents originally born outside the United States, at 72.4%. Of that percentage, 55.3% was from China and 12.4% was from Mexico. The median age was 37. A total of 53.6% of the households earned $20,000 or less per year, the third-largest percentage in Los Angeles County. Chinatown led with a large proportion of Asian residents, at 70.8%, followed by Monterey Park (61.1%), Cerritos (58.3%), Walnut (56.2%), Rowland Heights (51.7%), San Gabriel (48.9%), Rosemead (48.6%), Alhambra (47.2%), San Marino (46.8%), and Arcadia (45.4%).

There are a few schools in present-day Chinatown: a charter school, a public elementary school, a private Catholic Boy's School, and Evans Community Adult School, the largest stand-alone English as a second language (ESL) adult school in the nation. In the 2000 U.S. Census, only 8.3% of Chinatown residents aged 25 or older possessed a college degree.

Chinatown includes the Los Angeles State Historic Park, locally known as the Cornfield, which consists of an open space for outdoor recreation. Chinatown also features the Alpine Recreation Center, which offers indoor gymnasiums, two basketball courts, volleyball courts, and an area for children to play in. The Los Angeles Public Library includes a Chinatown branch. While there is no central religion in Chinatown, there are several temples. The Taoist Thien Hau Temple reopened in 2005 and is often used for dance performances and firecracker displays during Chinese New Year.

Traditional Chinese food, with glass displays of hanging duck, is still noticeable and special in present-day Chinatown, as well as boba cafés and dim sum and Cantonese seafood restaurants. Some Southeast Asian cuisines, especially Vietnamese pho restaurants, have grown in number. In Chinatown's Far East Plaza is Chef Roy Choy's Chego restaurant and Wing Hop Fung Ginseng & China Products Center, a two-story supermarket.

Chinatown contains art galleries, jewelry stores, clothing stores, restaurants, bakeries, bookstores, grocery stores, banks (Far East National Bank, East West Bank, Bank of America), a motel, clothing stores, furniture stores, an auto repair shop, printing/stationery stores, beauty products stores, stores for Oriental gifts and crafts, and herbal stores that sell authentic ginseng and other traditional Chinese medicinal herbs. Chinatown's Central Plaza contains a statue honoring Dr. Sun Yat-sen, the Chinese revolutionary leader who was the Republic of China's first president and is considered the "founder of modern China." More recently, on June 15, 2013, a seven-foot tall Bruce Lee statue was built. The long-standing Hop Louie pagoda has become a bar.

The bohemian art scene in Chinatown began around 1998 with the establishment of China Art Objects, a clubhouse gallery for students from Pasadena's Art Center College of Design, and Black Dragon Society, a hybrid international arts hangout and showcase for UCLA undergraduates. The number of art galleries rose sharply, but the economic crash of 2008 caused many to close or relocate. However, there are signs that low rents in Chinatown and other factors, are attracting artists to return, and there may be a recovery.

There are some community events that help Chinatown remain relevant. On June 28, 2008, a celebration of the 1938 founding of New Chinatown was held as Los Angeles Chinatown's 70th Anniversary Party. Other popular events that occur yearly include a Chinese New Year Parade, a mid-autumn Moon Festival, a Miss Los Angeles Chinatown Pageant, and a firecracker run and fun walk (recurring for the past 36 years). Also offered is an "Undiscovered Chinatown" Walking Tour. In 2014 and 2015, Chinatown held "Summer Night" events with food trucks and temporarily had California's first pop-up "Cat café" (a popular trend from Japan) where visitors could pet and adopt kittens while drinking coffee and tea. A fundraiser for radio station KCRW "Art Beyond the Glass" (in its fourth year) was held in Central Plaza in June 2015 outside long-standing Chinese restaurant General Lee's, with live music performances, art showcases, and exhibitions from top Los Angeles bartenders.

Challenges and Hope for the Future in Los Angeles Chinatown

Chinatown can look inward for one method of recovery by making use of the Chinese lottery system. Like the original founders of New Chinatown and business leaders in San Francisco Chinatown, everyone in the larger Chinese business association pools money, usually monthly, and one person is selected to receive the money to start a business. Los Angeles's Little Tokyo borrowed this system, and so has Los Angeles Koreatown, whose business owners pool money every month to expand their businesses literally across the block. The Chinese business community needs to fully invest itself in business and property ownership and build Los Angeles Chinatown into a more attractive destination for tourism, commerce, and a better home for Chinese Americans. Chinatown needs new immigrants to open businesses and participate in the area as a greater community. To that end, a proper community center funded by the community will help make Chinatown more hospitable for younger families. Institutions like an SAT tutoring/English tutoring center and expanded afterschool programs would help. Popular Chinese sports like basketball and volleyball could also bring the community together.

Chinatown can rebrand by taking some of what works in the San Gabriel Valley while preserving what is special to Chinatown. A new Chinese American Museum, in addition to or to replace the museum in El Pueblo, could help, modeled after the impressive Japanese American National Museum in Little Tokyo.

The public perception of Chinatown needs to improve. The area is gradually becoming safer with police bike patrols, and cultural events have the potential to draw residents from all corners of Los Angeles County. If Chinatown can rebrand to attract new immigrants and open more businesses owned by its residents, it can transform into a more vibrant community.

See also in California: Baldwin Hills (Los Angeles, California); Boyle Heights, Jewish Neighborhood (Los Angeles, California); Boyle Heights, Latino Neighborhood (Los Angeles, California); Cambodia Town (Long Beach, California); Chinatown (San Francisco, California); Chinatowns (Duplicates) (San Francisco, California); East Los Angeles, Mexican American Enclave (Los Angeles, California); El Monte, Latino Enclaves (California); Fillmore District (San Francisco, California); Gardena and Torrance (South Bay Region, Los Angeles County, California); Glendale, Armenian Enclave (California); Historic Filipinotown (Los Angeles, California); Historic South Central (Los Angeles, California); Indio, Mexican and Central American Communities (California); Japantown (San Francisco, California); Kingsburg and Sveadal, Swedish Enclaves (California); Koreatown (Los Angeles, California); Little Arabia (Anaheim, California); Little Armenia (Los Angeles, California); Little Ethiopia (Los Angeles, California); Little India/Pakistan (Artesia, California); Little Italy (Los Angeles, California); Little Italy (San Diego, California); Little Italy (San Francisco, California); Little Saigon (San Francisco, California); Little Saigon (San Jose, California); Little Saigon (Westminster, California); Little Tokyo (Los Angeles, California); Logan Heights, Mexican Enclave (San Diego, California); Los Angeles, Hawaiian Enclaves (California); Los Angeles, West Side and San Fernando Valley Jewish Enclaves (California); Mayan Corner/24th and Mission (San Francisco, California); Monterey Park, First Suburban Chinatown (California); Mount Washington, Mexican Enclave (California); National City (San Diego, California); Olvera Street/La Plaza (Los Angeles, California); Pico Rivera, Latino Enclave (California); Riverside, Mexican Enclave (California); San Bernardino, Mexican Enclave (California); San Pedro, Italian and Croatian Enclaves (California); Santa Ana, Mexican Enclaves (California); Sawtelle (Los Angeles, California); Silicon Valley, Indian and South Asian Communities (Santa Clara Valley/San Jose Region, California); Sin City (Fresno, California); Solvang, Danish Community (California); Sonoma County, Italian Enclave (California); Tehrangeles (Los Angeles, California); Temescal (Oakland, California); Thai Town (Los Angeles, California); Watts (Los Angeles, California); Yuba City, Sikh Enclave (California)

See also Chinese/Taiwanese Enclaves: Bridgeport (Chicago, Illinois); Chinatown (Boston, Massachusetts); Chinatown (Phoenix, Arizona); Chinatown (San Francisco,

California); Chinatown Historic District/A'ala (Honolulu, Hawaii); Chinatowns (Duplicates) (San Francisco, California); Chinatowns (Manhattan; Sunset Park East, Brooklyn; Flushing, Queens) (New York City); International District (Seattle, Washington); Monterey Park, First Suburban Chinatown (California); New Chinatown (Portland, Oregon); Tucson, Chinese and Southeast Asian Enclaves (Arizona)

Michael Masukawa

Further Reading

Berthelsen, Christian. "Frederic Hsieh Is Dead at 54; Made Asian-American Suburb." *New York Times*, August 20, 1999.

Bonus, Rick, and Trinh Vo, Linda. *Contemporary Asian American Communities: Intersections and Divergences*. Philadelphia, PA: Temple University Press, 2002.

"Chinatown Neighborhood in Los Angeles, CA 90212 Detailed Profile." Accessed October 14, 2016. http://www.city-data.com/neighborhood/Chinatown-Los-Angeles-CA.html.

Butterfield, Fox. "Chinese Organized Crime Said to Rise in U.S." *New York Times*, 1985.

Chen, Tony. "California's First Cat Café Is Coming to Chinatown in October." *LA Weekly*, September 15, 2014. Accessed October 14, 2016. http://www.laweekly.com/restaurants /californias-first-cat-caf-is-coming-to-chinatown-in-october-5078385.

Chin, Jeffrey Gee (writer, director, filmmaker) in discussions with the author, September 2015.

Cho, Jenny, and the Chinese Historical Society of Southern California. *Chinatown and China City in Los Angeles*. Charleston, SC: Arcadia, 2011.

Fong, Timothy P. *The First Suburban Chinatown: The Remaking of Monterey Park, California*. Philadelphia, PA: Temple University Press, 1994.

Gary, Jesse, and Brayton, Julie. "Population in Chinatown Shrinks." NBC Southern California, January 19, 2012. Accessed October 14, 2016. http://www.nbclosangeles.com/news /local/Population-in-Chinatown-Shrinks-137740378.html.

Harvey, Doug. "Like a Magic Candle, Chinatown Relights." *The International Herald Tribune*, April 16, 2011.

Hummer, Jody. "Filming in Old Chinatown Los Angeles." Accessed October 14, 2016. http:// www.oldchinatownla.com/film.html.

Juliano, Michael. "Things to Do in Chinatown: Tours and Attractions in the LA Neighborhood." *TimeOut*, August 12, 2013. Accessed October 14, 2016. http://www.timeout .com/los-angeles/things-to-do/things-to-do-in-chinatown-tours-and-attractions-in -the-la-neighborhood.

Mai, Randy, and Chen, Bonnie. "The State of Chinatown Los Angeles." UCLA Department of Urban Planning, May 2013. Accessed October 14, 2016. http://www.aasc.ucla.edu /research/pdfs/statect.pdf.

McMillan, Penelope. "Founders' Feast: Four 'New Chinatown' Creators Honored on 50th Anniversary." *Los Angeles Times*, June 6, 1988. Accessed October 14, 2016. http://articles .latimes.com/1988-06-06/local/me-3045_1_chinatown-residents.

Miller, Stuart Creighton. *The Unwelcome Immigrant: The American Image of the Chinese 1785–1882*. Berkeley and Los Angeles: University of California Press, 1969.

"Neighborhoods of the City of Los Angeles: Population and Race, 2010 Census." Accessed October 14, 2016. http://www.laalmanac.com/population/po24la.htm.

Sandmeyer, Elmer Clarence. *The Anti-Chinese Movement in California*. Chicago: Illini Books, 1973.

Sedek, Zuhaila. "Evolution of Chinatowns." *New Straits Times* (Malaysia), January 5, 2008.

See, Lisa. *Shanghai Girls: A Novel*. New York: Random House, 2009.

See, Lisa. *On Gold Mountain: The One-Hundred-Year Odyssey of My Chinese-American Family*. New York: Random House, 1995.

Yen, Hope, and Nuckols, Ben. "Urban Chinatowns Wane as Asians Head to Suburbs." *Huffington Post,* March 20, 2012. Accessed October 14, 2016. http://www.huffingtonpost.com/2012/01/19/urban-chinatowns-decline_n_1217122.html

Zesch, Scott. *The Chinatown War: Chinese Los Angeles and the Massacre of 1871*. New York: Oxford University Press, 2012.

CHINATOWN (PHOENIX, ARIZONA)

Phoenix, Arizona, harbored two thriving Chinatowns between the 1870s and the 1940s. The first enclave grew around the First Street and Adams intersection, but the Chinese were forced out and migrated south to First Street and Madison. The Chinese population of Phoenix has since largely scattered throughout the country, although there are a few restaurants and buildings that echo Phoenix's Chinese past.

After immigrating to the United States to work on the railroads in the 1860s, many Chinese immigrants chose to remain in the country. The first Chinese immigrants in the Arizona Territory arrived in the late 1860s. The 1870 U.S. Census listed just 21 Chinese people in the Arizona Territory. However, by the 1870s the construction of the Southern Pacific Railroad across Arizona brought more Chinese men to Tucson. Despite anti-Chinese prejudices, Chinese communities settled in a number of Arizona towns, opening restaurants, grocery stores, and laundries.

By 1880, the U.S. Census listed 110 people of Chinese ancestry living in Phoenix, comprising 4.6% of the town's population. They often accepted work that others refused and subsequently dominated those industries. According to an 1886 article in the *Arizona Gazette*, the Chinese of Phoenix controlled the gardening industry, domestic work, laundries, and restaurants, illustrating just how quickly and powerfully the Chinese established economic roots within the spaces allotted to them. They established lines of credit and trade with San Francisco and Los Angeles as well as their own credit institutions when banks refused to lend money to minority groups.

Socially isolated, the Chinese of Phoenix preserved their languages and traditions in order to maintain a familiar, supportive environment in a town that was frequently hostile to their presence. The most visible element of this was Chinese New Year. Each year, Chinese New Year transformed Phoenix's Chinatown into a massive celebration of festive music, entertainment, firecrackers, and bright, colorful dragons.

Chinatown migrated several blocks south by the end of 1895. Real estate developers who wanted to take over the buildings and the public's discontent with the visibility of the Chinese community forced them to relocate to First Street and

---

Chinese Cultural Center

Many Chinese immigrants settling in Phoenix today are settling in the city's spreading modern neighborhoods. Geographic mobility and dispersion has encouraged organizations such as the Chinese Chamber of Commerce and the Chinese Cultural Center to assume a centralizing leadership role in representing Chinese and Chinese American culture in the public life of Phoenix. The Chinese Cultural Center provides views of the original Chinatown construction of which few visible remnants remain today. As such, it preserves the historic memory of one of Phoenix's early ethnic enclaves that has been disappearing under the waves of rapid development and change.

Madison, where it remained until the enclave dissipated in the 1940s. Once again, the Chinese opened grocery stores, laundromats, boarding houses, and shops, with families living above their businesses. While most of Chinatown's early inhabitants were single men, families became more common as immigrants increasingly settled in Phoenix without intending to return to China permanently. The Chinese Chamber of Commerce, the Chinese Salvation Society, the Chinese Boy Scouts, the Chinese Baptist Church, and other social and welfare organizations supported this growing community.

With each successive generation, increased prosperity brought more educational opportunities and social mobility. Such trends encouraged greater acculturation and expansion, despite the persistence of racial prejudices and discrimination. Chinese families began adopting American customs and increasingly settled and did business elsewhere in Phoenix. By 1929, there were 53 Chinese businesses in Phoenix outside of Chinatown. Despite the economic downturn of the 1930s, Chinese Americans continued to move to other parts of Phoenix, seeking economic prosperity and distance from Chinatown's seedy reputation, leading to a fragmenting of the neighborhood by the late 1930s and early 1940s.

Today, the neighborhood is almost entirely gone, and two sports arenas occupy most of what was once Chinatown. A handful of establishments remain as unassuming reminders of Phoenix's Chinese enclave. The Sun Mercantile Building, built in 1929 by Tang Shing, was a warehouse for Tang's thriving grocery store empire, but the building has been vacant for years. Sing High Chop Suey House, founded in 1928, is one of the handful of Chinese restaurants in the area. The Chinese Cultural Center features traditional Chinese architecture, shops, and restaurants. The nonprofit Phoenix Chinese Week puts on annual Chinese New Year festivities, ensuring that Chinese Americans, as well as the rest of Phoenix, retain some reminder of the once thriving enclave.

See also in Arizona: Phoenix and Other Cities, Mexican Enclaves (Arizona); Tucson, Chinese and Southeast Asian Enclaves (Arizona)

See also Chinese/Taiwanese Enclaves: Bridgeport (Chicago, Illinois); Chinatown (Boston, Massachusetts); Chinatown (Los Angeles, California); Chinatown (San

Francisco, California); Chinatown Historic District/Aʻala (Honolulu, Hawaii); Chinatowns (Duplicates) (San Francisco, California); Chinatowns (Manhattan; Sunset Park East, Brooklyn; Flushing, Queens) (New York City); International District (Seattle, Washington); Monterey Park, First Suburban Chinatown (California); New Chinatown (Portland, Oregon); Tucson, Chinese and Southeast Asian Enclaves (Arizona)

Katherine Anderson

Further Reading

Luckingham, Bradford. *Minorities in Phoenix: A Profile of Mexican American, Chinese American, and African American Communities, 1860–1992.* Tucson, AZ: University of Arizona Press, 1994.

Phoenix Chinese Week. "About." Accessed December 7, 2016. http://www.phoenixchineseweek.org/about.

Provenzano, Ashley. "Local Restaurant City's Last Sign of Phoenix's Chinatown." *Downtown Devil*, July 6, 2012. http://downtowndevil.com/2012/07/06/28446/sing-high-chop-suey-chinatown.

Riccardi, Nicholas. "Pressure Is Building on Phoenix Warehouse." *The Los Angeles Times*, November 30, 2005. Accessed December 8, 2016. http://articles.latimes.com/2005/nov/30/nation/na-phoenix30.

CHINATOWN (SAN FRANCISCO, CALIFORNIA)

To comprehensively understand San Francisco, we must understand the city's Chinatown and its history. Born during the Gold Rush, Chinatown is one of San Francisco's oldest ethnic communities and has been firmly entangled with the city's development since then. As of 2015, the Chinese constitute 21.4% of the city's population (worldpopulation.com), making them its largest ethnic community.

San Francisco's Chinatown is the oldest permanent Chinese settlement and remained, for a long time, the largest Chinese community in the United States. Its creation and transformation stand as an epitome of the history of Chinese America. Chinatown featured prominently in the nation's imagination, especially in the realm of race and racial relations, becoming a focal point in the debate over Chinese immigration in the late 19th century and later a tourist destination. Chinatown's story, therefore, also constitutes an important chapter of American history.

The creation of Chinatown indicates the continued impact of memories of the world Chinese immigrants had left behind and paralleled experiences of many other ethnic groups. Place names like "New England," "Worcester," "Boston," and "Hartford" express early English colonists' remembrance of the Old World. Like the Chinese, large numbers of immigrants who came from Southern and Eastern Europe created urban enclaves, such as Little Italies and Greektowns. In contrast to the colonists, who entered the New World with few political difficulties, 19th-century immigrants found themselves entering a nation state that was increasingly hostile to immigration. The ethnic communities that they created were not merely a reflection

Historic buildings in San Francisco's famous Chinatown, one of the oldest ethnic communities in the United States. (Jerryway/Dreamstime.com)

of sentimental memories of their native land but also a means to deal with the difficulties and hostilities that they faced in the New World. Few other immigrant groups encountered the kind of discrimination that the Chinese had to endure in the late 19th and early 20th centuries.

The Chinese who came to California shortly after the discovery of gold were the first large immigrant group from Asia. Anti-Chinese sentiments surfaced soon thereafter and became institutionalized. In 1852, when the Chinese population increased to 25,116 from 7,370 a year earlier, California legislature reenacted the Foreigner Miners' tax, targeting the increasing number of Chinese miners. Institutional racism against the Chinese reached the climax with the passage of the 1882 Chinese Exclusion Act, the only federal immigration restriction measure targeting a particular ethnic group. This act not only banned Chinese labor immigration for 10 years but also reaffirmed the legal principle that Chinese immigrants could not become naturalized citizens. Sanctioned by such racist government policies, popular hostility against the Chinese spread and grew increasingly more violent. In the 1885 Rocksprings massacre in Wyoming, for example, 51 Chinese were killed, and all the culprits went unpunished. By the end of the 1880s, as Jean Pfaelzer informs us, "close to two hundred towns . . . had driven out their Chinese residents" (Pfaelzer 2007, p. 253). Following such incidences of anti-Chinese violence, many survivors went to live in San Francisco's Chinatown, which served as a safe haven for the Chinese. In the 1860s, Chinese San Francisco's population grew from 2,719 to 12,022, making it the largest Chinese community in America by 1870. But it would be a mistake to think of the large Chinatown in San Francisco merely as a passive response to racial discrimination. This thinking prevents us from properly appreciating the historical agency of the Chinese and the meaning and significance of Chinatown as a transpacific community.

The continued existence and expansion of Chinatown embodied the resilience of the Chinese in the face of the increasingly powerful anti-Chinese movement that sought to wipe out the Chinese presence in the United States. The vitality of Chinatown is contributable, first of all, to the geographical location of San Francisco as a gateway to the Pacific region. The city was the main intermediary trade center for Chinese travel between America and China until the second half of the 20th century, linking the emigrant communities in South China and New-World job opportunities in the mining areas and railroad construction sites. San Francisco's Chinatown also existed as a logistics center of Chinese America, through which goods vital for the Chinese—ranging from food to clothing—were imported from China. Meanwhile, it was also through Chinatown that Chinese Americans sent remittances and letters back to their loved ones on the other side of the Pacific.

Chinese immigrant pioneers started to construct permanent houses in San Francisco as early as 1849. By the mid-1850s, social organizations had emerged to organize life in the budding community and help those in need. Known as *huiguan* in Chinese, native place associations were the most important. From the beginning, such associations took on significant responsibilities for the community, providing medical assistance to the sick, burying the dead, offering help to those facing lawsuits, and assisting newcomers.

The native place associations later joined forces to create the "Chinese Consolidated Benevolent Association," commonly known as "the Six Companies," which represented all Chinese Americans, especially when fighting discrimination. This reminds us that until the dispersal of the Chinese population and the establishment of large Chinese communities in cities beyond the West, Chinese San Francisco remained the de facto capital of Chinese America.

Chinatown's centrality in Chinese America in its early history stemmed from its strength as a commercial center. In 1856, there were already 88 Chinese businesses in Chinatown, offering a wide range of goods and services that were culturally important for the Chinese. Of particular importance was traditional Chinese food, including rice, a major component of the Chinese diet, which was imported from China in large quantities. Chinese shoppers could also find other Chinese foodstuffs in the 33 Chinese-owned groceries, which outnumbered all other kinds of businesses. There were also Chinese restaurants in Chinese San Francisco from the beginning. In 1849, a journalist named Bayard Taylor of the *New York Tribune* came to California. In his popular book *Eldorado, or, Adventures in the Path of Empire*, he mentioned three Chinese restaurants: Kong-Sung's near the water, Whang-Tong's in Sacramento Street, and Tong-Ling's in Jackson Street. Besides these three, he added, "in Pacific Street another Celestial restaurant had been opened, and every vessel from the Chinese ports brought a fresh importation." (Taylor 1894, pp. 117, 165). Such food stores and restaurants would multiply over time, constituting a defining feature of Chinatown as a "food town." The existence of such Chinese businesses explains the enormous appeal of Chinatown to Chinese immigrants.

To understand this appeal, we must point out a fundamental characteristic of the early Chinese American population. Like other ethnic groups who came to California during the Gold Rush, the Chinese who arrived during the mid-19th century were predominantly male. The sex-ratio imbalance was also reflected in Chinese San Francisco. Historian Benson Tong reports that of the 2,954 Chinese residents in the city in 1852, only 19 were women (Tong 1994, p. 3). While more women joined men among members of other ethnic groups in subsequent decades, Chinese America remained a bachelor society for a much longer period of time. The male and female ratio was a stunning 26.8 to 1 in 1890 and nearly 4 to 1 in 1930. This is largely a result of America's discriminatory policies against Chinese immigration. The implementation of the exclusion acts and the Page Law of 1875 made it extremely difficult for legitimate Chinese immigrant women to enter the country.

For those Chinese men living and working in San Francisco and elsewhere in California, Chinatown provided in an environment in which to recreate and relive the experiences in their native communities in southern China. Restaurants, in particular, offered precious space for socializing and relaxing. Chinese enclaves were quite crowded, especially in the late 19th and early 20th centuries. A special committee was formed by 1885 by San Francisco's Board of Supervisors. Full of anti-Chinese animosity, its report nonetheless revealed the cramped living conditions in the Chinese community: "the Chinese herd together as compactly as possible, both as regards living and sleeping-rooms and sleeping-accommodations" (Farwell, 1885, p. 6). In an article about restaurants in San Francisco, Noah Brooks wrote in 1868: "They seize every possible occasion for a feast, and the restaurants of the race in this city are almost constantly lighted up with the banquets of their numerous customers" (Brooks 1868, p. 472).

In the late 19th century, Chinatown provided multiple forms of recreation at a level unrivaled by any other Chinese enclave. One such recreational activity was opium smoking, which had already evidently become prevalent in the community as early as the 1850s. It was so prevalent that in 1850s newspaper articles exhorted Chinese readers to stay away from the "unlawful," "unfilial," and "harmful" habit. Opium was available in specialty opium stores and other shops, as well as at numerous opium dens. Viewed widely by mainstream America as a Chinese vice, the widespread habit of opium use in China was fostered by British as well as American opium merchants in the 19th century. The preponderance of men in the Chinese American population resulted in still another kind of recreation in Chinatown: prostitution, which existed legally in California until 1917 when the state's 1913 Redlight Abatement Law took effect. The brothels that served Chinese immigrant men employed not only Chinese but also white prostitutes.

However, Chinatown in San Francisco offered other recreational activities that were deeply rooted in Chinese cultural traditions. These included Chinese dramatic performances, which constituted an important attraction for Chinese immigrants. While some other forms of recreation were available in smaller Chinese settlements, the Chinese immigrant theater was found exclusively in Chinese San Francisco until the establishment of other major Chinese communities, such as New York's Chinatown.

Chinese theater was an integral part of San Francisco's Chinese community from the beginning. As early as 1852, a Chinese dramatic company started to perform regularly. In 1853, another theater was opened. The theater groups evolved into a sizeable self-sufficient organization with its own hierarchy. The Sun Heen Lok Theatre Company in 1870 had 45 people altogether, for example, including five laborers, two carpenters, and three cooks. The manager, a man in his 40s named Lun Heen, owned $10,000 in personal property. In the mid-1870s, a golden period for the immigrant theater, there were 11 Chinese troupes in San Francisco, each having at least 28 players. The names of these players—printed in 1875 in *The Oriental*, a Chinese newspaper—reveal that a number were women. In the late 1870s and early 1880s, the Chinese American community supported four regular theaters in Chinatown, two located on Jackson Street and two on Washington Street.

Theater-going remained an affordable and therefore popular recreational activity. As late as the early 20th century, admission was only 20 cents (50 cents for non-Chinese), and the poor could attend for free. For immigrant bachelors, the theater was a site for socializing and recreation. Before the performance began, people in the audience were often found eating, drinking, and loudly chatting and exchanging jokes.

More than merely a form of recreation, the Chinese theater created a platform for sustaining immigrants' collective historical memory and cultural identity. Many performances reenacted ancient historical events in Chinese history, helping Chinese theatergoers stay connected their historical roots and identity.

Similarly, the Chinese restaurants in Chinatown were more than a site of relaxation. These establishments constituted a cultural institution, creating a familiar environment for expressing and reaffirming cultural identity. Beginning in the 1880s, as Chinese Americans were driven out of many occupations such as mining and manufacturing, restaurants gradually emerged as a vital economic lifeline of Chinatown. Around that time, the Chinese Exclusion Act had built a formidable wall against immigration from China, and Chinatown was no longer seen as a threat but became an increasingly popular tourist attraction and a notable characteristic of the city. Representing a striking feature of the landscape of Chinatown, both visually and olfactorily, Chinese restaurants played an important role in attracting non-Chinese tourists and provided employment opportunities for many Chinese Americans.

The 1906 earthquake and subsequent fire that destroyed Chinatown and most of the city were catastrophic. But Chinese San Franciscans took the rebuilding of Chinatown as an opportunity to renew their community, renovating the streets and stores in an effort to improve its image as a desirable place. Such efforts to rebuild Chinatown were accompanied by a growing nationalist desire to modernize China after the model of Western countries. Various political factions, including reformers and revolutionaries, were actively represented in Chinatown in the early 20th century, politically dividing the community. In spite of their disagreements, many political organizations came to share a common goal, namely, to modernize and strengthen China. This goal became the dominant political ideology of the Chinese community in San Francisco.

Founded at the end of the 19th century in San Francisco, the Chinese American Citizens League embodied the emerging presence and voice of the younger generation of Chinese Americans. Some young Chinese Americans questioned and even challenged the prevailing ideology, insisting on displaying their status as Americans. Nevertheless, transnationalism, characterized by a profound concern about China's future, continued to be a salient feature of the Chinese community's mentality.

Transnationalism culminated during the Chinese Pacific War in an opposition Japanese aggression in China, as the Chinese community mobilized to raise money to aid their compatriots. Among the numerous fund-raising organizations found in cities across the country from New York to Honolulu was the China War Relief Association of America (its Chinese name translates into "Association to Save China") in San Francisco's Chinatown, which could no longer claim to be the capital of Chinese America but retained its leadership position in the West. By the end of World War II, the association had collected at least 5 million American dollars, buying things like winter clothing, medicine, and ambulances for the wounded soldiers and others in China. During these years, there was hardly a moment when a fund-raising campaign for China wasn't ongoing in the community.

Like Chinese Americans elsewhere in the country, Chinese San Franciscans held large and festive fund-raising events in Chinatown, in a conscious effort to improve their relationship with mainstream society. In July 1838, for example, they held a "Chinatown Night," a festive fund-raiser that featured Chinese cultural traditions, such as dancing dragons, Chinese plays, and Cantonese music. An estimated crowd of 300,000 people attended the event. Chinese San Francisco had never been so close to and so friendly with their white neighbors.

During the Cold War, however, it became clear that transnationalism was a double-edged sword. The victory of the Communists in China in 1949, and especially the advent of the Korean War, rekindled public resentment and government hostility toward the Chinese. The American government increasingly placed them under close scrutiny. As the Cold War political climate cut off Chinese Americans' physical ties to mainland, the leadership of Chinatown in San Francisco and other major cities pledged their allegiance to the Nationalist government that had fled to Taiwan.

After World War II, San Francisco's Chinatown was no longer the main destination for Chinese newcomers. In the postwar era, New York City replaced San Francisco as the largest port of entry. The passage of the Immigration and Nationality Act of 1965 abolished the racist quota system under the 1924 immigration law, opening doors for large numbers of new Chinese immigrants from Taiwan. In 1979, immigration from mainland China resumed. Even for those who went to California, Chinatown in San Francisco lost its attraction as a destination. They settled increasingly in new communities elsewhere, most noticeably in suburban cities like Monterey Park, California.

As the opening of China demystifies Chinese culture in recent decades, Chinatowns in many major cities, such as Washington, D.C., and Los Angeles, have been losing their appeal as tourist attractions. Coupled with high real estate prices, the decline of Chinatown in San Francisco has become more obvious than ever and has accelerated. According to the 2010 U.S. Census, as David Leventi reports in "The End of Chinatown," the core areas of Chinatown showed a drop in population (Leventi 2015). To declare the end of Chinatown, especially in San Francisco, however, may be premature and may represent a misunderstanding of the concept of "Chinatown." The decline of Chinatowns in San Francisco and other major cities marks a new era in Chinese American history and the development of Chinese American communities.

Notable Chinese San Franciscans

Ah Toy (d. 1928)

Coming to San Francisco around 1848, 20-year-old Ah Toy (her name was also spelled Atoy and numerous other ways) quickly become the most famous Chinese woman in 19th-century American society. This was in part because she was the first Chinese prostitute in California. In addition, the tall, attractive, English-speaking woman was also assertive, independent, and enterprising. By 1851, after wealthy and prominent white patrons bought her freedom, she had turned herself into a madam and reportedly created San Francisco's first peep show. And she fought legal battles against men, including Norman Assing, a powerful Chinese restaurateur, who tried numerous times to deport her. After the 1850s, she disappeared from San Francisco and from the public eye. In 1928, she died at the age of 100 in Santa Clara County.

The Chinese community in the United States, including San Francisco, remained a "bachelor society" in the late 19th and early 20th centuries, and a significant percentage of Chinese women in the United States worked as prostitutes. Ah Toy's life is not representative of the experiences of most of these women but does serve as a reminder of an important episode in the history of the Chinese in San Francisco and elsewhere.

Ng Poon Chew (1866–1931)

There were four major Chinese-language dailies in early 20th-century San Francisco, showing the importance of Chinatown as a center in Chinese American life. One of them was Chung Sai Yat Po (meaning literally "Chinese Western Daily"), which was for a long time the only major newspaper not affiliated with any of the Chinese political factions that remained active in the city. It was founded by Ng Poon Chew (Wu Panzhao in Pinyin), one of most influential journalists and publishers in Chinese American history.

Ng Poon Chew was born in Taishan County in the Pearl River Delta in Guangdong Province in 1866. After immigrating to the United States in 1881, he studied English at a Presbyterian church in San Jose, California, where he converted to Christianity and worked as a domestic servant to support himself. In 1889, he enrolled in the San Francisco Theological Seminary and became the pastor of Chinatown's Presbyterian church in the city in 1892. The church later dispatched him to Los Angeles, where he stopped being a pastor after a few years to start a Chinese language periodical named Wa Mi San Po in 1898. Then he went back to San Francisco and launched Chung Sai Yat Po in 1900, which would remain one of the main and most respected sources of information among the Chinese in San Francisco and beyond for half a century.

In spite of his conversion, he remained deeply involved in community affairs as a leader and leading voice. The newspaper offered extensive coverage of events in the United States, China, and Chinese America, serving to mobilize the community for various political, socioeconomic, and charitable causes, including epic fund-raising campaigns to build a railroad in Ng Poon Chew's native county in the early 20th century and to aid victims of Japanese invasion in China in the 1930s. Before his death in 1931, he was one of Chinese America's most vocal voices against anti-Chinese racism. He went on numerous speaking tours across the nation, laboring tirelessly to introduce Chinese culture to American audiences.

Charlie Low and the Forbidden City Night Club

Born in Winnemucca, Nevada, where his parents operated a small store, Charlie Low moved to San Francisco with his family in 1922. Beginning in the late 1930s, he became one of the most famous Chinese among the non-Chinese population in the city. This was not because of his flamboyant lifestyle but because of the nightclub, the Forbidden City, that he opened on the edge of Chinatown on Sutter Street in December 1938. It featured an all-Asian cast of performers, including singers, comedians, dancers, strippers, magicians, and musicians and gave them a precious opportunity to display their artistic talent. It became the most famous Chinese nightclub, extremely popular in particular among servicemen who transited through the city in World War II. Its popularity gradually declined thereafter. In the early 1960s, Charlie sold the Forbidden City, which remained in business until 1970.

Charlie Low's success as the founder of the Forbidden City is attributable to a number of factors, including his personal charm and connections and his savvy business strategy. But perhaps most important of all is the social and political climate of the time. The late 1930s was a turning point in the relationship between mainstream American society and Chinese America, a development that became particularly apparent in San Francisco. Following the Marco Polo incident in 1937, when Japan started an all-out war of invasion against China, Chinese Americans accelerated their efforts to aid China and effectively turned those efforts into improving the relationship with white Americans. In July 1838, for example, Chinese San Franciscans held a public event called "Chinatown Night" to raise money to assist war victims in China, featuring Chinese cultural traditions and attracting an estimated crowd of 300,000 people. Never before had so many white San Franciscans been so openly supportive of their Chinese neighbors and friendly to Chinese culture. This new political environment made it possible and acceptable for the alleged all-Chinese performers in the nightclub to provide Western-style entertainment to white audiences.

Mamie Tape

Mamie Tape was probably the most famous Chinese American child in the 19th century. In 1884, when she was eight years old, her parents tried to enroll her in a public school in San Francisco—Spring Valley Elementary School, which rejected her. Her father, Joseph, was a Chinese immigrant, working first as a domestic servant before becoming a small businessman. Her mother, Mary McGladery Tape, grew up in an orphanage in Shanghai before coming to the United States at age 11. In San Francisco, she learned English at the Ladies' Relief Society as a child. A vocal and assertive Chinese woman, she publically criticized the school's decision to bar her daughter from the public school system, noting that her daughter was rejected because of hatred toward Chinese. The couple sued the principal of the school, Jenny Hurley, and took the case to the Supreme Court of California. In *Tape v. Hurley* (1885), the court ruled in favor of the Tapes. Mamie was unable to attend Spring Valley because the city's board of education created a segregated Chinese school. The case nevertheless was an extremely important and rare victory for a marginalized minority group in a society, where racial segregation in public education would remain the accepted norm for many decades.

Cecilia Sun Yun Chiang (c. 1920–)

Cecilia Sun Yun Chiang embodies the tremendous role that Chinese Americans have played in significantly enriching America's palate by transplanting and popularizing their cuisine. She also embodies the entrepreneurial spirit and perseverance of Chinese Americans, who strove to carve a space in the New World for themselves in spite of enormous adverse circumstances. Although she was born to a privileged family in China (as the seventh daughter of 12 children), her life was full of turmoil. After Japan launched a full-scale invasion of China in 1937, she was forced to seek exile with her family in Chongqing at the age of 22. In 1949, she was uprooted again, this time leaving her native land to settle in Tokyo, where she opened a Chinese restaurant called the Forbidden City. In 1960, she learned that her sixth sister had lost her husband and was penniless and isolated. That news prompted Chiang to move to San Francisco to be with her sister.

In 1961, she opened her legendary restaurant (the Mandarin) in San Francisco, becoming one of the first to introduce regional Chinese food—Beijing, Shandong, Sichuan, and Hunan—in a city where Chinese food had remained predominantly Cantonese. In 1968, she moved her restaurant to Ghirardelli Square, ignoring warnings that business owners there would not welcome a Chinese restaurant. The new 300-seat establishment emerged as a gastronomical landmark with a national reputation. Thus, she became one of the first to successfully introduce Chinese food as high-end cuisine. Moreover, her use of fresh and locally produced foods became a source of inspiration for culinary pioneers of the time, such as Alice Waters, who called her "a woman of real and lasting influence. . . . a role model, a mentor, and an inspiration." She has also had a lasting influence on the younger generation, including her son, Philip Chiang, cofounder of the P. F. Chang restaurant chain.

See also in California: Baldwin Hills (Los Angeles, California); Boyle Heights, Jewish Neighborhood (Los Angeles, California); Boyle Heights, Latino Neighborhood (Los Angeles, California); Cambodia Town (Long Beach, California); Chinatown (Los Angeles, California); Chinatowns (Duplicates) (San Francisco, California); East Los Angeles, Mexican American Enclave (Los Angeles, California); El Monte, Latino Enclaves (California); Fillmore District (San Francisco, California); Gardena and Torrance (South Bay Region, Los Angeles County, California); Glendale, Armenian Enclave (California); Historic Filipinotown (Los Angeles, California); Historic South Central (Los Angeles, California); Indio, Mexican and Central American Communities (California); Japantown (San Francisco, California); Kingsburg and Sveadal, Swedish Enclaves (California); Koreatown (Los Angeles, California); Little Arabia (Anaheim, California); Little Armenia (Los Angeles, California); Little Ethiopia (Los Angeles, California); Little India/Pakistan (Artesia, California); Little Italy (Los Angeles, California); Little Italy (San Diego, California); Little Italy (San Francisco, California); Little Saigon (San Francisco, California); Little Saigon (San Jose, California); Little Saigon (Westminster, California); Little Tokyo (Los Angeles, California); Logan Heights, Mexican Enclave (San Diego, California); Los Angeles, Hawaiian Enclaves (California); Los Angeles, West Side and San Fernando Valley Jewish Enclaves (California); Mayan Corner/24th and Mission (San Francisco, California); Monterey Park, First Suburban Chinatown (California); Mount Washington, Mexican Enclave (California); National City (San Diego, California); Olvera Street/La Plaza (Los Angeles, California); Pico Rivera, Latino Enclave (California); Riverside, Mexican Enclave (California); San Bernardino, Mexican Enclave (California); San Pedro, Italian and Croatian Enclaves (California); Santa Ana, Mexican Enclaves (California); Sawtelle (Los Angeles, California); Silicon Valley, Indian and South Asian Communities (Santa Clara Valley/San Jose Region, California); Sin City (Fresno, California); Solvang, Danish Community (California); Sonoma County, Italian Enclave (California); Tehrangeles (Los Angeles, California); Temescal (Oakland, California); Thai Town (Los Angeles, California); Watts (Los Angeles, California); Yuba City, Sikh Enclave (California)

See also Chinese/Taiwanese Enclaves: Bridgeport (Chicago, Illinois); Chinatown (Boston, Massachusetts); Chinatown (Los Angeles, California); Chinatown (Phoenix, Arizona); Chinatown Historic District/A'ala (Honolulu, Hawaii); Chinatowns (Duplicates) (San Francisco, California); Chinatowns (Manhattan; Sunset Park East, Brooklyn; Flushing, Queens) (New York City); International District (Seattle, Washington); Monterey Park, First Suburban Chinatown (California); New Chinatown (Portland, Oregon); Tucson, Chinese and Southeast Asian Enclaves (Arizona)

Yong Chen

Further Reading

Coolidge, Mary Roberts. *Chinese Immigration*. New York: Henry Holt, 1909.

Brooks, Noah. "Restaurant Life in San Francisco." *Overland Monthly* (November 1868): 465–73.

Chiang, Cecilia. *The Seventh Daughter: My Culinary Journey from Beijing to San Francisco*. Berkeley, CA: Ten Speed Press, 2007.

Dong, Arthur. *Forbidden City, USA: Chinatown Nightclubs, 1936–1970*. (Los Angeles: Deep-Focus Productions, 2015.

Farwell, Willard B. *The Chinese at Home and Abroad*. San Francisco, CA: A.L. Bancroft, 1885.

Leventi, David. "The End of Chinatown," *The Atlantic*, December 2011. Accessed October 14, 2016. http://www.theatlantic.com/magazine/archive/2011/12/the-end-of-china town/308732.

Pfaelzer, Jean. *Driven Out: The Forgotten War Against Chinese Americans*. New York: Random House, 2007.

Taylor, Bayard. *Eldorado*. New York: G. P. Putnam's Sons, 1894.

Tong, Benson. *Unsubmissive Women: Chinese Prostitutes in Nineteenth-Century San Francisco*. Norman, OK: University of Oklahoma Press, 1994.

Worldpopulation.com. Accessed October 14, 2016. http://worldpopulationreview.com/us -cities/san-francisco-population.

CHINATOWN HISTORIC DISTRICT/A'ALA (HONOLULU, HAWAII)

Chinatown Historic District/A'ala is a neighborhood in downtown Honolulu that encompasses Chinatown and the once thriving Japanese ethnic enclave around A'ala Park. Chinatown borders Beretania Street and Nu'uanu Avenue to the north and east, while Honolulu Harbor and Nu'uanu Stream serves as its natural boundaries to the south and west. The recently restored Hawaii Theatre is located on its eastern edge, now called the Arts District for its galleries and cultural events. A'ala Park was born in the 1890s, when the marshy section of Iwilei was reclaimed. The triangular park faces Nu'uanu Stream and Beretania and King Streets. Originally used for taro farming by the Hawaiians, the area is named after the "fragrant" white blossoms of the *hala* trees. In its prime, the park hosted a variety of activities for the city and surrounding community.

Hawaiians settled in the area from an early date. Nu'uanu Stream, running to Mamala Bay, provided fresh water and rich soil, while Waikiki allowed easy beaching of canoes and closer access to deep-sea fishing. True to its moniker, Honolulu offered the best anchorage in the Islands, "sheltered" from both wind and waves. By 1850, Honolulu became a thriving port town for Westerners engaged in Pacific trade.

The first Chinese came to Hawaii in 1788, many of them carpenters or smiths who accompanied English merchants en route from China. Within 50 years, 30 of the 40 foreigners living in Honolulu were Chinese. Starting in 1852, the Chinese arrived as contract laborers for the growing sugar industry. Most did not renew their five-year contracts, opting instead to work on smaller private farms or to find alternative work in the city. Of the 6,000 Chinese plantation laborers in 1866, less than a quarter remained in farm work in 1922. About 75% of Chinese businesses were concentrated in the 25 acres of downtown Honolulu bounded by Beretania, Hotel, and Maunakea Streets and Nu'uanu Avenue. Fronting Honolulu Harbor, the area first catered to the whaling trade, welcoming upwards of 4,000 sailors every spring and fall. In the late 1800s, over 300 prostitutes worked Chinatown's streets, while a lucrative opium trade lined the pockets of prominent local dealers. Whaling subsequently waned, but the sugar industry continued to boom for most of the 20th century. Referred to as the Big Five, a handful of firms collectively controlled the business from planting and harvesting cane, to processing and shipping sugar.

Chinatown came into being in the 1870s when the area's ancient fishpond was filled. Chinese grocery stores, temples, and restaurants started up in the vicinity, some serving double duty as banks, post offices, and lodging for compatriots from the same village. Within the next decade, the Chinese constituted 20% of Honolulu's population, occupying 24% of wholesale, 62% of retail, and 85% of restaurant licenses in Hawaii. By 1896, half of the city's 153 Chinese stores were located in Chinatown. Yet it was never exclusively Chinese. In 1823, up to 5,000 Hawaiians lived within a square mile of the harbor. Many Chinese men married Hawaiian women. On the weekend, the meat and produce market on Nu'uanu Avenue would draw a bustling crowd in the absence of a public park. Meanwhile, the city's upper elites fled the downtown for the suburbs.

The early Chinatown neighborhood was a labyrinth of narrow streets and alleyways. Garbage collection was virtually nonexistent. In 1886, a restaurant fire on the corner of Smith and Henry Streets quickly spread out of control. The fire burned for three days and consumed an eight-block stretch of 7,000 Chinese and 350 Hawaiian homes, causing $1.5 million in damage.

Chinatown quickly rebuilt itself, but the area remained dangerously congested. When a wave of bubonic plague struck Honolulu in 1899, 7,000 residents were quarantined. Following the deaths of 13 people, the Board of Health ordered the infected area to be cleansed by a series of "sanitary" fires. On January 20, 1900, a planned fire at Beretania between Nu'uanu and the old Kaumakapili Church spread to the wharf, destroying 38 acres and 4,000 homes of mostly Chinese and Japanese residents. In four months' time, Honolulu was deemed plague free. Many Chinese business owners, made homeless by the fire, moved elsewhere. Its Chinese population dropped from 75% in 1884 to 40%.

When Hawaii became a U.S. Territory under the 1900 Organic Act, the Islands were subject to the 1882 Chinese Exclusion Act, which suspended the importation of Chinese labor for the next 10 years. As the Chinese sought to make Hawaii their permanent home, they increasingly came under attack by the Hawaiians and *haoles*, an elite group of local Caucasians of American or British stock. Rising anti-Chinese sentiment prompted the founding of dozens of family societies and mutual-aid associations, often uniting the Chinese from the same province or family clan. Other organizations, such as the Hoong Moon, had political aims to overthrow the Qing and to bring back the Ming dynasty. The Chinese also launched their own newspapers, five appearing between 1886 and 1901, including the *New China Daily*.

In 1916, the Chinese started the Chinese-American Bank, followed by the Liberty Bank of Honolulu six years later.

The Japanese were the next group to arrive. Known as the *gannenmono*, 148 Japanese made their way to Hawaii in 1868, the first year of the Meiji period. Between 1885 and 1894, some 29,000 government contract laborers would emigrate, followed by 57,000 private contract laborers in the next six years. The sudden influx of young single men spurred the development of a "red light district" in Iwilei, where a majority of the 200-plus prostitutes were Japanese. During the Great Chinatown fire, more than 3,000 Japanese were displaced. When the Chinese abandoned their businesses and migrated to the city outskirts, the Japanese moved into the area upon the conclusion of their contracts. Annexation brought an additional 71,000 Japanese to the Islands, until the Gentlemen's Agreement of 1907 restricted Japanese immigration. The legal setback, in turn, paved the way for the arrival of 14,000 Japanese picture brides. By 1910, the Japanese made up a third of the city's population; 24,000 of them concentrated in Palama, and in the outlying areas of Kalihi, Pawa'a, and Moiliili.

As the Japanese left the plantations, the Filipinos arrived as a source of permanent labor. Between 1910 and 1932, more than 100,000 Filipino men came to work in the islands' cane and pineapple fields. In 1930, almost 90% of the 52,672 Filipinos in Hawaii were men. Of the 40% who were reportedly married, nearly three-fourths had left their wives in the Philippines. Few Filipinos were engaged in nonagricultural work until the Great Depression forced some to seek employment in the city.

Far smaller in number were the Koreans. About 7,500 Koreans arrived in the three-year period between 1902 and 1905, when the Japanese established a protectorate over Korea. Less than one-seventh had previous farming experience, thus accelerating their exodus to Honolulu. A sizable Korean community soon emerged in Liliha and Palama, where rent was low and within close range of the cannery. Others made their mark in small business. Not long after the Schofield Army Barracks and Wheeler Air Force Base were built in Wahiawa in 1912, the Koreans came to monopolize the local laundry and tailoring businesses. Similar to the Japanese *tanomoshi* or Chinese *hui*, the Koreans relied on a traditional system of rotating credit known as *kye* to start their businesses. By 1930, more Koreans worked in the pineapple industry than on the sugar plantations; more than 60% lived in or around Honolulu, and 10% were concentrated in Wahiawa.

Between World Wars I and II, Honolulu's population reached 200,000. Sugar and pineapple continued to dominate Hawaii's booming economy, but tourism and military would soon play larger roles. For the Japanese American community, this was a period of generational change just as the American-born nisei, or second generation Japanese, were taking over from their foreign-born issei parents. McKinley High School, Oahu's only public high school from 1910 to 1920, was already being called "Tokyo High" due to the high enrollment of nisei students. In 1921, Reverend Takie Okumura of the Makiki Christian Church began a six-year campaign to Americanize the issei, followed by a series of annual New American Conferences targeting nisei youth. Yet the 1920s also brought internal division amid the tide of anti-Japanese vitriol. Following the Strike of 1920, the Japanese were branded anti-American, and Japanese-language papers were considered agitators that stirred up planter-worker antagonism. The territorial government seized the opportunity to abolish the Japanese-language schools, accusing them of being un-American. Soga Yasutaro, the editor and publisher of the *Nippu Jiji*, urged compliance, while Fred Makino of the *Hawaii Hochi*, fought restriction. Only in 1927 did the Supreme Court declare the statutes unconstitutional. A year later, when Myles Yutaka Fukunaga, a Japanese youth, allegedly kidnapped and killed the son of a Caucasian business leader, the ethnic community hoped to dissociate themselves from the crime.

A'ala Park was a popular spot for political rallies, where 7,000 Japanese came together during the first major sugar strike of 1909. It was also the centerpiece of neighborhood life, featuring a bandstand and two baseball fields. The park attracted people of different ethnic backgrounds, including Filipinos who would congregate from the island to play checkers and *sepak raga*, or kick volleyball. It was a natural meeting place, within walking distance from the Oahu Railway and Land (ORL) train depot on King Street. Already the prime route of Honolulu Rapid Transit's electric streetcars, the introduction of motorbus service in 1925 brought more traffic to King Street. A number of taxi stands to and from rural Oahu operated on A'ala Street, while a cluster of Japanese hotels stood on Beretania Street across the park. The area's proximity to Honolulu Harbor allowed Japanese hotel operators, often from the same prefectures as their guests, to act as travel agents and pick up new arrivals from the ship or immigrant station. The Yamashiro Hotel, whose proprietor served as the treasurer of the Higher Wage Association during the sugar strike, was the site of many meetings.

By the 1920s, A'ala became in essence a "Japantown." A'ala Rengo, a merchant's association on North King Street, was one of four influential Japanese business districts in town. Serving as a one-stop shopping center, each business was individually owned and managed. Other smaller nearby Japanese shopping areas included the Ginza, also on North King Street on the other side of River Street, and Chuo Rengo on Beretania Street between Nu'uanu and Fort Streets. Whether Hawaiian Pine, California Packing Corporation, the American Can Company or the dockyards and lumberyards, people on their way to work would walk through the A'ala Rengo. The Rengo included a couple of Chinese businesses, but the majority was Japanese-run and carried traditional Japanese foods, cultural paraphernalia, and clothing. Sato Clothiers, with its beginnings as a hat-cleaning business in 1911, became the first and only proprietor to offer small-sized, ready-made wear in 1928 when the popularity of Panama hats began to wane. Since ready-made clothing was expensive, Japanese women learned to sew their own clothes, attending the city's sewing schools in the summer. The Hawaii Importing Company, a purveyor of yardage, not only advertised in the Japanese and Hawaiian dailies, but also on a weekly Japanese radio program. Amaguri Taro, which succeeded Chow Dry Goods in 1935, specialized in sweet roasted chestnuts imported from Tientsing, China, and stored its products at the Hawaiian Electric Company's cold storage plant across from Irwin Park.

The A'ala Market was located on the same block as A'ala Rengo, but fronting Queen Street between Iwilei Road and Nu'uanu Stream. Founded by a group of Chinese and Japanese merchants shortly after World War I, the fish auction stall was one of the first businesses to open at A'ala. The covered open market, with different specialties, encompassed almost the entire block of ORL property. At the Yamauchi tofu shop, pig keepers would buy *okara*, or soy pulp, for feed.

The 1930s ushered a period of economic depression, where mainland politics and diplomatic relations spilled over into Honolulu's Japanese American community. Responding to charges of unfair business practices from local competitors, the Japanese Chamber of Commerce launched its first National Recovery Administration (NRA) sales event in 1934, complete with the "We Do Our Part" motto and blue eagle insignia. Together with issei-led on-the-job training programs for nisei youth, older establishments tried to weather the storm by appealing to a younger generation of customers and employees. Japanese American business owners hit yet another low point during the Second Sino-Japanese War when news of San Francisco's boycott of Japanese goods reached Hawaiian shores. Protesters distributed pamphlets urging local hotels and restaurants to refrain from serving Japanese beer and liquor, though Chinese merchants downplayed the boycotts as futile attempts to disrupt the neighborhood peace. As business bounced back, the Otani Seafood Company bought the entire A'ala Market Place in 1938, only to lose three-fourths of the building to a fire. In 1941, the marketplace reopened with much fanfare, but its three-day celebration was cut short by an unexpected turn of events: the bombing of Pearl Harbor.

In the early afternoon of December 7, 1941, 13 arresting squads combed through Honolulu and forcibly removed Japanese aliens and citizens alike from their families and homes within a three-hour period. By next day, 391 Japanese Americans had been apprehended. A number of A'ala's prominent businessmen, including the proprietor of the Otani Seafood Company, were interned, as was the editor of *Nippu Jiji*. On the third day, half of the 200 internees held at the immigration station were taken to Pier 5, where the men were transported to Sand Island. A total of 1,466 were held, while 1,875 were sent to mainland internment camps. The remaining Japanese Americans, most of them laborers, were spared out of economic necessity.

Under the "Speak American" campaign, Japanese clubs and societies of all kinds were abandoned while English-language classes filled up. The Hawaiian Department of Military Intelligence imposed mandatory censorship upon the Island's newspapers and radio, a move that threatened to destroy the Japanese American press. The military quickly reversed its position as soon as it discovered that the best way to communicate with the issei was through the vernacular dailies. Japanese American advertisers also changed their tune, with patriotic messages calling on customers to show their support for the nation by buying war bonds.

The military buildup of the 1930s and World War II brought a huge military population to the Islands. Chinatown catered to the needs of up to 46,000 servicemen with 10 blocks of drinking establishments and houses of prostitution. Several black-owned businesses targeting black GIs blossomed on Smith Street. Coupled with the internment of its ethnic leaders and martial law restrictions on commercial activity, the A'ala district lost more than just foot traffic, but also its neighborhood character. The lack of goods in general and the discouragement and unpopularity of Japanese products had a devastating effect on the once lively community, save for a few that offered hardware, tools, and curios.

The founding of the Honolulu Japanese Junior Chamber of Commerce (HJJCC) in 1949 by nisei businessmen heralded a transitional period for the Japanese American community, a harbinger for larger things to come in the postwar era. In 1953, the HJJCC kicked off the first Cherry Blossom Festival and crowned its first Queen. From the start, sponsors and advertisers formed a crucial component of the pageant and the Hawaii Visitors Bureau was there to promote the entire event. During Hawaiiʻs own "Red Scare," in which the International Longshoremenʻs and Warehousemenʻs Union (ILWU) was accused of having Soviet connections, Japanese Americans were front and center of the territoryʻs campaign to showcase democracy in action. The ethnic enclaves were teeming with business activity, characterized by the transnational flow of goods and entertainment from a now "liberated" Japan. By the 1950s, the Japanese Americans constituted the largest single ethnic group in Hawaii, providing the critical mass necessary to turn its economic power into political clout. From the much decorated 442nd Regimental Combat Team and 100th Infantry Battalion, to the so called "Democratic Revolution of 1954," which ended over 50 years of Republican party rule in Hawaii, Japanese Americans played a pivotal role in spearheading the territoryʻs long-delayed statehood in 1959.

Yet the political success story was not without a price. After the war, the Aʻala district became run down and neglected, as the smaller mom-and-pop operations struggled to keep afloat in an otherwise booming economy. The cessation of rail service in 1947 was a devastating blow for Aʻala merchants, already hit hard by the shift in demand for automobile traffic and parking. Compounded by an aging issei population, older establishments found it increasingly difficult to meet changing consumer needs and competition. The opening of the Ala Moana Center in 1959 exacerbated the situation by turning commercial activity away from downtown Honolulu, as did newer developments in the suburbs. By the 1960s, Waikiki had become the center of Honoluluʻs business activity, offset by the growth in tourism and recreation. Those financially able to do so began to move out of Aʻala. As buildings deteriorated and fell into disrepair, dance halls, poolrooms, bars, and slum housing began to take over the neighborhood. It was not long before merchants and residents were notified that the area was in a redevelopment project. Some storeowners relocated while many others retired. The new park, although much larger, was now occupied by the homeless.

In Chinatown, a number of urban renewal projects were also underway. The construction of large-scale condominiums such as Queen Emma Gardens in 1963 displaced hundreds of Chinese families without any relocation compensation. By then, only 5% of Chinatown residents were Chinese. The construction of Kukui Plaza followed in 1976, as a mixed-use facility that combined residential housing with retail. As the city and private landlords pushed gentrification with Department of Housing and Urban Development (HUD) block grants, activists formed the People Against Chinatown Evictions (PACE) in the 1970s to fight mass eviction and to secure low-income housing. Many PACE members were elderly retired people with fixed incomes who were once active in their respective labor unions. PACE conducted educational programs with Chinatown tours and coordinated outreach to schools, unions, churches, ethnic clubs, and the University of Hawaii. Buoyed by demonstrations at city hall and the state courthouse, the PACE campaigns eventually led to the renovation and construction of over 500 government-subsidized rental housing units in Chinatown. Despite these housing victories, more store closures would follow in the 1980s, as the Board of Health regulated against smoke houses and exposed meats. By the time the Hawaii Theatre closed its doors in 1984, Chinatown's residential population had dropped to close to 40% while the rest of the city experienced 12% growth.

Meanwhile, community-based efforts to restore and preserve the history of Chinatown picked up in 1973 with the nomination of the neighborhood to the National Register of Historic Places. The Wo Fat Restaurant, founded in 1882 and moved to the Hotel Street location in 1906, promoted itself as Honolulu's oldest restaurant until it closed in 2005. Burned down twice during the Chinatown fires, the current structure was built in 1937. The Encore Saloon at Hotel and Nu'uanu was built in 1886 and was one of the few buildings to survive the fires. The Armstrong Building on North King Street was built in 1905 and was home to the Musashiya fabric store from the early 1930s to 1982. Its proprietor, Koichi Miyamoto, who made a name for himself through ad-man George Mellon's "Musa-shiya the Shirtmaker" ads, is credited with creating the first "aloha shirt." Other notable buildings include the Kuan Yin Temple, Honolulu's oldest since the 1880s, and the Toyo Theatre, built in 1938. There were at least four movie theaters in the area showing Japanese cinema in its heyday, where the *benshi* played an important role as narrator in the earlier days of the silent movie. The Yokohama Specie Bank building at the corner of Merchant and Bethel Streets was constructed in 1908. First confiscated by the Alien Property Custodian at the start of World War II, the army later converted the basement into a 250-person cell block for military personnel.

The recent designation of the area as an Arts District owes much to the reopening of the Hawaii Theatre in 1996. The ARTS at Marks Garage, responsible for launching the First Friday Gallery Walk, has attracted young artists and musicians to Chinatown since the early 2000s. Together with the Hawaii Heritage Center's guided walking tours, Chinatown has reinvented itself as a Preserve America community and a nationally important historic site. A steady flow of immigrant shopkeepers from Vietnam and other parts of Southeast Asia has also reinvigorated the neighborhood. A'ala Park has returned to its roots as a gathering place, partly made over as a concrete ramp for young skateboarding enthusiasts. In 2003, the Japanese Cultural Center of Hawaii organized an exhibit of photos and artifacts in its own tribute to A'ala.

Notable People

Honolulu's many "firsts" among Asian Americans include Hiram Leong Fong, who became the first Asian American senator in 1959. Daniel Ken Inouye, a wounded war hero, was the state's first Asian American congressman, and Patsy Takemoto Mink was the first Asian American woman elected to congress in 1964. In 1974, George Ryoichi Ariyoshi became the first Asian American governor. In popular culture, Honolulu Police Department detective Chang Apana was the inspiration for author Earl Derr Biggers's fictional character, Charlie Chan. Wo Fat, the fictional villain in the TV series *Hawaii Five-O* was named after the Chinatown restaurant. In 2007, the Chinatown Gateway Plaza at the corner of Hotel and Bethel Streets was renamed in honor of Dr. Sun Yat-sen, who received his early education in Honolulu and later led a revolutionary movement that ended China's dynastic rule in 1911.

See also in Hawaii: Kaka'ako (Honolulu, Hawaii); Los Angeles, Hawaiian Enclaves (California)

See also Chinese/Taiwanese Enclaves: Bridgeport (Chicago, Illinois); Chinatown (Boston, Massachusetts); Chinatown (Los Angeles, California); Chinatown (Phoenix, Arizona); Chinatown (San Francisco, California); Chinatowns (Duplicates) (San Francisco, California); Chinatowns (Manhattan; Sunset Park East, Brooklyn; Flushing, Queens) (New York City); International District (Seattle, Washington); Monterey Park, First Suburban Chinatown (California); New Chinatown (Portland, Oregon); Tucson, Chinese and Southeast Asian Enclaves (Arizona)

Shiho Imai

Further Reading

Chinatown Honolulu Culture and Arts District Association. Accessed October 14, 2016. www.chinatownhonolulu.org.

Fuchs, Lawrence H. *Hawaii Pono: An Ethnic and Political History.* Honolulu, HI: Bess Press, 1961.

Hukilau Network. Accessed October 14, 2016. http://www.hawaiihistory.org.

Imai, Shiho. *Creating the Nisei Market: Race and Citizenship in Hawai'i's Japanese American Consumer Culture.* Honolulu, HI: University of Hawai'i Press, 2010.

Niiya, Brian. *Encyclopedia of Japanese American History: An A-to-Z Reference From 1868 to the Present.* New York: Facts on File, 2001.

Okihiro, Michael M. *A'ala: The Story of a Japanese Community in Hawaii.* Honolulu, HI: Japanese Cultural Center of Hawai'i, 2003.

Patterson, Wayne. *The Ilse: First Generation Korean Immigrants in Hawai'i, 1903–1973.* Honolulu, HI: University of Hawai'i Press, 2000.

Tamura, Eileen. *Americanization, Acculturation, and Ethnic Identity: The Nisei Generation in Hawaii.* Urbana, IL: University of Illinois Press, 1994.

Wong, Joy. "Chinatown Residents Showed Us How to Stop Wrecking Balls." *The Honolulu Advertiser*, July 3, 2005.

Yano, Christine. *Crowning the Nice Girl: Gender, Ethnicity, and Culture in Hawai'i's Cherry Blossom Festival.* Honolulu, HI: University of Hawai'i Press, 2006.

CHINATOWNS (MANHATTAN; SUNSET PARK EAST, BROOKLYN; FLUSHING, QUEENS) (NEW YORK CITY)

According to the 2010 American Community Survey, approximately 12.2% of the total New York population reported Asian origins. The largest Asian subgroup is Chinese, including Taiwanese, accounting for 46.17% of all Asians. Boasting a long history in New York City, Chinese immigrants and their children have played an important role in the reshaping of many neighborhoods. This report provides a general profile of New York City's three Chinatowns: Chinatown in Manhattan, Sunset Park East in Brooklyn, and Flushing in Queens, which are the areas with the largest concentrations of Chinese residents and businesses in 2010. We will focus on their demography, history, economy, culture, and politics.

History of Manhattan's Chinatown

The original New York Chinatown is located in the borough of Manhattan, bounded by the Lower East Side to its east and Little Italy to its north. Chinese immigrants began to settle in this area after sequential immigration waves of Dutch, Irish, Italian, and Jewish immigrants. According to the sociologist Jan Lin (1998, p. 31): "the first New York Chinese began congregating in the southern periphery of the Lower East Side on what had been called the 'plow and harrow site' (where a farm and tavern were situated in the seventeenth century) around Mott, Pell and Doyers Streets. A general store operated by the merchant Wo Kee at 8 Mott Street became an early center of social and commercial life in the immigrant enclave."

Lower Manhattan saw its first Chinese immigrants, who were sailors, around the 1830s. The later massive arrivals of Chinese New Yorkers were largely due to the prosperity of the trade in tea and porcelain between China and the United States, which in turn shaped New York as the major port of the nation. The Chinese New

Shoppers and cars crowd New York's Chinatown district, a well established enclave. (trekandshoot/Dreamstime.com)

Yorkers changed their previous behaviors and habits over time, especially during the period of the emerging "commercial orientalism" (Tchen 1999, p. xxi), the commercial forms of orientalism characteristic of shaping and generating the representations of Chinese things, ideas, and people at that time. More Chinese involved themselves in the tea trade, married Irishwomen, and formed mutual aid organizations. They blended in with the neighboring citizens, forming a highly diverse community. However, by the end of the 1800s, the eclipse of the fascination with Chinese goods and the change in the image of the Chinese from "procapitalist, Protestant-like 'mandarins'" to a representative of "abject opium-smoking, rat-eating criminals" (Tchen 1999, p. xxiii), as well as servile and low-cost labor, drove the Chinese away from the mainstream society and labor market. The implementation of the Chinese Exclusion Act of 1882 aggravated the situation, which made more Chinese flee from the West to the East Coast for more job opportunities. This further solidified Chinatown as a segregated community in both a commercial and a residential sense.

As sociologist Min Zhou (1992, p. 33) has noted, the "emergence of Chinatowns in the United States involved both an involuntary and a voluntary process." On the one hand, the exclusion of Chinese from the larger labor market maintained the segregation involuntarily. The majority of the immigrants in Chinatown at that time were peasants. The similar background enabled them to collaborate with each other in an effort to defend themselves against hostile external forces. On the other hand, the segregation was kind of voluntary because they shared similar backgrounds. Most of the early residents in Chinatown came to New York from villages in the Sze Yap area, speaking Taishanese, and the greater Pearl River delta region of Guandong Province, speaking Cantonese, in the hope of making a "gold" fortune. They were willing to do the work that few Americans wanted, spoke little English and lacked marketable skills.

The Chinese Exclusion Act was repealed in 1943 due to China's alliance with the United States during World War II, along with Chinese Americans' efforts to fight for their own rights. However, the immigration quotas continued to be based on the 1890 and 1920 populations of foreign-born Chinese in the United States. This restriction was finally relaxed in 1965 and the "Family Reunification" provision allowed family and relatives of Chinese Americans to immigrate to the United States, which contributed to the most recent influx of Chinese immigrants since 1965.

Not only had the population begun to increase in 1960s but the land expanded as well. Land became available due to the downturn of New York's economy, which caused the shutdown of manufacturing factories and corporate offices and made previous New Yorkers move out of lower Manhattan. Consequently, many old buildings remained and made room for the growing Chinatown in Manhattan.

Historically, Chinese immigrants clustered in Chinatowns for three practical reasons. First, the earliest wave of Chinese immigrants included sojourners who did not intend to settle permanently. As a result, they had fewer incentives to learn English and to become Americanized. Second, Chinatowns provided plenty of employment opportunities for low-skilled workers, both in the hand laundry and the restaurant business. Third, Chinatowns also functioned as "social centers of support that gave the workers in an alien environment the illusion of home" (Zhou 1992, p. 35).

Chinatown residents in the earlier migration era were mainly from two regions: Guangdong and Fuzhou. Cantonese were among the first immigrants, partly as a result of the willingness to escape from the civil wars ignited by Taiping Rebellion (1850), which first began in Guangdong province. According to the sociologist Peter Kwong (1996), Cantonese are unique. Somehow—due to a particular dialect that was distinct from the languages in other parts of China, as well as their shrewdness in business, which was regarded as against traditional Chinese social core values—they historically relied on their own resources and maintained the strongest family ties among the Chinese immigrant population.

Since the 1980s, the massive influx of Fuzhouness (people from the Fuzhou region) was considered unwelcome at first. A significant number were undocumented, though some became legal immigrants due to the 1989 executive order that allowed Chinese already in the United States to apply for status adjustment due to the Tiananmen Massacre. However, Chinatown residents were wary of Fuzhouness because some of them were so desperate to earn money that they committed crimes such as ransom kidnapping. Because of cultural differences and ethnic stereotypes, Fuzhouness distinguished themselves from Cantonese and built their own sub-enclave in the area around East Broadway under the Manhattan Bridge and Lower East Side.

Today, Manhattan's Chinatown boasts a mosaic of Chinese from Hong Kong, Taiwan, and mainland China. Those from mainland China hail from diverse provinces such as Beijing, Shanghai, Hunan, and Sichuan, speaking different dialects, including Mandarin, Cantonese, and Fujianese.

Satellite Chinatowns: Sunset Park East (Brooklyn) and Flushing (Queens)

Over the last decade, Flushing and Sunset Park East have emerged as counterparts of the old Chinatown. Flushing, bordering Flushing Meadows–Corona Park to its west, Francis Lewis Boulevard to its east, Union Turnpike to its south and Willets Point Boulevard to its north, saw a massive influx of Chinese residents, the majority of whom were Taiwanese, in the 1970s. In the early days, Chinese were regarded as unacceptable by the previous residents, most of whom were Jewish, Irish, Italian, and German. However, white residents began to leave for the suburbs in the 1960s and left many apartments empty, which made room for the influx of Chinese. Today, Flushing is a middle-class Chinese and Korean enclave, bustling with ethnic businesses. It is also well known for its tolerance of different religions, witnessing a new influx of Afghani, Indian, Pakistani, and Bangladeshi immigrants as well.

Similar to Flushing, Sunset Park East was home to Polish and Scandinavian enclaves at the turn of the 20th century. After the departure of white ethnics, this neighborhood saw waves of new immigrants: first Dominicans, then Puerto Ricans, then Asians and Arabs. Most of the initial Chinese residents in Sunset Park East, similar to Chinatown, shared Cantonese backgrounds. They originally settled on Eighth Avenue, because the number eight was symbolic of prosperity in Chinese and also because of its convenient access to Chinatown. Chinese immigrants appreciated Sunset Park because housing prices are more affordable than in Manhattan's Chinatown or in Flushing. As a result, Sunset Park East is predominantly working-class, given the lower socioeconomic background of its residents. Most of the residents in Sunset Park East either work there or take the N train directly to Manhattan's Chinatown.

Beyond these three Chinatowns, there are several other neighborhoods in the city with the potential of emerging as "new" Chinatowns. Specifically, three other neighborhoods reported more than 30% of Chinese residents in their population in 2010, including Bensonhurst, East Flushing, and Queensboro Hill. All of them have experienced a sharp increase in Chinese residents during the last decade.

Demographic Profiles

According to the 2010 U.S. Census, Chinese comprised 60.1%, 48.2%, and 47.33% of the total population in Chinatown, Flushing, and Sunset Park East, respectively. Between 2000 and 2010, the increase of Chinese population in Flushing and Sunset Park East was substantial, whereas Chinatown had experienced a slight decrease, from 66% to 60.1%. In both Chinatown and Sunset Park East, Chinese comprised almost 90% of the total Asian population. In contrast, there were two other large Asian groups in Flushing, namely, Koreans and Asian Indians, which accounted for 13.3% and 8.9% of the total Asian population there in 2010, compared to 24.9% and 15.9% in 2000. That is why it is called Chinatown of Queens but is also otherwise known as Koreatown or Little India. Furthermore, the composition of Hispanics also differs across the three neighborhoods. Specifically, Puerto Ricans (5.7%) and Dominicans (3.9%) were the dominant groups in Chinatown, South Americans (6.5%) and Colombians (3.5%) were in Flushing, and Mexicans (12.4%) and Puerto Ricans (7.8%) were in Sunset Park East. All three neighborhoods saw a decrease in Hispanics from 2000 and 2010, although some Hispanic subgroups had increased slightly. Specifically, the share of Mexicans in the total population in Sunset Park East grew by 3.8% over the last decade. These varying compositions of Hispanics infuse these neighborhoods with unique intergroup dynamics. For example, Puerto Ricans, Dominicans, and Mexicans are rather segregated from Chinese at the block group level in Chinatown and Sunset Park East, whereas South Americans and Colombians are more integrated with Chinese in Flushing.

Educational Attainment

The overall educational profile for Flushing residents is significantly higher than those in Chinatown and Sunset Park East. This difference captures the social class composition of these neighborhoods, with Flushing residents more likely to be from a middle-class background. In 2010, the majority of adults in Chinatown and Sunset Park East did not have a high school diploma, and many adults had less than a ninth-grade education. Nearly 41.5% (15,685) of adults in Chinatown and 48% (21,736) of adults in Sunset Park East were not high school graduates. These rates are almost double the New York City average level (20.9%). At the next levels, 21.4% of adults in Chinatown and 25.7% of adults in Sunset Park East adults have a high school diploma, while 25.6% of adults in Chinatown and 15.4% in Sunset Park East hold a bachelor's degree. In contrast, only 23.3% of Flushing adults lacked a high school diploma, and a large proportion of Flushing adults, 45.4%, had a college degree or higher education, of which more than half (28.1%) held a bachelor degree or higher, although this is still slightly below the city's average (33.3%).

Median Household Income

On average, household incomes are lower in Chinatown compared to Sunset Park East and Flushing. A third of households in Chinatown reported earning $20,000 or less a year, whereas a third of households in Sunset Park East and Flushing reported annual earnings from $20,000 to $49,999. At the top of the income scale, 13.1% of all households in Chinatown, 12.8% in Flushing, and 10.3% in Sunset Park East earned more than $100,000. The median annual income is highest in Flushing ($40,351) whereas it is significantly lower in both Chinatown ($33,280) and Sunset Park East ($34,399). On average, the median annual income in Flushing is 18% higher than that in Chinatown and Sunset Park East. This difference reflects the social class compositions of these neighborhoods. The initial Chinese residents in Flushing are middle-class and well-educated Taiwanese, but most of the Chinese immigrants in Sunset Park East and Chinatown are working-class Cantonese and Fujianese. That said, all three neighborhoods have more households earning less than $20,000 than the city average (22.5%).

Culture and Religion

The most important celebration for Chinese New Yorkers is indisputably the Lunar New Year, or Spring Festival, usually starting in January or February, and ending on the full moon. It is the moment when Chinese get together to honor their family and celebrate the new beginning. A lot of people parade on the street until midnight along with dragon and lion dancers, steel drummers, and fireworks. The color red, representative of good luck, could be seen everywhere during the festival. The Mid-Autumn Moon Festival is another important celebration in Chinatown. It is celebrated at the mid-harvest full moon, the 15th day of the eighth month of the lunar calendar, in honor of the ancestors and the brightest moon of the year.

Chinese food plays an important role through all the celebrations. The Lunar New Year banquet features eight courses, not including rice, which are considered a positive number because the words for "eight" and "fortune" are homophones in Chinese. The food always converys positive meanings during the holiday, such as "niangao" for "annual advance," taro root cakes for "rising fortune," "jiaozi" for prosperity due to their gold-coin shape, and "gut jai" for luck. The Moon Mid-Autumn Festival is characterized by moon cakes, or round cakes with special fillings, indicative of the idea of family reunion.

Besides the traditional Chinese food, hundreds of restaurants serve Chinatown, Flushing, and Sunset Park East, providing typical Asian food. "Dim sum," for example, is a typical Chinese brunch, especially among Cantonese and Hong Kongers. Most of the dishes are deep fried or steamed and are often served in small steamer baskets to keep them warm. The traditional dishes include steamed creamy custard buns, steamed chicken "paws," and braised beef short ribs. A variety of regional Chinese dishes are available: soup dumplings and turnip cakes from Shanghai, seafood served with Fuzhou sauce from Fujian, shrimp rolls and beef balls from Chaozhou, Peking duck from Beijing, Kung Pao chicken and hot pot from Szechuan, and pickled Napa cabbage and vermicelli from Northeastern China. The variety of the food speaks to the diversity of individuals of Chinese origins living in New York City.

This unique fare could not survive without the special ingredients provided in Chinese supermarkets. Chinese and Southeast Asian condiments such as cumin, which are key to authentic flavor, are provided in these supermarkets. Items exclusive to the Chinese groceries include herbal remedies, dried goods, and every part of pork, live frogs, sea fungus, and dried lizards.

Besides food, other businesses in the three Chinatowns include herbal pharmacies, beauty spas, souvenir shops, and traditional Chinese dress shops. Besides the Chinese traditional goods, tattoos of Chinese characters are also popular among people of non-Chinese origin. An interesting phenomenon in Chinatown is that you can always find something at an unbelievably cheap price after haggling with the vendors.

In terms of religion, Chinatown has "the largest Chinese Catholic congregation in the United States." There are a lot of churches in Chinatown, such as Grace Faith Church. One of the oldest, The Church of the Transfiguration on Mott Street, has witnessed a drastic demographic change from the Irish to the Italians and then to Chinese over the last two centuries. Although most Chinese are not originally Catholics, many converted to Catholicism after arriving in the United States because religious institutions can provide an important source of support.

In contrast, Buddhist temples or pagodas, traditional religious landmarks in China, do not have a long history in Chinatown but have developed at a rapid pace. Unfortunately, a few of them function mostly as a place for fortune-telling and incense burning. For example, Mahayana Buddhist Temple, located on Canal Street and Bowery Street near the Manhattan Bridge, is the largest Chinese Buddhist temple in New York City, famous for its 16-foot high golden Buddha inside.

Ethnic Economy

Before the 1960s, Chinatown's economy mostly consisted of service-oriented business, such as hand laundries. However, it almost stagnated, threatened by the development in technology, for example, the widespread use of washers and dryers. This, in turn, led to the development of other businesses, including restaurants and garments, the two pillar industries of Chinatown economy for quite a long time. The restaurant industry largely benefited from the changing taste of Americans and their appreciation of the Chinese cuisine. In the 1960s, the garment industry became increasingly reliant on Chinese immigrant workers, who quickly replaced previous Italian and Western European workers reaching retirement.

In these two industries, the majority of employment was confined to the Chinese communities. The operation of the restaurant is typical of the vertical "Chinese" supply chain: raw materials sold by Chinese wholesalers and importers, noodles and dumplings made by Chinese factories, the Chinese-English menu translated by Chinese printing houses. Most Chinese garment workers worked in factories owned by Chinese. The reasons for the "insider" employment are threefold: the lack of English ability, the importance of ethnic networks in getting a job, and the flexible employment entry and exit. Today, restaurants still account for a large share of Chinatown's economy, with the dramatic transformation from shabby eateries to elegant restaurants. According to Volkwein (2007), there are more than 500 restaurants in Chinatown. However, the garment industry has shrunk, especially in the aftermath of 9/11. New businesses, such as weddings, bussing, hypermarkets, barbershops, and buffets, have mushroomed throughout Chinatown. In addition, many agencies provide professional services, including real estate and financial consulting and health care.

Similar to Chinatown, small businesses, with fewer than 10 workers, predominate in Flushing and Sunset Park East, and most of them maintain the tradition of employing coethnics. Another important constituent in the Chinatown economy is tourism. On any given Sunday afternoon, Chinatown is packed with tourists from all over the world, hoping to learn more about Chinese culture or to get a good taste of dim sum. Flushing and Sunset Park are more suitable for an authentic culinary exploration, as the restaurants there prioritize the needs of Chinese over Americans or tourists. In that same vein, Sunset Park East is more "Chinese" than Flushing. In fact, Sunset Park East does not have much tolerance for outside visitors. English is seldom used in this area where the goods and services provided are particularly geared toward the Chinese.

Political Life

In the 1970s, many social service agencies sprung up in response to the needs of the large influx of Chinese immigrants and to help them tackle racial discrimination and unemployment. The Chinese Consolidated Benevolent Association is one of the oldest organizations among them. Founded in 1883, it has developed into an umbrella organization of 60 member organizations representing a cross-section of New York's Chinese community. The Chinese American Planning Council, founded during the 1960s economic downturn, is another important representative. As the largest social welfare agency in Chinatown, it provides a variety of programs in job training, mental health, and English improvement. It is also active in lobbying the government to strive for more funds for the poor in Chinatown.

Today, Chinese immigrants are more likely to put down roots, and a sizeable Chinese "second generation" (i.e., children of immigrants) has come of age. Sojourning is no longer the priority of this ethnic group, and permanent settlement has encouraged the rise of other associations, including nonprofit organizations, career-training centers, educational consulting firms, and most recently, senior community centers to serve an aging population of post-1965 Chinese immigrants.

Chinese residents in Flushing are more likely to participate in local politics. The Chinese American Voters Association, for example, is an influential civic organization that works directly on the issues regarding common economic concerns and legislative rights. More and more Chinese faces in the New York City Council best illustrate Flushing's effort in improving their political participation.

As a result of increasing integration into American society, Chinese immigrants and their descendants have also become more active in electoral politics. In 2009, John Chun Liu, who immigrated to the United States from Taiwan when he was five years old, was the first Asian to be elected comptroller of the City of New York. Prior to that, he was the first Asian member of the New York city council from 2001 to 2009, representing District 20 in Queens. In 2013, he was the first Asian to run in a mayoral election; however, he lost the election and was plagued by financial scandals. Other notable faces in local politics include John Chun Liu's successor, Peter Koo, and Margaret S. Chin, representing lower Manhattan in the New York City Council—both of whom are immigrants from Hong Kong.

Social Problems

In the late 1900s, Chinatown was long plagued by the problem of gangs and *tongs*, a term literally meaning "meeting hall" and based on family ties. Such groups were notorious for extorting "protection money," running illegal gambling rings and sweat shops, selling heroin, lending out money on usury, smuggling, blackmailing merchants, and other similar activities. Different gangs had their own territory, and they would fight with each other for economic interest. Another reason for the rampant activities of gang and tongs is that local residents were reluctant to cooperate with the police for fear of the consequences. After years of increased policing, gangs and tongs are no longer the serious problem they used to be, but they still exist, although most of the time underground.

The more immediate issue is poverty in the three neighborhoods. According to the 2010 American Community Survey, 29% of people in Chinatown, 26% in Sunset Park East, and 17.3% in Flushing lived below the poverty line, which was higher than the city average (16.2%). Poverty among Chinese is driven, in part, by a low level of education and a lack of English proficiency, which limits employment opportunities. Furthermore, the ethnic economy in these neighborhoods is still vulnerable due to the most recent economic recession.

Another major challenge in Chinatown is housing and crowded living quarters. The majority of housing stock in Chinatown is a century old, without elevators, but with crumbling walls, ruined ceilings, and rotted floors. Renter-occupied housing is very common in both Sunset Park East and Chinatown, whereas owner-occupied housing is more prevalent in Flushing. Over the last five years, median rent has increased significantly, which leads to a shortage of affordable housing in all three Chinatowns and their adjacent areas. In fact, the development of Sunset Park East and Flushing were directly linked to the outgrowth of Manhattan's Chinatown, which initially led many Chinese to look for affordable housing in other outer boroughs.

Despite these challenges, New York City's Chinatowns are vibrant communities that are deeply rooted in the neighborhoods they are part of. Their presence in these neighborhoods has transformed them into diverse and integrated communities with both residential and commercial components. They are here to stay and are remaking their communities with remarkable creativity and tenacity. As the city's second-largest ethnic group, Chinese and their children are full-fledged participants in both the local economy and local politics.

Van Tran and Mengying Li

See also in New York: Bedford-Stuyvesant (Brooklyn, New York); Borough Park/ Williamsburg/Crown Heights, Jewish Enclaves (Brooklyn, New York); Brighton Beach-Sheepshead Bay (Brooklyn, New York); Brooklyn, West Indian Enclave (New York); Coney Island (Brooklyn, New York); Crown Heights, Jamaican Enclave (Brooklyn, New York); Five Points (New York City); Greenpoint (Brooklyn, New York); Greenwich Village (New York City); Harlem (New York City); Harlem, Senegalese Enclave (New York City); Hell's Kitchen (New York City); Jackson Heights (Queens, New York); Jackson Heights, South Asian Enclave (Queens, New York); Little Brazil Street (Manhattan, New York); Little India, Jackson Heights (Queens, New York); Little Italy (Manhattan, New York); Lower East Side (New York City); Sleepy Hollow, Ecuadorian Enclave (New York); Staten Island, Sri Lankan Enclave (New York City); Sunset Park West and North Corona (New York City); Washington Heights (New York City); Yorkville, German Enclave (New York City)

See also Chinese/Taiwanese Enclaves: Bridgeport (Chicago, Illinois); Chinatown (Boston, Massachusetts); Chinatown (Los Angeles, California); Chinatown (Phoenix, Arizona); Chinatown (San Francisco, California); Chinatown Historic District/A'ala (Honolulu, Hawaii); Chinatowns (Duplicates) (San Francisco, California); International District (Seattle, Washington); Monterey Park, First Suburban Chinatown (California); New Chinatown (Portland, Oregon); Tucson, Chinese and Southeast Asian Enclaves (Arizona)

Further Reading

Chin, Margaret M. *Sewing Women: Immigrants in the New York City Garment Industry*. New York: Columbia University Press, 2005.

Foner, Nancy. *One Out of Three: Immigrants in New York in the Twenty-first Century*. New York: Columbia University Press, 2013.

Kwong, Peter. *The New Chinatown*. New York: Hill and Wang, 1996.

Lin, Jan. *Reconstructing Chinatown: Ethnic Enclave, Global Change*. Minneapolis, MN: University of Minnesota Press, 1998.

Tchen, John Kuo Wei. *New York Before Chinatown: Orientalism and the Shaping of American Culture, 1776–1882*. Baltimore, MD: Johns Hopkins University Press, 1999.

Volkwein, Ann. *Chinatown, New York: Portraits, Recipes, and Memories*. New York: Collins Design, 2007.

Zhou, Min. *Chinatown: The Socioeconomic Potential of an Urban Enclave.* Philadelphia, PA: Temple University Press, 1992.

Zhou, Min. "Chinese: Diverse Origins and Destinies." In Nancy Foner, ed. *One Out of Three: Immigrants in New York in the Twenty-first Century.* New York: Columbia University Press, 2013, pp. 120–47.

CHINATOWNS (DUPLICATES) (SAN FRANCISCO, CALIFORNIA)

San Francisco's Chinatown is notable for many things. The annual Chinese New Year parade telecast to the world, both in Chinese and English, illustrates this. The Chinese New Year parade is the largest Chinese New Year spectacle in the North Americas and hands down the largest in California. It is a global festival watched by mainland Chinese and is linked to overseas Chinese communities around the world. Coupled with the parade's significance is Miss Chinatown USA. This pageant is sponsored by and held in San Francisco, which produces an activity that unites and connects Chinese across the United States. Similar to the Ms. America pageant, different Chinese communities across the United States send their local Miss Chinatown representatives to compete for the Miss Chinatown USA crown. Due to the abolishment of anti-Asian laws, new immigrants, and Asian international businesses, the 21st Century Chinatown in San Francisco as we know it is vastly different than the past. Today, San Francisco does not have just one Chinatown but three distinctive Chinese communities within its city's boundaries. Unlike most literature on this subject from an outsider's perspective, this article is derived from an insider insight with an East Asian studies lens.

What Is in a Name?

In America, ethnic communities are often branded as "little" for their settlement locality such as "Little Havana" for Cuban Americans in Miami and "Little Tokyo" for Japanese Americans in Los Angeles. These brandings are usually imposed by the majority society and become an accepted way of categorizing minority groups. However, the connotation of the word *little* has a negative implication. "Little" implies a contrast with "developed" or "successful." These negative connotations do not stop with the word *little*: The "Spanish Harlem" tag for the Puerto Rican community in New York is often automatically interpreted as similar to the infamously reputed Black Harlem. Similarly, the government also imposes an inherently discriminatory label for ethnic groups such as "Hispanic," a broad and inadequate category when used to refer to all Spanish-speaking peoples. By the same token, when the European colonists migrated to this continent, they proclaimed for themselves much more adequate names, such as New York and New England by the English-speaking settlers or New Amsterdam by the Dutch. Hence, the name *Chinatown* follows the pattern of labeling by the American public.

In the Chinese communities across the United States, particularly in the San Francisco Bay Area, many overseas office branches of Chinese language newspapers from Hong Kong, Taiwan, and China incorrectly report Chinatown as "China City (zhong guo cheng)." In the 1840s, pioneering Chinese referred to their respective community in San Francisco as "Tong Yan Gai (tang ren jie)," or Chinese Street (Chinn 1969, p. 10); local descendants continue to identify with this name. In the early days of the settlement in 1850s, the Chinese lived within only a few streets of the host city. Therefore the name "Tong Yan Gai" was appropriate for their new home. The use of "Tong" in context is better understood as "Cantonese Street," reflecting the early Cantonese pioneers to California. With the exception of the Cantonese, Chinese people generally refer to themselves as "Han" after the first united Chinese dynasty, the Han Dynasty. They often say "I am Han Yan (Han Ren)"; "I am the son/daughter of Han." Naturally, the People's Republic of China's largest nationality is Han. Although this applies to most of China, the southern part of China where native Cantonese reside was incorporated into the empire during the Tong Dynasty. Therefore, the Cantonese refer themselves as "Tong" Yan (tang ren) after the Tong Dynasty period, instead of "Han" from the Han Dynasty. This thus correlates with the local name "Tong Yun Gai."

The initial Chinese settlements in California had an array of names: China quarters, China camps, and even shrimp camp in 1897 for those who engaged in this type of trade off the Pacific Coast. The Chinatown we see today evolved in part because the anti-Chinese movement from 1865–1895 forced Chinese residents into urban cities. As the Chinese community developed, they formed family and district associations to better assist their countrymen. In the later part of the 19th century, San Francisco Chinatown's social and cultural institutions were well established and had been modeled after other urban Chinatowns. The Chinese then referred to San Francisco's Chinatown as "Tong Yun Fow" or "Town of Tong people" (Young 2006). But most Chinese simply referred to San Francisco's Chinatown as "Dai Fow," or big city; Sacramento City as "Yee Fow," or second city; and Stockton City as "Sam Fow," or third city (Fong 2001). Yee Fow came in second commercially to San Francisco's "Dai Fow," hence having the name "second city." At one time, there were more than 10,000 Chinese in the mother lode county. Of the three cities, Stockton's Chinatown is the smallest. The mecca of Chinese America is the 75-mile radius around San Francisco's Chinatown. It is replicated by other urban Chinatowns spanning from the West to the East Coast.

Insular Chinatown

Unlike other major cities in the United States, the city and county of San Francisco advertise Chinatown as a tourist destination. It is essentially a city within a city, having a hierarchical social structure governing representatives as well as representing Chinese voices, not only in San Francisco but also in the United States at large. Partly due to past anti-Chinese laws and ethnic segregation, family and district associations were formed. A major requirement for these two associations was that the family associations accepted only male members with the same surnames, and the district association's male members must be from the same district. Thus an umbrella organization was created, the Chinese Benevolent Consolidated Association, to serve as the official representative for the people in the foreign land as well as the leading governing body within Chinatown. The general public refers to it as the Six Companies, representing the six major districts of Guangdong Province where most of the Chinese immigrants migrated from. The social network is such that a person who had a complaint or dispute with an individual had the right to solicit the family association for help. The representative of the family association would contact the other individual's family association to resolve the problem. If for some reason the problem was not resolved, the complaint then could be addressed by the district association. If the issue was still not resolved, the Six Companies would then be given the task to find a solution. If the complaint was still not fixed to the person's satisfaction, the complainant could seek justice from the U.S. courts. However, due to linguistic and social restrictions, this last step rarely occurred. This process of internal resolution was steadily practiced until the late 1960s.

The Six Companies, the Tongs, and even an organization like the Chinese American Citizens Alliance (CACA) have stationed their headquarters in San Francisco. CACA was founded in 1895, emerging out of necessity in an era of ill treatment toward American-born Chinese citizens. It was the first civil rights organization; members had to be born in this country. By 1941, the CACA gained enough traction and began to open lodges throughout the United States. The organization also founded the *Chinese Times* in 1924, the first Chinese newspaper published by Chinese Americans, which continued publication until 1988. The Tongs, on the other hand, were considered a black-sheep organization, but one that played an important role in the community. The Tongs were born of the frustration of Chinese establishments where the influential family associations held sway in most disputes. The difference between the Tong and the family and district associations was that any Chinese could join, regardless of their family surname and what district they came from. The Tongs are infamously known for being caught up in criminal activities such as gambling, prostitution, and politics, but very few people have noted the other positive roles that the Tongs played in the Chinese community. For example, the Tongs often protected Chinese miners, who were away from Chinatown in isolated mining camps throughout California.

San Francisco's Chinatown is a thriving community that is sandwiched between the North Beach Italian enclave and the West Coast Wall Street, and is by no means an insular community. The Chinese community has its own educational system, Chinese language schools, modern hospitals, and theaters. From the 1950 to 1980s, Chinatown had five Chinese theaters, for the most part showing imported Hong Kong films. These films from Hong Kong were important to young Chinese Americans for identity formation, leisure, and social activity. Four out of the five theaters had a stage; three of the theaters had balcony seating and an overall seating capacity of more than 500 people. Unlike today's theaters, Chinese theaters would show two feature films with an intermission. The theaters served both Chinese and

American snacks like wah mui (salted/preserved plums), popcorn and soft drinks. Every Saturday and Sunday, at least two theaters were open until 2 a.m. These theaters were often rented to host community special events and performances. More importantly, these Chinese language films provided an alternative interpretation of Chinese history and also served as the model for what it meant to be Chinese.

San Francisco Chinatown played a pivotal role in the Asian American Movement during the late 1960s. It is well documented that most of the student leaders came from Chinatown and the community worked closely with the movement. A great example is Professor George Woo, who as a student protested for the creation and implementation of Asian American Studies at San Francisco State College and later agitated Asian American students at UC Berkeley to demand an Asian American Studies program. At that time, the Japanese community was not yet rebuilt and the Pilipino community was small and existed right next to Chinatown. Most Asian representation in the 1960s actually stemmed from the Chinese community. The Asian students at San Francisco State College (changed to San Francisco State University) were able to protest for curriculum inclusiveness of minority contributions in the country due to support from the Chinese community. As a result of such protests, the department of Asian American Studies was formed in 1967–68, and Mr. Him Mark Lai, the dubbed Dean of Chinese American Studies, taught a new Asian American course.

Duplicate Chinatown: Inner Richmond District

Currently, volumes of literature address the "New Chinatowns" in the San Gabriel Valley of Los Angeles; Flushing, New York; and elsewhere. This labeling is partially accurate and is a convenient marker to show this type of community expansion. A more appropriate label would be "duplicate Chinatown" where many elements of the original Chinatown have been duplicated to a new expansion site. Clearly, the adjective "new" implies contrast to "old." Chinatown in the Inner Richmond District does not fundamentally contrast with the insular Chinatown located in San Francisco. More importantly, the ongoing interactions between the insular Chinatown and East Asia for communication, family, and business purposes are the same. It is a microcosm or perhaps reflection of the traditional Chinatown, not a contrast.

The City of San Francisco is divided into "districts" for economic and political election identification. These districts, however, serve an additional service for the locals. The Mission District is locally known as a Mexican and Spanish speaking area. The Castro District is known as the "gay" neighborhood. Inner Richmond has been home to white Russian and other European immigrants. Russian Orthodox Churches located on Geary Boulevard and California Street, large and small, reflect a strong presence. There are three main factors that enabled a duplicate Chinatown in Inner Richmond: the Civil Rights movement, the migration of the Chinese American families, and the new Chinese immigrants from East Asia. Before the civil

Table 1   San Francisco Asian and Chinese Population

Years	SF Population	Asian Pop.	Percentage	Chinese Pop.	Percentage
2010	805,235	267,915	33.3%	172,181	21.4%
2000	776,733	239,565	30.8%	152,620	19.6%
1990	723,959	207,901	28.7%	130,753	18.1%
1980	678,974	149,269	22.0%	82,244	12.1%

Source: http://www.Bayareacensus.ca.gov/counties/SanFranciscoCounty.

rights struggle was initiated, Chinese were restricted to live in Chinatown, and/or were heavily discriminated against in non-Chinese areas; after the Civil Rights Movement, more and more families were able to move wherever they pleased in San Francisco. This lack of restriction allowed Chinese American families to move out of Chinatown, particularly to Inner Richmond. In natural sequence, Chinese businesses followed the internal migration, capitalizing on the business opportunities in new territory, finally leading to new Chinese immigrants in the 1990s. With more education and economic means, Chinese bought homes and settled in Inner Richmond.

As Table 1 shows, the Chinese population in San Francisco has increased each decade, starting in 1980 with 82,244 to 172, 181 in 2010. The notable change came when Clement Restaurant opened in the late 1970s within the Inner Richmond district. This restaurant was the first to serve Chinese dim sum, baked goods, and take out. The next oldest establishment is Cheung Hing Deli & Meat, which was the first to sell deli-style Cantonese roast duck, pork, and chicken in that area. These foods are a staple of the Chinese palate and served to attract Chinese residents to that area. The core of this duplicate Chinatown is more than 13 city blocks on Clement Street, starting from Clement and Arguello Streets to Twelfth Avenue. The side streets connecting to Geary Boulevard add to the core area. Geary Boulevard is a major thoroughfare for the host city, composed of six lanes, and is dotted with Chinese and other Asian businesses. This duplicate is mixed with Irish bars, European bakeries, and Russian grocery stores. San Franciscans identify Inner Richmond as a middle-class residential district as the duplicate Chinatown emerged to serve both non-Asians and Chinese residents.

With the exception of the traditional family and other mutual aid associations, Inner Richmond has everything that a typical Chinatown offers. The community features local, regional, and global Chinese banking options. The Chinese American regional bank, East West Bank, and the Industrial and Commercial Bank of China are situated at the heart of Inner Richmond Chinatown. In addition, there are numerous coffee shops and bakeries that cater to Chinese clients. There are many places for the Chinese youth to hang out, such as the dessert and boba cafés. For example, the recognized boba name brand, Quickly, is often crowded with teens from the local middle school. These boba shops complement instead of compete with the surrounding restaurants and snack shops. While there are distinctively

Chinese businesses such as herb shops and herbal doctors to provide health services, there is also the European-owned Toy Boat Café, which serves ice cream, coffee, and deli sandwiches. Unlike the insular Chinatown, the Inner Richmond Chinese community is more fully integrated with other non-Asian businesses, and more than a third of customers are not Chinese.

Duplicate Chinatown II: Outer Sunset District

Another duplicate Chinatown exists in Outer Sunset, stretching from Nineteenth to Twenty-Sixth Avenues on Irving Street. It is relatively more residential than Inner Richmond. On occasion, the public might witness a police officer or two, each on horseback, patrolling the streets. Most of San Francisco's neighborhoods in the past were exclusively white European, dominated by Irish and Italian immigrants. These neighborhoods remained segregated even after a landmark 1948 U.S. Supreme Court decision against restrictions allowing only Caucasians to own or rent apartments and houses until the 1970s. During the early 1980s, other non-European residents started to move into the neighborhood. As the decades continued, more noticeable changes occurred with Asian and Chinese businesses: Kieser's Colonial was a popular diner serving famous homemade ice cream. The business was sold in 1977 and later replaced by a Chinese-Vietnamese noodle house, Huynh Hiep 2. The former Roth's Drugs is now the Bank of the Orient, reflecting the increase Chinese presence in the Inner Sunset District.

The Chinese and the general public cannot nickname the Outer Sunset district "New Chinatown" because the name has already been accepted by the public for Inner Richmond. However, the young Chinese American population has their own unofficial name for this community—Boba Boulevard. The most visible sights on Irving Street are businesses related to Tapioca Milk Tea, where within seven blocks, 10 Asian businesses ranging from cafés, pho noodle houses, and bakery shops are serving boba. Boba shops are fusion-style cafés offering desserts, mix-teas, smoothies, and juices with the options of popular Asian fruits such as durian. These boba shops provide tasty beverages and draw young people to socialize. The explosion of boba-serving shops is largely due to the social environment that they offer. One could compare this phenomenon to the 1950s soda fountain, where the moment school let out every afternoon, students would flock to their favorite hang-out to grab a treat. In this way, the many young people that frequent duplicate Chinatown II before dinner and at night contribute a great deal to its growth.

The core business area on Irving Street is a mixture of suburban and urban lifestyles. The side-street businesses along the corridor rounded off the core area of Irving Street as duplicate Chinatown II. Without Chinese literacy, it is hard to realize that there are two temples on the side streets and that Vietnamese noodle houses are actually owned and operated by Chinese-Vietnamese from Vietnam. This mixture of suburban and urban life is best illustrated in the diverse coffee/bakery shops, including Sheng Kee bakery, that cater to the Chinese elderly, families, and young professionals. These coffee/bakery shops are gathering places, particularly for the elderly to gossip and play chess with their compatriots. With the exception of the Chinese-owned supermarket Sunset Super, most of the businesses are mom-and-pop stores. Even the global Asian bank, Hong Kong Shanghai, occupies a relatively small branch compared to the Chinese American regional Bank of Orient, which maintains a large branch about three times larger. Without question, the Outer Sunset Chinese community businesses draw from both Chinatown and Inner Richmond.

Unlike Inner Richmond, the Outer Sunset district features two Chinese business clusters located on Noriega Street: one core area is from Nineteenth to Twenty-Third Avenues and the other from Thirtieth to Thirty-Fourth Avenues. These two clusters mirror the early stages of Chinese community expansion and draw businesses from both Chinatown and Inner Richmond. As a restaurant with a Chinese-style deli, it is not surprising that Cheung Hing from Inner Richmond migrated to the Noriega Street area. The large number of Chinese middle-class residents and business opportunities made Sunset a great expansion area for Cheung Hing. Also, the Cheung Hing restaurant has a brand name and is recognized in the Chinese community for their quality roast duck and pork throughout the Bay Area. The Chinese global banks and Chinese American regional banking establishments followed Chinese migration into different San Francisco neighborhoods. The Industrial and Commercial Bank of China and two East West Chinese American regional banks, each operate a branch in these two Chinese areas. In time, the two clusters will join together and a third duplicate Chinatown will materialize in Noriega Street.

The formation of duplicate Chinatowns in Inner Richmond and Outer Sunset can be traced in part from the increase in the Asian population, particularly the Chinese in San Francisco. Table 1 shows the city's Asian population's four decades of growth from 1980 to 2010. Of all Asian groups, the Chinese growth is the largest. In Table 2, the data shows that the Asian residents in the overall Richmond District, Inner Richmond and Outer Richmond, are much more numerous. Similarly, the Asian population is much larger in Inner and Outer Sunset districts. As indicated in Table 1 census data, it is not surprising that a majority of the Asian population in both districts is Chinese, able to sustain and form duplicate Chinatowns. More importantly, the Chinese-language newspapers such as *Sing Dao Daily*,

Table 2 Selected San Francisco Districts' Asian Population

Chinatown District Population: 14,540	Asian Percentage: 84%
North Beach District Population: 14,860	Asian Percentage: 37%
Inner Richmond District Population: 38,690	Asian Percentage: 38%
Outer Richmond District Population: 28,370	Asian Percentage: 48%
Inner Sunset District Population: 26,520	Asian Percentage: 33%
Outer Sunset District Population: 45,670	Asian Percentage: 57%

Source: SF Neighborhoods Socio-Economic Profiles, 2005–2009.

World Journal, and the *China Press* link and bond the San Francisco Bay Area Chinese communities.

Conclusion

There are more than a few explanations for the appearance of "New Chinatowns." The most important one is the liberal stance of the City of San Francisco after the Civil Rights era, allowing people of color into new neighborhoods. This is followed by economic opportunities to start businesses outside of Chinatown. These demographic changes also reflect the decline of first- and second-generation European businesses due to clients with differing tastes. It is not surprising that homes and businesses are sold to these incoming clients, forming Inner Richmond's duplicate Chinatown and later the Outer Sunset community. It is safe to suggest that the main reasons are due to new immigrant, economic opportunity, and the departure of past Caucasian residents, also termed as "white flight."

Stephen Fong

See also in California: Baldwin Hills (Los Angeles, California); Boyle Heights, Jewish Neighborhood (Los Angeles, California); Boyle Heights, Latino Neighborhood (Los Angeles, California); Cambodia Town (Long Beach, California); Chinatown (Los Angeles, California); Chinatown (San Francisco, California); East Los Angeles, Mexican American Enclave (Los Angeles, California); El Monte, Latino Enclaves (California); Fillmore District (San Francisco, California); Gardena and Torrance (South Bay Region, Los Angeles County, California); Glendale, Armenian Enclave (California); Historic Filipinotown (Los Angeles, California); Historic South Central (Los Angeles, California); Indio, Mexican and Central American Communities (California); Japantown (San Francisco, California); Kingsburg and Sveadal, Swedish Enclaves (California); Koreatown (Los Angeles, California); Little Arabia (Anaheim, California); Little Armenia (Los Angeles, California); Little Ethiopia (Los Angeles, California); Little India/Pakistan (Artesia, California); Little Italy (Los Angeles, California); Little Italy (San Diego, California); Little Italy (San Francisco, California); Little Saigon (San Francisco, California); Little Saigon (San Jose, California); Little Saigon (Westminster, California); Little Tokyo (Los Angeles, California); Logan Heights, Mexican Enclave (San Diego, California); Los Angeles, Hawaiian Enclaves (California); Los Angeles, West Side and San Fernando Valley Jewish Enclaves (California); Mayan Corner/24th and Mission (San Francisco, California); Monterey Park, First Suburban Chinatown (California); Mount Washington, Mexican Enclave (California); National City (San Diego, California); Olvera Street/La Plaza (Los Angeles, California); Pico Rivera, Latino Enclave (California); Riverside, Mexican Enclave (California); San Bernardino, Mexican Enclave (California); San Pedro, Italian and Croatian Enclaves (California); Santa Ana, Mexican Enclaves (California); Sawtelle (Los Angeles, California); Silicon Valley, Indian and South Asian Communities (Santa Clara Valley/San Jose Region, California); Sin City (Fresno, California); Solvang, Danish Community (California); Sonoma County, Italian Enclave (California); Tehrangeles (Los Angeles, California); Temescal (Oakland, California); Thai Town (Los

Angeles, California); Watts (Los Angeles, California); Yuba City, Sikh Enclave (California)

See also Chinese/Taiwanese Enclaves: Bridgeport (Chicago, Illinois); Chinatown (Boston, Massachusetts); Chinatown (Los Angeles, California); Chinatown (Phoenix, Arizona); Chinatown (San Francisco, California); Chinatown Historic District/ A'ala (Honolulu, Hawaii); Chinatowns (Manhattan; Sunset Park East, Brooklyn; Flushing, Queens) (New York City); International District (Seattle, Washington); Monterey Park, First Suburban Chinatown (California); New Chinatown (Portland, Oregon); Tucson, Chinese and Southeast Asian Enclaves (Arizona)

Further Reading

Bay Area Census, San Francisco City and County, Census Data. 1970–1990. Accessed October 14, 2016. http://www.bayareacensus.ca.gov/counties/SanFranciscoCounty70.htm.

Chinn, Thomas W. *A History of the Chinese in California, A Syllabus.* San Francisco, CA: Chinese Historical Society of America, 1969.

Choy, Phillip P. *San Francisco Chinatown: A Guide to Its History and Architecture.* San Francisco, CA: City Lights, 2014.

Fagan, Kevin. "Asian Population Swells in Bay Area, State, Nation." *SFGate,* 2012.

Fong, Joe Chung. "Mecca of Chinese America in California: Dai Fow (San Francisco), Yee Fow (Sacramento), and Sam Fow (Stockton), Sacramento Chinese Culture Foundation/ Asian American Studies at UC Davis." Sacramento, CA: Sacramento Chinese Culture Foundation, 2001.

Fong, Stephen. "Boba Culture: An East Asian Stranger." *Journal of Undergraduate East Asian Studies.* Vol. 2. Tucson: University of Arizona East Asian Studies Department, 2014.

Fong, T. P. *The First Suburban Chinatown: The Remaking of Monterey Park, California.* Philadelphia, PA: Temple University Press, 1994.

Kwong, Peter. *The New Chinatown.* New York: Hill and Wang. 1996.

Laguerre, Michel S. "Minoritized Space: An Inquiry Into the Spatial Order of Things." Institute of Government Studies Press and the Institute of Urban and Regional Development. Berkeley, CA: University of California Berkeley, 1999.

Laguerre, Michel S. "The Globalization of a Panethnopolis: Richmond District as the New Chinatown in San Francisco." *GeoJournal* 64 (2005): 41–49.

San Francisco Planning Department. "San Francisco Neighborhoods Socio-Economic Profiles 2005–2009." San Francisco, CA: SF Planning Department, 2011.

Ungaretti, Lorri. *Then & Now: San Francisco's Sunset District.* Charleston, SC: Arcadia, 2011.

Young, Judy, and CHSA. *Images of America: San Francisco's Chinatown.* Charleston, SC: Arcadia, 2006.

U.S. Census Bureau. FactFinder: San Francisco County 2010 Demographic Profile Data. Accessed October 14, 2016. http://www.census.gov/prod/cen2010/doc/sfl.pdf.

U.S. Census Bureau. FactFinder: San Francisco County 2000 Demographic Profile Data. Accessed October 14, 2016. http://www.census.gov/prod/cen2000/doc/sfl.pdf.

CHINESE/TAIWANESE ENCLAVES. *See* Bridgeport (Chicago, Illinois); Chinatown (Boston, Massachusetts); Chinatown (Los Angeles, California); Chinatown (Phoenix, Arizona); Chinatown (San Francisco, California); Chinatown Historic District/A'ala (Honolulu, Hawaii); Chinatowns (Duplicates) (San Francisco, California); Chinatowns (Manhattan; Sunset Park East, Brooklyn; Flushing, Queens)

(New York City); International District (Seattle, Washington); Monterey Park, First Suburban Chinatown (California); New Chinatown (Portland, Oregon); Tucson, Chinese and Southeast Asian Enclaves (Arizona)

CONEY ISLAND (BROOKLYN, NEW YORK)

The Coney Island neighborhood is one of the 42 neighborhoods that constitute New York City, located on the southern end of the borough of Brooklyn. Today, Coney Island is best known as the site of historic amusement parks and a leisure destination, but it is also a highly populated residential area. The neighborhood is a diverse urban area and a prominent ethnic group living there today is comprised of Ukrainian and Russian-speaking people from the former Soviet Union. As of 2012, there were approximately 60,000 residents located within the 11224 zip code that generally indicates the bounds of this Brooklyn neighborhood. Coney Island has drawn large numbers of Ukrainians and other immigrants from the former Soviet Union in recent years especially due to its location just west of Brighton Beach, a traditionally working class neighborhood, home to the densest concentration of Russian-speaking people in United States.

Coney Island is located in the southwestern corner of Brooklyn, on the eastern side of Lower New York Bay. It is bordered by the neighborhoods of Sea Gate to the west, Gravesend to the north, Brighton Beach to the east, and the Atlantic Ocean to the south. This neighborhood is generally bounded by Coney Island Creek and Leif Ericson Drive to the north, Ocean Parkway to the east, the Atlantic Ocean to the south, and West Thirty-Seventh Street to the west. Neptune Avenue and Mermaid Avenue are two prominent streets that run east to west through the neighborhood. Overall, Coney Island covers about 442 acres or approximately .691 square miles of Brooklyn.

Coney Island is located on the westernmost edge of the barrier islands of Long Island and was once a distinct island separated from the Long Island mainland by Coney Island Creek, measuring about four miles long and a half-mile wide. This creek consisted partially of mudflats and was filled in at different times during the early 20th century, thus turning the island into more of a peninsula. The island became fully connected to the mainland in 1962 when a portion of the creek was filled during the construction of the Verrazano-Narrows Bridge connecting Brooklyn with Staten Island. Today, it is an island in name only.

The earliest known Native American inhabitants of Coney Island were the Canarsie Indians, a group who considered themselves part of the Lenape people. Lenape Indians referred to the island as Narrioch, which loosely translates to "the land without shadows," in reference to the fact that its east to west facing beach remained in the sunlight all day long. At the time of European arrival, the Natives of western Long Island subsisted on the land through agriculture, hunting game, and harvesting seafood. They seasonally occupied different encampments, which revolved around the weather and food sources. Like many other natives of the shoreline regions, the Canarsie produced wampum beads from quahog and whelk shells for ornamental and ritual purposes. The Florentine explorer Giovanni da Verrazzano may have been the first known European to visit the island around 1528. He was followed much later by the Dutch, who began to travel to the area in increasing numbers following Henry Hudson's voyage of 1609. It is thought that one of Hudson's crewmembers, John Coleman, was killed by natives on a beach that may have been located on Narrioch.

In 1624, the Dutch established the colony of New Netherland, and by 1638 they negotiated the purchase of lands on western Long Island from the Lenape, including present-day Coney Island. It was the Dutch who renamed the island from Narrioch to "Conyne Eylandt," which translated to "Rabbit Island." This name first appears on a 1639 Dutch map, and early accounts describe the area as containing beautiful beaches, many trees, and diverse species of rabbits. The island was originally part of the town of Gravesend, which was founded in 1643 by English religious dissenters from New England. The land was primarily used for livestock grazing, with little development occurring on the island by the Dutch with the exception of a saltworks that briefly operated in 1663. When the colony of New Netherland was lost to the English in 1664 and was renamed the Province of New York, English settlers continued to refer to the island on the southwestern tip of Long Island as "Coney Island." It was an obvious choice as *coney* was a popular English term for "rabbit." It first appeared on English maps as "Coney Isle" as early as 1690.

In 1733, the modern spelling of Coney Island was applied to area. Nominal farming flourished on the island as well as cattle grazing on the surrounding salt meadows. A road to the island was built in 1734 that connected it to the mainland across a shallow inlet. Thirty-nine farming lots were established on any arable land on the island. Agricultural activities including mowing salt grasses and grazing. Wood cutting continued on Coney Island throughout most of the 18th century. Around 1763, a second road was built along the northern end of the farming lots. During the American Revolution, Gravesend Bay, situated just north of Coney Island, was the site of the British invasion of Long Island on August 22, 1776. The subsequent British victory during the August 27, 1776, Battle of Long Island ensured their dominance over the New York City region. Coney Island remained firmly in British hands for the duration of the war. Following the American Revolution, it slowly developed into a popular destination for residents of New York and western Long Island.

Around 1820, a new and more direct road to Coney Island was proposed along the existing "shell road," and in 1829 a new road and bridge were completed. As increasing numbers of people made summer journeys to the island's beaches, hotels were constructed, the first being built in 1827. In 1844, a large circular platform and tent known as the "Pavilion" was erected, and it attracted many visitors. This was soon followed by a wharf, another hotel, and several bathing houses along the southern shore of the island. By 1847, only two farms remained on the original Coney Island lots, as the area slowly became a summer resort. A horsecar route along what would later become Coney Island Avenue was completed in the 1850s, along with a railroad line in the 1860s. Following the American Civil War, the area quickly developed. Numerous restaurants, saloons, and bathing houses spread out from the railroad station outwards along the shoreline. In 1868, Coney Island's beaches had a reputation as the best on the Atlantic Coast, and by 1873 it was attracting between 25,000 and 30,000 visitors on the weekends. Within a few years, the beach front was crowded by new businesses, all seeking to cash in on Coney Island's newfound popularity.

Between 1874 and 1880, Ocean Parkway was constructed, running north from the Prospects Heights neighborhood in Brooklyn and south to Coney Island, which allowed for a more direct route to the attractions. The amusement industry was first introduced in 1876 when a carousel was opened at a bath house that would later be known as Balmer's Pavilion. In 1878, an iron pier was built that also helped to facilitate travel to the newly developed neighborhood by steamship. The first roller coaster built in the United States was opened at Coney Island in 1884, which quickly encouraged others to be built. Another tourist attraction, known as the Elephant Colossus or the Elephant Hotel, was a seven-story building shaped like an elephant that stood along Surf Avenue from 1885 to 1896. Before it was destroyed by fire, it was said the Elephant Colossus of Coney Island was the first artificial structure visible to newly arriving immigrants upon entering New York harbor even before they were able to view the Statue of Liberty. The first enclosed amusement park, Sea Lion Park, was created in 1895. Although it only lasted until 1902, it inspired several other amusement parks, including Steeplechase Park (1897), Luna Park (1903), and Dreamland (1904).

Following the completion of Ocean Parkway, the island was divided in half and the area began to evolve into four distinct neighborhoods. The far eastern end was an upscale section of the island known as Manhattan Beach, followed by middle-class Brighton Beach to the west and the Ocean Parkway. To the west of the parkway was the working-class amusement section of the island known as West Brighton Beach, followed by the lower-class neighborhoods of the West End. Until around 1900, Coney Island referred to the entire five-mile stretch of beach but the designation soon came to refer only to the two-mile stretch of West Brighton Beach and its four great amusement parks. Around this time, the west end of the island became a fenced-in residential community known as Sea Gate, designed to separate itself from the busier amusement area. By 1910, the name of West Brighton was replaced on maps, official documents, and daily speech with Coney Island. After this time, the name Coney Island was never used to refer to the entire five-miles of island, but rather only to this specific neighborhood. The modern boundaries of the Coney Island neighborhood—consisting of the beach to the south, running east to Ocean Parkway, north to the Belt Parkway and Coney Island Creek, and west to West Thirty-Sixth Street—have remained this way for over a century.

Between 1910 and 1920, a permanent residential community developed in the western Coney Island neighborhood, consisting primarily of small houses and bungalows. Italian immigrants were the first to move into this area west of the Stillwell Avenue railroad terminal, Luna Park, and north of Steeplechase. To the east of Luna Park and north of the Dreamland amusement parks was an area of dilapidated housing known as "The Gut" which housed a growing community of African American laborers along with Jewish vendors and domestic servants. In the 1910s and 1920s New York City experienced an increase in construction projects, including new housing and an extension of the subway into Brooklyn. The completion of the subway extension allowed all classes of citizens to reach Coney Island for five cents, which earned the neighborhood the nickname of the "Nickel Empire." Whereas the amusement area was formerly visited primarily by the rich and later by the middle class, Coney Island was now affordable to lower-income people and recent immigrants who worked in New York City's factories and sweatshops. In 1923, the neighborhood's beaches were opened to the public. A new boardwalk was built along the shoreline that attracted hundreds of thousands of visitors to the area weekly. In the midst of tourists, 1930s and 1940s Coney Island was home to largely middle- and working-class Italian and Jewish enclaves.

Coney Island remained the region's premier amusement destination from the turn of the 19th century through World War II. In the postwar years, multiple factors contributed to a gradual economic decline as the automobile brought new attractions within driving distance of the American tourist. Luna Park suffered from fire in 1944, closing soon thereafter. The company that purchased the site demolished the former amusement park, then constructed Luna Park Houses, high-rise apartment complexes, in its place. The Housing Act of 1949 began a period of urban renewal in New York City whereby large areas west of the amusement area were scheduled for redevelopment. Throughout the 1950s, the amusement industry of Coney Island still proved profitable, to the point that Astroland Amusement Park was opened in 1954. An aquarium opened on the site of Dreamland, and millions of seasonal visitors were drawn to the neighborhoods beaches and amusements. In 1953, developer Robert Moses successfully had the entire Coney Island peninsula rezoned for residential use only in an attempt to demolish the less profitable amusements and construct public housing. However, public complaints led to a protected amusement zone designed to preserve and support the remaining amusement parks.

By the 1960s, a demographic shift began to occur. Many members of the long-standing Italian and Russian-Jewish communities began to move to new suburban developments outside of New York City. In 1964, Coney Island's last amusement park, Steeplechase Park, closed entirely, which was an economic blow to the community. At this time, the city awarded much of the land in the "The Gut" section of Coney Island, including Steeplechase, to developers, led by Fred Trump, for the construction of middle-income apartments. The largely African American and Hispanic residents of the area relocated to the west, closer to Sea Gate. In a short time, a series of 24-story apartment buildings were built on the site. Few of these displaced residents were able to afford rent in the new Trump Village. A total of six apartment complexes were built in Coney Island from 1967 to 1974. Additional migrants from Puerto Rico, plus African Americans from the south, continued to be drawn to the area. Jewish and some Italian residents began to vacate their old Coney Island neighborhood, renting or selling their property to the newcomers. By the 1970s, the western section of the Coney Island neighborhood was considered a poverty zone.

During this time, neighboring Brighton Beach experienced significant population growth as some 40,000 Soviet Jewish immigrants settled in the neighborhood between 1975 and 1980. This wave of Russian-speaking immigrants, many of whom originated in Ukraine, led Brighton Beach to become known as "Little Odessa." Thousands of these Ukrainian and Russian-speaking immigrants also migrated west of Ocean Parkway and took up residence within the eastern bounds of the Coney

Island neighborhood. This new demographic continued to rise throughout the 1990s as thousands more Ukrainians, ethnic Russians, and other Russian speakers arrived following the collapse of the Soviet Union. Coney Island's affordable housing, growing ethnic enclave, and close proximity to nearby Little Odessa led to rapid changes in the neighborhood. The growing Ukrainian and Russian immigrant populations soon established a number of Eastern European restaurants, delis, and bakeries. Two well-known Russian bakeries in Coney Island, New York Bread and Georgian Bread, bring in many visitors from Brooklyn's greater Russian community.

The 2000 U.S. Census stated that there were 51,205 people living in Coney Island. The majority of the residents live in 30 different apartment towers, much of which is public housing. Coney Island's main ethnic groups remain African American, Hispanic, and recently arrived Russian and Ukrainian immigrants. The 2000 U.S. Census determined that just under half of the residents of Coney Island were foreign born, coming from Ukraine, Russia, Mexico, and Puerto Rico. By the early 2000s, the Coney Island neighborhood was being referred to by local residents as the "Russian Amusement Park." The percentage of foreign-born residents dropped somewhat between 2007 and 2009, likely corresponding with the economic recession of the period. The majority of immigrants who did arrive originated from Ukraine, Russia, China, and Belarus. Immigrants from Ukraine and Russia continued to flock to both sides of Ocean Parkway in such large numbers that a 2009 report on the economic outlook for Coney Island and Brighton Beach found it difficult to distinguish between the communities. The report highlighted that nearly half of the populations of both neighborhoods were foreign born, with half of that figure consisting of Ukrainian and Russian immigrants. According to the U.S. Census Bureau, there were immigrants from 50 different countries in Coney Island and Brighton Beach, but by far the most numerous were from Ukraine (25.2%) or Russia (21.2%).

Throughout 2007, efforts continued by major developers to rezone Coney Island to include additional housing units, among which were numerous high-rise luxury apartments. In August of that year the mayor of New York officially rejected this proposal and halted any housing construction within Coney Island's historic amusement zone. In 2009, Coney Island was rezoned to foster additional residential spaces, neighborhood services, and retail development. Much of this new retail space and neighborhood development was planned along Surf and Mermaid Avenues. At this time a 27-acre amusement and entertainment district was created, encompassing a significant portion of the old amusement parks. The gentrification process of the sections of the Coney Island neighborhood near the amusement district continued.

However, these developing urban renewal projects came to a halt in 2012. The October 2012 hurricane known as Superstorm Sandy devastated all neighborhoods on Coney Island with damaging winds and storm surges that resulted in significant flooding. It took several months to fully restore water, heat, and electricity to all parts of the island. The storm caused significant damage to the amusement parks, the Aquarium, and businesses in Coney Island. Due to the large numbers of Russian and Ukrainian immigrants living in the affected area, the Federal Emergency Management Agency assigned fluent community relations limited

English proficiency specialists to assist hurricane survivors. Luna Park was able to reopen in March 2013, and Nathan's Hot Dog Eating Contest was held that summer as well.

Demographic data for 2013–2014 demonstrates a robust Russian and Ukrainian population in Coney Island. Along with the rising immigrant population in the neighborhood came new businesses in the process of becoming established, including the Black Sea Bookstore, Café Glechik, and the offices of Air Ukraine. It is difficult to determine the full extent of the Ukrainian, Russian, and Russian-speaking peoples living in the eastern end of Coney Island due to its immediate proximity to Little Odessa in Brighton Beach. Although the neighborhood's total population is dwarfed by that of Brighton Beach to the east, the demographic data is striking. In the old West Brighton section of Coney Island, where many of these immigrants have congregated, an estimated 31.4% of people are of Russian descent, while 10.5% are Ukrainian, followed by a remnant Italian community of 2.8%. The 2010 U.S. Census indicated that Coney Island's seven census tracts contained a population that was 39% African American, 29% Hispanic, 23% white, and 10% Asian. Of those who identified as white, a significant portion were likely of Ukrainian or Russian descent. Ethnic and cultural demographic shifts have affected the Coney Island neighborhood in many ways over the past century. In the 21st century, the neighborhood is primarily shared among African American, Hispanic, and Ukrainian/Russian immigrants. Of the area's diverse populations, the Ukrainian and Russian enclave continues to rapidly expand west into the Coney Island neighborhood.

See also in New York: Bedford-Stuyvesant (Brooklyn, New York); Borough Park/ Williamsburg/Crown Heights, Jewish Enclaves (Brooklyn, New York); Brighton Beach-Sheepshead Bay (Brooklyn, New York); Brooklyn, West Indian Enclave (New York); Chinatowns (Manhattan; Sunset Park East, Brooklyn; Flushing, Queens) (New York City); Crown Heights, Jamaican Enclave (Brooklyn, New York); Five Points (New York City); Greenpoint (Brooklyn, New York); Greenwich Village (New York City); Harlem (New York City); Harlem, Senegalese Enclave (New York City); Hell's Kitchen (New York City); Jackson Heights (Queens, New York); Jackson Heights, South Asian Enclave (Queens, New York); Little Brazil Street (Manhattan, New York); Little India, Jackson Heights (Queens, New York); Little Italy (Manhattan, New York); Lower East Side (New York City); Sleepy Hollow, Ecuadorian Enclave (New York); Staten Island, Sri Lankan Enclave (New York City); Sunset Park West and North Corona (New York City); Washington Heights (New York City); Yorkville, German Enclave (New York City)

See also Russian/Ukrainian Enclaves: Brighton Beach-Sheepshead Bay (Brooklyn, New York); Nikolaevsk, Russian Enclave (Alaska)

David J. Naumec

Further Reading

Denson, Charles. *Coney Island and Astroland*. Charleston, SC: Arcadia, 2011.
Geberer, Raanan. "Coney Island: The Residential Area Behind the Bright Lights." *Brooklyn Daily Eagle*, December 2, 2014. Accessed October 14, 2016. http://www.brooklyneagle .com/articles/coney-island-residential-area-behind-bright-lights.

Kasson, John F. *Amusing the Millions: Coney Island at the Turn of the Century.* New York: Hill and Wang, 1978.

Lobo, Arun Peter, and Joseph J. Salvo. *The Newest New Yorkers: Characteristics of the City's Foreign-born Population.* New York: New York City Department of City Planning, 2013.

Macaulay Honors College. "The Peopling of Coney Island!" Accessed October 14, 2016. http://macaulay.cuny.edu/eportfolios/aries2014coneyisland.

New York State Comptroller. "An Economic Snapshot of Coney Island and Brighton Beach." Report 8-2012, July 2011. Accessed October 14, 2016. http://www.osc.state.ny.us/osdc/rpt8-2012.pdf.

New York Rising Community Reconstruction Program. "Brighton Beach, Coney Island, Manhattan Beach, and Sea Gate: NY Rising Community Reconstruction Plan. March 2014. Accessed October 14, 2016. http://stormrecovery.ny.gov/sites/default/files/crp/community/documents/brightonbeach-coneyisland-manhattanbeach-sea_gate_nyrcr_plan.pdf.

Stockwell, Austin P., and William H. Stillwell. *A History of the Town of Gravesend and of Coney Island.* Brooklyn, NY: W. W. Munsell, 1884.

U.S. Department of Commerce, U.S. Census Bureau. *Profile of General Population and Housing Characteristics: 2010.* "Zip code 11224." Accessed October 14, 2016. http://factfinder2.census.gov.

U.S. Department of Commerce, U.S. Census Bureau. *State & County QuickFacts.* "Kings County (Brooklyn Borough), New York." Accessed October 14, 2016. http://quickfacts.census.gov/qfd/states/36/36047.html.

Weinstein, Raymond M. "Succession and Renewal in Urban Neighborhoods: The Case of Coney Island." *Sociation Today* 5, no. 2 (Fall 2007). Accessed October 14, 2016. http://www.ncsociology.org/sociationtoday/v52/coney.htm.

CROATIAN ENCLAVES. *See* San Pedro, Italian and Croatian Enclaves (California)

CROWN HEIGHTS, JAMAICAN ENCLAVE (BROOKLYN, NEW YORK)

Crown Heights is a neighborhood in central Brooklyn. It is roughly one mile wide and two miles long, bounded by Atlantic Avenue to the north, Washington Avenue to the west, Ralph Avenue to the east, and Empire Boulevard and East New York Avenue to the south.

During the colonial era, Crown Heights was called Crow Hill, supposedly a reference to the crows that filled the trees on the neighborhood's tallest hill. In 1873, the *Brooklyn Eagle* speculated that the name actually referenced the African American settlement in that area. Others suggested that the "crows" were a reference to the inmates in Kings County Penitentiary, which was located in Crown Heights from 1846 to 1907.

Jamaican immigrants have flocked to New York for decades and continue to comprise one of the largest immigrant groups today, with New York State being home to the largest concentration of Jamaicans in the United States. Crown Heights is home to 104,000 Jamaican and Afro-Caribbean people.

Dancer at the West Indian American Day Carnival and Parade in Crown Heights, Brooklyn. Crown Heights is home to 104,000 Jamaican and Afro-Caribbean people. (Rebekah Burgess/ Dreamstime.com)

The British had colonized Jamaica from 1655 to 1962, but in 1834 slavery was abolished and Jamaicans, many with in-demand skills such as carpentry, masonry, and the like, were able to immigrate to other countries. The wave of West Indian immigration to the United States that occurred between 1899 and 1928 included 138,615 individuals, the majority of whom were Jamaicans. When the U.S. stock market crashed in 1929, the Great Depression made for reduced labor demands. Prohibitive legislation made it more difficult to enter the United States, curbing yearly migration.

During that first immigration wave, however, West Indians, including Jamaicans, originally settled in Manhattan, primarily Harlem. The neighborhood saw enormous growth, with a large commercial center along 135th Street. It is believed that it was on 135th Street and Lenox Avenue that Jamaican-born politician and black nationalist, Marcus Garvey, spoke out against a police slaying of a black man. This act is said to have launched his career as an activist, or as he and his contemporaries were often derogatorily called, "rabble-rousers." By 1930, almost no whites lived in Harlem. Later, around the time of World War II, many West Indians left Harlem for the suburbs or Brooklyn, where Bedford-Stuyvesant was initially the settlement location of choice. "Bed-Stuy," like other neighborhoods, was often segregated by block. One block might be inhabited by Jamaicans, the next by Trinidadians, and the next by Barbadians.

The postwar years were good for blacks in Brooklyn. Unemployment rates were at their lowest, and blacks were beginning to be able to take part in what was traditionally considered middle-class white American norms, such as car and homeownership. By the 1970s, many West Indians were able to afford the expensive, Romanesque homes in Brooklyn's Fort Greene, a neighborhood just west of Bed-Sty.

Great Britain had also been a popular destination for Jamaican immigrants after World War II, but the Commonwealth Immigration Act of 1961 prohibited much of their movement, curtailing immigration. In this context, the Hart-Celler Immigration Act of 1965 allowed the redirections of West Indian immigration to the United States rather than Great Britain that is still strong today. In the years preceding the act, 1,500 West Indians immigrated to America each year. Between 1966 and 1975, that yearly average increased to 12,400, and 18,000 between 1976 and 1985 (these numbers account for documented immigrants).

For the past 30 years, Crown Heights has been the largest West Indian enclave in New York, with runner-up neighborhoods including the Bronx, Norwood, Baychester, Flatbush, Brownsville, and various areas in Queens. New York is a notoriously popular place to settle, with the majority of the more than 500,000 immigrants that came to the United States in the last 40 years remaining in New York. Between 1990 and 1998, 40% of the Jamaican immigrants legally admitted to the United States intended to stay in New York. In the 2000s, Jamaican immigrants expanded their enclaves into Flatlands and Canarsie in Brooklyn, both in the southeastern section of the borough.

Crown Heights displays particularly visible and strong emblems of Jamaican culture, from ethnic food stores and restaurants to accents heard in conversations on the street to churches. Reggae and calypso music plays on car radios, and restaurants advertise goat curry and jerk chicken, traditional Jamaican dishes.

Other Jamaican cultural mainstays have transferred to immigrant life in New York, as well, such as the jitney service. Typical in Jamaica are cars-for-hire or vans that provide group transportation between destinations, similar to public transit. Many Jamaican immigrants feel the public transport options in New York are too expensive, too infrequent, and do not service enough areas. Jitney services, owned and operated by immigrants typically, have sprung up to fill this gap. They are often criticized for being unsafe, but they remain fairly popular.

Interestingly, Jamaican women made up a majority of immigrants for a time, partly due to higher female unemployment rates in Jamaica, prompting them to seek opportunities abroad. In America, many pursue careers in health care as nurses or home health aides. With English being their first language, they have an advantage in the workforce over other non-English speaking immigrants. Since many families separate for a time in order for one member to establish roots in the United States before sending for the rest of the family, an industry has grown up around the practice of shipping barrels full of goods to loved ones back in Jamaica.

West Indians share Crown Heights with the Chabad-Lubavitch Hasidic movement and the Lubavitch world headquarters, located on Frederick Law Olmstead and Calvert Vaux-designed Eastern Parkway. Cultural tensions between the groups peaked during a three-day period in August 1991. A car accident involving the Lubavitch leader Rabbi Menachem Mendel Schneerson's police-escorted motorcade killed a seven-year-old Guyanese boy named Gavin Cato and injured his cousin, Angela. One of Rabbi Schneerson's cars that had been trailing the car in which the rabbi was riding collided with another vehicle at an intersection, veered onto the sidewalk where the children were playing, and caused a 600-pound stone slab to fall on them. The black community, fueled by a number of rumors, including Hetzolah's (a Hasidic volunteer EMT organization) refusal to assist the black children and comments by Reverend Al Sharpton, responded to the tragic event by looting several stores and killing one Jewish man, a doctoral candidate from Australia named Yankel Rosenbaum. Tensions and violence from both blacks and Jews continued for several days, prompted in part by then Mayor David Dinkins's hesitation to respond to the riots and Rabbi Schneerson's refusal to address the incident at all.

Those tragic days, however, caused the formation of anti-bias initiatives in the community, headed by black and Jewish organizers. Project CURE is an example. It aims to unite young men of different racial and ethnic backgrounds within the community to promote understanding, tolerance, and respect. Unity Day also occurs yearly and is attended by over 10,000 people each June. It celebrates cultural traditions and differences, and fosters unity.

There have also been noted tensions between Caribbean blacks and American blacks within the community. Jamaican culture specifically stresses education and success, two values that they are said to use to differentiate themselves from American blacks, which has led one group to resent the other, particularly when both groups share experiences with racism and the challenges that mainstream American society places on minorities. Second-generation West Indians are said to assimilate into mainstream black American culture. Additionally, many Jamaican immigrants do not expect the racism they are met with, as they came from a country where they are the majority. Their challenges in Jamaica are that their economies are resource poor, unemployment is high, and wealth is not distributed evenly. They seek a better life in America only to be met with discriminatory treatment based on their skin color. In a culture that emphasized education as a method to upward mobility, race has presented more challenges in the United States than many had anticipated.

Similarly, West Indians of one nation consider themselves culturally different from West Indians of other nations, but as immigrants in New York their cultural similarities are more evident, and this unites the West Indian communities more than it divides them. This is evident through the West Indian Labor Day parade. Since 1969, the West Indian Carnival parade has occurred each Labor Day in Crown Heights, extending down the neighborhood's main thoroughfare, Eastern Parkway. It draws more than two million attendees to celebrate the community's prominent Afro-Caribbean population and enjoy an elaborate parade with festive costumes, floats, and food. This pre-Lenten festival is typically celebrated in February in the West Indies. Jamaicans are generally underrepresented in these festivities because their culture does not have such strong carnival traditions as others. To foster

---

New York's Largest Cultural Celebration

Claimed to be New York's largest cultural celebration, the Western Indian Parade, also known as the West Indian Carnival, is held on the first Monday of September (Labor Day) in Crown Heights. The carnival is a colorful display of pan-Caribbean culture and cuisine. The celebration aims to pay homage to traditional culture and show pride in the achievements of Americans of Caribbean descent.

The carnival is also known for delicious Caribbean food. One of the most popular is the Jamaican patties—a thin, flaky crust with a spicy ground beef interior. "Doubles"—a street food in Trinidad and Tobago—is also popular. It is a type of sandwich made with a turmeric-hued fry filled with curried chick peas.

The carnival's economic impact is also felt in New York. So much so that other cities, such as Miami and Boston, have imitated it. According to some statistics, the carnival in New York is attended by 1 to 3 million people each year. Moreover, a 2003 study found that the carnival had an economic impact exceeding $154,000,000, while organizers claimed that figure was closer to $200 million. Nevertheless, the carnival is an assertion of pan-Caribbean pride that brings people not only from the Caribbean together, but people from all over the world.

---

community, however, Jamaicans have been encouraged to participate in the parade and now have a "reggae night" the Thursday before Labor Day.

Other New York City neighborhoods with smaller but still notable concentrations of Jamaican immigrant residents include Jamaica in Queens, Mount Vernon and Eastchester in Westchester County, and Hempstead and Uniondale in suburban Nassau County on Long Island.

Notable former residents of Crown Heights include Chris Rock, Clive Davis, and Dr. Susan McKinney Steward, the first African American woman to receive her medical degree in New York. The first children's museum in the United States is also located in Crown Heights and was constructed in 1899. Most of the museum is underground.

See also in New York: Bedford-Stuyvesant (Brooklyn, New York); Borough Park/Williamsburg/Crown Heights, Jewish Enclaves (Brooklyn, New York); Brighton Beach-Sheepshead Bay (Brooklyn, New York); Brooklyn, West Indian Enclave (New York); Chinatowns (Manhattan; Sunset Park East, Brooklyn; Flushing, Queens) (New York City); Coney Island (Brooklyn, New York); Five Points (New York City); Greenpoint (Brooklyn, New York); Greenwich Village (New York City); Harlem (New York City); Harlem, Senegalese Enclave (New York City); Hell's Kitchen (New York City); Jackson Heights (Queens, New York); Jackson Heights, South Asian Enclave (Queens, New York); Little Brazil Street (Manhattan, New York); Little India, Jackson Heights (Queens, New York); Little Italy (Manhattan, New York); Lower East Side (New York City); Sleepy Hollow, Ecuadorian Enclave (New York); Staten Island, Sri Lankan Enclave (New York City); Sunset Park West and North Corona (New York City); Washington Heights (New York City); Yorkville, German Enclave (New York City)

See also West Indian/Jamaican Enclaves: Brooklyn, West Indian Enclave (New York); Chicago, Mexican and Puerto Rican Enclaves (Illinois); Holyoke, Puerto Rican Enclaves (Massachusetts); Little Haiti ("La Petite Haiti"/Lemon City) (Miami, Florida); Little Havana (Miami, Florida); Little Havana on the Hudson (North Hudson, New Jersey); Washington Heights (New York City); Ybor City (Tampa, Florida)

Meridith Roy

Further Reading

"A Brief History of Jamaica." Accessed October 19, 2016. http://www.mtholyoke.edu/~beckf20s/classweb/History.html.

Foner, Nancy, ed. *New Immigrants in New York, Completely Revised and Updated.* New York: Columbia University Press, 2001.

Forde, F. Donnie. *Images of America: Caribbean Americans in New York City 1895–1975.* Charleston, SC: Arcadia, 2002.

Fraser, Lisa. "Newcomers Stir Crown Heights Melting Pot." *Newsday/am New York.* January 8, 2014. Updated January 9, 2014. Accessed October 19, 2016. http://www.newsday.com/travel/newcomers-stir-crown-heights-melting-pot-1.6757699.

Jackson, Kenneth T., ed. *The Neighborhoods of Brooklyn.* New Haven, CT: Yale University Press, 1998.

Logan, John R. et al. "Immigrant Enclaves and Ethnics Communities in New York and Los Angeles." *American Sociological Review* 2 (2002): 299–322.

"Population: The Newest New Yorkers, 2000 edition. "Executive Summary." Accessed October 19, 2016. www.nyc.gov/html/dcp/html/census/nny_exec_sum/shtlm.

Shapiro, Edward S. *Crown Heights: Blacks, Jews, and the 1991 Brooklyn Riot.* Lebanon, NH: Brandeis University Press, 2006.

Sutton, Constance R., and Elsa M. Chaney, eds. *Caribbean Life in New York City: Sociocultural Dimensions.* Staten Island, NY: Center for Immigrations Studies, 1992.

CROWN HEIGHTS, JEWISH ENCLAVE (BROOKLYN, NEW YORK).
See Borough Park/Williamsburg/Crown Heights, Jewish Enclaves (Brooklyn, New York); Crown Heights, Jamaican Enclave (Brooklyn, New York)

CZECH ENCLAVES.
See Little Bohemia (Omaha, Nebraska); Pilsen (Chicago, Illinois); Point Cadet (Biloxi, Mississippi); Tabor, Czech Enclave (South Dakota)

DALLAS, MEXICAN ENCLAVES (TEXAS)

Dallas, Texas, with a population of over 1.2 million by official census count, is the third most populous city in Texas and the ninth most populous in the United States. Located in north Texas, it is the largest city in the Dallas–Fort Worth–Arlington Metropolitan Statistical Area, which ranks fourth in the United States with a population

There are numerous Mexican, and Mexican-American neighborhoods, in the greater Dallas area. (Jensen Walker/Getty Images)

of nearly 7 million. Dallas's Hispanic/Latino population numbers just over half a million (about 40% of the city's population), placing Dallas seventh among all U.S. cities. People of Mexican ancestry, meanwhile, number over 450,000, accounting for nearly 90% of the city's Hispanics/Latinos (U.S. Census Bureau 2009–2013).

The City's Migrant History

Mexicans first came to Dallas in large numbers in the 1870s. Mexican workers were concentrated in railroads, and the first Mexican residential enclaves in Dallas grew up around the railroad yards north of downtown. Mexican migration to the area got a further push from the turmoil of the Mexican Revolution (1910–1920). By this period, the neighborhood that would come to be known as "Little Mexico" was coalescing north of downtown Dallas. What had been an Eastern European Jewish neighborhood was being transformed by the exit of prospering former residents to the more affluent south side of the city. The proximity to railroads and other "industrial use properties" (slaughterhouses, garbage dumps, etc.) meant both proximity to employment for Mexican newcomers and, presumably, affordable housing due to the neighborhood disamenities of "foul chemical and animal smells" and associated health hazards (Villasana 2011, p. 17). By the 1930s, the neighborhood was home to over 15,000 people.

Sol Villasana attributes the demise of Little Mexico both to resident relocation and to the pressures of "urban renewal." World War II took many working-age Mexican men out of the neighborhood, "leaving behind aging parents and a fragile economic structure" (Villasana 2011, p. 99). The relocation of employment away from the city center and the beginnings of postwar suburbanization, too, contributed to the exodus from Little Mexico. As early as the 1940s, city planners were identifying Little Mexico as a "blighted" area—foreshadowing the "urban renewal" that would ultimately doom the neighborhood. As Villasana notes, the neighborhood's longtime Mexican residents were pushed out, either by eminent domain or by outright swindling at the hands of unscrupulous real estate developers (Villasana 2011, p. 99).

The demise of Little Mexico at the hands of "urban renewal" resulted in the formation of a new Mexican center, in the neighborhood of Oak Cliff. (Oak Cliff, once an independent municipality, was absorbed into Dallas over a century ago. It is located south of downtown Dallas.) Starting in the 1960s, Oak Cliff became a destination both for Mexican residents—over three-fourths of the area's population is of Mexican ancestry—and businesses, many making the move from Little Mexico. "Over the years the district attracted the remnants of Little Mexico . . . ," writes journalist Claire Ballor, "[the latter] now a curtain of high rises that screens the city from surrounding neighborhoods." Oak Cliff is a vibrant center of Mexican culture—restaurants and clothing shops, street music and food vendors—with the main thoroughfare of Jefferson Avenue now the "heart and soul of the [neighborhood's] Latino community." With Oak Cliff "becoming a safer, more pedestrian-friendly neighborhood" and a new bridge linking it with downtown, private investors have started buying up properties in the neighborhood, prices have started to rise, and some residents are concerned about a repeat—via gentrification—of what happened in Little Mexico (Ballor 2014).

Undocumented Migration Today

Migration from Mexico to the United States, of course, continues to the present. Rachel Adler describes one current stream of Mexican migration—begun in the late 1960s—from the state of Yucatán to Dallas (2008, p. 46). Mexican migrants in Dallas hail from many different parts of Mexico. While Yucatecans in Dallas "are comfortable with other Mexican migrants and interact with them" at work and in the broader community, Adler notes, the groups of Yucatecans she studied "live and work together and spend most of their time with other Yucatecos" (2008, p. 33).

Yucatecans tend to cluster in particular residential areas, and those from particular cities tend to further cluster among themselves. Those from the city of Kaal, on which Adler focuses, are the "largest residentially concentrated group of Yucatecans in Dallas," many living together in a particular apartment complex in the city's Brookhaven neighborhood. A number of Yucatecans from a town near Kaal, meanwhile, live at an adjacent apartment complex (Adler 2008, pp. 33, 40). This pattern recalls that observed by McDonald and McDonald about Southern Italian immigration to eastern cities a century or more ago, with people from particular towns clustering together in particular neighborhoods, on particular streets, and even in particular apartment buildings (1964, pp. 92–93).

Adler estimates the percentage of Dallas Yucatecans who are undocumented at 90% (2008, p. 36). For most, the process of entering the United States (on foot, over the U.S.-Mexico border) is costly and dangerous. It is, Adler emphasizes, also a transformative experience in terms of community and identity. "Many migrants said that when they visit Kaal they feel like outsiders," she notes. "At the same time, the border crossing experience is a principal criterion for membership in the migrant community" (2008, p. 54).

Like others in their position, Yucatecan undocumented migrants in Dallas "have found their niche in the low end of the city's service industries" (Adler 2008, p. 37). Among men, work in restaurants and hotels predominates (with dishwashing the first rung on the occupational ladder); among women, work as domestics is common. In the late 1990s, the average wage for Yucatecans in these occupations was around $7 per hour (similar for men and women), with few receiving benefits, and some working off the books. As much as these jobs may seem like mirror images— the lower rungs for men and women, respectively, in the gendered division of labor—one major difference is that most Yucatecan men work alongside other Yucatecans, while most Yucatecan women do not. This pattern is, in part, a result of men getting work through recommendations from Yucatecan acquaintances. Causation also runs in the other direction: working with other Yucatecans gives men access to new, largely Yucatecan friendship networks.

Mexicans and Dallas Racial Politics

People of Mexican ancestry, in the words of Michael Phillips, have historically "occup[ied] an uncomfortable middle ground in the city's racial hierarchy between wealthy Anglos at the top and poor African Americans at the bottom" (2006, p. 8). Mexican immigrants came into a city dominated by an all-white power structure, with *de jure* segregation of schools and other public accommodations, and in which non-whites were "limited to low-wage jobs and . . . few opportunities for economic advancement" (Phillips 2006, p. 126). Into the mid-20th century, Mexican Americans in Dallas attended segregated (non-white) schools, received lower wages than whites for the same work, and disproportionately lived in the least desirable housing with the least access to basic public services like running water and sanitation.

The racial caste system (characterizing, of course, not only Dallas, but the state, region, and nation as a whole) also shaped Mexican American politics. The "uncomfortable middle ground" included not only subjection to segregation and discrimination, but also striving to lay claim to white privilege. Phillips puts this striving in the context of similar attempts by other immigrant groups, as described by Roediger and others (Phillips 2006, pp. 10–11). Mainstream Mexican American political organizations "sought to have the Anglo community accept Latin Americans as a white ethnic group rather than as a separate race" (Phillips 2006, p. 128). Groups like the League of United Latin American Citizens (LULAC) adopted racial segregationist policies (against African Americans) of their own, distanced themselves from Mexican cultural identity, and emphasized their "Americanness" (Phillips 2006, p. 129). Mexican Americans were, for purposes of segregationist policy, sometimes officially classified as non-white and sometimes as white. However, in practice, "few Mexican Americans in Texas were prosperous enough to enjoy an easy ticket to whiteness" (Phillips 2006, p. 126).

A major rupture in the assimilationist politics of mainstream Mexican organizations came in the 1960s with the rise of radicalized student movements. These students rejected the claim to white privilege, identifying instead with the blended European, African, and indigenous ancestry of *la raza cosmica* ("cosmic race"). They condemned the older generation's attempts to distance Mexicans from blacks, instead identifying with African American liberation struggles. They threw off the label "Mexican American" in favor of "Chicano," turning away from the assertion of "Americanness" and toward identification with worldwide struggles against "gringo imperialism." While centered in Houston and at universities like the University of Texas–Austin, this new political consciousness inspired Chicano activism in Dallas as well (Phillips 2006, pp. 164–66).

During the 1970s, Dallas, like other U.S. cities, went through the throes of white flight—a reaction to urban risings (themselves responses to white supremacism and police violence) and school desegregation (certainly a response to protests by both African American and Mexicans). The city became increasingly "black and brown," but the African American and Hispanic/Latino communities, in the view of Phillips, did not achieve a high degree of unity in "challenging the white power structure" (2006, p. 176).

See also in Texas: Houston, Mexican Enclaves (Texas); Little India, Hillcroft (Houston, Texas); Little Saigon (Houston, Texas); Muenster, German Enclave (Texas); New Braunfels, German Enclave (Texas); Serbin, German Enclave (Texas)

See also Hispanic Enclaves: Annandale, Latino and Asian Enclaves (Virginia); Boyle Heights, Latino Neighborhood (Los Angeles, California); Bridgeport (Chicago, Illinois); Chicago, Mexican and Puerto Rican Enclaves (Illinois); East Los Angeles, Mexican American Enclave (Los Angeles, California); El Monte, Latino Enclaves (California); Historic South Central (Los Angeles, California); Holyoke, Puerto Rican Enclaves (Massachusetts); Houston, Mexican Enclaves (Texas); Indio, Mexican and Central American Communities (California); Jackson Heights (Queens, New York); Langley Park, Latino Enclaves (Maryland); Lawrence, Latino Enclaves (Massachusetts); Little Havana (Miami, Florida); Little Havana on the Hudson (North Hudson, New Jersey); Little Lima (Paterson, New Jersey); Logan Heights, Mexican Enclave (San Diego, California); Mayan Corner/24th and Mission (San Francisco, California); Mexicantown (Detroit, Michigan); Mount Washington, Mexican Enclave (California); Olvera Street/La Plaza (Los Angeles, California); Phoenix and Other Cities, Mexican Enclaves (Arizona); Pico Rivera, Latino Enclave (California); Riverside, Mexican Enclave (California); San Bernardino, Mexican Enclave (California); Santa Ana, Mexican Enclaves (California); Sleepy Hollow, Ecuadorian Enclave (New York); South Federal Boulevard (Denver, Colorado); Sunset Park West and North Corona (New York City); Upper Fells Point (Spanish Town) (Baltimore, Maryland); Washington Heights (New York City); Watts (Los Angeles, California)

Alejandro Reuss

Further Reading

Adler, Rachel H. *Yucatecans in Dallas, Texas: Breaching the Border, Bridging the Distance*. Boston, MA: Pearson Education, 2008.

Ballor, Claire. "Latino Neighborhoods: Dallas' Oak Cliff Beats with Hispanic Heart, But Some Fear Gentrification." Fox News Latino, September 30, 2014.

Phillips, Michael. *White Metropolis: Race, Ethnicity, and Religion in Dallas, 1841–2001*. Austin, TX: University of Texas Press, 2006.

U.S. Census Bureau, American Community Survey, B03001: Hispanic or Latino Origin by Specific Origin, 2009–2013.

Villasana, Sol. *Dallas's Little Mexico*. Charleston, SC: Arcadia, 2011.

DANISH ENCLAVES. *See* Elk Horn, Danish Enclaves (Iowa); Solvang, Danish Community (California)

DEARBORN AND DETROIT, MIDDLE EASTERN ENCLAVES (MICHIGAN)

Michigan is home to the highest concentration of Arab Americans in the United States, due to the greater Detroit area being home to the country's largest and most diverse Arab American community. The Detroit metropolitan area has a reputation for its high level of diversity and also its successful cultural outreach, but simply

The Detroit suburb of Dearborn is home to one of the biggest populations of Muslims and Arabs in the United States. (NOVA SAFO/AFP/Getty Images)

stating that someone is of an Arab background is not enough: Arab Americans are a diverse group, coming from 22 countries that make up the Arab world. Arab Americans see their identities as unique and special, and census data reflects this. The following is a nonexhaustive list of countries that have been recorded by Arab Americans in Census data: Lebanon, Syria, Egypt, Iraq, Jordan, Palestine, Morocco, Kuwait, Libya, Oman, Qatar, Saudi Arabia, Tunisia, the United Arab Emirates, and Yemen (Michigan, *Arab American Institute*). Although immigration from the Middle East into metropolitan Detroit has been occurring for over 100 years, it is in the past 30 years that Arab Americans have transformed this city into the center of Arab American life in the United States.

This entry will not only focus on metropolitan Detroit as a whole but also on the city of Dearborn. Dearborn is located in Michigan's Wayne County, on the southwest edge of Detroit's metropolitan area. It is the eighth-largest city in Michigan. As of 2014, the population was 95,535. The racial and ethnic composition is 89.1% white, 4.8% black, 3.9% Hispanic. The remaining very small percentages are Asian and those who identify as being of two or more races. Arab Americans are categorized as "white" in the census collection data and are not officially recognized as a federal minority group. Thus it is difficult to determine the exact number of Arab Americans in the Detroit metropolitan area. However, it is estimated that 41.7% of the population of Dearborn is of Arab ancestry.

The Dearborn area was inhabited for thousands of years by various indigenous peoples. It was first settled by French farmers in the late 18th century. French colonists established a trading post and developed Detroit during the colonial period, and they traded regularly with numerous regional tribes. The community continued to grow with the establishment of the Detroit Arsenal on the Chicago Road linking Detroit and Chicago. The Detroit Arsenal's main purpose was to serve as a supply depot for the army for the storage, maintenance, and repair of arms and ammunition. The city is named after patriot Henry Dearborn, a general during the American Revolution and secretary of war under President Thomas Jefferson. 1927 was the year in which Dearborn was established as a city. The city boasts a campus of the University of Michigan, as well as Henry Ford Community College. The city of Dearborn was the home of Henry Ford's bustling epicenter of manufacturing and remains the location of the Ford Motor Company's world headquarters. The Ford manufacturing plant partially explains the Arab American population in the area but Arabs began coming into Southeast Michigan well before the consolidation of the auto industry.

Immigration took off in the early 1900s as the auto industry drew in people from all over the world. Since their first wave of immigration into the United States in 1870, the Arab American population has continued to grow. This is because people coming into the United States try to find an area that is hospitable, where people of their same culture live, and where familial and religious networks are already in place. The first Arab immigrants to the Detroit area came in the 1880s and were of Syrian and Lebanese origins. Most of the Lebanese were Christians, but there were also Maronites, Melkites, and Eastern Orthodox. Some immigrants were also Sunni and Shia Muslims, but these were in small numbers. The Lebanese and Syrian Christians were from the Mount Lebanon area, whereas later Lebanese were Shia and from the southern part of the country. In the late 1800s, Henry Ford employed thousands of Lebanese, Yemenis, and others to work in Dearborn in his River Rouge complex, which gave Middle Easterners their first foothold in the area. It has been said the first immigrants who sought jobs in the automotive industry were offered five dollars per day. Later in the 20th century, other immigrants from the Middle East came into the Dearborn area, such as Armenians, Assyrians, Syriacs, and Chaldeans. Almost all of the Chaldeans came from the village of Tel Kaif and nearby villages in northern Iraq. The Syrian and Lebanese Muslims' first home was Highland Park, where they erected their first mosque in 1916. A bit later, the majority of this group moved to Dearborn. Baydoun, an Arab American whose grandfather immigrated to the United States from Lebanon to work in an auto plant, states "We are American and we are proud of who we are. Many Lebanese started off by selling goods and small commodities and found successes in the auto industry. We love the principles of freedom, equality, opportunity, justice, all of the things my grandfather probably came here for, to work side by side with people from around the world and respect each other" (Warikoo 2014).

In 1929, President Calvin Coolidge signed the Immigration Act of 1924 which decreased the number of Arabs and other immigrants allowed into the country. In 1965, however, there were major changes in the immigration laws that made it easier for family unification to take place. During the second wave of Arab immigration, in the 1960s, the majority of people came from Syria, Palestine, Iraq, and Yemen. Christian Chaldeans, the Iraqi minority in a Muslim country, took advantage of the Immigration and Nationality Act of 1965. Before the passage of the act, there were about 1,000 Christian Chaldeans in Detroit. But after its passage, their numbers increased greatly. By 1974, this group accounted for one-seventh of Detroit's estimated 70,000 Arab Americans. This group currently is mostly concentrated in the Oak Park, Southfield, Sterling Heights, and Troy areas. The third wave of immigration took place in the 1980s when war and political unrest were driving many from Iraq and Lebanon into the United States. When civil war in Lebanon broke out in 1975, many left the country. "At that time, you had a lot of Lebanese Muslims coming from southern Lebanon. Entire families—almost entire villages—would come and resettle in Dearborn" (Cwiek 2014). To them, Michigan was a safe haven, much safer than living with the fear of bombs in Beirut. Since then, immigrants from Yemen, Iraq, and the Palestine territories, the majority of whom are Muslim, have joined them.

The majority of Palestinian Americans are from villages and small towns in the West Bank. The first Palestinians arrived in the early 1890s, but the majority arrived after the Arab-Israeli wars of 1948 and 1967. The south end of Dearborn is home to a concentration of Yemeni, as is the area of Hamtramck. Hamtramck is a historically Polish working-class neighborhood isolated by industrial factories. Masjid Mu'ath bin Jabal, the Yemeni mosque located in this area, is credited with turning around this rough, industrial area of Detroit. This Yemeni mosque has laid the foundation for the ethnically mixed, visible Muslim population.

The main driver of recent immigration has been conflict in the Middle East. About 3,000 new Arab immigrants to Michigan came from Iraq after the Gulf War of 1991. In 2010, the United States opened 25,000 special visas to accommodate people from the Middle East, and the vast majority of these people are Iraqis. Among the most recent arrivals to the Arab American population are Iraqi refugees, mostly Shia from the south and Kurds from Northern Iraq. Many had been expelled from Iraq and were in refugee camps in Turkey and Saudi Arabia. It is clear that immigration from the Middle East into the United States—and, more specifically, Dearborn—has resulted from political issues in Middle Eastern countries. It is interesting to note that over the waves of immigration into Detroit, the religious makeup of the immigrants has shifted. Before 1960, as many as 90% of Arab immigrants were Christian, but most recent immigrants are Muslim. Today, the Chaldean community is mostly concentrated around Nine Mile Road and Coolidge Street. It is estimated that by 2004, Metro Detroit was the home of the largest Chaldean Catholic diaspora community in the world. Most Chaldeans originate from northern Iraq and some from Iran, Syria, and Turkey.

Between 1990 and 2000, the Michigan Arab American community grew by 65%. As the Arab American population makes up more than 40% of the population in Dearborn today, it is said that in the future Arab Americans will make up the majority of the population. Arab Americans have stated that they believe that in the coming years the community will continue to grow and prosper in metropolitan Detroit. Metro Detroiters with roots in the Middle East have taken on leadership roles such as in the Wayne County government to the Michigan Supreme Court, where two justices have Lebanese ancestry. The chief justices of district courts are of Arab descent and Muslim. The Arab Americans are also expanding into places such as Dearborn Heights and Canton as well as Oakland and Macomb counties. This community's continued expansion will help it become an integral part of the region as the residents continue to assume prominent roles in the community, local government, and businesses.

Education is the key to success experienced by Arab Americans and will propel them to leadership roles in society. As a result of the large Arab population, the local schools have implemented bilingual Arabic-English programs for those students who wish to learn about their language and heritage. Detroit has a reputation for being a good place to raise children in the Arab tradition while simultaneously integrating into American society. Because, since the Gulf War, the Detroit area has served as a point of entry into the United States, the local school systems have been increasingly improving their internal programs to attract observant Muslims and make them feel at home. For example, there have been increases in Arabic language instruction, *halal* meals, and days off for Islamic holidays. The initiatives have increased to include Islamic history and culture classes and opportunities for prayer. Through working with school boards and social services, the Muslim population has implemented trans-communal politics that move through city lines and ethnic groups to create a comfortable living space for themselves.

The heart of the Arab business district is Warren and Schaeffer Streets, an area where one can find over 100 Arab stores, the majority of them owned by Lebanese. Arab Americans own many shops and businesses, offering services in both English and Arabic, and we must not forget the smaller groups of immigrants such as Palestinians, Jordanians, and Yemenis. The majority of immigrants from Yemen did not arrive until the 1960s. By then there was a well-established network of organizations catering to the needs of the community. These organizations range from social and economic to religious services. Examples include the Arab Community Center for Economic and Social Services (ACCESS), which is one of the largest and most active associations; the American Syrian Arab Association; the Arab American Arts Council; the Arab American & Chaldean Communities Social Services Council; and the American Arab Anti-Discrimination Committee, to name a few. Community involvement is extremely present, which is a result of the number of places of worship and also Arab media outlets. Aside from religion, leisure and entertainment activities and channels also serve the community. The Arab Network of America, TV Orient, United TV, as well as a number of radio stations and newspapers, serve the community. The Arab American National Museum (AANM) opened in Dearborn in 2005. It is the first museum in the world devoted to Arab American history and culture. The eastern section of Dearborn contains a thriving Arab American population, and the streets are filled with Arab businesses and stores containing Middle Eastern foods, hookah cafés, and Islamic clothing.

The larger the community gets, the more it draws others from the same parts of the world. The story of Arab Detroit did not begin just yesterday; for the past 100 years there has been a steady stream of immigrants into the Detroit area. New arrivals look for people of the same nationality and religion, for mosques and churches to pray in, and for social and business networks. They look for the culture that will make them feel the most at home. Immigrants arriving today are much better prepared than they were decades ago, which is a result of an increasingly globalized society, with much more information about contemporary American life spreading around the world.

The Arab Americans in Michigan make up the most visible and organized constituency in the country, and no matter the economic successes of its residents, Detroit remains a charged and racially demarcated cityscape. There are a few notable people coming from the metropolitan area of Detroit, including Arab American science fiction and fantasy writer and poet Saladin Ahmed. Rima Fakih is a Lebanese American actress, model and winner of the Miss USA beauty pageant in 2010. Kemal Amen "Casey" Kasem was an American music historian, radio celebrity, and voice actor. He has also been the voice of Shaggy Rogers in the *Scooby-Doo* franchise. Hassan Al-Qazwini, born in Iraq, is the former leader of the Islamic Center of America in Dearborn. Lebanese-born social entrepreneur and real estate expert Moose M. Scheib is the CEO of CBIG, an advisory firm that counsels American and Middle Eastern companies doing business with each other.

A notable site in Dearborn is the Islamic Center of America, a Shia mosque that is the largest mosque in North America. Although the institution dates back to 1962 (when founded by Jawad Chirri), the new mosque in Dearborn opened in 2005. The mosque operates the Muslim American Youth Academy, an Islamic elementary and middle school. Although well known, this mosque is not the oldest in Dearborn. The Dearborn Mosque belonging to the American Moslem Society was built in 1937 by the nascent Islamic community. In the year in which it was built, the nascent community was comprised mostly of Sunni Muslims of the Bekaa Valley in Lebanon. The number of people attending this mosque grew between the 1960s and 1980s. Between the 1980s and 1990s, a conservative form of Sunni Islam dominated the mosque. This changed in the 2000s when it became known as the Yemeni Zaydi Dearborn Mosque, after a Shia group coming from Yemen.

A prevalent stereotype held by many Americans is that all Arabs are Muslim, which is far from the truth. A core of local Middle Easterners are Christian, led by the early wave of Iraqi Catholics known as Chaldeans, many of whom fled Muslim persecution. Recent times have brought more Muslim immigrants to the area who have been displaced by war and are drawn into the United States by educational and economic opportunities. According to a Wayne State University Study, as of 2007, it has been recorded that the Arab American community in metropolitan Detroit produces as much as $7.7 billion annually in salaries and earnings. Many people around the world believe that Detroit is in decline, but Arab Americans believe in the future of this city. Detroit's metropolitan area has seen both Islamophilia, which is an attraction to Islam or Muslims, and also Islamophobia, which is a fear of Islam or Muslims. This divide in sentiments enters the realm of religion as well. There have been news reports describing violence between Muslims and Christians in the area.

Throughout immigration, the largest group of Muslims in Dearborn have been Lebanese Sunnis. Regardless of this heavy concentration of Arabs, tensions remain high, especially since the attacks of September 11, 2001. The fight for the preservation of traditions and culture is ever present. While becoming stronger and more prominent in society, the second and third generations of immigrants are becoming Americanized. Accepting the practice of Islam within American culture has been difficult, especially with the publicly worn hijab. Arab Americans face criticism from some Americans if they wear it, yet also from their own religious group if they do

---

Simon Baz

"In brightest day, in blackest night, no evil shall escape my sight. Let those who worship evil's might, beware my power, Green Lantern's light!"

Meet Simon Baz, a Lebanese American from Dearborn, Michigan. When he assumed the mantle of the Green Lantern character (DC Comics) in 2012, he became the first big-name Muslim superhero. In the first issue, Simon confronts what it means to be an American Muslim in a post-9/11 world. Creator Geoff Johns, a Detroit native who is half-Lebanese, collaborated on the script with the Arab American Museum in Dearborn. Johns uses the city as a backdrop, hoping to "create a really compelling character who's from Dearborn that people from Dearborn and the surrounding area are really proud of and excited about."

Baz is another step toward diversification in the comic book world as creators seek out overlooked perspectives. The new Spiderman is half-black, half-Latino, and the original Green Lantern, Alan Scott, was revealed to be gay. Though Simon Baz is not the first Muslim comic book character, he is the first one at the helm of a series. Simon's origins indicate that Dearborn is gaining recognition as a source of valuable, untapped American voices.

not wear it. However, there is a substantial number of Christian Arab Americans who have accepted and even embraced this Americanization, as to be more included and welcomed by the greater American society. Arab Americans are developing a power base in the Detroit area, most clearly seen by the election of Spencer Abraham, the first Arab senator in the state of Michigan. Tensions will remain, but established programs and organizations will continue to finance programs that ensure new residents are integrated successfully and that the Arab American community in metropolitan Detroit is as cohesive as possible.

See also in Michigan: Little Poland (Hamtramck, Michigan); Mexicantown (Detroit, Michigan)

See also Middle Eastern Enclaves: Gallup, Palestinian Enclave (New Mexico); Glendale, Armenian Enclave (California); Little Arabia (Anaheim, California); Little Armenia (Los Angeles, California); Little Poland (Hamtramck, Michigan); Tehrangeles (Los Angeles, California); Watertown, Armenian Capital (Massachusetts)

Stephanie Tercero

Further Reading

Cwiek, Sarah. "What Explains Michigan's Large Arab American Community?" Michigan Radio, July 9, 2014. Accessed October 16, 2016. http://michiganradio.org/post/what-explains-michigans-large-arab-american-community.

"Detroit's Arab Americans." *Detroit 2020.* August 16, 2011. Accessed October 16, 2016. http://detroit2020.com/2011/08/16/detroits-arab-americans/.

El-Badry, Samia. "Arab American Demographics." Allied Media Corporation. Accessed October 16, 2016. http://www.allied-media.com/Arab-American/Arab%20american%20Demographics.html.

"Michigan." Arab American Institute. Accessed October 16, 2016. http://www.aaiusa.org/page/file/f6bf1bfae54f0224af_3dtmvyj4h.pdf/MIdemographics.pdf.

Rignall, Karen. "Building an Arab-American Community in Dearborn." *The Journal of the International Institute* 5, no. 1 (Fall 1997). Accessed October 16, 2016. http://quod.lib.umich.edu/j/jii/4750978.0005.106?view=text;rgn=main.

Salloum, Habeeb. "Detroit—Arab Capital of North America." *Al Jadid Magazine* 4, no. 25 (Fall 1998). Accessed October 16, 2016. http://www.aljadid.com/content/detroit-arab-capital-north-america.

Shryock, Andrew. *Islamophobia/Islamophilia: Beyond the Politics of Enemy and Friend.* Bloomington, IN: Indiana University Press, 2010.

Truitt, Brian. "Meet Simon Baz, DC Comics' New Arab-American Green Lantern." *USA Today,* September 5, 2012. Accessed November 14, 2016. http://usatoday30.usatoday.com/life/comics/story/2012-09-05/Simon-Baz-Arab-American-Green-Lantern/57594766/1.

U.S. Census Bureau. "Quick Facts: Dearborn City, Michigan." Accessed October 16, 2016. http://www.census.gov/quickfacts/table/PST045215/2621000.

Warikoo, Nirak. "A Quarter Million Michiganders Have Roots in Middle East." *Detroit Free Press,* October 24, 2014. Accessed October 16, 2016. http://www.freep.com/story/news/local/michigan/wayne/2014/10/24/arab-american-chaldean-diversity-future-metro-detroit/17804861.

The Week Staff. "Meet the New Muslim-American Green Lantern." *The Week*, September 7, 2012. Accessed November 14, 2016. http://theweek.com/articles/472544/meet-new -muslimamerican-green-lantern.

DETROIT (MICHIGAN). *See* Dearborn and Detroit, Middle Eastern Enclaves (Michigan)

EAST LOS ANGELES, MEXICAN AMERICAN ENCLAVE (LOS ANGELES, CALIFORNIA)

Mexicans have been a major part of Los Angeles's history for centuries. From the days of Spanish colonialism, to California's inclusion as part of the United States, to the present, the city has remained a major center for Mexicans. As of 2010, almost half of Los Angeles's population is Latino, the majority of it Mexican. Los Angeles, in fact, is home to the largest number of Mexicans outside of Mexico. While the city has often been the recipient of more immigrants than any other U.S. city, its immigrant population has been less diverse, with most coming from Mexico, El Salvador, and Guatemala, because of its close proximity to the Mexican border. The last few decades of the 20th century witnessed an influx of new immigrant groups,

A Latino boy rides his scooter, East Los Angeles, California. East Los Angeles' history as a Mexican American neighborhood can be traced to its founding as part of New Spain in 1781. (Americanspirit/Dreamstime.com)

most notably from Asian countries. East Los Angeles, however, remains an almost exclusively Mexican enclave, despite frequent changes in other immigrant neighborhoods. Its population of 126,496 is over 97% Mexican (U.S. Census 2010). Although it is currently an unincorporated area east of the Boyle Heights district in Los Angeles County, East Los Angeles was, in fact, founded as a Mexican pueblo.

East Los Angeles's history as a Mexican neighborhood can be traced to its founding as part of New Spain in 1781. The Spanish Crown authorized Gaspar de Portolá to settle the flat lowlands between the Los Angeles River and the Rio Hondo and establish a mission nearby. The colonial army escorted farming families from Mexico to settle the region. Soon after, Spain granted several large parcels of land to Antonio Maria Lugo, who had served as a soldier in the Spanish army. The Lugo family, among the first Californios, or Spanish colonists, became known as the founding family of Los Angeles. Their landholdings included East Los Angeles, which remained a wilderness until the latter decades of the 19th century, when black laborers, Italians, Germans, Russians, French, and Chinese moved into the area. Despite the influx of newcomers, however, East Los Angeles remained predominantly Mexican, especially as the unrest caused by the Mexican Revolution in the 1910s sparked a wave of emigration to the United States. Additionally, discrimination in Los Angeles proper pushed Mexicans across the river to East Los Angeles where low rents and inexpensive houses were common. Many Mexicans in East LA today can trace their origins to the families that settled in East Los Angeles during this period.

By 1920, there were over 100,000 Mexicans in southern California. The Mexican American community in East Los Angeles became the largest ethnic neighborhood in the United States. Urban development, coinciding with the construction of the interurban railroad and the rise of the automobile, created jobs that, although low-paying, made living in California a better option for many than remaining at home. The first 40 or so years of the 20th century were a key period for establishing East Los Angeles as a Mexican barrio; they also coincided with Los Angeles's expansion from a city of 100,000 residents to a major metropolis of over one million (Romo 1983, pp. viii, 5). While the Great Depression halted migration, the *bracero* program sparked a new wave of immigration beginning in 1942. The program, named after the Spanish term for "manual laborer," was a series of diplomatic agreements between the United States and Mexico to ensure that the United States had enough agricultural workers during World War II. The end of the *bracero* program did not spell the end of immigration to East Los Angeles. Much of it has simply continued undocumented. It ebbs and flows according to the U.S. economy. Both recent immigrants and the Mexican families that have been in East Los Angeles for decades have created a community where Spanish-language billboards and newspapers, community organizations, neighborhood fiestas, and local businesses celebrate Mexican culture.

The Mexican community has a long history of political involvement in East Los Angeles. During the Mexican Revolution, it became a center for both supporters and opponents of the revolutionaries. The Partido Liberal Mexicano, led by Ricado Flores Magón, was the most active group, opposing the dictatorship of Proforio

Díaz. Other groups, too, however, advocated for social and political reforms in Mexico and for greater equality for Mexicans in Los Angeles through social organizations and Spanish-language news outlets. During the Civil Rights Movement of the 1960s, East Los Angeles became a major center for the Chicano Movement, in which Mexican Americans advocated for the restoration of land, rights for farm workers, and education reforms. Cesar Chavez, cofounder of the National Farm Workers Association, later to become the United Farm Workers (UFW), was the most famous leader of this movement; Cesar Chavez Boulevard in East Los Angeles is named after him. The neighborhood was the site for the Chicano Blowouts, a series of 1968 protests against unequal conditions in public schools, as well as social injustice, generally. While the strength of the movement petered out by the 1980s, social activism continued. In the mid-1980s, a group of 400 women calling themselves the Mothers of East Los Angeles organized to oppose the construction of California's first state prison in East Los Angeles. Many shared the experience of being forced to move in the 1950s to make way for the construction of the freeway through their neighborhood. After a successful campaign against the state prison, they also got involved in other issues in the central city, and mobilized members of the community to oppose, for example, the toxic waste incinerator in Vernon and an oil pipeline going through center of East Los Angeles.

One reason that activism has been common in East Los Angeles is that its residents have traditionally been the targets of anti-immigrant discrimination. During the Great Depression, Mexicans and other immigrant groups in the Los Angeles area became scapegoats for white Americans' hostility over job loss. But while discrimination has decreased over time for some immigrant groups in Los Angeles, such as Jewish residents, it has persisted for Mexican Americans. To some extent, Mexican Americans share similar experiences with African Americans. They have become more, not less, likely to live and work in areas segregated from whites and to experience discrimination against non-whites. Despite the fact that Mexicans have created a long-lasting community in East Los Angeles, they tend to occupy the lower rungs of the economic ladder. The median household income for Mexicans in East Los Angeles is $36,755 as of 2010, compared to $51,100 nationally, with 26.8% of the population living below the federal poverty line. Urban economic restructuring in Los Angeles has created a bifurcated job structure in which the highly educated receive high wages and stable employment and less skilled workers receive low wages and less stable employment. Workers with middle-level qualifications are increasingly excluded for job opportunities. Because of Los Angeles's job economy, Mexicans have limited employment opportunities. Many work in the low-wage agricultural sector, as opposed to Angelinos from Central America, who are more likely to work in domestic occupations. The *bracero* program and subsequent immigration legislation that makes exceptions for "special agricultural workers" from Mexico, such as the Immigration and Control Act of 1986, are testaments both to the fact that Mexicans typically occupy farm jobs and to the fact that the U.S. government expects them to (Waldinger and Bozorgmehr 1996).

Although the majority of Mexican Americans have historically worked in the low-wage agricultural sector, many have opened businesses in East Los Angeles. As early as 1922, there were 239 Mexican businesses in East Los Angeles. These varied from service stations to small factories to meatpacking plants. Since cuisine is a major feature of most cultures, many of these businesses have centered on food. Of the original group of Mexican-owned enterprises, for example, 66 were grocery stores. Yet early on, few local markets carried popular Mexican food products, such as pigs' feet, chicharrones (pork rind), or chorizo (pork sausage). This would change, however. In the 1940s, Mexican immigrant Mario López founded the Carmelita Provision Company in East Los Angeles, named for Carmelita Avenue, and began to produce chorizo and other popular Mexican pork items. His business benefitted from the postwar demand for familiar, good-quality food products by the rapidly growing Mexican community. This demand has not ceased. Today, East Los Angeles boasts a great number of Mexican restaurants that serve traditional fare, such as cochinita pibil (slow-roasted pork), gorditas, (savory corn cakes), queso fondido (melted cheese), flautas (rolled tortillas), grilled tostadas, chiles rellenos, stuffed poblanos, and pork stew. Tamayo's Restaurant is a landmark East Los Angeles establishment, founded in 1985, that often hosts Hollywood celebrities, city officials, and ordinary residents. One of its specialties is chicken mole, a delicate sauce originating in the Oaxacan region made of chile and chocolate and as many as 30 or more other ingredients. Trendy Mexican eateries offer traditional Oaxacan black mole, as well as red, green, and yellow moles and exotic moles, such as velo de novia and passion fruit. Popular dining options allow restaurant goers to watch soccer and eat barbacoa—barbecue's pre-Columbian ancestor. For dessert, restaurants serve arroz con leche (sweetened rice with milk), raspados (snow cones), and tres leches cake. Despite different offerings, the majority of dining establishments in East Los Angeles are locally owned, rather than chains.

As of the second decade of the 21st century, in fact, the neighborhood is one of the last areas of Los Angeles whose landscape is marked by mostly locally owned enterprises, small mom-and-pop shops, and historic storefronts, especially on César E. Chávez Avenue and East First. This sense of tradition and community is bolstered by other celebrations of Mexican culture. A highly visible form of this cultural celebration are the murals that East Los Angeles became famous for in the 1970s. Mural painting became popular in Mexico following the 1910 Mexican Revolution, as artists sought to visually express social and political messages and make art more accessible to the general public. The art form was then transplanted to Los Angeles by way of travelers and immigrants. In 1932, on Olivera Street, David Alfaro Siqueiros painted an 80-foot-long mural, entitled *America Tropical*, which depicted the workers' struggle. While it was painted over soon after its completion, it reemerged in the 1970s during the Chicano art movement, which was especially active in East Los Angeles. At the East Los Angeles public housing project Estrada Courts, Charles "Gato" Felix started a Mexican mural project to address issues of social and political justice, which became known as the "East Los" mural movement. Since 1973, more than 80 two-story murals have been painted at Estrada Courts, the first of which reflected pre-Colombian influences and focused on workers' rights, especially those of the United Farm Workers. Then in 1976, arts-activist Judy Baca expanded the mural movement and helped start the Social and

Public Art Resources Center (SPARC). At the end of the 1980s, SPARC introduced "Neighborhood Pride: Great Walls Unlimited," an initiative to raise funds to paint murals throughout the Los Angeles area (Social and Public Art Resource Center 2014). The program has continued ever since.

In addition to murals that depict Mexican culture and politics, citywide celebrations promote Mexican culture. East Los Angeles boasts the nation's oldest and largest Hispanic parade, which celebrates Mexican Independence Day. The holiday marks the pronouncement of the start of the War of Independence from Spain on September 16, 1810, and its celebration usually includes the public ringing of bells and the recitation of the *Grito de Dolores* (Shout of Dolores), which includes the phrase "Viva Mexico!" The East Los Angeles Parade is endorsed by the Consulate General and presented by Comité Mexicano Cívico Patriótico, an organization founded in 1931 to promote and maintain Mexican traditions and customs. It runs along Cesar E. Chavez Avenue from Mednik Avenue to Gage Avenue and is followed by a patriotic festival with musical performances, dancing, and the offering and consumption of traditional foods, such as pozole, a soup made of hominy and pork, and tlayuda, a large crispy tortilla topped with refried beans, corn, and chorizo. Other foods have the colors of the Mexican flag—red, white, and green, like chiles en nogada. East Los Angeles also hosts Cinco de Mayo celebrations to commemorate the Mexican victory against the French at the Battle of Puebla on May 5, 1862. Los Angeles holds the largest Cinco de Mayo street fair in the world and East Los Angeles College typically puts on a parade, as well as dance performances that represent Aztec culture.

Sports are another embodiment of Mexican tradition in East Los Angeles. While soccer is the most popular sport nationwide in Mexico, baseball, the most popular sport in the northwest and southeast region, is tremendously popular in East Los Angeles and has been since the early 20th century. Mexican American baseball enjoyed a "golden age" from 1920–1960, and over the decades, East Los Angeles formed hundreds of associational baseball teams. The most famous of these is Carmelita Provision Company's *Los Chorizeros* which has achieved great national acclaim. The team had its start in 1941 when Mario López, a native of Chihuahua, Mexico, who had played on several teams in both Mexico and California, sponsored a team under his business's name, Mario's Service Station. Six years later, he started Carmelita's Provision Company, which became the team's sponsor. Its team members included López's business associates, factory workers, and other amateur players from the neighborhood. Over the years, the team has won numerous city, county, community, and tournament championships and continues to be a point of pride for East Los Angeles.

Community pride is indeed one reason the Mexican American population in East Los Angeles has persisted and flourished for over a century. Residents have managed to maintain old traditions while creating new ones. Discrimination against Mexicans in the United States continues to exist, but the increasing Hispanic influence in the U.S. political landscape promises to further improve neighborhoods like East Los Angeles.

See also in California: Baldwin Hills (Los Angeles, California); Boyle Heights, Jewish Neighborhood (Los Angeles, California); Boyle Heights, Latino Neighborhood (Los Angeles, California); Cambodia Town (Long Beach, California); Chinatown (Los Angeles, California); Chinatown (San Francisco, California); Chinatowns (Duplicates) (San Francisco, California); El Monte, Latino Enclaves (California); Fillmore District (San Francisco, California); Gardena and Torrance (South Bay Region, Los Angeles County, California); Glendale, Armenian Enclave (California); Historic Filipinotown (Los Angeles, California); Historic South Central (Los Angeles, California); Indio, Mexican and Central American Communities (California); Japantown (San Francisco, California); Kingsburg and Sveadal, Swedish Enclaves (California); Koreatown (Los Angeles, California); Little Arabia (Anaheim, California); Little Armenia (Los Angeles, California); Little Ethiopia (Los Angeles, California); Little India/Pakistan (Artesia, California); Little Italy (Los Angeles, California); Little Italy (San Diego, California); Little Italy (San Francisco, California); Little Saigon (San Francisco, California); Little Saigon (San Jose, California); Little Saigon (Westminster, California); Little Tokyo (Los Angeles, California); Logan Heights, Mexican Enclave (San Diego, California); Los Angeles, Hawaiian Enclaves (California); Los Angeles, West Side and San Fernando Valley Jewish Enclaves (California); Mayan Corner/24th and Mission (San Francisco, California); Monterey Park, First Suburban Chinatown (California); Mount Washington, Mexican Enclave (California); National City (San Diego, California); Olvera Street/La Plaza (Los Angeles, California); Pico Rivera, Latino Enclave (California); Riverside, Mexican Enclave (California); San Bernardino, Mexican Enclave (California); San Pedro, Italian and Croatian Enclaves (California); Santa Ana, Mexican Enclaves (California); Sawtelle (Los Angeles, California); Silicon Valley, Indian and South Asian Communities (Santa Clara Valley/San Jose Region, California); Sin City (Fresno, California); Solvang, Danish Community (California); Sonoma County, Italian Enclave (California); Tehrangeles (Los Angeles, California); Temescal (Oakland, California); Thai Town (Los Angeles, California); Watts (Los Angeles, California); Yuba City, Sikh Enclave (California)

See also Hispanic Enclaves: Annandale, Latino and Asian Enclaves (Virginia); Boyle Heights, Latino Neighborhood (Los Angeles, California); Bridgeport (Chicago, Illinois); Chicago, Mexican and Puerto Rican Enclaves (Illinois); Dallas, Mexican Enclaves (Texas); El Monte, Latino Enclaves (California); Historic South Central (Los Angeles, California); Holyoke, Puerto Rican Enclaves (Massachusetts); Houston, Mexican Enclaves (Texas); Indio, Mexican and Central American Communities (California); Jackson Heights (Queens, New York); Langley Park, Latino Enclaves (Maryland); Lawrence, Latino Enclaves (Massachusetts); Little Havana (Miami, Florida); Little Havana on the Hudson (North Hudson, New Jersey); Little Lima (Paterson, New Jersey); Logan Heights, Mexican Enclave (San Diego, California); Mayan Corner/24th and Mission (San Francisco, California); Mexicantown (Detroit, Michigan); Mount Washington, Mexican Enclave (California); Olvera Street/La Plaza (Los Angeles, California); Phoenix and Other Cities, Mexican Enclaves (Arizona); Pico Rivera, Latino Enclave (California); Riverside, Mexican Enclave (California);

San Bernardino, Mexican Enclave (California); Santa Ana, Mexican Enclaves (California); Sleepy Hollow, Ecuadorian Enclave (New York); South Federal Boulevard (Denver, Colorado); Sunset Park West and North Corona (New York City); Upper Fells Point (Spanish Town) (Baltimore, Maryland); Washington Heights (New York City); Watts (Los Angeles, California)

Lindsay Schakenbach Regele

Further Reading

Balderama, Francisco E., and Richard A. Santillan. "Los Chorizeros: The New York Yankees of East Los Angeles and the Reclaiming of Mexican American Baseball History." Accessed November 4, 2016. http://sabr.org/research/los-chorizeros-new-york-yankees-east -los-angeles-reclaimingmexican-american-baseball#footnote7_ct07stp.

Charles, Camille Zubrinksy. *Won't You Be My Neighbor: Race, Class, and Residence in Los Angeles*. New York: Russell Sage Foundation, 2009.

Logan, John R., Wenquan Zhang, and Richard D. Alba. "Immigrant Enclaves and Ethnic Communities in New York and Los Angeles." *American Sociological Review* (2002): 299–322.

Lomeli, Francisco A., ed. *Handbook of Hispanic Cultures in the United States: Literature and Art*. Houston: Arte Publico Press, 1993.

Mackun, Paul J., Steven Wilson, Thomas R. Fischetti, and Justyna Goworowska. *Population Distribution and Change: 2000 to 2010*. Washington, DC: U.S. Department of Commerce, Economics and Statistics Administration, US Census Bureau, 2011.

Pardo, Mary. "Mexican American Women Grassroots Community Activists: Mothers of East Los Angeles." In Karen Hansen and Anita Ilta Garey, eds. *Families in the US: Kinship and Domestic Politics*. (Philadelphia: Temple University Press, 1998): 251–62.

Romo, Ricardo. *East Los Angeles: History of a Barrio*. Vol. 12. Austin: University of Texas Press, 1983.

"Social and Public Art Resource Center." Accessed November 4, 2016. http://sparcinla.org/.

Waldinger, Roger, and Mehdi Bozorgmehr, eds. *Ethnic Los Angeles*. New York: Russell Sage Foundation, 1996.

EL MONTE, LATINO ENCLAVES (CALIFORNIA)

El Monte, California, is a city in the San Gabriel Valley of Southern California. Located between the San Gabriel and Rio Hondo rivers, El Monte lies about 13 miles east of Los Angeles. It began as a community of agricultural settlements, as migrants and immigrants stopping along the Santa Fe trail opted to set down permanent roots. While remaining primarily a farm town for its first century, conditions brought about by the Depression and World War II helped to transition the area to the industrial and commercial center it is today. Although Asian Americans have had a long history in El Monte, it has traditionally been and remains today a majority Hispanic community, with Hispanic residents currently making up 69% of the city's total population of 113,475 (U.S. Census Bureau 2010).

Early communities in the San Gabriel Valley were populated by individuals traveling the Santa Fe trail, which served as a thoroughfare for those seeking economic opportunities in California. Gaining its name from an old Spanish word for "wooded place," the lush lands of El Monte seemed promising for those interested in agriculture (Wilson and Lynch 2015). Settlers populated the region as early as 1851, and in 1853 the Los Angeles County Board of Supervisors set aside 86,000 acres for El Monte. The construction of the town's first railroad in 1873 made El Monte an even more readily accessible destination for settlers. Many of El Monte's early residents were white, arriving from southern states further east to start small farms and ranches. Early accounts of the region during this period describe El Monte and the surrounding areas as hotbeds of vigilante activity, as individuals took it upon themselves to establish justice in the sparse, newly settled lands.

Beginning around 1910, the Mexican Revolution pushed a new population of immigrants to seek opportunity in California. Between 1922 and 1927, the area's Mexican population increased from 400 to over 2,000 as immigrants sought work in El Monte citrus farms. While Mexicans still only represented about 20% of El Monte's population by the 1930s, growers felt that enticing farm laborers to set down permanent roots would be crucial to continually sustained prosperity. As a result, El Monte growers invested in providing housing and education for the area's Mexican laborers. Accordingly, the Hicks, Medina Court, and Las Flores immigrant camps were established. When issues like overcrowding and civil neglect began to threaten the Mexican communities, residents responded by creating their own networks of support services, called *colonias*. *Colonias* allowed Mexican farm laborers to establish churches, transportation networks, skills training classes, and other civil and social services that the local government did not provide, while simultaneously strengthening the community along common ties of cultural identity.

Throughout the first few decades of the 20th century, El Monte's Asian American population remained rather small, particularly in proportion to the Mexican population. Japanese, Chinese, and Filipino immigrants arrived in the area during the late 19th century to work as unskilled laborers, although in smaller numbers than Mexican immigrants. However, the Depression placed considerable financial strain on El Monte farmers, pushing them to rent out their land to Japanese immigrants looking to profit as tenant farmers. These Japanese tenant farmers tended to live on the farms and set working conditions and thus had considerable interaction with the Mexican laboring population. In 1933, tensions became critical between these growers and the largely Mexican farm labor population during the El Monte Berry Strike. Although, in the end, the strike produced few net gains for the Mexican labor force, it did contribute considerably to pro-organization sentiment and social unification among the Mexican labor community.

As World War II brought increased manufacturing to the greater Los Angeles area, El Monte's economy shifted gradually from primarily agrarian to industrial. By 1947, Los Angeles County provided 241,000 manufacturing jobs, up from 6,600 at the turn of the century. Such a transition not only transformed El Monte economically but culturally as well. Legion Stadium was built in El Monte just before the 1932 Olympics, intended to serve as a home for conventions and sporting events. However, in the 1950s Legion Stadium instead became a critical center for culture, particularly for youth. Due to its location outside of Los Angeles city limits, El Monte was not subject to the same laws restricting underage gatherings as Los Angeles proper. As a result, teenagers and young people from Greater Los Angeles flocked to see rock-and-roll shows at Legion Stadium. Shows drew a racially and ethnically diverse crowds, uniting white, black, Mexican, and Asian teens around a shared youth culture. So notorious and impactful was the rock-and-roll scene at Legion Stadium that it was memorialized in the 1963 hit song "Memories of El Monte," written by Frank Zappa and recorded by The Penguins.

El Monte remains salient as a center for ethnic arts and culture in the present day. The San Gabriel Valley is somewhat unique in Los Angeles country in that ethnic minorities still make up population majorities as they have for decades, remaining unaltered by gentrification and subsequent displacement experienced by ethnic populations in Los Angeles proper. While many neighboring communities in the San Gabriel Valley have majority Asian American populations, El Monte remains a majority Hispanic community. As a result, it maintains preeminence in the area for Chicano art, producing in recent years a burgeoning scene of novelists, poets, and visual artists.

In recent years El Monte has not been as productive economically as it has been culturally. El Monte's slow economic growth was compounded by the 2008 recession, with 14% unemployment and a median income 40% below state average in 2013. However, recent increases in investments from overseas present the possibility for increased economic development in the area. Chinese investors have recently poured considerable investment into the San Gabriel Valley, bringing increased tourism as well as luxury homes and hotels to the area. El Monte has been slow to attract investors compared to neighboring communities due to its comparatively small extant Asian American population, but as of December 2014 over $720 million worth of development projects were being discussed or actively developed in El Monte. As a result, it stands that the economic, demographic, and cultural makeup of El Monte could undergo significant transformation in the next few years. However, even with the possibility for increasing investment and luxury development it is unlikely that in the near future El Monte will lose its identity as a salient location for economic, ethnic, and cultural diversity.

See also in California: Baldwin Hills (Los Angeles, California); Boyle Heights, Jewish Neighborhood (Los Angeles, California); Boyle Heights, Latino Neighborhood (Los Angeles, California); Cambodia Town (Long Beach, California); Chinatown (Los Angeles, California); Chinatown (San Francisco, California); Chinatowns (Duplicates) (San Francisco, California); East Los Angeles, Mexican American Enclave (Los Angeles, California); Fillmore District (San Francisco, California); Gardena and Torrance (South Bay Region, Los Angeles County, California); Glendale, Armenian Enclave (California); Historic Filipinotown (Los Angeles, California); Historic South Central (Los Angeles, California); Indio, Mexican and Central American Communities (California); Japantown (San Francisco, California); Kingsburg and Sveadal, Swedish Enclaves (California); Koreatown (Los Angeles, California); Little Arabia (Anaheim, California); Little Armenia (Los Angeles, California); Little Ethiopia (Los Angeles, California); Little India/Pakistan (Artesia,

California); Little Italy (Los Angeles, California); Little Italy (San Diego, California); Little Italy (San Francisco, California); Little Saigon (San Francisco, California); Little Saigon (San Jose, California); Little Saigon (Westminster, California); Little Tokyo (Los Angeles, California); Logan Heights, Mexican Enclave (San Diego, California); Los Angeles, Hawaiian Enclaves (California); Los Angeles, West Side and San Fernando Valley Jewish Enclaves (California); Mayan Corner/24th and Mission (San Francisco, California); Monterey Park, First Suburban Chinatown (California); Mount Washington, Mexican Enclave (California); National City (San Diego, California); Olvera Street/La Plaza (Los Angeles, California); Pico Rivera, Latino Enclave (California); Riverside, Mexican Enclave (California); San Bernardino, Mexican Enclave (California); San Pedro, Italian and Croatian Enclaves (California); Santa Ana, Mexican Enclaves (California); Sawtelle (Los Angeles, California); Silicon Valley, Indian and South Asian Communities (Santa Clara Valley/San Jose Region, California); Sin City (Fresno, California); Solvang, Danish Community (California); Sonoma County, Italian Enclave (California); Tehrangeles (Los Angeles, California); Temescal (Oakland, California); Thai Town (Los Angeles, California); Watts (Los Angeles, California); Yuba City, Sikh Enclave (California)

See also Hispanic Enclaves: Annandale, Latino and Asian Enclaves (Virginia); Boyle Heights, Latino Neighborhood (Los Angeles, California); Bridgeport (Chicago, Illinois); Chicago, Mexican and Puerto Rican Enclaves (Illinois); Dallas, Mexican Enclaves (Texas); East Los Angeles, Mexican American Enclave (Los Angeles, California); Historic South Central (Los Angeles, California); Holyoke, Puerto Rican Enclaves (Massachusetts); Houston, Mexican Enclaves (Texas); Indio, Mexican and Central American Communities (California); Jackson Heights (Queens, New York); Langley Park, Latino Enclaves (Maryland); Lawrence, Latino Enclaves (Massachusetts); Little Havana (Miami, Florida); Little Havana on the Hudson (North Hudson, New Jersey); Little Lima (Paterson, New Jersey); Logan Heights, Mexican Enclave (San Diego, California); Mayan Corner/24th and Mission (San Francisco, California); Mexicantown (Detroit, Michigan); Mount Washington, Mexican Enclave (California); Olvera Street/La Plaza (Los Angeles, California); Phoenix and Other Cities, Mexican Enclaves (Arizona); Pico Rivera, Latino Enclave (California); Riverside, Mexican Enclave (California); San Bernardino, Mexican Enclave (California); Santa Ana, Mexican Enclaves (California); Sleepy Hollow, Ecuadorian Enclave (New York); South Federal Boulevard (Denver, Colorado); Sunset Park West and North Corona (New York City); Upper Fells Point (Spanish Town) (Baltimore, Maryland); Washington Heights (New York City); Watts (Los Angeles, California)

Marena Cole

Further Reading

Cheng, Wendy. "East of East: The Global Cosmopolitans of Suburban LA." *Boom: A Journal of California* 5, no. 1 (2015): 20–28.

"City of El Monte," elmonteca.gov. Accessed October 16, 2016. http://elmonteca.gov /LinkClick.aspx?fileticket=u7kNUyyFAC8=&tabid=179.

Garcia, Matt. *A World of Its Own: Race, Labor, and Citrus in the Making of Greater Los Angeles, 1900–1970*. Chapel Hill, NC: University of North Carolina Press, 2001.

Mostrom, Anthony. "The Lore of Southern California Permeated Frank Zappa's Music and Self-Image." *Los Angeles Times*, January 9, 2011. Accessed October 16, 2016. http://articles.latimes.com/2011/jan/09/local/la-me-0109-then-20110109.

Parsons, James J. "California Manufacturing." *Geographical Review* 39, no. 2 (1949): 229–241, doi: 10.2307/211046.

Shyong, Frank. "San Gabriel Valley's El Monte Getting a Boost From Chinese Investors." *Los Angeles Times*, December 13, 2014. Accessed October 16, 2016. http://www.latimes.com/local/california/la-me-el-monte-chinese-20141213-story.html.

United States Census Bureau. "El Monte City, California." *U.S. Department of Commerce*. Accessed October 16, 2016. http://www.census.gov/quickfacts/table/PST045214/0622230,00.

Velazquez, Maritza. "A Look Back at El Monte: City Offers Historical Tours." *San Gabriel Valley Tribune*, September 20, 2012. Accessed October 16, 2016. http://www.sgvtribune.com/general-news/20120920/a-look-back-at-el-monte-city-offers-historical-tours.

Wilson, Karen, and Daniel Lynch. "Here Come the Monte Boys: Vigilante Justice and Lynch Mobs in 19th Century El Monte." *KCET.org*. June 25, 2015. Accessed October 16, 2016. http://www.kcet.org/socal/departures/columns/east-of-east/here-come-the-monte-boys-vigilante-justice-and-lynch-mobs-in-19th-century-el-monte.html.

Wollenberg, Charles. "Race and Class in Rural California: The El Monte Berry Strike of 1933." *California Historical Quarterly* 51, no. 2 (1972): 155–64.

ELK HORN, DANISH ENCLAVES (IOWA)

Elk Horn is a small city in Shelby County, Iowa. As of 2014, the population was 647. Elk Horn is known for its historic Danish population, and it is one of the two largest rural Danish settlements in the United States. Although Danish immigration to the area peaked in the late 19th century, in recent decades residents of Elk Horn have worked to revitalize their heritage and bring emblems of Danish culture to the community.

Danish immigration to Iowa largely began in the 1870s. Immigrants left Denmark at far lower rates than from other Scandinavian nations such as Sweden or Norway because the country typically had much better economic opportunities than its neighbors. One early push for Danes to immigrate to the United States was in the wake of conflict in the 1860s. War broke out between Denmark and neighboring Prussia. As a result, two Danish provinces, Schleswig and Holstein, were made part of Prussia. That did not sit well with some Danish citizens, who opted to move to the United States.

Immigration from Denmark increased between the 1880s and 1920s. Iowa in general, and its southeast corner in particular, was an attractive destination for Danes looking for work in farming. Many arriving Danes had worked as farmers in their native country, and so it was a popular occupation for members of the community once they had arrived in the United States. Compared to other areas in the region, Iowa's southeast had abundant farmland available to newcomers.

Danish windmill in Elk Horn, Iowa. Although Danish immigration to the area peaked in the late 19th century, in recent decades residents of Elk Horn have worked to revitalize their heritage and bring emblems of Danish culture to the community. (Benkrut/Dreamstime.com)

By 1875, Elk Horn was home to so many Danish immigrants that the Elk Horn Lutheran Congregation was established to serve the community. By 1876, the congregation adopted a constitution and bought 40 acres of land, a testament to the size and relative prosperity of the area's young Danish community.

The coming decades brought further development to the small but developing Elk Horn. In 1877, the town established its first school. Two years later, *The Dannevirke*, a newspaper, began publication. *The Dannevirke* was the first Danish-language newspaper west of the Mississippi River. In 1878, the town also established a folk school, dedicated to teaching children Danish language and culture. By 1914, Elk Horn had about 800 inhabitants, slightly more than at the present day.

In 1924, immigration began to slow as result of new, stricter federal restrictions. Country-specific quotas on immigration meant that for Danes, as with all other peoples, access to the United States was more difficult and limited than it had previously been. While immigration from Denmark to the United States would continue after 1924, Elk Horn's population would no longer grow.

While Danish immigration to Elk Horn has not been substantial since the beginning of the 20th century, the area still remains connected to its cultural heritage. Significantly, in recent decades Elk Horn has expanded upon its Danish heritage and practices, creating increasing public opportunity to celebrate and participate in expressions of Danish culture. For example, in 1976, Elk Horn became home to the first and only authentic Danish windmill in the United States. The windmill was manufactured in Norre Snede, a town in Denmark. The town of Elk Horn had the windmill shipped overseas, where it was reconstructed and still stands today as a popular tourist attraction.

Elk Horn's Danish Windmill

Some 60 feet tall, Elk Horn's traditional Danish windmill is the only authentic, functional Danish windmill in the United States. For the past four decades, visitors have been able to visit it and learn about the area's Danish history. The windmill that now stands in Elk Horn is a type known as a smock mill, built in Norre Snede, Denmark, in 1848. It was used to grind grain to make flour. Other windmills like it could be found all over Denmark, as grain was a staple of Danish diet and economy. While these windmills traditionally served a vital role in feeding the Danish people, in modern times they have largely fallen into disuse and disrepair.

Harvey Sornson, a farmer from Elk Horn, visited Denmark in 1975. He saw many dilapidated and unused windmills throughout the Danish countryside and became concerned that shortly many of these windmills would be destroyed. Thus, he hatched the idea to bring an authentic, traditional Danish windmill to Elk Horn to celebrate the town's bicentennial and honor its ethnic heritage.

Sornson pitched the idea in a town meeting. Within a few days, Elk Horn residents raised $30,000 to bring a windmill to the town. Quickly, a windmill in Norre Snede was selected and a Danish carpenter began work to dismantle it. Its pieces were carefully numbered, and it was shipped overseas.

The mill arrived in Elk Horn on February 4, 1976. Being in so many pieces, it would require considerable reconstruction work—but townspeople were eager to help. With the assistance of some 300 volunteers, the windmill was put together. Today, it stands just off the highway as an official Iowa Welcome Center, making it a popular attraction for locals and tourists alike.

Furthermore, Elk Horn also holds an annual Tivoli Fest, a festival devoted to the celebration of Danish culture. The festival has taken place every year since 1980. Attendees can expect to enjoy traditional Danish foods, such as smorrebrod, a type of Danish open-faced sandwich, aebleskiver, which are small, spherical pancakes, and medisterpolse, which is a variety of spicy sausage. Visitors can also go on tours of the windmill, as well as the Museum of Danish America.

Overall, Elk Horn, Iowa, is a small town with unique character. Although Danish immigration to the area is by and large a thing of the past, Elk Horn works to maintain much of its traditional cultural heritage. With festivals, museums, and an authentic Danish windmill, Elk Horn's dedication to preserving its Danish past still rings with authenticity.

See also in Iowa: Amana Colonies (Iowa)

See also Danish Enclaves: Solvang, Danish Community (California)

Marena Cole

Further Reading

"Danish Immigration." Museum of the Danish American. Accessed October 7, 2016. http://www.danishmuseum.org.

"Danish Villages." Marne & Elk Horn Telephone Company. Accessed October 7, 2016. http://www.danishvillages.com.

Hoehnle, Peter. "Danes." *Iowa Pathways, Iowa Public Television*. Accessed October 7, 2016. http://www.iptv.org/iowapathways/mypath.cfm?ounid=ob_000200.

Nelson, Nora Lange. "Elk Horn History." The Danish Windmill. Accessed October 7, 2016. https://www.danishwindmill.com/press_room/elk_horn_history.asp.

Petersen, Wava. "Danish Windmill." The Danish Windmill. Accessed December 3, 2016. https://www.danishwindmill.com/press_room/danish_windmill_history.asp.

"Windmill History." The Danish Windmill. Accessed December 3, 2016. http://www.danishwindmill.com/danish_windmill_history/history_overview.asp.

ELMHURST (QUEENS, NEW YORK). *See* Sunset Park West and North Corona (New York City)

ETHIOPIAN ENCLAVES. *See* Little Ethiopia (Los Angeles, California)